Introduction to the Economics of Financial Markets

Introduction to the Economics of Financial Markets

James Bradfield

OXFORD

UNIVERSITY PRESS

2007

OXFORD
UNIVERSITY PRESS

Oxford University Press, Inc., publishes works that further
Oxford University's objective of excellence
in research, scholarship, and education.

Oxford   New York
Auckland   Cape Town   Dar es Salaam   Hong Kong   Karachi
Kuala Lumpur   Madrid   Melbourne   Mexico City   Nairobi
New Delhi   Shanghai   Taipei   Toronto

With offices in
Argentina   Austria   Brazil   Chile   Czech Republic   France   Greece
Guatemala   Hungary   Italy   Japan   Poland   Portugal   Singapore
South Korea   Switzerland   Thailand   Turkey   Ukraine   Vietnam

Published by Oxford University Press, Inc.
198 Madison Avenue, New York, New York 10016

www.oup.com

Oxford is a registered trademark of Oxford University Press

Library of Congress Cataloging-in-Publication Data
Bradfield, James.
    Introduction to the economics of financial markets / James Bradfield.
        p. cm.
    Includes bibliographical references and index.
    ISBN-13 978-0-19-531063-4
    ISBN 0-19-531063-2
    1. Finance. 2. Capital market. I. Title.
    HG173.B67 2007
    332—dc22   2006011610

9 8 7 6 5 4 3 2 1
Printed in the United State of America
on acid-free paper

To my wife, Alice, to our children, and to their children

To the memory of Professor Edward Zabel,
a friend and mentor, who taught me the importance of
extracting the economic interpretations from
the mathematics, and who taught me much more.

Preface

This book is an introductory exposition of the way in which economists analyze how, and how well, financial markets organize the intertemporal allocation of scarce resources. The central theme is that the function of a system of financial markets is to enable consumers, investors, and managers of firms to effect mutually beneficial intertemporal exchanges. I use the standard concept of economic efficiency (Pareto optimality) to assess the efficacy of the financial markets. I present an intuitive development of the primary theoretical and empirical models that economists use to analyze financial markets. I then use these models to discuss implications for public policy.

The book presents the *economics* of financial markets; it is not a text in corporate finance, managerial finance, or investments in the usual senses of those terms. The relationship between a course for which this book is written, and courses in corporate finance and investments, is analogous to the relationship between a standard course in microeconomics and a course in managerial economics.

I emphasize concrete, intuitive interpretations of the economic analysis. My objective is to enable students to recognize how the theoretical and empirical results that economists have established for financial markets are built on the central economic principles of equilibrium in competitive markets, opportunity costs, diversification, arbitrage, and trade-offs between risk and expected return. I develop carefully the logic that supports and organizes these results, leaving the derivation of rigorous proofs from first principles to advanced texts. (Some proofs and technical extensions are presented in appendices to some of the chapters.) Students who use this text will acquire an understanding of the economics of financial markets that will enable them to read with some sophistication articles in the public press about financial markets and about public policy toward those markets. Dedicated readers will be able to understand the central issues and the results (if not the technical methods) in the scholarly literature.

I address the book primarily to undergraduate students. The selection and presentation of topics reflect the author's long experience teaching in the Department of Economics at Hamilton College. Undergraduate and beginning graduate students in programs of business administration who want an understanding of how economists assess financial markets against the criteria of allocative and informational efficiency will also find this book useful.

I have taught mainly in the areas of investments and portfolio theory, and in introductory and intermediate microeconomic theory. I also teach a course in mathematical economics, and I have written (with Jeffrey Baldani and Robert Turner, who are economists at Colgate University) the text *Mathematical Economics*, second edition (2005). I recently taught an introductory course and an advanced seminar in mathematical economics at Colgate.

Readers of this book should have completed one introductory course in economics (preferably microeconomics). Although I use elementary concepts in probability and statistics, it is not critical that readers have completed formal courses in these areas. I present in the text the concepts in probability and statistics that will enable a student with no previous work in these areas to understand the economic analysis. Students who have completed an introductory course in probability and statistics will be able to understand the exposition in the text more easily. I use graphs extensively, and I assume that students understand the solution of pairs of linear equations.

Acknowledgments

My greatest debt is to my wife, Alice, whose encouragement, understanding, and clear thinking about choices are indefatigable.

Most professors owe much to their students; I am no exception. I have learned much from the students who have taken the courses from which I have drawn this book. Several of those students read many drafts of the book, eliminated errors, and made valuable suggestions for additional examples and for clarity of exposition. I thank John Balio, Tierney Boisvert, Katherine E. Brogan, Matt Clausen, Mike Coffey, Kaitie Donovan, Matt Drescher, John Durland, Schuyler Gellatly, Young Han, Tom Heacock, Jason Hong, Danielle Levine, Brendan Mahoney, Abhishek Maity, Katie Nedrow, Quang Nguyen, Greg Noel, Cy Philbrick, Brad Polan, Eric Reile, Dan Rubin, Katie Sarris, Kevin St. John, Gregory Scott, Joseph P. H. Sullivan, and Kimberly Walker. I appreciate the work of Rachael Arnold, who used her skills as a graphic artist to create computerized drawings of the several figures.

I thank Dawn Woodward for the numerous times that she assisted me with the arcana of word processing, and for many other instances of secretarial assistance.

Five former students served (seriatim) as editorial and research assistants. I am grateful to Mo Berkowitz, Jon Farber, Gregory H. Jaske, Kathleen McGrory, and Mac Weiss for their industriousness, their intelligence, and their constant good cheer. Each of them contributed significantly to this book.

I extend appreciation especially to Dr. Janette S. Albrecht, who watched the progress of this book through periods of turbulence, and who added several dimensions to my understanding of sunk costs.

Mrs. Ann Burns, a friend of long standing from my days in the dean's office, cheerfully, speedily, and accurately typed numerous drafts of the manuscript, many of which I wrote by hand, with labyrinthian notes (in multiple colors) in the margins and on the back sides of preceding and succeeding pages. I wish Ann and her family well.

I thank Mike Mercier for his editorial encouragement and guidance during an earlier incarnation of this book.

My friend and colleague, Professor of English George H. Bahlke, who is an expert on twentieth-century British literature, helped me to maintain a greater measure of equanimity than I would have had without his support.

I am also indebted to my friend and colleague, Professor of History Robert L. Paquette, who has written extensively on the Atlantic slave trade, and with whom

I teach a seminar on property rights and the rise of the modern state. Among other valuable lessons, Professor Paquette reminded me on several occasions that the application of theoretical models in economics is limited by the prejudices of the persons whose behavior we are trying to explain.

I appreciate the confidence that Terry Vaughn, Executive Editor at Oxford University Press, expressed in my work, which culminated in this book. Catherine Rae, the assistant to Mr. Vaughn, helped me in numerous ways as I responded to referees' suggestions and prepared the manuscript. Stephania Attia, the Production Editor for this book, supervised the compositing closely, and I thank her for doing so. I also appreciate the attention to detail provided by Jean Blackburn of Bytheway Publishing Services. Judith Kip, a professional indexer, contributed significantly by constructing the index.

Contents

**Part VI The Informational and Allocative Efficiency of
Financial Markets: Applications**

Part I

Introduction

1 The Economics of Financial Markets

1.1 The Economic Function of a Financial Market

The economic function of a financial market is to increase the efficiency with which individuals can engage in mutually beneficial intertemporal exchanges with other individuals.[1]

This book is an introductory exposition of the *economics* of financial markets. We address three questions. First, we explain how financial markets enable individuals to make intertemporal exchanges. Second, we explain how economists assess how well a system of financial markets performs this function. Third, we develop the implications for public policy of our answers to the first two questions.

1.2 The Intended Readers for This Book

We address this book to students who have completed at least one course in economics. We assume that the reader has a rudimentary understanding of opportunity cost, marginal analysis, and how supply and demand produce equilibrium prices and quantities in perfectly competitive markets. A course in probability and statistics will be useful, but not necessary. We provide in chapter 7 the instruction in probability and statistics that the reader will need. Students who have completed a course in probability and statistics can easily omit this chapter or use it for review.

The economic analysis of financial markets is essential for the effective management of either a firm or a portfolio of securities. There are several texts that develop these implications. The present book, however, addresses the economics of financial markets; our objective is to explain how, and to what extent, a system of financial markets assists individuals in their attempts to maximize personal levels of lifetime satisfaction (or utility) through intertemporal exchanges with other individuals. Even so, students interested in managerial topics can benefit from this book; after all, financial markets affect managers of firms and portfolios in many ways.

1.3 Three Kinds of Trade-Offs

Individuals allocate their scarce resources among alternative uses so as to maximize their levels of lifetime satisfaction. To accomplish this, each individual must make three kinds of trade-offs:

1. Each year individuals must allocate their resources between producing goods and services for current consumption, and producing (this year) goods for expanded future consumption. Economists call the latter kind of goods *capital goods*. A capital good is a produced good that can be used as an input for future production. Capital goods can be tangible, such as a railroad locomotive, or intangible, such as a computer language. It is primarily through the accumulation of capital goods that a society increases its standard of living over time.

2. Individuals must allocate among the production of current goods and services the resources that they have reserved this year to support current consumption. Students who have completed an introductory course in microeconomics will be familiar with this trade-off. In its simplest form, this is the problem of maximizing utility by allocating a fixed level of current income between the purchases of Goods X and Y. In any of its forms, this second kind of trade-off is not an intertemporal allocation, and thus it does not involve financial markets. Therefore, we do not discuss this question.

3. Each person who provides resources to produce capital goods faces a trade-off created by the interplay of risk and expected future return.

In most cases, persons who finance the creation of capital goods do so with other persons. These persons jointly hold a claim on an uncertain future outcome. The future value of this claim, viewed from the day of its formation, is uncertain because the future productivity of the capital goods is uncertain. If the persons who finance the creation of capital goods differ in their willingness to tolerate uncertainty, then these persons can create mutually beneficial exchanges.

Consider the following example. Ms. Lyons and Ms. Clyde jointly provide the capital goods for an enterprise, which produces an income of either $60 or $140 in any given year. These two outcomes are equally likely, and the outcome for any year is independent of the outcomes for all previous years. Consequently, the average annual income is $100. If the two women share the annual income equally, each woman's average annual income will be $50; in any given year her income will be $30 or $70, with each possibility being equally likely.

If Ms. Lyons is sufficiently averse to uncertainty, she will prefer a guaranteed annual income of $35 to an income that fluctuates unpredictably between $30 and $70. That is, Ms. Lyons will trade away $15 of average income in exchange for relief from uncertain fluctuations in that income. Ms. Clyde, on the other hand, might be willing to accept an increase in the unpredictable fluctuation of her income in exchange for a sufficiently large increase in her average income. Specifically, Ms. Clyde might prefer an income that fluctuates unpredictably between $25 and $105, which would mean an average of $65 per year, to an income that fluctuates unpredictably between $30 and $70, for an average of $50. If the two women's attitudes toward uncertainty are as we have described them, the women can effect a mutually beneficial exchange. In exchange for a $15 increase in her own average income, Ms. Clyde will insulate Ms. Lyons against the uncertain fluctuations in her income.

When people allocate resources in the present year to produce capital goods, they obtain a claim on goods and services to be produced in future years. This claim is a *financial security*. Financial markets offer several kinds of claims on the uncertain future outcomes that the capital goods will generate. Each kind of claim offers a different combination of risk and expected future return. Therefore, the persons who finance the creation of capital goods, and thereby acquire financial securities, must choose the combination of risk and expected future return to hold.

We will restrict our attention to trade-offs between current and future consumption, in addition to trade-offs among various claims on uncertain future outcomes. These two kinds of trade-offs involve intertemporal allocation. Persons who conduct these two kinds of trade-offs use financial markets to identify and effect mutually beneficial intertemporal exchanges with other persons.

1.4 Mutually Beneficial Intertemporal Exchanges

A central proposition in economics is that persons who own resources can obtain higher levels of utility by engaging in mutually beneficial exchanges with other persons. Intertemporal exchanges are a subset of these exchanges. In part II, we explain how financial markets promote intertemporal exchanges by reducing the costs of organizing these exchanges. In this section, we describe three kinds of intertemporal exchanges that financial markets promote.

1.4.1 Mutually Beneficial Exchanges between Current and Future Consumption That Do Not Involve Net Capital Accumulation for the Economy

Consider the following example, in which two persons exchange claims to current and future consumption without increasing the stock of capital goods in the economy.

Both Mr. Black and Mr. Green are employed. Each man's income for the current year is the value of his contribution to the production of goods and services this year. Each man's income entitles him to remove from the production sector of the economy a volume of goods and services that is equal in value to what he produced during the year. Economists define *consumption* as the removal of goods and services from the business sector by households. If every person spent his entire income every year, the economy would not be able to accumulate any capital goods in the business sector.

Now suppose that Mr. Black wants to spend this year $x more than his current income. That is, he wants to remove from the business sector a volume of goods and services whose value exceeds by $x the value of what he produced during the current year. If Mr. Black is to consume this year more than he produced this year, someone else must finance this "excess" consumption by consuming this year a volume of goods and services whose value is $x less than what he currently produced. Suppose that Mr. Green agrees to do this, in exchange for the right to consume next year a volume of goods and services whose value exceeds the value of what he will produce next year. Mr. Black is now a borrower and Mr. Green is a lender.

Typically, the agreement requires the borrower to repay the lender with interest. For example, in exchange for a loan this year equal to $x, Mr. Black will repay $y to Mr. Green next year, and $y>$x. But the payment of interest is beside the point here.

Both Mr. Black and Mr. Green can increase their levels of lifetime utility by undertaking this mutually beneficial exchange. Mr. Black gains utility by reducing his consumption next year by $y, and increasing his current consumption by $x. Were this not so, Mr. Black would not have agreed to the exchange. Similarly, Mr. Green gains utility by reducing his current consumption by $x and increasing his consumption next year by $y. Both men gain utility because they are willing to substitute between current and future consumption at different rates.

Consider the following numerical example. At the present allocation of his income between spending for current consumption and saving for future consumption, Mr. Black is willing to decrease the rate of his consumption next year by as much as $125 in exchange for increasing his rate of consumption this year by $100. Mr. Green's present allocation between current and future consumption is such that he will decrease his current rate of consumption by $100 in exchange for an increase in his rate of consumption next year by at least $115. That is, Mr. Black is willing to borrow at rates of interest up to 25%, and Mr. Green is willing to lend at rates of interest no less than 15%. Obviously, the two men can construct a mutually beneficial exchange.

The rate at which a person is willing to substitute between current and future consumption (or, more generally, between any two goods) depends on the present rates of current and future consumption. In particular, Mr. Black would be willing to increase his level of borrowing from its current level, with no change in his level of income, only if the rates of interest were to fall. The maximal rate of interest at which a person is willing to borrow, and the minimal rate of interest at which a person is willing to lend, depends on that person's *marginal* value of future consumption in terms of current consumption foregone. Each person has his or her own schedule of these marginal values, which changes as that person's patterns of current and future consumption change.

One of the functions of a financial market is to reduce the cost incurred by Messrs. Black and Green to organize this exchange. We consider this function in chapter 2, where we examine how financial markets increase the efficiency with which individuals can allocate their resources.

1.4.2   Mutually Beneficial Exchanges between Current and Future Consumption That Do Involve Net Capital Accumulation for the Economy

Consider again Mr. Green and Mr. Black. In the preceding example, Mr. Green is a lender; he agrees to remove from the business sector this year a volume of goods and services whose value is less than the value that he produced this year. Mr. Green finances Mr. Black's "excess" consumption.

There is another possibility for Mr. Green to be a lender. If Mr. Green consumes less than his entire income this year, the economy can retain, in the production sector, some of the output that would otherwise be delivered to households. That is, Mr. Green could finance the accumulation of capital goods in the production sector.

Although the production sector could retain goods that are appropriate for households, this is not usually done.[2] Rather, if Mr. Green spends less than his current income, the economy can reallocate resources out of the production of goods and services intended for households and into the production of capital goods, such as railroad locomotives and computer languages. By accumulating these capital goods in the production sector, the economy can expand its ability to produce goods and services in the future, including goods and services intended for households.

We say that Mr. Green *saves* if he spends less than his current income. If his act of saving enables another person, like Mr. Black, to spend more than his current income, then Mr. Green can be repaid in the future when Mr. Black transfers some of his future income to Mr. Green. Alternatively, if Mr. Green's saving enables the economy to accumulate capital goods, then Mr. Green can be repaid out of the net increase in future production that the expanded stock of capital goods will make possible.

1.4.3 Mutually Beneficial Exchanges of Claims to Uncertain Future Outcomes

Intertemporal allocations always involve uncertainty because the future is uncertain. In this subsection, we present a simple example of how two persons, who differ in their willingness to tolerate uncertainty, can construct a mutually beneficial exchange.

Ms. Tall and Ms. Short operate adjacent farms that are identical in all respects. In particular, the annual productivity of each farm is subject to the same vagaries of nature. Each year the output of corn on each farm is equal to either 800 tons or 1,200 tons, depending on whether nature is beneficial or detrimental that year. The state of nature for any particular year is unpredictable. Over the longer run, however, each of the two states occurs with a probability equal to 50%. Therefore, each woman's annual product fluctuates unpredictably between 800 and 1,200 tons of corn. Her average annual product is 1,000 tons of corn.

The two women differ in their willingness to tolerate uncertainty. Ms. Tall is *risk averse*. She prefers to have a guaranteed annual product of 900 tons of corn, rather than tolerating unpredictable fluctuations between 800 and 1,200 tons of corn. That is, if Ms. Tall is guaranteed 900 tons of corn each year, she will accept a decrease of 100 tons of corn in her average annual product.

Ms. Short is *risk preferring*. She will accept an increase in the range over which her product fluctuates, if she can gain a sufficiently large increase in the average level of her product.

Ms. Tall and Ms. Short construct the following mutually beneficial exchange based on the difference in their attitudes toward uncertainty: they combine their farms into a single firm. In a year in which nature is beneficial, each farm will produce 1,200 tons of corn, so that output of the firm will be 2,400 tons. When nature is detrimental, each farm will produce only 800 tons, and the output of the firm will be 1,600 tons. The risk-averse Ms. Tall will hold a *contractual claim*: she will receive 900 tons of corn each year regardless of the state of nature. Ms. Short will absorb the vagaries of nature by holding a *residual claim*: each year she will receive whatever is left over from the aggregate output after Ms. Tall is paid her contractual 900 tons.

When nature is beneficial, Ms. Short will receive 2(1200) tons − 900 tons, or 1,500 tons. When nature is detrimental, Ms. Short will receive 2(800) tons − 900 tons, or 700 tons. Therefore, Ms. Short's annual income will fluctuate unpredictably between 700 tons and 1,500 tons; her average annual income is 1,100 tons.

In summary, the risk-averse Ms. Tall will reduce the level of her average annual income from 1,000 tons to 900 tons, in exchange for being insulated from unpredictable fluctuations in her income. The risk-preferring Ms. Short will accept an increase in the range over which her annual income will fluctuate, in exchange for an increase in the average level of her income. Notice that the average of the two women's average incomes remains at 1,000, which is what each woman had before she entered the agreement.

Ms. Tall and Ms. Short have created a mutually beneficial exchange that involves levels of average income (or product) and levels of unpredictable variation in that income. Financial markets facilitate these exchanges by enabling firms to offer different kinds of securities. The contractual claim that Ms. Tall holds is similar to a bond; the residual claim that Ms. Short holds is similar to a common stock. We discuss the properties of these securities in detail in chapter 2.

1.5   Economic Efficiency and Mutually Beneficial Exchanges

In the preceding section, we described briefly the three kinds of mutually beneficial intertemporal exchanges that involve combinations of present and future outcomes. Unfortunately, before any two persons can conduct these exchanges, they must meet several conditions. First, the two persons must find each other. Then, they must agree on the terms of the exchange. These terms must specify the price of the good or service to be exchanged, the quantity and the quality of the good or service to be exchanged, and the time and place of its delivery. Moreover, the terms usually specify the recourse that each party will have if the other party defaults. Intertemporal exchanges are particularly complicated because they involve the purchase today of a claim on the uncertain outcome of a future event. Therefore, the terms for an intertemporal exchange must take into account the probabilities of the possible outcomes.

In an economy that uses a complex set of technologies, and that serves a large number of persons who have widely diverse preferences, meeting these conditions can be costly. An essential function of any system of markets, including financial markets, is to reduce the costs of meeting these conditions.

In this section, we address the question of how well a system of financial markets enables individuals to increase their utility by conducting intertemporal exchanges. The critical concept for the analysis of this question is *economic efficiency.*

Definition of Economic Efficiency
Economic efficiency is a criterion that economists use to evaluate a particular allocation of resources. Specifically, an allocation of resources is economically efficient if there is no alternative allocation that would increase at least one person's utility without decreasing any other person's utility. Consequently, if an allocation of resources is economically efficient, there are no further opportunities for mutually beneficial exchanges. By extension of this definition, a system of markets is economically efficient if it enables persons who own resources to reach an economically efficient allocation of those resources.

We can also state the criterion of economic efficiency in terms of an *equilibrium configuration of prices and quantities.*

Definition of Equilibrium

An equilibrium configuration of prices and quantities (briefly, an equilibrium) is a set of prices and quantities at which no buyer or seller has an incentive to make further purchases or sales.

A system of markets contains forces that cause prices and quantities to move toward their equilibrium values. But the equilibrium is not necessarily economically efficient. To be economically efficient, the equilibrium must enable buyers and sellers to conduct all potential mutually beneficial exchanges, not just those that can be conducted at the equilibrium prices.

A simple example from introductory economics will demonstrate this point. Air Luker is an airline that offers passengers two direct, nonstop flights each day between Albany, New York, and Portland, Maine, in each direction. Air Luker has a monopoly on air service between these two cities. The willingness of consumers to pay for transportation by air between Albany and Portland constrains the profitability of Air Luker's monopoly. Passengers who want to travel between Albany and Portland have alternatives to traveling by air. They can drive or ride the bus. They can also travel between Albany and Portland less frequently, substituting communication by telephone, e-mail, videoconferencing, or conventional mail for personal visits. The passengers can also forego the benefits of more frequent communication and spend their time and money on other things. None of these alternatives is a perfect substitute for travel by air between Albany and Portland.

A standard proposition in economics is that consumers as a group will reduce the rate (per unit of time) at which they purchase any product if the price of that product increases relative to their incomes and the prices of imperfect substitutes for that product. Succinctly, Air Luker faces a trade-off between the prices of its tickets and the number of tickets that consumers will purchase per day. The graph in figure 1.1 describes the choices available to the owners of Air Luker. On the horizontal axis, we measure the number of passengers per day between Albany and Portland. On the vertical axis, we measure the price of a ticket. We also measure marginal revenue and marginal cost on that axis. The demand curve defines the trade-off between ticket prices and passengers per day. Each point on the horizontal axis designates a specific number of passengers per day. The height of the demand curve above that point is the maximal price that consumers will pay per ticket to purchase that quantity of tickets per day. For example, Point A on the demand curve indicates that P_A is the maximal price that Air Luker can charge per ticket and expect to sell Q_A tickets per day.[3]

The marginal revenue and marginal cost curves in figure 1.1 measure the rates at which Air Luker's total revenue and total cost (both measured per day) would change if Air Luker were to reduce the price of a ticket enough to sell one more ticket per day. For example, starting from Point A on its demand curve, if Air Luker were to reduce the price of a ticket enough so that daily ticket sales increased by one, Air Luker's total (daily) revenue would increase by the height of the marginal revenue curve at the quantity Q_A, and total (daily) cost would increase by the height of the marginal cost curve at the quantity Q_A.[4]

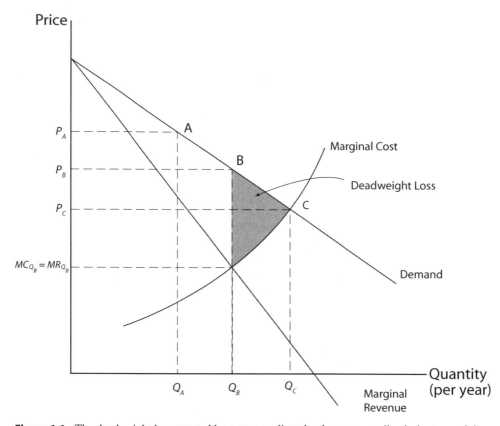

Figure 1.1. The deadweight loss created by a monopolist who does not use discriminatory pricing.

Air Luker will maximize its profit by setting the price of a ticket so that marginal revenue is equal to marginal cost at the number of tickets sold per day. The profit-maximizing price and quantity occur at Point B on the demand curve. At this point, the price paid by the consumers for a ticket exceeds the marginal cost incurred by Air Luker. Since the demand curve slopes downward, consumers would be willing to purchase tickets more frequently at a price that is both less than Air Luker's current price and greater than its marginal cost. If Air Luker could sell these additional units without reducing the price of a ticket, both Air Luker and the consumers could benefit. This potential, mutually beneficial, exchange requires that Air Luker charge (and the consumers pay) different prices for different units of the same good.

For example, on each day Air Luker could charge P_B per ticket for Q_B tickets, and a lower price, P_C, for $Q_C - Q_B$ tickets. For this scheme to work, Air Luker must be able to prevent those consumers who are willing to pay as much as P_B for ticket (rather than not fly on that day) from purchasing tickets at the lower price, P_C. That is, Air Luker must discriminate among consumers according to their willingness to pay. If the costs of doing this are too large, or if this is prohibited by law, then the equilibrium in the monopolist's market is economically *inefficient.*[5]

To be economically efficient, a system of financial markets must do two things: generate information that will enable persons to identify all potential opportunities for mutually beneficial intertemporal exchanges, and provide mechanisms through which persons can make these exchanges. To a considerable extent, financial markets accomplish both tasks by organizing trading in financial securities. There are, however, situations in which financial markets fail to create an efficient allocation of resources. Economists call these situations *market failures*.

Definition of a Failure of a Financial Market
A failure of a financial market is an allocation of resources in which there are opportunities for mutually beneficial intertemporal exchanges that are not undertaken.

1.6   Examples of Market Failures

There are three kinds of market failures that occur in the intertemporal allocation of resources: the problem of agency, the problem of asymmetric information, and the problem of asset substitution. We describe these problems briefly here. In chapter 13, we analyze these failures in detail and examine some of the ways that firms and investors use to mitigate them.

1.6.1   The Problem of Agency

An agency is a relationship in which one person, called the agent, manages the interests of a second person, called the principal. Ideally, the agent subordinates his or her own interests completely to the interests of the principal. The problem of agency is that if the interests of the agent are not fully compatible with those of the principal, and if the principal cannot costlessly monitor the actions of the agent, the agent might pursue his or her own interests to the detriment of the principal. The extent to which the principal suffers due to a problem of agency varies directly with the cost that the principal would incur to monitor the agent perfectly.

The problem of agency arises in a firm that is operated by a small number of professional managers who act as agents for a large number of diverse shareholders, none of whom owns a large proportion of the shares. It would be prohibitively costly for the shareholders to monitor perfectly the performance of their managers. First, the managers have superior access to relevant information. Second, it is difficult to organize a large number of diverse shareholders to act as a cohesive unit on every question. Third, the smaller the proportion of the firm that a shareholder owns, the smaller is the cost that he or she would be willing to incur for the purpose of monitoring the managers more closely.

An obvious example of the problem of agency is that managers might use some of the shareholders' resources to purchase excessively luxurious offices, memberships in clubs, travel on the firm's aircraft, and other perquisites rather than investing these resources in projects that will generate wealth for the shareholders.

A less obvious example of a problem of agency occurs because the managers are more willing to accept a lower expected return on the firm's investments in exchange for a lower level of risk than the shareholders would prefer to do. This problem arises if a significant proportion of the managers' future wealth depends on their reputations as managers. These reputations would be diminished were the firm to produce mediocre results, let alone fail. Shareholders can reduce the risk of mediocre earnings in any one firm by holding a diversified portfolio of investments in several firms.[6] Clearly, managers cannot reduce the risk to their reputations by working simultaneously for many firms. Since the shareholders can use diversification to reduce the risks of mediocre earnings in a single firm, the shareholders are more willing to have their firm undertake risky projects that have higher expected returns than their managers' less risky, reputation-preserving projects.

1.6.2   The Problem of Asymmetric Information

Both parties to a proposed transaction have information (and beliefs) about the possible future outcomes of that transaction. The information is asymmetric if one party has material information that the other party does not have. *Material information* is information that a person would pay to acquire before deciding whether to enter a proposed transaction. The problem of asymmetric information is that the inability of a party that possesses material information to transmit that information credibly to a second party can prevent what would otherwise be a mutually beneficial exchange.

An example of the problem of asymmetric information occurs if a firm lacks sufficient cash to finance a profitable new project. To raise cash for the project, the firm offers to sell newly created shares of stock. To the extent that investors who are not current shareholders purchase the new shares, the current shareholders will cede to the new shareholders a portion of the ownership of the firm. But the value of the firm will increase as a consequence of undertaking the new project. Whether the current shareholders gain or lose wealth depends on the amount by which the new project increases the value of the firm relative to the proportion of the firm that the new shareholders acquire.

Prospective new shareholders must decide what proportion of the firm they must acquire if they are to recover their investment. The larger the amount by which the new project will increase the value of the firm, the smaller the proportion of the firm the new investors must acquire. Further, the smaller the proportion of the firm that the new shareholders acquire, the larger the proportion of the firm that the current shareholders will retain, and the wealthier those current shareholders will be.

There is a conflict of interest between the current shareholders and the prospective new shareholders. If the firm's managers act in the interests of the current shareholders, the managers have an incentive to overstate the value of the new project so as to induce the prospective new shareholders to finance the project in exchange for acquiring a small proportion of the firm. Knowing the incentives of the managers, the prospective new shareholders might insist on acquiring so large a proportion of the firm that, even with the new project, the current shareholders will lose wealth to the new shareholders. If the managers expect that their current shareholders will lose wealth as a consequence of financing the project by issuing new shares, the managers will forego the project. Foregoing the profitable project is economically inefficient. By definition, a profitable project will generate sufficient earnings to allow the new shareholders who financed the project to recover their investment and to create a profit that can be shared by the current and the new shareholders.

A profitable project provides the potential for a mutually beneficial exchange. To realize the potential, the parties to the exchange must agree on terms that will be mutually beneficial. In the example described above, if the managers cannot credibly inform the prospective new shareholders about the value of the project, the current shareholders, acting through their managers, will be unable to effect a mutually beneficial exchange with the prospective new shareholders, even though the new project would be profitable.

1.6.3 The Problem of Asset Substitution

The problem of asset substitution is the incentive that a firm's managers have to transfer wealth from the firm's bondholders to its shareholders by substituting riskier projects for less risky ones. In section 1.4.3 of this chapter, we examined a simple model in which investors who differ in their willingness to tolerate uncertainty could effect a mutually beneficial exchange by choosing between contractual and residual claims to an uncertain outcome. In that example, there is no risk of default on the contractual claims because even in a bad year the output of the combined farms is sufficient to pay the contractual claims.

In a more realistic example, the residual claimants would be the shareholders, who would control the firm through their managers. The contractual claimants would be bondholders, who would have no right to participate in the management of the firm unless there is a default on the bonds. The market value of the bonds depends on the probability that the firm will default.

Suppose that the managers of the firm sell the two farms that comprise the firm, and use the proceeds to invest in a new project that has the same expected payoff as the former firm but a higher probability of a default on the bonds. For example, the minimal and maximal payoffs of the new project might be 400 tons and 3,600 tons of corn, respectively. The average payoff would remain at 2,000 tons ($[400 \times 3600])/2 = 2000$), but there is now a positive probability that the firm will not be able to make the contractual payment of 900 tons to the bondholders.[7]

The increase (from zero) of the probability of a default on the bonds will reduce the market value of those bonds. Since the average value of the annual payoff to the firm remains at 2,000 tons of corn, the market value of the entire firm will not change.[8] Since the claims of the bondholders and the claims of shareholders constitute the entirety of the claims on the firm, the market value of the shareholders' claim must increase.

We conclude that (at least under some conditions) the firm's managers can transfer wealth from the bondholders to the shareholders by substituting a riskier project for a less risky one.

Now suppose that a firm attempts to finance a risky new project by selling bonds. Recognizing that the firm's managers have an incentive to transfer wealth from bondholders to shareholders by substituting a riskier project for the project that the bondholders intended to finance, the bondholders might refuse to purchase the bonds. If the firm has no other way to finance the new project, the opportunity for a mutually beneficial exchange (between prospective bondholders and current shareholders) will be foregone, creating an economic inefficiency.

We conclude in chapter 18 by restating and consolidating, in the context of economic efficiency, the analyses of the earlier chapters.

Problems

1. Mr. Block's potato farm produces between 500 and 800 tons of potatoes each year if there is bad weather, and between 700 and 1,000 tons each year if there is good weather. The farm has several investors who together own a bond that entitles them to receive 600 tons of potatoes each year. Today there is .5 probability that weather will be good next year. If tomorrow that probability is changed to .4 for the succeeding year, what will happen to the price for which the investors could sell their bond?

2. ABC Furniture has been struggling to get customers into its store. In an attempt to increase sales, the firm has advertised that interest-free payments on furniture are not due until one year after the furniture is purchased. Under what condition would this be a mutually beneficial exchange between ABC Furniture and prospective new customers?

3. Mr. Brown wants to increase his current consumption by $100. The current interest rate paid by a bank for deposits is 10%, and the bank is willing to lend at 15%. If Mr. Brown can guarantee that he will repay a loan that he might obtain from Mr. Green, is it economically efficient for Mr. Green to keep $100 in the bank?

4. Ms. White and Ms. Black own farms next to each other. When the weather is good, each farm produces 2,000 tons of apples per year. When the weather is bad, each farm produces 1,000 tons per year. Ms. White is risk-averse. Ms. Black is willing to accept additional risk in exchange for a sufficient increase in her average rate of return. If good and bad weather occur with equal probability, and if Ms. White will accept a guaranteed return of 1,000 apples per year, can the two women effect a mutually beneficial exchange? What type of claim would each woman hold?

Notes

1. An intertemporal exchange is one in which the two sides of the exchange occur at different times. For example, Person A will give something of value to Person B at time 0 in exchange for a commitment by Person B to give something of value to Person A at a later time. In some cases, Person B will promise to deliver things of value at several future times. An essential property of an intertemporal exchange is the risk that Person B will be unable to make the promised delivery, or will refuse to do so. Another form of risk arises if what Person B promises to deliver depends on an outcome (such as the size of a crop) that will not be known until some future time.

2. Inventories of unsold consumption goods accumulated in the production sector increase the feasible levels of future consumption beyond what these levels would otherwise be. Therefore, these inventories are capital goods.

3. In more sophisticated models, the quantity of tickets that Air Luker could sell per day at a given price would be uncertain. In these models, the quantities on the horizontal axis would be the average (or expected) numbers of tickets sold per day at various prices. There is no

assumption that consumers are identical in their willingness to pay for tickets. Among those consumers who purchase tickets for a given day when the price is P_A, there could be some consumers who would have paid more than P_A for a ticket rather than not flying on that day. The height of the demand curve at Point A is the maximal price that Air Luker can charge per ticket and sell Q_A tickets per day. Equivalently, if Air Luker were to increase the price above P_A, some consumers would fly less frequently, with the result that Air Luker would sell fewer than Q_A tickets per day.

4. A more sophisticated analysis would recognize that the heights of the marginal revenue and the marginal cost curves at the quantity Q_A are the instantaneous rates at which total revenue and total cost would change in response to a change in quantity starting from Q_A.

5. The technical term for the value of the mutually beneficial exchanges foregone is *deadweight loss*. Most introductory texts in microeconomics explain how imperfect competition (of which a monopoly is only one example) creates deadweight losses. Some texts explain how firms and consumers can reduce deadweight losses by using devices such as discriminatory pricing. In chapter 13, we explain how firms can reduce deadweight losses by choosing the kinds of securities to issue.

6. To reduce her risk, the investor must diversify her portfolio across firms whose earnings are not highly correlated. We shall examine the question of optional diversification for an investor in chapters 8 (on portfolio theory) and 9 (on the capital asset pricing model).

7. If the firm has accumulated some reserves of corn, it could pay the bondholders even in bad years, but a sufficiently long consecutive run of bad years would exhaust the firm's reserves, producing a default.

8. The conclusion requires an assumption that investors are risk neutral.

9. A *hostile takeover* is an event in which a group of investors attempts to gain control of a firm against the opposition of the firm's current management. The means of gaining control is to acquire a sufficient number of the firm's shares to elect directors who will replace the current managers (and their policies) with a new set of managers (and policies).

10. A *supermajority provision* is a provision in a firm's corporate charter that requires approval of more than 50% of the directors or the shareholders before certain kinds of changes can be undertaken. A *poison pill* is a provision that would transfer wealth from new shareholders to the firm's current shareholders if the new shareholders acquire enough shares to dismiss the current management.

firm makes the final payment required by the bond. In other words, any time before the end of 2010, the investor can sell the bond to another investor. The second investor purchases from the first investor the right to receive the payments that remain in the sequence. Of course, the price that the second investor will pay depends on how many payments remain in the sequence, and on the second investor's alternative opportunities for investment. The fact that the bond is saleable to other investors makes it more attractive to any investor.

A bond is a contract between a borrower and a lender. The borrower could be a single person or a firm. Similarly, the lender could be a single person or a financial institution such as a bank, an insurance company, or a pension fund. The borrower is the *issuer* of the bond; the lender is the *owner* of the bond. The contract that defines the bond requires the issuer of the bond to make a specified sequence of payments to the owner of the bond, and to do things that protect the bond's owner against the possibility that the issuer might not make the promised payments on time. Typically, the borrower issues the bond to obtain funds to finance the purchase of an asset as an investment. For example, a railroad might issue a bond to purchase a set of new locomotives. To protect the interests of the lender, the borrower might be required to maintain insurance on the locomotives, and to allow only engineers certified by the Federal Railroad Administration to operate those locomotives.

By the definition of a bond, the obligations of the issuer of the bond to whoever owns the bond at the moment are guaranteed. But what is the nature of the guarantee? What recourse is available to the owner of the bond should the issuer fail to meet his or her obligations, for example, by failing to make the promised payments on time, or by failing to carry the required amount of insurance?

The legal term for a failure to meet one's contractual obligations specified by a bond is *default*.[1] If the issuer creates a default, the present owner of the bond acquires specified rights to the assets of the issuer. For example, should a railroad fail to make the required payments to the owner of the bond, that owner might acquire the right to ask a court to seize the locomotives, sell them, and use the proceeds to make the required payments to the owner of the bond.

The saleability of bonds enables investors to create mutually beneficial exchanges. Consider the following example of a bond issued by a person to finance the purchase of a house.

Homeowners frequently finance the purchase of a home by borrowing money from a bank. To induce the bank to make the loan, the homeowner issues a bond to the bank. The bond requires the issuer (the homeowner) to make a specified sequence of payments to the owner of the bond (the bank) and to do various things to protect the bank's interest, such as carrying fire insurance, paying the property taxes, and maintaining the home in good repair. The homeowner guarantees performance of these obligations by giving a mortgage to the bank. The mortgage is a lien on the property that entitles the bank to seize the property and sell it should the homeowner create a default.[2]

Banks that purchase bonds issued by homeowners usually sell those bonds to other investors, who form a pool of these bonds. These investors then issue securities that are saleable rights to the sequences of payments that the homeowners have promised to make. These securities are called *mortgage-backed securities*. Although the homeowners will make the payments directly to the banks that originated the loans, the banks will pass those payments to the investors who purchased the mortgaged loans, and those investors will, in turn, pass the payments to the persons who purchased the mortgage-backed securities. This process of creating mortgaged-backed securities is an example of a set of mutually beneficial exchanges. The banks specialize in originating loans, rather than purchasing rights to receive sequences of payments. The investors who purchase the loans from the banks specialize in creating diversified pools of loans, and thus reducing the risks borne by the persons who purchase the securities that are backed by this pool of loans.

The issuer of the bond borrows money by selling the bond to an investor, who thereby becomes a lender. The price that the investor will pay for the bond determines the cost that the investor pays for obtaining the loan. For example, suppose that a railroad wants to borrow $11,000,000 to purchase a locomotive. The railroad offers to sell 10 bonds at a price of $1,100,000 each. Each bond is a promise to pay $1,400,000 per year for 10 years. Over the 10 years, the investors will receive a total of $14,000,000 as a return on their investment of $11,000,000.

The railroad's attempt to raise $11,000,000 by selling 10 bonds for $1,100,000 each might not succeed. If investors believe that the railroad might be late with some of the promised payments, or might be unable to complete the payments, the investors might be willing to pay only $1,000,000 for each of the bonds. In this event, the railroad would have to sell 11 bonds (at $1,000,000 each) to raise the $11,000,000 required to purchase the locomotive. Over the term of the loan, the railroad would have to pay to the bondholders $1,400,000 on each of 11 bonds. The total that the railroad would repay for the loan of $11,000,000 would be (11 bonds)($1,400,000 per bond)=$15,400,000. When the railroad must sell 11 bonds to raise the $11,000,000 to purchase the locomotive, the investors who finance that purchase obtain a return of $15,400,000 on their investment of $11,000,000. The railroad must pay an additional $1,400,000 ($15,400,000−$14,000,000) to finance the locomotive because investors perceive a higher risk of late or missing payments.[3]

Since a bond is a saleable right to receive a sequence of payments, any investor can become a *lender in due course* by purchasing the bond from a previous owner. Consequently, the investor who became a lender by purchasing the bond from the issuer need not remain a lender until the issuer makes the final payment required by the bond. At any time while the issuer is paying off the loan, the original lender can recover at least a portion of the unpaid balance of the loan by selling the bond to another investor.[4]

Definition of Common Stock
A share of common stock is a saleable right to receive an indefinitely long sequence of future payments, with the size of each payment contingent on both the firm's future earnings and on the firm's future opportunities to finance new investment projects. These payments to the stockholders are called dividends.

Typically, a firm will pay a dividend on its common stock at regular intervals, such as semiannually or quarterly. Shortly before each date on which a dividend is scheduled, the firm's directors announce the size of the forthcoming dividend. The directors are free to choose whatever size of dividend they believe is in the longer-term interests of the investors who own the common stock.[5] The directors might retain some of the firm's earnings for use in financing future investment projects. In particular, the directors can decide to pay no dividend.

Unlike a bond, a share of common stock is not a contractual right to receive a sequence of payments. The owners of the common stock are the owners of the firm. As owners, the (common)[6] shareholders elect persons to the board of directors and thereby control the firm. The directors determine the size and the timing of the dividend payments. In particular, the directors can use some or all of the firm's earnings to finance new projects, rather than paying those earnings to the shareholders as dividends.

Payments to bondholders and shareholders depend on the firm's ability to generate earnings. As explained above, the bondholders have a contractual claim on those earnings. By contrast, the shareholders have a residual claim on the earnings. The directors may pay to the shareholders whatever earnings remain after the bondholders are paid, although the directors may retain some or all of those residual earnings to finance new projects.

Firms issue common stock to raise money to finance projects. Unlike the case of a bond, the investors who purchase newly issued shares of common stock from a firm do not have the right to get their money back at the end of some specified number of periods. These investors can, however, in effect withdraw their money by selling their shares to other investors, just as investors who own bonds can withdraw their money prematurely by selling bonds to another investor. Of course, the ability of an investor to withdraw money by selling a security depends on the current price of that security. That current price depends on all investors' current expectations of the ability of the firm to generate earnings over the future.

If common stocks were not saleable rights, firms would have difficulty financing new projects by selling common stock. To understand the economic significance of the saleability of rights, consider the decision to construct a new home. A house provides a stream of services over time. These services occur as protection from the elements, a commodious place in which to raise a family and to enjoy one's friends and relatives, and a safe place to store important possessions. It is difficult to construct a home that is both comfortable and that will not outlast the time when the owner either wants to move elsewhere (e.g., for retirement) or dies. Few persons would construct a comfortable home designed to last many decades if they did not have the right to sell or to rent that home to another person at any time in the future. The right to sell the home provides people who finance the construction with the ability to "disinvest" should they want to reallocate their resources in the future. It would be economically inefficient to prohibit transfers of ownership of existing homes. If such a prohibition were in effect, there would be far fewer homes built, and those that were built would be less comfortable and less durable. Moreover, the incentive to preserve the homes through timely maintenance would be diminished.

The same arguments apply to expensive and durable capital goods, such as a railway line. The investors who finance the construction of the line by purchasing securities from the railroad acquire a right to receive dividends based on the future earnings generated by the line. But few persons would purchase the new securities without the right to disinvest in the future by selling the securities to other investors.

Definition of a Callable Bond

A callable bond is a bond that the issuing firm has the right to cancel by paying to the bond's current owner a fixed price that is specified in the definition of that bond.

A firm might want to issue a callable bond to provide a quick way to refinance its debt should interest rates fall. Of course, the same callability that provides an advantage to the firm that issued the bond creates a disadvantage to an investor who holds that bond. Should the firm call the bond when interest rates fall, the owner of the bond will receive cash. With interests now lower, the former owner of the bond will have to accept a lower rate of return when he or she reinvests that cash. Therefore, to induce investors to hold callable bonds, the issuing firms will usually have to provide some incentive, such as setting the levels of the promised payments higher than they would be on a bond that is identical in all other respects, but that is not callable.

Consider the bond described at the beginning of this section. That bond requires the issuing firm to pay $100 to whoever owns the bond when a payment is due. The payments continue quarterly through the end of 2010. At that time, the firm makes a final payment of $10,000. In effect, the firm has borrowed $10,000 until the end of 2010. Until that time, the firm will pay interest at an annual rate of 4% ($400 per year/ $10,000=4% per year).[7]

Now suppose that interest rates fall. A bank will now lend $10,000 to the firm at only 2% per year. Suppose that the bond on which the firm is now paying $400 per year is callable at $10,050; that is, the firm can cancel the bond at any time by paying $10,050 to whoever owns the bond at that time. The amount of money that the firm must pay in order to cancel the bond is the *call price* of the bond. A simple calculation will show that the firm can improve its position by borrowing the call price of $10,050 from the bank, at 2%, and using that money to call the bond away from its current owner. In effect, the firm pays $50 for the opportunity to refinance the $10,000 loan at 2% rather than at 4%.

A loan that is secured by a mortgage on a residence is analogous to a callable corporate bond. To borrow from a bank, the homeowner sells a bond to the bank. The bond requires the homeowner to make regular payments to the bank. To guarantee the payments, the homeowner gives the bank a mortgage, which entitles the bank to acquire title to the house should the homeowner fail to make the required payments on time.[8] In most cases, the seller of the bond (the homeowner) has the right to cancel the bond at any time, without notice or penalty, by paying the balance due on the loan (including accrued interest, if any). The bond is thus callable by the homeowner, and the call price is the current outstanding balance on the loan. In the late 1990s and early 2000s, many homeowners refinanced their mortgaged loans as interest rates fell. In doing so, the homeowners called their existing bonds by paying off the balances of the loans, then issued new bonds (i.e., took out new mortgaged loans) at lower interest rates.

We conclude that small quantities of IBM common stock are highly liquid: the price of the asset will not be affected by the speed at which the transaction is conducted. But as the size of the transaction increases, the liquidity of the asset decreases.

Finally, consider a checking account in a bank. This account is defined in terms of dollars. A typical depositor can, without notice to the bank, redeem any part of the balance, or all of it, for cash. Compare this to a certificate of deposit at a bank. A certificate of deposit is an agreement by which a bank will pay a fixed rate of interest to a depositor who intends to leave a fixed amount of money on deposit for a fixed amount of time. In most cases, the depositor may withdraw the deposit (liquidate the certificate) only by forfeiting a portion of the interest that has accrued. Thus, certificates of deposit pay higher rates of interest than do checking accounts (many of which pay no interest), but certificates of deposit are less liquid.

There are two reasons why liquidity matters. One reason is that intertemporal exchanges involve claims on future payoffs, and the future is uncertain. The second reason is that some investment projects require large infusions of resources at the outset, and thereafter generate very long sequences of relatively small payments. The more liquidity financial markets provide, the larger the set of mutually beneficial intertemporal exchanges that individuals can conduct. Therefore, greater liquidity in financial securities increases the opportunities for individuals to increase their levels of lifetime utility.

Here is an example. The Mosquito Point Barge Company wants to purchase a new tugboat. With the new tugboat, the company can offer faster and more reliable service, and thus (it hopes) obtain higher profits. But the company does not have sufficient funds of its own to purchase the new tugboat.

Mr. Apple is willing to finance the Mosquito Point Barge Company's investment project by reducing his current consumption below his current income. He will obtain a financial security, which is a saleable claim on the uncertain sequence of future payoffs that the project will generate. But there is another source of uncertainty. Mr. Apple has aging parents. They might be able to care for themselves in their own home until they die, but they might not. Thus, Mr. Apple might want to purchase full-time care for them, and on relatively short notice. The more liquid the financial security offered by the barge company, the lower the cost that Mr. Apple will incur if he decides to sell the security on short notice. Thus, the more liquid the security, the more easily the barge company can finance its project. But any investment project involves an intertemporal exchange. We conclude that liquidity promotes intertemporal exchanges, and thus enables individuals to increase their levels of lifetime utility.

Consider another example. The Spring Lake Railroad wants to build a tunnel. The tunnel will enable the railroad to move freight trains more quickly between two major cities and thus generate a relatively small increase in profit each year. The tunnel will be extremely expensive to build, but it will last indefinitely with little maintenance. The railroad cannot finance the construction of the tunnel with its own funds.

No investor plans to live long enough to justify helping to finance the tunnel in exchange for a right to receive an indefinitely long sequence of relatively small payments. But if the investors can obtain financial securities, each investor can hold the security for some number of years, then sell it to a younger investor. The older is compatible with the *average* quality of the automobiles that are for sale. For example, suppose that the buyer is a taxicab company that purchases large numbers of used automobiles each year. If the quality ratings of the used automobiles offered for sale are uniformly distributed from 0 to 100, this company can expect that the average quality of the automobiles that it purchases each year will be equal to 50. Therefore, the price that the company will offer for any particular automobile will be based on the assumption that the quality of that automobile will be equal to 50.

Now consider the sellers of these used automobiles. Each seller knows the quality rating of each of his automobiles. Suppose that Mr. Black knows that the quality rating of his automobile is 75. Unless he can certify this quality to prospective buyers, he will have to accept a price based on a quality rating of only 50. The alternative is to withdraw his offer to sell the automobile. The same situation faces half of the prospective sellers, who know that the quality ratings of their automobiles exceed 50. In Akerlof's model, half of the prospective sellers will therefore withdraw from the market because they know that the market will underprice their automobiles. Consequently, the automobiles offered for sale have quality ratings that range from 0 to only 50. Although the prospective buyers cannot determine the quality of any particular automobile, they do know the distribution of quality ratings. Therefore, the buyers can anticipate that the average quality rating of the automobiles offered for sale will be equal to 25, not 50.

Buyers will then revise the price that they are willing to pay downward to a value that is compatible with a quality rating of 25. This downward revision of the buyers' prices will cause the sellers to withdraw those automobiles that have quality ratings between 25 and 50, and the price that buyers will offer will decrease further. This process is degenerative. In the limit, the market collapses because no seller can expect to obtain a fair price for an automobile.

In Akerlof's model, the market fails because there are potential mutually beneficial exchanges that are not realized. The failure of the market occurs because there is asymmetric information between buyers and sellers, and the sellers have no way to transmit their information credibly to the buyers.

Consider again Mr. Black, whose automobile has a quality rating of 75. Suppose that Mr. Black has a strong preference for new automobiles. Specifically, he is willing to sell his current automobile for a price that would be appropriate for a quality rating of 65, so that he could apply the proceeds of that sale toward the purchase of a new automobile. Ms. Green, on the other hand, would be willing to pay more than what Mr. Black is willing to accept if she can be certain that the quality rating of his automobile is 75. If Mr. Black could credibly transmit his information to Ms. Green, they could conclude a mutually beneficial exchange. But in the absence of a way to eliminate the asymmetry of the information, the potential for mutual gain will be foregone, and thus the market will fail. Only by eliminating the effects of the asymmetric information will the market be able to promote an efficient allocation of resources.

2.4.2 A Simple Example of Asymmetric Information and Economic Inefficiency for a Firm

We present a simple example of how asymmetric information between a firm and prospective new investors can create an inefficient allocation of resources. Assume first that the only kind of security that a firm can issue is common stock. Firms have prospective profitable projects but lack sufficient internal funds with which to finance them. Being profitable,[14] the new projects could provide a mutually beneficial exchange between new investors, who would finance the projects by purchasing newly created shares of common stock, and the firms' current shareholders. Before the firm sells newly created shares, the current shareholders own 100% of the firm.

By purchasing newly created shares, the new investors provide additional resources to the firm. In exchange, the new investors acquire a portion of the ownership of the firm from the current shareholders. Whether the new investors gain or lose wealth depends on (1) the value of the resources that the new investors transfer to the firm by purchasing the new shares, (2) the amount by which the value of the firm will increase once the new project is undertaken, and (3) the proportion of the ownership of the firm transferred from the current shareholders to the new investors. The prospective new investors have reason to fear that firms will exploit their superior information so that the combined effect of factors (1), (2), and (3) will transfer wealth from the new investors to the current shareholders, thus imposing a net loss on the new investors. Consequently, the prospective new investors will not purchase the new shares, the firms cannot undertake the projects, and the profit that could have been shared by the new investors and the current shareholders is foregone. Since potential mutually beneficial exchanges are foregone, resources are allocated inefficiently; there is a deadweight loss.

Consider another example. There is a large number of firms in the economy, half of which are strong firms and half of which are weak firms. Each firm will survive for exactly one more year, after which it will be rendered worthless. During that final year, each strong firm will generate earnings equal to $150 from its regular operations. Each weak firm will generate only $50 from its regular operations.

Each strong firm and each weak firm has an opportunity to invest in a new project that will increase that firm's earnings for its final year. The cost of the new project is $100 for each firm. A strong firm can use the new project to increase its earnings by $120. A weak firm can generate only $110 in additional earnings from the project. The management of each firm knows whether that firm is strong or weak. No one else can discover whether a particular firm is strong or weak until the end of the final year. Assume that the bank's interest rate is zero.[15] Since the project costs only $100, every firm has an incentive to undertake the project. Alas, each firm has paid out in dividends to its shareholders all of its earnings from previous years; consequently, no firm has any idle cash with which to finance new projects.

Because no firm has idle cash, a firm must sell new shares of stock to raise the $100 required to start the project. If a firm sells new shares and undertakes the project, two things will occur. First, the value of the firm will increase because the project is profitable. Second, once the new shares are issued, the proportion of the firm owned by the current shareholders will decrease by the proportion of the firm that the new shareholders acquire. The new shareholders will own a proportion of the *entire* firm, including the new project. Their claim is not limited to the earnings of that project. If the proportion of the firm acquired by the new shareholders is too large relative to the value of the new project, the current shareholders will lose wealth as a consequence of financing the project by issuing new shares.

We will now show that with the numerical values in the present example, current shareholders in a strong firm will forego the new project even though it is profitable. If an allocation of resources leaves a profitable project lying idle, that allocation is economically inefficient. There is at least one alternative allocation that would increase the wealth of some persons without decreasing the wealth of any person.

Due to the asymmetry of the information, the new investors will regard any firm that tries to finance a new project as if that firm were an average of a strong firm and a weak firm. Therefore, the proportion of the firm that the new investors will insist on acquiring will exceed the proportion that they would accept if they could be certain that the firm is a strong firm. The current shareholders in a strong firm will forego the new project because the proportion of the firm that they would have to cede to new investors (to induce them to finance the project) is so large that the new investors' claim on the firm's earnings would exceed the earnings of the new project.

The first step in demonstrating this result is to determine the total market value of a firm's shares. We will proceed by considering three alternate situations: in the first situation, no firm invests in the new project; in the second situation, each firm undertakes the new project and finances it by issuing bonds; and in the third situation, each firm attempts to finance the project by selling new shares. In all three situations, only the managers of each firm know whether that firm is strong or weak.

Consider the situation in which no firm undertakes the project. In this case, no firm will issue any new securities because there is no reason to raise additional financing. Therefore, each firm's current shareholders will have sole claim to the firm's earnings. The total market value of a strong firm's shares will be $150. A weak firm's shares will be worth $50. No investor can discover whether a firm is strong or weak until the end of the final year. Therefore, at the beginning of that year investors will evaluate each firm as if it were an average of strong and weak firms. Accordingly, if no firm undertakes the project, the total market value of a firm's shares will be (150+50)/2, or $100.

Next, suppose that every firm undertakes the project and finances it by selling $100 worth of bonds. Each firm will repay the bonds by using part of the earnings from the new project. The bonds will be riskless because even a weak firm can generate $110 from the project. The net earnings of a strong firm, after repaying the bondholders, will be $150+$120−$100=$170. The net earnings for a weak firm will be $50+$110−$100=$60. In each case, the net earnings will accrue to the shareholders. Since investors will evaluate each firm's shares as if that firm were an average of a strong and a weak firm, the total market value of a firm's shares at the beginning of the year will be ($170+$60)/2=$115.

The new project is profitable, whether it is undertaken by a weak firm or by a strong firm. The average profit across the two kinds of firms is:

$$\frac{(120-100)+(110-100)}{2} = \frac{20+10}{2} = 15. \tag{2.1}$$

Every investor knows that the average increase in the wealth of shareholders whose firms undertake the project and finance it with bonds will be $15. If investors believe that every firm will sell bonds and undertake the project, then competition among investors will set the total market value of each firm's shares equal to $115.

Finally, suppose that each firm attempts to finance the project by selling new shares. The new shareholders will acquire a claim to a proportion of the firm's total earnings, not just the earnings from the new project. A strong firm will generate earnings equal to $150+$120, or $270; a weak firm will generate $50+$110, or $160. For each firm, the new shareholders who contributed the $100 to finance the project will not recover their investment directly, as do the bondholders in the preceding case. Rather, the new shareholders must rely on obtaining a sufficiently large proportion of the ownership of the firm through their purchase of new shares.

When the firm sells new shares at the beginning of the year to finance the project, the value of those new shares is $100, because that is the amount of new financing raised. Again, investors will evaluate each firm as if it were the average of the two kinds of firms. Then the total value of all the shares, current and new, in a firm will be $(270+160)/2=215$. Therefore, the proportion of a firm that the new shareholders own is $(100/215)$; the old shareholders own the proportion $(115/215)$ of the firm. Therefore, to finance the new project by selling new shares, the old shareholders must cede $(100/215)$ of the firm to new investors. Of course, the firm is now more profitable because it has the new project. The question for the old shareholders is: will raising $100 by selling new shares allow the new investors to acquire such a large proportion of the firm that the old shareholders will lose wealth to the new shareholders? We address this question next.

If a strong firm does not undertake the new project, its earnings will be limited to its regular earnings of $150. Without the project, there is no need to sell new shares. Therefore, the old shareholders are the only shareholders. They will receive the entire $150, which appears in the upper right-hand corner of table 2.1. The zero in the lower right-hand corner indicates that there is no payment to new shareholders (because there are no new shareholders).

The left-hand column of table 2.1 records the payoffs to old and new shareholders in the case that the strong firm does undertake the project. To finance the project, the old shareholders must cede $(100/215)$ of the firm to new shareholders. The old shareholders will retain $(115/215)$ of the firm. Total earnings for the firm will be $150 from regular earnings plus $120 from the project, for a total of $270. The old shareholders will receive $(115/215)$ of $270, or $144.42. New shareholders will receive $(100/215)$ of $270, or $125.58. Reading from the top row in table 2.1, it is clear that the managers of a strong firm will serve their old shareholders better by declining the project.

Table 2.1
Payoffs for a Strong Firm

	Does Undertake the Project	Does Not Undertake the Project
Old shareholders	$\dfrac{115}{215}$ ($150 + $120) = $144.42	$150
New shareholders	$\dfrac{100}{215}$ ($150 + $120) = $125.58	$0

Table 2.2
Payoffs for a Weak Firm

	Does Undertake the Project	Does Not Undertake the Project
Old shareholders	$\dfrac{115}{215}$ ($50 + $110) = $85.58	$50
New shareholders	$\dfrac{100}{215}$ ($50 + $110) = $74.41	$0

In table 2.2, we report the payoffs for a weak firm. The top row in table 2.2 shows that managers of weak firms will serve their old shareholders better by accepting the project.

How do the new shareholders fare? The lower right-hand corners of tables 2.1 and 2.2 are irrelevant; if the firms do not undertake the project, there are no new shareholders.

New shareholders invest $100, whether the firm undertaking the new project is strong or weak. Comparing the lower left-hand corners of the two tables, we see that the investment of $100 in a strong firm returns $125.58; the same investment in a weak firm returns only $74.41. Unfortunately, new investors cannot distinguish between strong and weak firms when the new shares are offered. But if all firms, strong and weak, undertake the new project, then new investors who diversify across several firms can count on receiving an average of (approximately) $100, because ($125.58+$74.41)/2=$99.995.

Strong firms will not undertake the project; if a strong firm sells enough new shares to finance the project, the payoff to the old shareholders will decrease from $150 to $144.42. In a strong firm, the project will transfer wealth from the old shareholders to the new shareholders.

In a weak firm, the project will transfer wealth in the other direction, from new shareholders to old shareholders. The new shareholders invest $100 and receive only $74.41; the old shareholders increase their payoff from $50 to $85.58.

Although investors cannot distinguish between strong and weak firms, they can recognize that only the weak firms have an incentive to offer new shares to finance the project. Therefore, investors will evaluate any firm that offers new shares as a weak firm. The total market value of the old and new shares of a weak firm will be $60+$110=$170. Since the new shareholders will invest $100, the value of their shares will be $100, and therefore the new shareholders will own (100/170) of the firm. The payoff to the new shareholders will then be (100/170)(170), or $100. Since the new shareholders will just recoup their investment, with no profit, they will be indifferent to financing the project.

Strong firms will not be able to finance the project without transferring wealth away from their current shareholders. New investors will assume that any firm that offers to sell new shares is a weak firm. Therefore, new investors will insist on acquiring (100/170) of any firm in which they invest $100 by purchasing new shares. If a strong firm cedes the proportion (100/170) to new investors, the old shareholders will retain only (70/170) of the firm. Total earnings for the strong firm (including the project) will be $150+$120=$270. The old shareholders will receive

$(70/170)(\$270) = (.41)(\$270) = \$110.70$, which is less than the \$150 they will get if their firm declines the project.

We have now established that resources can be allocated inefficiently if there is asymmetric information between managers of firms and shareholders (both current and prospective). Strong firms cannot credibly identify themselves as strong firms to prospective investors. Consequently, projects that would return \$120 (in a strong firm) for an investment of only \$100 are foregone.

It is easy to show that a strong firm could increase profits for both old and new shareholders if the firm could communicate credibly with prospective investors, thereby eliminating the asymmetric information. Without the new project, the old shareholders will receive 100% of \$150. Let Z be the proportion of the firm that the old shareholders will retain after the firm raises \$100 by selling new shares. Total earnings for a strong firm with the project will be \$270. Consequently, the old shareholders will gain wealth even though new shareholders are present if $Z(\$270)>\$150$, or

$$Z > \frac{\$150}{\$270} = .556 \qquad (2.2)$$

If old shareholders retain the proportion Z of the firm, then new shareholders will acquire the proportion $1-Z$. Since the new shareholders will have invested \$100, they will gain wealth if

$$
\begin{aligned}
&(1-Z)(\$270) > \$100, \text{ or} \\
&\$270 - \$100 > Z\$270, \text{ or} \\
&\frac{\$270 - \$100}{\$270} > Z, \text{ or} \\
&.63 > Z
\end{aligned}
\qquad (2.3)
$$

We conclude that the managers of a strong firm can create a mutually beneficial exchange between old and new shareholders if the old shareholders retain more than 55.6%, but not more than 63%, of the firm.

2.5 The Problem of Agency

In the preceding section on asymmetric information, the market failed to realize some mutually beneficial exchanges because of an inability of some persons to transmit information credibly to other persons. If the firm's investors and its managers were the same persons, this asymmetry would not arise. In this section, we briefly consider a second problem that arises from the separation of investors and managers. This is the problem of agency.

Agency is a relationship between two persons, or groups of persons. One person, called the principal, provides the resources for an enterprise and employs a second person, called the agent, to operate the enterprise. The principal not only determines broad policies for the agent to follow but also allows the agent some flexibility in administering these policies. The problem of agency is that the agent might exploit the flexibility provided by the principal by administering the enterprise so as to favor his or her own interests rather than those of the principal.

For example, a principal purchases a motel and employs an agent to manage it. In addition to renting rooms and collecting revenue, the agent is obligated to find economical ways to purchase supplies and supervise the staff so as to maintain the reputation of the motel as clean, safe, and friendly. The principal allows the agent to illuminate the No Vacancy sign at a "reasonable" time. The principal pays the agent a fixed salary that does not depend on the motel's occupancy rate.

The agent has a conflict of interest with the principal. It is clearly unreasonable for the principal to expect the agent to remain awake every night until the last room is rented and then work regular hours the next day. Indeed, on some nights the motel will remain below full occupancy throughout the night. On the other hand, few principals would be satisfied to have the No Vacancy sign illuminated at 5:00 P.M. every day, regardless of how many rooms remain vacant. What will the agent do? What should the principal expect the agent to do? The agent's behavior will surely affect the principal's return on investment. It is naive to expect that the agent will resolve in the principal's favor every instance in which there is a conflict of interest. This fact will make any potential rate of return from the motel less attractive. If the problem of agency is sufficiently severe, the principal will not invest, with the possibility that some mutually beneficial exchanges will not be realized.

Consider a second example. In this example, the interests of a firm's managers will cause them to diversify the firm's investments across projects to an extent that is not compatible with the interests of the firm's shareholders.

Most investors diversify their holdings over several firms' securities. By doing so, investors can reduce the amplitude of the unpredictable variability of the rate of return on their invested funds, without reducing the average rate of return on those funds. This is possible because it is highly unlikely that every firm's earnings will increase by the same percentage or decrease by the same percentage in the same year. A firm's earnings are subject to two kinds of unpredictable forces. One kind of force affects single firms or single industries, without affecting the entire economy. An example of this would be a shift of consumers' preferences away from dining and entertainment outside of the home, in favor of spending more time in the home. The other kind of force affects all firms in the economy, but not to the same degree. An example of this would be a decision of the Federal Reserve Board to change interest rates.

Most large firms operate several investment projects simultaneously. Portfolio theory, which we present in chapter 8, indicates that these firms face a trade-off between the average rate of return on their capital and the variability of that rate of return. To a limited extent, a firm can decrease the variability of its rate of return, without decreasing its average rate of return, by choosing projects whose individual rates of return are not highly correlated with each other. But once the firm has chosen projects that will minimize the variability of its rate of return while producing a given average rate of return, any further decrease in variability requires that the firm accept a reduction in its average rate of return.

The firm's shareholders and its managers have a conflict of interest with regard to choosing the combination of the firm's average rate of return and the volatility of that rate of return. Managers' wealth consists of a portfolio of financial securities *and* the market value of their reputation as managers. The financial securities can generate income, either now or when the managers retire. Their reputations will affect their ability to secure another managerial position should they lose their current position or desire to move elsewhere. The greater the volatility of the firm's rate of return, the greater the risk that a manager could lose his or her position. Therefore, the greater the importance of the manager's reputation as a component of her wealth, the stronger the incentive to choose investment projects that will reduce the volatility of the firm's rate of return, even if this will reduce the firm's average rate of return.

For example, suppose the firm has debt in its capital structure. Debt requires that the firm make periodic payments of interest, regardless of whether the firm's earnings at the time that the interest payments are due are high or low. The greater the volatility of the firm's earnings, the greater the risk that the firm will have trouble making the interest payments. If the firm encounters this kind of difficulty, the manager's reputation might suffer.

A typical shareholder will not have his or her wealth as heavily concentrated in the firm as the firm's managers do, because reputation is not an issue for the shareholder. The shareholder will create an investment portfolio by purchasing the securities of several firms, just as a single firm will operate a portfolio of investment projects. Therefore, the shareholder is in a situation that is analogous, but not identical, to the situation of a single firm. Within limits, the firm can reduce the volatility of its rate of return by diversifying its investments across projects whose rates of return are not highly correlated. Similarly, shareholders can reduce the volatility of the rate of return on their portfolios by diversifying their investments across firms whose rates of return are not highly correlated. Both the firm and the shareholder can reduce the volatilities of their rates of return by accepting a decrease in their average rates of return.

Shareholders, however, enjoy a more favorable trade-off between the average rate of return and the volatility of the rate of return than does the firm. By making investments in several firms, shareholders can diversify their portfolios across the aggregate of all the projects undertaken by all of the firms. Since shareholders can diversify over a larger set of projects than any one firm can, they can reduce the volatility of their rate of return while incurring a smaller sacrifice in the average rate of return than a single firm can.

Since managers have a higher concentration of wealth, including their reputation, invested in the firm than the typical shareholders do, managers have a stronger incentive to reduce the volatility of the firm's rate of return than its shareholders do. Therefore, managers and shareholders will often have different preferences about the projects in which the firm should invest.

2.6   Financial Markets and Informational Efficiency

2.6.1   Information and Mutually Beneficial Exchanges

We have seen that the economic function of financial markets is to facilitate mutually beneficial intertemporal exchanges. One element of this function is to reduce the costs of learning about opportunities to make these exchanges. Financial markets reduce these costs by creating a set of equilibrium prices for an extensive variety of financial securities.

We know that a financial security is a saleable right to receive a sequence of payments. These sequences of payments are the results of intertemporal exchanges. Since the exchanges are intertemporal, the payments necessarily involve both waiting and risk. In equilibrium, the relative prices of these securities enable investors to evaluate the underlying intertemporal exchanges on the basis of waiting and risk. By extension, individuals can use the prices of existing financial securities to identify opportunities for new mutually beneficial exchanges.

In later chapters, we explain how individuals can use the relative prices of existing securities to identify prospects for new exchanges. For now, however, we will address the economic efficiency and the informational content of the prices of financial securities.

Any system of markets can be evaluated by its contribution to economic efficiency. We recall that economic efficiency is an allocation of resources in which there are no further opportunities for mutually beneficial exchanges. Financial markets contribute to economic efficiency by creating a set of relative prices for financial securities that contain information about mutually beneficial intertemporal exchanges. If financial markets are to be economically efficient, then the information about the potential costs and benefits in prospective intertemporal exchanges that is contained in the prices of financial securities must be comprehensive and accurate. That is to say, the information must be such that there are no potential beneficial exchanges that are foregone. We say that financial markets are *informationally efficient* if the information contained in the prices of securities is comprehensive and accurate in the sense just described.

2.6.2 The Efficient Markets Hypothesis

Definition of the Efficient Markets Hypothesis
The efficient markets hypothesis states that the current price of each financial security accurately reflects all the information that is known today about the sequence of future payments that will accrue to an investor who owns that security.

The information includes the distribution of those payments over time, and the amplitude of their unpredictable variability. If the efficient markets hypothesis is true, then each security will be priced so that its expected rate of return will provide an investor who holds that security with the equilibrium levels of compensation for waiting and for bearing risk. There will be no mispriced securities. Consequently, if the efficient markets hypothesis holds, it will be impossible for an investor to find a security whose rate of return will, on average, outperform the market after allowing for waiting and for bearing risk.

Consider this simple example of how the efficient markets hypothesis would affect the price of a security. The Mosquito Point Barge Company has a long record of paying its shareholders an annual dividend equal to $2 per share. Banks pay interest at the rate of 10% per year on deposits. An investor can, therefore, purchase an income equal to

$2 per year by depositing $20 in a bank. One share of common stock in the barge company will also generate an annual income equal to $2 per year. A straightforward application of opportunity cost then implies that the equilibrium price of a share in the Mosquito Point Barge Company will be $20. Since the two assets generate identical incomes, the prices of the assets must be equal.

Now suppose that the Mosquito Point Barge Company has unexpectedly received a contract with the Weedsport Fertilizer Plant that will enable the barge company to increase its annual dividend to shareholders from $2 to $3, beginning two years from now. Once the company begins paying dividends at the rate of $3 per year, the price of a share of its common stock will be equal to $30, because an investor would have to maintain in a bank a deposit equal to $30 to generate an annual income of $3. Although the higher dividend will appear two years from now, the information that the dividend will increase is available now. The efficient markets hypothesis requires that the price of a share in the barge company begin to increase immediately to reflect the information that the dividend will increase from $2 to $3 two years from now. The price of the share will not increase immediately from $20 all the way to $30 because the higher dividend rate will not appear immediately. Instead, the price will increase steadily from $20 to $30 during the time remaining until the new dividend comes into effect.

In the preceding example, the information about the new contract with the fertilizer company appeared all at once, not in small bits over time. Under the efficient markets hypothesis, investors must have been surprised by this information. Had investors anticipated the information, the price of the barge company's common stock would already have reflected the increase in future dividends.

Consider a second example of how the efficient markets hypothesis would affect the price of a security. Investors in the Mosquito Point Barge Company will recognize that the company's ability to pay dividends will depend on its ability to maintain contracts with its current customers and win new customers. Changes in taxes on profits and in the price of fuel will also affect the company's ability to pay dividends. Under the efficient markets hypothesis, the price of a share of common stock in the Mosquito Point Barge Company will reflect at each moment all the information then known about what might happen to future dividends. For example, suppose that the Spring Lake Railroad is competing with the barge company for the business of shipping fertilizer. If the efficient markets hypothesis holds, then the price of the barge company's common stock will change to reflect changes in the probabilities that the railroad will win the contract to ship the fertilizer.

2.6.3 The Joint Hypothesis

The efficient markets hypothesis states that the current prices of financial securities are such that the expected rate of return on each security will provide the equilibrium level of compensation for the waiting and the risk that an investor who holds that security must bear. This means that any empirical test of the efficient markets hypothesis is conditional on a second hypothesis that specifies the equilibrium relationship among expected rates of return, waiting, and levels of risk. Further, this second hypothesis must specify how we are to quantify these risks.

There are several alternative models of equilibrium in financial markets. The seminal model is the capital asset pricing model, which we will study in chapter 9. In this model, the quantity of risk in a security is measured by the correlation between its rate of return and the rate of return on a special portfolio that contains all the securities in the market. But the capital asset pricing model is only one of several alternatives that economists have studied as descriptions of equilibrium in financial markets.

The empirical test of the efficient markets hypothesis depends on whether security prices reflect information with sufficient accuracy so that investors cannot, on average, outperform the market by finding securities that will provide rates of return exceeding the equilibrium levels of compensation for waiting and for bearing risk. But the measurement of these equilibrium levels of compensation is conditional on the model of equilibrium that the economist chooses. Therefore, the efficient markets hypothesis is one part of a *joint hypothesis.* If investors could outperform the market by using a particular strategy, there are always two competing explanations between which the economist cannot distinguish. One explanation is that the efficient markets hypothesis does not hold; there is information about future earnings that is not accurately reflected in current prices. That is, investors can find securities that are mispriced. The competing explanation would be that the economist is using the wrong model to define the equilibrium relationship among expected rates of return, waiting, and risk.[16] We shall encounter the joint hypothesis throughout the later chapters in this book when we consider empirical studies of financial markets.

Problems

1. A firm has a reputation of highly volatile earnings. What incentive would an investor have to buy a convertible bond?

2. One year ago a firm issued bonds. Today, the Fed lowered the rates of interest. Why might it have been beneficial for a firm to have included a callable feature in the bonds that it issued last year?

3. Consider a market in which half of all firms are weak firms and the other half are strong. There is no way for an investor to distinguish between firms that are strong and firms that are weak. At the end of the present year, all firms will be liquidated.

Each firm currently has an investment opportunity. Assume that no firm has cash on hand to finance the investment.

The interest rate is zero. The structure of each firm is specified in the table below:

Firm Type	Liquidation Values Next Year without the Project	Liquidation Values Next Year with the Project	Cost of the Project
Strong	$150	$260	$90
Weak	$50	$150	$90

A. If each firm finances the project by selling bonds, determine for each firm the increase in its shareholders' wealth, and the total market value of the firm's shares.

B. If each firm could finance the project by issuing additional shares, which type of firm would undertake the project?

C. How could an investor use a firm's financing strategy to determine if that firm is strong or weak?

Notes

1. If the issuer of a bond creates a default, that issuer is said to be *in default* (of his obligations under the bond).

2. The term *mortgage* is commonly used, incorrectly, as a synonym for a loan to purchase a house. In fact, the mortgage is not the loan; the mortgage is a lien issued to the bank by the homeowner on the property as a means of guaranteeing that the homeowner will meet the obligations specified by the bond. A loan secured by a mortgage is a *mortgaged loan*.

3. The additional $1,400,000 is only a potential adjustment for the increase in risk. Should the railroad miss any of the promised payments, the investors would not receive the full $1,400,000. Should the railroad be late with any payments, the investors would lose the interest that they could have earned by depositing the payments in a bank, had the payments been made on time.

We conclude that the price that the railroad will have to pay to finance a locomotive will depend on the risks perceived by the investors to whom the railroad would sell the bonds. The higher the perceived risks, the more bonds the railroad will have to sell to raise the $11,000,000. Since each bond requires the railroad to repay $1,400,000 over 10 years, an increase in risk raises the cost to the railroad of financing the purchase of the locomotive. For a sufficiently high level of risk, purchasing the locomotive will cease to be a profitable investment project.

4. If there has been an increase in the risk perceived by investors generally between the time that the investor purchased the bond and the time that he wants to sell it, the price that the investor will have to accept for the bond might not be high enough to allow him to recover his investment fully.

5. We will see in section 2.5 and in chapter 13 that the inability of the shareholders to monitor the directors perfectly creates incentives for the directors to pursue their own interests to the detriment of the shareholders' interests. This conflict of interests, and the shareholders' attempts to mitigate it, is called the *problem of agency*.

6. A firm can have two kinds of stock, common and preferred. Owners of preferred stock have a contractual right to receive a specified sequence of payments subject to the adequacy of the firm's earnings to make those payments after the firm makes the payments promised to its bondholders. Unlike the bondholders, the owners of the preferred stock have no legal recourse in the event that the firm's earnings are insufficient to make the promised payments on the preferred shares. Further, the owners of the preferred shares (usually) do not have the right to vote for directors. Thus, bonds, shares of preferred stock, and shares of common stock form a hierarchy among investors who hold claims to the firm's earnings. The bondholders have the highest priority, owners of the preferred shares come next, and owners of the common stock come last. However, as contractual claimants, the owners of the bonds and the preferred stock have an upper limit on the payments that they can receive. As residual claimants, the owners of the common stock are entitled to whatever earnings remain after the other two classes of claimants

are paid. Therefore, once the earnings are sufficient to pay the contractual claims, any growth in the earnings accrues entirely to the owners of the common stock. Since bonds and preferred stock are both forms of a contractual claim, we shall not discuss preferred stock separately.

7. We ignore the effect of quarterly compounding on the calculation of the interest rate.

8. The mortgage is not the loan. The mortgage is the lien that the borrower places on the house to guarantee repayment of the loan.

9. Beginning several years ago, investors can also buy and sell many securities from dealers who operate during hours when the organized exchanges are closed. It is also possible to trade on foreign exchanges in the securities of American firms.

10. At 12:20 P.M. on June 23, 2004, the bid price for IBM was $90.52, and the asked price was $90.54. The spread between the bid and asked for IBM is low because the volume of trading in that stock is large.

11. Harold Demsetz introduced the term *predictable immediacy* in analyzing the economics of dealers on organized securities exchanges. H. Demsetz, "The Cost of Transacting," *Quarterly Journal of Economics* 82, no. 1 (1968): 33–53.

12. G. A. Akerlof, "The Market for 'Lemons': Quality Uncertainty and the Market Mechanism," *Quarterly Journal of Economics* 84, no. 3 (1970): 488–500.

13. S. C. Myers and N. Majluf, "Corporate Financing and Investment Decisions When Firms Have Information That Investors Do Not," *Journal of Financial Economics* 13 (1984): 187–221.

14. A *profitable* project is one that generates future earnings that are sufficiently large, and that occur sufficiently soon, to provide the investors who finance the project with returns that exceed what those investors could have obtained by financing alternative projects. The *value* of a firm is the amount of money for which a group of investors could purchase the entire firm, and thus obtain exclusive rights to all the firm's earnings. By undertaking a profitable investment, the firm will increase its value. We discuss the relationship between profitability and value in detail in chapter 3, where we explain the concept of net present value of a sequence of payments.

15. This unrealistic assumption simplifies the arithmetic without affecting the qualitative economic conclusion.

16. There is a third possibility: both the efficient markets hypothesis fails and the economist is using the wrong model of equilibrium.

Part II

Intertemporal Allocation by Consumers and Firms When Future Payments Are Certain

3 The Fundamental Economics of Intertemporal Allocation

3.1 The Plan of the Chapter

The fundamental economic objective of every person is to allocate her scarce resources among various alternatives so as to maximize her lifetime utility. These alternatives include producing goods and services for current consumption, and producing goods that can be used as inputs for the production of goods and services in future years. The allocation of resources each year between these two kinds of production is the essence of intertemporal allocation.

Even if a person were living on a desert island, without contact with other persons with whom he could cooperate or trade, that person would still have to decide how to allocate his resources between the production of consumption goods and capital goods if he wanted to maximize his lifetime utility. A benefit of living in a society of individuals who cooperate and trade is that each individual can use mutually beneficial exchanges to reach higher levels of lifetime utility than he could reach if he did not cooperate and trade. The function of financial markets is to organize those intertemporal exchanges.

In this chapter, we develop the fundamental aspects of economics that explain the existence and operation of financial markets. To focus on the fundamentals, we consider a sequence of simple situations. Each situation, although a simplification of reality, contains the elements of intertemporal allocation. By examining these simple models first, we will be able to recognize more easily the fundamental economic aspects in the more complex situations that we address in later chapters.

We first examine a primitive economy in which there is no trading between persons. We then introduce the possibility of trade, but without the convenience of markets. We conclude the chapter by developing the concepts of income, wealth, and present values. These concepts are essential to understanding the economics of financial markets.

3.2 A Primitive Economy with No Trading

We can develop the essence of the economics of financial markets by first considering a primitive society in which individuals produce and consume in isolation from other consumers. There are no markets in this society, because there are no exchanges among consumers. Each person in this society owns a limited set of resources, which she uses to produce goods for her own consumption. These resources consist of the 24 hours that she has each day, her ability to work, her levels of various skills, some land that she cleared in previous years, and a few simple tools that she built in those years.

There are two kinds of goods that she can produce each year. First, she can produce goods, such as food, that she can consume that year. We will call these goods *consumption goods*. Leisure is also a consumption good. She can "produce" leisure simply by using some of her time to do nothing. Second, she can produce goods this year that she can use as factors of production in future years. We will call these goods *capital goods*. Examples of capital goods include tools that will increase her productivity in harvesting food, and ditches to irrigate land and thereby increase its productivity.

In any year, each person's stock of resources is insufficient to produce all of the goods that she would like to have. This relative scarcity of resources requires her to make two kinds of choices each year. First, she must allocate her limited resources between producing consumption goods and producing capital goods. Second, she must decide which consumption goods and which capital goods to produce, and in what quantities. We assume that her only reason to produce capital goods is to increase the quantity of consumption goods that she can produce in future years. Therefore, these two kinds of decisions each year will determine the sequence of consumption goods that she can enjoy over her lifetime. We assume that she will allocate her scarce resources so as to maximize her lifetime utility.

Students should recall from their introductory course in economics that every choice involves an opportunity cost. To produce food this year is to forego an opportunity to produce something else this year. Clearly, the production of leisure also has an opportunity cost.

We are particularly interested in intertemporal opportunity costs. Any unit of consumption goods produced this year requires resources that could have been used to produce capital goods this year. The larger a person's stock of capital goods, the greater the volumes of all goods, including consumption goods, that she can produce in future years. Therefore, the opportunity cost of any unit of consumption goods produced this year is the increase in the quantities of consumption goods that she will forego in future years as a consequence of not producing capital goods this year. This relationship is reversible. The (intertemporal) opportunity cost of a given increase in the future production of consumption goods is the quantity of current consumption goods that must be foregone in order to release sufficient resources to produce the capital goods that will be required to produce those future consumption goods.

3.2.1 Stocks, Flows, and Intertemporal Allocation

In economic analysis, it is important to distinguish between mathematical entities that are measured as *stocks* and those that are measured as *flows*. An entity is measured as a stock if its numerical magnitude does not involve the passing of time. An entity is measured as a flow if its numerical magnitude is a rate at which the magnitude of a stock increases (or decreases) over time.

Consider the following examples. The current balance in your checking account is measured as a stock; the rate at which you are increasing that balance by making deposits is measured as a flow. The balance today could be $1,600, and the rate at which you are increasing that balance by making deposits could be $300 per month. To say that your balance is $1,600 per day would not make sense; similarly, to say that you are making deposits of $300 would be ambiguous without specifying the rate at which you are making those deposits. Your balance will grow more rapidly if you make deposits at the rate of $300 per day, rather than $300 per month.

The unpaid balance on a mortgaged loan is measured as a stock; the rate at which you are reducing that balance by making monthly payments is measured as a flow. The national debt is measured as a stock; the national deficit, which is the rate at which the debt is increasing per year, is measured as a flow. The value of a person's investment in shares of IBM common stock is measured as a stock; the dividends paid on those shares are measured as a flow.

Capital goods are stocks of resources that are used to produce flows of consumption goods. Some capital goods produce consumption goods indirectly by making other capital goods more productive. For example, an irrigation ditch is a capital good that can increase the output of corn per acre of cleared land. The cleared land is also a capital good.

An *accumulated stock* of consumption goods is a special case of a capital good. A person could use a portion of his resources this year to produce food that he then stores for future consumption. The maximal quantity of corn that a person can consume in any year is equal to the sum of what he produces during that year plus the stock of corn that he has accumulated and stored from production in earlier years. An accumulated stock of corn increases the quantity of corn that he can consume in a given year beyond what he produces that year. Therefore, we can regard the accumulated (and thus not yet consumed) stock of corn as a capital good.

We conclude that by producing capital goods the person can, in effect, transfer resources from the present to the future. The fundamental purpose of financial markets is to enable consumers to create mutually beneficial exchanges that involve these intertemporal transfers of resources. Therefore, we will be able to appreciate the economics of financial markets more easily if we pause to consider some of the ways in which a consumer can effect these intertemporal transfers even when he produces and consumes in isolation from other consumers.

3.2.2   Example: Transferring Consumption from the Present to the Future by Storing Current Output

Our first example is transparent. Suppose that Farmer Harold owns 10 acres of tillable land, and suppose that on each acre he can produce either 50 bushels of corn or 25 bushels of oats. Farmer Harold allocates resources between the production of corn and the production of oats for the current year simply by choosing the portions of his land to use for each crop. The opportunity cost of one bushel of oats is two bushels of corn, and the opportunity cost of one bushel of corn is one-half of a bushel of oats. Unless Farmer Harold has chosen to use all of his land to produce oats, he can obtain an additional bushel of oats for consumption this year by reducing his production of corn by two bushels. He decides to transfer some land from the production of corn to the production of oats, and thus he transfers some of his consumption from corn to oats.

Now suppose that Farmer Harold wants to transfer consumption from the current year to a future year. Obviously, he cannot transfer land from one year to the next. Land saved from the production of corn this year is available for the production of oats in the same year. But Harold cannot save land from one year to the next in the sense that by leaving one of his 10 acres unplanted this year, he will have 11 acres to plant next year. It is impossible to move an acre of land from the present to the future.

But it is possible to accomplish the same effect by storing the output of an acre of land from one year to the next. If he consumes this year the quantity of oats and corn that he produces on 9 of his 10 acres, and stores the output that he produces on the tenth acre, then next year he can consume all that he produces on his 10 acres, plus the stored output of 1 acre. In effect, he will have transferred one acre from the present to the future.

3.2.3   Example: Transferring Consumption from the Present to the Future by Producing Capital Goods

For our second example, we consider a case in which the consumer allocates some of his resources this year to produce capital goods. The capital goods will increase the productivity of her resources in future years.

The quantities of oats and corn that Harold can produce this year depend on how much time Farmer Harold allocates to weeding those crops during the growing season. Suppose that he reduces the time that he allocates to weeding and uses that time to improve the drainage of those acres. This reallocation of his time will increase the productivity of those acres for future years and decrease the quantities of oats and corn that he will produce during the current year. Harold will have traded a decrease in his level of consumption in the current year for an increase in the levels of consumption that his land will support in future years. Therefore, Harold will have transferred consumption from the current year to future years.

We have just seen two examples of how a person could transfer consumption from the present to the future. It is also possible to transfer consumption from the future to the present.

3.2.4   Example: Transferring Consumption from the Future to the Present by Consuming Capital Goods

Assume that the farmer has allocated some of his resources in previous years to improving the productivity of those resources. For example, he could have improved the drainage of his fields. Similarly, he could have created tools that would improve his productivity in harvesting, or he could have constructed shelters for storing crops. In each of these three cases, the improvements will require maintenance. Drainage ditches will eventually become clogged, tools will become dull or worn out, and shelters will require repairs. Assume that these improvements to his resources will increase their productivity by more than the productivity lost by maintaining them. That is, the improvements provide a net gain in productivity.

The farmer could now transfer some consumption from the future to the present by neglecting the maintenance of the improvements that he created in previous years.

By neglecting maintenance, he can allocate all of his resources to current consumption. In the short run, this will enable the farmer to increase his current level of consumption. Of course in the longer run, the neglect of maintenance will reduce the productivity of his resources, which will reduce the levels at which he can consume in future years.[1]

3.3   A Primitive Economy with Trading, but with No Markets

We have seen that a person who produces and consumes in isolation from other persons can reallocate consumption between the present and the future. But there are limits to the ability to do this. In any given year, the person must use some of her resources (which can include previously accumulated stocks of consumption goods) to provide consumption goods: otherwise she would starve or succumb to the elements. Therefore, she can allocate something less than 100% of her resources to the production of new capital goods. Similarly, the size of her stock of capital goods limits the extent to which she can increase her current consumption by neglecting to maintain those capital goods.

In this section, we examine how two or more persons can expand their opportunities to reallocate consumption between the present and the future by trading with each other.

3.3.1   Trade Based on Comparative Advantage

A fundamental concept in economics is that two persons can both gain by specializing in their production according to the theory of comparative advantage, and then trading.[2] Here is a simple example.

Ms. Black and Mr. Green can produce both oats and corn. The production possibility frontiers for each person appear in figure 3.1. The combined frontier defines the economically efficient combinations of oats and corn that Ms. Black and Mr. Green can produce jointly if they allocate their resources according to their comparative advantages. The vertical intercept of the combined production possibility frontier is at 400 units of corn, which is the sum of the maximal amounts of corn that both persons can produce.

We see that Mr. Green is more productive than Ms. Black because his frontier lies further from the origin than hers does. The critical difference, however, between the two persons is that their frontiers have different *slopes*.

Now suppose that the two persons want to produce some oats and minimize the quantity of corn foregone by doing so. For every unit of oats that Ms. Black produces, she must forego producing two units of corn. Therefore, her opportunity cost of one unit of oats is two units of corn. Mr. Green's farm is different. For every unit of oats that he produces, he must forego five units of corn. His opportunity cost of a unit of oats is five units of corn. In terms of opportunity costs, Ms. Black is more efficient in producing oats. We say that Ms. Black has a comparative advantage over Mr. Green in producing oats.

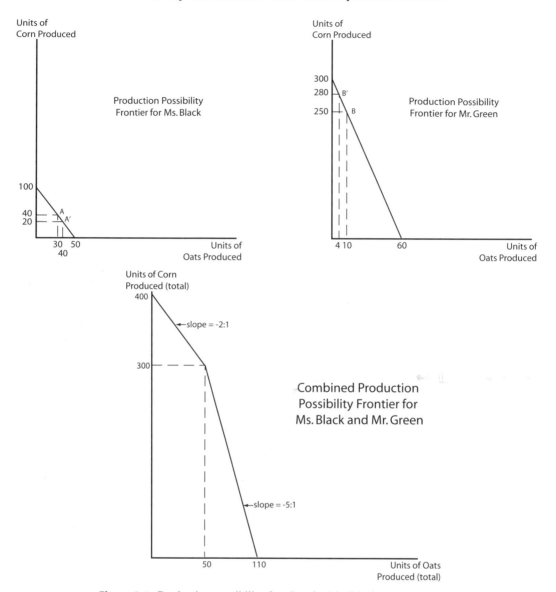

Figure 3.1. Production possibility frontiers for Ms. Black and Mr. Green.

Since Mr. Green's marginal cost of producing oats (in terms of corn foregone) is higher than the marginal cost that Ms. Black would incur to produce oats, Mr. Green should produce no oats unless Ms. Black has exhausted her capacity to produce oats. Therefore, the upper branch of the combined production possibility frontier in figure 3.1 is Ms. Black's frontier. Any increase in the quantity of oats produced beyond 50 units requires that Mr. Green produce some oats. Since Mr. Green's marginal cost for producing oats exceeds that of Ms. Black, the combined production possibility frontier becomes steeper at the point that corresponds to 50 units of oats.

A principle of comparative advantage is that if one person has a comparative advantage over a second person in producing oats (and foregoing corn), then the

Table 3.1
Marginal Costs for Ms. Black and Mr. Green to Produce Oats and Corn

Farmer	Marginal Cost of Oats (in Units of Corn)	Marginal Cost of Corn (in Units of Oats)
Ms. Black	2	$\frac{1}{2}$
Mr. Green	5	$\frac{1}{5}$

second person has a comparative advantage over the first person in producing corn (and foregoing oats). We have seen that Ms. Black has a comparative advantage in producing oats because her opportunity cost of oats is only two units of corn, and Mr. Green's opportunity cost of oats is five units of corn. By inverting these costs, we can see that Mr. Green has a comparative advantage in producing corn.

Mr. Green must forego five units of corn to produce one unit of oats. Conversely, he must forego one unit of oats to produce five more units of corn. Then by proportionality, he must forego only one-fifth of a unit of oats to produce one more unit of corn. Similarly, Ms. Black must forego one-half of a unit of oats to produce one more unit of corn. Since Mr. Green can produce one more unit of corn at a lower cost in terms of oats foregone than Ms. Black can, Mr. Green has a comparative advantage over Ms. Black in producing corn. In table 3.1 we show the comparative advantage of each farmer. Each farmer's marginal cost of producing oats is a constant quantity of corn foregone because that farmer's production possibility frontier is linear. Similarly, each farmer's marginal cost of producing corn is a constant quantity of oats foregone. The marginal costs for either good are different for the two farmers because the slopes of their frontiers are different.

It is easy to show that if Ms. Black and Mr. Green specialize in production according to comparative advantage, both persons can increase their consumption of both goods. Of course, this will require that the two persons trade.

Suppose that prior to specialization and trade, Ms. Black produces 30 units of oats and 40 units of corn each year. This allocation of her resources places her at Point A on her production possibility frontier in figure 3.1. Mr. Green allocates his resources to produce 10 units of oats and 250 units of corn each year, placing him at Point B on his frontier.

Now let Ms. Black move downward and rightward along her frontier to Point A′, where she will produce 40 units of oats and 20 units of corn. By moving from Point A to Point A′, Ms. Black increases her production of oats by 10 units and reduces her production of corn by 20 units. Mr. Green moves upward and leftward along his frontier to Point B′, where he will produce 4 units of oats and 280 units of corn. Mr. Green increases his production of corn by 30 units and reduces his production of oats by 6 units.

In table 3.2, we display the changes in the quantities of each good produced by each person. The bottom row of the table indicates that there are net increases in the quantities produced of both goods.

Table 3.2

Changes in Production and Consumption Made Possible by Reallocating Resources According to the Comparative Advantages of Ms. Black and Mr. Green

	Changes in Production		Possible Changes in Consumption	
	Oats	Corn	Oats	Corn
Ms. Black	+10	−20	+1	+7
Mr. Green	−6	+30	+3	+3
Net changes	+4	+10	+4	+10

There are several arrangements that will enable each person to consume a larger amount of each good. For example, Mr. Green could consume 3 of the 30 additional units of corn that he produces, and transfer to Ms. Black the remaining 27 units. Since Ms. Black reduced her production of corn by only 20 units, and receives 27 units from Mr. Green, she increases her consumption of corn by 7 units. Consequently, both persons increase their consumption of corn.

Simultaneously, both persons can consume larger quantities of oats. For example, if Ms. Black consumes 1 of the additional 10 units of oats that she produces, she can transfer to Mr. Green the remaining 9 units of oats. Since Mr. Green reduced his production of oats by 6 units, and receives 9 units from Ms. Black, he increases his consumption of oats by 3 units.

By reallocating their resources between the production of oats and corn in accordance with their comparative advantages, both Ms. Black and Mr. Green can enjoy higher levels of consumption of both goods without reducing their levels of consumption of any other good.

3.3.2 Trade Based on Differences in Intertemporal Marginal Rates of Substitution

If Ms. Black and Mr. Green differ in the rates at which they are willing to substitute between present and future consumption, they can also increase their levels of lifetime utility by borrowing and lending from each other.

Suppose that Ms. Black wants to transfer consumption from the future to the present by an amount that exceeds what her current resources will permit. She could accomplish this transfer by borrowing resources from Mr. Green this year. Next year (or in some future year, or several future years) Ms. Black will repay Mr. Green by transferring some of her resources to him. It is likely that Ms. Black will pay "interest" to Mr. Green by transferring to him a quantity of resources that exceeds the quantity that she borrowed.

Let X_1 be the maximal quantity of future consumption that Ms. Black is willing to forego for the privilege of increasing her current consumption by the quantity X_0. Similarly, let Z_1 be the minimal quantity of future consumption that Mr. Green is willing to accept as payment for decreasing his current consumption by X_0. If $Z_1 < X_1$, then Ms. Black and Mr. Green can both increase their levels of lifetime utility by

Table 3.3

A Mutually Beneficial Intertemporal Exchange between Ms. Black and Mr. Green at a Rate of Interest of 15%

	Ms. Black	Mr. Green
Current year	Borrows $100	Lends $100
Next year	Willing to repay $118	Willing to receive $110
	Does repay $115	Does receive $115
Net gains	$3	$5
Combined net gain: $3+$5=$8		

borrowing and lending. That is, Ms. Black and Mr. Green can undertake a mutually beneficial intertemporal exchange in which Mr. Green will transfer X_0 in current consumption to Ms. Black, and Ms. Black will transfer to Mr. Green a quantity of future consumption that is larger than Z_1 and less than X_1. The greater the difference between Z_1 and X_1, the greater the total amount by which the two persons can benefit from the exchange. The negotiations between Ms. Black and Mr. Green will determine the distribution of the total benefit between them.

Consider the following numerical example. Ms. Black wants to increase her current consumption to a level that exceeds her current income. To do so, she is willing to reduce her level of consumption next year by $118 in exchange for a $100 increase in her current level of consumption. Mr. Green is willing to forego $100 in current consumption in exchange for an increase of $110 in his level of consumption next year. Both Ms. Black and Mr. Green are willing to substitute between present and future consumption, but at different rates. Consequently, there can be a mutually beneficial intertemporal exchange. Let Mr. Green lend $100 to Ms. Black this year, and let Ms. Black repay the loan next year with interest that is greater than $10 and less than $18. Each person will substitute current and future consumption at a rate that is more favorable than the rate at which that person is willing to substitute. As a result, each person will benefit from the exchange. We represent these mutual benefits in table 3.3.

Ms. Black agrees to purchase a good from Mr. Green. The good is an increase of $100 in Ms. Black's current level of consumption. Mr. Green produces this good by reducing his current level of consumption by $100. Ms. Black is willing to pay for this good by reducing her future consumption by $118. Since Ms. Black and Mr. Green have agreed on a rate of interest of 15%, Ms. Black pays only $115 for a good that is worth $118 to her. Consequently, her net gain from the exchange is $3.

Mr. Green is willing to produce the $100 increase in Ms. Black's current consumption in exchange for a payment of only $110 in an increase in his future consumption. Since Mr. Green receives $115 for the good that he would have produced for only $110, his net gain from the exchange is $5.

Consequently, Ms. Black and Mr. Green have a combined net gain of $8, which is equal to $100 times the difference between the minimal rate of interest at which Mr. Green is willing to lend and the maximal rate at which Ms. Black is willing to borrow. The allocation of the $8 net gain between the two persons depends on their relative skills in bargaining.

Since both Ms. Black and Mr. Green gain by lending and borrowing $100 at 15%, we would expect both persons to expand the amount that they lend and borrow. As Ms. Black increases her current consumption at the expense of reducing her future consumption, we would expect her to reduce the maximal rate of interest that she is willing to pay. Similarly, as Mr. Green increases his future consumption at the expense of reducing his current consumption, we would expect him to increase the minimal rate of interest that he is willing to accept.[3] Equilibrium occurs when the two rates coincide. At that point, neither person has an incentive to undertake any further exchanges between present and future consumption.

If Ms. Black and Mr. Green are the only persons in the economy, they can probably locate and negotiate with each other directly. But in an economy that has a large population of persons who differ in their willingness to substitute between present and future consumption, financial markets can substantially decrease the costs of effecting intertemporal exchanges. Any reduction in the costs of producing a good will increase the quantity of that good produced and consumed. Mutually beneficial intertemporal exchanges are no exception. Consequently, the existence and operation of financial markets increase the welfare of those members of the society who participate, directly or indirectly, in mutually beneficial intertemporal exchanges.[4]

Consider, for example, the market for mortgaged loans used to finance the construction of new homes and the purchase of existing homes. The borrowers in this market pay interest to the lenders over many years. The interest is the price that a borrower pays for early access to a home,[5] rather than postponing access until he or she can accumulate enough savings to purchase a home without a loan. Thus, by paying interest a borrower substitutes an increase in present consumption for a decrease in future consumption. The lenders substitute in the opposite direction. By advancing the loan, the lenders reduce their current consumption. As the loan is repaid with interest, the lenders can increase their future consumption relative to what it would have been had they not made the loan.

The mortgaged loans effect mutually beneficial exchanges between the borrowers and the lenders. The lenders are the bank's depositors. Banks facilitate these exchanges by reducing the costs that the borrowers and the lenders would otherwise incur. One of the costs for a lender is the risk that the borrower might not repay the loan (or not repay on time). Banks reduce this cost for lenders partly by investigating the credit-worthiness of prospective borrowers and partly by enabling the lenders (the bank's depositors) to diversify their lending across several borrowers. Similarly, the cost incurred by a borrower to arrange a loan with a bank is lower than the cost he or she would incur if he or she negotiated with a set of lenders directly.

Without banks, many potential mutually beneficial exchanges would not be attempted because the costs of effecting these exchanges would exceed the benefits. The market for mortgaged loans is just one example.

We know that two persons can benefit from an intertemporal exchange only if they are willing to substitute between present and future consumption at different rates. We know also that the larger the difference in the rates at which two persons are willing to substitute between present and future consumption, the greater is the benefit that they can share.

We assume that every person is willing to forego some current consumption in exchange for a sufficiently large increase in future consumption. That is to say, every person would agree to lend if the rate of interest were sufficiently high. Similarly, every person is willing to increase current consumption in exchange for a sufficiently small decrease in future consumption. This means that every person would borrow if the rate of interest were sufficiently low. It is likely that the larger the number of persons in an economy, the larger will be the variation among those persons in the rates at which they are willing to substitute intertemporally. Therefore, the larger the number of persons in the economy, the greater the incentive for any one person to search for another person whose willingness to substitute differs substantially from his or her own. Financial markets reduce the costs of these searches, and thereby increase the extent to which the potential benefits from mutually beneficial intertemporal exchanges are realized.

3.3.3 The Rise of Markets

We have seen that individuals can increase their levels of lifetime utility by making intertemporal allocations of their scarce resources, and by entering agreements with other individuals for specialization and exchange according to the theory of comparative advantage. Individuals could do these two things without creating firms.

For most goods and services, however, the development of technology since the Industrial Revolution has enabled owners of resources to obtain the benefits of specialization and exchange more efficiently by pooling their resources in firms than by operating those resources separately. Part of the reason is that the opportunities for specialization have become more numerous and more sophisticated. Also, much of the new technology favors the use of production on a large scale. Over time, technology has become both more complex and more dependent on large commitments of capital for long periods of time. For these reasons, technological development has increased the demand for financial markets because these markets reduce the costs of organizing intertemporal exchanges and accumulating capital goods. Without financial markets, many potential mutually beneficial intertemporal exchanges would be foregone.

3.4   The Assumption That Future Payments Are Known with Certainty Today

Introductory students know that economists often use simplified models to concentrate on the essential aspects of a question. For example, to introduce the concept of real marginal opportunity costs, we assume that the economy produces only two goods, X and Y, and that the economy's production possibility frontier is smooth and concave. Most economies, however, can produce more than two goods; it would be remarkable if all production possibility frontiers were smoothly concave. Even so, the simple model of an economy that can produce only two goods provides a powerful introduction to critical analytical concepts. Indeed, this simplified model probably enables introductory students to grasp more quickly the essential idea that the cost of producing an additional unit of Good X is the quantity of Good Y that must be foregone, and that the marginal cost of producing Good X increases as the economy moves rightward and downward along the frontier.

We know that financial economics is a study of how consumers maximize lifetime utility by allocating resources among activities that will provide various levels of present and future consumption. The future outcomes of these activities cannot, in general, be known with certainty today. Individual consumers differ in their willingness to tolerate uncertainty. Therefore, consumers can increase their lifetime levels of utility by entering into exchanges that shift risk from one person to another. These exchanges are claims to future levels of consumption that are conditional on future outcomes of various productive activities. The analysis of the pricing of these conditional claims is critical to understanding the economics of financial markets. The analysis is also complex. We can understand the analysis of these conditional claims more easily by first considering how a financial market will organize mutually beneficial exchanges under the simplifying assumption that there is no uncertainty about future outcomes. We can then exploit several analogies between the case in which there is no uncertainty about future outcomes and the more realistic case in which there is uncertainty.

3.5   Abstracting from Firms

By organizing their resources within firms, consumers can more fully exploit the opportunities for specialization and exchange provided by modern technology. By issuing a variety of conditional claims on its future earnings, the modern corporation provides a rich set of opportunities for mutually beneficial allocations of risk. Financial markets provide linkages between consumers and the firms that use the consumers' resources to produce goods and services. Some of these linkages are informational; consumers want to know what kinds of transformations their firms can make between the input of resources and the output of goods and services. Consumers also want to be able to enter mutually beneficial exchanges of risk with other consumers who hold the firms' securities. The markets provide these linkages by organizing the trading, and thus the pricing, of a variety of financial securities.

The analysis of how, and how well, the financial markets provide these linkages is the central task of this book. But it is a complex task. We can proceed best by first abstracting from the fact that consumers use firms to organize the transformation of inputs into outputs of goods and services. Doing so will enable us to concentrate on the essential function of financial markets, which is to expand the range of mutually beneficial exchanges. By first abstracting from firms, we can more easily develop the analytical principles that we will use later when we do consider how financial markets link consumers and firms.

Of course, abstracting from firms will limit our analysis by excluding several important problems. These problems include asymmetry of information between a firm's owners and managers, and conflicts of interest between owners and managers. We consider these problems later, after we have developed the fundamental analytical concepts that are essential to study these problems beyond a conversational level.

The Distinction between Income and Wealth

The first step in the analysis of the intertemporal maximization of utility is to distinguish between income and wealth. Income is a flow of value, whereas wealth is a stock of value. If Ms. Brown works for someone else in exchange for the payment of money, her income is measured as a flow of dollars relative to some unit of time, such as one year. If she is self-employed producing potatoes, her income is measured as a flow of potatoes produced per year. Ms. Brown will probably sell some or all of the potatoes that she produces, thereby exchanging the form of her income from potatoes to money. But whatever the form in which she receives her income, that income is a flow, a measure of the value obtained (in some form) per year (or per some other unit of time).

Conversely, wealth is a stock of value. It is the result of an accumulation of income generated in the past or in the present. There are three forms in which Ms. Brown could hold wealth. The most primitive form of wealth is a stock of consumption goods. Ms. Brown could, for example, simply accumulate and store some of the potatoes that she produces each year. In any given year, the maximal quantity of potatoes that she could consume during that year (without borrowing from another consumer) would be equal to the total quantity of potatoes that she produces in that year, plus the volume of potatoes that she had accumulated during previous years. That is to say, assuming again that she does not borrow, her consumption would be constrained by her current income and her accumulated wealth. In this example, her consumption, her income, and her wealth are all measured in terms of potatoes.

The second form in which Ms. Brown could hold wealth is money. For example, she can sell her entire output of potatoes in a given year, thereby converting her income into money, and then save some of that income. That accumulation of income will increase her wealth. In future years, she can consume that wealth by spending the money to purchase goods and services.

The third, and most sophisticated, form in which Ms. Brown could hold wealth is an accumulation of claims on income to be generated in the future. For example, Ms. Brown could give some of her current output of potatoes to Mr. Black, who would then use them as seed potatoes to expand the scale on which he will produce potatoes next year. In exchange for allowing Mr. Black to use some of her current output of potatoes as an input for future production, Ms. Brown will obtain from Mr. Black a claim on a portion of his future output.

In a more sophisticated model of an economy, this claim would be saleable. Ms. Brown could sell the claim to someone else, rather than exercising it herself. This saleable claim would be a *financial security*. Financial markets would determine the price of this security by reconciling the willingness of households to divert income from current consumption and the ability of farmers like Mr. Black to use seed potatoes to expand future levels of output. As a result, Ms. Brown and Mr. Black could construct a mutually beneficial exchange.

In summation, the ideas to keep in mind are that income is a flow, and that wealth is a stock acquired by accumulating income that is not spent for consumption.

3.7	**Income, Wealth, and Present Values**

In the next section, we analyze a simple case in which a consumer uses a financial market to borrow or lend, and thereby to allocate resources between present and future consumption so as to maximize lifetime utility. To prepare for this analysis, we must first develop the concept of present value.

3.7.1 Present Value

A present value is a stock of wealth that is economically equivalent to a future flow of income. Precisely, the present value of a particular flow of income is that level of wealth that would enable a person to replicate that flow of income.

Consider the following examples. Mr. Green's income is $110 per year for two years. He will receive his first payment of $110 today, and he will receive his second and final payment of $110 one year from today. The present value of Mr. Green's sequence of income payments is the level of wealth that Mr. Green must have today if he is to replicate the sequence of income payments. If we ignore the possibility that Mr. Green can invest any wealth today and receive interest next year, the answer is simple. Mr. Green would have to possess $220 in wealth today in order to replicate two payments of $110 each.

But suppose that Mr. Green can earn interest at the rate of 10% per year by placing money on deposit in a bank. In this case, a deposit of $100 in a bank today will grow to $110 one year from today. Therefore, Mr. Green could provide for the payment of $110 next year by depositing only $100 in a bank today. Economists would say that Mr. Green could *fund* an opportunity to receive $110 one year from today by depositing $100 in a bank account today.

Our question: how much money must Mr. Green have today to enable him to replicate the flow of income that provides $110 today and a second $110 one year from today? The answer depends on the rate at which Mr. Green can earn interest by depositing money in a bank. If the interest rate is 10% per year, then Mr. Green will require $210 today if he is to replicate the payments of $110 today and a second $110 one year from today. Mr. Green would use $110 of the $210 to make the first payment. He would then deposit the remaining $100 ($210 − $110) in a bank today. One year from now, he could withdraw a total of $110, counting both the original deposit and the interest at the rate of 10% on that deposit. He could then use that $110 to make the second payment.

We conclude that if Mr. Green can earn interest at the rate of 10% per year, then $210 is the present value of the flow of income that pays $110 immediately and a second $110 one year from today. It is easy to see that the present value of a flow of income varies inversely with the interest rate. Suppose that the interest rate were 5% per year. Clearly Mr. Green would have to deposit more than $100 today if the account is to grow to $110 by next year. Let D_0 be the amount that must be deposited today to fund a payment equal to P_1 one year from today. Let r be the annual rate of interest paid by the bank. Then D_0, P_1, and r are related by

$$D_0(1+r) = P_1 \tag{3.1}$$

or

$$D_0 = P_1/(1+r). \tag{3.2}$$

For our example, if the bank pays interest at 5% per year, Mr. Green would have to deposit $110/(1+.05), or $104.76 today if he is to use this bank account to fund a payment of $110 one year from today.

We will now consider the concept of present value for two more general cases. In the first case, the flow of income consists of a sequence of payments that continues for a finite number of years into the future. In the second case, the sequence of payments continues forever.

3.7.2   A Sequence with Two Future Payments

Define P_i as the payment that will occur i years from now. The values of the index i are restricted to nonnegative integers. Thus, P_0 is the payment that will occur today and P_1 is the payment that will occur one year from today, and so on.

Let r be the annual rate of interest paid by a bank, and assume that this interest is compounded annually. Then a deposit today equal to D_0 will grow to $D_0(1+r)^1$ at the end of one year. Define this value as D_1. That is, $D_1 = D_0(1+r)^1$. If an amount of money equal to D_1 is deposited in a bank one year from now and allowed to accumulate interest at rate r for one year, then the account will grow to $D_1(1+r)^1$ at the end of two years from now. Define $D_2 = D_1(1+r)^1$. Then by substitution we have:

$$D_2 = D_1(1+r)^1 = D_0(1+r)^1(1+r)^1 = D_0(1+r)^2. \tag{3.3}$$

That is, if D_0 is deposited in a bank today and allowed to accumulate interest for two years at a compound annual rate equal to r, the value of the account at the end of two years will be $D_0(1+r)^2$. Of course, for the initial deposit of D_0 to grow to a value of $D_0(1+r)^2$ at time 2, the entire initial amount of D_0 must be left on deposit for the entire two years; there must be no withdrawal of any part of the initial deposit at time 1.

In general, if D_0 is deposited in a bank today and allowed to accumulate interest for i years at a fixed compound annual rate equal to r, and there are no withdrawals, the value of the account at the end of i years will be $D_0(1+r)^i$.

We can now invert the preceding relationships to calculate the present value of a future payment.

By definition, the present value of a flow of payments is the amount of current wealth that would enable a person to replicate the flow of payments. Suppose that the flow of payments consists of a single payment, namely, a payment equal to P_1 one year from now. Using our earlier calculations, we know that the present value of P_1 is $P_1/(1+r)^1$. That is, a deposit equal to $P_1/(1+r)^1$ today will grow to a value equal to $[P_1/(1+r)](1+r) = P_1$ one year from today. Therefore, the amount of wealth that a person would need today to replicate a payment equal to P_1 one year from today is $P_1/(1+r)^1$. We say that $P_1/(1+r)^1$ is the present value of P_1. Note that the person who is replicating this payment would withdraw from the bank one year from today both the initial deposit and the accumulated interest. There is no need to leave any money on deposit in the bank because there are no further payments to replicate after time 1.

Next consider a second sequence that has only one payment. This payment occurs two years from now. Call this payment P_2. We want to determine the size of the deposit that a person would have to make today in order to be able to withdraw an amount equal to P_2 two years from now. This deposit today, plus the interest accumulated over two years, would replicate the payment of P_2. Consequently, an investor should be indifferent between owning today a sequence that will pay P_2 two years from now, and owning today a bank account that will enable him or her to replicate that payment.

Let X be the amount of the bank deposit today that would enable a person to replicate the payment of P_2 two years hence. We know that a deposit equal to X today will grow in value to $X(1+r)^2$ two years from today if there are no withdrawals before that time. Setting the value to which the account will grow equal to the future payment that we want to replicate, we have $X(1+r)^2=P_2$. Therefore, $X=P_2/(1+r)^2$. That is, a deposit equal to $P_2/(1+r)^2$ today will grow to a value equal to $[P_2/(1+r)^2](1+r)^2=P_2$ at time 2. The person who makes the initial deposit of $P_2/(1+r)^2$ would make no withdrawal at time 1. At time 2, the person would withdraw the entire balance in the account. There is no need to withdraw any funds at time 1 because there is no payment to replicate then, and there is no need to leave any money on deposit after time 2 because there are no further payments to replicate after time 2.

Since a deposit of X today will enable the depositor to replicate the payment of P_2 two years from today, $X=P_2/(1+r)^2$ is the present value of P_2.

Now consider a third sequence. In this sequence there are two future payments, namely, a payment equal to P_1 at time 1, and a payment equal to P_2 at time 2. There are no further payments. It is easy to show that the present value of this sequence of payments is the sum of the present values of each of the two future payments considered separately. First, note that a person could replicate these two payments simply by making two deposits today in separate accounts. A deposit of $P_1/(1+r)^1$ in one account will grow to a value equal to P_1 at time 1. A deposit of $P_2/(1+r)^2$ in a second account will grow to a value equal to P_2 at time 2. The person who is replicating the two payments simply withdraws the entire balance from each account, including the accumulated interest, at the designated time.

We can accomplish the same result by depositing the sum of the two present values in a single account. At time 1 we will withdraw an amount equal to P_1 from the account. The amount remaining in the account will then grow in value to the amount of the second payment, P_2, at time 2. Following is a demonstration of this result.

Define B_0 as the balance in the account at time 0. Define B_i as the balance in the account at time i after taking into account (1) whatever withdrawals were made prior to time i, and (2) whatever interest has been allowed to accumulate. The withdrawals will be the two payments that we want to replicate, namely, P_1 at time 1, and P_2 at time 2. The balance at time 0, B_0, is the sum of the present values of the two payments. Thus,

$$B_0 = \frac{P_1}{(1+r)^1} + \frac{P_2}{(1+r)^2}. \tag{3.4}$$

At time 1 the balance will have grown to:

$$B_1 = \left[\frac{P_1}{(1+r)^1} + \frac{P_2}{(1+r)^2} \right](1+r)^1$$

$$= P_1 + \frac{P_2}{(1+r)^1}.$$

$$(3.5)$$

After withdrawing the amount P_1 at time 1 to make the first payment in the sequence, the balance in the account will be equal to $P_2/(1+r)^1$. This balance will accumulate interest from time 1 to time 2. Therefore, the balance at time 2, before any withdrawals at time 2, will be

$$B_2 = \frac{P_2}{(1+r)^1}(1+r)^1 = P_2. \qquad (3.6)$$

The balance remaining in the account at time 2 will be P_2, which is exactly what is required to replicate the final payment in the sequence. Withdrawing this amount will exhaust the account, which is appropriate because there are no further payments to replicate after time 2.

3.7.3   A Numerical Example

Consider the following example. Ms. Black finds a new job in which she will be guaranteed a series of income payments. Although she will receive no payment today, she will receive a payment of $150 one year from today, and a second payment of $180 two years from today. Following the second payment, Ms. Black will receive no further income.

What amount of money must Ms. Black possess today in order to replicate this sequence of payments? In the absence of investment opportunities, the answer is clear: she must have $330. However, suppose Ms. Black is presented with the following option: by depositing her money in a nearby bank, she can earn interest on her deposit at a rate of 5% per year. How much money must she have to replicate the sequence of payments provided by the job?

One method by which she could replicate this flow of income is to make two deposits today in separate accounts. As we learned in section 3.7.2, if Ms. Black deposits the present value of her first payment [$P_1/(1+.05)^1$ or $142.86], her balance will grow to $150 at time 1. Similarly, by depositing $163.27 [the present value $P_2/(1+.05)^2$ of her second payment], Ms. Black's balance will grow to $180 at time 2. Ms. Black need only withdraw the entire balance from each account at the appropriate time.

However, Ms. Black need not hold two separate accounts. Instead, she may open a single account with a balance that equals the sum of the present values of her two payments. Using equation (3.4), we know that balance at time 0 must be $306.13. With an interest rate of 5%, at time 1 the balance will have grown to $321.44.

At time 1, Ms. Black will withdraw the amount necessary to make the first payment, namely $150. Consequently, the remaining balance will be $171.44. This balance will continue to gain interest from time 1 to time 2. Before Ms. Black makes her second withdrawal, her account will contain $180, the exact amount of her second payment.

As there are no further payments necessary to replicate the sequence, Ms. Black has emptied her account.

We return to the original question. With the option to invest her money at an annual interest rate of 5%, how much money must Ms. Black have today if she is to replicate the sequence of payments? The answer is the sum of the present values of both payments: $306.13.

3.7.4   A Sequence with an Infinite Number of Uniform Payments

We finally consider a sequence in which the payments are uniform and continue forever. The sequence provides a constant payment at the rate of P per year, beginning one year from today and continuing forever. The present value of this sequence is the amount of current wealth that would enable a person to replicate the sequence. Since the sequence of payments continues forever, we can replicate it by maintaining a balance in a bank account on which the annual interest is equal to the annual payment that we want to replicate. If the rate of interest is constant over time, then the required balance in the account will be constant (after allowing for the annual withdrawal of interest).

Again, define B_0 as the amount of money to be deposited at time 0. If the annual rate of interest is r, the value of the account at time 1, prior to any withdrawals, will be $B_1 = B_0(1+r)^1 = B_0 + rB_0$. Obviously, the balance at time 1 consists of the initial deposit B_0 plus the interest for one year on that deposit, rB_0. If we withdraw only the interest at time 1, we will leave a balance equal to B_0 on which to earn interest from time 1 to time 2. The interest at time 2 will be the same as it was at time 1, namely rB_0, because the balance on which we can earn interest over the second year is the same as the balance on which we earned interest over the first year. In general, by depositing B_0 at time 0 and withdrawing only the interest each year, we can replicate an infinite sequence of payments equal to rB_0 per year. Therefore, the amount of current wealth B_0 that would enable us to replicate an infinite sequence of annual payments equal to P when a bank pays interest at a rate of r per year is determined by the equation $rB_0 = P$. The solution is $B_0 = P/r$.

A numerical example will make this transparent. If the bank pays interest at the rate of 10% per year and the annual payment in the sequence is equal to $100, then a deposit equal to $100/.10 = $1,000 will enable us to replicate the sequence. Leaving the $1,000 in the bank permanently will enable us to withdraw $100 per year forever, which is identical to the sequence that we want to replicate.

3.7.5   Present Values and Economic Equivalence

The present value of a sequence of future payments is also known as the *capitalized value* of that sequence. The reason is that the present value is the amount of financial capital required to replicate that sequence of payments. We know that the present value is the amount of current wealth that would enable a person to replicate the sequence. Wealth is a stock (rather than a flow). One of the forms in which a person can hold wealth is a bank account. The balance in the account is part of the person's financial capital. Hence, the capitalized value of a sequence of future payments is the stock of financial capital that would enable a person to replicate the sequence.

The present value of a sequence is a stock; it is the quantity of wealth that a person must have now if he or she is to replicate that sequence. The sequence itself is a flow; it is measured as payments per year (or per some unit of time) over some interval of years into the future. The future payments need not be equal from one year to the next, nor need they continue indefinitely into the future. As we saw earlier, the sequence could contain only one future payment.

We now introduce the concept of *economic equivalence* between sequences of payments. Two sequences are economically equivalent if they have the same present value. If two sequences are economically equivalent, an investor who owns either sequence, and who can borrow from and lend to a bank, can use the payments in that sequence to replicate the payments in the other sequence without committing any of his own funds. Therefore, an investor will be indifferent between owning sequences that are economically equivalent. As a particular application of this concept, note that using one's own money to purchase a sequence produces the same result as purchasing that sequence by using money borrowed from a bank.

The capitalized value (or present value) of a sequence of payments, and the sequence of payments itself, are economically equivalent in the sense that anyone who owns the right to receive the payments in the sequence can exchange that right for its capitalized value. The converse also holds. This concept of economic equivalence will be important throughout the book. For that reason, we pause here to provide two examples.

Let the annual interest rate be 10%, and consider the sequence of three payments specified by $P_1 = \$110$, $P_2 = \$121$, and $P_3 = \$133.10$. The capitalized value of this sequence is:

$$
\begin{aligned}
B_0 &= \frac{P_1}{(1+r)^1} + \frac{P_2}{(1+r)^2} + \frac{P_3}{(1+r)^3} \\
&= \frac{\$110}{(1+.10)^1} + \frac{\$121}{(1+.10)^2} + \frac{\$133.10}{(1+.10)^3} \\
&= \frac{\$110}{1.1} + \frac{\$121}{1.21} + \frac{\$133.10}{1.331} \\
&= \$100 + \$100 + \$100 \\
&= \$300.
\end{aligned}
\tag{3.7}
$$

A person who owns the right to the sequence that will pay $110 at time 1, $121 at time 2, and $133.10 at time 3 could sell the right to that sequence for $300. To show this, suppose that the person offered to sell the sequence for $290. A second person could borrow $290 from a bank and use that money to purchase the sequence. At time 1, the borrower would owe the bank the $290 plus interest for one year, or $290(1+.10)^1 = \$319$. But the borrower could use the first payment from the sequence to reduce his indebtedness to the bank. Doing this would reduce his debt to $319 − $110, or $209.

If the borrower used the second payment from the sequence to pay down the debt, he or she would owe the bank at time 2 the amount $209(1+.10)^1 − \$121 = \$229.90 − \$121 = \$108.90$.

At time 3, the debt will be $108.90(1+.10)^1 = \$119.79$, which is less than what the borrower will receive as the third (and final) payment in the sequence. Therefore, the borrower will obtain a net profit at time 3 equal to $133.10−$119.79=$13.31. This profit arises because, at $290, the sequence that pays $110 at time 1, $121 at time 2, and $133.10 at time 3 is underpriced, assuming that the interest rate is 10% per year. Competition among investors will drive the price of the sequence up to $300. The reader should be able to show that an investor could not make a profit by borrowing $300 from a bank and purchasing the sequence. Obviously (and the reader should be able to show this), the sequence would be overpriced at any price above $300; investors who purchased the sequence for more than $300 would incur a loss.

But what if the investor uses his or her own funds to purchase the sequence, rather than borrowing from a bank? Students of economics will immediately recognize that using one's own money to purchase the sequence, rather than depositing that money in a bank, incurs an opportunity cost in the form of interest foregone.

We have shown that an investor who owns a right to receive a sequence of payments can convert that right to its capitalized value. To show the converse, we recognize that an investor can convert the capitalized value of a sequence into the sequence itself by depositing the capitalized value in a bank, and then by replicating the sequence with a series of withdrawals. Using the preceding example, let the investor deposit $300 today. That balance will grow to $300(1+.10)^1=$330 at time 1. Withdrawing $110 at time 1 will leave $330−$110=$220 to accumulate interest between time 1 and time 2. At time 2, the balance in the account will be $220(1+.10)^1=$242. Withdrawing $121 at time 2 will leave $121, which will grow to $121(1+.10)^1, or $133.10 at time 3. This last amount can be withdrawn at that time to replicate the final payment in the sequence. This concludes our discussion of fundamental analytical concepts involved in the intertemporal allocation of resources. In chapter 4, we use these concepts in our presentation of the Fisher diagram of optimal intertemporal allocation.

Problems

1. LickIt Candy Company produces two types of candy: pops and gum. The company has two plants, East Plant and West Plant. In West Plant, each machine can produce 3 units of gum/hr or 2 units of pops/hr. In East Plant, each machine can produce 5 units of gum/hr or 1 unit of pops/hr. What is the marginal cost of producing 15 units of gum in East Plant? Which plant has a comparative advantage?

2. With Good X plotted horizontally, and Good Y plotted vertically, the slope of Ms. Tall's production possibilities frontier is −2:1 while the slope of Ms. Short's production possibilities frontier is −3:1. Who has a comparative advantage in terms of X and Y? Use a graph to explain your answer.

3. The First Bank is currently paying 10% interest compounded annually on all deposits. Mr. Smith deposits $100 at $t=0$. How much would he need to deposit one year later at $t=1$ to have $275 in the bank the next year, at $t=2$? By how much would he have to increase his deposit at $t=0$ in order to have $275 at $t=2$ without making a deposit at $t=1$?

4. Heart College charges students a different fee for each year of their education. The tuition for the first year is $2,200. Tuitions for the second, third, and fourth years are $2,420, $2,662, and $2,928.2, respectively. Each tuition payment is due at the end of the year for which it is paid. How much would Mr. Smith be willing to pay today to buy the full four-year package if the interest rate is 10%?

Notes

1. We assume that the farmer allocates to current production, rather than to leisure, the time that would have been spent on maintenance.

2. Most introductory courses in economics present the theory of comparative advantage. For that reason, we present only a simple example here.

3. These changes in the maximal and minimal rates of interest are an example of the axiom known as "diminishing marginal rate of substitution." Under this axiom, the marginal rate at which a person is willing to substitute less of Good Y for an increase of one unit of Good X decreases as the total quantity of Good X that the person has increases.

4. A carpenter who neither borrows nor lends will still benefit from the operation of financial markets if, by using those markets, the construction firm that employs her can more easily obtain loans with which to finance the construction of new homes.

5. The concept of interest as the price of early access to a good appears in A. Alchian and W. Allen, *Exchange and Production: Theory in Use* (Belmont, Calif.: Wadsworth, 1969), 265.

4 The Fisher Diagram for Optimal Intertemporal Allocation

4.1 The Intertemporal Budget Line

We will develop a graphical tool to explain how a consumer determines the levels of borrowing or lending to maximize lifetime utility.[1] We begin with a simple model in which a person has only two periods in which to consume. The problem is to determine the optimal allocation of resources between consumption this year and consumption next year. We will emphasize the informational function of financial markets that enables consumers to identify and create mutually beneficial intertemporal exchanges.

In figure 4.1, we measure levels of income and spending this year on the horizontal axis, and levels of income and spending next year on the vertical axis. Let time 0 be the present moment; let time 1 be the moment that is exactly one year from now; and let time 2 be the moment that is exactly two years from now. The current year begins at time 0 and ends at time 1; the following year begins at time 1 and ends at time 2. The consumer will die at time 2.

The consumer's flow of income consists of a sequence of payments, namely I_0 at time 0, followed by I_1 at time 1. We represent this sequence by $\{I_0, I_1\}$, which we plot in figure 4.1 as the point $\{I_0, I_1\}$.

Now define $\{C_0, C_1\}$ as the sequence of the consumer's spending. Unless the consumer is a miser, whom we would define as a person whose ultimate goal is to acquire money rather than goods and services, the consumer obtains utility only by using her income to acquire consumption goods. The consumer now has two problems. The first problem is intertemporal; she must allocate her spending optimally between the current year and the following year. The second problem is to allocate her spending for each year optimally among the various goods and services that are available to purchase within that year. We will abstract from this second problem, and analyze only the first problem.

The consumer's problem of intertemporal allocation arises because the sequence of expenditures for consumption, $\{C_0, C_1\}$, that will maximize her lifetime utility will not, in general, correspond to the sequence of her income flows, $\{I_0, I_1\}$. For example, if the consumer is a recent college graduate, her current income, I_0, is likely to be quite low relative to her future income, I_1. It is likely that she would prefer to reallocate some of her future income to the present so that she can have a better distribution of her lifetime income between consumption this year and consumption next year. In particular, she might prefer to use some of her future income to purchase a house now, and then

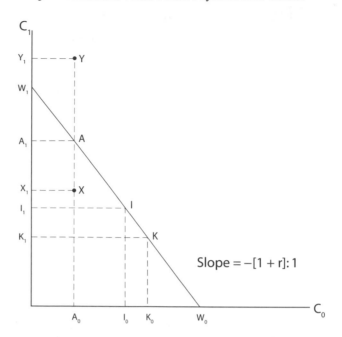

Figure 4.1. An intertemporal budget line.

next year spend less than her total income for that year. As a second example, most persons, once they are well established in a job, will allocate some of their current income to saving for retirement.

If the consumer can borrow and lend, she can exchange her present sequence of income payments for one of several alternative sequences. The object is to choose from those alternative sequences the one that will enable her to allocate consumption optimally between this year and next year. Our first step is to determine the set of alternatives from which the consumer can choose. The set of alternative sequences available to the consumer is determined by (1) her present sequence of income payments, and (2) the interest rates at which she can borrow and lend.

4.1.1 Economic Equivalence of Points on the Budget Line

In section 3.7.5 of the preceding chapter, we introduced the concept of economic equivalence for a sequence of payments and the capitalized value of that sequence. We can extend the concept of economic equivalence to two sequences of payments. Two sequences of payments are economically equivalent if a person who owns one of those sequences can obtain the other sequence by an appropriate combination of borrowing and lending. Assume that the consumer can either borrow from, or lend to, a bank at an annual rate of interest equal to r. Of course, the rate of interest that banks pay on deposits is less than the rate that they charge for loans. But our assumption that the two rates are the same will allow us to present more easily the fundamental principles of intertemporal allocation. For many analytical questions, this simplifying assumption does little harm. For other questions, the difference between the rates of interest that banks will pay on deposits or charge for loans is critical. To analyze those questions, economists use different models.

The straight line in figure 4.1 that passes through the point I is the set of alternative sequences of income payments that are economically equivalent to the sequence $\{I_0, I_1\}$. If the consumer can borrow or lend at an annual rate of interest equal to r, she can exchange any sequence of income payments that lies on this line for any other sequence that lies on the same line. This straight line is called the consumer's *intertemporal budget line*. The slope of this budget line is $-(1+r)$: 1.

There is a close analogy between a production possibility frontier for the economy and an intertemporal budget line for a consumer. Both a production possibility frontier and an intertemporal budget line define trade-offs that are conditional on levels of scarce resources. A production possibility frontier defines the alternative combinations of goods that an economy can produce in a single year, given the level of resources on which the economy can draw. These resources include tangible inputs, such as land and railroad equipment, and intangible inputs, such as technological knowledge and the level of technological sophistication in the labor force. An intertemporal budget line defines the alternative combinations of current and future consumption that a person can enjoy, given his or her current level of wealth and the interest rate. The level of resources available to the economy in a given year is analogous to the individual's level of wealth at the beginning of a year. The state of the technology is analogous to the interest rate. Technology specifies the rates at which the economy can substitute between goods by producing more of one and less of another. The interest rate specifies the rate at which an individual can substitute between current and future consumption either by borrowing or by lending.

Consider the sequence $\{A_0, A_1\}$ that lies at point A on the budget line. By lending, the consumer can trade her present sequence of income payments, $\{I_0, I_1\}$, for the sequence $\{A_0, A_1\}$. It is easy to see why this is true. The slope of the budget line is $-(1+r)$. Therefore, using the definition of slope as "rise over run":

$$\frac{A_1 - I_1}{A_0 - I_0} = 2(1+r), \tag{4.1}$$

so that

$$A_1 - I_1 = -(1+r)(A_0 - I_0), \tag{4.2}$$

and

$$A_1 = I_1 + (1+r)(I_0 - A_0). \tag{4.3}$$

In equation (4.3), the term $(I_0 - A_0)$ is the amount by which the consumer reduces her level of current consumption below her current income. If the rate of interest is r, the future value of $(I_0 - A_0)$ is $(1+r)(I_0 - A_0)$. Consequently, equation (4.3) states that the consumer's level of consumption next year, A_1, is equal to her future income I_1 plus $(1+r)(I_0 - A_0)$, which is the future value of the decrease in her current level of consumption. At time 1, the consumer supplements her income by withdrawing from the bank both her deposit of $(I_0 - A_0)$ and the accumulated interest of $r(I_0 - A_0)$. That is, the consumer can lend to a bank to move upward and leftward along her intertemporal budget line. In doing so, she is reallocating her resources from current consumption to future consumption.

Rewriting equation (4.3) produces

$$I_0 - A_0 = \frac{A_1 - I_1}{(1+r)}, \tag{4.4}$$

which states that the amount by which the consumer must decrease her current consumption is $(A_1 - I_1)/(1+r)$, or the present value of the amount by which she will increase her future consumption beyond her future income.

We have just seen how the consumer can use lending to a bank to move leftward and upward along her intertemporal budget line. Alternatively, the consumer can use borrowing (from a bank) to reallocate resources from future consumption to current consumption. That is, she can move rightward and downward along her budget line. Consider the sequence at point K. At point K the consumer spends on consumption the quantities K_0 this year and K_1 next year. Proceeding as before, we have:

$$\frac{K_1 - I_1}{K_0 - I_0} = -(1+r), \tag{4.5}$$

so that

$$\frac{K_1 - I_1}{-(1+r)} = K_0 - I_0, \tag{4.6}$$

and

$$\frac{I_1 - K_1}{(1+r)} = K_0 - I_0. \tag{4.7}$$

In equation (4.7), the term $(K_0 - I_0)$ is the amount that the consumer borrows today in order to increase her current consumption above her current income. Consequently, the term $(I_1 - K_1)$ is the amount by which she must decrease her consumption next year in order to pay off her loan. If the interest rate is r, then $(I_1 - K_1)$ must be the future value of $(K_0 - I_0)$. That is, $(I_1 - K_1) = (1+r)(K_0 - I_0)$. Students should note that it is also possible for the consumer to operate at point X, where she consumes X_0 in the current year and X_1 in the following year. This combination of consumption, however, is not favorable. The consumer is not using all of her resources, and thus not maximizing utility. Should she decide to only consume A_0 in the present year, her budget will allow her to consume more than X_1 in the next year, namely A_1. Conversely, it is not possible for her to function at a point such as Y. Even through borrowing and lending, she does not have enough resources to have the combination of present and future consumption represented by point Y.

4.1.2   Interpreting the Intercepts and the Slope of the Budget Line

To continue our graphical analysis of a consumer's intertemporal allocation between present and future consumption, we need an economic interpretation of the intercepts of the intertemporal budget line.

Let W_0 be the horizontal intercept of the intertemporal budget line in figure 4.1. Accordingly, W_0 is the maximal level of current consumption that the consumer can afford if she spends all of her current income, I_0, plus $I_1/(1+r)$, which is the present value of her future income. Proceeding as before, we have:

$$\frac{0-I_1}{W_0-I_0}=-(1+r),\tag{4.8}$$

so that

$$-I_1=-(1+r)(W_0-I_0),\tag{4.9}$$

and thus

$$\frac{-I_1}{-(1+r)}+I_0=\frac{I_1}{(1+r)}+I_0=W_0.\tag{4.10}$$

Let W_1 be the vertical intercept of the consumer's intertemporal budget line. Then W_1 is the maximal amount of future consumption that the consumer can afford if she spends none of her current income. If she deposits her entire current income of I_0 in a bank today, the value of her account at time 1 will be $I_0(1+r)$. At time 1, the maximal amount that she can spend is the sum of this bank balance, plus the income I_1 that she will have at time 1. Then $W_1=I_1+I_0(1+r)$. That is, her maximal level of consumption at time 1 is the sum of her income at time 1 plus the future value of her income at time 0.

We know that a sequence of payments and its present value are economically equivalent. This means that by either borrowing or lending, a person who has an amount of current wealth equal to the present value of the sequence can replicate that sequence, and conversely, a person who owns the right to receive the payments in the sequence can exchange that sequence for its present value. We can use this fact to interpret the intertemporal budget line in figure 4.1.

The horizontal intercept of the budget line represents a sequence of expenditures for consumption equal to $\{W_0, 0\}$. That is, the consumer spends in the current year her entire current income, I_0, and the present value of her future income, I_1. The present value of I_1 is $I_1/(1+r)^1$. A consumer who borrows $I_1/(1+r)^1$ from a bank today will owe the bank $[I_1/(1+r)^1](1+r)^1$, which is equal to I_1. Since the consumer will require her entire income next year to repay the bank, her level of consumption next year will be zero.

The economic interpretation of the vertical intercept of the budget line in figure 4.1 is analogous to the interpretation of the horizontal intercept. The vertical intercept is the maximal level of consumption that the consumer can achieve next year if she consumes nothing this year. Let W_1 be the value of the vertical intercept. Then the sequence of consumption expenditures that is represented by the vertical intercept is $\{0, W_1\}$. To achieve the consumption sequence $\{0, W_1\}$, the consumer must consume nothing this year and allocate her entire current income to investment. Specifically, the consumer deposits her current income, I_0, in a bank at time 0. Next year, at time 1, her balance at the bank will have grown to $I_0(1+r)^1$. Adding this balance to her income at time 1 will enable her to consume at time 1 at the level of $I_0(1+r)^1+I_1$. Therefore, W_1, which is the future value (at time 1) of the income sequence $\{I_0, I_1\}$, is equal to $I_0(1+r)^1+I_1$.

Two sequences of payments are economically equivalent if a person who has one of those sequences can obtain the other sequence by an appropriate combination of borrowing and lending. In general, if the consumer's income sequence is $\{I_0, I_1\}$, and if she can borrow or lend at an annual rate of interest equal to r, then the set of economically equivalent consumption sequences is defined by the straight line in figure 4.1 that passes through the sequence $\{I_0, I_1\}$ with a slope equal to $-(1+r)/1$. For example, starting from the income sequence $\{I_0, I_1\}$, the consumer can increase her current consumption by $1 by borrowing $1 against her future income. Next year, she will owe the bank $1(1+r)$. In figure 4.1, she will have moved from the point $\{I_0, I_1\}$ rightward by $1, and downward by $1(1+r)$. Similarly, by reducing her level of consumption by $1 today, she can increase her future consumption by $1(1+r)$.

4.1.3   A Numerical Example

Suppose that Mr. Ridge has just received a payment of $1,000 and will receive a second payment of $2,200 one year from now. Using these values, his income sequence is $\{I_0, I_1\} = \{\$1,000, \$2,200\}$. We have plotted this sequence as point R in figure 4.2. Mr. Ridge's intertemporal budget line is the straight line that passes through point R with a slope equal to $-(1+r)$, in which r is the rate of interest. If $r=.10$, then the slope of the intertemporal budget line is $-(1+.10)$.

The horizontal intercept of the intertemporal budget line in figure 4.2 is the present value of Mr. Ridge's income sequence. This present value, or wealth, is the maximal amount that Mr. Ridge could spend on consumption today, given his income sequence. His wealth is equal to his current income of $1,000, plus the amount that he can borrow

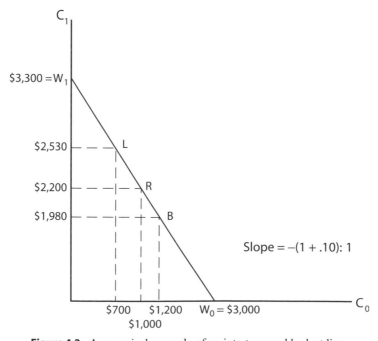

Figure 4.2. A numerical example of an intertemporal budget line.

today against the income that he will receive next year. The present value of this future income is \$2,200/(1+.10), or \$2,000. We conclude that Mr. Ridge's wealth is equal to \$1,000+\$2,200/(1+.10) = \$3,000. He can spend \$3,000 today by augmenting his current \$1,000 by borrowing \$2,000 from a bank; next year he will owe the bank \$2,200. Paying the bank will absorb his entire future income. Consequently, the cost that Mr. Ridge would incur to increase his current consumption by \$2,000 beyond his current income is that he must reduce his future consumption to zero.

The vertical intercept of Mr. Ridge's intertemporal budget line is the future value of his income sequence. This future value is the maximal level at which he can consume next year if he reduces his current consumption to zero. By depositing his entire current income of \$1,000 in a bank today, next year Mr. Ridge will have \$1,000(1+.10), or \$1,100, with which to augment his future income of \$2,200. We conclude that the maximal level of future consumption that his income sequence will support is \$1,000(1+.10)+\$2,200, or \$3,300, which is the value of the vertical intercept of the intertemporal budget line in figure 4.2.

Points B and L on the budget line in figure 4.2 designate two of the infinite number of alternative combinations of current and future consumption that Mr. Ridge can achieve when his income sequence is {\$1,000, \$2,200} and the interest rate is .10. Point B requires that he borrow, whereas point L requires that he lend. If Mr. Ridge neither borrows nor lends, he must accept the combination of present and future consumption that is identical to his income sequence. To choose the combination at point B, he would borrow \$200 from a bank today. Next year he would have to use \$220 of the \$2,200 that he would receive to repay the bank. Consequently, his future consumption at point B would be \$2,200−\$220=\$1,980. Notice that the rate at which Mr. Ridge must forego future consumption per dollar of increase in current consumption is (−)\$220/\$200, or −1.1, which we can write as −(1+.10)/1. The interest rate specifies the rate at which Mr. Ridge can substitute between future and current consumption by determining the slope of his intertemporal budget line.

Alternatively, to move from point R to point L, Mr. Ridge would lend. By spending only \$700 of his current income of \$1,000, he can deposit \$300 in a bank. Next year the bank account will be worth \$330, which will enable Mr. Ridge to consume at a level of \$2,200+\$330, or \$2,530.

4.2   Intertemporal Indifference Curves

The intertemporal budget line in figure 4.1 is the locus of the feasible combinations of current and future consumption that a consumer can achieve if her income sequence is $\{I_0, I_1\}$. We expect that the consumer is not indifferent among these combinations; some locations along the budget line will provide higher levels of lifetime utility (or satisfaction) than other locations. We now introduce *indifference curves*, which will enable us to analyze how the consumer will choose the combination on her intertemporal budget line that will maximize her lifetime utility.

In figure 4.3, we have plotted three intertemporal indifference curves for Ms. Black. An (intertemporal) indifference curve for Ms. Black is a locus of those combinations

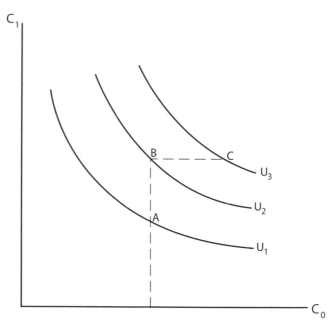

Figure 4.3. Three indifference curves.

of current and future levels of consumption that will provide Ms. Black with a fixed level of lifetime utility. Therefore, any indifference curve for Ms. Black is a set of alternative combinations of present and future consumption among which she is indifferent. An indifference curve is also known as a *constant utility curve*, because as Ms. Black moves along her indifference curve, she substitutes between current and future levels of consumption in such a way that the level of her lifetime utility remains constant.

Ms. Black's intertemporal budget line is a locus of combinations of current and future levels of expenditure that have the same present value. Any one of her indifference curves is a locus of combinations of current and future expenditures that provide the same level of lifetime utility. Accordingly, we can regard the intertemporal budget line as a locus of constant present value and any indifference curve as a locus of constant lifetime utility.

In our treatment thus far, we have collapsed the "future" into a single period, namely, "next year." This is not as restrictive as it might seem. We can resolve the problem of how to allocate resources optimally over time into a sequence of two-dimensional problems. The first problem is to make an optimal choice between spending now and spending later. We need not specify in the current period at what times in the future we will spend resources that we do not spend now. Resources not spent now are simply allocated to the future, which begins in the next period. When the next period arrives, we again make an optimal allocation between now and later, except that we make this allocation with whatever resources remain unspent from the current period. The important point is that at any moment we need consider only the choice between now and later.

4.2.1   Postulates That Govern Indifference Curves

Each of the three indifference curves in figure 4.3 corresponds to a specified, constant level of utility for Ms. Black. Let U_1, U_2, and U_3 denote the three levels of utility, and designate each indifference curve according to its level of utility. Economists use a set of postulates (or assumptions) to characterize the preferences of a typical consumer. These postulates are sufficiently plausible so that economists are willing to use them to construct theoretical models. More important, the models that are built on these postulates are quite successful in generating empirically verified predictions. That is, the postulates work; by using the postulates, economists can discover important insights into how consumers make choices. These postulates apply quite generally to the preferences of a typical consumer, not just to those preferences that involve intertemporal allocation. We will now use these postulates to justify the features of the indifference curves in figure 4.3.

One of the postulates states that a consumer is willing to substitute less of one good for a sufficiently large increase in another good. *Willing to substitute* means that the effect on the consumer's utility of the increase in her quantity of one good is exactly offset by the decrease in her quantity of the other good. In our case, the two goods are the levels of current and future consumption. The postulate states that for a sufficient increase in current consumption, the consumer is willing to forego some quantity of future consumption; the converse is also true. The willingness of a consumer to substitute between any Good X and any Good Y implies that an indifference curve for these two goods will have a negative slope.

A second postulate states that a consumer will gain utility if she acquires more of any good without decreasing the quantity of any other good that she has. This postulate is often known as "more is better than less." In figure 4.3, none of the three curves intersects with any other curve. Therefore, any two curves correspond to different levels of utility. Furthermore, if one curve lies above and to the right of a second curve, the first curve will correspond to the higher level of utility. This means that the three levels of utility satisfy the relationship $U_1 < U_2 < U_3$. Consider the points A, B, and C in figure 4.3. Points A and B provide the same level of current consumption and different levels of future consumption. Similarly, points B and C provide the same level of future consumption and different levels of current consumption. The postulate that more is better than less implies that the consumer's level of utility at point C is greater than her utility at point B, which in turn is greater than her utility at point A. More generally, the consumer's levels of utility increase as she moves rightward from indifference curve U_1 to indifference curve U_2 to indifference curve U_3.

We can use a third postulate to justify the convex shape of an indifference curve. This third postulate states that the rate at which Ms. Black is willing to forego future consumption in exchange for a one-unit increase in current consumption diminishes as she moves downward and rightward along any of her indifference curves. The rate at which Ms. Black is willing to substitute between current and future consumption is equal to the slope of the straight line that is tangential to an indifference curve at the point that corresponds to her present levels of current and future consumption. Clearly, the (absolute values of the) slopes of these tangential lines diminish as the consumer moves downward and rightward along any one of the indifference curves.

Mathematicians define as *convex* a curve that has the shape of the indifference curves in figure 4.3.[2]

Economists use postulates to construct models of economic phenomena. The value of a model is its ability to clarify thinking and to generate empirically verified hypotheses. By extension, a set of postulates is valuable if economists can build valuable models based on those postulates. We will not attempt to prove here that an individual's indifference curves are convex. We do offer the following example as a plausible rationale for this postulate.

Consider Mr. and Mrs. Saratoga, who enjoy dining in a certain class of restaurant with their two sons and their daughter. The cost of a typical meal for this family in these restaurants is $80. As a result, each time the Saratogas go to one of these restaurants, they must forego $80 worth of other goods and services that they could have purchased elsewhere. (Since this is a text on the economics of financial markets, it is important to recognize that among the goods that the Saratogas could have purchased are financial securities. That is, the Saratogas could have "saved" the $80, or any portion of it, by purchasing financial securities.) The question that arises from this situation is: how frequently per month will the Saratogas dine out if the cost of a meal is $80?

We can appreciate the implications of convexity of indifference curves if we restate the preceding question in the form of a marginal rate of substitution, as follows: How much spending on other goods and services will the Saratogas forego to increase by one the number of times per month that they dine in the restaurant? The postulate that indifference curves are convex implies that the amount of spending on alternatives that the Saratogas are willing to forego diminishes as the number of occasions on which they dine out per month increases.

For example, the family might be willing to pay at most $110 for the opportunity to dine out three times per month rather than two times per month. But the Saratogas are willing to pay at most $90 to dine out four times per month rather than three. Convexity of their indifference curves means that the marginal values of these occasions diminish as their frequency per month increases. Since the cost of each meal is $80, the Saratogas will dine out at least four times per month. In fact, this family will increase the frequency with which they dine out until the amount of spending on other goods that they are willing to forego decreases below $80. In technical language, the convexity of their indifference curves means that the marginal rate at which the Saratogas are willing to substitute away from other goods diminishes as the frequency of dining out increases.

4.2.2 The Marginal Rate of Intertemporal Substitution

Consider point D on indifference curve U_1 in figure 4.4. In a small neighborhood of point D, we can approximate movements along the indifference curve by movements along the straight line that is tangential to the indifference curve at point D. Designate this line as line D. Suppose that the slope of line D is $(-)4:1$. If Ms. Black is now at point D, then the maximal amount of future consumption that she can forego in exchange for an increase of $1 in current consumption without suffering a reduction in her level of utility is $4. If Ms. Black could obtain an increase of $1 in current consumption while giving up less than $4 in future consumption, she would obtain a net increase in her level of utility.

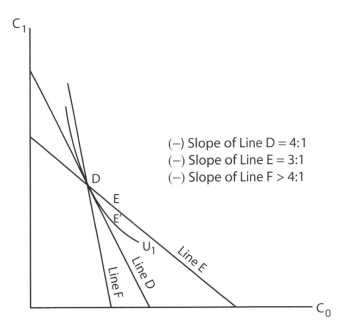

Figure 4.4. Intertemporal equilibrium and the marginal rate of substitution between future and current spending.

To understand this, consider the straight line labeled E that intersects indifference curve U_1 at point D. Line E slopes downward less steeply than 4:1. Therefore, to the right of point D, line E lies above indifference curve U_1. If Ms. Black were to move rightward along line E starting from point D, she could reach a point that lies above indifference curve U_1. Let point E be the combination of current and future consumption to which Ms. Black moves on line E, and let point E′ be a combination that lies directly below point E and on the same indifference curve that passes through point D. Points D and E′ provide the same level of utility because they lie on the same indifference curve. Compared to point E′, point E provides the same level of current consumption and a larger level of future consumption. Using our postulate that more is better than less, we conclude that Ms. Black will enjoy a higher level of utility at point E than at point E′. Because points D and E′ provide the same level of utility, point E also provides more utility than point D.

More generally, if, starting from point D, Ms. Black can substitute between current and future consumption at any rate that requires her to forego less than $4 in future consumption for a $1 increase in current consumption, then she can gain utility. Therefore, starting from point D, 4:1 is the maximal rate at which she can substitute less future consumption for more current consumption without suffering a reduction in utility.

It is instructive to examine the converse of the foregoing analysis. In figure 4.4, line F intersects indifference curve U_1 at point D with a slope that is steeper than 4:1. Starting from point D and moving leftward and upward along line F will enable Ms. Black to increase her level of utility for reasons analogous to our demonstration in figure 4.3. In general, if Ms. Black is now at point D, and she reduces her current consumption by $1 in exchange for an increase in future consumption that exceeds $4, she will gain utility. Therefore, if Ms. Black is now at point D, $4 is the minimal amount of additional future consumption that would offset the utility that she would lose by reducing her current consumption by $1. We conclude that 4:1 is Ms. Black's marginal rate of substitution between future consumption and current consumption when she is at point D.

Recall that our third postulate states that a consumer's marginal rate of substitution between future and current consumption diminishes as he moves rightward and downward along any of his indifference curves. Graphically, this means that the slopes of the tangential lines become less steep as one moves rightward and downward along any indifference curve. Consequently, indifference curves are convex, as drawn in figures 4.3 and 4.4.

4.3   Allocating Wealth to Maximize Intertemporal Utility

The simple model we have constructed has only two periods: this year and next year. To explain how the consumer will allocate resources between present and future consumption, we must combine two independent pieces of information. The first piece of information determines the set of intertemporal choices that the economy will permit the consumer to make. This set of feasible choices is specified by the consumer's intertemporal budget line. The second piece of information is the consumer's preferences regarding intertemporal substitution. The consumer's family of indifference curves specifies this information.

In figure 4.5, we have plotted the consumer's intertemporal budget line and three intertemporal indifference curves. Indifference curves that lie farther from the origin

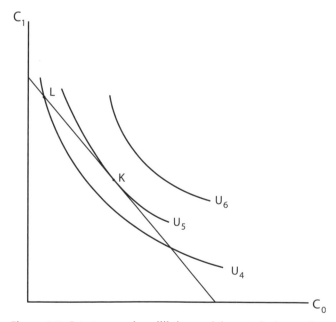

Figure 4.5. Intertemporal equilibrium and the marginal rate of substitution between future and current spending.

correspond to higher levels of utility. But the consumer can reach only those indifference curves that contain points that lie on or below the budget line. Since her indifference curves are convex, the highest curve that she can reach will be the curve that is tangential to the budget line. This curve, and its point of tangency with the budget line, will be unique because all of the indifference curves are convex and the budget line is linear.

The intertemporal budget line is a frontier that defines the maximal level of future consumption that the individual can afford, given her level of current consumption and level of wealth. Clearly, the individual would not choose a combination of current and future consumption levels that plot below her intertemporal budget line. Starting from any position below the budget line, an individual could increase her level of current consumption without foregoing any future consumption. She could also increase her level of future consumption without foregoing any current consumption. Moreover, she could increase both current and future consumption. We assume that the individual will not forego an opportunity to increase her level of consumption in one dimension if there is no cost in terms of a decrease in her level of consumption in another dimension. Therefore, an individual will always choose a position on, and not below, her intertemporal budget line.

Let the point of tangency be at K on indifference curve U_5 in figure 4.5. Then the slope of indifference curve U_5 at point K is equal to the (constant) slope of the budget line. Therefore, to maximize her lifetime utility, the consumer will choose the sequence of current and future consumption that lies on her budget line at a point where the rate at which she is willing to substitute between current and future consumption is equal to the rate at which the market will allow her to substitute by means of either borrowing or lending. Equating these two rates of substitution is an essential condition that the consumer must meet if she is to maximize her lifetime utility. We can appreciate this more fully by considering an allocation in which the consumer has not satisfied this condition.

Consider point L on the budget line in figure 4.5. Every point in the quadrant has precisely one indifference curve passing through it. Since the indifference curves are convex, and since indifference curve U_5 is tangential to the budget line at point K, that indifference curve cannot pass through L. Let U_4 be the indifference curve that passes through L. Then indifference curve U_4 must be lower than indifference curve U_5, and it must intersect the budget line at point L. Since the slope of the indifference curve is steeper than the slope of the budget line at point L, Ms. Black is willing to forego more in future consumption to obtain one more dollar in current consumption than the market requires.

For example, suppose that the slope of the indifference curve at point L is $(-)6:1$, and the slope of the budget line is $(-)2:1$. If Ms. Black has allocated her resources so that her sequence of current and future consumption is at L, then she is not maximizing her lifetime utility. Here is the reason: the market will allow Ms. Black to borrow $1 today if she will repay $2 next year. But at point L she is willing to repay as much as $6 next year if she can borrow $1 today. Clearly, Ms. Black should borrow. By borrowing, she can move rightward and downward along her budget line and thus move to a higher indifference curve.

We conclude that to maximize her lifetime utility, Ms. Black must allocate her resources so that the rate at which she is willing to substitute less future consumption for an extra $1 of current consumption is equal to the rate at which the market will allow her to do so.

We can put this conclusion another way. At point L, Ms. Black's marginal value of an additional $1 of current consumption exceeds her marginal cost. Both marginal value and marginal cost are measured in terms of the amount of future consumption foregone.

4.4   Mutually Beneficial Exchanges

In the preceding subsection, we determined how Ms. Black should allocate her resources if she can borrow or lend. Of course, Ms. Black does not lend to or borrow from the market. Rather, the market is a conduit through which Ms. Black can conduct mutually beneficial exchanges with other consumers. This market will be economically efficient if it enables consumers to identify and effect all the possibilities for mutually beneficial exchanges. We will examine this property of economic efficiency by considering two consumers, Ms. Black and Mr. Green. In what follows, we assume that these are typical of a large number of consumers, each of whom is too small to affect the interest rate at which they can borrow or lend. That is, we assume that the market is perfectly competitive.

Competition among consumers who want to maximize lifetime utility by borrowing or lending determines an equilibrium rate of interest, which in turn determines the slope of each consumer's intertemporal budget line. Since the market is perfectly competitive, every consumer will face the same interest rate. Consequently, every consumer's intertemporal budget line will have the same slope, namely $-(1+r)$. The fact that all consumers face the same interest rate is critical for showing that the market for borrowing and lending is economically efficient.

Although Ms. Black and Mr. Green face the same interest rate, these two consumers differ in two respects. First, the two persons have different levels of wealth. Their intertemporal budget lines lie at different distances from the origin. Second, the two persons have different preferences regarding substitution between current and future consumption. Therefore, Ms. Black's set of indifference curves will not have the same shapes as Mr. Green's indifference curves.

In figure 4.6 (a) and (b), we have drawn the budget lines and indifference curves for the two consumers. Ms. Black's sequence of income payments is located at point T in figure 4.6(a). She has a relatively small current income and a relatively large future income. Mr. Green has the opposite configuration of current and future incomes; his sequence of income payments lies at point Q in figure 4.6(b). The intertemporal budget line for each consumer is a straight line that passes through that consumer's income sequence and has a slope equal to $-(1+r)$. Ms. Black is wealthier than Mr. Green because her budget line lies farther out from the origin. If we were to plot both budget lines on the same graph, Mr. Green's budget line would lie between the origin and Ms. Black's budget line. Consequently, Ms. Black can afford any of the combinations of current and future consumption that Mr. Green can afford, and many combinations that he cannot afford; Mr. Green can afford only a subset of the combinations that Ms. Black can afford.

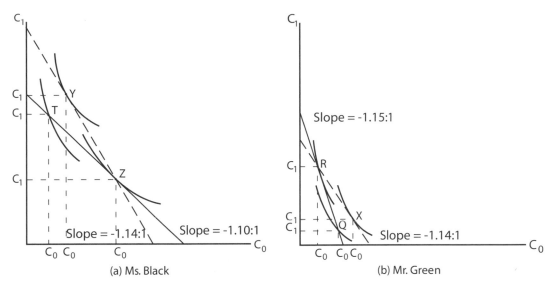

Figure 4.6. Optimal lending and borrowing by two consumers.

Every point in figure 4.6(a) represents a sequence of current and future consumption for Ms. Black. In particular, point T is that sequence of current and future consumption that is identical to her income sequence. If Ms. Black neither borrows nor lends, she would consume all of her income in the year that she receives it.

Every sequence of current and future consumption in figure 4.6(a) generates a specific level of utility for Ms. Black. Therefore, every point in figure 4.6(a) lies on one, and only one, of Ms. Black's indifference curves. Ms. Black's preferences between current and future consumption are such that the indifference curve that passes through her income sequence at point T intersects her budget line at that point. Moreover, the indifference curve is steeper than the budget line at that point. Therefore, Ms. Black will maximize her lifetime utility by borrowing, and she will move downward and rightward along her budget line until she reaches a point of tangency with an indifference curve. Let her optimal sequence of current and future consumption be at point Z in figure 4.6(a).

By contrast, Mr. Green's income sequence and preferences for current and future consumption mean that he should move upward and leftward along his budget line. Therefore, he lends that portion of his current income that will establish a tangency between his budget line and one of his indifference curves. Mr. Green's optimal location is at point R in figure 4.6(b).

The slope of the line tangential to a consumer's indifference curve at a specific point is that consumer's marginal rate of substitution of future consumption for an increase of \$1 in current consumption. Once both consumers have reached their optimal positions on their budget lines, each consumer's marginal rate of substitution between current and future consumption will be equal to the same value, namely $(1+r)$. Consequently, there will be no further opportunity for Ms. Black and Mr. Green to undertake a mutually beneficial exchange that involves current and future consumption.

To verify this last statement, suppose that Ms. Black faces an interest rate equal to .10 (per year), while Mr. Green faces an interest rate equal to .15. Then the budget lines for the two consumers would have different slopes. By reducing her consumption this year by $100, Ms. Black could increase her consumption next year by $110. But Mr. Green could increase his consumption next year by $115 if he reduced his consumption this year by $100. To maximize her utility, Ms. Black would choose a location along her budget line at which her marginal rate of substitution is equal to (1+.10):1. That is, once Ms. Black has allocated her resources optimally between current and future consumption, she will be willing to give up no more than $1.10 in future consumption in exchange for an additional $1.00 in current consumption. Conversely, Ms. Black would require at least $1.10 in additional future consumption in exchange for giving up $1.00 in current consumption.

Similarly, Mr. Green would choose a position along his budget line at which his marginal rate of substitution is equal to (1+.15):1.

There would now be a potential for a mutually beneficial exchange between the two consumers. Mr. Green would have a higher marginal value of current consumption, measured in terms of future consumption foregone, than would Ms. Black. Thus, both consumers could increase their levels of utility if Mr. Green were to borrow from Ms. Black.

Suppose that Mr. Green proposed to borrow from Ms. Black at an interest rate equal to .14. That is, Mr. Green would borrow $1.00 from Ms. Black today and repay her $1.14 next year. Mr. Green would gain utility because he would be willing to pay as much as $1.15 next year if he could increase his current consumption by $1.00. Similarly, Ms. Black would gain utility because she would be willing to reduce her current consumption by $1.00 in exchange for as little as $1.10 in additional consumption next year.

In figure 4.6(b), we show how Mr. Green could increase his utility by borrowing from Ms. Black. If he had no opportunity to borrow from Ms. Black, Mr. Green would be constrained to the choices represented by his budget line. Under this constraint, he would maximize his utility by locating his consumption sequence at point R, where his indifference curve is tangential to his budget line. Since the slope of his budget line is equal to −(1+.15), the slope of his indifference curve at point R would also be equal to −(1+.15). If Mr. Green could now borrow $1.00 and repay only $1.14 next year, he would move to a higher indifference curve. By paying interest at a rate equal to .14, he would move along a straight line whose slope is less steep than the slope of his budget line. That is, the straight line that represents his opportunities to borrow from Ms. Black would intersect his budget line at point R and would move above that budget line to the right of point R. Therefore, by borrowing from Ms. Black, Mr. Green could move to a higher indifference curve and maximize utility at point X.

In figure 4.6(a), we show in an analogous way that Ms. Black could move to a higher indifference curve by lending to Mr. Green. If she had no opportunity to lend to Mr. Green, Ms. Black would be constrained to a budget line whose slope is equal to −(1+.10). Suppose that, under this constraint, she chose point Z on her budget line. The slope of her indifference curve at this point would be equal to −(1+.10). If she could now lend to Mr. Green at an interest rate equal to .14, she could move upward and leftward from point Z along a straight line whose slope is equal to $-(1+.14)$. This straight line is steeper than her budget line. Therefore, by lending to Mr. Green, Ms. Black could move to a higher indifference curve; she would thus maximize utility by locating her consumption sequence at point Y, the point of tangency between her new indifference curve and new budget line.

We draw two conclusions. First, unless every consumer faces the same interest rate, there will be unrealized opportunities for mutually beneficial intertemporal exchanges. Second, if all consumers face the same interest rate, r, and maximize utility, then $(1+r)$ is the common marginal rate of substitution at which any consumer is willing to forego future consumption in exchange for a \$1.00 increase in current consumption. Equivalently, $(1+r)$ is the common minimal increase in future consumption that every consumer will require as compensation for reducing current consumption by \$1.00. This relationship between the interest rate and the rate at which consumers will substitute between current and future consumption is critical for determining the rate at which the economy should accumulate capital if consumers are to maximize their levels of lifetime utility. We consider the question of efficiency in the accumulation of capital in the next section.

4.5   The Efficient Level of Investment

We recall from chapter 1 that consumers can increase their stock of capital goods by diverting resources away from the production of consumption goods. This exchange of consumption goods for capital goods is called an investment.

By investing in one year, consumers can enjoy a larger volume of consumption goods in future years than would be possible without the investment. Therefore, an investment is an exchange of current consumption goods for an increase in the quantity of future consumption goods.

There is sometimes confusion between lending and investment. Borrowing and lending are obviously opposite sides of the same transaction. Whether an investment is made depends on whether or not the borrower uses the borrowed resources to construct capital goods. If she does, then the lender has financed investment by decreasing his current consumption. But if the borrower uses the resources to increase her own level of current consumption above her current income, there is no investment because there is no increase in the stock of capital goods. The lender and the borrower will simply have exchanged portions of their current and future levels of consumption.

To what extent will consumers invest? How do financial markets contribute to reaching an economically efficient resolution of the allocation of resources between current and future consumption? We can use the analysis of the preceding subsection to answer these questions.

We know that if a consumer can borrow or lend, she will move along her budget line until she establishes a tangency between that budget line and one of her indifference curves. At this point of tangency, her marginal rate of substitution of future consumption for an extra \$1.00 of current consumption will be equal to $(1+r):1$, if r is the rate of interest at which that consumer can borrow or lend. If every consumer faces the same interest rate, then every consumer's marginal rate of substitution will be equal to $(1+r):1$. Therefore, a consumer can move to a higher indifference curve if, and only if, that consumer can obtain more than $\$(1+r)$ in additional future consumption in exchange for a \$1.00 decrease in current consumption. Consequently, every consumer will invest if the ratio of the increase in future consumption to the decrease in current consumption that finances it exceeds the ratio of $(1+r):1$.

4.5.1 A Graphical Analysis

We want to show how the economically efficient choice of investment projects is determined by financial markets through the comparison of marginal rates of substitution and the rates of return on prospective investment projects.

In figure 4.7, we return to Ms. Black. Her initial income sequence is at point A. Assume initially that Ms. Black has no opportunity to invest in the accumulation of capital goods. Suppose that initially her opportunities for intertemporal allocation of resources are limited to borrowing from and lending to other consumers at the interest rate r. Under these conditions, her intertemporal budget line passes through point A with a slope equal to $-(1+r)$. To maximize her utility, Ms. Black uses lending to move along her budget line to point B, which lies on indifference curve U_1.

Now suppose that Ms. Black has an opportunity to finance an investment project. Specifically, by investing $\$H_0$ today, Ms. Black can receive $\$H_1$ next year. Ms. Black will employ a manager to run the project. The manager will purchase $\$H_0$ worth of resources today and use those resources to produce a capital good. Next year the manager can use that capital good to increase the production of a

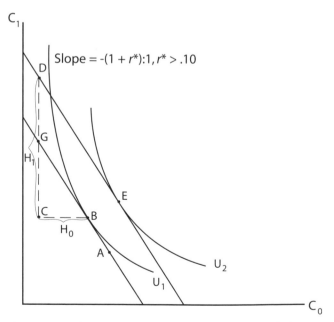

Figure 4.7. Using a profitable investment project to shift the intertemporal budget line.

consumption good, which he can sell for $\$H_1$. Assume that the manager's wage is included in $\$H_0$ and that the capital good lasts only one year. Then the full cost of the project is $\$H_0$, and the full benefit is $\$H_1$. Ms. Black incurs the cost in the form of a decrease in her consumption this year; she receives the benefit as an increase in her consumption next year.

Should Ms. Black undertake this project? If so, how should she finance it? If the ratio of $\$H_1$ to $\$H_0$ exceeds $(1+r)$, the answer is yes, because the project will enable Ms. Black to reach a higher indifference curve than the one that she currently occupies. If future payments are known with certainty, which is the assumption throughout this chapter, then the method that Ms. Black uses to finance the project will have no effect on the size of her gain from the project. This assertion follows from a consideration of opportunity costs.

Suppose that the ratio of $\$H_1$ to $\$H_0$ exceeds $(1+r)$, so that Ms. Black should undertake the project. In figure 4.7, we have shown the cost of the project, $\$H_0$, as a leftward movement from point B to point C. That is, Ms. Black finances the project by reducing her current consumption by the amount $\$H_0$. The payoff from the project is $\$H_1$, which we show as a vertical movement from point C to point D. By financing the project, Ms. Black moves from point B in the current year to point D in the next year. Since the ratio of $\$H_1$ to $\$H_0$ exceeds $(1+r)$, a straight line drawn between points B and D would be steeper than Ms. Black's budget line. Consequently, by financing the project she can reach a combination of current and future consumption that lies above the budget line that passes through her initial income sequence.

Investing in the project enables Ms. Black to reach the higher budget line that passes through point D. This budget line is parallel to her original budget line because the interest rate at which she can borrow or lend is still r. Therefore, once Ms. Black reaches point D on the higher budget line, she can borrow or lend her way to any other point on that line. Clearly, if Ms. Black can move to any point on the higher of the two budget lines, she can reach a higher indifference curve by investing in the project. The optimal point for Ms. Black on the higher indifference curve is, of course, point E, the point of tangency between the budget line and one of her indifference curves.

In drawing figure 4.7, we have assumed that Ms. Black's preferences regarding current and future consumption are such that this point of tangency on the higher budget line lies at point E, which is upward and rightward from the tangency at point B on her initial budget line. In this event, Ms. Black would maximize her utility by using the project to increase both her current and her future consumption. We need not have placed point E upward and rightward from point A. If the project has a positive net present value, then the ratio of H_1/H_0 will exceed $(1+.10)/1$. If this condition is satisfied, Ms. Black can use an investment in the project to reach a higher budget line than the line on which her initial sequence of income lies. Once on the higher budget line, she can use borrowing or lending to move along that line to a point of tangency with an indifference curve. The indifference curve that is tangential to the higher budget line necessarily represents a higher level of utility than the indifference curve that is tangential to the lower budget line. Therefore, investing in the project enables Ms. Black to increase her level of utility.[3]

4.5.2 **Profit versus Utility**

The conclusion in the preceding section bears further discussion. Some will argue that while a project is "profitable," consumers will not finance the project because it requires too large a reduction in current consumption. This argument is incorrect because it confuses profit with utility. The configuration of Ms. Black's indifference curves in figure 4.7 illustrates why this argument fails.

Since the ratio H_1/H_0 exceeds $(1+.10):1$, the project is profitable. We can identify the profit either as a payoff in dollars or as a rate of return.

Profit in Terms of Dollars

We first demonstrate that the payoff in dollars exceeds the opportunity cost. To finance the project, Ms. Black must reduce her current consumption by H_0, which is the horizontal distance between points B and D in figure 4.7. If Ms. Black invested $\$H_0$ in a bank today, next year she would have (including both principal and interest) an amount of money equal to the vertical distance between points B and G. But if she invests H_0 in the project today, her payoff next year will be the vertical distance between points B and D. Since point D is vertically above point G, the project more than covers Ms. Black's opportunity costs and is therefore profitable. Its payoff in dollars exceeds what Ms. Black could obtain from investing in a bank account.

Profit in Terms of Rate of Return

We can restate the preceding analysis by examining the rate of return on the project, rather than calculating the amount of the payoff in dollars. The rate of return on the project exceeds the rate of return at the bank. Investing in the project allows Ms. Black to move from point B to point D in figure 4.7. The slope of the straight line connecting these points is steeper than the original budget line. The slope of the budget line is $-(1+r):1$. Let the slope of a line connecting points B and D be $-(1+r^*):1$. Then r^* must exceed r. The project takes Ms. Black from point B to point D by generating a rate of return that exceeds the rate of return that she can get in a bank. That is, the project is profitable because its rate of return exceeds Ms. Black's opportunity cost.

A Numerical Example

Let the points B, G, and D in figure 4.7 have the following coordinates:

$$B = \{B_0, B_1\} = \{\$400, \$700\}$$

$$G = \{G_0, G_1\} = \{\$300, \$810\}$$

$$D = \{D_0, D_1\} = \{\$300, \$860\}$$

Let the interest rate, r, be .10 per year.

Points B, G, and D represent alternative sequences of payments. The horizontal distance between point B and point G, and between point B and point D, is $100. The vertical distance between point B and point G is $110. The vertical distance between point B and point D is $160.

Since points B and G lie on the same budget line, their sequences have the same present value. Since point D is vertically above point G, the project more than covers Ms. Black's opportunity costs and is therefore profitable. Since the interest rate is .10 per year, the slope of a budget line is $-(1+.10):1$, which is the rate at which Ms. Black can substitute between consumption next year and consumption this year. For example, if Ms. Black were at point B, she could move to point G by reducing her current consumption by $100 and investing that amount in a bank. Next year, her income will be $700 plus the $110 that she can withdraw from the bank. She could then consume next year at a level of $700+$110=$810. The net return on her investment would be ($110−$100)/$100=.10.

Instead of investing $100 in a bank, Ms. Black could invest in the project. To do this would be to move from point B to point D in figure 4.7. Next year her payoff from the project will be $160. Combining this payoff with the income of $700 that she will receive next year independently of the project, she could consume next year at a level of $700+$160, or $860. The net return on her investment would be ($160−$100)/$100, or .60. The slope of a straight line connecting points B and D would be $-(1+.60):1$.

We have established that the project is profitable, whether we measure profit in terms of dollars or in terms of rate of return. Now consider whether the project can enable Ms. Black to increase her utility.

In figure 4.7, point D lies below indifference curve U_1, which is the highest indifference curve that she could reach on her initial budget line. Therefore, Ms. Black will have less utility if she undertakes the project and moves to point D than she will have if she remains at point B. The project does not provide Ms. Black with a sufficient increase in future consumption to compensate her for the decrease in current consumption required to finance the project; therefore, Ms. Black will not finance the project.

But this argument ignores the fact that if Ms. Black has access to a financial market in which she can borrow and lend, she need not reduce her current consumption at all in order to finance the project. In fact, depending on her preferences for current and future consumption, she gains utility by financing the project *and* increasing her current consumption.

In figure 4.8, we demonstrate how Ms. Black could use an investment in the project to move directly from her initial income sequence to her optimal sequence of current and future consumption.

Ms. Black's initial income sequence is at point A. Then her initial budget line passes through point A with a slope equal to $-(1+.10):1$. The project requires an investment of H_0 dollars today and generates a return of H_1 dollars next year. The ratio $H_1/H_0 > (1+.10):1$. We can represent the project graphically by starting at any point on Ms. Black's initial budget line, moving leftward by a distance of H_0 and then upward by a distance of H_1. Starting from point A, Ms. Black could borrow the amount (E_0-Z_0). By construction, $(E_0-Z_0)=(E_0-A_0)+(A_0-Z_0)$, and $(A_0-Z_0)=H_0$, which is the amount by which Ms. Black must reduce her current spending to finance the project.

Ms. Black could use the (E_0-Z_0) that she borrows in the current year to finance the project, $H_0=(A_0-Z_0)$, and increase her spending on current consumption by the amount (E_0-A_0). Next year, Ms. Black's income will be Z_1, which is the sum of A_1, which she will receive independently of the project, plus the payoff, $H_1=(Z_1-A_1)$,

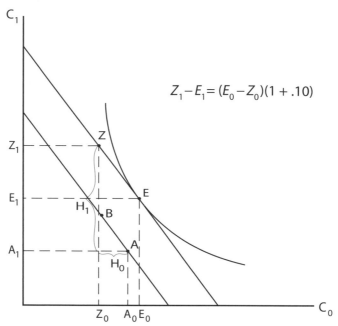

Figure 4.8. Using a profitable investment project to increase the maximal level of utility attainable.

that the project will generate. Since she borrows $(E_0 - Z_0)$ in the current year, she will owe the bank $(E_0 - Z_0)(1 + .10)$ next year. Since the slopes of the budget lines are equal to $-(1 + .10):1$, $(Z_1 - E_1) = (E_0 - Z_0)(1 + .10)$. Therefore, Ms. Black will have E_1 available for spending on consumption next year after paying off the loan (including the interest). By investing in the project, financed by borrowing from a bank, Ms. Black can convert her initial income sequence, located at point A, to the sequence located at point E. At point E, she can spend more on current consumption *and* on future consumption than she could at point A.

Again, the relative locations of points A and E are irrelevant so long as point E lies on a higher budget line than the budget line that contains point A. Point E will lie on a higher budget line if (and only if) the net present value of the project is positive. We conclude that there is no conflict between profit and utility. Economic efficiency requires that Ms. Black undertake every project that has a positive net present value. By extension, every firm in which Ms. Black is a shareholder should undertake every project that has a positive net present value.

4.5.3 Choice of Financing

When the future payments from a project are certain, the method chosen to finance the project is irrelevant to the effect of that project on the investor's utility. In section 4.5, we had Ms. Black finance the project initially by reducing her current consumption. But she then offset that decrease in her current consumption by borrowing from a bank. She could have borrowed from a bank at the outset, or she could have borrowed from another consumer; she could even have borrowed from herself. If she did, she would have incurred an implicit cost in the form of interest foregone. If she chooses to borrow from a bank or from someone else, she will incur an explicit cost in the form of the interest that she pays. Examining figure 4.7 will show that the indifference curve that Ms. Black can reach by investing in the project does not depend on her choice of how to finance the project.

We can easily demonstrate the foregoing result numerically in chapter 5, where we consider firms explicitly. In chapter 13 we will show that if future payments are not certain, the choice of the method of financing does have an effect on whether or not investors can gain utility by undertaking the project.

4.5.4 Summary of Efficient Investment

To achieve an efficient allocation of resources, consumers should finance all projects whose (net) rates of return r^* exceed the rate of interest r. Equivalently, consumers should finance all projects that are profitable in the sense that the (net) rate of return r^* on the funds invested exceeds the opportunity cost r incurred by not depositing those funds in a bank. This correspondence between maximizing profit and maximizing utility is a central principle in economics. We are not saying that profit and utility are identical; indeed, a person's utility usually depends on many considerations in addition to income, profit, or (monetary) wealth. We are saying that in a financial market, the allocation of resources that will maximize a person's profit is the same allocation that will maximize his or her utility.

At any moment, there will be several potential investment projects. We could rank these projects in descending order by the values of their rates of return. We know that consumers should finance all projects whose rates of return exceed the interest rate, r. Suppose that consumers begin to finance projects, choosing first the project that has the highest rate of return, and choosing additional projects in descending order of their rates of return. As consumers accept more projects, they increase the extent to which they are foregoing current consumption in exchange for increases in future consumption. By analogy to the argument in the preceding subsection, the convexity of indifference curves means that the common value of consumers' marginal rates of substitution will increase as consumers trade away more and more current consumption. This increase in the common value of the marginal rate of substitution will increase the equilibrium value of the interest rate, r. Thus, as more and more projects are undertaken, the rate of return of the marginal project will decrease, and the common value of the marginal rate of substitution will increase. The market will reach an equilibrium when the value of the interest rate and the value of the common marginal rate of substitution are equal.

4.6 The Importance of Informational Efficiency in the Prices of Financial Securities

We know that economic efficiency requires that individuals undertake all mutually beneficial exchanges. We also know that in a society that has both a large population and access to complex technologies, there are substantial costs in identifying and effecting all the possibilities for mutually beneficial exchanges. An essential function of a system of financial markets is to transmit information about investment projects and about the rates at which investors are willing to substitute present and future consumption. We say that a financial market is informationally efficient if the prices of financial securities contain all the information that investors need to identify and undertake all mutually beneficial exchanges.

If Ms. Black and Mr. Green are willing to substitute between present and future consumption at different (marginal) rates, they can effect a mutually beneficial exchange. In a modern economy, they would transmit information about their rates of substitution by the prices at which they are willing to buy or sell financial securities. But to achieve economic efficiency, these prices must accurately reflect marginal rates of substitution. If the prices do not do this, some potentially mutually beneficial exchanges will be foregone.

As another example, suppose that a firm has a project that will generate a rate of return equal to 16% per year. Prospective investors are willing to lend at 10% per year. If the investors can inspect the project and determine for themselves that it will pay 16%, then the firm (acting as an agent for current shareholders) and the new investors can create a mutually beneficial exchange. In a modern economy, the technological complexity and the scale of most projects precludes firms from raising the requisite financing from investors who will examine the plans for the project at the same level of detail as the firms have done. Rather, firms and investors will rely on the prices of financial securities to transmit information about proposed investment projects and about the willingness of investors to finance those projects. If the prices of securities do not transmit sufficient information about these projects, there will be an inefficient allocation of resources because some mutually beneficial exchanges will be foregone.

In some situations, a firm can transmit information about investment projects only by the firm's choice of which kind of security to offer to new investors. We briefly discussed an example of this in chapter 2 when we asserted that a firm could overcome a problem of asymmetric information by offering a convertible bond, rather than a straight bond or straight equity. A system of financial markets becomes more informationally efficient by increasing the variety of financial securities in which it organizes trading. The relative prices of these securities contain information for investors. Consequently, the richer the variety of financial securities, the greater is the extent to which all potential mutually beneficial exchanges will be undertaken. We consider in detail several cases of this assertion in chapters 13 and 14.

Notes

1. In keeping with the introductory level of this book, we develop the relevant properties of a utility function in sections 4.2 and 4.3 in the context of using a financial market to effect mutually beneficial intertemporal exchanges. Although our presentation of utility functions is rigorous in that context, we do not present a comprehensive treatment of utility functions.

2. Graphically, if $f(x)$ is a (strictly) convex function of x, then the chord between any two points on the graph of $f(x)$ lies below the graph of $f(x)$ between those two points.

3. Since indifference curves are convex, there can be at most one indifference curve that is tangential to a specific budget line. The postulate that more is better than less requires that indifference curves cannot intersect. Therefore, the indifference curve that is tangential to the higher budget line represents a higher level of utility.

5 Maximizing Lifetime Utility in a Firm with Many Shareholders

5.1 ## The Plan of the Chapter

We know that individuals enter mutually beneficial intertemporal exchanges as part of their strategies to maximize their levels of lifetime utility. The essential purpose of financial markets is to facilitate these exchanges by providing information and liquidity. Some economists would say that the essential purpose of financial markets (indeed, any market) is to reduce transaction costs. In the preceding two chapters, we made several simplifying assumptions to develop the fundamental principles defining the economics of financial markets. In particular, we abstracted from an explicit consideration of firms.

A firm has been described as a nexus of contracts through which owners of resources organize exchanges.[1] Most of these exchanges are based on the theory of comparative advantage reviewed in chapter 3. Since the Industrial Revolution, the technologies for production have become increasingly sophisticated, with the result that allocating resources according to comparative advantages requires increasingly narrow specialization of functions in the organization of production. Moreover, the implementation of these technologies requires large amounts of capital that are beyond the abilities of most individuals to finance. Consequently, individuals pool their resources in firms and employ professional managers to select and operate investment projects.

In the preceding chapter, we explained how individuals could use markets to conduct mutually beneficial intertemporal exchanges. We also explained how individuals would choose the projects in which to invest. We abstracted from firms, but, as just explained, most of these projects would be located within firms. In this chapter, we explain how financial markets provide information and incentives so that individuals who own resources can use firms to obtain the benefits of specialization and exchange. We conduct our analysis explicitly in terms of an individual who owns shares in a firm.

Recall from chapter 4 that individuals should undertake all investment projects whose rates of return exceed the rate of interest offered by a bank. By investing in these projects, they can move from their current intertemporal budget line to a higher budget line. Once on that higher budget line, they can use borrowing or lending to move along that line to a point of tangency with an indifference curve. That indifference curve corresponds to a higher level of utility than the highest indifference curve that they can reach from their initial budget line.

5.2   A Firm with Many Shareholders

When there are many owners of a firm, the same principle applies: the firm should undertake every project for which the rate of return exceeds the rate of interest offered by a bank. By doing so, the firm would be doing for its shareholders what they could do for themselves if they could undertake the same projects that the firm can undertake by pooling the shareholders' funds. A critical point in what follows is that the firm need not make any allowance for variation in its shareholders' willingness to substitute between present and future consumption. As is explained in chapter 4, in equilibrium, every consumer (and thus every shareholder) will allocate resources so that the marginal rate of substitution between future consumption and present consumption is equal to the interest rate. Therefore, all shareholders are identical at the margin. Consequently, the firm can increase the utility of all its shareholders by making decisions based on the (identical) marginal preferences of each shareholder. We demonstrate this assertion by means of several numerical examples.

5.2.1   The Value of a Single Share

The Spring Lake Railroad generates net earnings equal to $10,000,000 per year. We define net earnings to be the amount of money that the railroad could pay to its shareholders as dividends each year. Therefore, the $10,000,000 is what remains from the railroad's earnings each year after the railroad pays all of its costs. These costs include the immediate costs, such as wages, taxes, expenses for fuel and maintenance, and so on, plus provision for the periodic replacement of locomotives, freight cars, track, and so forth. That is, the railroad could pay $10,000,000 annually to its shareholders indefinitely into the future. Assume that the railroad does pay its entire net earnings to its shareholders in dividends each year. In this example, the railroad does not retain any of its annual earnings.

Note here that to retain earnings is to invest in the accumulation of cash balances (or assets such as U.S. government bonds that are "near cash" because they are highly liquid). Thus, by not retaining earnings, the Spring Lake Railroad incurs the opportunity cost of not investing. Nevertheless, for the purpose of simplicity we will continue to assume that the railroad pays its entire net earnings to its shareholders.

The Spring Lake Railroad has 1,000,000 shares of common stock outstanding; therefore, the annual dividend per share is $10. A person who owns one share has the right to receive $10 per year forever. Assume that the interest rate at a bank is equal to 10% per year. Drawing upon our work on present values in section 3.7 of chapter 3, we conclude that the market value of one share is equal to ($10 per year/.10 per year), or $100. The market value of a share is the amount of money that an investor would require to replicate the sequence of payments provided by the share. If the interest rate is .10, a deposit equal to $100 would enable the investor to withdraw $10 in interest each year forever, thus replicating the sequence of payments generated by the share.

5.2.2 Selling New Shares of Stock without Undertaking New Investment Projects

The only way that the railroad can increase the wealth of its shareholders is to undertake investment projects on which the rates of return exceed the rates of interest at which the shareholders can, acting on their own, borrow and lend in the financial markets. A good way to demonstrate this is to examine the effect on shareholders if the railroad were to sell new shares of stock and use the proceeds to pay an extra dividend to the shareholders.

In section 4.1 of chapter 4, we demonstrated that each consumer will have an intertemporal budget line that is determined by the consumer's sequence of current and future income and by the rate of interest. Consumers will use borrowing or lending to move along their intertemporal budget lines until they reach a point of tangency with an indifference curve. This is the highest indifference curve that consumers can reach, given their sequence of incomes and the rate of interest. The only way in which consumers can move to a higher indifference curve and thereby increase their level of utility, is to move to a higher budget line. The only way to move to a higher budget line is to undertake an investment project on which the rate of return exceeds the rate of interest.

If the railroad were to pay its shareholders a special dividend financed by selling new shares, the railroad would merely be moving each shareholder along his or her current budget line, rather than to a higher budget line. Neither the current shareholders nor the investors who purchased the new shares will gain utility. We will now demonstrate this result numerically.

Suppose that the railroad wants to pay an extra dividend, for one year only, equal to $15 per share. The railroad is already paying out in dividends its entire net earnings each year. Therefore, it must raise additional financing to pay the extra dividend. Since there are currently 1,000,000 shares outstanding, the railroad must raise $15,000,000 to pay the extra dividend. If the railroad raises this $15,000,000 by selling new shares, how many shares must it sell? The answer is *not* $15,000,000/$100, or 150,000 shares. The reason is that the price of a share will no longer be $100 once the railroad sells additional shares.

We specified that the railroad will use the $15,000,000 in additional financing solely to pay an extra dividend. In particular, the railroad will not undertake any new investment projects. Therefore, the railroad's net earnings will continue at $10,000,000 per year. At the moment, the regular dividend rate is $10 per year because there are only 1,000,000 shares outstanding. Once the railroad sells additional shares, the regular dividend rate will drop below $10 per year because there will be more than 1,000,000 shares over which to distribute the same $10,000,000 per year.

Let x be the number of additional shares that the railroad must sell to raise $15,000,000. At time 0, the railroad announces that it will raise $15,000,000 by selling x new shares immediately. There will now be $1,000,000 + x$ shares outstanding. There will be no distinction between a share that was outstanding before the announcement and a newly issued share. All outstanding shares have identical rights to receive future dividends, regardless of when the shares were issued. An investor who purchases any share at time 0 has the right to receive a sequence of dividends beginning one year from now and continuing forever.

Let D' be the dividend rate (per share) once the new shares are issued. Since the railroad's annual earnings will remain at \$10,000,000, while the number of shares will have increased to 1,000,000+1x, the new dividend rate, D', will be equal to \$10,000,000/(1,000,000+x). Let P' be the new equilibrium price of a share at time 0, after investors take into account the railroad's announcement. Since all shares are priced on an *ex dividend* basis,[2] the new price will be:

$$P' = \frac{D'}{.10} = \frac{\$10,000,000/(1,000,000+x)}{.10}. \tag{5.1}$$

Multiplying both sides of this equation by $(1,000,000+x)$ produces:

$$P'(1,000,0001x) = \$10,000,000/.10, \text{ or}$$
$$P'(1,000,000)1 P'x = \$100,000,000 \tag{5.2}$$

The railroad wants to raise \$15,000,000 by selling x new shares. We know that these shares will command a price equal to P'. Therefore, $P'x$ must equal \$15,000,000. Making this substitution in the last equation produces:

$$P'(1,000,000) + \$15,000,000 = \$100,000,000, \text{ or}$$
$$P' = \frac{\$100,000,000 - \$15,000,000}{1,000,000}, \text{ or} \tag{5.3}$$
$$P' = \frac{\$85,000,000}{1,000,000} = \$85.$$

As expected, the equilibrium price of a share falls in response to the announcement that the railroad will increase the number of shares outstanding without increasing the annual net earnings that will be available to pay dividends on those shares.

The number of shares that the railroad must issue to raise the \$15,000,000 is:

$$x = \$15,000,000/P' = \$15,000,000/\$85$$
$$= 176,471 \text{ shares.} \tag{5.4}$$

The new dividend rate is:

$$D' = \$10,000,000/(1,000,000+x)$$
$$= \$10,000,000/(1,000,000+176,471)$$
$$= \$10,000,000/(1,176,471) \tag{5.5}$$
$$= \$8.50.$$

We will now show that no investor will gain or lose utility as a consequence of the railroad's decision to finance a special dividend by selling new shares. To demonstrate this assertion, it is sufficient to show that no investor will move to a higher or lower budget line because no investor will either gain or lose wealth.

Consider first an investor who owns one share at time 0 before the railroad makes its announcement. That investor's wealth at time 0 is \$110, which consists of the current dividend of $10, plus the value of his share, which is $100. That is, this investor could liquidate his wealth at time 0 by cashing his dividend check for $10 and selling his share for $100; the horizontal intercept of his budget line is, therefore, $110.

Once the railroad makes its announcement at time 0, the price of this investor's share will drop from $100 to $85. His regular dividend of $10 will be unaffected, and he will receive the special dividend of $15. The decrease in the value of his share is just offset by the special dividend. Since his wealth at time 0 remains at $110, he remains on the same budget line and thus neither gains nor loses utility. Beginning at time 1, he will receive dividends at the rate of $8.50 per year, a reduction of $1.50 from what he would have received had the railroad not sold additional shares at time 0. But he can recover this $1.50 per year by investing the special dividend of $15 at time 0. A deposit of $15 in a bank at time 0 will enable him to withdraw $1.50 in interest per year forever. This procedure is known as creating a *homemade dividend*.

The railroad's action in selling new shares to pay a special dividend has no effect on investors who own shares before the announcement. The railroad has simply done for these investors what they could have done for themselves. By selling 176,471 new shares to raise $15,000,000, the railroad has, in effect, borrowed $15 for each of its original 1,000,000 shares. For an investor who owns one of the original shares, the railroad has borrowed $15. But this "loan" is not free. The investor "pays" for the loan by accepting a reduction equal to $1.50 in his regular dividend rate. That is, the investor pays "interest" at the rate of 10% per year.

Instead of investing his special dividend of $15 in a bank, the investor could use the special dividend to purchase $15 worth of additional shares. We know that the price of a share will drop to $85 once the railroad announces its plans. Therefore, the investor will be able to purchase $15/$85, or approximately .176 of a share. Beginning at time 1, the dividend rate per share will be $8.50. Therefore, the dividend on .176 of a share will be (.176)($8.50), which is approximately $1.50 per year.

We conclude that an investor who owns one share is not affected by the railroad's decision to issue a special dividend. Had the railroad not issued this special dividend, the investor could have financed his own special dividend by borrowing $15 from a bank, and then each year used $1.50 of his regular dividend of $10 to pay interest to the bank. Alternatively, if the railroad does pay the special dividend, the investor can undo the effect of the railroad's action on future dividends by creating a homemade dividend. The investor can do this either by depositing the special dividend in a bank and then drawing interest at the rate of $1.50 per year, or by using the special dividend to purchase an additional .176 of a share, which will pay an annual dividend of $1.50 per year.

We will now consider an investor who purchases one share at time 0, after the railroad announces the special dividend. It does not matter whether the investor purchases one of the newly issued shares or one of the shares that was already outstanding. Each share purchased at time 0 entitles its owner to receive a dividend equal to $8.50 per year, beginning next year and continuing forever. Since the price of one share will drop to $85 in consequence of the announcement, that investor will pay only $85 for one share. A dividend equal to $8.50 per year will just meet that investor's opportunity cost. The new investor neither gains nor loses wealth. By purchasing one share at time 0 after the announcement, she merely trades away $85 and acquires the right to a sequence of future payments whose present value is $85. She will not move to a different intertemporal budget line and therefore will neither gain nor lose utility.

5.2.3 Assets, Capital Gains, and Capital Losses

From our work in the preceding subsections, we conclude that a firm can increase its shareholders' levels of lifetime utility by undertaking any investment project whose rate of return exceeds the rate of interest that the shareholders can earn in a bank. The net present values of these projects are delivered to the shareholders initially as an increase in the price of their stock. This increase, called a *capital gain*, is the present value of the sequence of future dividends that the project will generate. In this section, we discuss briefly the meaning of assets, capital gains, and capital losses. Acquiring a working knowledge of these terms is important for understanding the literature of financial economics.

An asset is anything that will generate a flow of goods or services over time. Each asset has a value determined by the present value of the prices that consumers are willing to pay over time to obtain the goods or services that the asset will produce. However, not every asset has a market value. Some assets generate goods and services that are not bought or sold in markets. For example, a person's acquired ability to enjoy the works of Charles Dickens is valuable to that person in the sense that the person would presumably be willing to pay something to avoid losing that ability. The person might pay more to preserve his ability to read fine print than he otherwise would. But unless the person is able to use his ability to enjoy Dickens by producing public performances or readings, that person's asset will have no market value.

We might agree, then, that there is a difference between value and price In particular, the equilibrium price of any good is the marginal value of the equilibrium quantity of that good. For example, when the market for railroad locomotives is in equilibrium, a railroad is indifferent between purchasing one more locomotive or foregoing that purchase and spending the price of the locomotive on something else. Consequently, the marginal value of the locomotive is equal to its price.

Most of the assets of interest to economists do produce goods or services that pass through markets. These assets, therefore, do have market value. The market value of a railroad locomotive is the present value of the flow of earnings that it will produce for the railroad. A young woman's skill as a writer of computer software is an asset. If she could sell today a contract for her lifetime services as a software engineer, the price of that contract would be the present value of the sequence of salary payments that she could earn over her lifetime. If the markets for assets are perfectly competitive, the equilibrium price of an asset will be equal to its common marginal value across all of its uses.

For example, a railroad on which the marginal contribution of a locomotive to earnings is low will sell that locomotive to a railroad on which that locomotive can make a larger marginal contribution to earnings. Both railroads can gain from this exchange. As a railroad increases its stock of locomotives, the marginal contributions of these locomotives to earnings diminish. Similarly, as a railroad decreases its stock of locomotives, each successive locomotive sold will cause earnings to decrease by successively larger amounts. (Recall the law of diminishing marginal returns from your introductory course.) Railroads will buy and sell locomotives from each other until the marginal value of a locomotive is equal to a common value across all railroads.

Financial assets (or financial securities) are claims on the earnings of other assets. A capital gain (or loss) is a change in an investor's wealth consequent to an increase (or decrease) in the price of an asset that he or she owns. An increase in the market value of one's home creates a capital gain on that home. A decrease in the price of a security that one owns creates a capital loss on that security.

We need to address two more issues. The first issue is the distinction between realized and unrealized gains and losses. A *realized capital gain* is a gain that is converted into cash by selling the asset whose price has increased. Similarly, a *realized capital loss* is a loss that is converted into cash by selling the asset whose price has decreased. To realize a capital gain or loss is to sell the asset whose price has changed.

One often hears that a capital gain or a capital loss "doesn't count" unless it is realized. It is true that capital gains and losses are not included in the computation of one's taxable income until those gains and losses have been realized by selling the asset. To say that these gains and losses do not count until they are realized is misleading because that implies that an investor can, and should, ignore them when deciding how to allocate assets to maximize lifetime utility. Consider the following example.

Mr. Fox purchased a share of the ES&D Railroad several years ago when the price was $100. Since that time the railroad has paid minuscule dividends, and the price of a share has fluctuated unpredictably. Recently, the railroad has experienced a loss of business due to several derailments that have delayed shipments. The railroad has announced a temporary suspension of dividends so as to conserve cash and to finance a rebuilding of the roadbed to reduce the frequency of derailments. The price of a share is now $60. Both Mr. Fox and his wife agree that there is little prospect that the price of a share of the railroad will increase soon.

Air Luker is a new airline that offers direct, nonstop passenger service between Albany, New York, and Portland, Maine. There are no competitors on this route. Ticket sales are brisk, and customer satisfaction is high. Air Luker has begun to pay dividends. The price of a share in the airline is $20. Both Mr. and Mrs. Fox agree that at its current price an investment in the stock of Air Luker is promising, and that their investment in the railroad is unlikely to generate a profit in the foreseeable future. The Foxes disagree on whether to sell their investment in the railroad and invest the proceeds in the airline.

Mr. Fox holds that whatever they might gain by investing in the airline would be diminished by the loss of the $40 that they would incur by selling their stock in the railroad. Mrs. Fox claims that the loss of $40 has already occurred and that continuing to hold the stock in the railroad cannot avoid that loss. She argues that while the value of their investment in the railroad *was* worth $100 when they purchased the stock, that investment is *now* worth only $60. For her, the choice is whether to continue to hold the $60 in the form of one share of the railroad or three shares of the airline. Since the railroad is unlikely to recover from its difficulties within the near future, while the airline shows promise of continued growth, Mrs. Fox prefers to sell the stock in the railroad and invest in the airline.

Mrs. Fox is correct. One way of seeing this is to suppose that the Foxes recently received inheritances from Mr. Fox's Uncle Herbie and Mrs. Fox's Aunt Millie. From Uncle Herbie, the Foxes inherited a share of stock in the railroad that he had purchased for $100 some time before he died. From Aunt Millie, the Foxes inherited $60 in cash. Should the Foxes invest in Air Luker only the $60 that they inherited from Aunt Millie and continue to hold the stock in the railroad in order to avoid losing the $40 difference between what Uncle Herbie paid for the stock and the price for which the Foxes could sell the stock now?

Investors maximize lifetime utility by using borrowing or lending to move along their intertemporal budget lines until they reach a point of tangency with an indifference curve. Therefore, any event that shifts the budget line will affect lifetime utility. For any given rate of interest, the position of the budget line can be determined by its horizontal intercept, with the horizontal intercept being an investor's present value. Since this present value is contingent on the prices of the investor's assets, any capital gain or loss on these assets will shift the budget line, and thus affect lifetime utility.

5.3   A Profitable Investment Project

Our final topic in this chapter is the effect that a profitable investment project will have on an investor's utility. We show that if the railroad undertakes a profitable investment project, then the railroad's current shareholders will gain the entire benefit of the project, regardless of how the railroad finances that project. By *profitable*, we mean a project that has a positive net present value. In particular, if the railroad finances the project by selling new shares, the new shareholders will obtain a return that merely covers their opportunity costs. The conclusion that the railroad's current shareholders gain the entire value of the project regardless of the method of financing is a consequence of our assumption that all future payments are known with certainty. The value of examining this admittedly unrealistic case is that we can develop a model that will, by analogy, assist us when we consider the more realistic case in which the future is uncertain.

5.3.1   The Definition of a Profitable Investment Project

We define as profitable any investment project that will enable investors to shift their intertemporal budget lines outward and thereby increase their levels of lifetime utility. An investor's budget line will shift outward (parallel to itself if there is no change in the interest rate) if there is an increase in her wealth. Assume that her assets include one share of common stock in the railroad. Then her wealth includes her current dividends and the present value of her future dividends. Therefore, an investment project that will increase the sum of her current dividends and the wealth of her future dividends is profitable by our definition. This definition is useful because we assume that any investor will want to do whatever he can to increase his level of lifetime utility.

5.3.2   A New Locomotive

An investment project can be regarded as a sequence of payments in which some of the payments are negative and some are positive. Suppose that the railroad purchases a new locomotive. This locomotive is capable of pulling longer and heavier freight trains, at higher speeds, and with less time required for periodic maintenance than any of the railroad's present locomotives. The higher speeds and longer trains will enable the railroad to attract more shippers and deliver more freight per day, and consequently collect more revenue. The lower maintenance will enable the railroad to retain a larger share of its revenue as profit.

To keep the example simple (but without obscuring the essential economics involved), we assume that the cost of the new locomotive is $1,000,000 and that the entire cost must be paid on delivery, at time 0. Even with careful periodic maintenance, however, the new locomotive will not last forever. We assume that the railroad will set aside each year a portion of its new revenues against the time when the new locomotive will no longer be operable. Consequently, the railroad will have a sequence of these new locomotives in service indefinitely. We assume further that after allowing for periodic maintenance, and after setting aside funds each year for replacement of the locomotives, the net increase in the railroad's annual earnings as a consequence of the new locomotives is equal to $300,000. This will enable the railroad to increase its annual dividends to shareholders by the same amount. Is the project profitable? The answer depends on the investors' opportunity costs.

The investment project is a sequence of payments. At time 0 the payment is −$1,000,000 to purchase the locomotive. We use a negative sign to indicate that the railroad must pay this amount to someone else at time 0. Beginning at time 1, and continuing yearly thereafter forever, the payment is +$300,000. Here we use a positive sign because the railroad will receive this amount annually. In the notation of a sequence, the project is:

$$\{-\$1,000,000, \ +\$300,000, \ +\$300,000, \ +\$300,000, \ldots\}.$$

Drawing on our work in chapter 2, we know that the present value of this sequence is:

$$
\begin{aligned}
&-\$1,000,000 + \frac{\$300,000 \text{ per year}}{.10 \text{ per year}}\\
&= -\$1,000,000 + \$3,000,000 \qquad\qquad (5.6)\\
&= \$2,000,000.
\end{aligned}
$$

Recall that the present value (or capitalized value) of a sequence is the amount of money that would be required now (at time 0) to replicate the sequence. Applying this definition to the sequence above takes a bit of care because of the negative sign. If the first term in the sequence were zero, the sequence would be $\{\$0, \ +\$300,000, +\$300,000, \ +\$300,000, \ldots \}$, and the present value would be $(+\$300,000/\text{year})/(.10/\text{year})$, or $+\$3,000,000$. An investor would require $3,000,000 at time 0 to replicate a sequence of payments equal to $+\$300,000$ beginning next year and continuing forever. She could deposit the $3,000,000 permanently in a bank, and use the 10% interest each year to make the payments.

Including the initial payment to purchase the locomotive, the project is:

$$\{-\$1,000,000,\ +\$300,000,\ +\$300,000,\ +\$300,000,\ \dots\}.$$

To replicate this sequence is to pay $1,000,000 at time 0, and then receive $300,000 per year, beginning at time 1 and continuing forever. It is now clear that $2,000,000 is the amount of money that one must have at time 0 to replicate the sequence. Combining the $2,000,000 with the $1,000,000 that one will receive at time 0 from the sequence will produce $3,000,000 with which one could finance the annual payments of $300,000 that begin at time 1.

There is another interpretation of the net present value of the project. The net present value of a project is the maximal amount of money that an investor would be willing to pay for the right to undertake the project. Drawing on our example in section 5.2 regarding the equilibrium price of a security, suppose that an investor could purchase the right to invest in this project for $1,600,000. This investor could then make a profit equal to $400,000 immediately. Here is the procedure that would produce this profit.

The investor could borrow $3,000,000 from a bank at time 0. She would then use $1,000,000 to purchase the locomotive and $1,600,000 to pay for the right to invest in the project, and put the remaining $400,000 in her pocket. Beginning at time 1, and continuing yearly thereafter forever, the investor would pay the annual interest on the $3,000,000 by using the $300,000 of annual earnings that the project will generate.

But won't the bank want its $3,000,000 back? Not as long as the borrower makes the annual payments of interest. As is the case with any firm, the bank is in the business of producing earnings, and the bank's earnings are the interest that it collects on its loans. If the loans are repaid, the flow of interest (and thus the bank's earnings) ceases. Consequently, the bank will not want its funds back, unless it has doubts about the reliability of the borrower to continue paying interest.

In the preceding analysis, the railroad "overborrowed" from the bank. The railroad could have financed the locomotive by borrowing only $2,600,000 from the bank. If the railroad borrowed $2,600,000, the annual payments of interest to the bank would be $260,000. The annual revenue generated by the new locomotive is $300,000. After paying the annual interest to the bank, the railroad could increase the dividends to its shareholders by $40,000 per year. The net present value of $40,000 per year, discounted at .10 per year, is $400,000 ($40,000 per year/.10 per year = $400,000). In an application of a homemade dividend, shareholders could obtain the $400,000 today by borrowing that amount from a bank, using the $40,000 increase in their annual dividends to pay interest to the bank in perpetuity.

We conclude that shareholders will be indifferent to whether the railroad borrows $3,000,000 or only $2,600,000 from the bank to initiate the project. So long as the shareholders have access to a financial market in which they can borrow and lend, the shareholders can substitute between sequences of payments that are economically equivalent in the sense that they have the same net present value.[3]

5.4   Financing the New Project

We will now evaluate three alternatives for financing the project. We show that when there is no uncertainty about future payments, current shareholders will capture the entire net present value of the project regardless of how the firm finances it. If new shareholders or banks finance the project, they will obtain a return that is equal to their opportunity costs. Working through the following three cases will provide an understanding of how the market causes the price of a security to reflect the net present value of the sequence of future payments to which that security is a claim.

5.4.1 Financing the New Project by Borrowing from a Bank

This is the easiest case to demonstrate. We recall that the railroad's regular annual net earnings are $10,000,000. The entire earnings are paid as dividends to the 1,000,000 outstanding shares, making the annual dividend per share equal to $10. Since an investor who owns one share has the right to receive $10 per year forever, beginning one year after he purchases the share, the price of each share will be $100.

At time 0, the railroad borrows $1,000,000 and purchases the locomotive. Beginning at time 1 and continuing yearly thereafter forever, the railroad will owe $100,000 to the bank as interest on the loan. Annual earnings will increase from $10,000,000 to $10,300,000, with the increase of $300,000 produced by the new locomotive. After using $100,000 to pay interest to the bank, the total annual net earnings available for payment to shareholders as dividends will be $10,200,000. Since the railroad will not have issued any new shares, the dividend rate beginning at time 1 will be ($10,200,000 per year)/1,000,000 shares, or $10.20 per year. Since the interest rate is .10, the price of a share will increase at time 0 from $10.00/.10 to $10.20/.10. That is, the price of one share will increase from $100 to $102. Therefore, purchasing the new locomotive will deliver to each investor who owns one share a capital gain on that share equal to $2.

There will be no change in the dividend at time 0, which will remain at $10. Therefore, the investor will obtain at time 0 an increase in present value equal to the capital gain on his share, or $2. Since there are 1,000,000 shares outstanding, and the net present value of the project is $2,000,000, each investor who owns one share has a claim equal to 1/1,000,000 of $2,000,000, which is $2. He receives this increase in present value in the form of a capital gain on his share.

5.4.2 Financing the New Project by Issuing New Shares

As an alternative to borrowing from a bank, the railroad could raise the $1,000,000 required to purchase the new locomotive by issuing x new shares. From time 1 onward, the railroad's annual earnings will be $10,300,000. All of these earnings will be available for distribution as dividends to shareholders because there will be no loan on which to pay interest. However, the alert reader will anticipate that the railroad will have to pay sufficient dividends to the new shareholders to meet their opportunity costs. Otherwise, the railroad would not be able to sell the new shares. These opportunity costs are, of course, the interest that the new investors could have earned by depositing their money in a bank rather than by purchasing the new shares. Thus, the railroad will still have to pay interest, even though it has not borrowed from the bank.

Using the same argument that we used in section 5.2.2, we can calculate the new price of a share at time 0 as follows. Let the price of a share at time 0 be P''. The railroad must raise $1,000,000 by selling x new shares at a price of P'' each. Then we have:

$$P''x = \$1,000,000 \tag{5.7}$$

The preceding equation has two variables, P'' and x. We need a second equation containing the same variables to obtain a solution. We can obtain the second equation from the calculation of P'' as the capitalized value of the new sequence of dividends. The annual dividend rate before the new project is $10 per share. The new dividend rate will be different for two reasons. First, the new project will increase the railroad's net earnings available for distribution to shareholders. Second, there will be a larger number of shares over which to pay the dividends.

At time 1, and continuing forever, the net earnings available to pay dividends will be $10,300,000. The number of shares will be $1,000,000 + x$. Therefore, beginning at time 1 the dividend rate per share will be:

$$D'' = \frac{\$10,300,000 \text{ per year}}{[1,000,000 + x]} \tag{5.8}$$

Given *ex dividend* pricing, the price of a share at time 0 will be:

$$
\begin{aligned}
P'' &= \frac{D''}{.10} \\
&= \frac{\dfrac{\$10,300,000 \text{ per year}}{[1,000,000 + X]}}{.10 \text{ per year}}
\end{aligned} \tag{5.9}
$$

Multiplying both sides of the equation by $(1,000,000 + x)$ produces

$$P''(1,000,000 + x) = \frac{\$10,300,000}{.10} = \$103,000,000. \tag{5.10}$$

Using the fact that $P''x = \$1,000,000$ and substituting, we have:

$$P''(1,000,000) + \$1,000,000 = \$103,000,000. \tag{5.11}$$

so that

$$P'' = \frac{\$102,000,000}{1,000,000} = \$102.$$

Since $P''x = \$1,000,000$, the number of new shares that the railroad must issue is:

$$x = \$1,000,000/\$102 = 9,804 \text{ shares (approximately).} \tag{5.12}$$

Therefore, the new dividend rate, which will begin at time 1, is:

$$D'' = \$10,300,000/1,009,804 = \$10.20 \text{ (approximately).} \tag{5.13}$$

We can now show that the present value for an investor who owns one share at time 0 before the railroad announces the project will increase by $2. We can also show that the new shareholders will only cover their opportunity costs. They will not enjoy an increase in present value. Therefore, the new project will not enable them to shift their budget line outward. The new shareholders will not be able to increase their utility.

Consider first an investor who owns one share at time 0 before the railroad announces the project. We will call him an "old" shareholder. The price of his share at time 0 is $100. Once the railroad announces at time 0 that it will undertake the project by selling 9,804 new shares, the price of one share will change immediately to reflect this information. The new price at time 0 will be $P'' = \$102$. The new dividend rate will not take effect until time 1, when the new locomotive first produces the increase in earnings. Therefore, the dividend for one share at time 0 will remain at $10. The announcement at time 0 that the railroad will sell x new shares and purchase the locomotive will increase the present value of the old share by $2. This increase in present value is consistent with the fact that the new dividend rate that will begin at time 1 will be $10.20. Clearly, $2 is the present value of the increase in the rate at which the old shareholder will receive dividends beginning at time 1.

Now consider an investor who purchases one share at time 0 after the announcement. She will pay $102 for that share. She will receive dividends at the rate of $10.20 per year, beginning at time 1. These dividends will provide a rate of return equal to 10% on her investment. Thus she will meet her opportunity costs but make no net gain in present value.

The railroad sells 9,804 new shares at $102 per share to raise the $1,000,000 required to purchase the locomotive. The railroad pays each year in dividends to the new shareholders a total of ($10.20)(9,804), or $100,000. Equivalently, the old shareholders on whose behalf the railroad undertakes the project must pay $100,000 per year to the new shareholders. Thus, whether the railroad finances the project by borrowing $1,000,000 from a bank, and pays $100,000 per year in interest, or finances the project by "borrowing" $1,000,000 from new shareholders and paying them $100,000 in dividends, the old shareholders still pay 10% per year to finance the project.

We now make two more observations. Both observations support the assertion that the old shareholders will be indifferent to the method of financing the project.

Observation 1

We have shown that the new shareholders do not obtain any of the net present value of the new project. But what if the railroad has additional opportunities in the future to undertake profitable new projects? The shareholders who are new at time 0 will be old shareholders from time 1 onward. By letting these new shareholders into the firm at time 0, won't the railroad dilute the interests of the current (at time 0) old shareholders in the profits from whatever additional new projects that the railroad might discover in the future? Had the railroad financed the project by borrowing from a bank, the old shareholders would not have any competition for the profits from any projects that might arise in the future. The bank is entitled only to interest at the rate of 10% on the money that it lent to finance the initial project. The bank has no claim on any subsequent projects.

If the market is informationally efficient, admitting the new shareholders into the firm will not dilute the interests of the old shareholders. The reason is that the price of a share at time 0 will include the present values of all the new projects that investors expect will arise in the future. Competition among investors at time 0 will cause the price of a share at time 0 to reflect whatever investors expect, as of time 0, about the ability of the railroad to discover profitable projects in the future. Therefore, an investor who purchases a newly issued share will receive a sequence of dividends, including dividends from projects that will be begun in future years, that will just cover her opportunity costs.

The only way in which any investor, new or old, can obtain more than his or her opportunity costs is to hold shares when the railroad discovers a new project that the market did not anticipate; that is to say, the investor must hold the share when the market is surprised by new information. The reader should note that the term *new information* is a redundancy. In an efficient market, the price of each financial security reflects all that is known about the sequence of future payments that the owner of the security can expect. Therefore, any information that causes a change in the price of a security is new. When an efficient market receives information, there is an unanticipated change in the price of financial securities. Indeed, a more sophisticated definition of capital gains and losses than we offered earlier is a change in the price of an asset consequent to information about the ability of that asset to generate earnings in the future.

Some firms are regarded as growth firms because their earnings are expected to grow over time. Some persons believe that owning shares in these firms is profitable. But this is not correct. The reason, again, is opportunity costs.

Suppose that investors expect that the Spring Lake Railroad will be able to increase its earnings by 5% per year as the economy grows and as the technology for operating trains improves. This steady increase in net earnings does not depend on new projects. In this case, investors expect that the railroad's net earnings will be $10,000,000 at time 0; $10,500,000 at time 1; $11,025,000 at time 2; and so on. If the railroad does not issue any new shares, the dividend rate will steadily increase from $10.00 at time 0, to $10.50 at time 1, $11.025 at time 2, and so on. Then competition among investors will cause the price of a share at time 0 to be more than $100. Moreover, the price will be such that an investor who owns one of these shares, or who purchases one, will just cover his or her opportunity costs.[4] So long as the growth in the railroad's earnings is anticipated, the current price of a share will prevent any investor from beating the market by owning (or purchasing) a share. If information arrives that was not anticipated by investors, and thus was not reflected in the price of a share, then there will be either a capital gain or a capital loss on the share. An investor who owns a share before the information arrives will receive a gain or incur a loss.

Observation 2

The second point also turns on the difference between borrowing from a bank and selling new shares. The railroad can always get rid of its debt to the bank by using some of its earnings each year to pay down its debt to the bank. Eventually, the debt will be paid off. Some persons argue that the railroad's shareholders will be better off if the railroad pays off its debt. But this conclusion is not correct because it ignores opportunity costs. We have seen that if the railroad borrows from a bank, or sells new shares, it is merely borrowing money on behalf of the old shareholders. Those shareholders will have to pay for that loan, either by paying interest to the bank or by paying to the new share-holders in dividends what those investors could have earned for themselves by depositing the price of a share in a bank.

Suppose that the railroad were to use some of its earnings to pay off its debt at the bank or to repurchase (and cancel) shares that it previously issued as new shares. Of course, earnings used to pay off a debt or to repurchase some of the outstanding shares are earnings that the railroad could have paid out as dividends to the remaining share-holders. Consequently, those remaining shareholders will suffer a reduction in dividends, which they could have invested by themselves (in a bank) to earn 10% per year. So the question is, will the remaining shareholders gain or lose if the railroad uses some of its current earnings to pay off debt or to repurchase the previously issued new shares?

The answer, which again depends on opportunity costs, is that the remaining shareholders will neither gain nor lose. The railroad would merely be doing for the remaining shareholders what they could do for themselves.

Paying off the debt would enable the railroad to avoid paying interest to the bank. Repurchasing and canceling some shares would enable the railroad to avoid paying dividends on those shares. But both the interest on the debt and the dividends on the shares cost the railroad, and hence the old shareholders, 10% per year. By using some of its earnings to avoid paying interest to the bank or dividends on some of its shares, the railroad is investing in projects that pay 10% per year. But the remaining shareholders could have earned 10% per year by themselves by investing in a bank the money that the railroad invested by paying off the debt or repurchasing some of the shares.

5.4.3 Financing the New Project by Using Retained Earnings

The last method of financing that we consider is retained earnings. Retained earnings are a portion of net earnings. Net earnings are that portion of the railroad's revenues that it could pay to shareholders in dividends without jeopardizing its ability to continue its operations. For example, net earnings are equal to revenues from transporting freight and passengers, minus wages and salaries, interest payments on its bonds, taxes, and provisions for current maintenance and for replacement of equipment such as locomotives. Retained earnings are that portion of earnings that the railroad does not pay to its shareholders as dividends. Many firms retain a portion of their net earnings for the purpose of financing new investment projects. In some cases, a firm will use retained earnings to accumulate a stock of funds so as to be able to finance new projects that will appear in the future without having to choose between issuing new securities and foregoing the project. In chapter 13 we examine in detail this reason to accumulate retained earnings.

The railroad will purchase the locomotive at time 0 by reducing current dividends by a total of $1,000,000. The railroad will neither borrow from a bank nor issue new shares. The earnings available at time 0 for distribution as dividends will be $10,000,000−$1,000,000, or $9,000,000. Consequently, the dividend per share at time 0 will be $9,000,000/1,000,000, or $9.00.

Beginning at time 1 and continuing forever, the railroad's net annual earnings will increase to $10,300,000. Since there will be no interest to pay to a bank, and no new shareholders to participate in dividends, the dividend rate per shareholder beginning at time 1 will be $10,300,000/1,000,000, or $10.30 per year. The *ex dividend* price of a share at time 0 will be:

$$P''' = \frac{\$10.30 \text{ per year}}{.10 \text{ per year}} = \$103. \tag{5.14}$$

The new value for the price provides a capital gain, at time 0, equal to $3.00 per share.

It is now easy to show that an investor who owns one share at time 0 before the railroad announces the project will gain $2.00 in present value.

As in the cases of financing the project by borrowing from a bank or by issuing new shares, the wealth of an investor who owns one share before the announcement is the value of the current dividend plus the present value of the future dividends. The current dividend (before the announcement) is $10. The present value of the future dividends is the current price of a share, which is $100. Therefore, the investor's present value before the project is announced is $110. The announcement by the railroad has two effects: the dividend per share at time 0 falls by $1, and the price of a share increases by $3. The result is as follows: the wealth for an investor who owns one share increases by $2. We established earlier that the net present value of the project is $2,000,000. Since there are 1,000,000 shares, and since each share delivers to its owner an increase in wealth equal to $2, the current shareholders as a group acquire the entire present value of the project.

5.5   Conclusion

The profitability of a new project depends on the sequence of its net earnings and on the interest rate. A convenient measure of profitability is net present value, which is the maximal amount that an investor (or a group of investors, or a firm acting on behalf of its shareholders) would be willing to pay for the right to invest in the project. Equivalently, the net present value of a project is the amount by which investors could increase their wealth by undertaking the project. Graphically, the net present value of a project is the horizontal distance by which an investor could shift his or her intertemporal budget line outward as a consequence of undertaking the project.

A firm can increase the lifetime utility of its shareholders in only one way: by undertaking all investment projects that have a positive net present value. Moreover, if all future payments are known with certainty, then current shareholders (those investors who own shares before the firm makes a decision on whether to undertake the project) will be indifferent to the firm's choice of how to finance the project. If the project's net present value is positive, the current shareholders will acquire all of that net present value regardless of how the firm finances the project; any investor who purchases a share after the firm announces the project, or any bank that lends money to the firm, will obtain no more than their opportunity cost. Similarly, if the project has a negative net present value, the current shareholders will incur a loss equal to that net present value; banks and new investors will cover their opportunity costs. A firm cannot convert an unprofitable project into a profitable one simply by using the correct form of financing, nor can a firm convert a profitable project into an unprofitable one by using the wrong form of financing.

We have shown that if a firm finances a new project with funds provided by outsiders, be they either a bank or investors who purchase newly issued shares, the outsiders will not obtain any of the net present value of the project. The entire net present value is captured by the current shareholders because they own the firm, without which the project is worthless. No group of outsiders would finance the purchase of a new locomotive unless they had a railroad on which to operate the locomotive.

In more sophisticated models than the one presented in this chapter, current shareholders and outsiders would share the net present value of the project if both groups held some monopoly power. For example, the railroad might enjoy a monopoly in carrying freight between two cities; if investors want to participate in this freight business, they must do so through the railroad. Simultaneously, there might be a single bank, or a single group of collaborating outsiders, able to finance a locomotive. If the railroad does not have sufficient funds of its own to purchase the locomotive, the current shareholders will have to share with outsiders the net present value of the locomotive's contribution to earnings.

We have assumed throughout the chapter that banks lend and borrow at the same rate of interest. Again, more complex models allow for a gap between the rates of interest for borrowing and for lending. For managerial applications of finance, the gain in the ability of the model to produce useful results is worth the additional complexity. For most applications in economics, however, the simpler model is better.

The foregoing results depend on the existence of an informationally efficient market. In an efficient market, investors have expectations and information about the abilities of firms to discover profitable new projects in the future. In such an informationally efficient market, the current prices of all securities will reflect the consensus of investors' beliefs and expectations about the present values of all future opportunities for profit. Consequently, no investor can expect to gain more than his or her opportunity costs in any investment. Conversely, every investor can expect to cover all of the opportunity costs. The only way in which an investor will gain more than the opportunity costs (or fail to cover them) is if the market is surprised by new information while the investor is holding a security.

The assumption that all future opportunities are known with certainty today is clearly not realistic. Nevertheless, the conclusions that we have established about financing and investment in this chapter have analogies in models that do take uncertainty explicitly into account. Questions in which uncertainty is an important consideration will occupy us for most of the remainder of this book.

Problems

1. Captain Mo runs a commercial fishing unit consisting of a fleet of 20 boats. His regular net earnings per year are $15,000,000, and his company has 1,000,000 shares outstanding.

Suppose that he decides to purchase a newer, faster, and more productive fishing vessel. That is, his new boat can locate, catch, and stockpile more fish per hour, and do so with less time required for periodic maintenance, than any of his present boats. The new boat will enable the fleet to catch and deliver to the market more fish per day, and consequently collect more revenue.

The new boat costs $5,000,000, and this amount must be paid out in full at time 0. After allowing for periodic maintenance, the net increase in the fleet's annual earnings as a consequence of the new boat is equal to $800,000 starting at time 1.

The rate of interest is 10%/year.

Each year Captain Mo pays his entire net earnings to his shareholders as dividends, unless he uses a part of those earnings to finance a new project.

(a) What is the sequence of payments that Captain Mo will receive from the project?

(b) What is the net present value of the project?

(c) Describe how Captain Mo would finance the project by borrowing from a bank. What is the price per share before and after the project? What are the dividends per share before and after the project? What is the capital gain each shareholder will receive (per share) when Captain Mo purchases the new shipping vessel?

(d) Describe how Captain Mo would finance the project by issuing new shares. What is the price of a share at time 0? How many new shares must he issue? What will be the new dividend rate? How will the present value of a share held before Captain Mo announces the project change?

(e) Describe how Captain Mo would finance the project by using retained earnings. What will be the dividend per share at time 0? What is the *ex dividend* price of a share at time 0? What is the capital gain per share at time 0?

2. The DR motor car company has 100 shares of stock outstanding. The net earnings of the company are $5,000 per year, continuing forever. The firm announces that one year from now the company will have an opportunity to pay $1,000 to begin the construction of a new plant. One year after construction begins, the plant will generate additional net earnings equal to $330/year. These additional earnings will continue forever.

Determine:

(a) The net present value of the project.

(b) The new equilibrium price of a share if the firm finances the project by issuing new shares when the construction of the plant begins.

(c) The number of new shares that the firm must issue.

Notes

1. M. C. Jensen and W. H. Meckling, "Theory of the Firm: Managerial Behavior, Agency Costs, and Ownership Structure," *Journal of Financial Economics* (October 1976): 305–360.

2. The *ex dividend* price of a share at time 0 is the price that entitles the investor to receive dividends beginning at time 1. An investor who purchases the share *ex dividend* at time 0 does not receive the dividend paid at time 0 on that share. That dividend is paid to the investor who sold the share at time 0.

3. Our claim for shareholders as a group holds pro rata for an individual shareholder. Suppose that Adrian owns 1% of stock in the railroad. With the new locomotive in service, the increase in Adrian's annual dividend would be 1% of $40,000 per year, or $400 per year. The net present value of this increase in dividends is ($400 per year/.10 per year), or $4,000. Adrian could create a one-time homemade dividend of $4,000 by borrowing that amount from a bank today and using the extra annual dividend of $400 to pay the interest in perpetuity.

4. To continue to own is equivalent to deciding not to sell, which in turn is equivalent to deciding to purchase.

6   A Transition to Models in Which Future Outcomes Are Uncertain

6.1   A Brief Review and the Plan of the Chapter

In the preceding five chapters, we presented an elementary analysis by considering several models. Although these models are instructive, their usefulness is limited by the unrealistic assumption that consumers, investors, and managers of firms all know with certainty how the future will unfold. There will be no defaults by persons who borrow money today and promise to repay it later. Banks that promise to pay interest at rate r will do so, and there will be no unanticipated changes in the interest rate in future years. The sequences of future payments that could be generated by proposed investment projects are known with certainty today. In short, everyone knows how the future will develop.

By supposing that the future is certain, we can easily derive and explain the fundamental principles of the economics of financial markets. The first principle is that the purpose of these markets is to facilitate mutually beneficial intertemporal exchanges. Intertemporal exchanges involve sequences of payments over time. A second principle asserts that the equilibrium price of a security is the net present value of the sequence of payments associated with that security. A third principle holds that to maximize the welfare of its shareholders, a firm should undertake every investment project that has a positive net present value, and that the shareholders will be indifferent to the means by which the firm finances these projects. Many, but not all, of these principles hold by analogy for more realistic cases in which the future is not certain. For this reason, we can analyze the more realistic cases by using analogies with the case in which the future is certain.

But the analogies between the case in which the future is certain and the case in which the future is uncertain are not perfect. If we are to understand the economics of financial markets, we must take uncertainty explicitly into account. The present chapter provides a transition from what we have learned in the preceding five chapters to the analyses that we present in the remainder of the book. The critical question from here on is: how do financial markets adjust the prices of securities when the future is uncertain?

We show that the return to any investment has two components: a reward for waiting and a reward for bearing risk. The reward for waiting is the rate of return on a risk-free government bond. The bond is risk-free because the government can always use its power to tax (and its power to print money) to make the payments that it is obligated to make under the bond.[1] Specifying the reward for bearing risk is a difficult problem, but one on which economists have made much progress. In fact, several economists have been awarded Nobel Prizes for their contributions to this question. Their work is known collectively as *modern portfolio theory*.[2]

In equilibrium, the price of a security must be adjusted for risk because investors are risk averse. The typical investor will not hold a security whose rate of return fluctuates unpredictably unless the price of that security is low enough to compensate for the variability of its rate of return. The seminal contribution of modern portfolio theory is to explain the relationship between the average rate of return on a security and the variability of that rate of return.

In the following section, we present some general observations about risk and risk aversion. Then in section 6.3 we provide a synopsis of modern portfolio theory. In section 6.4, we examine a simple model of a firm whose future earnings are uncertain. In section 6.5, we use this model to show how financial markets can facilitate a mutually beneficial exchange between two investors who differ in their willingness to tolerate risk. In section 6.6, we use this example to explain how a risk-free bond and a risky stock are priced according to modern portfolio theory.

6.2   Risk and Risk Aversion

The term *risky* is used by some persons to describe a venture that has a high likelihood of failing, with the result being that investors lose everything that they invested in the project. Although economists recognize that form of risk, they usually reserve the term *risky* to describe any venture that will generate payments that fluctuate unpredictably over time. In this sense, *risky* is not synonymous with *foolhardy*.

Definition of Risk for a Financial Security
The risk of a financial security is the unpredictable fluctuation in the rate of return on that security.

Economists have established that the typical investor is risk averse. An investor is risk averse if the average rate of return that he or she must have to hold a security increases as the level of unpredictable variability in the rate of return on that security increases. A numerical example will make this clear.

Consider three securities: *A*, *B*, and *C*. The annual dividend on Security *A* is $100, and there is no fluctuation in that payment from one year to the next. The annual dividend on Security *B* is $100±$15. In any given year, the probability of receiving a dividend of $115 is 50%; consequently, the dividend will be $85 with a probability of 50%. The annual dividend on Security *C* is $100±$40, and the deviations of +$40 and −$40 occur with equal probabilities of 50%.

The average annual dividend on each security is $100, but the three securities differ in the ranges over which the dividends can fluctuate. The dividend on Security *A* never fluctuates; the dividend on Security *B* fluctuates over a range from $85 to $115; and the dividend on Security *C* fluctuates over a range of $60 to $140. At what prices will the three securities trade?

Suppose that the annual rate of interest at a bank is .10. From our work in chapter 3, we know that the price of Security A will be $100 (per year)/.10 (per year), or $1,000. Rewriting this equation, we see immediately that the annual rate of return on Security A is $100 (per year)/$1,000=.10 (per year). The rate of return on Security A is the same as the investor could get from a bank. This is appropriate because both Security A and the bank provide an annual payment that is riskless because there is no fluctuation.

What about the rates of return on Securities B and C? These two securities pay on average $100 per year just as does Security A. But if investors are risk averse, they will require a higher average rate of return to hold Security B, and a still higher average rate of return to hold Security C. This means that the price of Security B must be less than the price of Security A, and the price of Security C must be lower still.

For example, suppose that the price of Security B is $90. Then the average rate of return on that security will be $100 (per year)/$90, or 11.1 % (per year). Thus, an investor who holds Security B is compensated for the unpredictable variability by receiving an extra 1.1 percentage points in the average rate of return. The price of Security C must be even lower than $90 if the rate of return on that security is to exceed 11.1%, and thereby compensate investors for accepting the higher level of unpredictable variability in its rate of return.

In the next several sections, we present a simple version of the models that economists use to analyze the connection between the level of risk in a security and the rate of return that the security must offer if investors are to hold that security. If we can determine the equilibrium rate of return for a security, it is a simple step toward determining its equilibrium price.

First, we must have a measure of risk. We must be able to explain, for example, what we mean by saying that one security is twice as risky as another. Second, we must be able to explain the rate at which the market makes adjustments for risk. If we can agree that one security is twice as risky as another, what does that imply for the difference in the average rates of return on those securities? These two issues are the essence of modern portfolio theory.

6.3   A Synopsis of Modern Portfolio Theory

Modern portfolio theory addresses two questions. The first question is: how should rational, utility-maximizing investors allocate their wealth among holdings of financial securities? The answer is that investors will allocate their funds among securities so as to construct a portfolio in which the combination of average rate of return and risk is preferable to every alternative combination of average return and risk that they could obtain. Since investors are risk averse, they will not accept any portfolio, say Portfolio A, if there is an alternative Portfolio B for which the level of risk is the same or lower than that for Portfolio A, but the average rate of return is higher than Portfolio A. Equivalently, they will not accept Portfolio A if there is a Portfolio C for which the average rate of return is the same or higher than that of Portfolio A, but the level of risk is lower. But this answer is incomplete because it does not specify how investors are to construct portfolios so as to sort them according to our comparisons of Portfolios A, B, and C.

The second question for modern portfolio theory follows from the first. If investors behave rationally, what empirical relationships should economists observe among the prices of financial securities? Initially, the term modern portfolio theory was reserved for the models that address the first question. The models that address the second question were known as *capital market theory*. Over time, modern portfolio theory has come to be defined more expansively so that it now includes both kinds of models.

According to modern portfolio theory, each security will be priced so that its average rate of return provides separate rewards for waiting and for bearing risk. We discuss each of these rewards separately.

6.3.1   The Reward for Waiting

An investment necessarily requires waiting for a return on the resources invested.

The reward for waiting is the rate of return on a government bond that will mature at the end of the interval over which we are calculating the rate of return on the security. This rate of return is analogous to the interest rate at a bank that we have been using in the preceding chapters. We use the rate of return on a (U.S.) government bond as the reward for waiting because that rate is guaranteed for an investor who holds the bond until it matures.

For example, suppose that we are interested in explaining the 30-day rates of return on financial securities. To obtain a value for the reward for waiting, we would use a government bond that matures 30 days after it is issued. Let the bond have a face value equal to $1,000. The government makes no explicit payments of interest on this bond. Rather, an investor collects interest implicitly because the price of the bond at the beginning of the 30-day period is less than $1,000.[3]

If an investor can purchase the bond for $994 and receive $1,000 30 days later when the bond matures, she will earn $6 in implicit interest. The monthly rate of interest is $6/$994, or .006. This rate of interest is riskless because there is no chance that the U.S. government will not honor its commitment to pay $1,000 to the holder of the bond at the end of the 30 days. Since there is no risk on these bonds, we take their rate of return as the reward for waiting for the ensuing 30 days.

This reward for waiting is not constant over a sequence of months because the initial prices of these 30-day bonds change from month to month to reflect changes in the supply of, and the demand for, short-term loans. Consequently, future values of the (30-day) reward for waiting are outcomes for a random variable when considered as of the present moment.

6.3.2   Two Kinds of Risk

Financial economists recognize two kinds of risks that are borne by investors who own financial securities. The first kind of risk is *systematic risk*. The second kind of risk is *firm-specific* (or *idiosyncratic*) *risk*.

> ***Definition of Systematic Risk***
> *The systematic risk in a security is the unpredictable variability of the earnings of the firm that is attributable to events that are systemic to the macroeconomic system within which the firm operates.*

Definition of Firm-Specific (or Idiosyncratic) Risk
The firm-specific (or idiosyncratic) risk in a security is the unpredict-
able variability in the earnings of the issuing firm that is attributable to events
that are specific to that firm, rather than to systemic macroeconomic events.

Examples of systematic risk include the effect on a firm's ability to generate earnings of changes in the Federal Reserve Board's policy regarding interest rates, changes in the tax code for corporations, changes in the policy of the Department of Justice that affect the enforcement of the Anti-Trust Act with regard to proposed mergers and acquisitions, and changes in fiscal policy to stimulate or restrain the level of macroeconomic activity.

A firm's ability to generate earnings also depends on the prices that it pays for inputs, the strength of the demand for its products, litigation, resignations of critical executives, and the actions of regulatory authorities, to name just a few. These dependencies are examples of firm-specific (or idiosyncratic) risk.

In modern portfolio theory, the equilibrium average rate of return on a security depends only on the amount of systematic risk contained in that security; the amount of firm-specific risk is irrelevant. The reason is that an investor can eliminate the firm-specific risk contained in a security by holding that security as part of a diversified portfolio. In a large economy with many firms, instances of firm-specific risk are unlikely to be correlated across firms, especially for firms in different industries. By diversifying their investments over a large number of firms whose firm-specific risks are uncorrelated, investors can create a portfolio whose rate of return is independent of the levels of firm-specific risk of the securities contained in that portfolio. If one of the firms in which they invest suffers a negative judgment in a lawsuit, for example, a different firm in the portfolio might unexpectedly win a favorable decision in an application for a patent. The unexpected negative effect on the earnings of the first firm will be, to some extent, offset by the unexpected positive effect on the earnings of the second firm.[4] Since investors can avoid firm-specific risk, the financial markets need not provide any reward for bearing that risk. In chapter 9, we explain how investors should diversify their holdings to eliminate (almost) all of the effects of firm-specific risk on the rate of return on their portfolio.

But investors cannot diversify away from the macroeconomic system within which the firms whose securities they hold operate.[5] Therefore, the equilibrium average rate of return on a security will depend on the amount of systematic risk contained in that security.

Economists describe systematic risk as *rewardable risk* because an investor cannot eliminate that risk through diversification. Similarly, firm-specific risk is *unrewardable risk*.

6.3.3 The Reward for Bearing (Systematic) Risk

Since firm-specific risk is irrelevant to the price of a security,[6] from this point onward we use the term *risk* to mean *systematic risk* when the meaning of the term is clear from the context.

The reward for bearing risk by holding a particular security is the product of two terms. The first term is the *quantity of risk* contained in that security. The second term is the *market price of risk*.

The quantity of risk contained in a security is proportional to the sensitivity of the rate of return on that security to variations in the level of macroeconomic activity. Each security has its own quantity of risk because each security has its own degree of sensitivity to variations in the level of macroeconomic activity.

The level of macroeconomic activity is measured by the rate of return on a portfolio that represents the entire economy. Economists use several alternative approximations to this portfolio. A popular approximation is the rate of return on the S&P 500. This is a portfolio that contains 500 stocks chosen by Standard and Poor's Corporation to represent the American economy.

In chapter 9, where we present the Capital Asset Pricing Model, we will explain how to determine the quantity of risk in a particular security. For now, suppose that the quantity of risk for Security J is 2. Then, on average, the change in the rate of return on Security J from one year to the next will be two times the change in the rate of return on the S&P 500 over the same one-year period. Alternatively, suppose that the quantity of risk for Security K is 1.2. On the average, the change in the rate of return on Security K will be only 1.2 times the change in the rate of return on the S&P 500. In the context of modern portfolio theory, Security J is more risky than Security K because the rate of return on Security J is more sensitive than the rate of return on Security K to changes in the rate of return on the S&P 500. The changes in the rates of return on Securities J and K are expansions of changes in the rate of return on the S&P 500 because the quantities of risk on both securities are greater than 1. If a third security, Security L, has a quantity of risk equal to, say, .7, then the changes in the rate of return on Security L would be contractions of the changes in the rates of return on the S&P 500.

Economists use the term *systematic risk* to describe the sensitivity of the rate of return on a particular security (such as Security K) to fluctuations in the level of macroeconomic activity.

At any moment, the market price of risk is a constant that applies to all securities. This constant is the rate at which the market compensates an investor for bearing risk. Multiplying the quantity of risk in a security by the market price of risk determines the portion of that security's average rate of return that is the reward for bearing risk. As with the reward for waiting, the value of the market price of risk can vary over time.

6.3.4 Numerical Examples

Here are some examples of how modern portfolio theory determines the equilibrium average rate of return for a security as the sum of a reward for waiting and a reward for bearing risk.

Suppose that the interest rate on the government bond is .10. Suppose also that the market price of risk is equal to .04. Finally, suppose that, on average, the change in the rate of return on Security K from one year to the next is equal to 1.6 times the change in the rate of return on the S&P 500 over the same period. Then the quantity of risk in Security K is equal to 1.6. According to modern portfolio theory, the equilibrium average rate of return on Security K will be:

Equilibrium average rate of return for Security K

= Reward for waiting + Reward for bearing risk

= Reward for waiting + (market price of risk) (quantity of   (6.1)

   risk in Security K)

= .10 + [.04][1.6] = .164.

In equilibrium, an investor who holds Security K should receive an average rate of return equal to 16.4%. Ten percentage points of this rate of return are a reward for waiting; the investor could have received this return merely by placing his money in a government bond and waiting for one year to pass. To receive a rate of return greater than 10%, the investor must be willing to bear risk by holding a security whose rate of return is sensitive to the unpredictable variations in the level of macroeconomic activity. The sensitivity of the rate of return on Security K to changes in the rate of return on the S&P 500 is equal to 1.6. The market price of risk is equal to .04. Therefore, an investor who holds Security K is entitled to an increase of (.04)(1.6), or .064, in the average rate of return. That is, by holding Security K, the investor is entitled to a rate of return that is equal to 10 percentage points for waiting and an additional 6.4 percentage points for bearing risk.

If the investor wants a higher average rate of return, he must move his funds from Security K to a security whose rate of return is more sensitive to the level of macroeconomic activity. The market price of risk determines how much additional risk he must accept for each additional percentage point of average rate of return. Since the market price of risk is .04, each additional percentage point of average rate of return requires an additional quantity of risk equal to .01/.04, or .25. Therefore, if the investor wants to increase his average rate of return by one percentage point (.01), he must move his funds to a security whose quantity of risk is .25 higher than the risk on Security K.

Here is an example. Security K's quantity of risk is 1.6. Suppose that the quantity of risk in Security T is 1.85, which is .25 higher than the risk in Security K. The equilibrium average rate of return on Security T will be:

Equilibrium average rate of return for Security T

= Reward for waiting + Reward for bearing risk

= Reward for waiting + (market price of risk) (quantity of   (6.2)

   risk in Security T)

= .10 + (.04)(1.85) = .174,

which is one percentage point higher than the average rate of return on Security K.

With this brief exposition of modern portfolio theory in hand, we next present a simple model of a firm whose earnings are affected by both systematic and unsystematic risk. We use this model to illustrate how financial markets can facilitate mutually beneficial exchanges when future earnings are uncertain.

A Model of a Firm Whose Future Earnings Are Uncertain: Two Adjacent Farms

Intertemporal allocations always involve uncertainty because the future is uncertain. Here is a simple example of an exchange between two persons who differ in their willingness to tolerate uncertainty.

Ms. Tall and Ms. Short operate adjacent farms that are identical in all respects. Each farm produces only corn. The annual earnings of each farm fluctuate unpredictably for two reasons. First, the quantity of corn produced on each farm is subject to the same vagaries of nature. Second, the price at which each woman can sell her corn depends on the level of macroeconomic activity, which fluctuates unpredictably from one year to the next. We propose the following simple model of the annual earnings of each woman.

Suppose first that the level of macroeconomic activity is constant, with the result being that the price of corn is constant. Each year the output of corn on each farm will be high or low depending on whether nature is beneficial or detrimental that year. When nature is beneficial, each farmer will earn $1,200; when nature is detrimental, each farmer will earn only $800. The state of nature for any particular year is unpredictable. Over the longer run, however, each of the two states occurs with a probability equal to 50%. Therefore, if the price of corn is constant, each woman's annual earnings will fluctuate unpredictably between $800 and $1,200; her average annual earnings will be $1,000.

Now suppose that the level of macroeconomic activity fluctuates unpredictably from one year to the next. We will measure that activity by the rate of return on the S&P 500. Specifically, let the rate of return on the S&P 500 take the values $\{-.02, -.01, .00, +.01, +.02, +.03, +.04\}$ according to the probabilities in table 6.1.

We can see from the probability distribution in table 6.1 that the rate of return on the S&P 500 is symmetrically distributed around its central value of .01. That is, over the longer run, the average value for the rate of return will be .01. Further, deviations equal to the same number of percentage points above and below the average of .01 are equally likely.[7]

Table 6.1
Hypothetical Probability Distribution for the Rate of Return on the S&P 500

Rate of Return on the S&P 500	Probability
−.02	.05
−.01	.10
.00	.15
.01	.40
.02	.15
.03	.10
.04	.05
	1.00

Assume that the price of corn is positively correlated with the rate of return on the S&P 500. When the level of economic activity is high, consumers increase their willingness to pay high prices for fresh vegetables, with the result that the price of corn is high. Similarly, when economic activity is low, the price of corn is low; consumers begin to economize, with the result that they are less willing to pay for fresh corn.

The earnings of Ms. Short and Ms.Tall will vary positively with both the level of economic activity (through its effect on the price of corn) and with the state of nature. We model this joint dependence as follows. Let the earnings on each farm in a given year t be determined by the following equation:

$$E_t = \$1,000 \pm \$200 + 2(\$100)[100(S_t - .01)], \tag{6.3}$$

in which E_t is the level of earnings on one farm for the year t, S_t is the rate of return on the S&P 500 for year t, and 2 is the constant that measures the sensitivity of the farm's earnings for year t to the level of macroeconomic activity in that year.

Equation (6.3) states that the earnings on a farm for year t will be equal to $1,000, plus an adjustment to allow for the effect of nature in that year, plus a further adjustment to allow for the effect of the level of macroeconomic activity that year. The adjustment for the effect of nature is $+\$200$ or $-\$200$, depending on whether or not nature has a beneficial or a detrimental effect on the production of corn that year.

The adjustment for the level of macroeconomic activity is determined by the amount by which the rate of return on the S&P 500 deviates in year t from its average, and by the sensitivity of the farm's earnings to variations in the level of macroeconomic activity. The deviation of the rate of return on the S&P 500 from its average fluctuates unpredictably from year to year according to the probabilities specified in table 6.1. The term $(S_t - .01)$ is the deviation in year t of the rate of return on the S&P 500 from its average value of .01 The term 100 inside the square brackets converts this deviation to the equivalent number of percentage points. The sensitivity of the farm's earnings to fluctuations in macroeconomic activity is measured by the constant 2. On average, every variation of one percentage point in the rate of return on the S&P 500 leads to a change in the level of the farm's earnings equal to (2)($100), or $200. The term $100 converts deviations in the rate of return on the S&P 500 to deviations in the level of earnings on the farm.

Note that the average level of annual earnings on the farm is equal to $1,000, because the average adjustment for nature and the average adjustment for macroeconomic activity are both equal to zero. Since beneficial and detrimental effects of nature occur with equal frequency, the adjustments of $+\$200$ and $-\$200$ average to zero. The distribution of values for the rate of return on the S&P 500 are symmetrically distributed around the value .01. Consequently, the average value of the term $(S_t - .01)$ is also equal to zero.

The range over which the annual earnings can fluctuate runs from a low of $200 to a high of $1,800. Earnings for year t will take their minimal value of $200 if in that year nature is detrimental and the rate of return on the S&P 500 takes its lowest value, which is $-.02$. The detrimental effect of nature will depress earnings by $200. A rate of return on the S&P 500 for year t equal to $-.02$ is a negative deviation of three percentage points from its average value. The low level of macroeconomic activity will depress earnings on the farm by (2)($100)(3), or $600. Then the combined effect in year t of nature and the macroeconomy will be to depress earnings on the farm by $800.

Table 6.2
Examples of How Variations in the State of Nature and the Level of Macroeconomic Activity Affect the Level of Earnings on the Farm

	Effect of Nature in Year t	Rate of Return on S&P 500 in Year t	Earnings for the Farm in Year t
1	+$200	.00	$1000+$200+2($100) [100(.00−.01)]=$1000
2	+$200	.02	$1000+$200+2($100) [100(.02−.01)]=$1400
3	−$200	.04	$1000−$200+2($100) [100(.04−.01)]=$1400
4	−$200	−.02	$1000−$200+2($100) [100(−.02−.01)]=$200
5	+$200	.04	$1000+$200+2($100) [100(.04−.01)]=$1800
6	−$200	.01	$1000−$200+2($100) [100(.01−.01)]=$800

Similarly, if nature is beneficial and if the rate of return on the S&P 500 takes its maximal value in that year, the earnings on the farm for that year will be $1,000 plus $800, or $1,800.

In table 6.2, we provide some examples of how variations in the state of nature and in the level of macroeconomic activity affect the level of earnings on a farm. In row (1) of table 6.2, the farm's earnings are equal to their average level of $1,000. The beneficial effect of nature, which added $200 to earnings, was exactly offset by the effect of a weak economy; the rate of return on the S&P 500 was one percentage point below its average of .01. In row (2), the rate of return on the S&P 500 was one percentage point above its average and nature was beneficial. Each effect increased the farm's earnings by $200 above the average of $1,000, making earnings for that year equal to $1,400. In row (3), nature is detrimental, but the economy is strong; the rate of return on the S&P 500 is three percentage points above its average. The effect of nature is to decrease the farm's earnings by $200, and the effect of the economy is to increase those earnings by $600. The net effect on earnings is to increase them by $400 above the average, to a level of $1,400.

In row (4) of table 6.2, both nature and the economy depress the farm's earnings. The former decreases earnings by $200; the latter decreases earnings by $600 because the rate of return on the S&P 500 is three percentage points below its average value. In row (5), nature is beneficial and the economy is as strong as it can be. Consequently, the farm achieves its maximal level of earnings, $1,800. Finally, in row (6), nature is detrimental, which decreases earnings on the farm by $200 from the average of $1,000. Since the economy is operating at its average level, there is no further effect on the farm's earnings, which are $800.

6.5   Mutually Beneficial Exchanges: A Contractual Claim and a Residual Claim

At the beginning of the preceding section, we stated that Ms. Tall and Ms. Short differ in their willingness to tolerate uncertainty. We will now show how these two women can create a mutually beneficial exchange by exchanging different kinds of securities.

One security is a contractual claim. Its owner agrees to a reduction in the average return that she could have had in exchange for being insulated against the unpredictable fluctuations in her rate of return from one year to the next. The other security is a residual claim. Its owner insulates the holder of the contractual claim against risk. In exchange, the holder of the residual claim receives both a higher average rate of return and a higher volatility of that rate of return. In a more general model, investors could trade levels of risk by exchanging securities issued by firms that have different sensitivities to fluctuations in the level of macroeconomic activity.

Consider the two adjacent farms that we described in section 6.4. Ms. Tall owns one farm; Ms. Short owns the other. The annual earnings on each farm fluctuate unpredictably between a low of $200 and a high of $1,800. The average annual earnings on each farm are $1,000.

Ms. Tall is highly risk averse; specifically, she would prefer to have a guaranteed annual income of $600, rather than an annual income that has an average of $1,000.

Ms. Short is less risk averse than her neighbor. If she can have the total of the incomes from both farms each year, then she will guarantee an annual income of $600 to Ms. Tall. Under this arrangement, Ms. Short's average annual income will be equal to $1,400, which is a gain of $400 over what her average income would be if she depended only on her own farm and did not provide a guaranteed annual income to Ms. Tall. Here is the reason: the income on each farm varies over the interval from $200 to $1,800. Therefore, the sum of the incomes from the two farms will vary over the interval from $400 to $3,600. Since both the firm-specific variations and the systematic variations are symmetric, the average of the sum of the annual incomes will be ($400+$3,600)/2, or $2,000. Allowing for the $600 that Ms. Short will pay to Ms.Tall each year, Ms. Short's average annual income will be $1,400.

In gaining an increase of $400 in her average annual income, Ms. Short must accept an increase in the range over which her income will vary. If she depends only on her own farm and makes no guarantee to Ms.Tall, Ms. Short's income will vary over the range from $200 to $1,800. When Ms. Short enters the new arrangement, her income will vary over the interval from −$200 to $3,000. Note that the average over this range is (−$200+$3,000)/2 = $2,800/2 = $1,400.

The lowest value for Ms. Short's income will be −$200. This will occur if the income on each farm takes its lowest value, which is $200. In that event, the sum of the farms' incomes will be $400, and Ms. Short will have to borrow (either from a bank or from herself) $200 to make the guaranteed payment of $600 to Ms. Tall. The maximal value that Ms. Short's income can take is $3,000. This will occur if each farm produces its maximal income, which is $1,800. In that event, the sum of the farms' incomes will be $3,600. After paying the guaranteed $600 to Ms. Tall, Ms. Short will have an income of $3,000.

The two women have made a mutually beneficial exchange. The highly risk-averse Ms. Tall trades away $400 of her average annual income of $1,000 in exchange for a guarantee against unpredictable fluctuations in her income. The less risk-averse Ms. Short accepts an increase in the range over which her income will fluctuate, in exchange for an increase of $400 in her average income.

Ms. Tall holds a contractual claim; she will receive $600 each year regardless of both the state of nature and the level of macroeconomic activity. Ms. Short will absorb the vagaries of both nature and the macroeconomy by holding a residual claim; each year she will receive whatever is left over from the aggregate income of the two farms after Ms. Tall is paid her contractual $600.

Ms. Tall and Ms. Short have created a mutually beneficial exchange that involves the levels of their average incomes and ranges over which their annual incomes vary. Financial markets facilitate these exchanges by enabling firms to offer different kinds of securities. The contractual claim that Ms. Tall holds is analogous to a bond; the residual claim that Ms. Short holds is analogous to a common stock.

6.6   The Equilibrium Prices of the Bond and the Stock

6.6.1   Equilibrium Values for Prices and Rates of Return

We know from the preceding chapters that when future payments are certain, there is an equilibrium relationship between the sequence of payments generated by a security, the price of that security, and the rate of return that an investor can earn by holding that security. This equilibrium relationship is determined through the application of opportunity costs. Specifically, given the level of earnings generated by the security, the price of the security must be such that the rate of return investors can earn by holding the security will just offset the opportunity cost they incur by not placing their money in a bank.

The equilibrium price of a security is the present value of the sequence of future payments associated with that security, using the bank's rate of interest to discount the future payments. If the interest (or discount) rate changes, the price of the security will change in a way to maintain equality between the opportunity costs of holding the security or holding a bank account of equal value. That is, corresponding to a bank's interest rate (which is determined mainly by macroeconomic conditions), there is an equilibrium value for the price of the security.

There is an analogous relationship when future payments are uncertain. There is an equilibrium relationship between the price of a security and the risk-adjusted discount rate for the future payments generated by that security. The value for the risk-adjusted discount rate is determined by the market price of risk and by the quantity of risk contained in that security.

In the next two subsections, we derive the equilibrium price and discount rates for the bond held by Ms. Tall and for the stock held by Ms. Short.

6.6.2   The Equilibrium Price of the Bond

The bond is a contractual claim on the income generated by the firm formed by combining the two farms. The holder of the bond, Ms. Tall, is entitled to receive $600 per year regardless of instances of firm-specific risk or systematic risk. We shall suppose that all investors regard the bond as riskless. That is, investors believe that Ms. Short will always pay the guaranteed $600 per year, even if in a given year she must borrow (either from a bank or from herself) to do so. This assumption is tantamount to assuming that investors believe that Ms. Short will use her high average earnings to accumulate a balance in the bank that is sufficient to honor the guarantee in those (relatively infrequent) years when the earnings of the firm are less than $600. Remember, the earnings will be never be less than $400, and that will occur only if during the same year the conditions for growing corn are poor and the level of macroeconomic activity takes its minimal value.

If investors regard the bond as riskless, then the appropriate discount rate is the bank's interest rate. If this rate is .10, then the equilibrium price of the bond is:

$$P_B = (\$600 \text{ per year})/(.10 \text{ per year}) = \$6,000. \tag{6.4}$$

6.6.3 The Equilibrium Price of the Stock

The stock is a residual claim on the firm's earnings. Ms. Short, who holds the stock, is entitled each year to whatever remains of the firm's earnings after Ms. Tall is paid $600. As we established in section 6.4, Ms. Short's average annual income is $1,400. Her income in any year will fluctuate due not only to the vagaries of nature but also to the unpredictable fluctuations in the level of macroeconomic activity. The vagaries of nature contribute firm-specific risk to Ms. Short's annual income. But firm-specific risk is diversifiable, and thus not rewardable. We can ignore it in determining the rate of return that Ms. Short can expect to earn by holding the stock.

The sensitivity of the rate of return on Ms. Short's stock to the unpredictable fluctuations in the level of macroeconomic activity is the systematic risk for that stock. Ms. Short cannot eliminate this risk by holding her stock as part of a diversified portfolio.[8] Therefore, the quantity of systematic risk associated with her stock will affect its equilibrium rate of return.

The contribution of the systematic risk associated with Ms. Short's stock to the equilibrium rate of return on that stock is determined by the sensitivity of the firm's earnings to variations in the level of macroeconomic activity. In our example, the level of this sensitivity is 2. Since the market price of risk is .04, the equilibrium risk-adjusted rate of return on the stock is the reward for waiting plus the reward for bearing risk, or:

$$
\begin{aligned}
&\text{Equilibrium } \textit{risk-adjusted} \text{ rate of return on the stock} \\
&= \text{Reward for waiting} + \text{Reward for bearing risk} \\
&= \text{Reward for waiting} + (\text{market price of risk}) (\text{quantity of risk}) \\
&= .10 + [.04][2] = .10 + .08 = .18.
\end{aligned}
\tag{6.5}
$$

In equilibrium, Ms. Short should receive an average rate of return equal to 18%, which consists of 10% as a reward for waiting and 8% as a reward for bearing risk. If Ms. Short is to receive an average rate of return equal to 18%, then the price of the stock must be the present value of her average earnings from the stock, discounted at the rate of 18%. Since her average annual earnings will be equal to $1,400, we conclude that the equilibrium price of the stock is:

$$
\begin{aligned}
&\text{Equilibrium price of the stock} = [\$1400 \text{ per year}]/[.18 \text{ per year}] \\
&= \$7,777.78.
\end{aligned}
\tag{6.6}
$$

Note that the equilibrium price of the stock is less than $14,000, which is the result we would obtain if we were to capitalize the average earnings of $1,400 per year by the bank's interest rate of .10 per year. Ms. Short's average annual earnings from her stock are $1,400. Since her earnings are sensitive to changes in the level of macroeconomic activity, and thus fluctuate unpredictably around this average, it is inappropriate to discount the average of these risky earnings by using the risk-free discount rate. The appropriate discount rate to calculate the price of the stock is determined by the sensitivity of the earnings on the stock to changes in the level of macroeconomic activity. Ms. Short is compensated for bearing risk (and thereby insulating Ms. Tall from risk) by being able to purchase the right to receive an average of $1,400 per year by paying less than $14,000. Using the concept of opportunity costs, it is easy to show that competition among investors seeking a risk-free profit will ensure that the price of a right to receive a guaranteed annual income of $1,400 will be $14,000, when banks pay interest at the rate of .10 per year.

Suppose that the price of a security that pays a guaranteed $1,400 per year were $13,500. An investor could purchase the security using $13,500 borrowed from a bank. One year later, the investor would realize a profit equal to $50 because he would receive $1,400 from the security and owe only $1,350 in interest to the bank; (.10)($13,500)=$1,350. If the bank were willing to leave the principal of the loan outstanding and collect only the interest each year, the investor would realize a profit of $50 per year. If the bank insisted on having the loan paid off at the end of one year, the investor could do so by selling the security for $13,500. Whether or not the investor pays off the loan at the end of the first year, he still realizes a profit of $50 for that year. Competition among investors seeking this profit will force the price of the security up to $14,000. At this price, investors cannot obtain a profit by purchasing the security using funds borrowed from a bank that charges interest at .10 per year.

The reader should replicate the foregoing argument for the case in which the price of the security is above its equilibrium value of $14,000.

6.7   Conclusion

A financial security is a saleable right to receive a sequence of future payments. In the preceding chapters, we restricted our attention to cases in which all investors know with certainty today what those future payments will be. Under this restriction, we explained that the current price of a security is the present value of the future payments that will accrue to the investor who holds that security. That present value is calculated by discounting each future payment by the interest rate that banks will pay on deposits.

In the present chapter, we have shown that the principles that govern the pricing of financial securities when there is no uncertainty about future payments have analogous applications when future payments are uncertain. To allow for uncertainty, we use a risk-adjusted discount rate. Under modern portfolio theory, the adjustment for risk depends only on the sensitivity of the rate of return on that security to the level of macroeconomic activity. The justification for this is that rational investors can avoid firm-specific risk by holding well-diversified portfolios. But investors cannot escape the effects on a security's rate of return of the unpredictable volatility in the level of macroeconomic activity. This effect is systematic risk. Economists measure the level of macroeconomic activity by the rate of return on a diversified portfolio such as the S&P 500.

In the preceding chapters, we also examined how financial markets promote mutually beneficial intertemporal exchanges, again assuming that there is no uncertainty about future payments. We stated that economic efficiency in the allocation of scarce resources requires that the financial markets are informationally efficient. In particular, managers of firms need to know the rates at which investors are willing to substitute between present and future consumption. Similarly, investors need accurate information about the rates at which proposed investment projects will generate future earnings. These observations apply also to an economy in which there is uncertainty about future earnings. To examine how, and how well, financial markets allocate resources under uncertainty, we need to develop models of how the markets set the prices of securities when future earnings are uncertain.

How could managers determine the rates at which an investor is willing to substitute between present and future consumption, and between the average rate of return on a project and the volatility of that rate of return? How should managers choose investment projects and methods of financing them if investors have different rates at which they are willing to substitute between the present and the future, and between average return and volatility?

The answers are analogous to questions we raised (and answered) in chapter 4. In that chapter, we concluded that in equilibrium every investor would allocate her wealth between present and future consumption so that the marginal value of present consumption is equal to $1 + r$ (where r is the rate of interest). That is, in equilibrium, the marginal value of one more dollar of present consumption is equal to an additional $(1 + r)$ dollars in future consumption. Since every investor faces the same value for the interest rate, r, all investors place the same marginal value on present consumption. Therefore, managers should undertake all projects whose rates of return exceed the interest rate.

When future payments are uncertain, managers should use risk-adjusted interest rates to determine which projects to undertake. We explain how to obtain these risk-adjusted interest rates in part IV, where we derive modern portfolio theory.

In part III, we present those elements of probability and statistics that we use in part IV to derive modern portfolio theory and its empirical implications for the prices of financial securities. Then in part V, we use these tools to address specific questions about the efficacy of financial markets in promoting economic efficiency.

Problems

1. Suppose that the interest rate on a government bond is .10, and that the market price of risk is equal to .05. In addition, suppose that, on average, the change in the rate of return on Security K from one year to the next is equal to 2.5 times the change in the rate of return on the S&P 500 over the same period.

(a) What is the reward for waiting? What is the quantity of risk in Security K?

(b) According to the capital asset pricing model, what is the equilibrium average rate of return on Security K?

(c) How much additional risk must an investor accept for each additional one percentage point of average rate of return? Describe how the investor should restructure his portfolio to gain an additional one percentage point of average rate of return.

2. Suppose that the price of a security that is guaranteed to pay $2,000 per year is $19,000. Explain how an investor could purchase the security using funds borrowed from a bank (at a rate of .10 per year) and make a risk-free profit of $100 per year? If the price of the same security were $21,000, what would the investor do?

Notes

1. In fact, the bond does carry the risk that the government might inflate the general level of prices by printing too much money relative to the supply of goods and services. In this event, the bondholders would suffer a loss of purchasing power. To address this problem, the government now offers bonds on which the payments of interest are periodically adjusted for inflation.

2. The names of the Nobel laureates and a selected bibliography of their works appear at the end of the book.

3. A bond whose issuer makes no periodic payments of interest is called a *zero coupon bond*. Until the early twentieth century, bonds were issued as certificates, the borders of which were divided into coupons. Each coupon bore a date on which a payment of interest was due. When an interest payment came due, the owner of the bond would clip the appropriate coupon and present it to the bank that made the payments of interest as an agent of the firm that issued the bond. The *coupon rate* of a bond was the percentage of the bond's face value that the issuing firm was obligated to pay annually as interest. Investors who owned bonds were known as coupon clippers. Bond certificates no longer have coupons. It is more efficient, and safer, to record the name of the owner of a bond and make payments electronically than to rely on the mailing and storage of physical coupons. The term *coupon rate* survives, however, as the percentage of a bond's face value that is to be paid annually as interest. Hence, a zero coupon bond, or a zero, is a bond on which there are no annual payments of interest. The owner of the bond receives interest implicitly because the bond is sold initially (by the issuing firm) at a price that is less than the bond's face value that the issuer must pay at the maturity date of the bond.

4. The net effect on the investors' earnings will depend on the relative amounts of money that they have invested in the two firms. We explain this in chapter 8.

5. By including securities of both American and foreign firms in their portfolios, investors can eliminate some of the risk that they would bear if they held only American securities. For a portfolio that is diversified across several countries, the relevant macroeconomic system is the world economy. The level of systematic risk for a security in this portfolio is the sensitivity of the rate of return on that security to unpredictable fluctuations in the rate of return for the world economy. The calculation of this rate of return is problematic; we do not pursue this matter further.

6. The asset pricing models in modern portfolio theory hold that the equilibrium price of a security does not depend on the amount of firm-specific risk in that security. In some of the more recent (and more complicated) models, the equilibrium price of a security does depend on the firm-specific risk in that security.

7. Sometimes there is confusion between a percentage and a percentage point. Suppose that a bank increases the rate of interest that it pays on deposits from .04 per year to .05 per year. The increase in the rate of interest by one percentage point, from .04 to .05, is a 25% increase in the rate of interest, since $(.05-.04)/.04=.25$.

8. Holding the stock as part of a properly diversified portfolio will, however, minimize the firm-specific risk. We define a properly diversified portfolio in chapter 8.

Part III

Rates of Return as Random Variables

7 Probabilistic Models

7.1 The Objectives of Using Probabilistic Models

Financial markets promote mutually beneficial intertemporal exchanges by reducing the costs for individuals to buy and sell financial securities. The securities are rights to receive sequences of future payments. The economics of financial markets is a systematic study of how, and how well, these markets promote mutually beneficial exchanges. To answer these questions, economists must first explain the principles that govern how financial markets set the prices of securities.

In the preceding chapters, we analyzed a simple version of this question by assuming that there is no uncertainty about either the timing or the size of any future payment. Using this assumption, we could easily develop the concepts of present value and opportunity cost. These concepts underlie the central principle that governs the prices of financial securities. This principle is that competition among investors and firms causes the relative prices of securities to adjust so that investors have no incentive to reallocate their funds among securities, and firms have no incentive to change their decisions on which securities to issue and which projects to undertake. If the relative prices of securities have adjusted so as to produce these effects, the market has produced an *equilibrium configuration of prices*. In this equilibrium, the price of each security is the present value of its associated sequence of future payments, and this present value is equal to all the costs, including the opportunity costs, that an investor must incur to purchase the right to receive that sequence of payments.

In reality, of course, future payments are not certain. Some borrowers renege on their promises to pay. The unpredictable variations in firms' future earnings creates a greater problem. A firm relies on its future earnings to pay interest and dividends on its securities. Few firms can predict their earnings with certainty. A firm's earnings will be affected by variations in the demand for its products and in the costs of its inputs. In particular, variations in interest rates will affect a firm's earnings by changing the costs of carrying inventories.[1]

The price of a financial security takes into account any unpredictable variation in future payments. Economists do this by using the concept of a random variable. A random variable is a variable that takes values according to a probabilistic process. A probabilistic process is a process that generates values according to the unpredictable outcomes of an experiment. For example, define the random variable Y as the total number of red cards that one will obtain after drawing one card from each of two decks. The possible values for Y are 0, 1, and 2. Suppose that it is equally likely to draw either a red card or a black card from a given deck. Further, suppose that the two draws are independent in the sense that the outcome of the draw from one deck has no effect on the outcome of the draw from the other deck. Under these conditions, Y will take the value 0 with probability 0.25, the value 1 with probability 0.5, and the value 2 with probability 0.25.[2]

In chapters 1 through 5, we conducted our analyses in terms of the prices of financial securities rather than in terms of their rates of return. This was convenient because, under the assumption that there is no uncertainty about future payments, there is, in equilibrium, only one rate of return. This is the rate of interest paid by banks. In equilibrium, the difference between the prices of any two securities will compensate investors for the differences in the timing and the sizes of the payments generated by the two securities. Competition among investors will adjust the price of each security so that investors who receive the sequence of payments generated by that security will receive a rate of return equal to the rate of interest that they could receive by depositing their money in a bank.

In chapter 6, we considered a simple model in which future payments are uncertain. In that case, investors will create mutually beneficial exchanges based on their differences in willingness to bear risk. In equilibrium, competition among investors will adjust the prices of securities so that their average rates of return will compensate investors for the levels of risk in those securities. Since securities differ in their levels of risk, they will differ in their average rates of return. We saw an example of this in chapter 6 in the difference between the average rate of return on the bond held by Ms. Tall and the average rate of return on the stock held by Ms. Short.

For much of the analysis in the remainder of this book, it will be more convenient to focus on the probability distribution of the rates of return on a security, rather than on its price. We define equilibrium in a financial market as a set of alternative combinations of risk and average rate of return that are available to investors. Competition among investors will adjust the probability distribution of the rate of return on each security so that each security offers one of the equilibrium combinations of average rate of return and risk.

To understand the concept of equilibrium as a set of alternate combinations of risk and average rate of return, we represent the rate of return on a security as a random variable, and develop properties of the probability distribution of that random variable.

7.2   Rates of Return and Prices

In this section, we explain the relationship between the rate of return on a security and the price of that security. Assume that securities can be bought or sold only at discrete times. Let t designate any one of these times, and let t take the values $t=0$, $t=1$, $t=2$, and so on. The present moment is $t=0$. Payments of dividends or interest occur only at these times. An investor who purchases a security at time t will not receive any dividend or interest that is paid on that security at time t. He will not be eligible to receive dividends or interest on that security until time $t+1$. The investor who sells the security at time t receives whatever interest or dividend is paid at that time. We say that securities are sold *ex dividend*, or *ex interest*.[3]

The rate of return on a security over one period of time is the change in its price over that period plus the dividend or interest paid during or at the end of that period. For convenience, we consider only stocks, so that the only payment that can occur is a dividend.

Let $r_{i,t}$ be the rate of return on Security i from time $t-1$ to time t. Let $P_{i,t-1}$ be its price at time $t-1$, and $P_{i,t}$ be its price at time t. Finally, let $D_{i,t}$ be the dividend paid (per share) during the period that ends at time t. If the firm pays no dividend during that period, then $D_{i,t}$ will be zero.[4]

The rate of return $r_{i,t}$ is defined by:

$$r_{i,t} = \frac{(P_{i,t} - P_{i,t-1}) + D_{i,t}}{P_{i,t-1}}. \tag{7.1}$$

The variable $r_{i,t}$ is the rate at which an investment in Security i will change in value from time $t-1$ to time t, with the rate of change measured per dollar invested in Security i at time $t-1$. The difference in prices, $P_{i,t} - P_{i,t-1}$, is the capital gain or loss, and $D_{i,t}$ is the dividend. Clearly, the rate of return can be negative if the price falls from time $t-1$ to time t by an amount that exceeds the size of the dividend.

The definition of the rate of return $r_{i,t}$ does not require that the investor purchased Security i at time $t-1$; she could have purchased it earlier. Nor does the definition require that she sell Security i at time t. Consistent with the concept of opportunity costs, the definition of rate of return in equation (7.1) recognizes that an investor who purchased Security i prior to time $t-1$ had the opportunity to sell it at that time for $P_{i,t-1}$ in cash. A decision at time $t-1$ to continue to hold a share of Security i that the investor bought at an earlier time is economically equivalent to a decision to purchase a share of Security i at time $t-1$.[5] Either decision is a decision to hold wealth from time $t-1$ to time t in the form of a share of Security i rather than in the form of a quantity of cash equal to $P_{i,t-1}$. To decide not to sell at time $t-1$ a share acquired previously is an implicit decision to forego holding $P_{i,t-1}$ in cash. To decide to purchase a share at time $t-1$ is an explicit decision to forego holding the cash.

The same logic applies at time t. The critical point is to distinguish between the *level* of the investor's wealth and the *form* in which the investor holds that wealth.

Consider at time t two investors, Mr. Croton and Ms. Harmon. Mr. Croton owns one share of Security i, and Ms. Harmon owns an amount of cash equal to $P_{i,t}$. Both investors hold the same level of wealth at time t; they differ only in the forms in which they hold their wealth. The share of stock and the quantity of money are interchangeable. At time t, a decision by Mr. Croton to continue holding his wealth in the form of one share of Security i is economically equivalent to a decision by Ms. Harmon to purchase one share of Security i. Again, we see an instance of opportunity cost and the distinction between implicit and explicit expenditures. By choosing not to sell his one share of Security i, Mr. Croton has implicitly chosen to forego the opportunity to increase his holdings of cash by the amount $P_{i,t}$. Analogously, by purchasing one share of Security i at the price $P_{i,t}$, Ms. Harmon has explicitly chosen to decrease her holdings of cash by that amount.[6]

We conclude from equation (7.1) that an investor's rate of return on Security i from time $t-1$ to time t does not depend on whether he purchased that security at time $t-1$ or at some earlier time. Similarly, his rate of return from time $t-1$ to time t does not depend on whether he sells the security at time t or whether he decides to hold it beyond that time. The calculation of the rate of return $r_{i,t}$ requires only that the investor hold the security during the interval from time $t-1$ to time t.

In summary, an investor's rate of return does not require that the investor purchases the security at the beginning of the period or sells it at the end of the period. This assertion often causes trouble for introductory students. For that reason, we present the following three numerical examples.

7.2.1 First Numerical Example

Consider the following data for Security i:

$$P_{i,t-1} = \$100,$$
$$P_{i,t} = \$105, \qquad (7.2)$$
$$D_{i,t} = \$10.$$

Using equation (7.1), the rate of return on Security i is

$$
\begin{aligned}
r_{i,t} &= \frac{(P_{i,t} - P_{i,t-1}) + D_{i,t}}{P_{i,t-1}} \\
&= \frac{(\$105 - \$100) + \$10}{\$100} = .15.
\end{aligned}
\qquad (7.3)
$$

An investor who owns one share of Security i at time $t-1$ has, in that one share, a level of wealth equal to $100. How, when, or at what price he acquired that share is irrelevant for the purpose of calculating his rate of return over the interval from time $t-1$ to time t. The investor's decision at time $t-1$ is whether to continue to hold his $100 of wealth in the form of one share of Security i, or to sell that share and hold his wealth in the form of $100 in cash.

Suppose that he decides to continue holding the share. At time t, the level of his wealth will be $115. He will own a share of stock that he could sell for $105, and he will hold a dividend check that he could cash (or deposit in his bank account) for $10. Whether he sells his share at time t or continues to hold it beyond that time is irrelevant.[7] The fact remains that the increase in the price of Security i from $100 at time $t-1$ to $105 at time t increased the level of his wealth by $5. This increase in the value of his share from time $t-1$ to time t, plus the $10 dividend paid at time t, is a rate of return of .15 (or 15%) on his level of wealth at time $t-1$.

Sometimes students are tempted to conclude that the $5 gain in wealth caused by the increase in the price of the share does not "really count" because the gain is "only on paper." Economists do not take this view because it confuses the form of the investor's wealth with its level. The $5 gain in wealth is really there. In fact, if the investor can sell fractional shares, he could obtain the $5 gain by selling 5/105 of his now more valuable share. He would then hold his $115 of wealth at time t in the form of $5 in cash raised by selling 5/105 of a share, $10 in cash from the dividend, and 100/105 of a share. That fractional share would be worth (100/105)$105 = $100.[8]

7.2.2 **Second Numerical Example**

Suppose that the price of Security i decreases from \$100 at time $t-1$ to \$90 at time t. The investor's wealth in this case decreases by \$10. We do not conclude that the loss of \$10 does not count because it is only on paper. At time $t-1$, the investor who owned a share of Security i could have sold it for \$100. At time t, the share can be sold for only \$90. It is not true that the share is "really" worth \$100 at time t. The value of any asset at a specific time is the amount of money for which the owner can, in fact, sell it at that time. The price at which the investor bought the asset at some earlier time is irrelevant.[9] Similarly, any of the prices at which the asset could have been bought or sold at times prior to time t are irrelevant to the value of the asset at time t. Finally, if an investor who owns Security i at time t believes that it is "really" worth more than its current price of \$90, he should continue to hold that security, and sell it only after other investors discover that it is underpriced at \$90 and bid its price up.

Of course, the price of a security is an outcome of competition among investors, all of whom are free to increase their investment in that security (by reallocating funds from other securities) or to decrease their investment in that security. Each of these investors has an idea about what the security is "really" worth. Some of these investors have assiduously collected detailed information with which they form their estimates; some of the investors might even have inside information. Corporate insiders are not prohibited by law from buying, selling, or holding securities issued by their firms. The insiders are only prohibited from buying or selling on inside information. But an insider is likely to evaluate the publicly available information better than an outsider can. Moreover, an insider can affect the price by choosing not to trade, because the absence of the insider's trade will reduce the volume of buy orders or sell orders for the security.

The fact that the price of Security i reflects competition among investors, many of whom have information about the firm that issued the security, and some of whom have excellent information, should give pause to the typical outsider who believes that he knows that the current price of Security i is not what that security is "really" worth.

7.2.3 **Third Numerical Example**

Suppose that the data are:

$$P_{i,t-1} = \$100,$$
$$P_{i,t} = \$98,$$
$$D_{i,t} = \$5.$$

(7.4)

Again, from equation (7.1), the rate of return is:

$$r_{i,t} = \frac{(P_{i,t} - P_{i,t-1}) + D_{i,t}}{P_{i,t-1}}$$
$$= \frac{(\$98 - \$100) + \$5}{\$100} = .03.$$

(7.5)

In this case, the capital loss of \$2 is more than offset by the \$5 dividend.

Why would a security that pays a dividend suffer a decrease in price? This is an easy question if we recall that the price of a security is the present value of anticipated future dividends. The decrease in price could have been caused by the arrival of information after time $t-1$ and before time t that caused investors to revise downward their expectations about future dividends.

The rate of return defined in equation (7.1) is called the total rate of return because it combines both the change in the capital value (gain or loss) and the payment of the dividend. Resolved into these parts, the total rate of return becomes:

$$r_{i,t} = \frac{(P_{i,t} - P_{i,t-1}) + D_{i,t}}{P_{i,t-1}}$$

$$= \frac{P_{i,t} - P_{i,t-1}}{P_{i,t-1}} + \frac{D_{i,t}}{P_{i,t-1}}.$$

(7.6)

The first quotient is the rate of capital gain (or loss, if negative); the second quotient is the dividend yield. Both are calculated as a rate of return per dollar invested as of time $t-1$.

7.3   Rates of Return as Random Variables

A random variable is a variable whose value is determined by a probabilistic process. The random variable could be the number of spots on the uppermost face of a six-sided die. In this case, the probabilistic process is the rolling of the die. Alternatively, the random variable could be the number of red cards obtained by drawing one card from each of two decks. The probabilistic process in this case is to shuffle the decks (separately), and then to draw one card from each deck.

The essence of a random variable is the description of the probabilistic process that generates its values. The values generated by the process are known as the outcomes of the process or, synonomously, the outcomes for the random variable. The outcome generated by any single operation of this process is unpredictable. But (usually) we know enough about the process to determine the relative frequency with which we expect to observe particular outcomes during a large number of repetitions of the process.[10]

The following are two examples of random variables that illustrate the distinction between the unpredictability of a specific outcome and the predictability of relative frequencies of specific outcomes over large numbers of trials.

Let Y be the random variable defined as the number of dots showing on the uppermost face of a six-sided die. Accordingly, Y may take any of the values in the set $\{1, 2, 3, 4, 5, 6\}$. Each of the six sides of the die is equally likely to be on the upper face of the die after a roll. Since the die has no memory and no consciousness, there is no reason to believe that the die would or could "try" to display any particular outcome on any roll, based on the pattern of outcomes on previous rolls. Therefore, the probability of obtaining a 4, for example, on any given roll is 1/6. Even if a 4 has occurred much less, or much more, frequently than 1/6 of the preceding several rolls, the probability of obtaining a 4 on the next roll is still 1/6.

A good way to understand this assertion that the probability of obtaining a 4 on a given roll is equal to 1/6 is to appeal to the law of large numbers. Obviously, in any given roll we either will, or we will not, obtain a 4. There is no sense in which we can obtain one-sixth of a 4. The law of large numbers is a statement about relative frequencies in large numbers of trials. In the present case, a trial is one roll of the die. For this case, the law states that as the number of trials increases without limit, the difference between the proportion 1/6 and the proportion of the total number of trials that result in a 4 will approach zero. This is the sense in which we should interpret the probability 1/6 as the likelihood of obtaining a 4 on a given roll.

Suppose that we were operating a casino in which we offer customers an opportunity to pay $1.00 for the privilege of rolling a six-sided die once. If a 4 turns up, we will pay the customer $4.00. If the outcome of the roll is anything other than a 4, the customer gets nothing.

We have no way of predicting the outcome of a given roll. Nor do we care, so long as we stimulate enough interest in this game to have a large number of rolls. Here is the reason. The probability of a customer rolling a 4 is 1/6. By the law of large numbers, the difference between the fraction 1/6 and the proportion of the total number of trials (or rolls) that will generate a 4 will approach zero as the number of trials increases without limit. Let N be the number of times that customers play this game per week. The larger the value of N, the more confidence we can have that the proportion of rolls that produce a 4 will be within a given interval around the proportion 1/6. For sufficiently large N, the number of occasions on which we must pay $4.00 to customers will be $(1/6)N$, to a close approximation. The casino's total payout will be $(1/6)N(\$4.00)$ per week. Since we charge customers $1.00 for each roll, our revenue will be $N(\$1.00)$ per week. The casino's weekly profit for this game will be approximately:

$$N(\$1.00) - (1/6)N(\$4.00)$$
$$= N(\$1.00 - \$0.67) \qquad (7.7)$$
$$= N(\$0.33).$$

This is a good place to discuss more precisely the concepts of confidence and approximation. Suppose that we are interested in predicting the casino's weekly profit from this game to within an error of plus or minus five percentage points. The law of large numbers asserts that the larger the value of N, the more confidence we will have that our weekly profit will be within the interval:

$$(.95)N(\$0.33) \leqq \text{Weekly Profit} \leqq (1.05)N(\$0.33). \qquad (7.8)$$

If we can persuade customers to play this game only 100 times per week, we predict that our weekly profit will be 100($0.33), or $33.00, using equation (7.7). We can have some level of confidence that the actual profit for a particular week will lie within a 10% interval centered on $33.00. That is, the actual profit will lie within the interval from (.95)100($0.33) to (1.05)$N$($0.33), or, since $N=100$, from $31.35 to $34.65.

If we are more successful in stimulating interest in this game, with the result that our customers roll the die 10,000 times per week, then our weekly profit will be approximately 10,000($0.33), or $3,300.00, again using equation (7.7). A 10% interval around this estimate would run from $3,135.00 to $3,465.00. The relative sizes of the

10% intervals centered on the estimates of $33.00 and $3,300.00 are obviously the same; although the absolute sizes of the two intervals are different, both intervals are 10 percentage points wide relative to their center points. But the law of large numbers asserts that the likelihood that the weekly profit will lie within 10% of $3,300.00 when the number of trials is 10,000 is greater than the likelihood that the weekly profit will lie within 10% of $33.00 when the number of trials is only 100.

To continue this example would require that we develop further the probabilistic model that governs the outcomes from rolling dice. Rather than doing that, we next examine normal probability distributions, which are good approximations of the rates of return on common stocks.[11]

7.4   Normal Probability Distributions

In the preceding sections of this chapter, we presented examples of random variables whose outcomes are limited to a discrete set of values. Such random variables are called discrete random variables. The possible outcomes generated by rolling a six-sided die are $\{1, 2, 3, 4, 5, 6\}$. For the number of red cards obtained in one draw from each of two decks, the outcomes are $\{0, 1, 2\}$.

Discrete random variables are not convenient for analyzing rates of return because rates of return can take any one of an infinite number of values along a continuum. A continuous (or continuously distributed) random variable may take any of an infinite number of values along a continuum. Since the number of possible outcomes is infinite, it is awkward to speak of the probability of a specific outcome. Rather, we speak of the probability that the random variable will take a value that lies within a specific interval. Usually, the interval of interest is a subinterval of the interval that contains all the possible outcomes.

7.4.1   The Normal Density Function

Every random variable is defined by the probabilistic mechanism that generates values (or outcomes) for it. Let the rate of return on Security i from time $t-1$ to time t be the normally distributed random variable $\tilde{r}_{i,t}$, characterized by the normal probability density function, shown in figure 7.1.

The bell-shaped curve in figure 7.1 is the probability density function for the normally distributed random variable $\tilde{r}_{i,t}$. All probability density functions are scaled so that the area between the horizontal axis and the graph of the density function is equal to 1.0. A normal probability density function has the symmetrical shape of a bell, as shown in figure 7.1.

We can now define the probability of an outcome for $\tilde{r}_{i,t}$. Since $\tilde{r}_{i,t}$ is a continuous random variable, we define an outcome in terms of an interval in which the value generated for $\tilde{r}_{i,t}$ will lie. Let r_A and r_B, with $r_A < r_B$, be fixed values that define an interval of potential values for $\tilde{r}_{i,t}$.

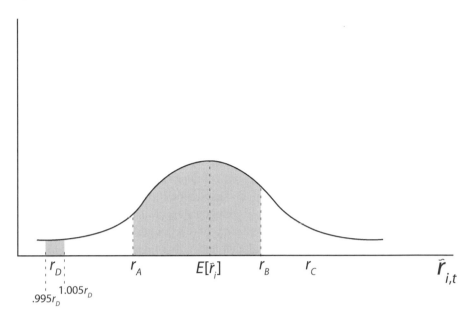

Figure 7.1. A normal probability density function.

Definition: The probability that a single trial will generate an outcome for the random variable $\tilde{r}_{i,t}$ that will lie within the interval (r_A, r_B) is equal to the area between the horizontal axis and the probability density function over that interval.

The shaded area in figure 7.1 is the probability that a single trial will generate a value for $\tilde{r}_{i,t}$ that will satisfy $r_A \leqq \tilde{r}_{i,t} \leqq r_B$.

The fact that the area under the entire probability density function is equal to 1.0 ensures that the probability that $r_A \leqq \tilde{r}_{i,t} \leqq r_B$ will be less than 1.0, unless the interval (r_A, r_B) includes the entire range of values that $\tilde{r}_{i,t}$ can take.

We need to use some care in interpreting the probability density function graphed in figure 7.1. The height of the density function at a particular value for $\tilde{r}_{i,t}$ is an approximation of the probability that $\tilde{r}_{i,t}$ will lie within a small interval around that value. The probability that $\tilde{r}_{i,t}$ will take that particular value is zero. The explanation follows.

We know that a random variable takes values according to outcomes generated by a probabilistic process. We know also that a continuous random variable, such as a rate of return on a security, can take any of an infinite number of values. Let r_C in figure 7.1 be one of the possible outcomes for $\tilde{r}_{i,t}$. The probability that $\tilde{r}_{i,t}$ will take the specific value r_C is equal to the area under the density function and over the single value r_C. But this area is equal to zero because the width is equal to zero. Consequently, the probability that $\tilde{r}_{i,t}$ will take exactly the value r_C is equal to zero. A nonzero probability requires a nonzero area under the density function.

By contrast, consider the interval from $.995r_D$ to $1.005r_D$ in figure 7.1. We have now centered on the single value r_D, an interval that is one percentage point wide $(1.005 - .995 = .01)$. The probability that $\tilde{r}_{i,t}$ will take a value within the interval from

.995r_D to 1.005r_D is equal to the area under the density function and over that interval. Since the interval has (nonzero) width, the area, and hence the probability, that $\tilde{r}_{i,t}$ will take a value such that .995$r_D \leq \tilde{r}_{i,t} \leq 1.005r_D$ is nonzero. The probability that $\tilde{r}_{i,t}$ will take the value r_D itself (or any other single value) is zero.

7.4.2 A Brief Digression on Parameters and Variables

A *parameter* is a variable whose value is fixed in order to specify a particular element in a set of elements that have one or more common property. The distinction between parameters and variables is critical in probabilistic models in finance. For that reason, we pause here to develop this distinction through an analogy.

In figure 7.2, we have graphed three functions. The common property of these functions is that they are all straight lines. A particular straight line is fully determined by its slope and its vertical intercept, both of which are specified by the numerical values of the two parameters in its equation.

Let x and y be variables whose values can be any of the real numbers, which include whole numbers and fractions, both positive and negative numbers, and zero. On a coordinate system in which the values of y are plotted vertically and the values of x are plotted horizontally, the general form of an equation for a straight line is:

$$y = mx+b, \tag{7.9}$$

in which m is the parameter whose value specifies the slope of the line, and b is the parameter whose value specifies the line's vertical intercept. A particular straight line is fully determined by specifying fixed values for the parameters m and b. By holding the parametric values for m and b fixed, the variables x and y may take any values that satisfy equation (7.9). That is, the combinations of values for x and y are constrained to move along a *specific* straight line. By changing the parametric values for m and b,

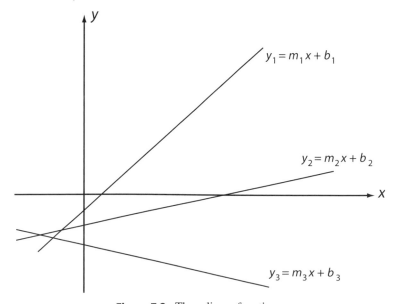

Figure 7.2. Three linear functions.

we allow the combinations of values for *x* and *y* to move along a *different* straight line. We now apply this distinction between parameters and variables to our consideration of normal probability density functions.

7.4.3 The Expected Value and the Standard Deviation of a Normally Distributed Random Variable

There is an infinite number of distinct normal probability density functions. A particular normal density function is fully specified by the values assigned to its expected value and its standard deviation, which are its only two parameters. The expected value of a random variable is the sum of the values that the variable can take, with each value weighted by the probability that the variable can take that value. For a normally distributed random variable, the numerical value of its expected value is the center point of its symmetric probability density function. The standard deviation of a random variable is the positive square root of the sum of squared deviations that the variable can take from its expected value, with each deviation weighted by the probability that it can occur. The numerical value of the standard deviation determines the spread of the density function. In this subsection, we develop some of the properties of the expected value and the standard deviation for a normal density function.[12] First we explain why these parameters are important.

The probabilities with which a rate of return will take values within various intervals are determined by the probability density function for that rate of return. If there is a change in the values of either of the parameters that define the density function, there will be changes in the probabilities that govern the outcomes for the rate of return.

A fundamental property of modern portfolio theory is that an individual investor can, within limits, choose the values of the expected value and the standard deviation of the probability density function that governs the rate of return on the portfolio. An investor can do this by altering the allocation of funds among the individual securities in the portfolio. By changing the values of the expected value and the standard deviation for the rate of return on the portfolio, an investor can change the probabilities that the rate of return will lie within various intervals.

The expected value is a fixed value of the random variable. The expected value of a normally distributed random variable is the center point of its symmetric density function. In figure 7.1, the expected value is E_r.

The second parameter is the standard deviation, the value of which determines the spread, or dispersion, of the density function around its expected value. Unlike the expected value, the standard deviation is not a specific value of the random variable. The standard deviation is a measure of dispersion that is defined in the same units as the random variable. If the random variable is a rate of return, which is defined as a percentage, then the standard deviation is measured in terms of percentage points.

By definition, 68% of the area under a normal density function is contained within an interval that extends from one standard deviation below the expected value to one standard deviation above the expected value. An interval that extends from two standard deviations below the expected value to two standard deviations above it contains 95% of the area under the density function. In figure 7.3, we have drawn some examples of normal probability density functions.

Figure 7.3. Normal probability density functions.

7.5
7.5 A Joint Probability Distribution for Two Discrete Random Variables

Since our primary use of probability theory will be to study the characteristics of portfolios of securities, we must explicitly consider the probabilistic interactions among securities. Accordingly, we now introduce the concept of a joint probability distribution of the rates of return on two securities. To preserve the accessibility of this book for introductory students, we present a simple joint distribution of discrete rates of return for two securities. For our purposes, the analogies between discrete and continuous rates of return are sufficiently close to warrant the simplification.

We will now construct a numerical example to show how the set of combinations of expected return and standard deviation that an investor can choose for a portfolio are determined by the expected returns, the standard deviations, and the correlation coefficient for Securities A and B. The objective of this exercise is to derive the locus of the available combinations of expected return and standard deviation from a joint probability distribution for Securities A and B.

7.5.1 A Joint Probability Distribution for the Rates of Return on Securities A and B

In table 7.1, we have created an extremely simple joint probability distribution for the rates of return on Securities A and B. Consider first the 3×3 matrix in the upper left-hand corner of table 7.1.

Each of the two rates of return may take one of three values. For Security A, the rate of return for a given period will be $-.10$, $.20$, or $.50$. For Security B, the possible outcomes are $.05$, $.10$, and $.15$. The nine entries in the 3×3 matrix are the joint probabilities for the nine possible combinations of values for $\tilde{r}_A$ and $\tilde{r}_B$. For example, the entry in the cell located in the first row and the first column indicates that the combination of $\tilde{r}_A=-.10$ and $\tilde{r}_B=.05$ will occur with a probability equal to $.1$. Similarly, the probability is also $.1$ that $\tilde{r}_A$ will take the value $.50$ (third column), and simultaneously $\tilde{r}_A$ will take the value $.10$ (second row). The nine combinations of values for $\tilde{r}_A$ and $\tilde{r}_B$ are the only outcomes that can occur. Therefore, the nine probabilities in the 3×3 matrix must sum to 1, as they do.

Now consider the single column of three cells located to the right of the 3×3 matrix. The entries in these three cells are the probabilities for the three possible

Table 7.1
Joint Probability Distribution for $\tilde{r}_A$ and $\tilde{r}_B$

		Possible Outcomes for $\tilde{r}_A$			Probabilities for $\tilde{r}_B$ Independent of the Value of $\tilde{r}_A$	Possible Outcomes for $\tilde{r}_B$
		−.10	.20	.50		
Possible outcomes for $\tilde{r}_B$	.05	.1	0	0	.1	$\tilde{r}_B = .05$
	.10	.1	.6	.1	.8	$\tilde{r}_B = .10$
	.15	0	0	.1	.1	$\tilde{r}_B = .15$
Probabilities for $\tilde{r}_A$ independent of the value of $\tilde{r}_B$		.2	.6	.2		
Possible outcomes for $\tilde{r}_A$		$\tilde{r}_A = -.10$	$\tilde{r}_A = .20$	$\tilde{r}_A = .50$		

outcomes for $\tilde{r}_B$, without any restrictions on the value taken simultaneously by $\tilde{r}_A$. We call these entries the unconditional probabilities for $\tilde{r}_B$.

Consider the outcome in which $\tilde{r}_B=.05$. The ways in which this outcome can occur are indicated by the probabilities in the top row of the 3×3 matrix in table 7.1. The only positive entry occurs for the joint outcome in which $\tilde{r}_B=.05$ and $\tilde{r}_A=-.10$. The probability for this joint outcome is .1. Since this joint outcome is the only way in which $\tilde{r}_B$ can take the value .05, the probability that $\tilde{r}_B=.05$ is .1. This is recorded in the top row of the single column on the right in table 7.1.

The entry in the second row of the single right-hand column in table 7.1 is the probability that $\tilde{r}_B$ will take the value .10. The probability of this outcome is the sum of the probabilities of the separate ways in which $\tilde{r}_B$ can take the value .10. The middle row of the 3×3 matrix has positive entries in all three cells. Therefore, $\tilde{r}_B$ will take the value .10 if any one of three joint outcomes occur. These three joint outcomes are $\tilde{r}_B=.10$ and $\tilde{r}_A=-.10$; $\tilde{r}_B=.10$ and $\tilde{r}_A=.20$; and $\tilde{r}_B=.10$ and $\tilde{r}_A=.50$. The sum of the probabilities of the joint outcomes in which $\tilde{r}_B$ takes the value .10 is .8, which is recorded in the middle row of the single right-hand column. Finally, the probability that $\tilde{r}_B$ takes the value .15 is .1, which is the sum of the probabilities across the third row of the 3×3 matrix.

The entries in the single row located in table 7.1 below the 3×3 matrix are the unconditional probabilities for the three outcomes for $\tilde{r}_A$. Following our argument establishing the unconditional probabilities for $\tilde{r}_B$, the entry in each cell of the single row below the 3×3 matrix is the sum of the entries in the corresponding column of the matrix.

The expected return and the standard deviation of any portfolio that contains Securities A and B will depend on the proportions in which the investor allocates her funds between those two securities, and on the values of the five parameters that specify the joint probability distribution for the two securities. Those parameters are the expected return and the standard deviation of Security A, the expected return and the standard deviation of Security B, and the correlation coefficient between the rates of return on those securities. Next, we obtain the values of those parameters, beginning with the expected returns and the standard deviations.

7.5.2 The Expected Returns and the Standard Deviations for Securities A and B

For the joint probability distribution in table 7.1, each security's rate of return is symmetrically distributed about its expected value. We can verify this by examining the unconditional distributions that are recorded in the single column to the right of the 3×3 matrix and in the single row below that matrix. The column on the right indicates that for $\tilde{r}_B$, the lowest and the highest possible outcomes are equidistant from the middle outcome. Moreover, $\tilde{r}_B$ will take these two outlying outcomes with equal probabilities. Therefore, the expected return for $\tilde{r}_B$ is its middle value, .10. Similarly, the expected return for $\tilde{r}_A$ is its middle value, .20.

Recall that the standard deviation is a probability-weighted average of the distances by which the values for a random variable can deviate from its expected value. More precisely, the standard deviation is the positive square root of the probability-weighted average of the squares of distances from the expected value.[13]

Using the entries in the 3×3 matrix in table 7.1, and the expected values that we have just calculated for Securities A and B, the value of the standard deviation for Security A is:

$$
\begin{aligned}
\sigma_A &= \sqrt{\sigma_A^2} \\
&= \sqrt{[(-.10-.20)^2(.2)+(.20-.20)^2(.6)+(.50-.20)^2(.2)]} \\
&= \sqrt{[(-.30)^2(.2)+(0)^2(.6)-(.30)^2(.2)]} \\
&= \sqrt{[2(.2)(.09)]} \\
&= \sqrt{.036} \\
&= .1897.
\end{aligned}
\tag{7.10}
$$

Similarly, the value of the standard deviation for Security B is:

$$
\begin{aligned}
\sigma_B &= \sqrt{\sigma_B^2} \\
&= \sqrt{[(-.05)^2(.1)+(.05)^2(.1)]} \\
&= \sqrt{2(.1)(.0025)} \\
&= \sqrt{(.2)(.0025)} \\
&= \sqrt{.0005} \\
&= .0224.
\end{aligned}
\tag{7.11}
$$

Note that the standard deviation for Security A is larger than the standard deviation for Security B. There are two reasons for this. First, the distance from E_A to either of the two outlying values for $\tilde{r}_A$ is greater than the distance from E_B to either of the two outlying values for $\tilde{r}_B$. Second, the probabilities that $\tilde{r}_A$ will take either of its outlying values are greater than the probabilities that $\tilde{r}_B$ will take either of its outlying values.

7.5.3 The Covariance and the Correlation Coefficient between the Rates of Return on Securities A and B

To develop portfolio theory in chapter 8, we need two additional parameters. These are the covariance and the correlation coefficient between the rates of return on Securities A and B. The covariance is the probability-weighted sum of all possible products of deviations of the rates of return on Securities A and B from the expected values for those securities. The correlation coefficient between the rates of return on Security A and B is equal to the covariance between those securities divided by the product of their standard deviations. The correlation coefficient is, therefore, a scaled covariance. The effect of the scaling is to restrict the possible values for the correlation coefficient to the interval from -1 to $+1$, including the endpoints.

We begin with the covariance. The covariance between any two random variables is the probability-weighted average of the products of the distances by which each random variable can deviate from its expected return. To calculate the covariance between $\tilde{r}_A$ and $\tilde{r}_B$, we must first identify all the possible combinations of the deviations that the two random variables can take from their expected returns. Define C_{AB} as the covariance between the rates of return on Securities A and B. The joint probability distribution for $\tilde{r}_A$ and $\tilde{r}_B$ specified in table 7.1 is so simple that there are only two terms in the calculation of C_{AB}. These terms are generated by the cell in the top row of the first column and by the cell in the bottom row of the third column.

We can ignore the four cells whose entries are zero. Since C_{AB} is a probability-weighted average, the combinations of outcomes corresponding to these four cells do not enter the calculation of C_{AB}. We can also ignore the entire middle row of table 7.1. The covariance involves products of deviations from expected returns. The entire middle row of table 7.1 pertains to the three outcomes in which $\tilde{r}_B$ takes the value of its expected return. Therefore, the deviation of $\tilde{r}_B$ from E_B is equal to zero for each of these three outcomes. Consequently, for each of the outcomes corresponding to the middle row of table 7.1, the products of the deviations from the expected returns will be equal to zero.

Now that we have eliminated from consideration all but the cells in the upper left and the lower right corners of the matrix in table 7.1, we can calculate the covariance between $\tilde{r}_A$ and $\tilde{r}_B$ as:

$$
\begin{aligned}
C_{AB} &= (.1)(-.10-.20)(.05-.10)+(.1)(.50-.20)(.15-.10) \\
&= (.1)(-.30)(-.05)+(.1)(.30)(.05) \\
&= .003.
\end{aligned}
\tag{7.12}
$$

The value of the covariance between $\tilde{r}_A$ and $\tilde{r}_B$ depends on the combinations of the deviations of $\tilde{r}_A$ from E_A and $\tilde{r}_B$ from E_B. If both random variables frequently take values on the same sides of their respective expected values, the covariance will be positive. The joint probabilities in table 7.1 indicate that $\tilde{r}_A$ and $\tilde{r}_B$ cannot simultaneously take values on opposite sides of their expected returns. Therefore, C_{AB} must be positive. The value of C_{AB} is quite small because the probabilities of the possible deviations are small.

Using equation (7.12) and the definition of the correlation coefficient, we find:

$$\rho_{AB} = \frac{C_{AB}}{\sigma_A \sigma_B}$$

$$= \frac{.003}{(.1897)(.0224)} \tag{7.13}$$

$$= .706.$$

In this subsection, we have calculated the values of the covariance and the correlation coefficient for a very simple joint distribution of two random variables. The definitions of these parameters for continuous random variables are analogous to the case for discrete variables.[14]

7.6   A Summary Thus Far

The probabilities with which the monthly rate of return on a specific security takes various values are normally distributed. A normal probability density function is fully determined by the fixed values of its two parameters, namely, the expected value and the standard deviation. The investor cannot control, or predict, the outcome of the random rate of return for a given month, nor can he or she control the values of the two parameters that define the density function for that security's rate of return.

The investor's primary concern, however, is with the density function that governs the probabilities for the rate of return on a portfolio of securities. That rate of return is also a random variable, because the rate of return on the portfolio is a weighted average of the rates of return on the securities contained in that portfolio. An investor cannot control, or predict, the rate of return on ther portfolio for a given month any more than he or she can control the rates of return on the constituent securities. But the expected value and the standard deviation of the density function for the portfolio depend on how the investor allocates funds among the securities in that portfolio. Consequently, the investor can, within limits, choose the density function for the portfolio.

We show in chapter 8 how the alternative combinations of values for the expected value and standard deviation for a portfolio depend on the expected values and the standard deviations of the constituent securities, and on the correlation coefficients between pairs of those securities. We also show in chapter 8 how the investor can choose the density function that will govern the rate of return on the portfolio by choosing the proportions in which she allocates her funds among the constituent securities.

7.7   The Effect of the Price of a Security on the Expected Value of Its Rate of Return

Consider the rate of return on Security i from time $t-1$ to time t. Recall from equation (7.1) that this rate of return is:

$$r_{i,t} = \frac{(P_{i,t} - P_{i,t-1}) + D_{i,t}}{P_{i,t-1}}. \tag{7.14}$$

As of time $t-1$, this rate of return is a random variable because the values of $P_{i,t}$ and $D_{i,t}$ are not yet known. We recognize this by using tildes to rewrite equation (7.14) as:

$$\tilde{r}_{i,t} = \frac{(\tilde{P}_{i,t} - P_{i,t-1}) + \tilde{D}_{i,t}}{P_{i,t-1}}. \tag{7.15}$$

We now rewrite equation (7.15) to express the random rate of return $\tilde{r}_{i,t}$ as a sum of two random variables, minus the constant 1:

$$\tilde{r}_{i,t} = \frac{\tilde{P}_{i,t}}{P_{i,t-1}} + \frac{\tilde{D}_{i,t}}{P_{i,t-1}} - 1. \tag{7.16}$$

The numerator, $\tilde{P}_{i,t}$, of the first term on the right side of equation (7.16) is the present value, as of time t, of the payments that will accrue from time $t+1$ onward to investors who hold Security i from time t onward. (Recall our assumption that all securities are priced *ex dividend* or *ex interest*.)

The future payments represented by $\tilde{P}_{i,t}$ can be either explicit or implicit. Dividends are explicit payments. Capital gains (or losses), which are increases (or decreases) in the price of Security i, are implicit payments.

For example, suppose that there is an increase in the price of Security i from time $t-1$ to time t. The higher price occurs because at time t, investors expect that future dividend payments will be higher than investors had expected at time $t-1$. Had investors believed at time $t-1$ what they now believe at time t, the price at time $t-1$ would have been higher, and there would be no revision in the price between times $t-1$ and t. Recall from section 7.2 that an investor can convert capital gains to explicit dividends by selling a portion of his or her investment in Security i.

The numerator, $\tilde{D}_{i,t}$, of the second term on the right side of equation (7.16) is also a random variable because the size of the dividend (if any) that will be paid at time t is a random variable when viewed from time $t-1$.

We will now show how a change in the price of Security i at time $t-1$ affects the expected value of the probability density function that will generate a value for the rate of return on Security i at time t.

Define $E[\tilde{r}_{i,t}]$ as the expected value of the rate of return on Security i as of time t. It is important to remember that while $\tilde{r}_{i,t}$ is a random variable, $E[\tilde{r}_{i,t}]$ is a parameter. Since $\tilde{r}_{i,t}$ is normally distributed, $E[\tilde{r}_{i,t}]$ is the center point of the density function for $\tilde{r}_{i,t}$.

A theorem in probability theory states that if one random variable is defined as a constant multiplied by a second random variable, then the expected value of the first random variable is equal to that same constant multiplied by the expected value of the second random variable. Let $\tilde{x}$ be a random variable, let k be a constant, and define the random variable $\tilde{y}$ by:

$$\tilde{y} = k\tilde{x}. \tag{7.17}$$

Then by the theorem just stated, the expected values of $\tilde{x}$ and $\tilde{y}$ are related as:

$$E(\tilde{y}) = E(k\tilde{x}) = kE(\tilde{x}). \tag{7.18}$$

In a sense, the theorem allows us to pull the constant k through the expected value operator, E.

A second theorem states that if one random variable is defined as the sum of two (or more) random variables, then the expected value of the first random variable is the sum of the expected values of the two (or more) random variables. Let $\tilde{x}$, $\tilde{y}$, and $\tilde{z}$ be random variables, and let $\tilde{z}$ be defined by:

$$\tilde{z} = \tilde{x} + \tilde{y}. \tag{7.19}$$

Then the expected values are related by:

$$E(\tilde{z}) = E(\tilde{x}) + E(\tilde{y}). \tag{7.20}$$

Finally, a constant can be treated as a random variable whose probability density function is concentrated at a single point. That is, the standard deviation of a constant is equal to zero. If we were to draw a graph of the probability density function of a constant, that density function would be a vertical line whose horizontal intercept would be the value of that constant.[15]

Applying these two theorems and the property of a constant just stated to equation (7.16), the expected value as of time $t-1$ of the random rate of return $\tilde{r}_{i,t}$ is:

$$
\begin{aligned}
E[\tilde{r}_{i,t}] &= E\left[\frac{\tilde{P}_{i,t}}{P_{i,t-1}} + \frac{\tilde{D}_{i,t}}{P_{i,t-1}} - 1\right] \\
&= E\left[\frac{\tilde{P}_{i,t}}{P_{i,t-1}}\right] + E\left[\frac{\tilde{D}_{i,t}}{P_{i,t-1}}\right] + E[-1] \\
&= \frac{E[\tilde{P}_{i,t}]}{P_{i,t-1}} + \frac{E[\tilde{D}_{i,t}]}{P_{i,t}} - 1.
\end{aligned}
\tag{7.21}
$$

We now use equation (7.21) to explain one aspect of how competition among investors causes the prices of financial securities to take values that establish an equilibrium configuration of probability density functions. Each density function governs the probabilistic outcomes for the random rate of return on a particular security.

The expected value and standard deviation of the rate of return on an investor's portfolio are determined by (1) the expected values and standard deviations of the securities that the investor includes in the portfolio, (2) the correlations among the rates of return on those securities, and (3) the proportions in which the investor allocates the invested funds across those securities. The critical point for the present discussion is that the attractiveness of a given Security i for inclusion in an investor's portfolio will depend on the estimates of the expected value and the standard deviation of the density function that governs Security i's rate of return.[16]

The expected value of the rate of return on Security i from time $t-1$ to time t is defined by:

$$E\left[\tilde{r}_{i,t}\right] = \frac{E(\tilde{P}_{i,t})}{P_{i,t-1}} + \frac{E(\tilde{D}_{i,t})}{P_{i,t-1}} - 1. \tag{7.21, repeated}$$

At time $t-1$, the value of $\tilde{r}_{i,t}$ is a random variable because the values of $\tilde{P}_{i,t}$ and $\tilde{D}_{i,t}$ will not be known until time t. But at time $t-1$, an investor can estimate the expected value of $\tilde{r}_{i,t}$ by estimating the expected values of $\tilde{P}_{i,t}$ and $\tilde{D}_{i,t}$, and then by substituting these expected values, and the observed value for $P_{i,t-1}$, into the right-hand side of equation (7.21).

Notice that $P_{i,t-1}$ occurs only in the denominators on the right side of equation (7.21). Therefore, an increase in the price of Security i at time $t-1$ will reduce the investor's estimate of $E(\tilde{r}_{i,t})$. Since the expected value is the center point of a normal probability density function, an increase in the price of Security i at time $t-1$ will shift leftward the investor's estimate of the density function that governs the outcome for $\tilde{r}_{i,t}$.

At time $t-1$, each investor will decide, based on the estimate of $E(\tilde{r}_{i,t})$, whether to increase his holdings of Security i, decrease those holdings, or make no change. Suppose that the total number of shares sought by investors who want to increase their holdings of Security i exceeds the total number of shares offered for sale by those investors who want to reduce their holdings of Security i. Then at the current value of $P_{i,t-1}$, the total quantity of Security i that some investors attempt to purchase exceeds the total quantity that other investors offer to sell. Competition among investors attempting to add shares of Security i to their portfolios at time $t-1$ will create upward pressure on $P_{i,t-1}$. As the value of $P_{i,t-1}$ rises, each investor will revise downward the estimate of $E(\tilde{r}_{i,t})$, since $P_{i,t-1}$ appears only in the denominators on the right side of equation (7.21).

Investors need not agree on their estimates of $E(\tilde{r}_{i,t})$ because each investor makes his or her own estimates of $E(\tilde{P}_{i,t})$ and $E(\tilde{D}_{i,t})$ at time $t-1$. Nevertheless, an increase in the value of $P_{i,t-1}$ will be observed by all investors at time $t-1$. Every investor will then reduce his or her estimate of $E(\tilde{r}_{i,t})$. As these estimates of $E(\tilde{r}_{i,t})$ fall, investors who previously sought to increase their holdings of Security i will now be less eager to do so. For analogous reasons, investors who were previously willing to sell some of their holdings of Security i will now be more eager to do so. In fact, there could be some investors who, as $P_{i,t-1}$ rises, will switch from buyers of Security i to sellers.

Competition among investors at time $t-1$ causes the value of $P_{i,t-1}$ to adjust so that the quantity of shares of Security i that investors offer for sale is equal to the quantity that other investors seek to buy. Equivalently, the value of $P_{i,t-1}$ will adjust so that, after all trading at time $t-1$ is concluded, each investor will hold at time $t-1$ the quantity of shares of Security i that he or she wants to hold. That is, there is an equilibrium distribution among investors of the existing shares of Security i.

The mechanism that produces this equilibrium at time $t-1$ is implied by equation (7.21). At time $t-1$, each investor has estimates of $E(\tilde{P}_{i,t})$ and $E(\tilde{D}_{i,t})$, and, using equation (7.21), an estimate of $E(\tilde{r}_{i,t})$. The configuration among investors of these estimates of $E(\tilde{r}_{i,t})$ creates an excess demand for shares of Security i, or an excess supply, or neither. If there is an excess demand, competition among investors seeking to increase their holdings will force the value of $P_{i,t-1}$ up. Through equation (7.21), the increase in $P_{i,t-1}$ will reduce each investor's estimate of $E(\tilde{r}_{i,t})$, thus reducing the excess demand. The value of $P_{i,t-1}$ will have reached its equilibrium when it has increased far enough to eliminate the excess demand. Similarly, if the initial value of $P_{i,t-1}$ creates an excess supply of Security i at time $t-1$, competition among investors who seek to reduce their holdings of Security i will force the value of $P_{i,t-1}$ down, and hence the value of each investor's estimate of $E(\tilde{r}_{i,t})$ up, until the excess supply is eliminated.

7.8   The Effect of the Price of a Security on the Standard Deviation of Its Rate of Return

The standard deviation of a random variable is the positive square root of the variance of that random variable. For some purposes, it is more convenient to work with the variance.

Repeating equation (7.16), the rate of return is

$$\tilde{r}_{i,t} = \frac{\tilde{P}_{i,t}}{P_{i,t-1}} + \frac{\tilde{D}_{i,t}}{P_{i,t-1}} - 1. \tag{7.22}$$

The rate of return for Security i is equal to the sum of two random variables, each of which is multiplied by the constant $1/P_{i,t-1}$, minus a constant. To calculate the variance of $\tilde{r}_{i,t}$, we use the following property of the variance of a sum of random variables. Let $\tilde{x}$, $\tilde{y}$, and $\tilde{z}$ be random variables, and define the random variable $\tilde{w}$ by:

$$\tilde{w} = a\tilde{x} + b\tilde{y} + c\tilde{z}, \tag{7.23}$$

in which a, b, and c are constants. Then

$$\sigma_{\tilde{w}}^2 = a^2 \sigma_{\tilde{x}}^2 + b^2 \sigma_{\tilde{y}}^2 + c^2 \sigma_{\tilde{z}}^2$$
$$+ 2ab C_{\tilde{x},\tilde{y}} + 2ac C_{\tilde{x},\tilde{z}} + 2bc C_{\tilde{y},\tilde{z}} \tag{7.24}$$

in which $C_{\tilde{x}\tilde{y}}$ is the covariance between $\tilde{x}$ and $\tilde{y}$, and $C_{\tilde{y}\tilde{z}}$ and $C_{\tilde{x}\tilde{z}}$ are defined similarly. Defining $a = b = 1/P_{i,t-1}$, $c = 1$, and $\tilde{z} = 1$, and applying (7.24) to (7.22), we may write the variance of the rate of return on Security i as:

$$\sigma_{\tilde{r}_{i,t}}^2 = \frac{\sigma_{\tilde{P}_{i,t}}^2 + \sigma_{\tilde{D}_{i,t}}^2 + 2C_{\tilde{P}_{i,t-1},\tilde{D}_{i,t-1}}}{(P_{i,t-1})^2} \tag{7.25}$$

In obtaining (7.25), we used the facts that the variance of $\tilde{z}$ and any covariance involving $\tilde{z}$ are zero. This is true because every term in a variance, and every term in a covariance, is a deviation of the value of a random variable from its expected value. Sinze $\tilde{z}$ is a constant (equal to 1), when we apply (7.24) to (7.23), every term in the variance of $\tilde{z}$, and every term in any covariance between $\tilde{z}$ and any other random variable, is equal to zero.

We conclude from (7.25) that the effect on the variance of $\tilde{r}_{i,t}$ of a change in $P_{i,t-1}$ is ambiguous because the covariance ($C_{\tilde{P}i,t,\tilde{D}i,t}$), between the price and the dividend at time t, can be either positive or negative.

7.9   A Linear Model of the Rate of Return

To prepare for work on portfolio theory in chapter 8, and on capital market theory in chapters 9 and 10, we present here a linear probabilistic model for the rate of return on a security. The central idea is that as the rate of return on a special portfolio changes from one period to the next, the probability density function for the rate of return on Security i shifts rightward or leftward along the horizontal axis in figure 7.1. Usually, this special portfolio is constructed so that it represents either the entire economy or some sector of the economy. Consequently, the coefficient in the linear equation that determines the expected value for the rate of return on Security i measures the sensitivity of the probability density function for the rate of return on Security i to changes in the level of macroeconomic activity.

The model that we present is an amplification of the model that we sketched toward the end of chapter 6. In chapters 8, 9, and 10, we discuss alternatives for constructing this portfolio. In fact, the various asset pricing models are distinguished by the structure of the portfolio, or portfolios, whose rates of return at time t locate the expected value of the density function for the rate of return on Security i.

7.9.1 Conditional Density Functions

A portfolio is a collection of securities. Suppose that Portfolio M contains 100 securities, and let j be an index that takes any of the values 1, 2, . . . , 100. Assigning one of these values to j specifies a particular security in Portfolio M. When we speak in general of Security j, we are making a statement that applies to any of the 100 securities.

Portfolio M has a rate of return that is derived from the rates of return of its constituent securities. If the rates of return on these securities are normally distributed, then the portfolio's rate of return will also be normally distributed. In fact, the expected value and standard deviation of the portfolio's density function will be determined by (1) the expected values and standard deviations of the rates of return on the constituent securities, (2) the correlation coefficients among those rates of return, and (3) the proportions in which the portfolio's total funds are allocated among those constituent securities. We explain this relationship in more detail in chapter 8.

Let Security i be any security. Security i might, or might not, be a member of Portfolio M. Let $\tilde{r}_{m,t}$ be the rate of return on Portfolio M for time t.

Consider the following linear model. For any time t, the rate of return on Security i is generated by:

$$\tilde{r}_{i,t} = \alpha_i + \beta_i \tilde{r}_m + \tilde{\varepsilon}_i. \tag{7.26}$$

In equation (7.26), the terms i and β_i are constants specific to Security i. The term $\tilde{\varepsilon}_i$ is a random variable that is specific to Security i.

We impose two restrictions on the model in equation (7.26). First, we require that for all securities, $\tilde{\varepsilon}_i$ is normally distributed and has an expected value equal to zero. Then:

$$E(\tilde{\varepsilon}_i) = 0 \text{ for all Securities } i, \ i = 1, 2, \ldots, 100. \tag{7.27}$$

Second, we require that the random variables $\tilde{r}_M$ and $\tilde{\varepsilon}_i$ are independent for all securities. We discuss the meaning of independence between random variables in more detail in section 7.12 on correlation. For now, it is sufficient to state that independence between $\tilde{r}_m$ and $\tilde{\varepsilon}_i$ means that an outcome for either random variable has no influence on the probabilities with which the other random variable will take specific values.

The model in equation (7.26) asserts that the rate of return on Security i depends on two sets of forces. One set of forces is generated by the behavior of the macroeconomy in which Firm i does business. For example, the general level of interest rates, the rate of inflation, whether consumers fear the onset of a recession, the level and the structure of corporate and personal income taxes, and the levels of prices in financial markets will affect the ability of Firm i to generate earnings. The model in equation (7.26) uses the value of $\tilde{r}_{m,t}$ as an index of the state of the economy in which Firm i operates. Note that the subscript i on the coefficient β_i in equation (7.26) indicates that a change in the state of the economy, as measured by a change in the value of $\tilde{r}_{m,t}$, will not affect all firms equally. The effect on $\tilde{r}_{i,t}$ of a change in $\tilde{r}_{m,t}$ will depend on the parameter β_i, which is specific to Firm i. If Firm i's rate of return is highly sensitive to the state of the macroeconomy, then the value of β_i will be large and postive.[17]

The second set of forces that affect $\tilde{r}_{i,t}$ is specific to Firm i. These forces include, for example, variations in the efficiency of the firm's management, progress or delays in bringing the firm's new products to market, favorable or unfavorable resolution of lawsuits involving the firm, changes in the costs of the firm's inputs, and changes in the strategies employed by the firm's competitors. These forces are called firm-specific or idiosyncratic forces. Their effects on $\tilde{r}_{i,t}$ are transmitted through $\tilde{\varepsilon}_i$.

At any time t, the effect of the firm-specific forces on $\tilde{r}_{i,t}$ may be either positive or negative. These effects are random. Thus the outcome for $\tilde{\varepsilon}_i$ at any time t is modeled as an outcome from a normal density function. For analytical and graphical convenience, we define $\tilde{\varepsilon}_i$ so that $E(\tilde{\varepsilon}_i)=0$.

The constant α_i is that part of Firm i's average rate of return that does not depend on the state of the macroeconomy. For example, if Firm i is in a sector of the economy that investors expect to have rapid growth of earnings, such as Internet firms, then the value of α_i will be large. If the expected value of the firm-specific term, $\tilde{\varepsilon}_i$, were nonzero, we would incorporate this expected value of $\tilde{\varepsilon}_i$ into the value of $\tilde{\alpha}_i$ and then redefine $\tilde{\varepsilon}_i$ so that its expected value is zero.

Reading from left to right in equation (7.26), for any time t, the rate of return on Security i is equal to α_i adjusted by two disturbances. The value of the macroeconomic disturbance is $\beta_i \tilde{r}_{m,t}$ and the value of the microeconomic (or firm-specific) disturbance is $\tilde{\varepsilon}_{i,t}$. We can interpret this model easily by presenting it graphically as a probability density function for Security i that shifts rightward or leftward with changes in the level of macroeconomic activity. The value of the sensitivity coefficient for Security i, β_i, determines the distance by which a change in the level of macroeconomic activity shifts the density function for Security i.

Suppose that at time t the outcome for the rate of return on Portfolio M is the particular value r_A. Then the only variability in $\tilde{r}_{i,t}$ will be caused by the random outcome for the firm-specific disturbance $\tilde{\varepsilon}_i$. Note the absence of a subscript t on the random variable $\tilde{\varepsilon}_i$. The probability density function for $\tilde{\varepsilon}_i$ does not shift from one time to the next. With the outcome for $\tilde{r}_{m,t}$ fixed at r_A, the outcome for $\tilde{r}_{i,t}$ will be the sum of the constants α_i and $\beta_i r_A$, plus the random outcome for $\tilde{\varepsilon}_i$. Using the theorems for expected value, and our assumption that $E(\tilde{\varepsilon}_i)=0$, the expected value for $\tilde{r}_{i,t}$, given that $\tilde{r}_{m,t}$ has taken the value r_A, is

$$E(\tilde{r}_{i,t}|\tilde{r}_{m,t}=r_A)$$
$$=\alpha_i+\beta_i r_A+E(\tilde{\varepsilon}_i)$$
$$=\alpha_i+\beta_i r_A. \tag{7.28}$$

The symbol $E(\tilde{r}_{i,t}|\tilde{r}_{m,t}=r_A)$ is read as "the conditional expected value of (the random variable) $\tilde{r}_{i,t}$, under the condition that (the random variable) $\tilde{r}_{m,t}$ takes the value r_A. The outcome for $\tilde{r}_{m,t}$ determines the location along the horizontal axis of the probability density function that will then generate an outcome for $\tilde{r}_{i,t}$. Therefore, a change in the outcome for $\tilde{r}_{m,t}$ will shift the conditional density function for $\tilde{r}_{i,t}$.

7.9.2 Graphical Examples

Figure 7.4 is a three-dimensional diagram.[18] If the pages of this book were three-dimensional, we would have three independent axes. We could plot values for $\tilde{r}_{m,t}$ on one axis that would run horizontally across the page from left to right. Values for $\tilde{r}_{i,t}$ would be plotted on a second axis that would run vertically from the bottom of the page to the top. The third axis would intersect the page perpendicularly. The portion of this axis containing positive values would rise out of the page toward the reader. Negative values on this axis would be plotted below the page, away from the reader. The values that we plot on this third axis are probability densities for $\tilde{r}_{i,t}$. Since probability densities cannot be negative, we can ignore that part of the diagram that is below the page.

In figure 7.4, the upward-sloping straight line in the plane of the page is the graph of

$$E(\tilde{r}_{i,t}|\tilde{r}_{m,t}) = \alpha_i + \beta_i \tilde{r}_{m,t}. \tag{7.29}$$

This straight line is the locus of conditional expected values for $\tilde{r}_{i,t}$, conditional on $\tilde{r}_{m,t}$.

The conditional expected values for $\tilde{r}_{i,t}$ depend on the outcomes for $\tilde{r}_{m,t}$. Once the outcome for $\tilde{r}_{m,t}$ is determined, the outcome for $\tilde{r}_{i,t}$ will be drawn from a density function centered at a value determined by equation (7.29), which is graphed in figure 7.4. From equation (7.29), we conclude that this conditional density function is simply the density function for $\tilde{\varepsilon}_i$. The contributions of $\tilde{\alpha}_i$ and $\beta_i \tilde{r}_{m,t}$ to $\tilde{r}_{i,t}$ are represented by the

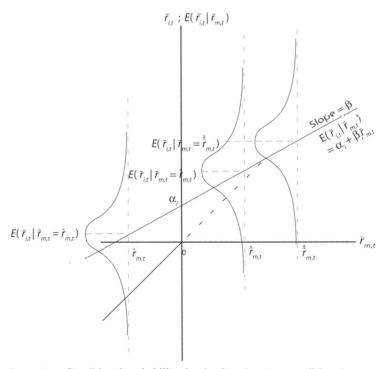

Figure 7.4. Conditional probability density functions ($r_{i,t}$ conditional on $r_{m,t}$).

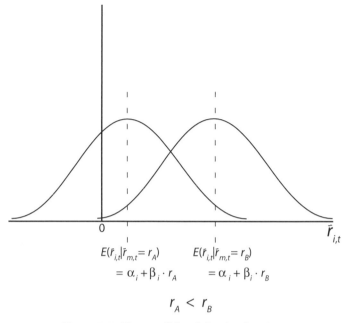

Figure 7.5. Two conditional density functions.

height of the straight line at the outcome for $\tilde{r}_{m,t}$. The only remaining contribution to $\tilde{r}_{i,t}$ is the firm-specific random variable $\tilde{\varepsilon}_i$.

In figure 7.5, we have displayed the conditional density functions for two alternative cases in which $\tilde{r}_{m,t}=r_A$ and $\tilde{r}_{m,t}=r_B$. Each of these density functions is identical to the density function for $\tilde{\varepsilon}_i$, except for the location of its expected value. In the model defined by equation (7.29), the outcome for the macroeconomic variable, $\tilde{r}_{m,t}$, determines the expected value of the density function for $\tilde{r}_{i,t}$, for that time t. Once $\tilde{r}_{m,t}$ is known, the outcome for $\tilde{r}_{i,t}$ is equal to its conditional expected value, $\tilde{\alpha}+\beta_i\tilde{r}_{m,t}$, plus or minus the firm-specific disturbance given by the outcome for $\tilde{\varepsilon}_i$.

7.10   Regression Lines and Characteristic Lines

7.10.1   Regression Lines

The main purpose of linear regression is to construct a straight line whose slope and vertical intercept summarize the relationship between paired values for two variables. Consider the following example.

In table 7.2 are hypothetical data for the rates of return on Securities i and j for times $t=1$ through $t=10$. In figure 7.6, we have plotted the data from table 7.2. This plot is called a scatter diagram. Note that the 10 data points are not colinear. The diagram does, however, exhibit an upward slope from left to right. We could say that, in general, or on the average, higher values for $r_{i,t}$ occur contemporaneously with higher values for $r_{j,t}$. Alternatively, an increase in the return on Security i is likely to occur at the same time as an increase in the return on Security j. The sense in which we can interpret the term

Table 7.2
Hypothetical Paired Values for $r_{i,t}$ and $r_{j,t}$

Time t	1	2	3	4	5	6	7	8	9	10
$r_{i,t}$	.04	.07	.01	.03	.07	−.02	.00	.05	.03	.06
$r_{j,t}$	−.01	.02	.03	.00	.04	−.05	.01	.04	.01	.02

likely is this: the forces that produce an increase in the return on Security i will shift the probability density function for Security j rightward, thereby increasing the probabilities with which Security j will take values above its expected value.

Economists use regression to approximate and summarize the relationships among the data for $r_{i,t}$ and $r_{j,t}$. In figure 7.6, we construct a straight line that minimizes the sum of the vertical distances between the data points and the straight line. The resulting line is called the regression line of r_j on r_i. The regression line, being linear, is fully determined by the values of its intercept, α, and its slope, β.

Now suppose that we believe that the rate of return on Security i is generated by the linear probabilistic model defined by equation (7.26). We can regard the data in the first row of table 7.2 and their scatter diagram in figure 7.6 as 10 random draws from this model. Further, for each value drawn for $\tilde{r}_{m,t}$, the corresponding value for $\tilde{r}_{i,t}$ can be regarded as a draw from the conditional probability density function for $\tilde{r}_{i,t}$, given the value drawn for $\tilde{r}_{m,t}$. We take the height of the regression line above the value drawn for $\tilde{r}_{m,t}$ as an estimate of the conditional expected value for $\tilde{r}_{i,t}$, given the value drawn for $\tilde{r}_{m,t}$. That is, the regression line is a locus of estimates of the center points of the conditional density functions from which outcomes for $\tilde{r}_{i,t}$ are generated. Under this interpretation, data points lying above the regression line indicate that,

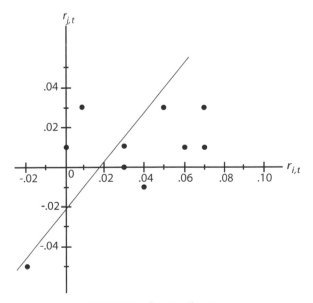

Figure 7.6. Scatter diagram.

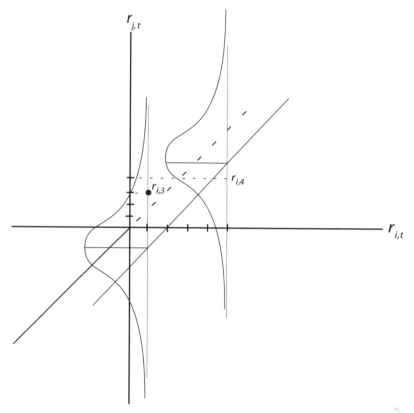

Figure 7.7. The conditional density functions for $\tilde{r}_{i,3}$ and $\tilde{r}_{i,4}$.

given the outcome for $\tilde{r}_{m,t}$, the outcome for $\tilde{\varepsilon}_{i,t}$ was positive, so that the outcome for $\tilde{r}_{i,t}$ came from the upper half of its conditional distribution.

In figure 7.7, we have redrawn figure 7.6 as a three-dimensional diagram to show the conditional density functions for $\tilde{r}_{i,3}$ and $\tilde{r}_{i,4}$. Since the outcome for $\tilde{r}_{i,3}$ lies above the regression line, we infer that at time 3, the contribution to $\tilde{r}_{i,3}$ for firm-specific risk, $\tilde{\varepsilon}_{i,3}$, was positive. Similarly, at time 4, there was a negative contribution from firm-specific to the return on Security i because the data point for time 4 lies below the regression line.

We can now see the economic significance of β, the slope of the regression line. The value of β is the sensitivity of the conditional expected value of $\tilde{r}_{i,t}$ to changes in $\tilde{r}_{m,t}$.

7.10.2 Characteristic Lines

The regression line between the rates of return on Security i and Portfolio M is called the characteristic line for Security i (relative to Portfolio M). This regression line characterizes Security i in the sense that the line shows how the conditional expected return for Security i is affected by the value for the rate of return on Portfolio M. In particular, the slope of Security i's characteristic line, which is the value of β_i, is the rate at which the conditional density function for Security i will shift whenever the rate of return on Portfolio M increases by one percentage point.

7.11 The Parameter β_i as the Quantity of Risk in Security i

As we sketched in chapter 6 and show in chapters 9 and 10, the value of β_i is the quantity of risk contained in Security i. Here is a brief statement of the rationale that supports this interpretation of β_i.

A central objective of portfolio theory is to explain how an investor should allocate funds among individual securities to create a portfolio that will maximize the expected rate of return, given a fixed level of risk in that portfolio. In chapter 8, we show that an equivalent objective is to minimize the level of risk in the portfolio, given a fixed level of expected return. Of course, each of these objectives requires that we specify how risk is to be measured.

The measurement of risk will occupy much of our attention in chapter 8. There we explain why economists measure the level of risk in a portfolio as the standard deviation of the rate of return on that portfolio. The measure of risk for an individual security is more complicated, but the reasoning is both clear and persuasive. We show that a prudent investor will allocate funds across a diversified portfolio of securities, rather than placing all funds in a single security. Therefore, we measure the level of risk that an investor bears by holding any particular security by the effect of that security on the standard deviation of the portfolio in which the investor holds that security. This contribution from portfolio theory is the basis for capital market theory, which generates hypotheses about the equilibrium relationship between the level of risk in a security and the expected value of its rate of return.

In chapter 8, we show that the standard deviation of a portfolio is equal to a weighted sum of the beta values of its constituent securities. The weights in this sum depend on the proportions in which the investor allocates funds across the securities in the portfolio. Consequently, the level of risk that an investor incurs by including Security i in his or her portfolio is proportional to the value of Security i's beta. Further, the marginal effect of Security i on the standard deviation of the portfolio is proportional to the β_i. The higher the value of a security's beta, the more volatile will be a portfolio in which that security is held. Therefore, the higher the beta for any Security i, the lower must be the price of Security i if an investor is to include that security in the portfolio.

When the word *risk* is introduced into a discussion of investments and financial markets, some students think of an outcome in which the investor loses all, or substantially all, of the investment. However, as we show in the next chapter, there are strong reasons to believe that an investor who holds a properly diversified portfolio faces a negligible probability of losing the entire investment, or even most of it.[19]

The more significant risk for an investor is the volatility of the rate of return on the portfolio. Consider an investor who depends on investments to generate income to meet current obligations.[20] This investor might be a retired person who is relying on investment income to meet living expenses. Alternatively, the investor might be a college, a hospital, or a charity such as the Salvation Army, whose trustees rely on investment income to meet some of their regular, ongoing expenses. All of these investors could be harmed if the rates of return on their investments were highly, and unpredictably, volatile.

Investors who do not rely on their investments to generate current income are less sensitive to unpredictable volatility, but they are not indifferent to it. Consider the investor who is trying to accumulate capital to finance a child's education at college or the construction of a retirement home. This investor can tolerate variations in the rate of return from one year to the next, especially in the early years. But the wider the fluctuations in the rates of return, and the higher the probability of an extended sequence of low rates of return, the higher is the risk that the investor will not have accumulated sufficient capital to send his daughter to college or to build his retirement home.

For all of these reasons, investors are sensitive to the volatility in the rate of return on their portfolios. In the next chapter, we explain in detail how the probabilistic behaviors of the rates of return on individual securities interact to determine the volatility of the rate of return on the portfolio in which an investor holds those securities. Then in chapter 9, on capital market theory, we explain how economists use the relationship between individual securities and portfolios to create a model of the trade-off that financial markets will establish between the expected return and the risk on individual securities. This model, the capital asset pricing model, is one of the seminal contributions to the economics of financial markets.

7.12   Correlation

7.12.1   General Observations

The regression line in figure 7.6 is the straight line that best fits the scatter diagram according to the criterion of minimizing the sum of (squared) vertical deviations from the data points to the regression line. Correlation is a measure of how closely the data points are distributed above and below the regression line. For an initial glance at the difference between correlation and regression, consider figure 7.8. Although the data points in (b) are more widely dispersed than those in (a), both scatter diagrams have identical regression lines. The two scatter diagrams are constructed so that the straight line that best fits the data in (a) has the same pair of values for its slope and intercept as the line that best fits the data in (b).[21]

The two scatter diagrams differ in the average proximity of their data points to their regression lines. The correlation coefficient for a set of data points is a measure of the average proximity of the data points to their regression line. Sometimes, the correlation coefficient is described as a measure of closeness of fit.

By definition, the correlation coefficient takes a value between -1 and $+1$. For a given scatter diagram, the sign of the correlation coefficient will be the same as the sign of the slope of the regression line for that scatter diagram. The more closely the

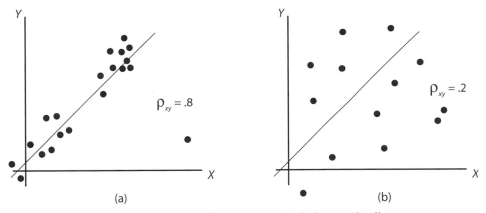

Figure 7.8. Two scatter diagrams with identical regression lines.

data points are located to their regression line, the closer the value of the correlation coefficient will be to -1 or $+1$. If the data points are collinear, all the data points will lie on the regression line. If this regression line for a set of collinear data points slopes downward, the correlation coefficient will take the value -1. If the regression line for collinear data points slopes upward, the value of the correlation coefficient will be $+1$.

More generally, if the regression line for a scatter diagram slopes upward, then the correlation coefficient for that set of data points will be positive. The more tightly the data points are concentrated around their regression line, the closer the correlation coefficient will be to $+1$. The same relationship holds for regression lines that slope downward, except that the correlation coefficient is negative.

A special case occurs if the scatter diagram is such that its regression line has a slope of zero. In this case, the correlation coefficient is zero, and the proximity of the data points to the regression line has no effect on the value of the correlation coefficient.

In figure 7.8, note that, except for regression lines that have a slope of zero, the slope of the regression line controls only the sign of the correlation coefficient. The magnitude of the correlation coefficient is determined by the dispersion of the data points around the regression line.

7.12.2 Correlation and Prediction

The value of the correlation coefficient between two variables is a measure of the precision with which we can use the outcome for one of the variables to predict the outcome of the other variable. For any one of the scatter diagrams in figure 7.8, we can use the regression line to predict the value for y, if we know the value for x. If the value for x is such that the data point lies close to the regression line, then our error in predicting the value of y will be small. Consider panel (a) of figure 7.8. Since most of the data points are close to their regression line, the average size of the error in using the regression line to predict the value of y given the value of x will be small.

Analogously, if the data points are widely dispersed around their regression line, as in panel (b), then the average error will be large.

For any scatter diagram, the absolute value of its correlation coefficient is determined by the dispersion of the data points around their regression line. Therefore, the absolute value of the correlation coefficient is a measure of the value of knowing the slope and the vertical intercept of the regression line if one is interested in using the value of x to predict the value of y. For example, if we wanted to predict y from x, and we knew that the absolute value of the correlation coefficient is high, as in panel (a), then we would be willing to pay a higher price to discover the equation of the regression line than we would if the absolute value of the correlation coefficient is low, as in panel (b). The absolute value of the correlation coefficient can also be regarded as a measure of our confidence in using the regression line as a basis for predicting the value of y, given the value of x.

7.13   Summary

The market for financial securities establishes an equilibrium configuration of prices at each moment. Specifically, at time $t-1$ the price of each security will adjust so that the probability distribution for the rate of return on that security (for the interval that ends at time t) will be such that the quantities of that security that investors want to buy and sell will be equal. Consequently, at the conclusion of trading at time $t-1$, each investor will hold the configuration of securities that will produce the combination of expected return and standard deviation that he or she wants for the rate of return on the portfolio. If new information arrives between time $t-1$ and time t about the abilities of firms to generate earnings, or if investors change their attitudes toward risk, then the prices of securities will change to create a new equilibrium distribution of securities among investors at time t.

Problems

1. Consider the following data for Security A:

$$P_{A,t-1} = \$1,000$$

$$P_{A,t} = \$1,100$$

$$D_{A,t} = \$50$$

(a) Calculate the rate of capital gain (or loss) over the interval from time $t-1$ to time t.

(b) Over that interval, what is the dividend yield?

(c) What is the total rate of return on Security A over the interval from time $t-1$ to time t?

2. Consider the following joint probability distribution for the rates of return on Securities A and B:

		Possible Outcomes for $\tilde{r}_A$			Probabilities for $\tilde{r}_B$ independent of the value of $\tilde{r}_A$
		0	.30	.60	
Possible	.07	.1	.2	.1	.4
outcomes for $\tilde{r}_B$	.14	.1	0	.1	.2
	.21	.1	.2	.1	.4
Probabilities for $\tilde{r}_A$ independent of the value of $\tilde{r}_B$		.3	.4	.3	

What are the values of the standard deviations for Securities A and B?

Notes

1. Firms typically maintain inventories of inputs, finished outputs, or both. Firms that finance these inventories by borrowing from banks on lines of credit incur explicit costs for interest. Firms that have used their own funds to finance these inventories incur opportunity costs because these funds could have been invested elsewhere. These firms could, for example, pay down some of their debt, thus avoiding explicit interest costs. The firms could also invest their funds in short-term bonds, thus receiving interest income.

2. To calculate the probability of obtaining two red cards, we enumerate the possible outcomes of drawing one card from each deck. There are four possible outcomes: (1) red from the first deck and red from the second deck; (2) red from the first deck and black from the second deck; (3) black from the first deck and red from the second deck; and (4) black from the first deck and black from the second deck. Each of these four outcomes is equally likely; only one of the four has two red cards. Therefore, the probability of obtaining two red cards in one draw from each of the two decks is 1/4, or 0.25. Analogously, the probability of obtaining no red cards is also 0.25, since obtaining no red cards is equivalent to obtaining two black cards. Finally, there are two ways to obtain a total of one red card. One way is to draw a red card from the first deck and a black card from the second deck. The probability of this joint outcome is (0.50)(0.50), or 0.25. The second way to obtain one red card is to draw it from the second deck, while drawing a black card from the first deck. Since each of these outcomes is equally likely, the probability of obtaining a total of one red card in two draws is the sum of the two probabilities, or 0.25+0.25=0.50. Once the two draws are made, the probability that the random variable Y will take precisely one of the values 0, 1, or 2 is 100% or 1.0. Therefore, the probabilities of these mutually exclusive and exhaustive outcomes for Y must sum to 1.0, as they do, because 0.25+0.50+0.25=1.0.

3. This is the standard procedure on organized exchanges.

4. Most firms that pay dividends do so every three months. If we are modeling monthly rates of return, $D_{i,t}$ will be nonzero at most only one time out of three. (The firm could skip a

dividend due to poor earnings.) If we are modeling daily rates of return, $D_{i,t}$ will be zero most of the time.

5. We ignore brokers' commissions, taxes, and the spread between dealers' bid prices and asked prices.

6. The foregoing discussion of the interchangeability of cash and securities holds only if there are no commissions or other costs (transaction costs) incurred when buying and selling securities, no taxes imposed on realized capital gains, and no deductions allowed for realized capital losses.

7. Remember, we are assuming that there are no transaction costs and no taxes on capital gains.

8. Mutual funds and some firms will redeem fractional shares. The relevance of fractional shares diminishes, of course, as the total number of shares that the investor owns increases. For example, an investor who owned 100 shares at time $t-1$ would see the value of her wealth increase from $10,000 to $10,500 as the price per share increases from $100 at time $t-1$ to $105 at time t. This investor could liquidate the $500 gain in her wealth by selling 10 full shares.

9. This price is only relevant in the calculation of the capital gains tax when the investor sells the asset.

10. Assertions about relative frequencies of particular outcomes in a large number of repetitions of a probabilistic process are known as laws of large numbers. There are several such laws, all of which assert properties of the limits that probabilities approach as the number of repetitions of the process increases without bound. The following example of a simple version of these laws of large numbers is sufficient for this book: let Z_N be the number of times that a red ace is drawn from a deck of playing cards in N successive draws. After each draw, the drawn card is returned to the deck, which is reshuffled. The proportion of N draws in which a red card appears is Z_N/N. Since there are 2 red aces in the deck of 52 cards, the probability of obtaining a red ace on a single draw is 2/52 or 1/26. A law of large numbers asserts that the difference between the probability, 1/26, of getting a red ace and the actual proportion, Z_N/N, of red aces obtained in N draws will approach zero as the number, N, of repetitions increases without bound. To put this law in a different way: as the number of repetitions gets larger, the likelihood that the actual proportion of red cards, Z_N/N, will deviate from the theoretical proportion, 1/26, by more than a specified amount steadily decreases.

11. In fact, it is the logarithms of the rates of return that are normally distributed. More important, economists have known for some time that there are important phenomena in the financial markets for which the rates of return are not normally distributed. In particular, some distributions have "fatter tails" than the normal distributions. Recently, economists have conducted analyses based on these nonnormal distributions. These analyses are beyond the scope of this book, mainly because they have not yet been incorporated into a comprehensive model of asset pricing.

12. The definition of the expected value of a random variable as the probability-weighted sum of the values that it can take is appropriate only for a discrete random variable. For a continuous random variable, r, such as a rate of return, the expected value is the integral, $\int rf(r)dr$, over the entire range of the density function, $f(r)$. Analogously, the standard deviation of r is the positive square root of $\int (r-E_r)^2 f(r)dr$, in which E_r is the expected value of r.

13. Recall that the definition of the standard deviation involves the squares of distances so that negative and positive distances will not offset each other. If squares of distances were not used, the standard deviation would understate the dispersion of the probability density function around the expected return.

14. For continuous variables, the covariance and the correlation coefficient are defined in terms of integrals. For discrete variables, the definitions use sums. See note 12.

15. If k is a constant, $E(k)=k$.

16. The attractiveness of Security i also depends on the values of the correlation coefficients between the rate of return on Security i and the rates of return on all of the other securities that the investor could hold. We explain this relationship in chapter 8.

17. The reader should create examples to demonstrate this.

18. In fact, since the page is only two-dimensional, Figure 7.4 is a two-dimensional representation of a three-dimensional diagram.

19. Investors who held diversified portfolios, such as mutual funds, did not lose all of their wealth even during the bear market of 1972–74 or during the crash of 1987.

20. Income could come from realizing capital gains or from dividend payments.

21. That is, best fits against the criterion of minimizing the sum of the squared vertical distances between the data points and the regression line.

Part IV

Portfolio Theory and Capital Asset Pricing Theory

8 Portfolio Theory

8.1 Introduction

8.1.1 Definition of Portfolio Theory

A portfolio is a collection of securities. Portfolio theory is a formal analysis of the relationship between the rates of return on a portfolio of risky securities and the rates of return on the securities contained in that portfolio. The rate of return on a portfolio is a random variable. The probability distribution that generates values for the rate of return on the portfolio is a compilation of the probability distributions that generate the rates of return on the securities contained in that portfolio. In this chapter, we develop an elementary version of portfolio theory. We then use that theory to explain how a rational investor would allocate funds among risky securities to create a portfolio that best suits his or her preferences regarding alternative combinations of risk and expected return.

8.1.2 The Uses of Portfolio Theory in the Economics of Financial Markets

Economists use portfolio theory to derive empirically testable models of how financial markets set the prices of individual securities. The seminal application of portfolio theory to this question created the capital asset pricing model, which we study in detail in the next chapter. Economists derived this model by determining what the equilibrium prices of individual securities would be if all investors used the principles of portfolio theory to construct their personal portfolios. Understanding the derivation of the capital asset pricing model from portfolio theory will contribute much to the reader's understanding of financial economics. The same exercise will also increase the reader's sophistication in microeconomic theory.

By leading to the creation of asset pricing models, portfolio theory has also contributed in several ways to our ability to analyze the economic efficiency with which financial markets allocate scarce resources. Addressing these questions of efficiency is important for the scientific purpose of understanding how the markets work. This analysis is also important as a basis for public policy toward financial markets.

Financial markets allocate scarce resources in several ways. We evaluate the performance of these markets against the criterion of economic efficiency that we developed in chapter 2. Recall that we defined economic efficiency in terms of mutually beneficial exchanges. Most exchanges require that at least one of the parties in the exchange bears risk; therefore, we must have a theory of how financial markets quantify risk and determine the reward for bearing risk if we are to assess the economic efficiency of these markets. The models of asset pricing that economists have derived from portfolio theory enable us to integrate risk into our analyses of exchanges among investors. We next discuss briefly four ways in which financial markets allocate resources.

First, financial markets promote exchanges between investors who are willing to accept lower expected rates of return in order to avoid some risk, and investors who are willing to bear higher levels of risk in order to gain higher expected rates of return. We considered an example of this in chapter 6, where we considered the exchanges of financial securities between Ms. Tall and Ms. Short, each of whom has different tolerances for risk.

Second, financial markets guide the allocation of investible funds among potential new projects by providing both corporations and individual investors with mechanisms for evaluating the levels of risk and expected rates of return on these projects.

Third, under some conditions financial markets can enable managers of firms to eliminate an asymmetry of information between themselves and potential new investors from whom the firm seeks additional capital to undertake new projects. If the conflict created by asymmetric information is not resolved, the firm's current investors and the potential new investors will forego a mutually beneficial exchange; foregone mutually beneficial exchanges create an economically inefficient allocation of resources. In chapter 13, we show that when managers have a variety of kinds of securities to offer to new investors, the managers can credibly transmit their superior information to new investors by the choice of the security they offer.

The fourth way in which portfolio theory contributes to the analysis of the efficiency of financial markets involves the governance of the modern corporation. A firm's managers act as agents of the shareholders, who own the firm's capital. Among other things, the managers must decide how to allocate the firm's earnings between investing in new projects and paying dividends. In chapter 13, we examine the incentives that can lead managers to make choices that decrease the shareholders' wealth. Economists call this phenomenon the problem of agency. We also explain how financial markets can mitigate this problem by means of offering different kinds of securities.

All four uses of portfolio theory have implications for public policy. Public policy should enhance the ability of the markets to promote economic efficiency. In particular, public policy should mitigate the inefficiencies created by asymmetries of information and by problems of agency. But in order to construct public policies that will promote an efficient allocation of resources, we must understand how markets affect the allocation of resources. To do so, we need a theory of capital asset pricing. Portfolio theory has made substantial contributions to the development and testing of alternative theories of capital asset pricing.

8.1.3 The Plan of the Chapter

In the remainder of this chapter, we show how the expected returns, standard deviations, and correlation coefficients of individual securities determine the set of combinations of expected return and standard deviation that an investor can choose for a portfolio. We first consider in detail portfolios that contain only two securities. We show how the value of the correlation coefficient between these two securities determines the set of combinations of expected return and standard deviation (i.e., risk) that the investor can obtain for his or her portfolio.

A particularly transparent use of portfolio theory occurs when two risky securities have perfectly correlated rates of return. In this situation, an investor can construct a riskless portfolio. Competition among investors will ensure that the rate of return on this riskless portfolio will be equal to the rate of return on any single riskless security, such as a bank account or a government bond. In chapter 15, we use this fact to derive the equilibrium prices of derivative securities, such as options.

The trade-off between the expected return and the standard deviation for portfolios that contain more than two securities is analogous to the case in which the portfolio contains only two securities. We summarize that analogy without the detail in which we analyze portfolios that contain only two risky securities.

8.2 Portfolios as Synthetic Securities

A portfolio is a synthetic security that an investor creates by purchasing a combination of elemental securities. An elemental security is a security, such as a common stock or a bond, issued by a firm or a governmental agency.

The rate of return on a portfolio is a weighted average of the rates of return on its constituent securities. We know that the rate of return on a security is a random variable whose value is generated by a probability density function. Therefore, the rate of return on the portfolio is also a random variable, and the value of the portfolio's rate of return is generated by a probability density function that is a composite of the density functions for the constituent securities.

The expected return and standard deviation for the portfolio's rate of return are determined by the expected returns, standard deviations, and correlation coefficients of the securities contained in the portfolio, and by the proportions in which the investor allocates funds across those securities. The investor cannot choose the rate of return on the portfolio because that rate of return is a random variable. By choosing the proportions in which to allocate funds across those securities, the investor can, however, within limits, choose the expected value and the standard deviation of the probability density function that will govern the rate of return on the portfolio. This is the sense in which a portfolio is a synthetic security.

Here is an example. Consider two simple portfolios. Portfolio 1 contains only Security A; Portfolio 2 contains Securities A, B, and C.

To construct Portfolio 1, the investor allocates 100% of the funds to Security A. To purchase Security A is to purchase the right to receive a rate of return whose value will be generated by Security A's probability density function. Let σ_A and E_A be the standard deviation and expected return of this density function. When an investor purchases Security A, he or she purchases the combination of parameters (σ_A, E_A) for the density function that will generate the rate of return. Since Portfolio 1 contains only

Security A, the expected rate of return on Portfolio 1 is, obviously, E_A, and the standard deviation of that rate of return is σ_A.

Portfolio 2 contains Securities A, B, and C. The values for the rate of return on this portfolio will be generated by a probability density function that is a composite of the density functions for Securities A, B, and C. Let E_2 and σ_2 be the expected return and the standard deviation for Portfolio 2. By varying the proportions in which to allocate funds across Securities A, B, and C, the investor can choose from many alternative combinations of values for the parameters E_2 and σ_2 that will govern the rate of return on Portfolio 2. The fact that an investor can choose among several combinations of values for E_2 and σ_2 by altering the allocation of funds among individual securities is fundamental to understanding the economics of financial markets.

8.3   Portfolios Containing Two Risky Securities

8.3.1   Risky Securities

A risky security is a security whose rate of return will deviate randomly from its expected value. Therefore, the probability density function for a risky security will have a nonzero value for its standard deviation. In portfolio theory, *risky* does not mean inadvisable, highly speculative, or anything else that would imply that the security is a poor investment. Rather, *risky* simply means *not riskless*.

A riskless security is one whose rate of return is guaranteed never to deviate from a known constant. The probability density function for a riskless security has a standard deviation equal to zero. The graph of this density function is a single vertical line erected at the value of the expected return.

8.3.2   The Rate of Return on the Portfolio

Let W be the amount of money that an investor uses to form a portfolio that contains only two securities, A and B. Let X_A and X_B be the proportions in which the investor allocates funds to these securities. Since the portfolio contains no securities other than A and B, then:

$$X_A + X_B = 1. \tag{8.1}$$

For example, if $W = \$1,000$, and the investor chooses .7 as the value for X_A and .3 as the value for X_B, then he or she forms the portfolio by purchasing \$700 worth of Security A and \$300 worth of Security B. Let the random variables $\tilde{r}_A$ and $\tilde{r}_B$ be the rates of return on Securities A and B, and let the random variable $\tilde{r}_P$ be the rate of return on the investor's portfolio. The rate of return on the portfolio is related to the rates of return on its constituent securities by:

$$\tilde{r}_P = X_A \tilde{r}_A + X_B \tilde{r}_B. \tag{8.2}$$

The rate of return on the portfolio is a weighted average of the rates of return on the constituent securities, with the weights being the proportions X_A and X_B that determine the structure of the portfolio. Note that the aggregate amount of funds, W, does not appear in equation (8.2). The rate of return on the portfolio is determined solely by the rates of return on the constituent securities and by the proportions in which the investor allocates funds between those securities.

Suppose that in a given month the outcomes for the rates of return on Securities A and B are $r_A = .10$ and $r_B = .18$. If the investor formed a portfolio by setting $X_A = .7$ and $X_B = .3$, then the rate of return on the portfolio for that month would be:

$$\tilde{r}_P = X_A \tilde{r}_A + X_B \tilde{r}_B$$
$$= (.7)(.10) + (.3)(.18) \tag{8.3}$$
$$= .07 + .054 = .124.$$

Therefore, the value of the investor's portfolio would have increased by 12.4% over the month. If he or she had committed a total of $W = \$1,000$ to the portfolio at the beginning of the month, then the value of the portfolio at the end of the month would be:

$$(1 + \tilde{r}_P)W = (1 + .124)\$1,000$$
$$= \$1,124. \tag{8.4}$$

Had the investor committed \$2,000 to the portfolio and used the same values for X_A and X_B, the second portfolio would have been twice the size of the first portfolio, but the two portfolios would have identical *structures*. Therefore, the rate of return on the two portfolios would be equal, namely $r_P = .124$. But the value of the larger portfolio at the end of the month would be \$2,248, twice the ending value of the smaller portfolio.

8.3.3 Short Positions

We digress briefly to consider portfolios in which the investor takes a short position in one of the two securities. We do this because in some cases we can discover the equilibrium prices of risky securities by examining portfolios that contain these securities and also contain short positions in one or more related securities. In chapter 15, we use this procedure to analyze the equilibrium prices of options.

In the numerical example in the preceding section, the investor constructed a portfolio by purchasing quantities of both Securities A and B. We know this because the allocative proportions X_A and X_B both have positive values. We say that the investor had *long* positions in both securities. If an investor is long in both securities, then the total dollar amount that she can invest in either security must be less than W, which is the aggregate value of the invested funds. If, however, the investor sells one of the securities short, she can use the proceeds of that short sale to increase her investment in the other security to an amount greater than W. If the investor does take a short position in one security, the allocative proportion for that security will be negative, and the proportion for the other security will be greater than 1. The sum of the two proportions must still be equal to 1.

Consider the following example. The investor takes a short position in Security A by an amount equal to 40% of her total funds, W. To do this, she sets $X_A = -.4$. Since

$X_A + X_B = 1$, the proportion of her total funds that she will allocate to Security B will be $X_B = 1 - X_A = 1 - (-.4) = 1.4$. If $W = \$1,000$, she will borrow \$400 worth of shares of Security A, sell them, and combine the proceeds of \$400 with the \$1,000 of her own money that she has committed to the portfolio. She will then purchase \$1,400 worth of shares of Security B, so that she has a long position in that security equal to \$1,400. Her long position of \$1,400 in Security B exceeds by 40% the total amount of money, \$1,000, that she has committed to the portfolio.

The investor's position in Security B is long by \$1,400 because that is the amount of money that she could raise if she were to liquidate her position in Security B. Since she owns \$1,400 worth of Security B, liquidating her position in that security would require selling \$1,400 worth of that security, thus raising \$1,400.

The investor's position in Security A is equal to $X_A W$. Since $X_A = -.4$ and $W = \$1,000$, her position in that security is $-\$400$, which is a short position. Her position in Security A is short by \$400 because that is the amount of money that she would have to pay to liquidate that position. Since she initially borrowed \$400 worth of Security A, she would have to spend \$400 to repurchase a sufficient number of shares of that security to extinguish her debt to owners of Security A.

In the preceding paragraph, we assumed that the prices of neither security change after the investor constructs the portfolio. Under this assumption, liquidating the portfolio would raise $\$1,400 + (-\$400) = \$1,000$, which is exactly what she invested. If the prices of the two securities changed between the time that she constructed the portfolio and the time that she liquidated it, then the portfolio could, of course, be worth more than \$1,000, or less than \$1,000.

8.4   The Trade-Off between the Expected Value and the Standard Deviation of the Rate of Return on a Portfolio That Contains Two Securities

8.4.1   The Equations for the Expected Return and the Standard Deviation of the Portfolio

We shall now develop the relationship between the investor's choice of values for X_A and X_B and the values of the expected return and the standard deviation on her portfolio.

The expected value of the rate of return, E_P, and the standard deviation of that rate of return, σ_P, on the investor's portfolio are determined by the proportions, X_A and X_B, in which she allocates funds to Securities A and B, and by the five parameters that define the probability density functions for those securities. These parameters are the expected return and the standard deviation for Security A, the expected return and the standard deviation for Security B, and the correlation coefficient between the rates of return on those securities. Specifically, E_P and σ_P are determined by:

$$E_P = X_A E_A + X_B E_B, \tag{8.5}$$

and

$$\sigma_P = \sqrt{\sigma_P{}^2} = \sqrt{(X_A{}^2 \sigma_A{}^2 + 2\rho_{AB}\sigma_A\sigma_B X_A X_B + X_B{}^2 \sigma_B{}^2)}. \tag{8.6}$$

The term under the square root sign on the right-hand side of equation (8.6) is the variance of the rate of return on the portfolio. For portfolios, it is often convenient to work with the variance rather than the standard deviation.

8.4.2 Parameters, Decision Variables, and Independent Variables

It will be helpful to sort the many symbols that appear in the equations above into three groups, as follows.

Parameters: E_A, σ_A, E_B, σ_B, ρ_{AB}.

The investor has no control over the probability density functions that generate outcomes for the rates of return on Securities A and B. These probability density functions are fully defined by the values of the five parameters. The values of these parameters depend on the operational and financial decisions made by the managers of Firms A and B, and on the relationships between the operations of these firms and the performance of the macroeconomy in which these firms participate.

Decision variables: X_A, X_B.

The investor chooses the values X_A and X_B to specify the proportions in which she will allocate funds between Securities A and B. Since these securities are the only candidates for the portfolio, $X_A + X_B = 1$. Either X_A or X_B can be positive, negative, or zero depending on whether the investor takes a long position, a short position, or no position in that security.

Dependent variables: E_P, σ_P.

The investor's portfolio is a synthetic security that she creates by holding Securities A and B in a certain proportion. The rate of return on the portfolio is governed by a probability density function that the investor constructs by choosing values for the proportions X_A and X_B. But the portfolio's density function is fully defined by the values of its expected return and its standard deviation. Equivalently, the investor chooses the combination of values for the expected return and the standard deviation on her portfolio by choosing the proportions, X_A and X_B, that define her portfolio. The relationship between the investor's decisions on X_A and X_B, and the consequent values for E_P and σ_P, is specified by equations (8.5) and (8.6).

8.4.3 Economic Interpretations

Here are the economic interpretations of the several terms in equations (8.5) and (8.6). From equation (8.5), we see that the expected return for the portfolio is a weighted average of the expected returns of the two constituent securities. The weights are the allocative proportions, X_A and X_B. If the investor allocates most of her funds to Security A, and only a small proportion to Security B, then the average rate of return on the portfolio will be closer to the average rate of return on Security A than to the average rate of return on Security B. The right-hand side of equation (8.5) ensures this. Note from equation (8.5) that E_P, the expected return on the investor's portfolio, does not depend on the correlation coefficient, ρ_{AB}.

The portfolio's standard deviation, σ_P, is defined by equation (8.6). The first and third terms under the square root sign on the right-hand side of equation (8.6) are analogous to the two terms that define E_P in equation (8.5). When calculating E_P, we put on the expected return for each constituent security a weight that is equal to the proportion of the funds allocated to that security. When calculating the standard deviation for the portfolio, we square the weighted standard deviations of Securities A and B.

The standard deviation for the portfolio is also affected by the interaction between the rates of return on Securities A and B. The effect of this interaction is measured in equation (8.6) by the middle term, which contains the correlation coefficient, ρ_{AB}. The reason is easy to understand.

The standard deviation for any random variable measures the dispersion of values that the random variable can take above and below its expected value. More precisely, the standard deviation is a probability-weighted measure of dispersion around that expected value. Therefore, the standard deviation for the portfolio will increase if the rates of return on Securities A and B interact in a way that increases the probability that the rate of return on the portfolio, $\tilde{r}_P$, will take values far above, and far below, its expected value, E_P. Similarly, if the interaction between Securities A and B decreases the probability that $\tilde{r}_P$ will take values from E_P, then including those two securities in the portfolio will decrease the standard deviation of the rate of return on the portfolio.

The value and the sign of the correlation coefficient between the rates of return on Securities A and B is a measure of the effect of those securities on the probabilities that the rate of return on the portfolio will take values far above and far below E_P. Here is the reason.

Suppose that the value of the correlation coefficient is large and positive. For example, suppose that $\rho_{AB}=.9$. Then in any given month, the rates of return on Securities A and B are highly likely to be on the same sides of their respective expected values. Moreover, the number of Security A's standard deviations by which r_A is displaced from E_A is highly likely to be equal to the number of Security B's standard deviations by which r_B is displaced from E_B. That is, the rates of return for the two securities will lie the same standardized distance away from their respective expected values.

For example, suppose that in a given month the rate of return for Security A lies above E_A by a distance of $2.5\sigma_A$. Then the fact that $\rho_{AB}=.9$ means that there is a high probability that the rate of return for Security B for that month will lie above E_B by a distance of $2.5\sigma_B$. If ρ_{AB} were equal to $+1$, which is the maximal value that a correlation coefficient can take, then the probability would be 1 (100%) that r_B will take the value of $E_B+2.5\sigma_B$ whenever r_A takes the value $E_A+2.5\sigma_A$.

Similarly, suppose that in a given month r_A takes a value below E_A. If $\rho_{AB}=.9$, there is a high probability that the number of Security B's standard deviations by which r_B lies below E_B will be equal to the number of Security A's standard deviations by which r_A lies below E_A.

Finally, if the correlation coefficient, ρ_{AB}, is large and negative, there is a high probability that in any given month the rates of return on Securities A and B will lie on opposite sides of their respective expected rates of return at distances equal to the same number of their respective standard deviations.

We can now see the effect of the value of ρ_{AB} on the size of the standard deviation of the rate of return on a portfolio that contains both Securities A and B. The standard deviation for the portfolio, σ_P, measures the dispersion of values for the rate of return on the portfolio above and below the expected rate of return on the portfolio, E_P. From equation (8.5), we know that the value of E_P is a weighted average of the expected rates of return, E_A and E_B, on the constituent securities. In any given month, the rate of return on the portfolio is a weighted average of the rates of return on Securities A and B for that month. If the rates of return on both securities are simultaneously above (or below) their respective expected rates of return, then the two securities will reinforce each other in moving the rate of return on the portfolio above (or below) its expected rate of return. In particular, if the rates of return on Securities A and B are simultaneously far above (or far below) their expected rates of return, then the rate of return on the portfolio will be far above (or far below) its expected rate of return. The higher the value of the correlation coefficient, ρ_{AB}, the higher the probability that the rates of return on Securities A and B in a given month will lie on the same sides of their respective expected rates of return by the same number of their respective standard deviations. Consequently, the higher the value of ρ_{AB}, the higher the probability that the interaction between Securities A and B will amplify the dispersion of values for the rate of return on the portfolio. Therefore, the larger the value for ρ_{AB}, the larger the value for σ_P.

Using analogous reasoning, we conclude that if the value of the correlation coefficient is large and negative, the probability is high that the inclusion of Securities A and B in the portfolio will have offsetting effects on the rate of return on the portfolio. Therefore, the smaller (more negative) the value for ρ_{AB}, the smaller the value for σ_P.

8.4.4 The Locus of Combinations of Expected Returns and Standard Deviations for Portfolios

We will now use a graph to increase our understanding of how an investor can alter the combination of expected return and standard deviation on a portfolio. Each point in figure 8.1 represents a specific combination of expected return and standard deviation on a portfolio. Expected return is measured in the vertical dimension, and standard deviation is measured in the horizontal dimension. We want to draw a locus of those combinations of expected return and standard deviation that the investor can construct. From our discussions of equations (8.5) and (8.6), we know that the combinations of expected return and standard deviation that the investor can choose for a portfolio are determined by the values of the five parameters E_A, σ_A, E_B, σ_B, and ρ_{AB}. To construct an example of a locus, suppose that the values of the first four parameters are $E_A = .20$, $\sigma_A = .06$, $E_B = .10$, and $\sigma_B = .02$. We will leave the value of the correlation coefficient unspecified for the moment.

The investor constructs a portfolio by choosing an allocation of funds between Securities A and B. One of her choices is to allocate 100% of her funds to Security A, and none to Security B. To do this, she would set $X_A = 1$ and $X_B = 0$. If she holds only Security A in her portfolio, then the rate of return on her portfolio will be simply the rate of return on Security A; the rate of return on Security B will be irrelevant. Then the expected return, E_P, and the standard deviation, σ_P, on the investor's portfolio will be equal to the expected return and the standard deviation on the only security in that portfolio. That is, $E_P = E_A$ and $\sigma_P = \sigma_A$.

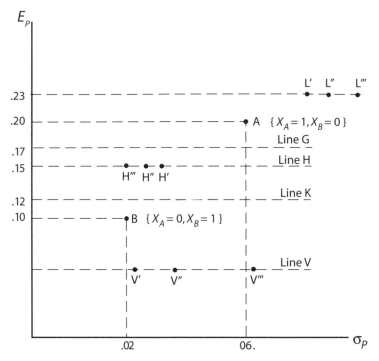

Figure 8.1. Combinations of expected rate of return (E_p) and standard deviation (σ_p) on portfolios.

In figure 8.1, Point A designates the combination of expected return and standard deviation that the investor can obtain by setting $X_A=1$ and $X_B=0$. Similarly, by setting $X_A=0$ and $X_B=1$, the investor can obtain the combination of expected return and standard deviation located at Point B. In this case, her portfolio will contain only Security B.

Suppose that the investor splits her funds equally between the two securities. Designate the resulting portfolio as Portfolio H, and define X_A^H and X_B^H as the proportions in which the investor must allocate her funds to Securities A and B to construct Portfolio H. If the investor allocates equal amounts of money to Securities A and B, then $X_A^H = X_B^H = .5$.

The expected return on Portfolio H is obtained easily from equation (8.5). Substituting the values $E_A=.20$, $E_B=.10$, $X_A^H=.5$, and $X_B^H=.5$ into the right-hand side of equation (8.5), we have:

$$E_H = X_A^H E_A + X_B^H E_B$$
$$= (.5)(.20)+(.5)(.10) \qquad (8.7)$$
$$= .15.$$

The expected return on Portfolio H is a simple average of the expected return on Securities A and B because the investor constructed Portfolio H by splitting her funds equally between those two securities.

What about the standard deviation on Portfolio H? From equation (8.6), we see that the standard deviation on a portfolio depends on the correlation between the rates of return on Securities A and B through the middle term, $2\rho_{AB}\sigma_A\sigma_B X_A{}^H X_B{}^H$. But the correlation coefficient, ρ_{AB}, does not appear in equation (8.5), which determines the value for E_H. Therefore, E_H will be equal to .15 regardless of the value of ρ_{AB}. We conclude that the combination of expected return and standard deviation in Portfolio H will lie along Line H in figure 8.1. The vertical intercept of Line H is at $E_P = .15$.

We next consider two other portfolios, which we will call Portfolio G and Portfolio K. To construct Portfolio G, the investor allocates 70% of her funds to Security A, and the balance to Security B. Define $X_A{}^G$ and $X_B{}^G$ as the allocative proportions that define Portfolio G. Then $X_A{}^G = .7$ and $X_B{}^G = .3$. Using equation (8.5), the expected return on Portfolio G will be:

$$E_G = X_A{}^G E_A + X_B{}^G E_B$$
$$= (.7)(.20) + (.3)(.10) \tag{8.8}$$
$$= .17.$$

As in the case of Portfolio H, the correlation coefficient between the rates of return on Securities A and B will affect the standard deviation on Portfolio G but not the expected return on that portfolio. Therefore, in figure 8.1 the combination of expected return and standard deviation for Portfolio G will lie on the horizontal line labeled Line G, whose vertical intercept is at $E_P = .17$.

Finally, let Portfolio K be defined by the allocative proportions $X_A{}^K = .2$ and $X_B{}^K = .8$. The combination of expected return and standard deviation for Portfolio K will lie on Line K in figure 8.1. The vertical intercept of this line is $E_K = .12$, which result we obtain by using equation (8.5) and using the values $X_A{}^K = .2$ and $X_B{}^K = .8$ for the allocative proportions.

8.4.5 The Effect of the Correlation Coefficient ρ_{AB} on the Expected Return and the Standard Deviation of the Portfolio

We know from equation (8.5) that the value of the correlation coefficient between the rates of return on Securities A and B has no effect on the expected return of Portfolio H (or any portfolio). The correlation coefficient does, however, affect the standard deviation for Portfolio H through the middle term in equation (8.6); this term is $2\rho_{AB}\sigma_A\sigma_B X_A{}^H X_B{}^H$ once we substitute $X_A{}^H$ and $X_B{}^H$ for X_A and X_B.

Portfolio H contains positive investments in both Securities A and B because both $X_A{}^H$ and $X_B{}^H$ are positive. The two standard deviations, σ_A and σ_B, are also positive. Therefore, the value of the term $2\rho_{AB}\sigma_A\sigma_B X_A{}^H X_B{}^H$ varies directly with the value of the correlation coefficient, ρ_{AB}. Consequently, for any fixed allocation of funds between Securities A and B, the smaller the value of the correlation coefficient between the rates of return on Securities A and B, the smaller the standard deviation of the portfolio.

Consider three alternative values for the correlation coefficient, as follows:

$$\rho_{AB'} = .8; \quad \rho_{AB''} = .1; \quad \rho_{AB'''} = -.6. \tag{8.9}$$

Each of these three alternative values for ρ_{AB} generates a value for the standard deviation on Portfolio H. Let $\sigma_{H'}$ be the standard deviation for Portfolio H for the case in which $\rho_{AB}=\rho_{AB'}=.8$. Similarly, let $\sigma_{H''}$ and $\sigma_{H'''}$ be the standard deviations for Portfolio H when ρ_{AB} takes the values $\rho_{AB}=\rho_{AB''}=.1$, or $\rho_{AB}=\rho_{AB'''}=-.6$. Since ρ_{AB} affects the standard deviation on Portfolio H only through the term $2\rho_{AB}\sigma_A\sigma_B X_A{}^H X_B{}^H$ in equation (8.6), and since σ_A, σ_B, $X_A{}^H$, and $X_B{}^H$ are all positive numbers, we conclude that the three alternative values for the standard deviation on Portfolio H, corresponding to the three alternative values for the correlation coefficient, satisfy the ranking:

$$\sigma_{H'} > \sigma_{H''} > \sigma_{H'''}. \tag{8.10}$$

In figure 8.1, three points are plotted on the horizontal line labeled Line H. Each point designates a combination of expected return and standard deviation for Portfolio H that corresponds to one of the three alternative values for ρ_{AB}. Point H′ corresponds to the case in which $\rho_{AB}=\rho_{AB'}=.8$. Similarly, Points H″ and H‴ correspond to the cases in which $\rho_{AB}=\rho_{AB''}=.1$, or $\rho_{AB}=\rho_{AB'''}=-.6$. The points H′, H″, and H‴ lie at the same height because the value of ρ_{AB} has no effect on the expected return for Portfolio H. From equation (8.6), we know that the standard deviation on Portfolio H decreases as the value of ρ_{AB} decreases. Therefore, as ρ_{AB} decreases from .8 to .1 to $-.6$, the combination of expected return and standard deviation for Portfolio H moves horizontally leftward along Line H from Point H′ to Point H″ to Point H‴.

Our analysis of the effect of the value of ρ_{AB} on the combination of expected return and standard deviation for Portfolio H also holds for Portfolios G and K. As the value of ρ_{AB} decreases, the points in figure 8.1 that designate the combinations of expected return and standard deviation for Portfolios G and K move horizontally leftward along the lines labeled Line G and Line K.

Thus far we have considered portfolios in which the investor either holds positive quantities of both Securities A and B, or places 100% of the funds in one of those securities and holds none of the other security. The combinations of expected return and standard deviation that characterize these portfolios lie on a line in figure 8.1 that passes from Point A to Point B. We know that the locus must pass through these points because two of the portfolios that the investor can construct consist of placing 100% of the funds in one security and none of the funds in the other security.

The degree of curvature of the locus increases as the value of the correlation coefficient between the rates of return on Securities A and B decreases from $+1$ to -1. In section 8.6, we show that when ρ_{AB} takes its maximal value, $+1$, the combinations of expected return and standard deviation on portfolios that contain only Securities A and B all lie on the straight line that connects Points A and B. That is, when $\rho_{AB}=+1$, the locus of combinations of expected return and standard deviation has no curvature at all. As ρ_{AB} decreases, the locus becomes more sharply curved to the left. If ρ_{AB} takes its minimal value, -1, then the locus becomes two straight lines that intersect on the vertical axis at a point between $E_B=.10$ and $E_A=.20$. One of these lines slopes upward from this point on the vertical axis to Point A. The other line slopes downward from this point to Point B.

We now consider the combinations of expected return and standard deviation that the investor can choose for a portfolio by taking a short position in one of the two securities.

Suppose that the investor constructs Portfolio L by taking a short position in Security B equal to 30% of her initial funds. To do this, she sets the value of $X_B{}^L=-.3$. Since Securities A and B are the only securities in her portfolio, we must have $X_A{}^L+X_B{}^L=1$. This condition, and her choice that $X_B{}^L=-3$, means that $X_A{}^L=1-X_B=1-(-.3)=1.3$. For example, suppose that the investor's initial funds were \$100. She would then purchase \$130 worth of Security A, financing this purchase by using \$100 of her own funds augmented by the \$30 that she raises by selling borrowed shares of Portfolio B. The expected return on Portfolio L will be:

$$
\begin{aligned}
E_L &= X_A{}^L E_A + X_B{}^L E_B \\
&= (1.3)(.20)+(-.3)(.10) \\
&= .23.
\end{aligned}
\tag{8.11}
$$

Notice that the expected return on Portfolio L lies outside the interval between $E_B=.10$ and $E_A=.20$. Since the correlation coefficient ρ_{AB} has no effect on the expected return on a portfolio, the combination of expected return and standard deviation for Portfolio L will lie somewhere on Line L in figure 8.1. The height of this line is .23.

Now consider the effect of ρ_{AB} on the standard deviation for Portfolio L. Recalling our earlier work, the correlation coefficient will affect σ_L through the middle term of:

$$
\sigma_L = \sqrt{[(X_A{}^L)^2 \sigma_A{}^2 + 2\rho_{AB}\sigma_A\sigma_B X_A{}^L X_B{}^L + (X_B{}^L)^2 \sigma_B{}^2]}.
\tag{8.12}
$$

In Portfolio L, the investor holds Security A long and Security B short. Therefore, $X_A{}^L X_B{}^L$ is negative. In our numerical example, $X_A{}^L X_B{}^L=(1.3)(-.3)=-3.9$. Since the product $\sigma_A\sigma_B$ is positive, the term $2\rho_{AB}\sigma_A\sigma_B X_A{}^L X_B{}^L$ will increase as the value of ρ_{AB} decreases from $+1$ to -1. In figure 8.1, let the points L′, L″, and L‴ designate the three combinations of expected return and standard deviation for Portfolio L that correspond to the alternative values for ρ_{AB}, namely $\rho_{AB'}=.8$, $\rho_{AB''}=.1$, and $\rho_{AB'''}=-.6$. Then the corresponding three values of the standard deviation for Portfolio L must be ordered as follows:

$$
\sigma_{L'} > \sigma_{L''} > \sigma_{L'''},
\tag{8.13}
$$

so that in figure 8.1, Point L′ lies farthest to the left on Line L, and Point L‴ lies farthest to the right on that line.

Next consider Portfolio V, in which the investor holds a short position in Security A. For Portfolio V, $X_A{}^V<0$ and $X_B{}^V>1$. Following an argument analogous to the one we used for Portfolio L, we can conclude that the expected return on Portfolio V is less than the expected return on Security B. Therefore, the combination of expected return and standard deviation for Portfolio V lies somewhere on the horizontal line labeled Line V in figure 8.1. Further, since $X_A{}^V<0$ and $X_B{}^V>1$, the product $X_A{}^V X_B{}^V$ is negative. Therefore, as is the case with Portfolio L, the standard deviation of Portfolio V increases as the value of ρ_{AB} decreases from $+1$ to -1. The points V′, V″, and V‴ on Line V in figure 8.1 designate the three combinations of expected return and standard deviation for Portfolio V that correspond to the three alternative values for ρ_{AB}.

We can summarize our analysis thus far by considering the three loci in figure 8.2. Each locus is a set of alternative combinations of expected return and standard

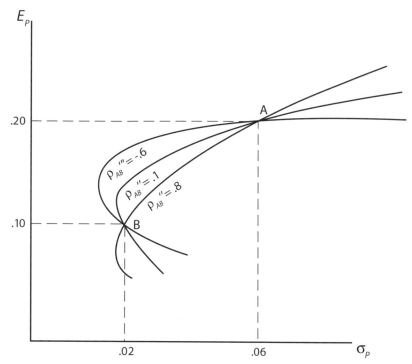

Figure 8.2. Combinations of expected rate of return (E_P) and standard deviation (σ_P) for portfolios for three alternative values for the correlation coefficient between Securities A and B.

deviation that correspond to a particular fixed value for ρ_{AB}. We have set these values at $\rho_{AB'}=.8$, $\rho_{AB''}=.1$, and $\rho_{AB'''}=-.6$. For any one of the fixed values of ρ_{AB}, the investor can move the combination of expected return and standard deviation for the portfolio along the locus corresponding to that value of ρ_{AB} by altering the proportions in which funds are allocated between Securities A and B.

All three loci pass through Point A and Point B because the investor can always allocate 100% of the funds to one of the two securities. If the investor does so, the expected return and standard deviation on the portfolio will (obviously) be equal to the expected return and standard deviation on the only security in that portfolio; the value of ρ_{AB} will be irrelevant. To verify this, note that if $X_A=1$, then $X_B=0$, and $X_AX_B=0$. Then from equations (8.5) and (8.6), the expected return on the investor's portfolio will be equal to E_A, and the standard deviation will be equal to σ_A. The value of ρ_{AB} will be irrelevant because the middle term in equation (8.6) will disappear in consequence of $X_AX_B=0$.

The locus corresponding to $\rho_{AB'}=.8$ is the least sharply curved of the three loci, and the locus corresponding to $\rho_{AB'''}=-.6$ is the most sharply curved. Consequently, for any fixed allocation of funds between Securities A and B in which the investor holds positive amounts of both securities, the standard deviation on the investor's portfolio decreases as the value of the correlation coefficient between the rates of return on the two securities decreases. Equivalently, for any fixed level of expected return on an investor's portfolio, the value of the standard deviation for that portfolio decreases as the correlation between the two securities decreases. Using our work in section 8.4.3, we will show why this is true.

If the correlation coefficient is large and positive, there is a high probability that in any given month the values for the rates of return on Securities A and B, $\tilde{r}_A$ and $\tilde{r}_B$, will lie on the same sides of their expected values. Moreover, whenever the rate of return for either of the securities takes a value that is far from its expected return in one direction, there is a high probability that the rate of return on the other security will take a value that is far from its expected return and in the same direction. If the investor holds positive amounts of both Securities A and B in the portfolio, and if the correlation between these securities is large and positive, then the random values of the two rates of return are likely to reinforce each other in their effects on the volatility of the rate of return on the portfolio.

If Securities A and B are mutually reinforcing in their effects on the volatility of the rate of return of the portfolio, then the standard deviation of the portfolio will be relatively large. Alternatively, if the correlation coefficient is large and negative, then there is a high probability that in any given month the values for $\tilde{r}_A$ and $\tilde{r}_B$ will lie on opposite sides of their expected values. Moreover, whenever the rate of return for either security deviates far from its expected return in one direction, the rate of return for the other security will be highly likely to deviate far from its expected return in the opposite direction. Therefore, if the investor holds positive amounts of both securities, and if the correlation coefficient is large and negative, the random variations in the two rates of return are likely to offset each other in their effects on the standard deviation of the portfolio.

Imagine two inexperienced paddlers sitting in a canoe. Suppose that each paddler is inclined to shift his weight unpredictably to one side or the other. If the two paddlers shift their weights with a large and positive correlation, then the random shifts of the two paddlers are likely to reduce the stability of the canoe (perhaps leading to a capsizing). But if the two paddlers shift their weights with a large and negative correlation, the random shifts are likely to increase the stability of the canoe.

The preceding analysis applies to portfolios in which the investor holds positive quantities of both securities. For all of these portfolios, the expected returns lie within the interval bounded by E_A and E_B. If the investor has a short position in one security (and thus a long position in the other), then the product $X_A X_B$ will be negative. Consequently, the expected return on the portfolio will lie either above E_A or below E_B. Moreover, for these portfolios, the middle term for the standard deviation in equation (8.12), $2\rho_{AB}\sigma_A\sigma_B X_A X_B$, will vary inversely with the value of the correlation coefficient. Therefore, for any fixed allocation of funds between Securities A and B in which the investor holds a short position in one of those securities, an increase in the value of ρ_{AB} will cause the standard deviation on the portfolio to increase.

The effect of ρ_{AB} on the combinations of expected return and standard deviation that the investor can construct by using Securities A and B is summarized by the three loci in figure 8.2. For reasons previously discussed, all three loci pass through Points A and B. For portfolios in which the investor holds fixed positive amounts of both securities, a decrease in the value of ρ_{AB} will reduce the standard deviation on the portfolio, thus shifting the locus leftward. For portfolios in which the investor holds a fixed short position in one of the securities (and thus a fixed long position in the other security), a decrease in the value of ρ_{AB} will increase the standard deviation on the portfolio, thus shifting the locus rightward. In neither case will a change in ρ_{AB} affect the expected return on the portfolio. Since all loci must pass through Points A and B, a decrease in the value of ρ_{AB} will cause a locus to become more sharply curved.

8.5   A Simple Numerical Example to Show the Effect of ρ_{AB} on the Trade-Off between Expected Return and Standard Deviation

In section 7.7 of chapter 7, we calculated the expected values, the standard deviations, and the correlation coefficient for a simple numerical example of a joint probability distribution of the rates of return on Securities A and B. The values of those parameters are shown in table 8.1. In chapter 7, we explained that the correlation coefficient between the rates of return on two securities governs the amount by which the conditional probability density function for one security shifts in response to a specific outcome for the rate of return on the other security. Let the rate of return on Security B for month t take a value that is displaced from its expected return by a distance equal to $\hat{\delta}$ times the standard deviation for Security B. The value of $\hat{\delta}$ can be positive, negative, or zero. Then, using the values of the parameters of the joint distribution of Securities A and B, the conditional expected return and standard deviation for Security A for month t are:

$$E(\tilde{r}_A | \tilde{r}_B = E_B + \hat{\delta}\sigma_B) = E_A + \rho_{AB}\hat{\delta}\sigma_A$$
$$= .20 + (.706)\hat{\delta}(.1897)$$
$$= .20 + .1339\hat{\delta},$$

and

$$(8.14)$$

$$\sigma(\tilde{r}_A | \tilde{r}_B = E_B + \hat{\delta}\sigma_B) = \sqrt{\sigma_A{}^2[1 - (\rho_{AB})^2]}$$
$$= \sqrt{(.1897)^2[1 - (.706)^2]}$$
$$= \sqrt{.018049}$$
$$= .1343.$$

In words, the unconditional probability density function for Security A is centered on the value .20; the standard deviation of this density function is .1897. We have drawn this density function in figure 8.3. But the value drawn for the rate of return on Security A in a given month is connected to the rate of return drawn for Security B in that month through the correlation coefficient between Securities A and B.

Table 8.1
Values of the Parameters for Securities A and B for the Joint Probability Distribution in Table 7.1

$$E_A = .20; \ \sigma_A = .1897$$
$$E_B = .20; \ \sigma_B = .0224$$
$$\rho_{AB} = .706$$

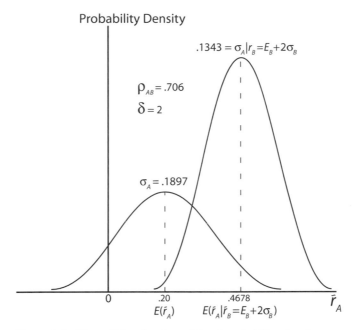

Figure 8.3. Unconditional and conditional probability density functions for Security A.

Specifically, if in month t the rate of return drawn for Security B is displaced from the expected return for that security by a distance equal to $\hat{\delta}$ times the standard deviation for that security, then the density function from which a value will be drawn for Security A in month t will shift a distance of $.1339\,\hat{\delta}$, and the standard deviation of the density function will decrease from .1897 to .1343. We have drawn this conditional density function in figure 8.3 for the case in which $\hat{\delta} = 2$.

Using the values for E_A, E_B, σ_A, σ_B, and ρ_{AB} from table 8.1, we can now determine the locus of combinations of expected return and standard deviation for the investor's portfolio. In figure 8.4, we plot the value for the portfolio's standard deviation horizontally, and the value for its expected return vertically. The curve is the locus of alternative combinations of expected return and standard deviation from which the investor may choose by varying the proportions, X_A and X_B, in which funds are allocated between Securities A and B. Points A, B, C, and D represent four of these combinations. Since each combination of expected return and standard deviation characterizes a unique portfolio, we shall refer to Points A, B, C and D as portfolios.

Portfolio A is formed by allocating 100% of the investor's funds to Security A. To construct Portfolio A, the investor sets $X_A^A = 1$ and $X_B^A = 0$. Similarly, setting $X_A^B = 0$ and $X_B^B = 1$ will construct Portfolio B.

Consider next Portfolio C. In figure 8.4, we have located Portfolio C so that its expected return is .16. We can now use equation 8.5 to calculate the values of the allocative proportions for Portfolio C as follows:

$$E_C = X_A^{\ C} E_A + X_B^{\ C} E_B. \tag{8.15}$$

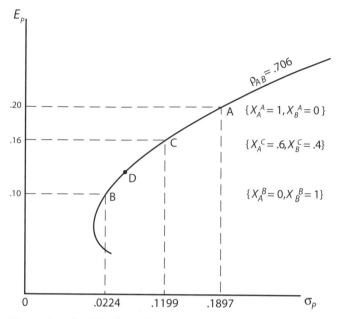

Figure 8.4. Combinations of expected rate of return and standard deviation for portfolios containing only Securities A and B. The value of the correlation coefficient is ρ_{AB} 5 .706.

Substituting the values .16 for E_C, .20 for E_A, and .10 for E_B, and using the fact that $X_A{}^C + X_B{}^C = 1$ (so that $X_B{}^C = 1 - X_A{}^C$), we can rewrite (8.15) as:

$$.16 = X_A{}^C (.20) + (1 - X_A{}^C)(.10), \tag{8.16}$$

which shows that:

$$X_A{}^C = .6, \quad \text{and} \quad X_B{}^C = .4. \tag{8.17}$$

The solution in equation (8.17) is easy to understand by recognizing from equation (8.5) that the expected return on a portfolio is a simple weighted average of the expected returns on its constituent securities with the weights given by the proportions in which the investor allocates funds to those securities. The expected return on Security A is .20, and the expected return on Security B is .10. Since the expected return on Portfolio C, .16, lies between .10 and .20, Portfolio C will contain positive amounts of both securities. Therefore, both $X_A{}^C$ and $X_B{}^C$ must lie between 0 and 1. Moreover, since .16 lies closer to .20 than to .10, the investor must allocate a larger proportion of her funds to Security A than to Security B. Therefore $X_A{}^C$ will be larger than $X_B{}^C$. Finally, note that on the vertical axis in figure 8.4, the expected return on Portfolio C, .16, lies 6/10 of the distance from E_B to E_A. If the investor had wanted a portfolio whose expected return is .10, she would allocate all of the funds to Security B. Similarly, to construct a portfolio whose expected return is .20, she would allocate all of the funds to Security A. To construct a portfolio whose expected return lies 6/10 of the distance from the expected return on Security B toward the expected return on Security A, the investor must move

6/10 of her funds out of Security B and into Security A, and thus the allocative proportions that define Portfolio C are $X_A{}^C = .6$ and $X_B{}^C = .4$.

The standard deviation of Portfolio C is determined by equation 8.6, which we repeat below.

$$\sigma_C = \sqrt{[X_A{}^C \sigma_A]^2 + 2X_A{}^C X_B{}^C \rho_{AB} \sigma_A \sigma_B + (X_B{}^C \sigma_B)^2}. \tag{8.18}$$

It is important to remember that the investor chooses only the values for $X_A{}^C$ and $X_B{}^C$. These are the only variables on the right-hand side of equation (8.18). The symbols σ_A, σ_B, and ρ_{AB} are parameters, not variables. The values for σ_A, σ_B, and ρ_{AB} emerge as a consequence of the competition among all investors as they buy and sell securities. The resulting values of σ_A, σ_B, and ρ_{AB} in equation (8.18), like the values of E_A and E_B in equation (8.5), are not within the individual investor's control.

The values of the parameters in equation (8.18) are $\sigma_A = .1897$, $\sigma_B = .0224$, and $\rho_{AB} = .7060$. Substituting these values and the values .6 for $X_A{}^C$ and .4 for $X_B{}^C$ on the right-hand side of equation (8.18), we obtain the standard deviation for Portfolio C:

$$\sigma_C = .1199. \tag{8.19}$$

We conclude that if the rates of return on Securities A and B are jointly distributed according to table 8.1, and if the investor allocates the funds in the proportions 60% to Security A and 40% to Security B, then the probability density function for the rate of return on the portfolio will have an expected return equal to .16 and a standard deviation equal to .1199. This result is indicated by the location of Point C in figure 8.4.

An investor who constructs Portfolio C by allocating 60% of the funds to Security A and 40% to Security B has chosen a particular probability density function to govern the rate of return on the portfolio. We have displayed this density function in figure 8.5. There is a correspondence between Figures 8.4 and 8.5 that is useful for

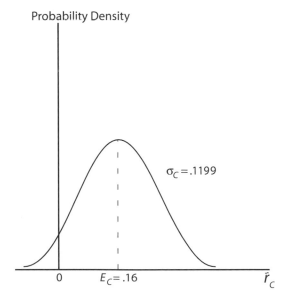

Figure 8.5. Probability density function for Portfolio C, constructed by allocating 60% of funds to Security A and 40% of funds to Security B.

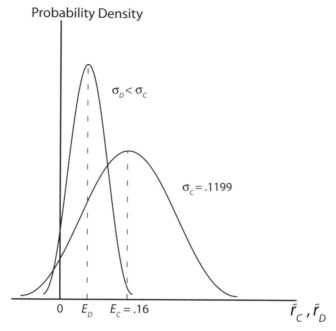

Figure 8.6. Probability density functions for Portfolios C and D. Relative to Portfolio C, Portfolio D has a larger allocation of funds to Security B and a smaller allocation of funds to Security A.

understanding the implications of portfolio theory for the ways in which financial markets allocate resources. Each point in figure 8.4 designates a specific combination of values for the expected return and the standard deviation of a probability density function; two of these density functions are shown in figure 8.6. If the investor were to change the allocation of funds to proportions other than 60% to Security A and 40% to Security B, he or she would change the expected value and the standard deviation of the probability density function that will govern the rate of return on the portfolio.

Now consider Portfolio D. Portfolio D provides a different combination of standard deviation and expected return, compared to the combination offered by Portfolio C. By constructing Portfolio D rather than Portfolio C, the investor accepts a lower average rate of return on the investment, in exchange for a higher probability that the actual rate of return in any given month will lie within a narrow interval around that average. This trade-off is illustrated in figure 8.6 by the difference between the two probability density functions.

The center point of the density function that generates values for the rate of return on Portfolio C lies to the right of the center point of the density function for Portfolio D. However, the density function for Portfolio D is more tightly compressed around its central value than is the case for Portfolio C. In general, an investor can change the combination of average rate of return and dispersion that governs the rate of return on the portfolio by changing the proportions in which funds are allocated among the securities contained in the portfolio. Economists call this opportunity to choose among alternative combinations of the average rate of return and dispersion the *risk-return trade-off.*

Suppose that an investor wants to create a portfolio whose expected return exceeds the expected return on Security A. To do this, she must augment her initial funds by selling Security B short, then invest the borrowed funds plus her own funds in Security A. For such a portfolio, X_A will exceed 1, and X_B will be negative.

For example, suppose that the investor wants to construct a portfolio whose expected return is equal to .22. Call this Portfolio L. Proceeding as before with equation (8.5), we have:

$$E_L = .22 = X_A{}^L(.20) + X_B{}^L(.10). \tag{8.20}$$

Using the fact that $X_B{}^L = 1 - X_A{}^L$, we can solve for the allocative proportions as follows:

$$.22 = X_A{}^L(.20) + (1 - X_A{}^L)(.10)$$

$$X_A{}^L = \frac{.22 - .10}{.20 - .10} = \frac{.12}{.10} = 1.2,$$

and

$$X_B{}^L = 1 - X_A{}^L = 1 - 1.2 = -.2. \tag{8.21}$$

To construct Portfolio L, the investor borrows a quantity of shares of Security B worth 20% of the investor's initial funds, and sells these shares short. She then purchases a quantity of shares of Security A worth 120% of her initial funds. The expected return on Portfolio L is .22, which is equal to the expected return on Security B plus 120% of the difference between the expected return on Security A and the expected return on Security B. Therefore, to move from a portfolio that contains only Security B to Portfolio L, the investor would move into Security A 120% of the funds that she now holds in Security B. This would require selling 100% of what she now owns in Security B, plus selling short in Security B 20% of that amount.

We turn finally to the role of the correlation coefficient, ρ_{AB}, in determining the combinations of expected return and standard deviation that an investor can choose for a portfolio. For convenience, we repeat equations (8.5) and (8.6):

$$E_p = X_A E_A + X_B E_B, \tag{8.5, repeated}$$

and

$$\sigma_P = \sqrt{\sigma_P{}^2} = \sqrt{(X_A{}^2 \sigma_A{}^2 + 2\rho_{AB}\sigma_A\sigma_B X_A X_B + X_B{}^2 \sigma_B{}^2)} \tag{8.6, repeated}$$

Recall that the correlation between the rates of return on Securities A and B has no effect on the expected return of the investor's portfolio because ρ_{AB} does not appear in equation (8.5). The expected return on a portfolio depends only on the expected returns of its constituent securities taken separately. The interaction between the two rates of return has no bearing on the average rate of return on the portfolio. But ρ_{AB} does affect the standard deviation on the investor's portfolio through the middle term on the right-hand side of equation (8.6), $2\rho_{AB}\sigma_A\sigma_B X_A X_B$.

In table 8.2, we have calculated the combinations of expected return and standard deviation for each of six alternative portfolios that the investor can construct using

Table 8.2
Combination of Expected Return and Standard Deviation for Six Portfolios Created by Using Securities A and B

Portfolio	X_A^P	X_B^P	E_P	σ_P
L	1.2	−.2	.22	.2245
M	.2	.8	.12	.0522
N	.4	.6	.14	.0859
O	.6	.4	.16	.1203
P	.8	.2	.18	.1550
Q	−.2	1.2	.08	.0269

only Securities A and B, whose rates of return are jointly distributed as shown in table 8.1. As we know, the value of the correlation coefficient for that joint distribution is .7060. Each portfolio is designated by a point in figure 8.7, whose coordinates indicate the combination of expected return and standard deviation offered by that portfolio. The curved locus, identified by ρ_{AB}=.706, designates all of the combinations of expected return and standard deviation that the investor could construct by varying the allocation of funds between Securities A and B.

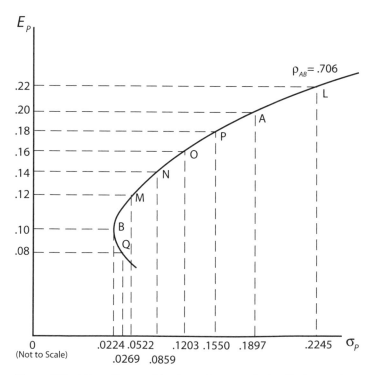

Figure 8.7. Alternative combinations of expected rate of return and standard deviation for portfolios containing only Securities A and B when ρ_{AB} = .706.

The Special Cases of Perfect Positive and Perfect Negative Correlation

We know that the standard deviation of the rate of return on a portfolio that contains two risky securities depends on the value of the correlation coefficient between the two securities. We also know that the value of the correlation coefficient is confined to the interval from -1 to $+1$, including the endpoints. If the correlation coefficient between two securities is equal to -1, we say that those two securities are perfectly negatively correlated. (More precisely, the rates of return on the two securities are perfectly negatively correlated.) Similarly, if the correlation coefficient between the two securities is equal to $+1$, then their rates of return are perfectly positively correlated. If the rates of return on two securities are perfectly correlated, either positively or negatively, an investor can use those two securities to construct a riskless portfolio. This portfolio will be riskless because its rate of return will be generated by a probability density function whose standard deviation is equal to zero. Consequently, the rate of return on the portfolio will be a constant that is equal to the expected value of the density function. The graph of the density function will be a single vertical line erected over the expected value.

In sections 8.6.3 and 8.6.4, we show how an investor can construct a riskless portfolio that contains two perfectly correlated risky securities. First we explain the analytical significance of riskless portfolios.

8.6.1 The Analytical Significance of Riskless Portfolios

If the rates of return on two risky securities are perfectly correlated, we can determine the equilibrium prices of those securities by using the fact that the rate of return on the riskless portfolio that we can construct with those securities must be equal to the interest rate at a bank. The most impressive use of this analytical technique is to determine the equilibrium prices of put options and call options. In 1973, Fischer Black and Myron Scholes used this fact to derive a formula for pricing options.[1] The universal acceptance by investors of this formula created a voluminous expansion in the trading of options. Put options and call options are sophisticated securities, which are called derivatives because their values are derived from the values of other, related securities. We discuss options and the models for determining their equilibrium prices in chapter 15.

Here is a synopsis of the technique for using a riskless portfolio to determine the equilibrium prices of risky securities whose rates of return are perfectly correlated. The fundamental idea is that in equilibrium all riskless securities must have the same rate of return. If two riskless securities offer different rates of return, investors will reallocate funds from one security to the other until the relative prices of the securities change so that their rates of return become equal. Consider the following example.

Suppose that the rates of return on Securities A and B are perfectly correlated. Then, as we show in sections 8.6.3 and 8.6.4, an investor could use those securities to create a riskless portfolio. Suppose that the rate of return on this portfolio is .16, and the interest rate at a bank is .10. At time t_0, an investor could borrow $100 from the bank and invest that money in the portfolio. At time t_1, he will owe the bank $110, and he can liquidate his portfolio for $116. After paying the bank, he will have a profit of $6.

It is important to recognize that this $6 is a profit that is net of opportunity costs. To see this, suppose that at time t_0 the investor decides to divert $100 of his salary into an investment. If he purchases a bank account at time t_0, the value of that account at t_1 will be $110. But if he invests that $100 in the riskless portfolio, the value of that portfolio at time t_1 will be $116. The net gain from choosing the portfolio is $6, after allowing for the interest foregone by investing the $100 in the portfolio rather than in a bank account.

In equilibrium, two riskless assets must pay the same rate of return. In our present example, one of these assets is a bank account, and the other asset is a riskless portfolio that contains Securities A and B. We know that the expected return on the portfolio is a weighted average of the expected returns on Securities A and B. From chapter 4, recall that the expected return on a security is inversely related to the current price of that security. In equilibrium, the current prices of Securities A and B must be such that the weighted average of the expected returns on these securities is equal to the bank's interest rate. In our present example, the weighted average of the rates of return on Securities A and B is .16, which exceeds the rate of return on a bank account. The fact that the portfolio offers a higher riskless portfolio than does the bank means that the rates of return on Securities A and B are too high relative to the interest rate. Since the rate of return on a security is inversely related to its price, we conclude that the prices of Securities A and B are too low. Investors will move money out of banks and into Securities A and B to exploit the difference between the rate of return at the bank and the rate of return on the riskless portfolio that contains Securities A and B. This reallocation of funds by investors will force the prices of Securities A and B up, and consequently their rates of return down, until the rate of return on the riskless portfolio decreases to equality with the interest rate. In the next section, we provide a numerical example of this process.

For the preceding example, we assumed (implicitly) that the investor forms the riskless portfolio by holding positive amounts of both Securities A and B; that is, he has long positions in both securities. In section 8.6.4, we explain the effect on the prices of Securities A and B for the case in which creating the riskless portfolio requires that the investor take a short position in one of the securities.

8.6.2   Perfect Negative Correlation

The rates of return on two securities can be inversely related to each other because the two rates of return react oppositely to a common influence. For example, suppose that Firm A is an airline and Firm B sells camping equipment. The earnings of both firms could react oppositely to changes in the price of crude oil. Vacations that require flying to distant places and vacations that involve camping nearby are, to some extent, substitute goods. It is conceivable that an increase in the price of crude oil could encourage consumers to substitute camping for air travel. If so, a change in the price of crude oil could cause the rates of return on Firms A and B to change in different directions.

We know that the correlation coefficient between the rates of return on Securities A and B is one of the factors that determine the combinations of expected return and standard deviation that an investor can choose by constructing portfolios containing only these two securities. In this section, we derive the locus of combinations of expected return and standard deviation for portfolios that contain two securities whose rates of return are perfectly negatively correlated.

First, we briefly review the meaning of perfect negative correlation. Suppose that the rates of return for two securities are perfectly negatively correlated. If the outcome for one of the securities is displaced from its expected return by a distance equal to z of its standard deviations, the outcome for the other security will be a distance equal to z of its standard deviations away from its expected return in the opposite direction. For example, suppose that the rates of return on Securities H and K are perfectly negatively correlated and have the following values for their expected rates of return and standard deviations:

$$E_H = .06, \quad \text{and} \quad \sigma_H = .03;$$
$$E_K = .12, \quad \text{and} \quad \sigma_K = .05. \tag{8.22}$$

Now suppose that in January the rate of return on Security H is equal to .09. This outcome lies above the expected return for Security H by one of that security's standard deviations. That is, $.09 = .06 + (1).03$. Since $\tilde{r}_H$ takes a value that is one of its standard deviations above its expected return, perfect negative correlation between the rates of return on Securities H and K means that the value of $\tilde{r}_K$ will be one of its standard deviations below its expected return. In this case, $\tilde{r}_K = .12 - (1)(.05) = .07$. Similarly, suppose that in February $\tilde{r}_K = .045$. Expressing this outcome for Security K in terms of its expected return and standard deviation, we have $.045 = .12 - (1.5)(.05)$. Since $\tilde{r}_K$ has taken a value that lies 1.5 of its standard deviations below its expected return, the value for $\tilde{r}_H$ in February must lie 1.5 of its standard deviations above its expected return. That is, in February, $\tilde{r}_H = E_H + (1.5)\sigma_H = .06 + (1.5)(.03) = .105$.

8.6.3 Riskless Portfolios That Contain Two Risky Securities Whose Rates of Return Are Perfectly Negatively Correlated

Suppose that the rates of return on Securities U and V are perfectly negatively correlated. Let X_U^R and X_V^R be the proportions in which an investor allocates funds between these two securities to construct Portfolio R. We shall now determine the values of X_U^R and X_V^R that will make Portfolio R riskless.

If Portfolio R is to be riskless, then the investor must choose X_U^R and X_V^R so that $\sigma_R = 0$. From equation 8.6, we have:

$$\sigma_R^2 = (X_U^R)^2 \sigma_U^2 + 2\rho_{UV} \sigma_U \sigma_V X_U^R X_V^R + (X_V^R)^2 \sigma_V^2. \tag{8.23}$$

Since the rates of return on Securities U and V are perfectly negatively correlated, $\rho_{UV} = -1$. Using this fact, we may rewrite equation (8.23) as:

$$\sigma_R^2 = (X_U^R)^2 \sigma_U^2 - 2\sigma_U \sigma_V X_U^R X_V^R + (X_V^R)^2 \sigma_V^2$$
$$= [X_U^R \sigma_U - X_V^R \sigma_V]^2. \tag{8.24}$$

The first line above is the expanded form of the square of the difference between $X_U^R \sigma_U$ and $X_V^R \sigma_V$.

The standard deviations σ_U and σ_V on the right-hand side of equation (8.24) are parameters; their values are not within the investor's control. But the investor does choose the values for $X_U{}^R$ and $X_V{}^R$. To ensure that Portfolio R will be riskless, the investor must choose values for these allocative proportions so that the term within parentheses on the right-hand side of equation (8.24) is equal to zero. Using the fact that $X_U{}^R = 1 - X_V{}^R$, and setting the term $X_U{}^R \sigma_U - X_V{}^R \sigma_V$ equal to zero, we have:

$$(1 - X_V{}^R) \sigma_U - X_V{}^R \sigma_V = 0. \tag{8.25}$$

Solving equation (8.25) for $X_V{}^R$ produces:

$$X_V{}^R = \frac{\sigma_U}{\sigma_U + \sigma_V},$$

and

$$X_U{}^R = 1 - X_V{}^R = \frac{\sigma_U + \sigma_V}{\sigma_U + \sigma_V} - \frac{\sigma_U}{\sigma_U + \sigma_V}$$

$$= \frac{\sigma_V}{\sigma_U + \sigma_V}. \tag{8.26}$$

We conclude that if the investor allocates the funds between Securities U and V in the proportions specified by equation (8.26), and if $\tilde{r}_U$ and $\tilde{r}_V$ are perfectly negatively correlated, then the standard deviation on Portfolio R will be equal to zero. Therefore, Portfolio R will be riskless.

The guaranteed rate of return on Portfolio R will be its expected return. Using equations (8.5) and (8.26), this expected return is

$$E_R = X_U{}^R E_U + X_V{}^R E_V$$

$$= \frac{\sigma_V}{\sigma_U + \sigma_V} E_U + \frac{\sigma_U}{\sigma_U + \sigma_V} E_V. \tag{8.27}$$

Consider the following numerical example. Let the expected returns, the standard deviations, and the correlation coefficient for Securities U and V be as follows:

$$E_U = .02; \quad \sigma_U = .01$$
$$E_V = .06; \quad \sigma_V = .04 \tag{8.28}$$
$$\rho_{UV} = -1.0.$$

Then from equation (8.26), the structure of riskless Portfolio R is:

$$X_V{}^R = \frac{\sigma_U}{\sigma_U + \sigma_V} = \frac{.01}{.01 + .04} = .2,$$

$$X_U{}^R = \frac{\sigma_V}{\sigma_U + \sigma_V} = \frac{.04}{.01 + .04} = .8,$$

$$E_R = X_U E_U + X_V E_V$$
$$= (.8)(.02) + (.2)(.06) = .028, \tag{8.29}$$

and

$$\sigma_R = (X_U{}^R \sigma_U - X_V{}^R \sigma_V)$$
$$= (.8)(.01) - (.2)(.04) = 0.$$

Following are two examples to show that the rate of return on Portfolio R can not deviate from .028, even though the rates of return $\tilde{r}_U$ and $\tilde{r}_V$ on the constituent securities are random variables.

Suppose that in March the outcome for $\tilde{r}_V$ is equal to .14. The number of Security V's standard deviations by which the outcome of .14 is displaced away from the expected return for Security V is:

$$\text{Number of standard deviations} = \frac{.14 - E_V}{\sigma_V} = \frac{.14 - .06}{.04} = 2. \qquad (8.30)$$

Since $\sigma_V = .04$, the outcome of .14 for $\tilde{r}_V$ lies 2 of Security V's standard deviations above the expected return for Security V.

The rates of return on Securities U and V are perfectly negatively correlated. Therefore, whenever $\tilde{r}_V$ takes a value that lies 2 of its standard deviations above its expected return, $\tilde{r}_U$ must take a value that lies 2 of its standard deviations below its expected return. Thus, whenever $\tilde{r}_V = .14$, the rate of return on Security U will be:

$$\begin{aligned} \tilde{r}_U &= E_U - 2\sigma_U \\ &= .02 - 2(.01) = 0.00. \end{aligned} \qquad (8.31)$$

When $\tilde{r}_V = .14$ and $\tilde{r}_U = 0.00$, the rate of return on Portfolio R will be:

$$\begin{aligned} \tilde{r}_R &= X_V{}^R \tilde{r}_V + X_U{}^R \tilde{r}_U \\ &= (.2)(.14) + (.8)(-0.00) \\ &= .028 - 0 = .028. \end{aligned} \qquad (8.32)$$

Consider a second numerical example. Suppose that in April the rate of return on Security V is equal to .03. In this case, the outcome for $\tilde{r}_V$ lies 3/4 of one of its standard deviations below its own expected return, because:

$$(.03 - E_V)/\sigma_V = (.03 - .06)/.04 = -.75. \qquad (8.33)$$

The perfect negative correlation between $\tilde{r}_V$ and $\tilde{r}_U$ ensures that whenever $\tilde{r}_V$ takes a value that lies 3/4 of one of its standard deviations below its expected return, the value for $\tilde{r}_U$ for that month will lie 3/4 of one of its standard deviations above its expected return. That is,

$$\begin{aligned} \tilde{r}_U &= E_U + (.75)\sigma_U \\ &= .02 + (.75)(.01) = .0275. \end{aligned} \qquad (8.34)$$

When the rates of return on Securities V and U are $\tilde{r}_V = .03$ and $\tilde{r}_U = .0275$, the rate of return on Portfolio R will be:

$$\begin{aligned} \tilde{r}_R &= X_V{}^R \tilde{r}_V + X_U{}^R \tilde{r}_U \\ &= (.2)(.03) + (.8)(.0275) \\ &= .006 + .02200 = .028. \end{aligned} \qquad (8.35)$$

Perfect negative correlation between the rates of return on Securities U and V ensures that in any given month the two securities will take values that lie on opposite sides of their respective expected returns by the same number of their respective standard deviations. The structure of Portfolio R exploits this fact. Recall from equation (8.31) that the values for the proportions $X_V{}^R$ and $X_U{}^R$ that define Portfolio R are based on a relationship between the values of the standard deviations σ_V and σ_U.

We encourage the reader to replicate the result that Portfolio R will always produce a rate of return equal to .028 by trying other pairs of values for $\tilde{r}_V$ and $\tilde{r}_U$, making sure that these values lie on opposite sides of their expected returns by the same number of their own standard deviations.

8.6.4 Riskless Portfolios That Contain Two Risky Securities Whose Rates of Return Are Perfectly Positively Correlated

If the rates of return on two securities are perfectly positively correlated, then in any given month the outcomes for these rates of return will lie on the same sides of their expected returns by the same number of their own standard deviations. An investor can create a riskless portfolio by exploiting this fact. As in the case of perfect negative correlation that we examined in the preceding section, the allocation of funds between the two securities will be based on a relationship between their standard deviations. When the correlation is perfectly negative, the investor exploits the fact that the two rates of return will always lie on opposite sides of their respective expected returns. When the correlation is perfectly positive, the investor creates perfect negative correlation by taking a short position in one of the securities.

Let the rates of return on Securities W and Z be perfectly positively correlated. Then $\rho_{WZ} = +1$. Let Portfolio T be defined by allocating funds to Securities W and Z in proportions X_W^T and X_Z^T. The variance on Portfolio T is

$$
\begin{aligned}
\sigma_T^2 &= (X_W^T)^2 \sigma_W^2 + 2\rho_{WZ}\sigma_W\sigma_Z X_W^T X_Z^T + (X_Z^T)^2 \sigma_Z^2 \\
&= (X_W^T)^2 \sigma_W^2 + 2(1)\sigma_W\sigma_Z X_W^T X_Z^T + (X_Z^T)^2 \sigma_Z^2 \\
&= [X_W^T \sigma_W + X_Z^T \sigma_Z]^2,
\end{aligned}
\tag{8.36}
$$

in which the second line follows from the first by using the fact that $\rho_{WZ} = +1$. The second line is then the expansion of the square of the sum of $X_W^T \sigma_W$ and $X_Z^T \sigma_Z$, which is the third line in (8.36). To make Portfolio T riskless, the investor chooses values for the allocative proportions X_W^T and X_Z^T so that the term $X_W^T \sigma_W + X_Z^T \sigma_Z$ is equal to zero. Using the fact that $X_W^T + X_Z^T = 1$, and thus that $X_W^T = 1 - X_Z^T$, we write:

$$
X_W^T \sigma_W + X_Z^T \sigma_Z = (1 - X_Z^T)\sigma_W + X_Z^T \sigma_Z = 0.
\tag{8.37}
$$

Solving for X_Z^T produces:

$$
X_Z^T = \frac{-\sigma_W}{-\sigma_W + \sigma_Z} = \frac{-\sigma_W}{-(\sigma_W - \sigma_Z)} = \frac{\sigma_W}{\sigma_W - \sigma_Z}
$$

and

$$
\begin{aligned}
X_W^T = 1 - X_Z^T &= \frac{\sigma_W - \sigma_Z}{\sigma_W - \sigma_Z} - \frac{\sigma_W}{\sigma_W - \sigma_Z} \\
&= \frac{-\sigma_Z}{\sigma_W - \sigma_Z}.
\end{aligned}
\tag{8.38}
$$

From equation (8.38) it is clear that one of the two allocative proportions for Portfolio T is negative and the other exceeds 1.[2] That is, to construct a riskless portfolio using two securities whose rates of return are perfectly positively correlated, the investor takes a short position in one of the securities and invests more than 100% of her wealth in the other security. If $\sigma_W > \sigma_Z$, then $\sigma_W/(\sigma_W - \sigma_Z) > 1$, and $-\sigma_Z/(\sigma_W - \sigma_Z) < 0$. Then $X_Z^T > 1$ and $X_W^T < 0$. To form the riskless Portfolio T, the investor sells Security W short, and invests the proceeds of that short sale plus all of her own funds in Security Z. Conversely, if $\sigma_W < \sigma_Z$, then $X_Z^T < 0$ and $X_W^T > 1$. In this case, the investor takes a short position in Security Z and invests more than 100% of her funds in Security W.

By taking a short position in one of the two securities, the investor creates a portfolio in which the rates of return on the two positions are perfectly negatively correlated. We demonstrated in the preceding section that perfect negative correlation between two rates of return allows the investor to construct a riskless portfolio.

Consider the following numerical example. Let the rates of return on Securities W and Z be governed by the following parameters:

$$E_W = .09; \qquad \sigma_W = .04$$
$$E_Z = .15; \qquad \sigma_Z = .10 \qquad\qquad (8.39)$$
$$\rho_{WZ} = +1.0.$$

From equation (8.38), we can now form Portfolio T by setting

$$X_Z^T = \frac{\sigma_W}{\sigma_W - \sigma_Z} = \frac{.04}{.04 - .10} = -4/6 = -2/3,$$

and

$$X_W^T = \frac{-\sigma_Z}{\sigma_W - \sigma_Z} = \frac{-.10}{.04 - .10} = \frac{-10}{-6} = 5/3. \qquad (8.40)$$

The investor sells Security Z short in an amount equal to 2/3 of her initial funds. She then purchases Security W in an amount equal to 5/3 of her initial funds.

The guaranteed rate of return on Portfolio T is

$$E_T = X_W^T E_W + X_Z^T E_Z$$
$$= (5/3)(.09) + (-2/3)(.15) \qquad (8.41)$$
$$= .15 - .10 = .05$$

Consider the following example. An investor begins with $1,200. If she invests this $1,200 in Portfolio T, then one period later the value of her portfolio should be $1,200(1 + .05) = $1,260 regardless of the outcomes for either Security W or Security Z considered individually. Can this rate of return of .05 be guaranteed?

To construct Portfolio T at the beginning of, say, June, the investor takes a position in Security Z equal to $(X_Z^T)(\$1,200)$. Since $X_Z^T = -2/3$, the investor's initial position in Security Z is $(-2/3)(\$1,200) = -\$800$. That is, the investor sells short $800 worth of Security Z.

The investor's initial position in Security W is $(X_Z^T)(\$1,200)=(5/3)(\$1,200)=$ $2,000$. She finances this position by using $1,200 of her own funds augmented by $800 of funds that she borrows by selling Security Z short.

We will now calculate the value of the investor's position at the end of June. Let h be any number. Suppose that at the end of June the rate of return for Security W is h of its standard deviations away from its expected return. Then we can express the rates of return on Securities W and Z for the month of June as:

$$\tilde{r}_W = E_W + h\sigma_W \tag{8.42}$$

and

$$\tilde{r}_Z = E_Z + h\sigma_Z. \tag{8.43}$$

Since $\tilde{r}_W$ and $\tilde{r}_Z$ are perfectly positively correlated, in any given month they must take values that lie on the same sides of their respective expected returns at distances that are equal to the same number (h) of their respective standard deviations. If h is positive, then the rates of return on both securities take values that lie above their expected returns. If h is negative, both rates of return are below their expected returns; if $h=0$, both rates of return are at their expected returns.

The value of the investor's portfolio at the end of June is the sum of the values of her positions in Securities W and Z. The ending value of each position is equal to the initial value of that position multiplied by one plus the rate of return on that position for June. Using equations (8.42) and (8.43), the ending value of her position in Security Z is:

$$\begin{aligned} -\$800(11\tilde{r}_Z) &= -\$800(1+E_Z+h\sigma_Z) \\ &= -\$800[1+.15+(h)(.10)] \end{aligned} \tag{8.44}$$

The investor's ending position in Security W is:

$$\begin{aligned} &+\$2,000[1+E_W+h\sigma_Z] \\ &= 1\$2,000[1+.09+(h)(.04)]. \end{aligned} \tag{8.45}$$

The net value of the investor's portfolio at the end of June is the sum of the values of her ending positions in the two securities. Using equations (8.44) and (8.45), this value is:

$$\begin{aligned} &-\$800[1+.15(h)(.10)] \\ &+\$2000[1+.09+(h)(.04)] \\ &= -\$800(1.15)+\$2000(1.09) \\ &\quad +h[-\$800(.10)+\$2000(.04)] \\ &= -\$800(1.15)+\$2000(1.09) \\ &\quad +h[-\$80+\$80] \\ &= -\$920+\$2180=\$1260. \end{aligned} \tag{8.46}$$

We have demonstrated that regardless of the value of h, the ending net value of the investor's portfolio will be $1,260. Since she began with $1,200, she has obtained a rate of return equal to .05, because ($1,260-$1,200)/$1,200=$60/$1,200=.05$.

8.6.5 Arbitrage and Equilibrium When Two Risky Securities Have Perfectly Correlated Rates of Return

In equilibrium, any two securities that investors regard as comparably risky must have equal expected returns. If this were not so, investors would sell, or sell short, the security with the lower expected return, and purchase the security with the higher expected return. This reallocation of funds will cause a change in the relative prices of the two securities, which will eliminate the discrepancy between the two expected returns.

This property of equilibrium has an immediate application to determining the equilibrium prices of two risky securities whose rates of return are perfectly correlated. We know that an investor can construct a riskless portfolio by using two securities whose rates of return are perfectly correlated. Whether the perfect correlation is positive or negative affects only the structure of the portfolio; either kind of perfect correlation can be used to obtain a guaranteed rate of return. An alternative for an investor who wants a guaranteed rate of return is to deposit money in a bank. In equilibrium, the rates of return offered by the bank and by a riskless portfolio must be equal. If they are not equal, we can predict which way the prices of the risky securities that are contained in the riskless portfolio will move.

Consider the earlier example of Securities U and V, whose rates of return are perfectly negatively correlated. We established that we could use these two securities to construct Portfolio R, whose guaranteed rate of return would be .028. Suppose that the rate of return offered by a bank were .01. Then investors would withdraw, or borrow, money from the bank and form Portfolio R. But Portfolio R requires positive positions in both Securities U and V because X_U^R and X_V^R are both positive. Therefore, investors will attempt to increase their holdings of both Securities U and V, which will force the prices of these securities upward. As the prices of these securities rise, their expected returns will fall. Further, as banks continue to lose deposits and grant loans, the interest rate might increase.[3]

Next, consider Securities W and Z, whose rates of return are perfectly positively correlated. We established that by taking a short position in Security Z and purchasing Security W, the investor could construct Portfolio T, whose riskless rate of return would be equal to .05. If the interest rate at the bank is again .01, investors will move funds out of banks and construct Portfolio T. Specifically, an investor will use the money borrowed from a bank, augmented by funds raised by selling Security Z short, to purchase shares of Security W. Selling Security Z short will force its price down, and buying Security W will force its price up. Consequently, the expected return on Security Z will increase and the expected return on Security W will decrease. Since the investor holds a negative position in Security Z, an increase in its expected return will decrease the rate of return on her portfolio. Similarly, by holding a positive position in Security W, a decrease in its expected return will decrease the rate of return on her portfolio. This process will continue until the discrepancy between the rate of return on Portfolio T and the rate of return at the bank is eliminated.

In chapter 14, we show how perfect correlation can be used to derive (a simple version of) the Black-Scholes formula for pricing options.

| 8.7 | **Trade-Offs between Expected Return and Standard Deviation for Portfolios That Contain _N_ Risky Securities** |

In section 8.5, we established that if the rates of return on Securities A and B are not perfectly correlated $(-1 < \rho_{AB} < +1)$ then the locus of efficient combinations of expected return and standard deviation that an investor can construct is concave. This locus passes through the points (σ_A, E_A) and (σ_B, E_B) that designate the two securities. The curvature of the locus depends on the magnitude of the correlation coefficient. The closer the value of ρ_{AB} is to -1, the more severely the locus will be curved toward the vertical axis, while still passing through the points (σ_A, E_A) and (σ_B, E_B).

If the investor has N securities from which to construct a portfolio, and if no pair of those securities has their rates of return perfectly correlated (either positively or negatively), the locus of efficient combinations of expected return and standard deviation is a concave curve that does not touch the vertical axis. Let the point (σ_i, E_i) designate one of the N securities. If $N > 2$, it is not necessarily the case that (σ_i, E_i) will lie on the locus. Typically, (σ_i, E_i) will lie below and to the right of the locus (that is, inside the locus). The economic significance of this result is that if an investor has more than two securities over which to diversify funds, it is unlikely that the investor can minimize the standard deviation of the portfolio, given a fixed expected return on that portfolio, by allocating 100% of the assets to a single security. Put another way, if the investor can diversify across three or more securities, it is usually possible to increase the expected return on the portfolio, without also increasing the standard deviation on that portfolio,[4] by taking advantage of the correlations among the several securities.[5]

| 8.8 | **Summary** |

A portfolio is a collection of financial securities. A defining characteristic of a particular portfolio is the set of proportions in which the investor's funds are allocated among the constituent securities. The rate of return on a portfolio is a normally distributed random variable whose probability density function is a composite of the density functions of the constituent securities. By changing the proportions in which funds are allocated among the constituent securities, an investor can change the expected rate of return and the standard deviation on the portfolio. The feasible combinations of expected rate of return and standard deviation for the portfolio depend on the expected rates of return and the standard deviations of the individual securities, and on the correlation coefficients between the rates of return on those securities.

If the rates of return on two securities are perfectly correlated (positively or negatively), the set of feasible combinations of expected rate of return and standard deviation for the portfolio lie on a pair of straight lines that intersect at the vertical axis. (We measure the expected rate of return on the vertical axis, and the standard deviation on the horizontal axis.) Consequently, an investor can use two perfectly correlated securities to construct a riskless portfolio. In equilibrium, the rate of return on that portfolio must be equal to the rate of interest at a bank. Consequently, given perfect correlation, an equilibrium consists of a configuration of values for the expected rates of return, the standard deviations, and the interest rate.

In the general case, the rates of return on two securities will not be perfectly correlated. Given imperfect correlation, the set of feasible combinations of expected rate of return and standard deviation lie on a concave locus that does not reach the vertical axis. In the following chapter, we use this result to construct the capital asset pricing model, which asserts that in equilibrium the expected rate of return and the risk of a security are linearly related. An essential characteristic of this model is that the risk of an individual security is not measured by the standard deviation of its rate of return. Rather, the risk of a security is the marginal effect of that security on the standard deviation of the portfolio in which the investor holds that security.

Problems

1. Suppose that in January the outcomes for the rates of return on Securities H and B are .09 and .15, respectively.

(a) If an investor had formed his portfolio (worth a total of $1,000) by allocating 60% of his funds to Security H (X_H=.60) and 40% of his funds to Security B (X_B=.40), what is the rate of return on his portfolio for January?

(b) Suppose the investor had constructed his portfolio by taking a short position in Security H equal to 20% of his initial funds. Calculate the rate of return on the portfolio for January.

(Remember, since Securities H and B are the only securities in his portfolio, we must have $X_H+X_B=1$.)

2. If F_A=.35, σ_A=.1622, E_B=.35, σ_B=.0436, and ρ_{AB}=.668, what are the conditional expected return and standard deviation for Security A?

3. If the expected rates of return for Security H and Security B are .09 and .15, respectively, calculate the values of the allocative proportions for a portfolio whose expected rate of return is 13%.

4. Let Portfolio P contain Security H and Security K, which are perfectly negatively correlated. Let the expected returns, the standard deviations, and the correlation coefficient for Securities H and K be as follows:

$$E_H=.08 \qquad \sigma_H-.04$$
$$E_K=.010 \qquad \sigma_K=.08$$
$$\rho_{HK}=-1.0$$

If Portfolio P is to be riskless, what must be its structure, and what is the value of its guaranteed rate of return?

Notes

1. F. Black and M. Scholes, "The Pricing of Options and Corporate Liabilities," *Journal of Political Economy* 81, no. 3 (1973): 637–654.

2. The formula in equation (8.38) is not defined if $\sigma_W = \sigma_Z$, because in that case the denominator would be equal to zero.

3. Investors will continue to move funds out of the bank and into Securities U and V until the riskless rate of return on Portfolio R and the interest rate at the bank are equal.

4. Alternatively, by increasing the number of securities over which the portfolio is diversified, it is usually possible to decrease the standard deviation of the rate of return on the portfolio without decreasing the expected return.

5. For an advanced treatment of portfolio theory, including portfolios that contain N securities, consult E. J. Elton, M. J. Gruber, S. J. Brown, and W. N. Goetzmann, *Modern Portfolio Theory and Investment Analysis*, 6th ed. (New York: Wiley, 2003).

9 The Capital Asset Pricing Model

9.1 ## Introduction

In this chapter, we use portfolio theory to derive the capital asset pricing model. This model, abbreviated CAPM in the literature, is the seminal model created by economists to address the following question: what empirical relationships should we observe among the prices of financial securities if investors allocate their funds according to the principles of portfolio theory? In particular, when financial markets are in equilibrium, what will be the relationship between the average rate of return offered by a security and the quantity of risk that must be borne by an investor who holds that security? Of course, to answer these questions we must first decide how to measure the risk in a security.

In the 1960s, the economists William Sharpe and John Lintner, drawing on the seminal work of Harry Markowitz, provided an initial answer to these questions. Their work became known as the capital asset pricing model.[1] The CAPM asserts that in equilibrium the market will adjust the price of each security so that the average rate of return on that security will be equal to the sum of a reward for waiting and a reward for bearing risk. Here is the intuition for this result. A financial security is a saleable right to receive a sequence of future payments. These payments might be guaranteed, as in the case of interest payments on a bond, or they might be subject to unpredictable fluctuations, as in the case of dividend payments on common stock. Whatever the security, the investor who holds that security must wait for the future payments. An investor can avoid unpredictable fluctuations in future payments by holding a government bond. This investor would receive a guaranteed rate of return simply by waiting for the government to make the scheduled payments. In the CAPM, that part of a security's average rate of return that is the reward for waiting is equal to the rate of interest on a government bond.

Investors are risk averse. Consequently, investors must be rewarded for bearing risk if they are to hold securities whose future payments fluctuate unpredictably. In the CAPM, the reward for bearing risk by holding a particular security is equal to a constant market price of risk that applies to all securities, multiplied by the quantity of risk contained in that security. The market price of risk is the increase in the average rate of return on an efficient portfolio that investors can obtain if they accept an increase of one percentage point in the standard deviation of the rate of return on that portfolio.

For example, suppose that both Portfolio U and Portfolio W are efficient. Recall that an efficient portfolio is one for which there exists no alternative portfolio that has a higher expected return without also having a higher standard deviation. Suppose further that the standard deviation for Portfolio W is one percentage point larger than the standard deviation for Portfolio U. Then if the market price of risk is equal to 3, the expected return on Portfolio W will be three percentage points higher than the expected return on Portfolio U.

The market price of risk is a constant; as a price of risk, it does not depend on the quantity of risk that the investor chooses to bear. Rather, the value of the market price of risk is determined by a complicated average of investors' willingness to substitute between alternative combinations of the average rate of return and the standard deviation of the rate of return on their portfolios. Later in this chapter, we explain the derivation of the market price of risk.

The quantity of risk, on the other hand, varies among individual securities. The quantity of risk for a particular security is proportional to the covariance between the rate of return on that security and the rate of return on a special portfolio that serves as an index for the performance of the macroeconomy. The larger the value of this covariance for a particular security, the more sensitive is the rate of return on that security to unpredictable fluctuations in the performance of the macroeconomy. Under the CAPM, the more sensitive a security's rate of return to fluctuations in the performance of the macroeconomy, the higher is that security's quantity of risk. The reward for bearing risk by holding a particular security is then equal to the quantity of risk contained in that security multiplied by the market price of risk. Therefore, the more sensitive a security's rate of return to fluctuations in the macroeconomy, the higher will be the equilibrium value of that security's expected return under the CAPM.

The CAPM quickly generated strong and broad interest among financial economists for three reasons. First, the model is simple. It is defined by three linear equations, which we derive later in this chapter. Second, these equations have transparent intuitive interpretations that reflect the standard principles of microeconomic theory. Third, the initial empirical tests of the CAPM were very encouraging.

It is common in an empirical science that a seminal theoretical model that has generated empirically testable hypotheses for a set of phenomena will be succeeded by more sophisticated models that explain those phenomena more accurately, or explain a larger set of phenomena, or both. The history of the CAPM in financial economics is no exception. As economists extended their empirical tests of the CAPM, several anomalies arose. For example, the CAPM predicted that the financial market systematically underprices the securities of small firms. Consequently, investors could apparently obtain excess average rates of return, even after allowing for risk, by forming portfolios of securities issued by small firms. Economists addressed this and other anomalies by constructing and testing new models of equilibrium for the prices of financial securities. These new models differ from the CAPM primarily in how they adjust the equilibrium value of the expected rate of return on a security for the quantity of risk in that security.

Although the CAPM has been supplanted by asset pricing models that are both more comprehensive and more accurate, the CAPM remains seminal in its contribution to the way economists think about the pricing of capital assets. The CAPM is the conceptual forefather of the newer models. For that reason alone, it is important to understand the derivation of the CAPM.

In the CAPM, each security has a single quantity of risk. This quantity of risk is proportional to the covariance between the rate of return on that security and the rate of return on the market portfolio. In the newer models, each security has several quantities of risk. Each quantity of risk is proportional to the covariance between the rate of return on that security and the rate of return on a special portfolio that represents a particular aspect of the macroeconomy. Each quantity of risk has its own market price of risk. The equilibrium value for the expected rate of return on a particular security is equal to the interest rate on a government bond plus a sum of adjustments for risk. Each term in this sum is equal to the quantity of a specific kind of risk contained in that security multiplied by the market price of risk for that kind of risk.

Here is a simple example of the newer models. Suppose that a model asserts that, in equilibrium, the expected rate of return on a security depends on the rate of return on a risk-free government bond, plus the covariances between the rate of return on that security and:

1. The rate of return on the market portfolio
2. The difference in the average rates of return of small firms and large firms
3. The difference between the rate of return on the risk-free asset and the average of the rates of return on high-grade corporate bonds

In this model there are three sources of risk, each measured by a covariance between the rate of return on the security and the rate of return on a portfolio. The first source of risk, (1), which is the covariance of the security with the market portfolio, measures the sensitivity of the return on the security to unpredictable fluctuations in the level of macroeconomic activity.

We may call the second source of risk, (2), the *size factor*. For any period t, the magnitude of the size factor is the difference between the average rate of return on a portfolio of, for example, the 100 smallest firms in the economy and the average rate of return on a portfolio of the 100 largest firms. For any security, the magnitude of the size factor for that security is the covariance between the rate of return on that security and the difference between the average rate of return of the smallest firms and the average rate of return of the largest firms. The rationale for including a size factor as a source of risk is to allow the model to recognize that the size of a firm might have some effect on the probability density function of its rate of return. For example, the value of the covariance between the rate of return of a firm and the size factor might depend on the size of the firm. If changes in the performance of the macroeconomy affect small firms differently than large firms, including the size factor might improve the accuracy of the asset pricing model.

The third source of risk, (3), is known as the *default factor*. The rate of return on high-grade corporate bonds depends on the likelihood, as perceived by investors, that the firms will default on those bonds.[2] If investors perceive an increase in the likelihood of defaults, the investor will refuse to purchase bonds unless they offer a higher rate of return. Thus, in any period t, the difference between the rate of return on the risk-free asset and the average rate of return on high-grade corporate bonds is a measure of investors' assessment, at period t, of the likelihood of defaults in the future. The covariance between the rate of return on a security and the size of the default factor is a measure of the sensitivity of that security's performance to the risk of defaults in the corporate sector. Including a default factor in an asset pricing model as a source of risk for individual securities might improve the accuracy of that model in explaining the difference in average rates of return across different securities.

Following are (in verbal form) equations that describe the difference between the CAPM and a three-factor asset pricing model for Security i (which represents any security). Define the following:

$$E_i = \text{the equilibrium average rate of return on Security } i$$

$$R_{rf} = \text{the rate of return on the risk-free asset}$$

$$R_i = \text{the rate of return on Security } i$$

$$R_{\text{Factor } j} = \text{the rate of return on Factor } j$$

$$\text{Cov}(R_i, R_{\text{Factor } j}) = \text{the covariance between the rates of return on Security } i$$
$$\text{and Factor } j$$

$$PR_{\text{Factor } j} = \text{the price of risk for risk attributable to sensitivity to unpre-}$$
$$\text{dictable variability in the rate of return on Factor } j$$

The CAPM states that:

$$E_i = R_{rf} + (PR_{\text{macroeconomy}})[\text{Cov}(R_i, R_{\text{macroeconomy}})]. \tag{9.1}$$

The three-factor model described above would state that:

$$\begin{aligned}
E_i = R_{rf} &+ (PR_{\text{macroeconomy}})[\text{Cov}(R_i, R_{\text{macroeconomy}})] \\
&+ (PR_{\text{size factor}})[\text{Cov}(R_i, R_{\text{size factor}})] \\
&+ (PR_{\text{default factor}})[\text{Cov}(R_i, R_{\text{default factor}})].
\end{aligned} \tag{9.2}$$

The newer models of the equilibrium relationship between expected return and risk in financial markets are more sophisticated than the CAPM. But the seminal insight of the CAPM has survived in these newer models. The adjustment of the expected rate of return on a security for the riskiness of that security is determined by the covariances between that security's rate of return and the rates of return in specific sectors of the economy.

In section 9.2, we indicate briefly the connection between portfolio theory and capital market theory. In section 9.3, we present an intuitive exposition of the CAPM. We emphasize the ways in which that model is built on the fundamental principles of microeconomic theory that support the analysis of markets in general, not just financial markets. Then in section 9.4 we discuss, again on an intuitive level, the three equations that define the CAPM. We present formal derivations of two of the equations in sections 9.5 and 9.6. (The third equation is a set of regression lines. The technical discussion of regression lines appeared in chapter 7.) In section 9.7, we explain why the quantity of risk associated with a security in the CAPM is the marginal contribution of that security to the standard deviation of the rate of return on the investor's portfolio. A brief summary of the chapter appears in section 9.8.

9.2 Capital Market Theory and Portfolio Theory

A financial market is, after all, a market. The analysis of equilibrium in a financial market is fundamentally the same as the analysis of equilibrium in any market. The primary function of a market is to establish prices that will effect mutually beneficial exchanges. If the markets are efficient, then the prices are such that all opportunities for mutually beneficial exchanges are undertaken. For this to occur, the prices must accurately reflect all relevant marginal costs and marginal benefits.

Consider the following example. In an introductory microeconomics course, students learn that a pure monopolist is economically inefficient because price exceeds marginal cost at the profit-maximizing rate of output. The monopolist and her customers could create mutually beneficial exchanges if she increased her rate of output to the point at which price equals marginal cost. In the absence of some form of discriminatory or multipart pricing, an increase in the rate of output beyond the point at which marginal revenue is equal to marginal cost will transfer wealth from the monopolist to the customers. Therefore, creating a mutually beneficial exchange requires some departure from conventional pricing. But the fact remains that, under conventional pricing, a monopolist allocates resources in a way that foregoes some opportunities for mutually beneficial exchanges.

The analysis of equilibrium in a financial market is a particular application of microeconomics. The fundamental principles of microeconomics, such as marginal analysis, opportunity costs, and the zero-profit condition for long-run equilibrium in perfect competition, apply to the analysis of a financial market just as they do to any market. We can strengthen our understanding of the CAPM, and the more sophisticated models that have followed it, if we first develop an intuitive appreciation of how these models are generated by application of the fundamental principles of microeconomics.

In the preceding chapter on portfolio theory, we derived the set of feasible combinations of expected return and standard deviation that an investor could create for his personal portfolio. Each combination of expected return and standard deviation is associated with a specific portfolio. We demonstrated how an investor could form a particular portfolio by choosing the proportions in which he allocated his funds among individual securities. In the present chapter, we analyze how investors will allocate their funds among financial securities if these investors use the results of portfolio theory. The result of this analysis is the CAPM.

We know that investors are risk averse. They will accept an increase in the standard deviation of the rate of return on their portfolio only if they are compensated for the additional risk by receiving a sufficiently large increase in the average rate of return on their portfolio. Individual investors differ in their willingness to accept higher values of standard deviation as the cost of obtaining higher values of average return. Therefore, investors as a group will demand a variety of portfolios, with each portfolio offering its own combination of average return and standard deviation.

9.3   The Microeconomic Foundations of the CAPM

In this section, we present an intuitive exposition of the CAPM. We begin with a discussion of the microeconomic foundations of the CAPM. A fundamental result of microeconomics is that in a competitive market the equilibrium value of the price of anything is equal to the value of its marginal contribution to some objective, such as the maximizing of profit, or utility. Consider the following example.

There is a restaurant in a small town. Some residents of the town dine at the restaurant frequently, some occasionally, and some not at all. The monthly frequency with which a resident dines at this restaurant is determined by that person's marginal utility schedule and by the price of a typical meal. Suppose that each person's marginal utility decreases as the monthly frequency of his visits to the restaurant increases. Then each person will increase the number of his visits per month to a level such that the value of his marginal utility would decrease below the price of a meal if he were to increase the number of his visits further.

Suppose that the price of a meal is $15, and that Mr. Black dines at the restaurant eight times per month (on the average). We would conclude that dining in the restaurant eight times per month rather than seven times per month is worth at least $15 to Mr. Black. If this were not true, then he would not have chosen to dine eight times per month. Similarly, dining nine times per month rather than eight is worth less than $15 to Mr. Black; otherwise he would have chosen to dine nine times rather than eight.

Consumers differ in their preferences for dining at this restaurant. Each consumer has his own schedule of marginal utilities. But in equilibrium, each consumer will adjust the frequency with which he dines at this restaurant so that the value of his marginal utility is (approximately) equal to $15. Thus, in equilibrium all consumers will have the same marginal utility, and the price of the good will be a measure of this common marginal utility.

We can apply this concept to the pricing of financial securities, and in particular to the CAPM. The central idea of the CAPM is that in equilibrium investors will adjust the levels of expected return and standard deviation on their portfolios by choosing the proportion in which to split their funds between a risk-free government bond and a unique efficient portfolio that contains all the risky securities in the economy. Each investor's position in risky securities will consist of an investment in this unique portfolio. We will show that the price of each security will be determined by its marginal contribution to the expected return and the standard deviation of that unique portfolio.

The unique efficient portfolio of the CAPM is called the market portfolio. Recall from chapter 8 that every portfolio has an expected return and a standard deviation. A portfolio is efficient if there is no alternative portfolio that has a larger expected return without also having a larger standard deviation. We also recall that a portfolio is defined by the proportions in which the investor's funds are allocated across the securities contained in that portfolio.

The market portfolio contains every risky security in the economy. The proportion in which a particular security appears in the market portfolio is equal to the proportion of the total value of the outstanding shares of that security relative to the sum of the total values of the outstanding shares of all the risky securities in the economy.

Here is a simple example. Suppose that IBM, GE, and the Burlington Northern Railway were the only firms in the economy. Suppose also that the current price of a share of IBM stock is $100, and that there are 1,000,000 shares of IBM stock outstanding. Then the total value of the outstanding shares of IBM is $100,000,000. Consequently, an investor could purchase the entire IBM Corporation for $100,000,000.[3] Similarly, suppose that the total value of the outstanding shares of GE stock is $300,000,000, and that the total value of the outstanding shares of the Burlington Northern Railway is $200,000,000.

Recall from chapters 5 and 6 that the price of a share of stock issued by a firm is the (risk-adjusted) present value of the sequence of earnings that investors expect the firm to generate per share.[4] By extension of this interpretation of the price of a share, the total value of a firm's outstanding shares is the present value of the total of the earnings that investors expect the firm to generate. Define the production sector of the economy as the set of all firms. Then the aggregate value of all firms' shares is the present value of the total of the earnings that investors expect the economy to generate.

In our present example, the sum of the values of the outstanding shares of IBM, GE, and the Burlington Northern Railway is $100,000,000 + $300,000,000 + $200,000,000, or $600,000,000. These values are based on the prices of the shares in the three firms, and the price of a share in any firm reflects investors' expectations of the ability of that firm to generate earnings. Therefore, investors expect that IBM will generate $100,000,000/$600,000,000, or 1/6 of the (risk-adjusted present value of the) earnings generated by the economy. Similarly, investors expect GE to generate 1/2 of the earnings, and the Burlington Northern Railway to generate 1/3 of the earnings.

According to the CAPM, investors will construct portfolios by using a portion of their wealth to purchase risk-free government bonds and using the balance of their wealth to construct a portfolio of risky securities. The portfolio of risky securities is a scaled-down version of the market portfolio. That is, an investor constructs a portfolio of risky securities by purchasing the securities contained in the market portfolio in the same proportions that define the market portfolio.

Here is a numerical example. Mr. Amsterdam has $10,000 in wealth. Based on his willingness to tolerate an increase in risk in exchange for an increase in expected return, he decides to allocate 20% of this wealth to a (risk-free) government bond, and the remaining 80% to a scaled-down version of the market portfolio. The market portfolio contains IBM, GE, and the Burlington Northern Railway in the proportions 1:3:2. To construct the risky part of his portfolio, Mr. Amsterdam would allocate $8,000 across IBM, GE, and the Burlington Northern Railway in the proportions 1:3:2. That is, he will invest 1/6 of $8,000, or $1,333.33, in shares of IBM, 3/6 of $8,000, or $4,000 in shares of GE, and 2/6 of $8,000, or $2,666.66 in shares of the Burlington Northern Railway.

9.4   The Three Equations of the CAPM

The CAPM defines an equilibrium by two linear relationships between risk and expected return. A third linear relationship defines the quantity of risk in any particular security.

The first linear relationship, which is called the capital market line, defines the set of alternative combinations of risk and expected return for efficient portfolios. The quantity of risk in an efficient portfolio is defined as its standard deviation. The second linear relationship, which is called the security market line, defines the set of alternative combinations of risk and expected return for individual securities. The third linear relationship is a set of regression lines, one for each security. Each regression line is obtained by regressing the rate of return for a particular security on the rate of return for the market portfolio. The quantity of risk in a particular security is the slope of that regression line. This slope is equal to the covariance between the rates of return on the particular security and the market portfolio, divided by the variance of the rate of return on the market portfolio. We will show that, in the CAPM, the quantity of risk in an individual security is the marginal contribution of that security to the standard deviation of the σ market portfolio.

9.4.1 The Capital Market Line

Let K designate any efficient portfolio, and let E_K and σ_K designate the expected return and the standard deviation on Portfolio K. The rate of return on a security depends on its price. If the CAPM is the correct model of equilibrium, then the financial market will set the prices of all securities, including those contained in Portfolio K, so that the values of E_K and σ_K satisfy the following equation:

$$E_K = R_f + \frac{(E_M - R_f)}{\sigma_M} \sigma_K, \tag{9.3}$$

Where R_f is the rate of return on a (risk-free) government bond, E_M is the expected return on the market portfolio, and σ_M is the standard deviation on the market portfolio. The term $(E_M - R_f)/\sigma_M$ is the market price of risk. Then equation (9.3) states that in equilibrium the expected rate of return on an efficient portfolio is equal to a reward for waiting plus a reward for bearing risk. In an efficient portfolio, the quantity of risk is measured by the standard deviation of the rate of return on that portfolio. (The quantity of risk in an individual security is the ratio of the covariance between the rates of return on that security and the market portfolio, divided by the variance on the market portfolio.)

The reward for bearing risk is the second term in equation (9.3). The risk borne by holding a portfolio is the unpredictable variation in its rate of return. We measure this risk by the standard deviation. Since investors are risk averse, the higher the portfolio's standard deviation, the higher its expected return must be in order to induce investors to hold that portfolio. The term $(E_M - R_f)/\sigma_M$ in equation (9.3) defines the equilibrium trade-off between the values of the expected return and the standard deviation for efficient portfolios. Specifically, if both Portfolio H and Portfolio K are efficient portfolios, then the difference in the values of their expected rates of return will be equal to $(E_M - R_f)/\sigma_M$ times the difference in the values of their standard deviations.

We can state this result algebraically in a way that will provide a further interpretation of $(E_M - R_f)/\sigma_M$ as the market price of risk. If both H and K are efficient portfolios, their combinations of expected return and standard deviation must satisfy equation (9.3). Therefore, we can write:

$$E_H = R_f + \frac{(E_M - R_f)}{\sigma_M} \sigma_H, \tag{9.4}$$

and

$$E_K = R_f + \frac{(E_M - R_f)}{\sigma_M} \sigma_K. \tag{9.5}$$

Subtracting (9.5) from (9.4), we have:

$$(E_H - E_K) = \frac{(E_M - R_f)}{\sigma_M} (\sigma_H - \sigma_K) \tag{9.6}$$

and thus

$$(E_H - E_K)/(\sigma_H - \sigma_K) = \frac{(E_M - R_f)}{\sigma_M}. \tag{9.7}$$

The last two equations state that for any two efficient portfolios, the difference between their expected rates of return per unit of difference between their standard deviations must be equal to the constant $(E_M - R_f)/\sigma_M$. For this reason, economists define $(E_M - R_f)/\sigma_M$ as the market price of risk for efficient portfolios.

In figure 9.1, we show graphically how the capital market line resolves the rate of return on any efficient portfolio into a reward for waiting and a reward for bearing risk. The straight line in figure 9.1 is the capital market line defined by equation (9.3). The reward for waiting is defined by the constant R_f, which fixes the vertical intercept of the capital market line. Investors who want to avoid all risk will place all of their money in government bonds. The standard deviation on their portfolios will be zero, and the expected return will be equal to R_f.

The reward for bearing risk in an efficient portfolio is determined by the quantity of risk in that portfolio, and by the market price of risk. The quantity of risk is the value of the portfolio's standard deviation, which is measured on the horizontal axis. The market price of risk is $(E_M - R_f)/\sigma_M$, which is the slope of the capital market line. The market price of risk is the additional amount of expected return that the market must provide to induce investors to accept an increase of one unit in the standard deviation in their portfolio. Since investors are risk averse, $(E_M - R_f)/\sigma_M$ will be positive, and the capital market line will slope upward. The reward for risk on a particular portfolio is equal to its quantity of risk, as measured by its standard deviation, multiplied by the market price of risk, which is the constant $(E_M - R_f)/\sigma_M$.

Consider the three efficient portfolios whose combinations of expected return and standard deviation are indicated by the points J, H, and K in figure 9.1. The expected return on each portfolio is equal to the reward for waiting, plus an adjustment for bearing risk. Portfolio J has a zero standard deviation, so its expected return is limited to the reward for waiting. Therefore, point J coincides with R_f at the vertical intercept of the capital market line. Since both Portfolios H and K have positive values for their standard deviations, their expected rates of return will exceed the reward for waiting

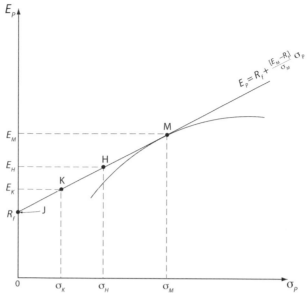

Figure 9.1. The capital market line.

by an adjustment that depends on the magnitudes of their standard deviations and on the market price of risk. To determine the adjustments for risk for Portfolios H and K, we start at the vertical intercept of the capital market line and move rightward and upward at a slope of $(E_M - R_f)/\sigma_M$ until we reach the point that corresponds to the value of the standard deviation for the portfolio under consideration. Since Portfolio K has a larger standard deviation than does Portfolio H, the equilibrium expected return for Portfolio K will exceed that for Portfolio H.

We pause here to consolidate our understanding of the CAPM thus far. We will then be in a position to address the second equation of the CAPM, which is the security market line.

The capital market line, as defined by equation (9.3) and displayed in figure 9.1, establishes the trade-off between standard deviation and expected return that is available to investors who choose efficient portfolios. The equilibrium rate of return on any portfolio is equal to the sum of a reward for waiting and a reward for bearing risk. The reward for waiting is the rate of return on a government bond. This rate of return establishes the vertical intercept of the capital market line.

The reward for bearing risk in an efficient portfolio is the product of the quantity of risk in that portfolio and the market price of risk. The portfolio's standard deviation is its quantity of risk. The market price of risk is $(E_M - R_f)/\sigma_M$. This price specifies the rate at which the investor can obtain an increase in the expected return on investment by accepting an increase in the standard deviation of that rate of return. If the investor were to reallocate the funds among securities so that the standard deviation on the portfolio increased by .01 (one percentage point), then he or she would enjoy an increase equal to $(E_M - R_f)/\sigma_M$ (.01), or $(E_M - R_f)/\sigma_M$ percentage points, in the expected return on the portfolio. Therefore, $(E_M - R_f)/\sigma_M$ is the trade-off between expected return and standard deviation on efficient portfolios.

9.4.2 The Security Market Line

The security market line is the second relationship that the CAPM uses to define the equilibrium in a financial market. In contrast to the capital market line, which defines the equilibrium trade-off between risk and return for efficient portfolios, the security market line defines the equilibrium trade-off between risk and return for correctly priced securities. The difference between the security market line and the capital market line is in the adjustment for risk. The capital market line measures the risk of an efficient portfolio by the standard deviation of that portfolio. We show in section 9.7 that the security market line measures the risk of an individual security by the marginal contribution of that security to the standard deviation of the market portfolio.

The rationale for defining the risk of a security as its marginal contribution to the standard deviation of the market portfolio is as follows. A rational investor will construct a portfolio by dividing funds between a government bond and the market portfolio.[5] Since the market portfolio contains all the risky securities in the economy, each investor will necessarily place a portion of the funds in each risky security. Conversely, any rational investor who places funds in a risky security will hold that security only as part of the investment in the market portfolio. Since the risky part of the investor's portfolio consists of the investment in the market portfolio, the standard deviation on the portfolio will be equal to the standard deviation of the market portfolio multiplied by the proportion of funds allocated to that portfolio. Therefore, the marginal contribution of any particular risky security to the standard deviation of the investor's portfolio will be proportional to the marginal contribution of that security to the standard deviation of the market portfolio.

The equation for the security market line defines the equilibrium expected return for any correctly priced security as the sum of a reward for waiting plus a reward for bearing risk. Therefore, the security market line does for correctly priced individual securities what the capital market line does for efficient portfolios. Let Security j be any risky security. The equation of the security market line is:

$$E_J = R_f + (E_M - R_f)/\beta_J, \tag{9.8}$$

in which

$$\beta_J \equiv \frac{\mathrm{Cov}(R_J, R_M)}{\sigma_{M^2}}. \tag{9.9}$$

The term R_f in equation (9.8) is the reward for waiting. The second term is the reward for bearing risk by holding Security j. As in the capital market line, the reward for bearing risk is the product of two terms. The first term of this product, $(E_M - R_f)$, is the market price of risk for individual securities. The second term, β_J, is the quantity of risk for Security j. In section 9.4.3, we explain how economists obtain an estimate of the value of $\beta_{j,}$ and why β_j measures the marginal contribution of Security j to the standard deviation of the market portfolio.

The market price of risk for individual securities, $(E_M - R_f)$, that appears in the equation for the security market line is proportional to $(E_M - R_f)/\sigma_M$, which appears in the equation for the capital market line as the market price of risk for efficient portfolios. The difference between the two prices of risk is due only to scaling; it need not concern us here.

The security market line in equation (9.8) states that, in equilibrium, the levels of expected return and risk on any security are linearly related. In particular, suppose that the value of β_j is zero. Then Security j makes no contribution to the standard deviation of the market portfolio. The standard deviation of any investor's portfolio is equal to the standard deviation of the market portfolio multiplied by the proportion of the funds allocated to the market portfolio. Therefore, if Security j makes no contribution to the standard deviation of the market portfolio, it makes no contribution to the standard deviation of any investor's personal portfolio. Thus, if β_j is equal to zero, the expected return for Security j will be limited to the reward for waiting, namely the term R_f in equation (9.8).

In our discussion of the capital market line, we showed, in equation (9.7), that the ratio of the difference between the expected returns on two efficient portfolios to the difference between their standard deviations is equal to $(E_M - R_f)/\sigma_M$, which is the market price of risk for efficient portfolios. The security market line establishes an analogous proportionality for correctly priced securities. Consider Security X and Security Y. In equilibrium, the expected rates of return for both securities must satisfy the security market line, which requires:

$$E_X = R_f + (E_M - R_f)(\beta_X), \tag{9.10}$$

and

$$E_Y = R_f + (E_M - R_f)(\beta_Y). \tag{9.11}$$

Subtracting the second equation from the first produces:

$$\frac{(E_X - E_Y)}{(\beta_X - \beta_Y)} = (E_M - R_f). \tag{9.12}$$

The security market line requires that the difference in the expected rates of return for Securities X and Y be proportional to the difference in their levels of risk. The constant of proportionality, $(E_M - R_f)$, is the market price of risk for individual securities.

The graph of the security market line appears in figure 9.2. Notice the difference between figures 9.1 and 9.2. In figure 9.1, the variable on the horizontal axis is σ_P, which is the measure of risk for a portfolio. In figure 9.2, the variable on the horizontal axis is β_i, which is the measure of risk for an individual security. The capital market line in figure 9.1 is the locus of combinations of risk and expected rate of return for efficient portfolios. The security market line in figure 9.2 is the locus of combinations of risk and expected rate of return for correctly priced securities.

9.4.3 The Characteristic Lines

The third relationship that defines the CAPM is a set of equations. Each security has its own characteristic line that defines the conditional expected return on that security for period t as a linear function of the rate of return on the market portfolio for period t. The equation of the characteristic line for Security i is:

$$E(\tilde{r}_{i,t}|r_{m,t}) = \alpha_i + \beta_i r_{m,t}. \tag{9.13}$$

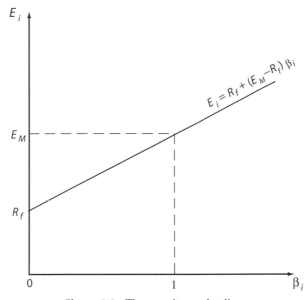

Figure 9.2. The security market line.

According to equation (9.13), the center point of the probability density function for the rate of return on Security i for period t depends on the rate of return on the market portfolio for that period. A change in the rate of return on the market portfolio will *shift* the density function for Security i. Specifically, if the rate of return on the market portfolio increases by one percentage point from period t to period $t+1$, then the density function for Security i for period $t+1$ will shift rightward by $\beta_i(.01)$ from its position in period t. Put another way, β_i measures the sensitivity of the expected rate of return on Security i to changes in the rate of return on the market portfolio.

Note that equation (9.13) specifies only the center point of the density function for Security i in period t. The rate of return on Security i for period t will be:

$$\tilde{r}_{i,t} = E[\tilde{r}_{i,t}|r_{m,t}]+\tilde{e}_{i,t}$$
$$= \alpha_i +\beta_i r_{m,t} +\tilde{e}_{i,t}, \tag{9.14}$$

in which $\tilde{e}_{i,t}$ is the value in period t of the random error term for Security i.[6] The value and the sign of $\tilde{e}_{i,t}$ determines the magnitude and the direction of the displacement of the rate of return on Security i for period t from its conditional (on $r_{m,t}$) expected value for that period.

The significance in the CAPM of the characteristic line for Security i is that the slope, β_i, of that characteristic line determines the equilibrium location of Security i along the security market line. Recall from section 9.4.2 that the security market line is the locus of equilibrium combinations of risk and expected return for correctly priced securities. The quantity of risk in an individual security is the value of β for that security. Values of β are plotted on the horizontal axis for the security market line. Hence, the slope of the characteristic line for Security i determines the location of that security along the horizontal axis for the security market line. The security market line then determines the equilibrium expected return for Security i that is compatible with the quantity of risk contained in Security i. The values of α_i and β_i in the characteristic line for Security i are estimated by using historical data to regress r_i on r_m.

9.5   A Summary of the Intuitive Introduction to the CAPM

The CAPM defines equilibrium for both efficient portfolios and for correctly priced individual securities. In each case, the equilibrium expected rate of return is equal to a reward for waiting plus a reward for bearing risk. The reward for waiting is the interest that an investor foregoes by not having money in a government bond. This opportunity cost is the same for efficient portfolios and for correctly priced securities. It is the constant that appears as the first term in both the capital market line and the security market line.

With regard to risk, each investor is ultimately interested in the unpredictable variability of the rate of return on his or her personal portfolio. Therefore the investor's reward for bearing risk, whether at the level of the portfolio or at the level of an individual security held in that portfolio, depends on the standard deviation of the portfolio. In either case, the reward for bearing risk is equal to a market price of risk multiplied by a quantity of risk. These market prices of risk establish the trade-offs that the investor can make between an increase in the level of risk and the increase in the level of expected return that the market will provide as compensation for that increase in risk.

For the investor's personal portfolio, the quantity of risk is equal to the proportion of funds in the market portfolio multiplied by the standard deviation on the market portfolio. For an individual security, the quantity of risk is equal to that security's marginal contribution to the standard deviation of the market portfolio, because every investor places some funds in the market portfolio, and the market portfolio contains every risky security.

The fact that both the capital market line and the security market line are linear makes it easy to obtain clear economic interpretations of the equilibrium that the capital asset pricing model predicts for a financial market. We shall examine these interpretations in detail later in this chapter. These economic interpretations are useful for understanding how financial markets allocate resources between production for the present and production for the future. We can then use this understanding to analyze questions of public policy regarding financial markets.

The usefulness of theoretical models, particularly as a guide to policy, depends on empirical verification of those models. The empirical implications of the capital asset pricing model are relatively easy to test empirically because the equations for the capital market line and the security market line are linear. Economists have conducted a large number of empirical studies of the CAPM. We shall see that the results of these tests have contributed much to our understanding of how financial markets set the prices of securities. We shall also see how the failures of the CAPM to explain certain phenomena (such as the relationship between risk and expected return for small firms) have led to more sophisticated models of asset pricing.

| 9.6 | **The Derivation of the Capital Market Line** |

9.6.1 The Assumptions

The derivation of the capital market line is based on several assumptions. As with any economic model, we should judge the CAPM not by the realism of its assumptions, but by its ability to organize thinking, to produce insights, and to generate empirically testable hypotheses. The assumptions are as follows:

1. There is a risk-free asset that provides a guaranteed rate of return.
2. There are no restrictions against selling short.
3. There are no transaction costs or taxes.
4. Every investor evaluates a portfolio solely on the basis of its combination of expected return and standard deviation.
5. Investors are risk averse in the following sense. If two portfolios have the same value for their expected returns, investors will prefer the portfolio that has the lower value for its standard deviation. Similarly, if two portfolios have the same value for their standard deviations, investors will prefer the portfolio that has the higher value for its expected return.
6. All investors have the same beliefs about the values of the expected returns and the standard deviations for all individual securities, and the correlation coefficients between all pairs of securities. Therefore the locus of combinations of expected return and standard deviation for efficient portfolios is the same for all investors.

9.6.2 A Digression on the Use of Assumptions in Economics

There is frequently a misunderstanding about why economists make assumptions. Since the derivation of capital market theory is also based on assumptions, we digress for a moment to discuss the use of assumptions in economics.[7]

The ultimate objective in microeconomic theory is to establish knowledge about how markets set prices. This means that we must be able to identify the fundamental variables that determine prices. We must also be able to predict how the market will change those prices if the values of those fundamental variables change. There is an important distinction here that is frequently ignored, or at least misunderstood, by persons who have not studied economics formally. The object of economics is not to predict the values of the fundamental variables and thus the values of the prices. Rather, the object is to explain the relationship between the fundamental variables and the prices.

For example, suppose that the market for apples is perfectly competitive. Suppose also that the demand curve for apples slopes downward, and the supply curve for apples slopes upward (their usual shapes). Economic theory should be able to answer the question: "What would be the effect on the price of apples of a tax on suppliers equal to $2 per bushel of apples sold?" Economic theory is not responsible for predicting the price of apples. The theory is responsible for only predicting the change in the price of apples if the tax is imposed.

The operation of a market economy in setting prices and allocating resources is highly complex. The number of individuals involved is large, and these individuals differ in the quality of their information, their objectives, and their personal resources. The complexity of the markets makes it difficult for economists to generate hypotheses that are both highly detailed and empirically testable. A highly detailed description of an individual investor, for example, might be very interesting, but the very complexity of the detail that makes the description interesting also inhibits analysis. A model that is realistic is usually too complex to allow the economist to answer questions that take the form, "What would happen to X if Y were to change?"

To analyze a market system (or any system) is to answer questions that take the form: "What would happen if . . ." In analyzing a market system, economists manage the problem of complexity by basing their initial analysis on assumptions on how individuals make choices. In making these assumptions, we are not attempting to describe the conscious thought processes of every individual, although it would certainly be useful (and fascinating) if we could do so. Rather, the purpose of the assumptions is to enable economists to use the powerful methods of mathematics to derive empirically testable hypotheses about how markets set prices. The validity of these assumptions is determined not by how accurately they describe how an individual would explain how he or she makes choices. Rather, the validity of a set of assumptions depends on the success with which economists, using these assumptions, can derive hypotheses that are eventually verified by empirical testing.

Starting with their tentative assumptions about how individuals make choices generally, economists use logic, usually by analyzing formal mathematical models, to derive theoretical propositions to describe how an individual's specific choices would be related to specific factors beyond his or her control. The next step is to determine what would happen if all individuals in a given market made their choices in this way. The final step is to derive empirically testable hypotheses based on the behavior predicted by the theory. If the hypotheses are supported by the empirical tests, then economists can place some confidence in the initial assumptions from which the theory, and then the empirical hypotheses, were derived.

9.6.3 Constructing the Capital Market Line

We can now construct the capital market line, which will define the equilibrium trade-off between expected return and standard deviation for efficient portfolios. The first step is to represent a portfolio as a point in a two-dimensional space.

Associated with any portfolio is the probability density function that generates values for the rate of return on that portfolio. That probability density function is completely defined by the values of its expected return and standard deviation. Therefore, we can represent a particular portfolio by a single point in a graph in which the standard deviation is measured along the horizontal axis, and the expected return is measured along the vertical axis.

Let there be a total of N risky securities in the economy. In figure 9.3, the curved locus is the boundary of the combinations of expected return and standard deviation that an investor can obtain by constructing portfolios that contain only risky securities. We explained in chapter 8 why this locus is concave. Portfolios such as D, which lie

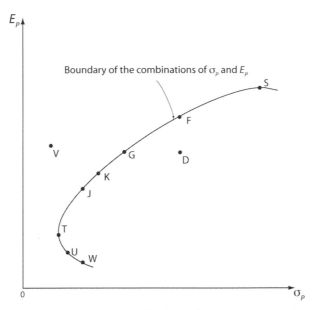

Figure 9.3. Alternative combinations of expected return and standard deviation for portfolios containing *N* risky securities.

below and to the right of the boundary, are feasible, but inefficient. An investor who holds Portfolio D could, by changing the proportions of risky securities, move to Portfolios such as F or G. From Assumption 5, we know that any investor will prefer either F or G to D. Of course, all the portfolios that lie along the boundary between F and G are also preferable to Portfolio D because each of these portfolios provides both a higher expected return and a lower standard deviation than Portfolio D.

We know that all portfolios that are plotted below and to the right of the boundary are inefficient. We also conclude that any portfolio, such as U or W, that is located on a negatively sloped portion of the boundary is also inefficient. For example, Portfolio J is superior to Portfolio W. Therefore, Assumption 5 applied to figure 9.3 implies that each investor will hold one of the portfolios that lie along the positively sloped portion of the boundary T and S.

This last statement is important because it reduces the number of portfolios that we should expect to see in equilibrium. Therefore, if we are to construct a model of equilibrium in a financial market, the model need be concerned only with the port-folios that lie along the boundary in figure 9.3 between points T and S.

A portfolio such as V, whose combination of expected return and standard devia-tion lies above and to the left of the boundary, is unobtainable. The relationships among the expected returns, the standard deviations, and the correlation coefficients of the risky securities will not permit an investor to construct a portfolio whose com-bination of expected return and standard deviation lies at point V.

To construct any one of the portfolios on the efficient boundary in figure 9.3, the investor commits all of the funds to the purchase of risky securities. This is not to say that the investor must hold every risky security in the portfolio. There could be some portfolios along the boundary that require that the investor purchase some, but not all, of the risky securities.

We now consider the risk-free asset. The risk-free asset is usually a U.S. government bond. Let R_F be the guaranteed rate of return on this asset. We can think of the rate of return on the risk-free asset as being generated by a probability density function whose expected rate of return is equal to R_F and whose standard deviation is equal to zero. We can thus regard the risk-free asset as a portfolio represented by the point R_F on the vertical axis in figure 9.4.

Now suppose that the investor allocates a portion of her funds to the risk-free asset and allocates the remaining portion of the funds to the Portfolio K of risky assets that lies on the efficient boundary in figure 9.4.

Let Z be any portfolio that the investor could construct by allocating her assets partly to the risk-free asset and partly to Portfolio K. The expected return and the standard deviation for Portfolio Z are determined by: (1) the proportions in which the investor allocates funds between Portfolio K and the risk-free asset, (2) the expected returns and standard deviations on Portfolio K and the risk-free asset, and (3) the correlation coefficient between the rates of return on Portfolio K and the risk-free asset. By changing the proportions in which funds are allocated between the risk-free asset and Portfolio K, the investor can change the combination of values for the expected return (E_Z) and the standard deviation (σ_Z) on Portfolio Z. That is, as the investor changes the allocation of her funds between the risk-free asset and Portfolio K, the point in figure 9.4 determined by the coordinates for σ_Z and E_Z will move. We will

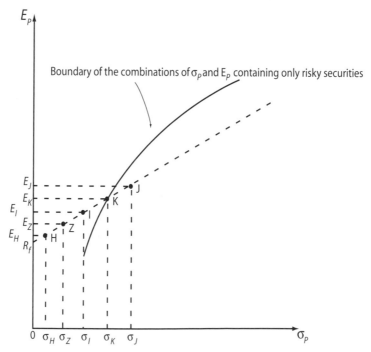

Figure 9.4. Alternative combinations of expected return and standard deviation for portfolios containing the risk-free asset and Portfolio K.

now derive the equation that specifies the trade-off between values for the expected return and values for the standard deviation on Portfolio Z.

Let X_{rf} and X_k be the proportions in which the investor allocates funds between the risk-free asset and Portfolio K in order to form Portfolio Z. We have $X_{rf}+X_k=1$ because Portfolio Z contains only the risk-free asset and Portfolio K.

In chapter 8, we used equations (8.5) and (8.6) to obtain the expected return and the standard deviation for a portfolio that contains two securities. Repeating those two equations here, and applying them to Portfolio Z, we have:

$$E_z=X_{rf}E(r_f)+X_kE_k, \tag{9.15}$$

and

$$(\sigma_Z)^2=(X_{rf}\sigma_{rf})^2+2X_{rf}X_k\,\rho_{rf,k}\sigma_{rf}\,\sigma_k+(X_k\sigma_k)^2. \tag{9.16}$$

The middle term in equation (9.16) contains the expression $\rho_{rf}\sigma_{rf}\sigma_k$. By definition of a correlation coefficient, we have $\rho_{rf,k}=\mathrm{Cov}(r_f,r_k)/\sigma_{rf}\sigma_k$, in which $\mathrm{Cov}(r_f,r_k)$ is the covariance between the rates of return on the risk-free asset and the market portfolio. Since the standard deviation on the risk-free asset, σ_{rf}, is equal to zero, the correlation coefficient between the risk-free asset and Portfolio K is undefined. For this reason, we rewrite equation (9.16) as

$$(\sigma_Z)^2=(X_{rf}\sigma_{rf})^2+2X_{rf}X_k\mathrm{Cov}(r_f,r_k)+(X_k\sigma_k)^2. \tag{9.17}$$

By definition, the standard deviation of the risk-free asset is equal to zero. The covariance between the rate of return on the risk-free asset and the rate of return on Portfolio K is also equal to zero. A covariance is a measure of the relationship between changes in one variable and changes in a second variable. Specifically, the covariance between the rates of return on the risk-free asset and Portfolio K is a probability-weighted sum of products. Each product is a deviation of the rate of return on the risk-free asset from the expected rate of return on that asset, multiplied by a deviation of the rate of return on Portfolio K from the expected rate of return on Portfolio K. But by definition, the rate of return on the risk-free asset never deviates from its expected value. Therefore, every product in the sum that defines the covariance between the risk-free asset and Portfolio K contains a zero. Hence the entire sum, and thus the covariance between the risk-free asset and Portfolio K, is equal to zero.

Since both the standard deviation of the risk-free asset and the covariance between the risk-free asset and Portfolio K are equal to zero, the first two terms on the right-hand side of equation (9.17) are equal to zero. Taking the positive square roots on both sides of (9.17) produces:

$$\sigma_z=X_k\sigma_k. \tag{9.18}$$

Solving (9.18) for X_k, we obtain:

$$X_k=\alpha_z/\sigma_k. \tag{9.19}$$

Since $X_{rf}+X_k=1$, we can write $X_{rf}=1-X_k$. Using $X_k=\sigma_z/\sigma_k$, we can write:

$$\begin{aligned} X_{rf} &=1-X_k \\ &=1-\sigma_z/\sigma_k \\ &=(\sigma_k-\sigma_z)/\sigma_k. \end{aligned} \tag{9.20}$$

Finally, using (9.15) and (9.20), we can rewrite (9.15) as:

$$E_z = \left[\frac{\sigma_K - \sigma_Z}{\sigma_K}\right]R_f + \left[-\left[\frac{\sigma_K - \sigma_Z}{\sigma_K}\right]\right]E_K \tag{9.21}$$

$$E_z = R_f + \frac{(E_k - R_f)}{\sigma_k}\sigma_z. \tag{9.22}$$

Equation (9.22) is the equation of a straight line. The variables are the expected return and the standard deviation of a portfolio constructed by allocating funds between the risk-free asset and Portfolio K. Three of these portfolios are designated by the points H, I, and J in figure 9.4. The relative locations of these points indicate how the three portfolios differ in their dependence on the risk-free asset and Portfolio K. Specifically, let X_h, X_i, and X_j be the proportions of the investor's initial funds allocated to the risk-free asset to form Portfolios H, I, and J. Using equations (9.22) and (9.19), we can show that $1 > X_h > X_i > X_j$.

Consider Portfolio H, and let E_H and σ_H be the expected rate of return and the standard deviation on that portfolio. Since Portfolio H lies strictly between point R_f and point K in figure 9.4, we have $R_f < E_H < E_K$. Since the expected return and the standard deviation for Portfolio H must satisfy (9.22), we have:

$$R_f < R_f + \left[\frac{E_K - R_f}{\sigma_K}\right]\sigma_H < E_K. \tag{9.23}$$

In figure 9.4, $E_K > R_f$. Then the inequality on the left in equation (9.23) requires that $\sigma_H/\sigma_K > 0$, and the inequality on the right requires that $\sigma_H/\sigma_K < 1$. Then equation (9.19) requires that $1 > X_h > 0$. Similar arguments will establish that $1 > X_h > X_i > 0 > X_j$.

Since Portfolios H, I, and J contain only the risk-free asset and Portfolio K, the proportions of the investor's initial funds allocated to Portfolio K in each case are equal to 1 minus the proportions allocated to the risk-free asset. Then the relative positions of Portfolios H, I, and J in figure 9.4 imply that $1 - X_j > 1 > 1 - X_i > 1 - X_h > 0$.

To form either Portfolio H or Portfolio I, the investor holds long positions in both the risk-free asset and in Portfolio K. Portfolio J lies beyond point K in figure 9.4. To form Portfolio J, the investor must sell the risk-free asset short and allocate to Portfolio K 100% of the initial funds plus the funds raised from the short sale of the risk-free asset.

The next step in constructing the capital market line is to recognize that the concavity of the efficient frontier of portfolios that contain only risky securities means that there is a unique optimal portfolio of risky securities that an investor should combine with the risk-free asset. This portfolio is located at the point of tangency between the straight line that emanates from R_f on the vertical axis and that is tangential to the efficient boundary for portfolios that contain only risky securities. This tangential line is the capital market line, which we have drawn and so labeled in figure 9.5. Designate the point of tangency as point M, which corresponds to a specific portfolio of risky securities known as the market portfolio.

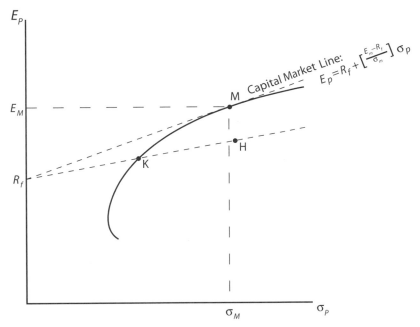

Figure 9.5. Alternative combinations of expected return and standard deviation for portfolios containing the risk-free asset and either Portfolio K or the market portfolio M.

That the market portfolio is the optimal portfolio of risky assets to combine with an investment in the risk-free asset is obvious from the fact that the line from R_f to the point of tangency at M has a greater slope than a line from R_f to any other portfolio of risky securities. Consider the line through point K. For any portfolio, such as Portfolio H, which lies on the line through point K, there is a set of portfolios that lie on the line through point M at locations that are above and to the left of Portfolio H. Each of these portfolios has either a larger expected return than Portfolio H, a smaller standard deviation than Portfolio H, or both. Given our assumptions about investors' preferences, no investor would choose Portfolio H on the line through point K when he or she could instead form any of the portfolios that lie above and to the left of Portfolio H on the line through point M.

9.7   The Derivation of the Security Market Line

9.7.1   The Economic Rationale

The security market line defines the equilibrium relationship between the expected rate of return and the quantity of risk for any individual security. Specifically, in equilibrium the relative prices of individual securities must be such that each security provides a combination of expected rate of return and beta that lies on the security market line.

The economic rationale underlying the security market line is analogous to the rationale that supports the capital market line. In equilibrium, there will be no opportunities for investors to obtain an expected rate of return that exceeds the reward for waiting plus the reward for bearing risk. The capital market line is the locus (or frontier) of efficient combinations of expected rate of return and risk for portfolios.

The connection between the capital market line and the security market line is through the market portfolio. The allocation of an investor's funds among risky securities and the risk-free asset determines the expected rate of return and the standard deviation on that investor's portfolio. In constructing their portfolios, all investors hold risky securities in the proportions determined by the market portfolio. In equilibrium, an investor cannot construct a portfolio that lies above the capital market line by holding risky securities in proportions other than the proportions defined by the market portfolio. The algebraic consequence of the investor's inability to move above the capital market line by holding risky securities in proportions other than those that define the market portfolio is the equation of the security market line. The risk of an individual security is the value of beta for that security. Then in equilibrium the combination of expected rate of return and beta for each security must lie on the security market line.

Next we provide a sketch of the algebraic derivation of the security market line.[8]

9.7.2 The Derivation

The derivation of the security market line uses the *tangency condition* for equilibrium that is familiar to students who have completed an introductory course in microeconomics. In general, the tangency condition states that an economic actor should choose the values of the variables that are under his or her control so that for each variable, the marginal benefit is equal to the marginal cost. In the case of the security market line, the variables under consideration are the allocations of an investor's funds among the risky securities. The marginal benefit of increasing the proportion of funds allocated to any Security i is the effect on the expected rate of return of the investor's portfolio; the marginal cost is the effect on the standard deviation of that portfolio, multiplied by the market price of risk. In equilibrium, the marginal benefit and the marginal cost of increasing the allocation of funds to Security i will be equal. Put differently, in equilibrium, the ratio of the marginal effect of an allocation to Security i on the expected rate of return of the investor's portfolio to the marginal effect on the standard deviation of that portfolio will be equal to the market price of risk.

The equality between the marginal benefit and the marginal cost to the investor's portfolio of increasing the proportion of funds allocated to Security i means that the investor can only move along the capital market line, rather than to a position above that line. Alternatively, if the marginal benefit is not equal to the marginal cost associated with an allocation to Security i, the investor can construct a portfolio that will lie above the capital market line by changing the allocation of funds to Security i.

In figure 9.6, we plot combinations of standard deviation and expected rate of return on portfolios. The concave locus is the efficient set of portfolios that contain only risky securities. The capital market line is the straight line that emanates from the risk-free rate of return on the vertical axis to the point of tangency with the concave locus. The coordinates of the point of tangency are the standard deviation and the expected rate of return for the market portfolio. Point M in figure 9.6 is the market portfolio.

Recall that an individual security is a special case of a portfolio. Therefore, each individual security is represented by a point whose coordinates are the standard deviation and the expected rate of return for that security. We know that by diversifying funds across several securities, the investor can reduce the standard deviation on the portfolio without reducing the expected rate of return. Therefore, any portfolio that contains only one security cannot be efficient. Consequently, each individual security will be represented in figure 9.6 by a point that lies below and to the right of the concave locus.

Let Security 1 be represented by point 1 in figure 9.6. We want to determine the conditions under which an investor, whom we will call Abigail, could use Security 1 to construct a portfolio that lies above the capital market line. Of the funds that Abigail allocates to risky securities, let X_1 be the proportion that she places directly in Security 1 and $1 - X_1$ be the proportion that she places in the market portfolio. Since the market portfolio contains all risky securities, including Security 1, her total allocation to Security 1, as a proportion of the funds that she allocates to risky securities, will exceed X_1.[9]

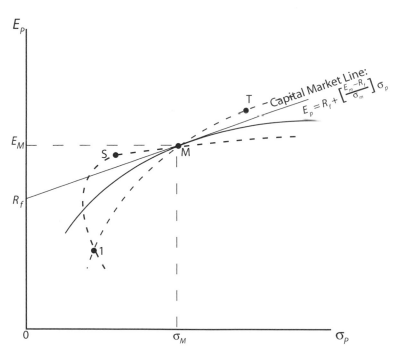

Figure 9.6. Examples in which Security 1 is underpriced (locus contains point S) or overpriced (locus contains point T).

Recall our work on portfolio theory in chapter 8. The combinations of standard deviation and expected rate of return that an investor can obtain by allocating funds between two securities whose rates of return are not perfectly correlated lie on a concave locus. This locus passes through the two points that represent the expected rates of return and the standard deviations of the two securities. Let Security 1 be one of the two securities, and let the market portfolio be the other security. (Just as we can regard an individual security as a special case of a portfolio, we can regard a portfolio as a synthetic security.)

The concave locus that connects Security 1 and the market portfolio must pass through point 1, because Abigail could allocate to Security 1 100% of the funds that she places in risky securities. In this case, X_1 would be equal to 1; she would allocate no funds to the market portfolio because $1 - X_1$ would be equal to 0. Similarly, the locus must pass through point M because Abigail could allocate to the market portfolio 100% of the funds that she places in risky securities. In this case, she would set X_1 equal to 0, and thus make no direct investment in Security 1. She would hold Security 1 only as part of the market portfolio. By choosing a value for X_1 strictly between 0 and 1, Abigail can obtain any of the combinations of standard deviation and expected rate of return that lie on the locus between point 1 and point M. As the value of X_1 decreases from 1 toward 0, the combination of standard deviation and expected rate of return on Abigail's portfolio moves upward along the locus from point 1 toward point M.

It is a consequence of probability theory that the combinations of standard deviation and expected rate of return for portfolios that contain an investment in the market portfolio and a direct investment in Security 1 lie on a concave locus that passes through point 1 and point M. There is no economic content in this fact. The economic content arises from whether the locus between point 1 and point M is tangential to the capital market line at point M, or intersects the capital market line at point M. We will show that equilibrium requires a tangency at point M between the locus and the capital market line, and that the algebraic consequence of a tangency is the equation of the security market line.

The easiest way to show that equilibrium requires a tangency is to show that a lack of tangency provides an opportunity for investors to construct portfolios that lie above the capital market line. There are two possibilities.

Suppose that the locus between Security 1 and the market portfolio intersects the capital market line at point M from above when moving from left to right. This is one of the two cases shown in figure 9.6. Let point S be a point on the locus that lies above the capital market line and between Security 1 and the market portfolio. Then point S represents a portfolio that Abigail constructs by choosing a value for X_1 that is between 0 and 1. Let the portfolio at point S be Portfolio S. If Abigail can create the portfolio whose standard deviation and expected rate of return are above the capital market line, then she can achieve any combination of standard deviation and expected rate of return that lies on a straight line that runs from the risk-free rate of return through point S. That is, by allocating her funds between the risk-free asset and the portfolio at point S, she can obtain combinations of standard deviation and expected rate of return that lie above the capital market line. But the capital market line is, by definition, the locus of efficient combinations of standard deviation and expected rate of return. We conclude that, in equilibrium, the locus between Security 1 and the market portfolio can have no points such as point S that lies above the capital market line between point 1 and point M. Therefore, the locus cannot intersect the capital market line from above at point M.

An analogous argument will show that the locus between Security 1 and the market portfolio cannot intersect the capital market line at point M from below, when moving from left to right. That is, a point like point T in figure 9.6 contradicts the definition of the capital market line. Consequently, the locus must be tangential to the capital market line at point M.

Before we demonstrate why tangency at point M produces the equation for the security market line, we consider two numerical examples, one for the portfolio at points S and one for the portfolio at point T.

A Numerical Example for the Portfolio at Point S

Suppose that Abigail has $16,000 to invest. Of this amount, she reserves $6,000 for the risk-free asset, leaving $10,000 for allocation to risky securities. She must now decide how to allocate the $10,000 among the risky securities in the economy. According to the CAPM, she should allocate the $10,000 across all the risky securities in the economy in the proportions determined by the values of those securities relative to the aggregate value of all the risky securities. For this example, let there be four firms in the economy, each of which issues common stock. For each firm, we list the price per share, the total numbers of shares outstanding, and the total value of the firm's securities in table 9.1. We also show the proportions for the market portfolio implied by the relative values of the firms.

Table 9.1

Price Quanities of Shares and Values of Firms; Proportions That Define the Market Portfolio

Firm	Price	Quantity of Shares	Value of Firm
1	$100	80,000,000	$8,000,000,000
2	$50	100,000,000	$5,000,000,000
3	$40	500,000,000	$20,000,000,000
4	$10	1,700,000,000	$17,000,000,000
		Aggregate value of the firms	$50,000,000,000

Firm	Proportions That Define the Market Portfolio
1	$8,000,000,000 / $50,000,000,000 = 8/50 = .16
2	$5,000,000,000 / $50,000,000,000 = 5/50 = .10
3	$20,000,000,000 / $50,000,000,000=20/50 = .40
4	$17,000,000,000 / $50,000,000,000=17/50 = .34
	Total 1.00

Table 9.2

The Dollar Amounts in Which Abigail Holds the Four Risky
Securities and the Risk-Free Asset to Construct Portfolio S

Funds allocated to the risk-free asset	$6,000
Funds allocated to the four risky assets held in Portfolio S	$10,000
Total funds invested	$16,000

In figure 9.6, point S lies more than half of the distance from point 1 toward point M along the locus that connects the two points. The relative location of point S suggests that to construct Portfolio S, Abigail must allocate to Portfolio M more than half of the funds that she places in risky securities. Suppose that to construct Portfolio S, the proportion of funds allocated to the market portfolio is .70. Since Abigail has $10,000 to allocate to risky securities, she places (.70)$10,000, or $7,000 in the market portfolio. The remaining .30 of the $10,000, or $3,000, goes directly into Security 1. Since the market portfolio contains Security 1, Abigail makes two investments in that security. One of her investments in Security 1 is direct; the other is indirect through the market portfolio.

In table 9.2, we show the dollar amounts that Abigail invests in the four risky securities to construct Portfolio S. More significant for our argument is a comparison of the proportions in which she holds the four securities compared to the proportions in which those securities appear in the market portfolio (tables 9.3 and 9.4).

A comparison of the data in tables 9.1 and 9.4 indicates two ways in which the structures of Portfolio S and the market portfolio differ. First, in Portfolio S, .412 of the funds are allocated to Security 1; the remaining .588 of the funds is allocated to Securities 2, 3, and 4. In the market portfolio, Security 1 gets only .16 of the funds; Securities 2, 3, and 4 together account for .84 of the funds. Thus, Portfolio S has a heavier emphasis on Security 1 and a lighter emphasis on Securities 2, 3, and 4, compared to the market portfolio. Second, the relative emphases among Securities 2, 3, and 4 are the same in the two portfolios. The proportions among Securities 2, 3, and 4 in Portfolio S are .07:.28:238. In the market portfolio, the proportions are .10:.40:.34. The proportions for Securities 2, 3, and 4 in Portfolio S are .7 times the corresponding

Table 9.3

The Dollar Amounts in which Abigail Allocates $10,000 among
the Four Risky Securities to Construct Portfolio S

	Direct	Indirect Through the Market Portfolio	Total
Security 1	$3,000	(.16) $7,000 = $1,120	$4,120
Security 2	0	(.10) $7,000 = $700	$700
Security 3	0	(.40) $7,000 = $2,800	$2,800
Security 4	0	(.34) $7,000 = $2,380	$2,380
			$10,000

Table 9.4
The Proportions in which Abigail Allocates
$10,000 among Four Risky Securities to
Construct Portfolio S

Security 1	$4,120 / $10,000 = .412
Security 2	$700 / $10,000 = .07
Security 3	$2,800/ $10,000 = .28
Security 4	$2,380/ $10,000 = .238
Total	1.000

proportions in the market portfolio. Therefore, Abigail's holdings of Securities 2, 3, and 4 in Portfolio S are a scaled-down version of what her holdings of those securities would have been in the market portfolio.

The fact that the locus between Security 1 and the market portfolio intersects the capital market line at the market portfolio means that Abigail can obtain a combination of standard deviation and expected rate of return that lies above the capital market line. Since the locus intersects the capital market line from above as it moves from Security 1 toward the market portfolio, Abigail should reduce her investment in the market portfolio and increase her investment in Security 1. Since the market portfolio contains Security 1, Abigail restructures her portfolio of risky securities by reducing her investments in Securities 2, 3, and 4 and increasing her investment in Security 1. In the present example, she reduces her investment in Securities 2, 3, and 4 to 70% of the amounts that she would have held in the market portfolio, and reallocates that money to Security 1.

We conclude that if the locus between Security 1 and the market portfolio intersects the capital market line at the market portfolio from above when moving from left to right, Security 1 is underpriced[10] relative to Securities 2, 3, and 4. A security that is underpriced offers an expected rate of return that is too high relative to its risk. The measure of risk for an individual security is the value of its beta. Then the combination of expected rate of return and beta for an underpriced security plots above the security market line. As investors shift funds out of Securities 2, 3, and 4, and into Security 1, the price of Security 1 will rise relative to the prices of the other securities. An increase in the price of Security 1 will force its expected rate of return downward, moving its combination of expected rate of return and beta toward the security market l.[11]

A Numerical Example for the Portfolio at Point T

In figure 9.6, the locus between Security 1 and the market portfolio intersects the capital market line at point M from below as that locus moves from left to right. Consequently, the locus moves above the capital market line after it reaches point M. As in the preceding example, if the locus intersects the capital market line at point M, Security 1 is mispriced. In the preceding example, where the locus intersects the capital market line from above, Security 1 is underpriced. Abigail exploits this error by constructing Portfolio S. Graphically, this means moving some funds out of the market portfolio and into Security 1. In terms of the structure of her portfolio, Abigail decreases her investment in Securities 2, 3, and 4 and places those funds in Security 1.

In the present example, the situation is reversed. The fact that the locus between Security 1 and the market portfolio intersects the capital market line at point M from below means that Security 1 is overpriced.[12] Abigail exploits the overpricing of Security 1 by moving funds out of Security 1 and into Securities 2, 3, and 4. Graphically, she sells short Security 1 held directly, and places the proceeds of that short sale into the market portfolio. By doing so, she constructs Portfolio T. Since the market portfolio contains Security 1, selling short Security 1 held directly has the effect initially of reducing her position in Security 1 and placing those funds into Securities 2, 3, and 4.[13]

We conclude that if the locus between Security 1 and the market portfolio intersects the capital market line from below when moving from left to right, Security 1 is overpriced. The combination of the expected rate of return and the beta for Security 1 lies below the security market line; Security 1 provides too low an expected rate of return for its beta. Investors will exploit this situation by moving funds out of Security 1 and into Securities 2, 3, and 4. As the investors do so, the price of Security 1 will fall, causing its expected rate of return to increase. As the expected rate of return on Security 1 increases, the combination of its expected rate of return and beta will move upward toward, and in equilibrium to, the security market line. With regard to the capital market line, the locus between Security 1 and the market portfolio will change so that the locus is tangential to the capital market line at the market portfolio.

The Algebra

Recall from chapter 8 that the value of the correlation coefficient between the rates of return on a security and the market portfolio controls the curvature of the locus between that security and the market portfolio. According to the CAPM, Security 1 is correctly priced if and only if the locus in question is tangential to the capital market line at the market portfolio. Tangency means that the slope of the locus at point M is equal to the slope of the capital market line at that point. The slope of the capital market line is the market price of risk, which is the constant $(E_M - R_f)/\sigma_M$. At point M, the slope of the locus between Security 1 and the market portfolio is equal to $(E_M - R_f)\sigma_M/\mathrm{Cov}(r_1 r_M)$. Equating the two slopes and rearranging terms produces the equation of the security market line evaluated for Security 1, namely:

$$E_1 = R_f + (E_m - R_f)\beta_1, \qquad (9.24)$$

in which

$$\beta_1 = \mathrm{Cov}(r_1 r_M)/\sigma_{M^2}. \qquad (9.25)$$

The demonstration that we sketched for Security 1 applies to any risky security. Each security has its own locus of alternative combinations of standard deviation and expected rate of return that an investor can obtain by combining an investment in that security with an investment in the market portfolio. Each of these loci must pass through point M because the investor could hold each security only as part of the market portfolio. In equilibrium, each locus must be tangential to the capital market line at the point that represents the market portfolio. The algebraic consequence of the common tangencies of these loci at point M is the equation of the security market line, namely:

$$E_i = R_f + (E_m - R_f)\beta_i, \tag{9.26}$$

in which

$$\beta_i = \text{Cov}(r_i r_M)/\sigma_{M^2}, \text{ for } i = 1, \dots, N, \tag{9.27}$$

and in which N is the number of risky securities in the economy.

9.8 Interpreting β_i as the Marginal Effect of Security i on the Total Risk in the Investor's Portfolio

In this section, we show that the value of β_i is the marginal effect of Security i on the standard deviation of the market portfolio. This fact supports the intuitive appeal of the CAPM as being compatible with a fundamental principle of microeconomics. The principle is that the optimal value of any variable satisfies the condition that the marginal benefit attributable to that variable is equal to its marginal cost. Accordingly, an investor should adjust the proportion of funds allocated to Security i so that the marginal benefit and the marginal cost attributable to holding that security are equal.

9.8.1 The Economic Rationale

For an investor, the marginal benefit of holding Security i is the effect on the expected rate of return of the portfolio, net of the return on the risk-free asset, of a small increase in the proportion of funds allocated to that security. (We subtract the return on the risk-free asset because an investor can obtain that rate without holding any of Security i, or any risky asset.) The marginal cost of holding Security i is the effect of that security on the standard deviation of the portfolio multiplied by the market price of risk. We multiply by the market price of risk to make the marginal effect on the standard deviation commensurate with the marginal effect on the expected rate of return.[14]

According to the CAPM, each investor allocates funds between the risk-free asset and the market portfolio in a proportion determined by that investor's tolerance for risk. The standard deviation and the expected rate of return on the investor's portfolio are equal to the standard deviation and the expected rate of return on the market portfolio multiplied by the proportion of funds allocated to that portfolio. Consequently, the marginal effects of Security i on the expected rate of return and the standard deviation of the investor's portfolio are proportional to the marginal effects of Security i on the expected rate of return and the standard deviation of the market portfolio. Therefore, after making an allocation to the risk-free asset, the proportion of funds that the investor should allocate to Security i should equate the marginal effect of that security on the expected rate of return of the market portfolio to the marginal effect of that security on the standard deviation of the market portfolio multiplied by the market price of risk.

9.8.2 Establishing That β_i Is the Marginal Quantity of Risk for Security i

The equation of the security market line is

$$
\begin{aligned}
E_i &= R_f + (E_M - R_f)\beta_i \\
&= R_f + (E_M - R_f)\mathrm{Cov}(r_i, r_M)/\sigma_M{}^2 \\
&= R_f + \frac{(E_M - R_f)}{\sigma_M}\mathrm{Cov}(r_i, r_M)/\sigma_M,
\end{aligned}
\tag{9.28}
$$

in which the first term is the reward for waiting and the second term is the reward for bearing risk. We recall that the term $(E_M - R_f)/\sigma_M$ is the market price of risk from the capital market line. We can show that the marginal effect of Security i on the standard deviation of the rate of return on the market portfolio is $\mathrm{Cov}(r_i, r_M)/\sigma_M$.[15]

Subtracting R_f from both sides of equation (9.29), we have:

$$
E_i - R_f = \frac{(E_M - R_f)}{\sigma_M}\mathrm{Cov}(r_i, r_M)/\sigma_M.
\tag{9.29}
$$

In words, equation (9.29) states that in equilibrium the marginal benefit of holding Security i (net of the reward for waiting) is equal to the marginal cost of holding that security.

9.9 Summary

The capital asset pricing model is the seminal model for the pricing of risky financial assets. The theoretical foundation for the CAPM is the work of Harry Markowitz, who published in 1959 his work on how investors should construct portfolios to maximize the expected rate of return for a given value of the standard deviation (or minimize the standard deviation for a given value of the expected rate of return). Markowitz's work is known as portfolio theory. Building on portfolio theory, William Sharpe and John Lintner published in 1964 a model to answer the question: what empirical relationships should we observe among the prices of financial securities if investors used the results of Markowitz's portfolio theory to construct their personal portfolios? The result of the work by Sharpe and Lintner is the CAPM.

The central result of the CAPM is that the risk of an individual security is not equal to the standard deviation of its rate of return. Rather, the risk of an individual security is equal to the covariance between the rate of return on that security and the rate of return on the market portfolio, divided by the variance of the rate of return on the market portfolio. The market portfolio contains investments in every risky security in the economy; the proportion in which Security i appears in the market portfolio is equal to the total market value of the outstanding shares of Security i, divided by the sum of the total market values of the outstanding shares of all securities. Thus, the structure of the market portfolio reflects the importance of each risky security relative to the economy. Approximately speaking, the market value of Security i is the risk-adjusted net present value of the future sequence of earnings that will accrue to investors who hold that security.[16] Under this interpretation of the price of Security i multiplied by the number of its shares outstanding, the structure of the market portfolio reflects the relative ability of firms to generate earnings.

The central equation of the CAPM is the security market line, which we repeat here:

$$
\begin{aligned}
E_i &= R_f + (E_M - R_f)\beta_i \\
&= R_f + (E_M - R_f)\mathrm{Cov}(r_i, r_M)/\sigma_{M^2}.
\end{aligned}
\tag{9.30}
$$

To emphasize the relationship between the security market line and the capital market line, the security market line is sometimes written in the form:

$$
E_i = R_f + \frac{(E_M - R_f)}{\sigma_M}\mathrm{Cov}(r_i, r_M)/\sigma_M,
\tag{9.31}
$$

in which the term $(E_M - R_f)/\sigma_M$ is the slope of the capital market line. The slope of the capital market line is the market price of risk.

The term β_i is the quantity of risk in Security i. Graphically, β_i is the amount by which the conditional probability density function for Security i shifts for every one percentage point by which the rate of return on the market portfolio changes. Algebraically, β_i is the marginal effect of Security i on the standard deviation of the rate of return on the market portfolio. The security market line states that the equilibrium expected rate of return for Security i is equal to a reward for waiting plus a reward for bearing risk, in which the reward for bearing risk is equal to the quantity of risk in Security i, multiplied by the market price of risk that applies to all securities.

The security market line is derived from the capital market line, which defines the equilibrium trade-off between the expected rate of return and risk for efficient portfolios. Every efficient portfolio is a combination of the risk-free asset and the market portfolio. Accordingly, the equation for the capital market line is:

$$
E_p = R_f + \frac{(E_M - R_f)}{\sigma_M}\sigma_p,
\tag{9.32}
$$

in which the subscript p designates any efficient portfolio.

The quantity of risk for an efficient portfolio is the standard deviation of its rate of return. The quantity of risk for an individual security is the marginal contribution of that security to the standard deviation of the market portfolio because, in equilibrium, all investors hold risky securities only as part of the market portfolio.

Problem

Kaitie has $60,000 to invest. Of this amount, she reserves $15,000 for risk-free assets, leaving $45,000 for allocation to risky securities. There are only three firms in the economy, each of which issues common stock. The following are the price per share, the total number of shares outstanding, and the total value of each firm's securities.

Firm	Price	Quantity of Shares	Value of Firm
1	$150	70,000,000	$10,500,000,000
2	$80	93,750,000	$7,500,000,000
3	$25	1,000,000,000	$25,000,000,000
		Aggregate value of the firms	43,000,000,000

According to the capital asset pricing model, in what proportions should Kaitie allocate the $45,000 across the risky securities in the economy if she is to construct the "market portfolio?"

How much money will Kaitie allocate to each security?

Notes

1. W. F. Sharpe, "Capital Asset Prices: A Theory of Market Equilibrium under Conditions of Risk," *Journal of Finance* 19 (1964): 425–442; J. Lintner, "The Valuation of Risk Assets and the Selection of Risky Investments in Stock Portfolios and Capital Budgets," *Journal of Economics and Statistics* 47 (1965): 13–37; H. Markowitz, *Portfolio Selection: Efficient Diversification of Investments* (New York: Wiley, 1959).

2. Failing to make payments is not the only way to create a default. A firm will create a default if it is late in making the promised payments to the bondholders.

3. In fact, an attempt to purchase all 1,000,000 shares of IBM would likely drive the price per share above $100, so that an investor would have to pay more than $100,000,000 to purchase the IBM Corporation. The foregoing assertion is an example of the difference between a marginal value and an average value. This distinction is critical in economics; a failure to understand it is the cause of many errors in understanding economic phenomena. The price of any consumption good is the marginal value of that good to consumers. Consider the quantity demanded of meals in a restaurant. Suppose that Maria dines at Andrew's Café three times per month, on average, and typically pays $20 for a meal there. It is an error to conclude that the value to Maria of dining at Andrew's Café three times per month is $60. The $20 price for one meal is the maximal price that Maria is willing to pay to dine at Andrew's three times per month *rather than* two times per month. If Andrew were to increase the price of a meal at his café, Maria would reduce the frequency with which she dines there. Only if Andrew increased the price above the maximal amount that Maria would pay to dine there once per month, rather than not at all, would Maria discontinue her patronage. The total value to Maria of dining at Andrew's Café three times per month is (approximately) the sum of the maximal amounts of money that she would pay to dine there once per month (rather than not at all), plus the maximal

amount she would pay to dine there twice per month (rather than once), plus the maximal amount she would pay to dine there thrice per month (rather than once). Unless marginal utilities are constant, a given quantity of a good multiplied by the price of the good will not be equal to the total value of that quantity of the good to the consumer. The foregoing analysis applies also to a financial security. The price of the security measures the marginal value of that security to the investor who owns it. That is, the price of a share of IBM stock is the maximal amount of money that an investor would pay to have one more share of that stock in her portfolio. (Equivalently, the price of the share is the minimal amount of money that the investor would accept to reduce the quantity of IBM stock in the portfolio.) The price of a share of IBM is the marginal value of IBM to investors, not its average value. The smaller the frequency of her dining at Andrew's Café, the higher is the marginal value to Maria of dining there. Analogously, the marginal value of an IBM share in an investor's portfolio increases as the number of shares of IBM in the portfolio decreases. Consequently, the minimal price that an investor would require to release one share of IBM from her portfolio increases as the number of shares of IBM that remain in the portfolio decreases. This explains why an attempt by a person to purchase all the shares of IBM would require paying a price per share well above the current price.

4. The shareholders receive the earnings either explicitly as dividends or implicitly as capital gains. Recall that the shareholders can realize these capital gains by creating homemade dividends. The values of the capital gains are the (risk-adjusted) net present values of the projects in which the firm invests its retained earnings.

5. We exclude from consideration investors who place all of their funds in a government bond. Since these investors avoid risk entirely (other than the risks associated with inflation of the prices of goods and services), their effect on the prices of risky securities is limited to their effect on the interest rate offered by the government bond.

6. In most asset pricing models, the error term for Security i, $\tilde{e}_i$, is distributed identically across periods and independently of $\tilde{r}_m$.

7. For an excellent introductory treatment of the use of assumptions (or postulates) in economic theory, see "Attributes of Economic Analysis," in A. A. Alchian and W. R. Allen, *Exchange and Production: Competition, Coordination, and Control*, 3rd ed. (Belmont, Calif.: Wadsworth, 1983), 9–10.

8. The formal derivation of the security market line requires calculus. The economics of the derivation is an application of marginal analysis from introductory microeconomics. Since we do not require a knowledge of calculus for reading this book, we provide an intuitive sketch of the argument. For a formal derivation, consult E. F. Fama and M. H. Miller, *The Theory of Finance* (New York: Holt, Rhinehart, and Winston, 1972), 284–285. See also E. J. Elton, M. J. Gruber, S. J. Brown, and W. N. Goetzmann, *Modern Portfolio Theory and Investment Analysis*, 6th ed. (New York: Wiley, 2003), 300.

9. In the market portfolio, the proportion of funds allocated to Security i is $P_i N_i / \Sigma_{j=1}^{N} P_j Q_j$, in which P_j is the price of one share of Security j, Q_j is the number of shares of that security outstanding, and there are N risky securities in the economy. Then Abigail allocates to Security 1 the proportion $[X_1 + (1-X_1)P_1 N_1 / \Sigma_{j=1}^{N} P_j Q_j]$ of the funds that she places in risky assets.

10. Relative to Securities 2, 3, and 4.

11. The effects of an increase in the price of Security 1 on the values of beta and the standard deviation for that security is beyond the scope of this text. We can say that if the CAPM is the correct model of expected rate of return and risk, the price of that security must move the combination of its expected rate of return and beta to a position that lies on, and not above (or below), the security market line. With regard to the capital market line, the price of Security 1 adjusts the values of the expected rate of return, the standard deviation, and the correlation coefficient between the rates of return on Security 1 and the market portfolio so that the locus

between Security 1 and the market portfolio is tangential to (i.e., does not intersect) the capital market line at the market portfolio.

12. Again, relative to Securities 2, 3, and 4.

13. If Point T in figure 9.6 lies far enough to the right of the market portfolio, Abigail will have a net short position in Security 1.

14. Recall that the market price of risk is the number of additional percentage points of expected rate of return that an investor can obtain by accepting one additional percentage point of standard deviation. Therefore, the market price of risk converts percentage points of standard deviation into the economically equivalent number of percentage points of expected rate of return. Derivations of the interpretation of beta as the marginal quantity of risk appear in many advanced textbooks in finance. The derivation here is based on the exposition in Fama and Miller, *The Theory of Finance*, 284–285. See also Elton, Gruber, Brown, and Goetzmann, *Modern Portfolio Theory and Investment Analysis*, p. 300. The formal derivation requires calculus, which is not a prerequisite for this text. Accordingly, we use the term *marginal effect* in place of the term *partial derivative*. This substitution should suffice for a reader who has completed an introductory course in microeconomics.

15. That is, let X_i be the proportion of funds that the investor allocates to the market portfolio. Then $\partial \sigma_M / \partial X_i = \mathrm{Cov}(r_i, r_M)/\sigma_M$.

16. Recall from section 4.2.1 in chapter 4 that since prices are marginal values, not average values, we must be cautious in interpreting the product of price times quantity.

10 Multifactor Models for Pricing Securities

10.1 Introduction

Multifactor models are analogous to, and inspired by, the CAPM. In the CAPM there is a single source of risk for each security; that source of risk is the unpredictable variation in the rate of return on the market portfolio. Each security has a single quantity of risk, which is the sensitivity of that security's rate of return to the rate of return on the market portfolio. In a multifactor model, there are two or more sources of risk for each security. Each source of risk is the unpredictable variation in the rate of return on a portfolio identified with that source of risk. Each security has more than one quantity of risk, and each quantity of risk is the sensitivity of that security's rate of return to the rate of return on the portfolio identified with that source of risk.

In the CAPM, the quantity of risk in a security is the amount by which the expected rate of return for that security shifts when the rate of return on the market portfolio changes. That is, the center point of the probability density function for a particular security is conditional on the rate of return of the market portfolio. In a multifactor model, each security has a separate quantity of risk for each of the factors in the model. Consequently, in a multifactor model the center point of the probability density function for a particular security is conditional on the rates of return of each of the factors in the model.

In both the CAPM and a multifactor model, the equilibrium expected rate of return on a security is equal to the sum of a reward for waiting and a reward for bearing risk. In both models, the reward for waiting is the same for every security and is equal to the rate of return on a government bond. In the CAPM, the reward for bearing risk in a given security is a single term, because there is only one source of risk. In a multifactor model, the reward for bearing risk in a given security is a sum of terms, one term for each source of risk.

A "factor" in a multifactor model is a portfolio. The CAPM is a single-factor model; the factor is the market portfolio. Economists developed multifactor models in an attempt to improve on the empirical record of the CAPM by allowing the expected rate of return on a security to depend on more than one source of risk. The fundamental contribution of the CAPM has, however, survived in the multifactor models. Namely, each source of risk for a security is the degree to which the probability density function for that security will shift when the rate of return on a factor changes. In the CAPM, the quantity of risk for Security i, β_i, is the covariance between the rates of return on Security i and the market portfolio, divided by the variance of the rate of return on the market portfolio. In a multifactor model, the quantity of risk for Security i with respect to Factor j is the covariance between the rates of return for Security i and Factor j, divided by the variance of the rate of return on Factor j. The challenge is to define the factors so that the model will predict accurately the relationship between expected rate of return and risk that the financial markets will establish in equilibrium.

In section 10.2, we present a hypothetical, and simple, two-factor asset pricing model. In section 10.3, we present the three-factor model developed by Eugene Fama and Kenneth French to explain the relationship between expected return and risk for stocks. This three-factor model retains beta from the CAPM and adds two additional factors for risk. One factor is based on the size of the firm; the second factor is based on the ratio of the book value of the firm to the market value of the firm's outstanding common stock. The empirical record of this three-factor model is superior to the record of the CAPM, which relies only on beta as a measure of risk.

Fama and French augmented their three-factor model by adding two factors to explain the returns on bonds. The resulting five-factor model recognizes that in an integrated financial market (in which investors can include both stocks and bonds in the same portfolio) there should be a single relationship between expected return and risk, rather than separate relationships for different kinds of assets. We discuss the five-factor model in section 10.4.

In section 10.5, we present a brief description of the arbitrage pricing theory (APT), which is a special kind of multifactor asset pricing model. We conclude with a summary in section 10.6.

10.2   Analogies and an Important Distinction between the Capital Asset Pricing Model and Multifactor Models

The CAPM is the intellectual forebear of multifactor models, including the arbitrage pricing model, for several reasons. While there are close analogies between the CAPM and the multifactor models, there is an important difference. Like most analyses in economics, the CAPM is derived from first principles by applying logic to a set of postulates within a specified empirical context.[1] In particular, economists derived the CAPM by using logic to determine how a rational, utility-maximizing investor would allocate investible funds among securities. As we know, the most important outcomes of this application of logic are as follows:

1. There is an equilibrium trade-off between expected rate of return and risk that governs the pricing of all securities.
2. Only systematic risk affects the expected rate of return on a security.
3. The measure of systematic risk of a security is the covariance between the rate of return on that security and rate of return on the market portfolio.[2]

The multifactor models and the arbitrage pricing model share with the CAPM the properties in (1) and (2) above. Further, the CAPM and the multifactor models define the quantities of the systematic risks for a security as the covariances between the rate of return on that security and the rates of return on specified portfolios. The critical difference between the CAPM and the newer models is that the portfolios that define the systematic risks for a security are not derived from first principles. In the multifactor models, economists use intuition to identify likely candidates for portfolios to define systematic risks and then select portfolios for inclusion as factors on the basis of how well the portfolios explain the differences in average rates of return across individual securities. For the arbitrage pricing model, the factors are selected strictly by an empirical process that begins with an arbitrary initial set of portfolios, then systematically revises those portfolios to improve the ability of the model to explain expected rates of return.[3]

The place of the CAPM as an intellectual foundation for the construction and interpretation of multifactor asset pricing models will be transparent as we proceed to present these models in the following sections.

10.3 A Hypothetical Two-Factor Asset Pricing Model

10.3.1 Factors as Sources of Risk

A factor is a portfolio of securities. Each factor is a source of risk for each security in the economy. In a two-factor model, each security has two quantities of risk, one for each of the factors. Each quantity of risk is the degree to which the expected rate of return on that security will change when the rate of return on the corresponding factor (or portfolio) changes by one percentage point. Define the two factors as follows.

Factor 1: A portfolio containing equally weighted positions in the common stocks issued by the 10 largest firms in the transportation sector of the economy. To construct this portfolio with an investment of $1,000,000, the investor would purchase $100,000 worth of the common stock of each of the 10 firms.

Factor 2: A portfolio containing equally weighted positions in the common stocks issued by the 10 largest firms in the financial services sector of the economy.

Since each factor is a portfolio, each factor has a probability density function that generates values for the rate of return on that portfolio. The hypothesis underlying a factor model is that the rate of return of each security is related to the rates of return on the factors. More specifically, the probability density function that generates values for the rate of return on Security i shifts as the rates of return on the factors change. The dependence (or sensitivity) of the probability density function for Security i to changes in the rate of return on a factor is the quantity of risk for Security i for that factor.

10.3.2 Quantities of Risk for Security 16

Consider Security 16, a specific security. (Whether Security 16 is included in one of the two factors is irrelevant.) Define $\beta_{16,1}$ as the quantity of risk contained in Security 16 with respect to Factor 1. Then $\beta_{16,1}$ is the degree to which the expected rate of return for Security 16 will change when the rate of return on Factor 1 changes by one percentage point. For example, suppose that $\beta_{16,1}$ is equal to 3. Then if the rate of return on Factor 1 were to increase by one percentage point, the probability density function for Security 16 would shift to the right by three percentage points.

Similarly, define $\beta_{16,2}$ as the quantity of risk contained in Security 16 with respect to Factor 2. Then $\beta_{16,2}$ is the degree to which the expected rate of return for Security 16 will change when the rate of return on Factor 2 changes by one percentage point.

The measurement of each quantity of risk in a two-factor model is analogous to the measurement of the single quantity of risk in the CAPM. In that model, the only source of risk for a security is the degree to which the expected rate of return for that security will change when the rate of return on the market portfolio changes by one percentage point. In chapter 9, we would have used the symbol β_{16} to represent the quantity of risk for Security 16. We would not have needed a second subscript for β because in the CAPM there is only one source of risk.

10.3.3   Equilibrium in the Hypothetical Two-Factor Model

The equation that defines the equilibrium relationship between expected return and risk for individual securities in a two-factor model is analogous to the equation for the security market line in the CAPM. For ease of reference, that equation is:

$$E_i = R_f + (E_m - R_f)\beta_i, \tag{10.1}$$

which states that the equilibrium expected return on Security i is equal to the reward for waiting plus a reward for bearing risk. The quantity of risk is β_i. The reward for bearing risk is $(E_m - R_f)$, which is proportional to the market price of risk that appears in the equation for the capital market line.

The equation in a two-factor model that is analogous to the equation for the security market line in the CAPM is:

$$E_i = R_f + \lambda_1 \beta_{i,1} + \lambda_2 \beta_{i,2} \tag{10.2}$$

Equation (10.2) states that the equilibrium expected return for Security i is equal to the reward for waiting plus a sum of two terms. Each term is the product of the quantity of risk relative to one of the factors multiplied by the market price of risk for that factor. The values for the betas and lambdas are slopes of regression planes. The procedure for obtaining these slopes is sketched in an appendix to this chapter.[4]

Consider the following numerical example, in which we compare the equilibrium values of the expected rates of return for Security 16 and Security 24. Suppose that the two quantities of risk for each of the securities, and the two market prices of risk, have the values shown in table 10.1. In the first line of table 10.1, the values of the betas are

Table 10.1
Values for the Quantities of Risk and the Market Prices of Risk

$\beta_{16,1} = 2$	$\beta_{16,2} = .5$
$\beta_{24,1} = 3$	$\beta_{24,2} = 1$
$\lambda_1 = .08$	$\lambda_2 = .22$

the quantities of risk contained in Security 16. Recall that Factor 1 is an equally weighted portfolio of common stocks issued by the 10 largest firms in the transportation sector of the economy. The quantity of risk in a particular security with respect to this factor is the sensitivity of the expected rate of return on that security to changes in the average rates of return for these firms. The value of 2 for $\beta_{16,1}$ means that the expected rate of return for Security 16 will increase by two percentage points whenever the average rate of return on the transportation sector increases by one percentage point.

Factor 2 is an equally weighted portfolio of common stocks issued by the 10 largest firms in the financial services sector. The value of .5 for value for $\beta_{16,2}$ means that the expected rate of return for Security 16 will change by one-half of one percentage point (in the same direction) for each one percentage point change in the average rate of return for the 10 largest firms in the financial services sector.

The second line in table 10.1 shows the values for two quantities of risk for Security 24. The value of 3 for $\beta_{24,1}$ indicates that the expected rate of return for Security 24 will change by three percentage points in the same direction for each change of one percentage point in the average rate of return for the transportation sector. Similarly, the value of 1 for $\beta_{24,2}$ indicates that the expected rate of return for Security 24 will change by one percentage point for each change of one percentage point in the average rate of return for the financial services sector.

The values for the lamdas in the third line of table 10.1 are the values for the two market prices of risk. The easiest way to interpret these values is to compare the adjustments for risk between securities 16 and 24.

Each security has two quantities of risk, one for each factor. The market rewards investors for bearing risk in a particular security by adjusting the expected rate of return for that security. For each security, the size of the adjustment for the risk generated by a specific factor depends on the quantity of that type of risk contained in that security, and on the market price for that type of risk. The market price of risk for a given factor is the value of the lambda for that factor. As a market price of risk, the function of a lambda is to convert a quantity of risk into an adjustment in the expected rate of return. For example, the value of .08 for λ_1 means that for each percentage point of risk generated in a security by Factor 1, the market will increase the expected rate of return on that security by .08 percentage points. Similarly, the value of .22 for λ_2 means that for each percentage point of risk generated in a security by Factor 2, the market will increase the expected rate of return on that security by .22 percentage points.

In table 10.1, the values for λ_1 and λ_2 are different because (for some reason) investors regard risk generated by Factor 2 as more burdensome than risk generated by Factor 1. We cannot say anything more definite than this without a more sophisticated model. But the following observation is pertinent. In most asset pricing models, we assume that individual investors are perfect competitors. Consequently, each investor must take the values of the parameters as fixed. But it is the competition among investors, as they trade securities to form their portfolios, that determines the values for the parameters. For example, the expected rate of return on Security 16 is the standard deviation of that rate of return and the correlation coefficients between the rate of return on Security 16 and the rates of return on all other securities depending on the relative prices of all securities. Competition among investors determines the relative prices of securities. Therefore, competition among investors determines the values of the parameters of the probability density functions that generate the rates of return on these securities. An equilibrium is established when competition among investors sets the values of the expected rates of return, the standard deviations, and the correlation coefficients so that the Security Market Line in equation (10.2) is satisfied for each security.

Since the values for the betas and the lambdas are the slopes of regression lines that involve rates of return, it is competition among investors that determines the values of the betas and the lambdas. Consequently, if the value for λ_2 exceeds the value for λ_1, we infer that investors regard the risk generated by the sensitivity of a security's rate of return to fluctuations in the rate of return on Factor 2 as more burdensome than the risk generated by Factor 1.

We will now use the values for the parameters in table 10.1 to calculate the expected returns for Securities 16 and 24. Assume that the rate of return on the government bond is .04. Then using the rate of return on the government bond, the values for the two lambdas in table 10.1, and the values for the two betas for Security 16 from table 10.1, and equation (10.2), we have:

$$
\begin{aligned}
E_{16} &= .04 + (.08)(2) + (.22)(.5) \\
&= .04 + .16 + .11 \\
&= .31.
\end{aligned}
\tag{10.3}
$$

The preceding equation states the risk-adjusted equilibrium expected rate of return for Security 16 is 31% (per year). Four percentage points of this rate of return are the reward for waiting; the remaining 27 percentage points are an adjustment for bearing risk. Also, 16 percentage points of the adjustment for risk are attributable to the sensitivity of the rate of return on Security 16 to unpredictable variations in the rate of return on Factor 1. The remaining 11 percentage points compensate for the sensitivity of the rate of return on Security 16 to unpredictable variations in the rate of return on Factor 2.

Similarly, the equilibrium expected rate of return on Security 24 is:

$$
\begin{aligned}
E_{24} &= .04 + (.08)(3) + (.22)(1) \\
&= .04 + .24 + .22 \\
&= .50.
\end{aligned}
\tag{10.4}
$$

The risk-adjusted equilibrium expected rate of return for Security 24 is 50% (per year). As in the case of Security 16, four percentage points of this rate of return are the reward for waiting. The adjustment for bearing risk by holding Security 24 is equal to 46 percentage points, of which 24 are attributable to risk generated by Factor 1, and 22 are attributable to risk generated by Factor 2.

We can increase our understanding of the two-factor model by comparing the adjustments for risk for Securities 16 and 24 in equations (10.3) and (10.4). Consider the difference in the adjustments to the expected rates of return on the two securities for the sensitivities of those securities to Factor 1. Security 16 has an adjustment of 16 percentage points for sensitivity to Factor 1, while the adjustment for Security 24 for Factor 1 is 24 percentage points. This is because Security 16 has only two-thirds of the sensitivity to Factor 1 that Security 24 has to that factor. Both the probability density function for Security 16 and the probability density function for Security 24 will shift when the rate of return on Factor 1 changes. Since $\beta_{16,1}=2$ and $\beta_{24,1}=3$, the density function for Security 16 will shift only two-thirds as far as the density function for Security 24 will shift. Consequently, the adjustment to the expected return for Security 16 is only two-thirds of the adjustment to the expected return for Security 24.

The market prices of risk are also important in determining the adjustments for risk. We can see this by examining the set of values in table 10.1. From the second line in that table, we see that the quantities of risk contained in Security 24 are equal to three for Factor 1 and one for Factor 2. This means that the probability density function for Security 24 is three times as sensitive to changes in the rate of return on Factor 1 as it is to changes in the rate of return on Factor 2. But the adjustment for risk attributable to Factor 1 is not three times the adjustment for risk attributable to Factor 2. In fact, the adjustment for Factor 1 is 24 percentage points and the adjustment for Factor 2 is 22 percentage points. The reason is the difference in the values of the two market prices of risk. The price of a unit of risk based on Factor 1 is only .08; the price of a unit of risk based on Factor 2 is .22. The price of risk for a factor is the number of percentage points by which the equilibrium expected rate of return on a security will increase for each percentage point by which the expected value (or center point) of the security's probability density function shifts. The security's density function shifts when the rate of return on a factor shifts.

10.4 The Three-Factor Model of Fama and French

Although early empirical tests of the CAPM were encouraging, subsequent and more sophisticated tests revealed anomalies. Perhaps the most celebrated of these anomalies is the size factor, according to which investments in portfolios of small firms outperformed the market, after allowing for risk. The combinations of expected rate of return and beta for portfolios in general were scattered randomly above and below, but close to, the security market line of the CAPM. But the combinations of expected rate of return and beta for portfolios that were restricted to small firms plotted above the security market line more frequently than could be attributed to chance. The implication of this anomaly was that either the market consistently underprices the securities of small firms, or that the CAPM is not correct as a model of the equilibrium relationship between expected rate of return and risk.

Fama and French addressed this and other anomalies by augmenting the CAPM to include two factors in addition to the market factor. One of the new factors adjusts the equilibrium expected rate of return for a firm based on the size of the firm. The second factor is an adjustment based on the ratio between the book value of the firm and the market value of its common stock. We consider the new factors in the next two sections.

10.4.1 The Factor for Size

The combinations of expected rate of return and beta for small firms are located above the security market line of the CAPM more frequently than chance would suggest. Therefore, according to the CAPM, the securities of small firms are underpriced; the

expected rate of return on a small firm is too high given the level of its risk as measured by beta. The existence of excessive expected rates of return for small firms suggests that there are some aspects of risk in small firms that are not reflected in the values
of the betas for those firms. Under this hypothesis, the CAPM does not set the prices of
small firms too low relative to the levels of risk in those firms. Rather, the CAPM under-
states the levels of risk in small firms by using only beta to measure that risk.

To allow for the effect of the size of a firm on its equilibrium expected rate of
return, Fama and French proposed a size factor. Recall that a factor is a portfolio.
Fama and French measure the size of a firm by the market value of its equity, that is,
the price of a share of the firm's common stock multiplied by the number of shares
outstanding. The authors then rank firms according to size and form two portfolios.
Portfolio S contains those firms that rank in the bottom half of all firms ranked by
size; Portfolio L contains the firms in the top half. For each month t, the rate of return
for the size factor is defined as the rate of return on Portfolio S minus the rate of return
on Portfolio L.

To interpret the size factor, consider the following hypothesis. Suppose that the
earnings of a small firm are more sensitive to unpredictable changes in interest rates
than the earnings of large firms. Since it is difficult to predict the course of interest
rates, investors who hold the securities of a small firm bear more risk (of unpredictable fluctuation in the rate of return on their portfolio) than they would if they
avoided those securities. Then to induce investors to hold the securities of small firms,
the market must provide a higher expected rate of return on the securities of small
firms. For a specific firm, the quantity of risk due to the size effect is the sensitivity of
the rate of return of that firm to changes in the rate of return on the size factor. We will
pursue this interpretation further in section 10.4.3, where we discuss the security market plane for the three-factor model.

10.4.2   The Factor for the Ratio of Book Equity to Market Equity

The second additional factor proposed by Fama and French depends on the ratio of
book equity to market equity of a firm. The book equity of a firm is (approximately)
the amount of money that the firm could raise by selling all its assets, minus the firm's
indebtedness to its contractual claimants. For example, if the firm has both bonds and
common stock outstanding, the book value of equity would be the amount of money
that the firm could pay to its shareholders after liquidating its assets and paying off the
bondholders.

The market value of equity is simply the market price of a share multiplied by the
number of shares outstanding. The book value of the entirety of a firm's assets is the
amount of money for which the firm could sell those assets. The prices that the assets
would bring in the market reflect the consensus of investors about the ability of those
assets to generate earnings in alternative employment. Therefore, the book value of
the firm's assets is the opportunity cost of those assets. Consider, for example, a
railroad that owns (rather than leases) its cars. The book value of those cars is their
value, as perceived by investors, of their most valuable alternative use. If other railroads have profitable opportunities to use additional cars, the book value of the cars

will be high. But if there is a surplus of cars among railroads, the book value of the cars will be low.

The market value of the railroad's common stock is the greater of (1) the (risk-adjusted) present value of the earnings that the railroad's current management can generate with the railroad's assets, or (2) the book value of the railroad's assets. Therefore, the market value of the railroad's common stock is equal to the book value of its assets plus whatever net value the management can add by using those assets profitably. Of course, profit must be calculated net of opportunity costs, and one of those opportunity costs is the book value of the equity. If the management is incompetent (or dishonest), the market value of the common stock could be less than the book value of equity. In this case, the shareholders could increase their wealth by replacing the current managers, because the most profitable use of the railroad's assets is their current use, given competent managers.

Alternatively, suppose that the managers are competent but that shippers and passengers switch to other modes of transportation. Once again, the market value of equity could be less than the book value of that equity. But in this case, the shareholders would increase their wealth by liquidating the firm.

Either of the two examples described above could lead to a corporate takeover of the railroad. If the current shareholders are unable or unwilling to fire the current managers or liquidate the firm, a new set of investors could obtain a profit equal to the difference between the book value and the market value of equity. The new investors could purchase the railroad's common shares at their market value, then use their new authority as owners of the railroad either to replace the managers or liquidate the firm.

The market value of a firm's equity depends on the price of the firm's common stock. Therefore, the market value of equity reflects investors' beliefs about the ability of that firm to generate earnings. The book value of a firm's equity is more difficult to measure because, unlike the firm's shares of common stock, the firm's assets are not being continually priced on an organized exchange. Nevertheless, the ratio of the two values of equity has empirical significance for asset pricing models and for other uses.

Define the book value of equity as BE, and the market value of equity as ME. Fama and French argue that a firm that has a high BE/ME ratio is a firm that investors expect to have relatively low (or slowly growing) earnings in the future. If investors expect future earnings to be low, they will be willing to purchase or hold the firm's stock only at low prices. The low prices will create a low market value of equity, and hence a high BE/ME ratio. Similarly, investors will bid up the price of the stock of a firm that they expect will produce large earnings. The high price of the firm's stock will create a low BE/ME ratio for that firm.

Fama and French create a BE/ME factor as follows. First, the authors calculate the BE/ME ratios for each firm over some historical period. They then rank the firms by their historical BE/ME ratios. Next, they create two portfolios. The first portfolio contains the firms in the upper half of the list of BE/ME ratios. The second portfolio contains the firms in the lower half of the list. The value of the BE/ME factor for month t is equal to the average rate of return over firms in the first portfolio for that month, minus the average rate of return over firms in the second portfolio for that same month.

10.4.3 The Security Market Plane for the Three-Factor Model

Define the following:

$R_{m,t} - R_{f,t}$ = the rate of return on the market portfolio minus the rate of return on the risk-free asset, both for month t

$R_{\text{Size},t}$ = the average of the rates of return on small firms minus the average of the rates of return on large firms, for month t

$R_{\text{B/M},t}$ = the average of the rates of return on firms with BE/ME ratios in the lower half of the list of all firms, minus the average of the rates of return on firms with BE/ME ratios in the upper half of the list, for month t.

Let R_i be the rate of return on Security i. Then the three quantities of risk for Security i are:

$$
\begin{aligned}
\beta_{i,M} &= \text{Cov}(R_i, R_M)/\sigma_M^2; \\
\beta_{i,\text{Size}} &= \text{Cov}(R_i, R_{\text{Size}})/\sigma_{\text{size}}^2; \\
\beta_{i,\text{B/M}} &= \text{Cov}(R_i, R_{\text{B/M}})/\sigma_{\text{B/M}}^2.
\end{aligned}
\tag{10.5}
$$

The beta values are the slopes of the plane obtained by regressing the rate of return on Security i against the rates of return on the three factors. Therefore, each beta value is the marginal effect of a factor on the conditional expected rate of return of Security i.[5]

Finally, let the three market prices of risk be λ_M for the market factor, λ_{Size} for the size factor, and $\lambda_{\text{B/M}}$ for the BE/ME factor. The values for the lambdas are the slopes of the plane obtained by regressing the expected rates of return of all the securities against the beta values for those securities.

The three-factor model of Fama and French asserts that the equilibrium relationship between expected rate of return and risk is:

$$
E_i = \text{Constant} + \lambda_M \beta_{i,M} + \lambda_{\text{Size}} \beta_{i,\text{Size}} + \lambda_{\text{B/M}} \beta_{i,\text{B/M}}.
\tag{10.6}
$$

Equation (10.6) for the three-factor model of Fama and French is analogous to equation (10.2) in section 10.2 for the security market plane for our hypothetical two-factor model. The constant term is an estimate of the reward for waiting. Each term that is a product of a lambda and a beta is an adjustment for risk.

10.4.4 The Size Factor and the Book-to-Market Factor as Predictors of Earnings

The rationale for including the market factor in the CAPM is clear. The market factor arises naturally in that model as a logical consequence of rational investors using the principles of portfolio theory to allocate their funds among risky securities. We would like to have similar rationales for the size factor and the book-to-market factor that Fama and French include in their three-factor model. The fact that the three-factor model has a good empirical record is welcome. We can have even more confidence in that model because Fama and French provide a strong economic rationale for the inclusion of these factors as determinants of the expected rates of return on stocks. That rationale is that the two factors are predictors of a firm's earnings. Since expected rates of return depend on investors' beliefs about the firm's future earnings, it is logical that investors would pay attention to any variables that have some power to predict future earnings.

10.5 The Five-Factor Model of Fama and French

10.5.1 An Integrated Market for Stocks and Bonds

Fama and French augmented their three-factor model by adding two factors to explain the expected rates of return on bonds. The augmented model has a total of five factors. The five-factor model explains the equilibrium relationship between expected rate of return and risk for both stocks and bonds with a single equation. The rationale for this equation is that, although stocks and bonds are different kinds of assets, both stocks and bonds are risky securities.[6] The rates of return on these securities are governed by probability density functions. Therefore, we ought to be able to explain the relationship between the expected rate of return and the risk on these securities with a single equation.

A good economic model will define a general principle that applies to a class of phenomena. Any particular item in that class of phenomena conforms to the general principle as a special case. Consider, for example, the common stocks of IBM and the Union Pacific Railroad. These two firms are quite different, but there is a unifying characteristic. An investor who holds a share of the stock of either firm owns a saleable right to receive an uncertain sequence of payments. The expected rate of return on each security depends on investors' beliefs about the probability density function that governs that firm's earnings. Obviously, it would be unsatisfactory to have one asset pricing model to explain the expected rate of return and risk for IBM, and a separate model to explain the expected rate of return for the Union Pacific Railroad. Nor do we want one asset pricing model for firms whose business is transportation and a different model for firms in the computer industry. We want a single model that is sufficiently general to accommodate both types of firm.

The same reasoning applies to stocks and bonds. Both are financial securities whose rates of return are governed by probability density functions. We want a single model that will explain the equilibrium relationship between expected rate of return and risk for both kinds of securities.

10.5.2 The Factor for the Term Structure of Interest Rates

The first factor that Fama and French added to enable their model to explain the expected rates of return on bonds is designed to recognize that one source of risk for bondholders is unexpected changes in the interest rates offered by alternative securities. Interest rates are, of course, a form of opportunity costs. Fama and French call their proposed factor TERM, which they define as:

$$\text{TERM}_t = \text{rate of return on a long-term government bond for month } t$$
$$- \text{rate of return on a one-month U.S. Treasury bill for month } t.$$

The value of the factor TERM_t is a proxy "for the deviation of long-term bond returns from expected returns due to shifts in interest rates."[7]

10.5.3 The Factor for the Risk of Default

The second factor proposed by Fama and French is designed to capture the risk that the firm might fail to make the required payments on interest and principal on time. Fama and French call this factor DEF because it is a proxy for the risk of default. The default factor is defined by:

$$\text{DEF}_t = \text{rate of return on a portfolio of long-term corporate bonds for month } t$$
$$- \text{ rate of return on a long-term U.S. government bond for month } t.$$

Since no one expects the federal government to default on its bonds,[8] changes in the value of the DEF factor measure changes in the risk of default on corporate bonds. Specifically, an increase in the value of the DEF factor from month t to month $t+1$ would occur if investors require a larger premium to hold bonds issued by corporations rather than bonds issued by the government. A plausible reason for an increase in the difference between the rates of return on the two kinds of bonds is that investors expect a higher probability of default on corporate bonds.

10.5.4 The Security Market Plane for the Five-Factor Model

Define the quantity of risk for Security i for the TERM factor as:

$$\beta_{i,\text{TERM}} = \text{Cov}(r_i, r_{\text{TERM}})/\sigma^2_{\text{TERM}}. \tag{10.7}$$

Then $\beta_{i,\text{TERM}}$ is the sensitivity of the rate of return on Security i to changes in the value of the TERM factor. That is, $\beta_{i,\text{TERM}}$ is the amount by which the conditional probability density function for Security i shifts when the value of the TERM factor increases by one percentage point.

Similarly, the quantity of risk for Security i for the DEF factor is:

$$\beta_{i,\text{DEF}} = \text{Cov}(r_i, r_{\text{DEF}})/\sigma^2_{\text{DEF}}. \tag{10.8}$$

The five-factor model proposed by Fama and French for the equilibrium relationship between the expected rate of return and risk on both stocks and bonds is:

$$E_i = \text{Constant} + \lambda_M\beta_{i,M} + \lambda_{\text{size}}\beta_{i,\text{size}} + \lambda_{\text{B/M}}\beta_{i,\text{B/M}} + \lambda_{\text{TERM}}\beta_{i,\text{TERM}}$$
$$+ \lambda_{\text{DEF}}\beta_{i,\text{DEF}}, \tag{10.9}$$

in which λ_{TERM} is the market price of risk for the TERM factor, and λ_{DEF} is the market price of risk for the DEF factor.

For any particular security, the values of one or more of the betas could be zero. For example, if Security i is a common stock for which the risk of default on corporate bonds has no bearing, the value of $\beta_{i,\text{DEF}}$ will be zero.

10.6 The Arbitrage Pricing Theory

10.6.1 A Brief Statement

The APT is a special case of a multifactor model. The distinguishing feature of the APT is that the factors are generated endogenously by an empirical technique called factor analysis. As is the case with any multifactor model, each factor is a portfolio of securities. But these portfolios, or factors, are not chosen by the investigator on the basis of inferences drawn from economic theory or from previous empirical studies. Rather, factor analysis chooses the factors based on the ability of the resulting model to explain differences in the expected rates of return on individual securities by using differences in the securities' quantities of risk with respect to the factors. Following is a brief summary of how a model based on the APT is constructed.

Factor analysis is an empirical procedure that generates a sequence of iterations. Keep in mind that a factor in an asset pricing model is a portfolio of securities. Each iteration of the factor analysis produces a set of factors to define a specific multifactor model of the relationship between the quantities of risk and expected rates of return for individual securities. Each multifactor model is then tested to determine how closely its predictions fit the data. Based on the results of the test for closeness of fit, the next iteration produces a revised set of factors, and hence a revised multifactor model. The process continues until it produces a model that satisfies a threshold for closeness of fit chosen by the investigator.

Here is an example of how the technique of factor analysis works. An investigator begins with historical data on the rates of return for a large set of securities. For example, she might use data on every security in the S&P 500 for the past 20 years. Using these data, the investigator uses factor analysis to construct an initial set of portfolios to use as factors. The composition of these initial portfolios need not detain us. For the purpose of example, suppose that there are four factors. Factor 1 might be a portfolio in which 20% of the investment is allocated to IBM, 70% to GE, and 10% to Union Pacific Railroad. Factor 2 could be a portfolio in which funds are distributed equally over the five largest airlines in the economy. Factor 3 might be a portfolio in which funds are distributed over the largest 20 firms that have an unbroken record of paying dividends over the last 10 years. In this portfolio, the funds are allocated across the 20 firms in proportion to the relative market values of those firms' outstanding common stock. Finally, Factor 4 might require an investment in 20 firms that have no discernible property in common. A distinguishing property of factor analysis is that the empirical procedure is free to define the factors in any way that produces a model that, for whatever reason, satisfies a threshold for closeness of fit.

Once the portfolios (factors) are chosen for a given iteration of the procedure, the next step is to calculate the quantities of risk for each security for each of the factors. These quantities of risk have the same interpretation as the quantities of risk in the multifactor models examined earlier in this chapter.

Next, the procedure calculates the market prices of risk for each factor. Again, as in any multifactor model, these prices of risk are determined by regression, using a criterion of closeness of fit.

Finally, using the quantities of risk for each security for each factor, and the market prices of risk for each factor, the resulting multifactor model is tested for its ability to predict the relationships between expected rates of return and quantities of risk for each security. A measure of closeness of fit is obtained. Based on this measure, the factor analysis generates a revised set of factors, and thus a revised factor model, subject to the condition that the revised model will produce a closer fit between expected rates of return and quantities of risk.

In some applications of factor analysis, the investigator chooses the number of factors that the empirical procedure may select; in other applications, the empirical procedure is free to vary the number of factors. But in any case, the objective is to produce a multifactor model that will explain the observed relationship across securities between expected rates of return and quantities of risk.

10.6.2 A Simple Comparison of an Arbitrage Pricing Model and a Factor Pricing Model

The following equation is an example of an arbitrage pricing model that has four factors:

$$E_i = \text{Constant} + \lambda_1 \beta_{i,\text{Factor 1}} + \lambda_2 \beta_{i,\text{Factor 2}} + \lambda_3 \beta_{i,\text{Factor 3}} + \lambda_{\text{Factor 4}} \beta_{i,\text{Factor 4}} \qquad (10.10)$$

A comparison of equation (10.10) with equation (10.9) shows that the structure of an arbitrage pricing model (with four factors) is identical to that of any specific multifactor asset pricing model that also has four factors. Each model states that the equilibrium expected rate of return on Security i is equal to a constant (which could be the reward for waiting) plus four adjustments for risk. In each model, each adjustment for risk is the product of two terms; those terms are a quantity of risk and the market price of that type of risk. Each quantity of risk is a covariance between the rate of return on Security i and the rate of return on a specific portfolio. The difference between the two models is that the four types of risks in the model of equation (10.9) are specified in advance by the researcher, whereas in the arbitrage pricing model of equation (10.10), the four types of risk are determined within the model (endogenously) by an algorithm that maximizes the closeness of fit.

10.6.3 Additional Observations about Arbitrage Pricing Models

A disadvantage of factor analysis is that the portfolios that are generated for the factors can be difficult to interpret. It is unlikely, for example, that any of the factors that will emerge from an application of factor analysis will contain securities with the kinds of common properties that we see in Factors 1, 2, and 3 in our example above. More likely, each factor will be like Factor 4, in which the constituent securities do not have any obvious property in common. It is then not clear what the quantities of risk, or the market prices of risk, in the model mean. One can say that the model works in the sense of producing a certain closeness of fit. But one cannot easily provide an intuitive rationale for why the model works, as one can with the three-factor model and the five-factor model of Fama and French.

Finally, a word about the term *arbitrage* in the arbitrage pricing model.[9] Most models of equilibrium in financial economics (and in several other areas of economics as well) rely on the process of arbitrage to enforce the predicted equilibrium relationship between prices and quantities. We have seen this in the derivation of the security market line in the capital asset pricing model in chapter 9. If the values of the parameters for Security i and the market portfolio enable an investor to construct a portfolio that lies above the capital market line, then competition among investors (acting as speculators) to exploit this opportunity will cause the price of Security i to change.

As the price of Security i changes, the values of the parameters of that security will change so as to eliminate the opportunity to use Security i to create a portfolio that lies above the capital market line. The same reliance on arbitrage occurs both in the multifactor models studied earlier in this chapter and in the arbitrage pricing model. Arbitrage, as part of the rationale for explaining why a model works, is not limited to the arbitrage pricing model.

10.7 Summary

The fundamental contribution of the CAPM is that the quantity of risk in a security is proportional to the covariance between the rate of return on that security and the rate of return on a special portfolio. We know that, for the CAPM, the special portfolio is the market portfolio. Unfortunately, the empirical record of the CAPM is not satisfactory. Among the several anomalies is the size effect, according to which the market (that is, investors) systematically underprices the securities of small firms.

Fama and French address the empirical shortcomings of the CAPM by presenting two models. Each model augments the CAPM by adding factors. In addition to the market factor from the CAPM, the three-factor model has a factor for size and a factor for the BE/ME ratio. For Security i, the quantity of risk associated with the size factor is the covariance between the rate of return on Security i and the difference between the rates of return on a portfolio of small firms and a portfolio of large firms. Similarly, the quantity of risk for the book-to-market factor is the covariance between the rate of return on Security i and the difference between the rates of return on a portfolio of firms that have high BE/ME ratios and a portfolio of firms that have small BE/ME ratios. Each factor has its own market price of risk. Fama and French demonstrate (empirically) that the size and book-to-market factors are proxies for future earnings, which provides an economic rationale for augmenting the CAPM by these factors.

Since both stocks and bonds are risky securities, and since investors can use the markets for both securities in constructing their portfolios, we should be able to explain the expected rates of return on both stocks and bonds with a single equation. To do this, Fama and French add to their three-factor model two factors to recognize the sources of risk that apply particularly to bonds. One of these factors captures the risk of default; the second factor is a proxy for the risk of unexpected changes in interest rates. The resulting five-factor model has a good empirical record.

The central contribution of the CAPM survives in the models of Fama and French. The risk of a security is measured by one or more covariances between the rate of return on that security and the rates of return on one or more portfolios.

Appendix: Estimating the Values of β and λ for a Two-Factor Model

Let there be N risky securities indexed by $i = 1, \ldots, N$. In a two-factor model, the equilibrium expected rate of return for Security i is:

$$E_i = R_f + \lambda_1 \beta_{i,1} + \lambda_2 \beta_{i,2}, \tag{10.11}$$

in which E_i is the expected rate of return on Security i, R_f is the rate of return on the risk-free asset, λ_1 and λ_2 are the market prices of risk associated with Factors 1 and 2, and $\beta_{i,1}$ and $\beta_{i,2}$ are the quantities of risk associated with Factors 1 and 2 for Security i. To use equation (10.11), we need values of $\beta_{i,1}$ and $\beta_{i,2}$ for each of the N securities. We also need values for λ_1 and λ_2.

We use a two-stage multivariable regression to estimate the values of the two lambdas and the $2N$ betas. We estimate the values of the betas first.

For each Security i, we estimate the values of $\beta_{i,1}$ and $\beta_{i,2}$ by regressing the rate of return for Security i on the rates of return of the two factors for some historical period. The estimated values for $\beta_{i,1}$ and $\beta_{i,2}$ are the slopes of the (three-dimensional) regression plane in the dimensions that represent the two factors.

Suppose that we are using monthly rates of return over a period of five years. Then for each month we have a three-dimensional data point. To visualize the three-dimensional regression, draw one axis across this page from left to right. Draw a second axis from the bottom of the page to the top. Make the two axes perpendicular to each other. Finally, draw a third axis perpendicular to the plane of the page and passing through the intersection of the first two axes. We measure the rate of return of Factor 1 on the first axis, the rate of return of Factor 2 on the second axis, and the rate of return on Security i on the third axis. Then for each month the rates of return of the two factors and the rate of return on Security i are the coordinates of a point located in the three-dimensional space that contains the plane of the page. Suppose that in a given month the rate of return of Factor 1 is positive, the rate of return of Factor 2 is negative, and the rate of return of Security i is positive. Then the three-dimensional point for that month will lie to the right of the second axis (that runs from the bottom of the page to the top), below the first axis (that runs from left to right across the page), and above the plane of the page. Since we are using monthly data over a period of five years, we will have 60 data points in the three-dimensional space that contains this page.

To regress the rate of return of Security i on the rates of return of the two factors, we fit a plane to the set of 60 data points. As in ordinary regression, we choose the plane that minimizes the sum of the squared distances from the data points to the regression plane. If we were to regress the values for a variable y on a variable x, we would fit a straight line to a set of two-dimensional data points. We would choose the intercept and the slope of that line to minimize the sum of squared vertical distances from the data points to the line.

We can define a straight line by specifying the value of its intercept with one axis (usually the vertical axis) and the value of its slope with respect to the other axis (usually the horizontal axis). Analogously, we can define a plane by specifying the value of its intercept with one of the three axes and the values of its slopes with respect to the other two axes. In the regression for Security i against the two factors, the value of $\beta_{i,1}$ is the slope of the plane with respect to the axis that runs across the page from left to right. The value of $\beta_{i,2}$ is the slope of the plane with respect to the axis that runs from the bottom of the page to the top.

To interpret these slopes as quantities of risk, consider a typical data point. The coordinates of this point for the two factors locate the point on the page; the coordinate for the rate of return of Security i determines the height of the data point above this page. This height above the page is the expected rate of return on Security i conditional on the rates of return on the two factors.

Suppose that the rates of return of Factors 1 and 2 are F_1 and F_2. Let these rates of return be the coordinates of Point H on the plane of this page. Then the height of the regression plane over Point H is the conditional expected rate of return for Security i, if the rate of return of Factor 1 is F_1 and the rate of return of Factor 2 is F_2. Suppose that the rate of return of Factor 1 increases by one percentage point, while the rate of return of Factor 2 does not change. Let Point J on the plane of this page represent the new coordinates. Then Point J will lie horizontally to the right of Point H by .01. The difference in the heights of the regression plane over Points H and J is the marginal effect of Factor 1 on the conditional expected rate of return of Security i. Therefore, the slope of the regression plane with respect to Factor 1, which is the value of $\beta_{i,1}$, is the marginal effect of Factor 1 on the conditional expected rate of return of Security i. Similarly, the value of $\beta_{i,1}$ is the marginal effect of Factor 2 on the conditional expected rate of return of Security i.[10]

To estimate the values of the lambdas, which are the market prices of risk, we need one final regression. In the CAPM there is a single source of risk, namely the volatility of the rate of return on the market portfolio. Consequently, there is a single market price of risk that applies to all securities. In a two-factor model, the two sources of risk are the volatilities of the rates of return with respect to changes in the values of the two factors. Consequently, there are two market prices of risk that apply to all securities. These market prices of risk are λ_1 for Factor 1 and λ_2 for Factor 2. To estimate the values of the two lambdas, we regress the values of the historical average rates of return on the N securities against the N pairs of values of betas for those securities.

Let the axis that runs across this page from left to right represent Factor 1, the axis that runs from the bottom of this page to the top represent Factor 2, and the axis that is perpendicular to the page represent the historical average rate of return on a security. For this regression, we have N data points, one for each security. The coordinates of the data point for Security i are $(\beta_{i,1}, \beta_{i,2}, E_i)$. We plot the first coordinate on the axis that runs across the page, the second coordinate on the axis that runs from the bottom to the top of the page, and the third coordinate on the axis that is perpendicular to the page. We then fit a plane to the N data points. The slope of the plane in the dimension corresponding to Factor 1 is the value of λ_1, and the slope of the plane in the dimension corresponding to Factor 2 is the value of λ_2.

Note that each security has its own values for the two betas. Therefore, to estimate the values for the betas we need N regressions, one for each security. But there is only one pair of values for the market prices of risk. Therefore, we need only one regression to estimate the values of the lambdas.

Problem

Consider the following numerical example in which we compare the equilibrium values of the expected rates of return for Security 19 and Security 84 in a two-factor model:

The two quantities of risk for each of the securities, and the two market prices of risk, have the following values:

$$\beta_{19,1}=5 \qquad \beta_{19,2}=.8$$
$$\beta_{84,1}=7 \qquad \beta_{84,2}=3$$
$$\lambda_1=.11 \qquad \lambda_2=.25$$

(a) Interpret each of the values.
(b) Assume that the rate of return on the government bond is .10. Using this value, the values for the two lambdas, and the values for the two betas for Security 19 and Security 84, calculate the *risk-adjusted* equilibrium expected rates of return for Security 19 and Security 84.

Notes

1. The postulates are axiomatic assertions about properties of any person's choices. These postulates include: more of any Good X is better than less of that good, given no changes in the quantities of any other good; willingness to forego some amount of any Good Y (per unit of time) in order to gain an additional unit of another Good X (willingness to substitute between Goods X and Y); and willingness to substitute between Goods X and Y at a diminishing marginal rate (the larger the quantity of Good X that a person has, the smaller the quantity of Good Y he is willing to forego to obtain one additional unit of Good X). For the derivation of the CAPM, the context includes assertions such as the rates of return on (almost) any two securities are imperfectly correlated.

2. In fact (as we know) the measure of risk for a security is proportional to the covariance because the beta for a security is equal to the covariance between the rate of return on that security and the rate of return on the market portfolio, with that covariance divided by the variance of the rate of return on the market portfolio.

3. For an excellent discussion and application of the choice of factors for a multifactor model, see N. R. Chen, R. Roll, and S. Ross, "Economic Forces and the Stock Market," *Journal of Business* 59, no. 3 (1986): 383–403; E. Fama and K. French, "Common Risk Factors in the Returns on Stocks and Bonds," *Journal of Financial Economics* (February 1993): 3–56.

4. Let y and x be variables. The regression of y on x will produce a straight line of the form $\hat{y}=\hat{\alpha}+\hat{\beta}x$, in which $\hat{y}$ is the estimated (or predicted) value for y given the value for x. The terms $\hat{\alpha}$ and $\hat{\beta}$ are parameters whose values are determined by minimizing the sum of squared differences between the actual and the predicted values for y given the values for x. The slope of the regression line is $\hat{\beta}$, whose value is the increase in the predicted value for y given an increase of one unit in the value for x. If we were to regress the variable y on the two variables x and w, we would obtain a plane defined by the equation $y'=\alpha'+\beta'x+\gamma'w$. The terms β' and γ' are parameters whose values are the slopes of the plane in the directions parallel to the axis on which the values for x and w are plotted. For example, the value for β' is the increase in the predicted value for y given an increase of one unit in the value for x, holding the value of w constant.

5. The plane obtained by regressing rate of return on Security i on the three factors will be a (hyper)plane in four-dimensional space. We will not attempt to visualize this plane. Nevertheless, the interpretation of the betas as the marginal effects of factors on the conditional expected rate of return of Security i holds. The procedure is analogous to that described in note 4 for the hypothetical two-factor model.

6. Although a bond is a contractual claim on the firm's earnings, the bond is a risky security because the market price of the bond can change at any time prior to the maturity date. A change in the current price of the bond creates a capital gain or loss for the investor who holds that bond. The rate of return on any security held from time t to time $t+1$ depends, in part, on the change in the price of that security over that interval. The price of a bond can change for two reasons. First, the firm might fail to make the required payments of interest and principal on time. Changes in investors' beliefs about the probability that the firm will not make the required payments will change the current price of the bond. Second, the rates of interest offered by other securities, such as U.S. Treasury bonds or certificates of deposit at a bank, might change. Changes in the interest rates offered by alternative securities change the opportunity cost of holding a firm's bond, which will change the current price of the bond. Investors who purchase bonds are not committed to holding those bonds to their maturity any more than investors who purchase stocks are committed to holding those stocks as long as the firm exists. In both cases, the typical investor is concerned about the capital gains and losses from period to period, as well as payments of interest and dividends.

7. Fama and French, "Common Risk Factors in the Returns on Stocks and Bonds." (See citation in Note 3.)

8. We must distinguish between a *nominal default* and a *purchasing power default*. A nominal default would occur if the government failed to pay the amounts of money on the schedule promised by the bond. No one expects a nominal default, so the bonds are riskless in this sense. The government might (through monetary policy) inflate the price level, which would reduce the purchasing power of the promised payments of money. Recently, the government has offered bonds whose payments are indexed to the price level. These bonds are fully riskless because investors are protected against both kinds of default.

9. Arbitrage is a process in which an investor obtains a risk-free profit, net of opportunity costs, by simultaneously purchasing an underpriced security and selling an overpriced security. In many cases one or both securities are portfolios constructed by the investor. Sophisticated examples of arbitrage appear in chapter 15 on options.

10. Since we are estimating the values of $\beta_{i,1}$ and $\beta_{i,2}$ with linear multivariable regression, the result of the regression is a plane. The two slopes of a plane are constants. Therefore, the estimated marginal effects of the two factors are constants.

Part V

The Informational and Allocative Efficiency of Financial Markets: The Concepts

11 The Efficient Markets Hypothesis

11.1 Introduction

11.1.1 The Efficient Markets Hypothesis Defined

The efficient markets hypothesis is "the simple statement that security prices fully reflect all available information."[1] Empirical tests of this hypothesis require a precise definition of the term *fully reflect*. A security is a saleable right to receive a sequence of payments. Both the amounts and the timing of these payments can be uncertain. The price of a security fully reflects all available information about the sequence of payments associated with that security if the marginal profit that an investor could earn by collecting additional information is zero.

The preceding definition of the term *fully reflects* has two implications that are important in discussions of the efficient markets hypothesis. The first implication is that so long as the costs of collecting information are positive, there will be some information about sequences of future payments that is not reflected in the prices of securities. The second implication is that to obtain a profit by collecting and trading on information, an investor must have a marginal cost for collecting information that is low relative to the marginal cost for a typical investor.

Consider the first implication. If the marginal cost of collecting and trading on information about future values of prices were zero, then competition among investors would cause current prices to reflect this information. If this were not so, any investor could obtain a profit by trading in the securities whose prices do not fully reflect the information. For example, consider the models in chapter 5, where we examined the effect on the price of a firm's stock when the firm announces a new project. In that chapter, we assumed that all future payments are known with certainty today. We also ignored transaction costs such as brokers' commissions and the opportunity cost of an investor's time. Then the marginal cost of collecting and acting on information is zero. Competition among investors causes the current prices of securities to reflect all information about future payments. In particular, prices will change to reflect immediately any new information, such as the announcement of a new project.

Instead of using the assumptions in chapter 5, suppose that investors must incur costs to assess the accuracy of a firm's announcement of a new project. Then the price of the firm's stock would reflect the information about the project only to the point at which the marginal profit of collecting more (or more accurate) information and trading on it is equal to zero. As long as the marginal costs of collecting and trading on information are positive, there will be some information that is not reflected in the prices of securities.

In chapter 9, we defined the risk-adjusted residual on a security as that portion of the security's rate of return that cannot be attributed to the rewards for waiting and for bearing risk.[2] In the CAPM, the residual is the vertical distance between the rate of return and the characteristic line. The residuals should be random, which means that they should not be predictable from one period to the next. There is, however, some evidence that the residuals are, to a small degree, predictable. The predictability of residuals would be sufficient to invalidate the efficient markets hypothesis only if the marginal costs of collecting and trading on information were zero. Since these costs are not zero, a certain degree of predictability of residuals is consistent with the efficient markets hypothesis.

This brings us to the second implication of our definition of the term *fully reflects* in the statement of the efficient markets hypothesis. The efficient markets hypothesis states that the prices of securities fully reflect all information about future sequences of payments. If this hypothesis holds, then no investor can obtain a profit by collecting information and trading on it. But clearly some investors do obtain profits by identifying mispriced securities. The existence of these investors is taken by some persons as conclusive evidence that the efficient markets hypothesis is false. This conclusion is unwarranted. The existence of some investors who can identify mispriced securities is compatible with the efficient markets hypothesis because investors differ in the marginal costs that they incur to collect, analyze, and trade on information. Investors who have a comparative advantage in identifying mispriced securities will specialize in doing so. The activities of these investors will cause prices to contain more information than they otherwise would. But so long as even these investors incur positive marginal costs, the prices of securities will not fully reflect all information about sequences of future payments.

11.1.2 The Weak, the Semistrong, and the Strong Forms of the Efficient Markets Hypothesis

As first exposited in 1972 by Eugene Fama, the efficient markets hypothesis was partitioned into three concatenated forms: the weak, the semistrong, and the strong.[3] Each form was defined for a specific set of information.

The Weak Form

The weak form of the efficient markets hypothesis was limited to historical information about the prices of securities and the volumes at which those securities were traded. The weak form stated that the current prices of securities fully reflected all information contained in the history of the prices and the volumes of trading. Consequently, the net marginal benefit to an investor of collecting information from past prices and volumes of trading for the purpose of predicting the future prices of securities is zero.

As an empirical fact, there is some serial correlation in the prices of securities. Therefore, there is some information in the past values of prices and volumes of trading that is useful in predicting the future values of prices if an investor can collect and analyze that information at a zero cost. But these costs are not zero for anyone, especially if one includes the opportunity costs incurred by spending time trying to predict the prices of securities rather than exploiting one's comparative advantage in other pursuits. Those whose comparative advantage does lie in predicting the prices of securities by examining data on past prices and volumes of trading should do so. These persons have lower marginal costs for predicting future prices from past data than the rest of us do.[4] In equilibrium, competition among these persons should improve the extent to which current prices reflect the information contained in past prices and volumes to the point at which the net marginal benefit for the rest of us falls to zero or below.

The presence of *statistically* significant serial correlation in the prices of securities is not equivalent to the presence of *economically* significant serial correlation, unless everyone can collect and analyze information, and trade on that information, at zero marginal costs. For most persons, the net marginal benefit of analyzing historical information is zero or negative. Thus, for most of us the weak form of the efficient markets hypothesis holds, even in the presence of empirically detectable serial correlation among prices of securities.

The Semistrong Form

The semistrong form of the efficient markets hypothesis states that the current prices of securities fully reflect all *public* information about the future values of those prices. Public information includes everything that one could learn from reading the public press and attending meetings that are open to the public. Since the public press reports historical information on prices and volumes of trading, the set of information for the weak form is contained within the set of information for the semistrong form.

The implication of the semistrong form of the hypothesis is analogous to the implication of the weak form, namely that the marginal benefit of analyzing public information in an attempt to predict the future prices of securities is zero. Once again, comparative advantages in analyzing public information differ across persons. And, as in the case of the weak form, we would expect that those persons whose marginal costs are relatively low would specialize in analyzing public information to the extent that the net marginal benefit for the rest of us in doing so is zero or negative. There is substantial empirical evidence that this is so. The ability of mutual fund managers consistently to outperform the market, after allowing for the levels of risk in their portfolios, and after subtracting the costs incurred to operate the mutual funds (which costs include the salaries paid to their financial analysts), is (close to) zero.[5]

The Strong Form

Finally, economists include the strong form of the hypothesis for logical completeness. The strong form states that the current prices of securities fully reflect all information about the future values of those securities. The set of information for the strong form includes all private, as well as all public, information. For example, the minutes of boards of directors and the reports of biologists employed by pharmaceutical firms would be part of the set of private information. No one believes that the efficient markets hypothesis holds in the strong form. Numerous empirical studies demonstrate conclusively that corporate insiders do possess material information about the future prices of securities, and that these insiders do trade on that information.[6]

11.1.3   Random Walks and the Efficient Markets Hypothesis

There is often confusion between the efficient markets hypothesis and the hypothesis that the prices of securities are governed by a random walk. A random walk is a particular kind of stochastic process. A stochastic process is a process that generates a sequence of values for some variable by taking draws from a sequence of probability distributions. In the general case, the parameters of the probability distribution that generates the value at time t depend on the values generated at times prior to time t. That is, the distribution that governs the process at any specific time depends on the evolution of the process up to that time. A random walk is a stochastic process in which the probability distribution that generates the outcomes does not depend on the evolution of the process. In the simplest case of a random walk, the probability distribution never changes throughout the process.[7]

There is considerable evidence that the changes in the prices of stocks follow a random walk with a positive drift. The positive drift reflects the growth of the economy over the longer term. In an efficient market, the current prices of securities fully reflect all current information about the abilities of the issuing firms to generate earnings over the future. Hence, the current prices reflect all current information about the future values of those prices. Prices change over time because new information becomes available. New information, by definition, is unpredictable. Some information arrives at predictable times, such as a firm's quarterly announcement of its earnings, but the information itself is unpredictable with certainty. Other information, such as a decision by a federal court in an antitrust case, is unpredictable both in its timing and in its content. It is the unpredictability in the arrival and the content of information that causes the prices of securities to change unpredictably.[8]

Some persons misinterpret the term *random walk* to mean that the prices of securities are random in the sense that there is no logical relationship between those prices and the ability of the issuing firms to generate earnings. This is incorrect. There is a discernible logic with which one can explain the prices of securities in terms of information about firms and the economy. This logic is defined by the various asset pricing models that we have studied. It is not the prices of securities that are random. Rather it is the sequence of *changes* in the prices that is random, because the arrival of information is random.

The efficient markets hypothesis states that once information arrives, the market immediately, and without bias, adjusts the prices of securities to reflect that information so as to eliminate opportunities for risk-free profits for speculators net of transaction costs. The efficient markets hypothesis makes no claim about the timing or the significance of new information. A random walk of changes in the prices of securities is consistent with the efficient markets hypothesis.[9]

11.1.4 The Significance of the Efficient Markets Hypothesis for Economic Efficiency

The efficient markets hypothesis also has a critical bearing on the question of the efficacy of financial markets in promoting an efficient allocation of resources. In an efficient allocation of resources, all opportunities for mutually beneficial exchanges are realized. Put another way, in an efficient allocation there are no further opportunities to increase the welfare of any person (or persons) without decreasing the welfare of some other person (or persons). To allocate resources efficiently, the economy must first identify the potential mutually beneficial exchanges and then transmit information about these opportunities to the persons who own the resources. A market economy uses prices to transmit this information. Consequently, to achieve an efficient allocation of resources the prices must fully reflect the benefits and the costs of all possible exchanges.

Financial markets promote intertemporal exchanges by facilitating the trading of financial securities. In a typical intertemporal exchange, one person pays money now to acquire a financial security from a second person. The second person is often a group of persons acting through a firm, and the payments in the sequence are usually uncertain.

The price of the security is the risk-adjusted net present value of the associated sequence of payments. The prices of securities must fully reflect these net present values if the financial markets are to achieve an efficient allocation of resources.

We conclude that the efficient markets hypothesis is much more than an interesting empirical question. The hypothesis has implications for the regulation of financial markets. If the prices of securities do not fully reflect the information about sequences of payments, there will be an inefficient allocation of resources. Alternatively, if the hypothesis is correct, so that security prices do fully reflect the relevant information, then regulation of financial markets could impede an efficient allocation of resources.

The efficient markets hypothesis is a claim about informational efficiency. Economic efficiency is a criterion by which we evaluate an allocation of resources. In a complex market economy, informational efficiency is a necessary condition for economic efficiency.

11.2 Informational Efficiency, Rationality, and the Joint Hypothesis

11.2.1 The Joint Hypothesis and the Equilibrium Values of Prices

The efficient markets hypothesis is one part of a joint hypothesis that involves (1) the claim that security prices fully reflect all the information about the associated sequences of payments, and (2) a claim that prices are equal to a particular set of equilibrium values. To test the efficient markets hypothesis is to test jointly the claim that prices are at their equilibrium values and the claim that we know what the equilibrium values are.

11.2.2 A Simple Example from Introductory Economics

Consider the following heuristic example. A perfectly competitive industry is in long-run equilibrium, and the long-run industry supply curve is upward sloping. The government asks economists to predict the effect on the equilibrium price paid by consumers if a tax were imposed on each firm equal to $4 for each unit produced and sold. The economists predict that the equilibrium price to consumers would increase, but by less than $4, and that the elasticities of demand and supply would determine the size of the increase. This prediction is an elementary application of the theory of the firm. But this theory is based on several assumptions, one of which is that firms attempt to maximize profits. It is easy to show that (unless firms' marginal cost curves are horizontal) a profit-maximizing firm will not attempt to pass on the full amount of the tax to consumers in the form of a higher price.[10]

Suppose that empirical tests of the economists' predictions show that imposing a unit tax imposed on perfectly competitive firms causes the price to increase by the full amount of the tax. We could interpret this empirical result in at least two ways. First, we could conclude that the tax does increase the long-run equilibrium value of the price by less than the tax, but that the market inefficiently adjusts the price to its new equilibrium value. In particular, the market initially increases the price by the full amount of the tax, and then adjusts the price downward toward its new equilibrium value only very slowly over time. That is, the price that appears immediately after the tax is imposed does not fully reflect the information that the new (long-run) equilibrium price has increased by less than the amount of the tax.

The second possible interpretation is that firms do not attempt to maximize profits. For example, suppose that firms set prices by adding a certain markup to average total cost. In this case, imposing on each firm a tax equal to $4 for each unit produced and sold does increase the equilibrium price by $4. Under this interpretation, when the price increases by the full amount of the tax it does fully reflect the information about the new equilibrium price. In this case, the market is informationally efficient; the economists used the wrong model to predict the effect of the tax on the equilibrium price.

We conclude that any test of the effect of a tax on the equilibrium price in a competitive industry is necessarily a test of a joint hypothesis. A test of whether the price increases by less than the tax is simultaneously a test of the efficiency with which the market transmits information through prices and a test of the assumptions that underlie the economists' model of the firm. If the price increases by the full amount of the tax, it is impossible to distinguish which of the two hypotheses failed. Alternatively, suppose that the empirical tests show that the price increases by less than the tax. We cannot know whether the market is informationally efficient (because we have the correct model of the firm to predict the new equilibrium price) or whether the market is inefficient (because we are using an incorrect model of the firm).

In financial economics, the joint hypothesis is that the market quickly adjusts security prices to reflect changes in information about their equilibrium values, and that we are using the correct model to define the equilibrium values of the prices relative to the information. Recall that under the CAPM the only risk that is relevant to the equilibrium expected rate of return for a security is systematic risk relative to the market portfolio. But the CAPM might not be the correct model. Consequently, if the market fails to adjust prices to values determined by the CAPM, we cannot unambiguously conclude that the market is informationally inefficient. We shall return to the joint hypothesis frequently throughout this section.

11.2.3 Fundamental (or Intrinsic) Values of Prices

Both in the scholarly literature and in the popular press, one sees reference to the fundamental value (or the intrinsic value) of a security. The implied argument is that the market is working properly if prices are equal to their fundamental values. Of course, this argument requires a definition of fundamental value, and at this point we encounter the joint hypothesis.

We propose that the most useful definition of the fundamental value (or intrinsic value) of a security is the equilibrium value of the price of that security. Throughout economics, the equilibrium price of a good is the price at which quantity demanded is equal to quantity supplied. There is no reason to use a different definition of equilibrium price for a financial security. Arguments about the difference between the market price of a security and the *real* value of that security are specious. The real, or intrinsic, or fundamental value of any good is the value for which a person can, in fact, purchase or sell a unit of that good.[11]

By assumption, persons undertake exchanges to increase their utility. For the purpose of analyzing the prices in financial markets, we can say that persons undertake exchanges to increase their risk-adjusted levels of wealth. Leaving aside for a moment the question of adjusting for risk, recall our analysis in chapter 5 of the optimal decisions of a firm in selecting and financing investment projects. We established that in equilibrium all investors face identical marginal trade-offs between present and future consumption. Consequently, the equilibrium price of a security is the price at which any investor is indifferent between holding his or her current portfolio and changing that portfolio to include one more unit of the security (and an equivalent decrease in the holdings of other securities). In particular, the equilibrium price of a security is the net present value of the sequence of payments associated with that security.

We now extend our argument to allow for risk. In the equilibrium defined by the CAPM, all investors face the same marginal trade-off between the expected rate of return and the quantity of risk in a security. Consequently, in equilibrium no investor has an incentive to hold risky securities in proportions other than those defined by the market portfolio.

We conclude that the fundamental value of a security is the equilibrium risk-adjusted price of that security. Since there is still some disagreement among economists about the correct model to adjust for risk, the fundamental value of a security is conditional on the investigator's choice of an asset-pricing model.

11.2.4 Rationality, Changes in Prices, and Informational Efficiency

Economic actors behave rationally if they make choices that are optimal relative to their objectives. We will examine the implications of this statement for informational efficiency in financial markets.

Assume that each actor's objective is to maximize utility. The first step is to allocate wealth between consumption and investment. Specifically, actors should equate the marginal rate at which they are willing to substitute between current consumption and the risk-adjusted present value of future consumption to the marginal rate at which they can substitute between those two goods in the financial markets. For the case in which future payments are certain, the foregoing statement is analogous to our analysis of utility maximization in chapter 3. The actor's next step is to construct a portfolio of financial securities so as to maximize the expected rate of return for the level of risk that he or she is willing to bear.

What are the implications for rationality of the foregoing statements? If there is no uncertainty about future payments, a rational actor will purchase any security whose price is less than the net present value of the sequence of payments associated with that security. Similarly, the actor will sell (or sell short) any security whose price exceeds the net present value of the sequence of payments. Consequently, competition among rational economic actors will force security prices to their equilibrium values. Or rational behavior will force prices to reflect their fundamental (or intrinsic) values. By extension of this argument, security prices will change whenever new information arrives to change the net present value of the sequences of payments associated with those securities. If the interest rate rises (or if investors expect the interest rate to rise in the near future), security prices will fall. If a firm unexpectedly reports good news about the future payments that its investors can expect, the price of that firm's security will increase to equality with the upwardly revised net present value of the future payments.

We have the same conclusion when future payments are uncertain if we modify the term *net present value* with the qualifier *risk-adjusted*. Competition among rational economic actors will force security prices to equality with the risk-adjusted net present values of the associated sequences of payments. By extension, prices will change whenever new information causes investors' perceptions to reevaluate the risk-adjusted net present values of the future payments.

In summary, rational movements in security prices are movements that realign the prices to reflect new information about the associated sequences of payments. By implication, a market is informationally efficient if security prices change rationally and without delay. The longer the market takes to adjust prices to new information, the longer the prices fail to reflect the risk-adjusted net present values of the underlying sequences of payments.

11.2.5 Bubbles

Finally, what about bubbles? We suggest that a good definition of a bubble is a departure of a price from the risk-adjusted net present value of the associated sequence of payments. Under this definition of a bubble, competition among rational investors will eventually force the price back to the risk-adjusted net present value, thus "bursting" the bubble. The amount of time required for rational investors to burst the bubble is a measure of the informational efficiency of the market. A perfectly efficient market would prevent bubbles entirely. Using our definition of a bubble, the phrase *irrational bubble* is a redundancy.

There is a temptation (which is irresistible for many commentators in the popular press) to classify as a bubble any rapid increase in the price of a security (or the general level of security prices) that is subsequently abruptly reversed. We have here another instance of the joint hypothesis. One explanation for a rapid increase of prices followed by an abrupt reversal is that investors perceived some information that warranted their reevaluating risk-adjusted net present values, and then subsequently perceived some information that led to a reversal of their earlier evaluations. Information, even accurate information, can be volatile. Think of a sportscaster reporting by radio on the progress of an athletic contest in which the lead between the competing teams changes abruptly and frequently. In a market in which sports fans bet on the outcome of the contest, the odds offered by bookies could change frequently to reflect the volatility of information about the abilities of the contestants. One might be tempted to identify bubbles in such a market.

A competing explanation for an abruptly reversed movement in a price is that after observing an increase in a price, which increase could have been a rational response to new information, investors continued to submit buy orders simply because prices are rising. This behavior is not rational as we have used the term here; the behavior is rather an instance of "monkey see, monkey do." Without knowing much more about the reasons why investors place orders, it is risky to conclude that sharp movements in prices are bubbles.

11.3   A Simple Example of Informational Efficiency

In this section, we present an extremely simple model of the adjustment of the price of a security to new information. An informationally efficient market keeps the price of each security at its equilibrium value. When new information arrives that changes the equilibrium price, an efficient market will adjust the price immediately to its new equilibrium value. Since we define informational efficiency in terms of the equilibrium values of prices, we must have a model that defines these equilibrium values. We will use a simple version of the CAPM to define equilibrium.

11.3.1   Risk-Adjusted Residuals and Informational Efficiency

As stated in earlier chapters, most of the analysis of the prices of financial securities is conducted by examining the rates of return on the security, rather than by examining the prices themselves. The rate of return on a security is the sum of the current dividend (or payment of interest, in the case of a bond) and any change in the price of the security. If at time t the market adjusts the price of a security to reflect new information, then part of the rate of return on that security for time t is attributable to the new information. To evaluate the informational efficiency of a market, economists disaggregate the rate of return on a security into the sum of the equilibrium rate of return for that security and an excess or residual rate of return. The excess rate of return (which can be positive, negative, or zero) on a security is that part of the rate of return that cannot be attributed to a reward for waiting or to a reward for bearing risk. In a perfectly efficient market, nonzero residuals occur only when the market adjusts prices to reflect new information. Moreover, since informational efficiency requires that the adjustment is immediate, nonzero residuals must not persist for any appreciable time after the information arrives. By definition, a residual is the amount by which the rate of return differs from the (risk-adjusted) equilibrium rate of return.

Therefore, a persistence of nonzero residuals means a persistence of the price of the security away from its equilibrium value. Consequently, economists evaluate the efficiency of a market by examining the behavior of residuals around the times when new information arrives.

11.3.2 Using the Capital Asset Pricing Model to Define Equilibrium

For the present example, we use the CAPM to define the equilibrium prices. Suppose that the earnings of the ES&D Railroad are uncorrelated with the behavior of the macroeconomy. Consequently, the value of the CAPM beta for the railroad is zero. Then the equilibrium expected rate of return for the common stock issued by the railroad is equal to the rate of return on the risk-free asset. Assume that this (annual) rate of return is equal to .10. Let the annual earnings per share be $10. Then the equilibrium price of a share of the ES&D Railroad is $10/.10, or $100. To keep the example simple, assume that all the earnings are paid out in dividends each year.

Let time t be the beginning of year t. Let P_t be the price of a share at time t, and let D_t be the dividend per share paid at time t. Assuming that securities are priced *ex dividend*, the rate of return for an investor who holds a share of the railroad's stock during year t is:

$$RR_t = (P_{t+1} + D_{t+1} - P_t)/P_t$$
$$= (\$100 + \$10 - \$100)/\$100 \tag{11.1}$$
$$= .10.$$

Under the CAPM, the equilibrium expected rate of return on Security i for year t, conditional on the rate of return on the market portfolio for that year, is:

$$RR_t^e = R_f + (R_{M,t} - R_f)\beta_i, \tag{11.2}$$

in which R_f is the rate of return on the risk-free asset, $R_{M,t}$ is the rate of return on the market portfolio for year t, and β_i is the slope of the characteristic line for Security i.

Since the value of beta for the ES&D Railroad is equal to zero, the equilibrium expected rate of return on its common stock for year t is:

$$RR_t^e = R_f + (R_{M,t})0$$
$$= .10. \tag{11.3}$$

Define the excess (or residual) rate of return for the railroad for year t as:

$$X_t = RR_t - RR_t^e$$
$$= RR_t - .10. \tag{11.4}$$

For any year t, the residual rate of return for the railroad is the excess of the rate of return for that year over the equilibrium (according to the CAPM) rate of return for the railroad for that year.

In the absence of new information about the railroad's future earnings, the price of its stock will not change from one year to the next. Consequently, the rate of return will be constant at .10, and the excess rate of return will be constant at 0.

Now suppose that at time $t+1$ investors learn that the earnings per share have increased from $10 to $12, and that the railroad can sustain this higher level of earnings permanently. The new equilibrium price for a share is $12/.10, or $120, and the rate of return for year t is:

$$RR_t = (P_{t+1} + D_{t+1} - P_t)/P_t$$
$$= (\$120 + \$12 - \$100)/\$100 \qquad (11.5)$$
$$= \$32/\$100 = .32.$$

Using equation (11.4), we can resolve this rate of return into the equilibrium rate of return and the excess rate of return:

$$X_t = RR_t - RR_t^e$$
$$= .32 - .10 \qquad (11.6)$$
$$= .22.$$

An investor who held a share during year t enjoyed a rate of return that is 22 percentage points above the equilibrium rate of return. Two percentage points of this excess are attributable to the unexpected increase of $2 in the dividend for time t. The unexpected $2 at time $t+1$ provides an excess rate of return on the investor's investment of $100 at time t equal to $2/$100, or .02. Similarly, 20 percentage points of the excess return arise because the price of the share increased by $20, which is the present value of the permanent increase in the dividend rate. The $20 increase in the value of the share provides a rate of return for the investor of $20/$100, or .20.

Unless there is additional information that arrives after time $t+1$, the price of the share will remain at $120. Since the dividend will remain at $12, the rate of return from time $t+1$ onward will be:

$$RR_{t+1} = (P_{t+2} + D_{t+2} - P_{t+1})/P_{t+1}$$
$$= (\$120 + \$12 - \$120)/\$120$$
$$= \$12/\$120 \qquad (11.7)$$
$$= .10,$$

and the excess rate of return will be:

$$X_{t+1} = RR_{t+1} - RR_{t+1}^e$$
$$= .10 - .10 \qquad (11.8)$$
$$= 0.$$

11.3.3 Efficient Changes in Prices When There Is New Information

If the market is perfectly efficient, the residuals of the rates of return over time should be zero except for those times when investors learn new information. On those occasions, the residuals should be large enough so that the price of the security adjusts instantaneously and fully to the new information.

In figure 11.1, we have plotted the residuals for the rate of return for the ES&D Railroad on the vertical axis. On the horizontal axis, we measure time relative to the time at which a well-defined event occurs. Usually, the event is the first appearance of the new information. Economists use the term *event time* to describe this organization

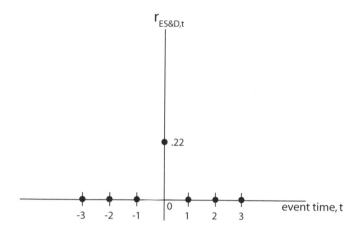

Figure 11.1. Efficient adjustment to new information.

of time. Thus, in our example, the information that the earnings per share will increase permanently from $10 to $12 appears at event time 0. The point 1 on the horizontal axis is event time 1, which is one period after the new information appears. The point −3 on the horizontal axis is event time −3, which occurs three periods before the new information appears. In our example, the new information appears at calendar time *t*.

In figure 11.1, we have plotted the residuals for the case in which the market is perfectly efficient. Before investors learn at event time 0 that earnings will increase, the equilibrium price of a share of the railroad is $100, the rate of return is .10, and the residuals are zero. At event time 0, the new information arrives. Competition among investors forces the price immediately to $120. The increase of $20 in the price of the share and the increase of $2 in the current dividend provides a residual (or excess) rate of return equal to .22, as we explained in the preceding section. Since the price of the share is fully adjusted at event time 0 to the new information, there is no further adjustment to that price in subsequent periods. Consequently, the residuals return to 0 beginning in event time +1 and remain at 0 unless an additional piece of new information arrives.

In an informationally efficient market, there is no opportunity to obtain an excess rate of return by watching the pattern of the residuals. Since beta is equal to zero for the railroad, the opportunity cost for holding the share is the rate of return on the risk-free asset. Investors who purchase shares after observing the positive residual at event time 0 will earn no more than their opportunity costs because the market has already adjusted the price fully to the new information. In order to earn more than the opportunity cost, an investor must obtain positive residuals after event time 0. But in an efficient market, the residuals will be zero after event time 0.

What about purchasing the security prior to event time 0? Investors who can anticipate that a positive residual will occur at event time 0 can earn more than their opportunity costs. But the existence of such an investor is incompatible with an efficient market. To anticipate the positive residual is to know about the new information prior to event time 0. If the information is available to anyone prior to event time 0, a perfectly efficient market must adjust the price of the security prior to event time 0.

In the following section, we consider implications for residuals for cases in which some investors acquire new information before other investors do.

11.3.4 Inefficient Changes in Prices When There Is New Information

A financial market is informationally efficient if the price of each security is always equal to the risk-adjusted net present value of the sequence of payments associated with that security. Consequently, an efficient market will adjust prices immediately to new information. Any delay in the adjustment of prices means that investors cannot rely on those prices to measure the net present values of the associated investment projects. Accurate information about the sequences of earnings is essential if the markets are to allocate resources efficiently.

If there is a delay in the adjustment of a security's price to new information, there will be a persistence of nonzero residuals around the time that the new information appears. Consider again the example of the preceding section. At calendar time t, there is information that the dividends per share have increased from $10 to $12 and that the higher rate will persist indefinitely. Figure 11.2 illustrates a delayed (and thus inefficient) adjustment of the price. Suppose that the market requires four periods to adjust the price from $100, which represents the old information, to $120, which represents the new information. In panel (a) we show the adjustment of the price. Since the adjustment occurs over three periods, the nonzero residuals persist over those three periods. In panel (b) we show the residuals that correspond to the adjustments of the price. In each case, we calculate the residual using equations (11.1) through (11.4).

Figure 11.3 illustrates a second example of an inefficient adjustment of the price of a share of the ES&D Railroad. In this case, the market first delays the adjustment of the price and then overadjusts the price. The overadjustment requires a subsequent correction. After the new information appears, the first residual is positive, which is followed by two negative residuals. The residuals return to zero only after the market finally establishes the price at $120, with no further adjustments. We show the

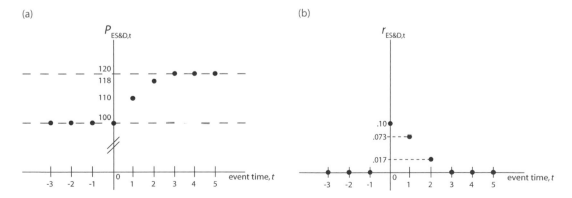

Figure 11.2. Inefficient (delayed) adjustment to new information: (a) the behavior of the price; (b) the behavior of the residuals.

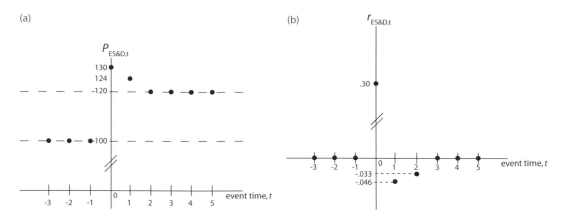

Figure 11.3. Inefficient adjustment to new information (an overadjustment, followed by a delayed correction): (a) the behavior of the price; (b) the behavior of the residuals.

pattern of the prices in panel (a) of figure 11.3; we exhibit the corresponding residuals in panel (b).

By definition, a residual is a rate of return that exceeds the investor's (risk-adjusted) opportunity costs. Therefore, the persistence of nonzero residuals displayed in figures 11.2 and 11.3 provides opportunities for investors to earn economic profits. An investor obtains economic profits by purchasing a security in advance of positive residuals and selling (or selling short) a security in advance of negative residuals.

In the case of the delayed adjustment displayed in figure 11.2, the first appearance of a positive residual is a signal that positive residuals will continue because the market has not fully adjusted the price to the new information. (In terms of changes in the price, the first change in the price signals that there will be a continuation of changes in the same direction.) In the case of the overadjustment displayed in figure 11.3, the investor first purchases shares in the railroad in anticipation of positive residuals. Once the residuals become negative, the investor then sells those shares, and perhaps sells short additional shares, in anticipation of further negative residuals.

The alert reader is likely to be skeptical about the procedure just described for obtaining economic profits. There are good reasons for skepticism. First, there is the problem of the joint hypothesis. In calculating the risk-adjusted residuals, we have assumed that the CAPM is the correct model to adjust for risk. If investors use the wrong model to calculate residuals, then the investors will incorrectly estimate the equilibrium price to which the market will (should) eventually adjust the price.

Consider the following example. Suppose that an investor plans to purchase a gasoline filling station at a price based on the profit that the current owner is receiving. Shortly before the sale is concluded, the government announces an increase in the tax per gallon. Although the demand for gasoline is highly price-inelastic, the demand function for gasoline still slopes downward. Consequently, the dealer cannot (except in the relatively short run) increase the price per gallon by the full amount of the increase in the tax without suffering a reduction in the volume of gasoline sold per week. Some of the costs of operating a gasoline station are fixed (such as property taxes, the opportunity cost of the capital invested in the land, etc.). The greater the fixed costs, the more important the volume of sales in the generation of a profit. If the investor assumes that the full amount of the tax can be passed on to the consumer with no loss in sales, she is using the wrong model. Using the wrong model will lead her to pay too high a price for the station. Her revenue could fall short of her opportunity costs, making her profit negative.

The second problem in using residuals as the basis of an investment strategy is that calculating residuals is costly. Explicit costs are incurred to collect the data and perform the calculations, and opportunity costs are incurred to analyze those data.

Third, the strategies implied by figures 11.2 and 11.3 require frequent purchases and sales. Each of these transactions incurs costs in the form of brokers' commissions and taxes.

Finally, an investor who trades in anticipation of nonzero residuals must hold a portfolio that is inefficient in the context of modern portfolio theory. According to the CAPM, the investor should hold risky securities in the proportions determined by the market portfolio. An investor who temporarily purchases or sells securities in pursuit of nonzero residuals necessarily holds a portfolio that does not offer an efficient combination of expected rate of return and risk. Consequently, an investor who pursues excess profits by trading on residuals incurs a cost in the form of accepting a lower expected rate of return on the portfolio given the level of risk in that portfolio.

11.4   A Second Example of Informational Efficiency: Predictability of Returns—Bubbles or Rational Variations of Expected Returns?

The early empirical tests of the efficient markets hypothesis supported the proposition that risk-adjusted rates of return are not predictable (aside from a small upward drift imparted by the historical tendency of the economy to grow over long periods of time). In the CAPM, each security's beta has a constant value over time. After allowing for changes in the rate of return on the market portfolio from one period to the next, any variation in the rate of return on a security is attributable solely to firm-specific risk, which is unpredictable. The efficient markets hypothesis stimulated a large amount of empirical work, which demonstrated that to some extent rates of return are predictable, even after adjusting for risk. Consequently, the major current issue in the debate about the efficient markets hypothesis is whether the predictability of rates of return is evidence of (irrational) bubbles or a consequence of rational variations in expected returns. That is, are we predicting (risk-adjusted) rates of return even though each security's beta is constant over time, or are we in fact predicting shifts in the values of beta for those securities? In this section, we discuss this question in the context of a simple example based on the relationship between the size of a firm and its expected rate of return.

11.4.1 The Size Effect as an Example of a Rational Change in Expected Returns

Early empirical tests of the CAPM were encouraging. The average rate of return on a security appeared to be linearly related to the value of the beta for that security. Equivalently, the difference in the average rates of return for any two securities was proportional to the difference in the beta values for those securities, just as the security market line of the CAPM predicts. Of course, no one would expect a linear model as simple as the CAPM to predict exactly the empirical relationship between the levels of risk and the average rates of return across all securities. Thus, economists were not surprised to find some dispersion of the data points for beta and average rate of return around the security market line.

Subsequent and closer examination of the empirical tests of the CAPM revealed that the dispersion of the data points around the security market line was not random. There is a systematic relationship between the size of a firm and the location of the data point for that firm relative to the security market line. The size of a firm is the aggregate market value of its outstanding securities. (In the simplest applications, the size of a firm is the price of its common stock multiplied by the number of shares outstanding.) The data points for small firms were more likely to be above the security market line than below it.

The height of the security market line over a given value of beta is the equilibrium value of the average rate of return that an investor should receive in exchange for bearing the level of risk represented by that value of beta. Consequently, a security is underpriced if the point representing its beta and its average rate of return is located above the security market line. (The average rate of return on that security is too high relative to the level of risk in that security.) According to the CAPM, the market systematically underprices the securities of small firms. Economists call this phenomenon the size effect.

The size effect has two competing implications that correspond to the two parts of the joint hypothesis. The first implication is that the market is systematically inefficient because the securities of small firms are underpriced. The second implication is that the CAPM is an incorrect specification of the relationship between risk and average return.

An essential property of equilibrium in any market is that no one has an incentive to change the allocation of her resources. Applied to a financial market, equilibrium requires that the relative prices of securities are such that no investor can obtain an excess risk-adjusted return by holding the securities of small firms in proportions larger than those which appear in the market portfolio. But this condition is violated if the market systematically misprices the securities of small firms. If the combinations of beta and average return for small firms lie above the security market line, then the combination of risk and average return for a portfolio of small firms will lie above the capital market line. A portfolio that lies above the capital market line offers an excess risk-adjusted average return, in violation of the definition of equilibrium.

Just as nature abhors a vacuum, economists abhor the notion that a market can be systematically out of equilibrium. One way to resolve an apparent disequilibrium is to reexamine the model used to define the equilibrium.

As we saw in chapter 10, Eugene Fama and Kenneth French proposed and tested multifactor asset-pricing models that include a factor for the size of the firm. These models have resolved several of the anomalies in the empirical testing of the CAPM.

11.4.2 A Change in the Size of a Firm as an Example of a Rational Change in the Expected Return

In this section, we present a simple example of how what might appear to be a predictable nonzero residual for a security could, in fact, be a rational variation in the risk-adjusted expected rate of return for that security. Suppose that investors regard small firms as riskier than large firms. Specifically, the expected rate of return that investors require to hold the security of a given firm depends both on the beta for that firm and on the size of the firm. If two firms have the same value for beta, investors will require a higher expected rate of return to hold the security of the smaller firm. Consider the following simple adjustment to the expected rate of return based on the size of the firm.

Let P_i be the price per share of the stock of Firm i, and let N_i be the number of shares outstanding. Then the size of Firm i is:

$$S_i = P_i N_i. \tag{11.9}$$

Let S_{ave} be the average size of the firms in the economy. Let δ be a positive constant. Suppose that the equilibrium expected rate of return for Firm i is:

$$E_i = R_f + (E_M - R_f)\beta_i + \delta(S_{\text{ave}} - S_i), \tag{11.10}$$

The first two terms on the right side of equation (11.10) are the equation for the security market line of the CAPM. The third term on the right side of (11.10) is the adjustment to the expected rate of return based on the size of Firm i relative to the average size of firms in the economy. Since δ is positive, the term $\delta(S_{\text{ave}} - S_i)$ adjusts the equilibrium expected rate of return upward for firms that are smaller than the average size of firms, and downward for firms that are larger than the average.

We emphasize that the model specified by equation (11.10) is only an example of how one might construct an alternative to the CAPM in an attempt to eliminate the risk-adjusted residuals that are systematically related to the size of firms in that model. In chapter 10 we discussed the three-factor model proposed by Fama and French that adjusts the equilibrium returns defined by the CAPM by adding terms for the size of the firm and for the ratio of the firm's book equity to its market equity.

Predictable risk-adjusted residuals are incompatible with an informationally efficient market. We will now use the model in equation (11.10) to present an example of how the existence of predictable residuals could be reconciled with an efficient market.

The model in equation (11.10) states that the expected rate of return for Firm i will change if the size of that firm changes (relative to the average size of firms). Suppose there is evidence that some variable, call it Z, is correlated with subsequent values of residuals under the CAPM. Specifically, let $Z_{i,t}$ be the value of Z for Firm i at time t. Let $X_{i,t}$ be the risk-adjusted residuals for Firm i at time t according to the CAPM. Finally, suppose that for some $\tau > 0$, the variable $Z_{i,t}$ is highly correlated with the values of $X_{i,t+1}, \ldots, X_{i,t+\tau}$. Then an investor could use information about $Z_{i,t}$ to predict the residuals for Firm i during the interval from time $t+1$ through time $t+\tau$. This ability to predict residuals violates the efficient markets hypothesis under the CAPM. But suppose that the modified CAPM in equation (11.10) is the correct model of equilibrium. Then the apparent ability to predict residuals by using the variable Z is specious. Let $Z_{i,t}$ be correlated with future changes in the size of Firm i. If equation (11.10) is the correct model of equilibrium, then information about $Z_{i,t}$ is information about the future expected rate of return for Firm i. An informationally efficient market is rational in the sense that the prices of securities reflect the available information about the values of the correctly risk-adjusted net present values of the associated sequences of payments. Nonzero residuals can be a rational response to new information.

11.5   Informational Efficiency and the Predictability of Returns

In this section, we provide a brief review of the main issues in the literature on the efficient markets hypothesis. For a rigorous and comprehensive treatment of this literature, readers should work through the paper by Eugene Fama, cited earlier, and the literature that has appeared subsequent to that paper.

11.5.1   A Brief Synopsis of the Debate

Following Fama, the debate about the efficient markets hypothesis is between those who argue that the predictability of returns (or equivalently, the predictability of residuals) is evidence of rational adjustment of expected rates of return to new information, and those who argue that the predictability of returns indicates bubbles. The debate has two dimensions. One dimension is the predictability of returns for given securities over time. The other is the predictability of returns across securities at a given time. The economists on each side of the debate have sophisticated empirical studies to support their positions. Nevertheless, as we explained earlier in this chapter, all tests of informational efficiency involve the joint hypothesis, and consequently many questions cannot be finally resolved.

11.5.2   The Challenge from Thaler and deBondt

The economists Richard Thaler and Werner deBondt raised a challenge to the Efficient Markets Hypothesis by presenting evidence of irrational behavior by investors.[12] Specifically, investors systematically form incorrect expectations about the continuation of recent movements in security prices. This research has led to a new set of hypotheses called *behavioral finance*, in which psychological considerations compete with theoretical asset pricing models to explain the empirical behavior of rates of return.[13]

Thaler and deBondt show that stocks that have abnormally high rates of return over a period of years have abnormally low rates of return over a subsequent period of years, and that the converse is also true.[14] These economists suggest that investors irrationally project recent movements too far into the future. Consequently, investors purchase stocks that have recorded high returns in the expectation that the high returns will persist. These (irrational) purchases of recent winners in pursuit of a continuation of the high returns forces the prices of these stocks far above their equilibrium values. The ensuing correction brings prices back down, causing abnormally low, or even negative, returns until the market reestablishes the prices at their equilibrium values.

Similarly, investor sell (or sell short) stocks whose recent returns are abnormally low, forcing the prices of these stocks far below their equilibrium values. The subsequent correction creates abnormally high returns until the prices regain their equilibrium values.

Of course, an "abnormal" rate of return is a return that differs from the risk-adjusted rate of return predicted by an asset pricing model. But which model is the correct one? Other economists claim that the phenomenon reported by Thaler and deBondt is attributable to a failure to adjust the returns correctly for risk, particularly for the sizes of the firms. Thaler and deBondt disagree, and the question is clouded by the joint hypothesis.

11.5.3 The Challenge from Summers and Shiller

There is evidence that residuals are autocorrelated. That is, information about current or past residuals is of some value in predicting the future values of those residuals. An investor can use these autocorrelations to obtain excess returns if the transaction costs are low enough. Some economists argue that, although the correlations are reliable, they are too close to zero to overcome the transaction costs, and thus the statistical relationship among the residuals has no economic significance.[15]

Summers and Shiller reject the argument that the market can be informationally efficient even in the presence of reliable, but small, autocorrelations.[16] These economists "present simple models in which prices can take large slowly decaying swings away from fundamental values (fads or irrational bubbles) but short-horizon returns have little autocorrelation."[17] If prices do take large departures from fundamental values, and return only slowly to those values, then the market is informationally inefficient, because investors cannot rely on security prices to provide accurate information about the net present values of sequences of payments.

11.5.4 Conclusion Thus Far

In this subsection, we have presented a brief context for the debate on the implications of the predictability of returns for the efficient markets hypothesis. The literature in this area is so voluminous and specialized that a comprehensive survey is far beyond the scope of this book.

Three conclusions are probably safe, however. First, however the debate proceeds from its current state, the CAPM has generated both theoretical and empirical research that has significantly advanced our knowledge of how financial markets set the prices of securities. In particular, both academics and professionals have accepted the principle that the correct measure of risk of a security involves a correlation between the rate of return on that security and the rates of return on one or more special portfolios.

The second conclusion is that after taking transaction costs into account, the market is efficient enough to eliminate all opportunities for excess returns except for investors who either have very low transaction costs or who have a strong comparative advantage in acquiring and analyzing new information rapidly and accurately.

The third conclusion addresses the value created by speculators. Readers should recall from their introductory courses that the basis of a mutually beneficial exchange of a good is that two (or more) persons differ either in the marginal costs at which they can produce that good, or in the marginal values that they place on that good, or both. The good in question can be an informationally efficient financial market. All investors benefit from an efficient market. Some investors specialize in discovering prices that do not fully reflect the information about the net present values of the associated sequences of payments. Economists define as speculators the investors who search for these incorrect prices. Competition among speculators forces prices to reflect the information that the speculators have acquired. Thus speculators produce a good by making markets more efficient than they would otherwise be.

What about the investors whose comparative advantage in speculating is so weak that they trade in the wrong direction, creating pressure on prices to depart further from net present values? These adverse movements of prices create even more opportunities for the more competent speculators to gain profits. The actions of the competent speculators will imposes losses on the incompetent ones, thus weeding them out.

11.6 Informational Efficiency and the Speed of Adjustment of Prices to Public Information

Public information is information that is available to the typical investor at little or no cost to that investor. Examples of public information include announcements by firms of projected or realized earnings, changes in financial structure, changes in senior management, and the status of litigation. Announcements by governmental agencies such as the Federal Reserve and the Departments of Commerce and Labor are also public information. In short, public information includes everything that the typical investor can obtain for the price of a newspaper or the cost of turning on a television set.

The efficient markets hypothesis requires that "prices reflect information to the point where the marginal benefits of acting on information (the profits to be made) do not exceed the marginal costs."[18] The empirical tests of the efficient markets hypothesis with respect to public information involve event studies, which we present in the next chapter. The consensus among economists is that the efficient markets hypothesis is verified with respect to public information. Consequently, unless an investor has an unusually strong comparative advantage in obtaining public information quickly, analyzing correctly its likely effect on prices, and trading quickly on that information at low transaction costs, it is highly unlikely that the investor will obtain profits that cover the marginal costs.

Informational Efficiency and the Speed of Adjustment of Prices to Private Information

The most demanding form of the efficient markets hypothesis is that the prices of securities fully reflect all information, including private information.[19] Under this form of the hypothesis, even persons with access to private information, such as officers of corporations and principals of investment banks, could not obtain (risk-adjusted) excess returns. Unsurprisingly, the empirical evidence does not support the efficient markets hypothesis with respect to private information. In this section, we provide a brief review of the evidence.

11.7.1 Insider Trading

There is strong evidence that corporate insiders do trade on private information, and that they do so profitably.[20] To trade profitably requires purchasing (or selling) a security in advance of the market's adjusting the price of that security to positive (or negative) information. That is, the insiders are able to predict nonzero risk-adjusted residuals. Since predictable residuals violate the efficient markets hypothesis, the market is not efficient with respect to private information.

That the market does not fully reflect private information did not surprise economists. What did surprise economists was evidence presented by Jeffrey Jaffe that investors who are not corporate insiders could also obtain nonzero residuals by mimicking the trades of the insiders for up to eight months after the insiders' trades became public knowledge.[21] This is a violation of the less demanding form of the efficient markets hypothesis, namely that security prices fully (and immediately) reflect all public information.

The Securities and Exchange Act of 1934 defines insiders as the senior officers and the directors of corporations, and persons who hold more than 10% of the stock. The act requires insiders to report their trades to the Securities and Exchange Commission by the tenth day of the month following the month in which the trade occurred. (Most insiders report their trades within a few days of the trades.) The commission publishes these reports one day after receiving them. Any investor can use these public reports to mimic the insiders' trades. If the market is efficient with respect to public information, the prices of the securities in which the insiders traded should fully reflect the information on which the insiders traded. Consequently, it should be impossible for outsiders to obtain nonzero residuals by mimicking the insiders' trades.

Economists treated as anomalous the market's apparent failure to adjust security prices to reflect the insiders' information soon enough to prevent opportunities for outsiders to mimic insiders profitably. As is usual with anomalies, economists diligently searched for explanations. The resolution is an example of the confounding effect of the joint hypothesis. Specifically, the anomaly arises because the distribution of insiders' purchases and sales is systematically related to the sizes of firms, and the CAPM has no adjustment for the size of the firm.

Purchases of securities by insiders are more likely to occur in small firms, while sales by insiders are more likely to occur in large firms. Jaffe used the CAPM to measure residuals. Recall that the CAPM systematically underprices small firms. Using these facts, N. Nejat Seyhun demonstrated that the ability of outsiders to obtain risk-adjusted residuals by mimicking insiders depends on using the CAPM to measure the residuals.[22] That is, the anomaly is not robust with respect to the choice of model to define equilibrium.

11.7.2 Security Analysts

The question here is, can security analysts identify mispriced securities with sufficient precision to allow their clients to obtain excess (risk-adjusted) returns net of transaction and opportunity costs? There is strong evidence that the answer is no, although there are a few anomalies. The apparent ability of the Value Line Investment Survey to identify mispriced securities is best known of these anomalies. The anomaly has been the subject of many empirical tests. Some economists argue that the residuals that investors can predict by using Value Line are not, in fact, excess returns. Rather, these residuals are indications of rational changes in risk-adjusted expected returns.

There is no clear resolution to the Value Line anomaly. Significantly, one economist "reports that the strong long-term performance of Value Line's group 1 stocks is weak after 1993. Over the 6.5 years from 1984 to mid-1990, group 1 stocks earned 16.9% per year compared with 15.2% for the Wilshire 5000 index. During the same period, Value Line's Centurion Fund, which specializes in group 1 stocks, earned 12.7% per year—live testimony to the fact that there can be large gaps between simulated profits from private information and what is available in practice."[23]

The preponderance of the evidence is that investors cannot obtain excess returns by relying on analysts. Quoting again from Fama:

> The evidence is that Value Line and some security analysts have private information that, when revealed, results in small but statistically reliable price adjustments. These results are consistent with the "noisy rational expectations" model of competitive equilibrium of Grossman and Stiglitz (1980). In brief, because generating information has costs, informed investors are compensated for the costs they incur to ensure that prices adjust to information. The market is then less than fully efficient (there can be private information not fully reflected in prices), but in a way that is consistent with rational behavior by all investors.[24]

The term *rational behavior* includes the condition that it is only excess returns net of opportunity costs (including transaction costs) that should count as evidence against the efficient markets hypothesis.

We conclude this section with some disturbing evidence against the hypothesis that investors are rational. Economists Brad M. Barber and Terrance Odean examined the performance of a large sample of investors who managed their own portfolios rather than investing indirectly through mutual funds and pension funds. According to these economists, in 1996 almost one-half of the common stocks in the United States were owned directly by households. The evidence is that the majority of these households traded so frequently that they did significantly less well than they would have done if they held more passive portfolios, such as they could have done by investing in mutual funds that track the major indexes. Barber and Odean titled the article "Trading Is Hazardous to Your Wealth." Quoting from the abstract:

> Individual investors who hold common stocks directly pay a tremendous performance penalty for active trading. Of 66,465 households with accounts at a large discount broker during 1991 to 1996, those that trade most earn an annual return of 11.4%, while the market returns 17.9%. The average household earns an annual return of 16.4%, tilts its common stock investment toward high-beta, small, value stocks, and turns over 75% of its portfolio annually. Overconfidence can explain high trading levels and the resulting poor performance of individual investors. Our central message is trading is hazardous to your wealth.[25]

11.7.3 Professional Portfolio Management

Finally, we briefly review the tests of the efficient markets hypothesis regarding mutual funds and pension funds. The question is whether the professional managers of these funds possess private information that enables them to outperform the market. Since we measure performance on a risk-adjusted basis, the empirical work on this question necessarily encounters the problems of the joint hypothesis.

Michael Jensen performed the seminal work on this question in 1968 and 1969.[26] In his study of mutual funds, and using the CAPM to define risk-adjusted rates of return, Jensen found that the average returns to investors in mutual funds, after subtracting the management fees and other expenses that the funds assess on their investors, fall about 1% below the security market line.[27] "Jensen concludes that mutual fund managers do not have private information."[28]

Studies subsequent to that of Jensen have presented evidence that mutual fund managers can generate returns gross of expenses that lie above the security market line, and therefore do have private information that the market has not reflected in security prices. At the level of the individual investor, however, it is returns net of expenses that matter. The evidence supports the conclusion that the expenses, which include the compensation of the managers, absorb the value of the managers' private information, leaving the net returns close to the security market line. There is also some evidence that any excess returns obtained by mutual funds are negatively related to expenses and turnover. This result suggests that the managers of these funds invest too much of the investors' funds in the search for mispriced securities.

11.8 Information Trading, Liquidity Trading, and the Cost of Capital for a Firm

In this subsection, we explain the relationship among the informational efficiency of a financial market, the liquidity of a firm's securities, and the firm's cost of capital. The first step is to explain the concept of the cost of capital for a firm.

11.8.1 The Cost of Capital for a Firm

The cost of capital for a firm is the rate of return that the firm must offer to investors to induce them to finance a project. The firm can infer the value of its cost of capital from the ratio of its earnings per share to the market price of a share. For example, suppose that the earnings per share of the ES&D Railroad are $12, and the price of a share of the railroad's stock is $100. Then the investors who hold the railroad's stock receive a rate of return of .12 on their investment. We conclude that the rate of return of .12 covers the investors' opportunity costs, because otherwise competition among the investors to sell their shares and invest the funds elsewhere would drive the price of the share down from $100. As the price of the share decreases, the ratio of the railroad's earnings per share to the price of a share increases until the rate of return for investors who hold those shares covers their opportunity costs.

We know that a firm can increase the wealth of its shareholders by undertaking any project that has a positive net present value. If the railroad issues new securities to finance a project, those securities become additional claims on the earnings of the entire firm. That is, both the new securities and the previously issued securities are claims to the earnings of the railroad's portfolio of projects. Usually, the firm cannot (or does not) issue securities that are claims to the earnings of a specific project.[29] Consequently, when calculating the net present value of a proposed project, it is critical that the firm use the cost of capital implied by the price of the firm's shares to discount the future earnings expected from the project. If a firm uses a discount rate that is less than its cost of capital when calculating the present value of a project, the firm will overstate the effect on its shareholders' wealth of undertaking that project. If the overstatement is sufficiently large, undertaking that project will cause the shareholders to lose wealth.[30]

Consider the following example. Prior to the unexpected imposition of a tax on the earnings of railroads, the ES&D Railroad planned to improve its roadbed to permit an increase in the speeds at which trains can operate. The railroad planned to finance the project by selling new securities. As we explained above, the price of the railroad's shares implied that the railroad's cost of capital is .12. Using that rate of return, the proposed project had a positive net present value. Therefore, had the tax not been imposed, the railroad could have increased its shareholders' wealth by undertaking the project.

The imposition of the tax reduces the railroad's earnings per share from $12 to $10, and as a result the price of a share falls from $100 to $83.33. At the lower price per share, the shareholders are again receiving a (net of tax) rate of return of .12. Had there been no change in the price of the railroad's outstanding securities to reflect the effect of the tax, the investors who hold the railroad's securities would have suffered a reduction in the rate of return on their investment. These investors would then have had an incentive to sell their shares in the ES&D Railroad and invest their funds in the securities of other firms whose earnings are not subject to the tax. But no investors would purchase the railroad's securities unless their price fell by enough to offset the effect of the tax. Consequently, the announcement of the tax will reduce the price of a railroad's outstanding securities. Moreover, if the market is informationally efficient, the price of the share will change immediately from $100 to $83.33.[31]

Since the additional earnings created by the project will be subject to the new tax, the net present value of the project will be less than it would have been without the tax. If the net present value of the project inclusive of the tax is negative, the railroad can no longer undertake the project profitably.

In effect, the imposition of the tax increases the firm's cost of capital. Without the tax, the net present value of the project is positive when the future earnings of the project are discounted at a rate of .12. That is, the project generates a rate of return that is greater than .12. If the railroad's cost of capital were, say, .15, the project would have to generate earnings at a rate greater than .15 if its net present value is to be positive. Since the net present value varies inversely with the rate at which the future payments are discounted, increasing the discount rate sufficiently would cause the net present value of the project to become negative. If the tax is high enough to make the net present value negative, the effect of the tax is the same as an increase the firm's cost of capital. Namely, the project must generate earnings at a higher rate if its net present value is to be positive. In the following section, we explain how a decrease in the liquidity of the firm's securities increases the firm's cost of capital, just as a tax on the firm's earnings has the effect of increasing the cost of capital.

As a second example, suppose that investors believe that the railroad's earnings will become more sensitive to unpredictable fluctuations in the performance of the macroeconomy. Under the CAPM, the railroad's beta will increase, which will require an increase in the expected rate of return on the railroad's securities. In the absence of an increase in the expected earnings of the railroad, the price of its securities must fall if the expected rate of return is to increase. Suppose that the price of a share falls from $100 to $80. Then the rate of return increases from $10/$100, or .10, to $10/80, or .125, and consequently the railroad's cost of capital increases to .125. Before investors revised their beliefs about the value of the railroad's beta, the firm could have profitably undertaken a project whose rate of return is equal to .11. Subsequent to the revision in investors' beliefs, that project is no longer profitable.

11.8.2 Liquidity and the Bid-Asked Spread

Liquidity is a measure of the effect on the price of an asset of an increase in the speed or the size of a transaction in that asset. A small number of shares of IBM stock is a highly liquid asset. An attempt to purchase or sell 5,000 shares immediately, without notice to prospective investors on the other side of the transaction, would have no measurable effect on the price at which the transaction is executed. But an offer to purchase or sell 50,000,000 shares immediately would have an effect on the price. Unlike the stock of IBM, the stocks of small firms are traded infrequently. For these firms, an attempt to purchase or sell 5,000 shares immediately would likely affect the price at which the transaction is executed.

It is common to hear the remark that a house is an illiquid asset because one cannot sell it quickly. "It takes time to sell a house." That statement is not true. The author could likely sell his house in a morning by accepting a sufficiently low price. Similarly, there are likely many houses that one could purchase in an afternoon by credibly offering to pay a sufficiently high price. Houses are not difficult to sell (or to purchase) quickly. But the effect on the price of allowing time to search for prospective buyers, and to allow those buyers to collect information about the house, is significant. That is the reason why most persons choose not to sell their homes quickly. A house is an illiquid asset because the *cost* of insisting on a speedy transaction, or of attempting to purchase or sell a large quantity, is significant.

Any asset, including a financial security, can be characterized in terms of its liquidity. In many contexts it is sufficient to speak of the price of a security. In fact, however, each security has two prices: a bid price (or bid) at which dealers will purchase shares for addition to their inventories, and a higher asked price (or asked) at which they will sell shares out of their inventories. Speaking generally, the economic function of a dealer in any good is to maintain a bid price at which the dealer stands ready to purchase the good without prior notice, and an asked price at which he or she will sell the good without notice. Harold Demsetz has stated that the essential function of a dealer is to provide predictable immediacy.[32]

A dealer is the owner of a particular kind of firm. Accordingly, economists analyze dealers by assuming that they will choose the values of their bid and asked prices to maximize profit.[33] To maximize profit is to maximize the difference between revenues and costs. The dealer's revenues include the markup between the bid price and the asked price. On a given day, a dealer might purchase several shares from some investors by paying his bid price, and subsequently resell those same shares to other investors at his asked price. The dealer will set his bid and asked prices so that the quantities of shares that he purchases over several hours during a typical day, or over a few days in a typical week, will be equal to the quantities of shares that he sells. If the dealer does not adjust his bid and asked prices to equate the quantities supplied to him with the quantities demanded from him, the level of his inventory will either increase or decrease to levels that he is not willing to tolerate.[34]

Capital gains are another source of revenue for the dealer. Dealers will obtain a capital gain if they can purchase shares in advance of the publication of positive information about the net present value of the sequence of payments associated with those shares. If dealers can obtain this information before the typical investor does, they can purchase the shares at a bid price that does not reflect the information, and later resell those shares at an asked price that does reflect the information. Once the positive information becomes public knowledge, dealers can increase both the bid and the asked prices. In fact, once the information becomes public, dealers must increase their prices to avoid a depletion of inventory to unacceptable levels.[35] A dealer can also obtain a capital gain if he can sell the security in advance of negative information.

Just as capital gains are a source of revenue for the dealer, capital losses are a source of costs. The dealer will incur a capital loss if he fails to adjust his bid and asked prices before the publication of new information that will affect the quantities of the security that investors want to hold in their portfolios. For example, suppose that the volume of sell orders exceeds the volume of buy orders between 10:00 and 10:15 A.M. on a given day. If this excess supply of shares to the dealer is caused by a random fluctuation in the difference between the volumes of buy and sell orders, the fluctuation in the size of the dealer's inventory will be temporary, and he will soon gain revenue by reselling at his asked price the excess of shares that the purchases at his bid price.[36]

But suppose that the excess of sell orders over buy orders is based on negative information that the dealer does not yet have. In this case, the dealer will have purchased shares that he cannot subsequently resell at a higher asked price once the information becomes public.[37]

We conclude that to maximize profit, the dealer in a security must choose bid and asked prices that are compatible with all the information about the net present value of the sequence of future payments that are associated with that security. To pursue this question, we must distinguish between information trading and liquidity trading.

11.8.3 Information Trading, Liquidity Trading, and the Bid-Asked Spread

Information trading is trading by investors who believe that the current bid price or the current asked price of a security do not correctly reflect the risk-adjusted net present value of the sequence of payments associated with that security. To the extent that their information is correct, competition among information traders will cause the prices of securities to reflect net present values more accurately. Thus, information trading increases the level of informational efficiency of the market, and thereby the level of economic efficiency.

Liquidity trading is trading by investors to adjust either the size or the level of risk in their portfolios. Persons typically increase the size of their portfolios to effect intertemporal exchanges. For example, most persons who are currently earning income divert a portion of that income away from current consumption and into the purchase of financial securities. In later years, these persons will sell some (or all) of those securities to augment their income during those years. A person who is saving for retirement or to pay for college educations for children or grandchildren will typically purchase financial securities (rather than accumulating cash under the mattress). Similarly, a person will sell financial securities to provide income during retirement, or to finance large expenditures, such as purchasing a house or sending children to college.

Persons may want to change the level of risk in their portfolios as their circumstances change. As they approach retirement, or move further into retirement, they might want to reduce their level of risk. In the context of the CAPM, such a person would move some funds out of the market portfolio and into the risk-free asset. Similarly, a person who becomes wealthier, or whose source of income becomes more secure, would move funds out of the risk-free asset and into the market portfolio.

At any moment, the investors who want to purchase a security at the dealers' asked price will typically include both information traders and liquidity traders.[38] Similarly, there are both information traders and liquidity traders offering to sell securities to the dealer at his bid price. The dealer cannot perfectly distinguish between the two kinds of traders. To the extent that the dealer is transacting with information traders, he is likely to incur a capital loss because those investors are trading on superior information. That is, the information traders offer to purchase the security at the dealers' asked price, or sell at his bid price, because they know that the dealers' prices do not fully reflect the traders' information.

Dealers will seek to protect themselves against losing to the information traders in two ways. First, they will increase the spread between their bid and asked prices. Second, they will reduce the depth at those prices. Depth is a measure of the quantity that dealers will offer to purchase at their bid price and sell at their asked price.

For example, a dealer might quote a bid price of $100.00 and an asked price of $100.86. But unless his inventory of shares is unacceptably low, he might purchase only 1,000 shares at his bid price. Should an investor offer to sell 10,000 shares, the dealer might take only 1,000 shares at $100.00 and offer substantially less for the remaining 9,000 shares. Similarly, the dealer might back away from his asked price if traders offer to purchase a large volume of shares at that price.

If a dealer in a security widens the spread between his bid and asked prices, the liquidity of that security decreases. Think of the markup between the wholesale and the retail prices of used automobiles. The larger the spread between these prices, the greater the cost incurred by a consumer who purchases an automobile and plans to trade it in on a newer model sometime later. Similarly, if the dealer reduces the depth that he provides at his bid and asked prices, the liquidity of the security decreases.

11.8.4   The Effects of Information Trading and Liquidity Trading on Economic Efficiency through Their Effects on the Cost of Capital

The price that investors are willing to pay for a security is inversely related to its liquidity. Recently married couples planning to make a down payment on a house are likely to hold some of their assets in liquid securities, like government bonds, rather than illiquid securities like the stock of a small firm, even if the long-term prospects of that firm are highly favorable. Parents who anticipate paying for college tuition for their children within the next year are also likely to be sensitive to the liquidity of a security.

If dealers perceive that the number of information traders is increasing relative to the number of liquidity traders, the dealers are likely to increase the spread between their bid and asked prices, or decrease the depth that they are willing to provide at those prices, or both. The same result will occur if the dealers believe that the information traders are increasing the quality of their information. In either case, the decrease in the liquidity of the security will depress the price of the security and thus increase the firm's cost of capital. The firm's cost of capital increases because the lower the price of its securities, the greater is the proportion of ownership that the current shareholders must cede to new investors in order to finance a new project. An increase in the cost of capital means that some his projects that were profitable will no longer be so.

The net effect of information traders on economic efficiency is ambiguous. To the extent that information traders increase the informational efficiency of the financial markets, they increase the level of economic efficiency. But to the extent that information traders increase firms' cost of capital by decreasing the liquidity of their securities, information traders decrease the level of economic efficiency. We revisit this question in chapter 16, where we discuss the issue of insider trading.

11.9   Distinguishing among Equilibrium, Stability, and Volatility

Discussions about financial markets are often inhibited by a confusion among the terms *equilibrium*, *stability*, and *volatility*. This confusion is especially damaging to an informed discussion of the efficient markets hypothesis. In this section, we offer a distinction among these three terms that can eliminate (or at least reduce) the confusion.

11.9.1 Equilibrium

An equilibrium is a configuration of prices and quantities at which the quantity supplied of each good is equal to the quantity demanded. An efficient equilibrium is one that offers no opportunities for further mutually beneficial exchanges. If a financial market is in an efficient equilibrium, no investor has an incentive to reallocate funds among securities. In an informationally efficient market, the equilibrium price of a security is the risk-adjusted net present value of the sequence of payments associated with that security. Consequently, if there is new information about the sequence of payments, or about the marginal rate at which investors are willing to substitute between current and future consumption, or between risk and expected rate of return, then the efficient equilibrium values of prices will change to reflect that new information.

The current price of a security is not necessarily its efficient equilibrium price. That is, although quantities supplied and demanded of that security might be equal, the current price need not be the risk-adjusted net present value of the associated sequence of payments. In particular, the arrival of information that changes the equilibrium price of a security does not necessarily mean that the current price will change to reflect the new information. The market might not be informationally efficient. This brings us to the definition of stability.

11.9.2 Stability

Stability is a criterion that economists use to classify equilibria. An equilibrium is stable if prices are always close to their equilibrium values. We define *close* to mean that the difference between the current price and its equilibrium value is sufficiently small, or sufficiently brief, that the typical investor cannot obtain a profit by speculating in that security. This definition of stability requires that, upon the appearance of new information, the market must adjust prices to their new equilibrium values quickly enough to eliminate opportunities for speculation for the typical investor. Of course we recognize that it is not the market that adjusts the prices. Rather, it is the competition of speculators trading on the new information that forces prices to their new equilibrium values quickly enough to eliminate opportunities for the typical investor to speculate profitably. No one will speculate unless he or she can expect to obtain a profit. Consequently, the stability of an equilibrium requires the existence of speculators who have a sufficiently strong comparative advantage to cover their marginal costs.

11.9.3 Volatility

Volatility is a measure of the magnitude and the rate at which the price can change unpredictably. Here we must be careful to distinguish between an equilibrium price and the efficient equilibrium price. There is a one-to-one correspondence between the efficient equilibrium price of a security and the information about the sequence of future payments associated with that security. Consequently, a change in the information will change the efficient equilibrium price. By definition, new information is unpredictable. If new information is also volatile, in the sense that the arrival of the information and the significance of the information are highly unpredictable, then the efficient equilibrium price of the security will be commensurately volatile. Whether the market is efficient is a separate question, and this question bears on the confusion among equilibrium, stability, and volatility. Consider the following examples.

Example 1. The prices of U.S. government bonds depend critically on the announcements of the Federal Reserve Board regarding monetary policy. The market immediately and correctly adjusts the prices of these bonds to announcements by the Fed. Suppose that the Fed were to change its policy frequently and in ways that have large effects on the prices of the bonds. Suppose also that the market cannot predict the Fed's announcements. In this situation the market is informationally efficient, because the equilibrium prices immediately and correctly reflect the new information. The bond market is also stable, because the actual prices are always close to their equilibrium values. But bond prices are volatile, not because the market is inefficient, but because the information to which the market responds efficiently is volatile.

Example 2. Suppose that the government imposes a large tax on short-term trading in foreign currencies. The tax discourages speculators, with the result that prices change slowly in response to new information. In this situation, large discrepancies can develop between current prices and the efficient equilibrium values of those prices. An unsophisticated observer might describe this market as stable, meaning that prices are not volatile, when in fact the market is unstable by our proposed definitions.

We conclude that stability and informational efficiency are closely related. A stable market is one in which prices are kept close to their equilibrium values, even if those prices are highly volatile because the information that determines those equilibrium prices is highly volatile.

11.10   Conclusion

In this chapter, we have discussed the importance of informational efficiency for an economically efficient allocation of resources. We examined some of the empirical work that addresses the extent to which financial markets are informationally efficient. The empirical work is constrained by the joint hypothesis, which requires that every empirical test of informational efficiency is necessarily also a test of the model of equilibrium that the investigator uses to measure abnormal returns (risk-adjusted residuals). There is evidence that residuals are reliably predictable, which would appear to violate the efficient markets hypothesis except for two considerations. First, it is unclear whether the predictability of residuals is a consequence of an inefficient market or evidence of rational changes in the risk-adjusted equilibrium expected rates of return. The joint hypothesis creates difficulties that, at this stage of our understanding of financial markets, are insurmountable. Second, there is a distinction between statistically significant and economically significant predictability. An informationally efficient market will cause prices to reflect information up to, but not beyond, the point at which the marginal benefit from predicting residuals is equal to the marginal cost of doing so. Consequently, so long as transaction and other opportunity costs are positive and sufficiently large, we are likely to find evidence of statistically significant predictability of residuals.

All the above being said, the financial markets are remarkably efficient. A succinct statement of the current state of the efficient markets hypothesis is this quotation from Fama: "It is a disappointing fact that, because of the joint hypothesis problem, precise inferences about the degree of market efficiency are likely to remain impossible. Nevertheless, judged on how it has improved our understanding of the behavior of security returns, the past research on market efficiency is among the most successful in empirical economics, with good prospects to remain so in the future."[39]

Appendix: The Effect of a Unit Tax in a Competitive Industry

Figure 11.A1 displays the effect of imposing a unit tax on the firms in a competitive industry. Let DD be the market demand curve for the good produced by the firms in this industry. The short-run industry supply curve is SS. In the absence of a unit tax, the equilibrium price (per unit) paid by consumers and received by firms is P_E; the equilibrium quantity produced and sold is Q_E.

To understand the effect of a unit tax on the equilibrium values of price and quantity in perfect competition, it is critical to recognize that the industry supply curve is a marginal cost curve. Consequently, the height of the industry supply curve at a given quantity is the minimal price that will induce firms in that industry to produce

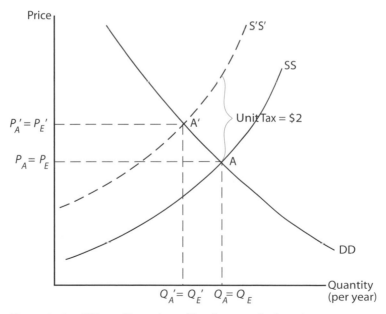

Figure 11.A1. Effect of imposing a $2 unit tax on the firms in a competitive industry.

that quantity.[40] To understand this interpretation, consider the following brief review of profit maximization by firms in a perfectly competitive industry.

In a perfectly competitive market, every firm behaves as if it could sell an unlimited quantity of its output at the market price. To maximize its profit, each firm will produce and sell the quantity of its output at which the marginal cost incurred by that firm is equal to the market price. Consequently, the marginal cost at a given quantity, say q_1, is the minimal price per unit that will induce that firm to produce q_1 units (per unit of time). By definition, the marginal cost at the quantity q_1 is the additional cost that the firm would incur to produce q_1 units of output (per unit of time) rather than $q_1 - 1$ units (per unit of time). If the firm's marginal cost curve is upward sloping, producing a quantity for which marginal cost is equal to the price assures the firm of a profit on each unit produced except the final (or the marginal) unit.[41] The profit gained from q_1 units (per unit of time) rather than $q_1 - 1$ units is zero. Were the firm to increase the rate of output beyond q_1, the profit on that final unit would be negative, and thus the firm's total profit would not be as large as it would be had the firm produced at the rate q_1.[42]

A consequence of the preceding analysis of the individual firm is that the height of the industry supply curve at any given quantity is the minimal price that the industry will require to produce that rate of output. Consider Point A on the supply curve, SS. If the price is P_A, each firm will produce a rate of output for which that firm incurs a marginal cost equal to P_A. Therefore, if each firm's marginal cost curve slopes upward, no firm will increase its rate of output unless the market price increases. For any firm to do so would cause a decrease in that firm's total profit. Therefore, P_A is the minimal price required by the industry to produce Q_A units.

The sum of the quantities supplied by all firms in the industry, when the price is P_A, will be Q_A. The marginal cost for the industry is the increase in total cost that all firms in the industry together would incur if the rate of output of the industry were to increase by one unit. The industry can increase its rate of output by one unit simply by having any one firm increase its output by one unit (with the other firms making no changes in their rates of output). When the market price is P_A, the marginal cost for every firm in the industry is P_A. Therefore, when the market price is P_A, the marginal cost for the industry is also equal to P_A.[43]

Now suppose that the government imposes on each firm a unit tax equal to $2. The imposition of this tax requires each firm to pay to the government $2 for each unit sold. Whether a firm passes all of this tax, some of it, or none of it to consumers in the form of a higher price is a matter of indifference to the government. The government only requires that each firm pay to the government $2 for each unit that that firm produces. In effect, the $2 tax is a fee that the government charges each firm for the right to produce a unit of the product.

Consider again Point A on the supply curve SS. We established that the price P_A is the minimal price that will induce firms in the industry to produce the quantity Q_A. If the government now charges a fee equal to $2 for the right to produce each unit of the product, then each firm will increase by $2 the minimal prices that it will accept to produce various quantities of its product. By extension, the imposition of a $2 unit tax will increase by $2 the minimal prices required for the industry to produce various quantities. In particular, a $2 unit tax will increase to $P_A + \$2$ the minimal price required for the industry to produce the quantity Q_A. Since the foregoing argument applies to any point on the supply curve, we conclude that the imposition on producers of a \$2 unit tax will shift the industry supply curve vertically upward by \$2.

What about the demand curve? A demand curve for Good X is a locus of maximal prices that consumers are willing to pay to purchase Good X at various rates (per unit of time). Consider Point A′ on the demand curve. The price $P_{A'}$ is the maximal price that consumers will pay if they are to purchase $Q_{A'}$ units of Good X per unit of time. If the price were to increase above $P_{A'}$, consumers would reduce the rate at which they purchase Good X. When deciding the rate at which to purchase Good X, consumers do not care why the price of Good X is whatever it is.[44] They are concerned only with how much of other goods they must forego if they purchase one more unit of Good X.

We conclude that the imposition of a unit tax on producers will shift the industry supply curve vertically upward by the full amount of the tax and will have no effect on the position of the demand curve.

The curve S′S′ in figure 11.A1 is the industry supply curve when the government imposes on producers a unit tax equal to \$2. The S′S′ curve is parallel to the SS curve; the vertical distance between the two curves at any rate of quantity produced is \$2. The imposition of the tax causes the equilibrium price to increase from P_E to $P_{E'}$, and the equilibrium quantity to decrease from Q_E to $Q_{E'}$. The sizes of the changes in the equilibrium price and quantity depend on the elasticities of the supply and the demand curves.[45]

We leave the reader to show that the effect of a unit tax on the equilibrium price and quantity does not depend on whether the government imposes the tax on producers or on consumers. That is, whether it is producers or consumers who deliver the tax to the government is immaterial.

Notes

In this chapter we draw substantively and extensively on the article by E. F. Fama, "Efficient Capital Markets: II," *Journal of Finance* 46 no. 5 (December 1991).

1. Ibid., 1575.

2. Recall that the size of the risk-adjusted residual depends on the investigator's choice of an asset pricing model.

3. E. F. Fama, "Efficient Capital Markets: A Review of Theory and Empirical Work," *Journal of Finance* 25, no. 2 (1970): 383–417.

4. Among the reasons why some persons will have lower marginal costs are: speedier access to data, lower costs for analyzing those data, lower costs for trading securities, better access to credit, and an absence of more lucrative alternatives. A Park Avenue psychiatrist, for example, would forego income from a lucrative practice were she to allocate to the analysis of data from the financial markets time that she could have used to treat neurotic patients. Even if the psychiatrist's superior intelligence would enable her to predict future prices better than the typical securities analyst, her comparative disadvantage in the analysis of securities, rather than neuroses, would make her net marginal benefit in predicting future prices of securities negative.

5. Perhaps financial analysts of high quality might work for mutual funds only if their salaries are sufficiently high to pay the fees of Park Avenue psychiatrists.

6. See, for example: N. H. Seyhun and M. Bradley, "Corporate Bankruptcy and Insider Trading," *Journal of Business* 70, no. 2 (1997); N. H. Seyhun, "Why Does Aggregate Insider Trading Predict Future Stock Returns?" *Quarterly Journal of Economics* 107, no. 4 (1992): 1303; N. H. Seyhun, "The Effectiveness of the Insider-Trading Sanctions," *Journal of Law and Economics* 35 (April 1992); N. H. Seyhun, "The Information Content of Aggregate Insider Trading," *Journal of Business*, 61, no. 1 (1988): 1–24; N. H. Seyhun, "Insiders' Profits, Costs of Trading, and Market Efficiency," *Journal of Financial Economics* 16, no. 2 (1986); N. H. Seyhun, *Investment Intelligence from Insider Trading* (Cambridge: MIT Press, 1998).

7. A common example of a random walk is the path taken by a person who meanders about in a desert according to the following process. First, the person attaches a ball to a string, whirls the ball around his head at a randomly determined speed, and releases the string at a randomly determined time. Once the string is released, the ball flies off and lands in a spot in the desert. The person then walks to that spot and whirls the string at a random speed, releasing it at a random time. Again the ball flies off, to land in a new spot. The path followed by the person who conducts this process is called, appropriately, a random walk. The walk is random in the sense that the direction in which the person will next walk, and the distance that he will walk in that direction, cannot be predicted from the path that he has followed to get to his present location. A more humorous example of a random walk is the path taken by a drunken person wandering about on a soccer field looking for his wallet. A theorem in probability theory states that the most likely place to find a person known to be following a random walk is the point from which the person began the walk. See, for example, W. K. Ching and M. S. Lee, "A Random Walk on a Circular Path," *International Journal of Mathematical Education in Science and Technology* 36, no. 6 (2005): 680–683.

8. For bonds that have a maturity date, the price of the bond will approach the (fixed) face value of the bond as the maturity date approaches. The path over which the price approaches the face value is, however, not predictable. The price of the bond at any given time is the present value of the payments of interest over the remaining life of the bond, plus the present value of the bond's face value. Since the present value of a sequence depends on the interest rate, and since the path of the interest rate over time is unpredictable, the path that the price of the bond will follow in its convergence with the face value of the bond is also unpredictable.

9. For an instructive, and humorous, discussion of random walks and the efficient markets hypothesis, see S. E. Landsburg, "Random Walks and Stock Prices," in *The Armchair Economist: Economics and Everyday Life* (New York: Free Press, 1993), 188–196.

10. The appendix to this chapter presents a standard diagram of this result.

11. Of course we recognize that prices are marginal values, and that there is a distinction between value in use and value in exchange. Transactions occur between persons whose marginal values in use differ from market prices, which are values in exchange. See note 4 in chapter 1.

12. W. deBondt and R. Thaler, "Does the Stock Market Overreact?" in *Advances in Behavioral Finance*, ed. R. H. Thaler (New York: Russell Sage Foundation, 1993).

13. For a recent discussion of this debate, see J. E. Hilsenrath, "Stock Characters: As Two Economists Debate Markets, The Tide Shifts; Belief in Efficient Valuation Yields Ground to Role of Irrational Investors; Mr. Thaler Takes On Mr. Fama," *Wall Street Journal*, October 18, 2004, p. A1.

14. A rate of return is abnormally high (or low) if the risk-adjusted residual is positive (or negative).

15. Under some stochastic models, the autocorrelation coefficient between the residuals for Security i for periods t and $t+1$ is the proportion of the residual observed in period t that will be

observed in the residual for period $t+1$. Suppose that the autocorrelation coefficient is .001. Then an investor would expect that only 1/1,000 of the residual observed in period t would (on averge) carry over to period $t+1$. Although an autocorrelation coefficient of .001 might be statistically significant, there is no economic significance for an investor due to transaction costs.

16. L. H. Summers, "Does the Stock Market Rationally Reflect Fundamental Values?" *Journal of Finance* 41 (1986): 591–601; R. J. Shiller, "The Volatility of Long-Term Interest Rates and Expectations Models of the Term Structure," *Journal of Political Economy* 87 (1979): 1190–1219.

17. Fama, "Efficient Capital Markets: II," 1580.

18. M. C. Jensen, quoted in Fama, "Efficient Capital Markets: II," 1575.

19. This subsection is a brief synopsis of Section VI (Tests for Private Information) in ibid., 1603–1607.

20. In chapter 16, we will discuss the implications of insider trading for economic efficiency.

21. J. Jaffe, "Special Information and Insider Trading," *Journal of Business* 47, no. 3 (1974): 410.

22. Seyhun, *Investment Intelligence from Insider Trading.*

23. Quoted in Fama, "Efficient Capital Markets: II," 1604–1605, in describing the work by M. Hulbert, "Proof of Pudding," *Forbes*, December 10, 1990, 316.

24. Fama, "Efficient Capital Markets: II," 1605.

25. B. M. Barbour and T. Odean, "Trading Is Hazardous to Your Wealth: The Common Stock Investment Performance of Individual Investors," *Journal of Finance* 55, no. 2 (2000): 773–806.

26. M. C. Jensen, "Risk, the Pricing of Capital Assets, and the Evaluation of Investment Portfolios," *Journal of Business* 42, no. 2 (1969): 167.

27. Loads were not subtracted. A front-end load is a sales charge that the investor pays to purchase shares of the fund. The load is usually paid to a broker who represents the fund. A typical front-end load is 8%. Thus, an investor who has $1,000 to invest will pay $80 to a broker in exchange for purchasing $920 worth of shares in the fund. Some funds also impose a back-end load when the investor redeems the shares. Most mutual funds today are no-load funds; investors purchase shares in these funds by communicating directly with the funds. Some funds, however, impose 12b-1 fees in addition to their expenses for managing the fund. These extra fees, which are named for the section of the Securities and Exchange Act that allows funds to designate themselves as no-load and still impose these fees, have the effect of a load.

28. Fama, "Efficient Capital Markets: II," 1605.

29. A common method of issuing securities that are claims to the earnings of a specific project is to create a separate corporate entity to operate the project and have that new corporate entity issue the new securities. "Spinning off" a division of the original firm is an example of creating a new corporate entity.

30. We could state this result in terms of an internal rate of return. The internal rate of return of a project is the rate of interest that would equate the net present value of the project to zero. Since net present values vary inversely with interest rates, if the rate of interest is less than the project's internal rate of return, the net present value of the project will be positive, and conversely. Consequently, the internal rate of return of a project is the marginal effect of that project on the rate of return on the firm's portfolio of projects. If the firm undertakes a project whose internal rate of return is less than the firm's cost of capital, the price of the firm's securities will fall to restore rate of return received by the firm's investors to equality with their opportunity costs.

31. Of course, any investor who held a share when the tax was announced would have incurred a capital loss of $16.33. But this capital loss does not affect the (expected) rate of

return from the time of the announcement forward. An investor who purchases a share after the announcement, and an investor who, having held the share when the announcement was made, and who continues to hold that share, will receive a rate of return equal to .12.

32. H. Demsetz, "The Cost of Transacting," *Quarterly Journal of Economics* 82, no. 1 (1968): 33–53.

33. We abstract here from the distinction between maximizing profit in a given period and maximizing wealth, which is the risk-adjusted net present value of the sequence of profits over several future periods.

34. As the dealer's inventory in the security increases, his portfolio becomes riskier because he is less well diversified. Moreover, he might have to borrow funds to finance the net purchases of securities. Similarly, he also incurs more risk as the size of his inventory decreases, particularly if he has to take a short position in the security in order sell more shares than he purchases.

35. See the preceding note.

36. Recall that *random* means unpredictable. In particular, in the present context random means that there is no information that would enable the dealer (or anyone else) to predict the imbalance of orders between 10:00 and 10:15 A.M.

37. Upon publication of the information, the dealer must reduce both his bid and asked prices to avoid a continuation of an excess of sell orders over buy orders, with the result that his inventory will increase to unacceptable levels. Even if his new asked price is higher than his former bid price, the difference between his former bid price and his new asked price will be less than his typical spread. He will lose revenue relative to what he would have obtained had he adjusted his prices before the new information became public.

38. On exchanges that use the specialist system, the dealer in each security is (with few exceptions) a monopolist. The New York Stock Exchange and the American Stock Exchange use the specialist system. Many stocks are traded on the over-the-counter exchange, which is a network of independent dealers. Competition among these dealers reduces the differences among their bid prices and among their asked prices.

39. Fama, "Efficient Capital Markets: II," 1576.

40. It is critical to distinguish between price and revenue. The price is the amount of money that a consumer pays per unit of a good purchased. Similarly, the price is the amount of money that a firm receives per unit of the product sold. Revenue (or total revenue) is price times quantity.

41. The profit to which we refer is (economic) profit before subtracting the fixed costs.

42. Students occasionally wonder why the firm should increase the rate of output to q_1, rather than stop at $q_1 - 1$, since the marginal unit contributes nothing to profit. Part of the answer is that the profit is the same whether the firm produces $q_1 - 1$ or q_1. More important is that the rule that requires the profit-maximizing firm to choose a rate of output for which price equal marginal cost serves to locate the profit-maximizing rate of output. The level of the firm's maximal profit is a separate consideration.

43. There is no requirement that the firms in a perfectly competitive industry have identical structures of costs. In particular, the marginal cost curves for the various firms might be different. The marginal cost curve for a low-cost firm would be close to the horizontal axis and have a shallow slope, while a high-cost firm's marginal cost curve would lie farther above the horizontal axis and have a steeper slope. Two firms that have different marginal cost *curves* will produce different rates of output even though both firms sell their output at the same market price (per unit of output). But in equilibrium, each firm will produce a rate of output at which that firm's marginal cost is equal to the common market price.

44. Consider your decision on how many gallons of gasoline to purchase per month. Suppose that the price per gallon is $2.80, which includes a federal excise tax equal to $0.50 per gallon.

It would be a rare consumer who would regard the price of a gallon of gasoline as being "really" only $2.30, because the $0.50 tax (somehow) doesn't count. The composition of the price is of no interest to consumers. If they want a gallon of gasoline, they must pay $2.80 that they could have spent on something else. It would be absurd to argue that they "really" pay only $2.30. In the shorter run, you would likely purchase fewer gallons per month, perhaps by carpooling, consolidating trips to shopping malls and grocery stores, or changing your habits in other ways. In the longer run, when your automobile deteriorates to the point that you no longer want to own it, you might replace it with a more fuel-efficient vehicle than you would purchase if the price of gasoline had not risen. It would be a rare consumer who would not, at least in the longer run, change the rate at which he or she purchases gasoline when the price rises. Now suppose that the government repeals the tax, but the price of a gallon remains at $2.80 (perhaps because a disruption in supplies coming from the Middle East offsets the elimination of the tax). The composition of the price has changed, but the price itself has not. Would you not argue that the price of a gallon of gasoline has "really" increased by $0.50 from its earlier value of $2.30, and that therefore we should expect consumers to purchase less of it? Whether the price paid by consumers increases because of a tax or because of a disruption in the Middle East is irrelevant to the quantity that consumers will choose to purchase (per unit of time).

45. All standard introductory and intermediate textbooks in microeconomics present an analysis of the effect of the tax on the size of change in the equilibrium price. This analysis is known as the incidence of the tax.

12 Event Studies

12.1 Introduction

An *event study* is an empirical technique designed to determine the direction and the magnitude of the effect of a specific piece of information on the equilibrium price of a security. The event study also measures the speed and reliability with which the market adjusts the price of the security to that information.[1] The second matter is, of course, the essence of the efficient markets hypothesis. We discussed the use of event studies briefly in the preceding chapter. In this chapter, we present a more thorough development of the technique and discuss five specific applications. For a more advanced and comprehensive treatment, the reader should consult the survey article by MacKinlay.[2]

12.2 Risk-Adjusted Residuals and the Adjustment of Prices to New Information

A risk-adjusted residual is that part of the rate of return on a security that cannot be attributed to a reward for waiting or to a reward for bearing risk. If the rate of return for Security A in month t exceeds the sum of the reward for waiting and the reward for bearing risk by holding that security during that month, the residual will be positive. Conversely, if the rate of return fails to compensate the investor for waiting and for bearing risk, the residual for Security A will be negative in that month. Economists use residuals in event studies to measure the efficiency of the market in adjusting the prices of securities to information about the sequences of payments that will accrue to investors who hold those securities.[3] To appreciate the use of residuals in event studies, we briefly review some aspects of the equilibrium prices of securities.

The equilibrium prices of securities depend on the economist's choice of an asset pricing model. An asset pricing model specifies an equilibrium in a financial market as a set of alternative combinations of expected rate of return and risk. In equilibrium, each security will offer one of the combinations of expected return and risk permitted by that model.

The expected rate of return and the risk of a security depend on the current price of that security and on the probability distributions that govern the future payments that will accrue to an investor who holds that security. Consequently, the equilibrium price of a security depends on the probability distributions for that security's future payments. Specifically, in equilibrium the market (hypothetically) adjusts the price of each security relative to the probability distributions for that security's future payments so that the security offers one of the equilibrium combinations of expected return and risk permitted by the asset pricing model.

The arrival of information about the probability distributions of a security's future payments will, in general, change the equilibrium value of the price of that security. In an informationally efficient market, the price of the security will change immediately to its new equilibrium value once the information arrives.

Consider the following simple example. Security A is riskless. The simplest way in which this could occur is for the probability distribution for the future payments to Security A to have a zero standard deviation. Security A would also be riskless if its beta value were zero even though its standard deviation were positive. Let the rate of return on the risk-free asset be .05 per year, and let the future payments for Security A be $10 per year. Since Security A is riskless, its equilibrium expected rate of return must be .05. Then the equilibrium price of Security A is $200 (because $10/$200=.05). Now suppose that new information arrives; the future payments to Security A will increase, beginning next year, to $20 per year. In response to the new information, the equilibrium price of Security A will increase to $400 (because $20/$400=.05). In an informationally efficient market, the price of Security A will increase immediately from $200 to $400 upon the arrival of the information.

To provide a more substantive example of how the equilibrium price of a security adjusts to information about its future payments, we use the CAPM to define equilibrium. Under that model, the equilibrium price of a security must create one of the alternative combinations of expected rate of return and risk that lie on the security market line. The slope of a security's characteristic line determines the position of that security along the security market line. For example, an increase in the slope of the characteristic line for a security would indicate an increase in risk for that security in the sense that the rate of return on that security is more sensitive to changes in the rate of return on the market portfolio. Therefore, an increase in the slope of the characteristic line would move that security rightward and upward along the security market line, increasing the expected rate of return on that security to a level commensurate with the increase in the risk of that security.[4]

If we plot the historical rates of return for Security A against the historical rates of return for the market portfolio, we will get a collection of data points that are scattered randomly above and below the characteristic line for Security A. In fact, the characteristic line is the straight line that best fits the scatter diagram.[5] The random deviations of the data points around the characteristic line are a consequence of firm-specific risk.

The horizontal coordinate of a data point for a given period is the rate of return on the market portfolio for that period; the vertical coordinate is the rate of return for Security A. The height of the characteristic line above the rate of return on the market portfolio is the sum of the reward for waiting and the reward for bearing risk. The residual for Security A is the vertical distance between the data point and the characteristic line. If the data point lies above the characteristic line, the rate of return on Security A exceeds the sum of the reward for waiting and the reward for bearing risk, and thus the residual corresponding to that data point is positive. Similarly, the residual is negative if the data point lies below the characteristic line.

Now suppose that new information indicates that the expected future payments to holders of Security A will increase with no increase in the sensitivity of the rate of return on Security A to the rate of return on the market portfolio. With no change in the sensitivity of Security A to the market portfolio, the position of Security A along the security market line will not change, and therefore the equilibrium expected rate of return for Security A will not change. The rate of return, and hence the expected rate of return, for Security A depend (negatively) on its price.[6] Therefore, if the combination of expected rate of return and risk offered by Security A are to remain unchanged, as required for equilibrium, the price of Security A must increase to offset the higher prospective payments to holders of Security A.

If the price of Security A does not change, the future data points for Security A will be located predominantly above Security A's characteristic line, rather than randomly scattered above and below that line. To preserve equilibrium, the price of Security A must increase so that the future data points will be randomly distributed above and below the characteristic line for Security A.

An informationally efficient market will adjust prices immediately to new information so that the data points for each security remain randomly distributed above and below that security's characteristic line. Equivalently, in an efficient market the average of the residuals for each security will be close to zero except for days on which new information arrives for that security. An event study assesses the informational efficiency of the market by studying the behavior of the residuals around the time that new information arrives.

| 12.3 | **The Structure of an Event Study** |

12.3.1 Definition of an Event

An event is an occasion on which a discrete piece of information becomes public. An event study is an analysis of the risk-adjusted residuals that occur within an interval of a few time periods before and after the event. Usually the period is a day on which the security is traded, and the interval covered by the study consists of a few days. In some cases, the period is as short as 15 minutes, and the interval covered is a span of several 15-minute periods that bracket the time when the information becomes public.

To qualify for an event study, the occasion on which the information becomes public must be sufficiently brief so that we can prevent other pieces of information from confounding the analysis. For example, an announcement by the Federal Reserve Board at 9:15 in the morning (before the major markets in New York begin trading) would qualify as an event. Similarly, an announcement by a firm at 5:00 in the afternoon (after the close of trading on the New York Stock Exchange) regarding projected earnings would qualify. An announcement that House Ways and Means Committee has voted to send a new tax bill to the floor of the House for a vote would qualify as an event suitable for an event study. Alternatively, a running commentary throughout the day on a case being argued before the Supreme Court would not qualify as an event because it would be too difficult to isolate distinct pieces of information.

12.3.2   Calendar Time and Event Time

In an event study, we measure time relative to the occurrence of the event under investigation. In most event studies, the unit of time is one day on which the organized stock exchanges are open.[7] For example, if a firm announced on Monday, June 7, 2004, that it will undertake a new project, we would define that day as Day 0 in event time. June 8, 2004, would then be day $+1$, and June 9 would be day $+2$. Days prior to the day of the event would have negative numbers in event time. The trading day next preceding the day of the event is Friday, June 4, 2004; in event time this would be day -1. Similarly, day -2 would be June 3, 2004.

We use event time rather than calendar time so that we can construct commensurate data across firms. If several firms announce new projects at various times throughout a five-year period, it would be meaningless to compare the rates of return for the firms on a given calendar date. Rather, we want to compare these firms on a given day relative to the date that the event occurred for that firm. For example, each firm has a rate of return on the third day following the date of the event for that firm. We could compare the rate of return on event day $+3$ for a particular firm to the average rate of return for event day $+3$ across all the firms that had similar events.

12.3.3   Risk-Adjusted Residuals and the Joint Hypothesis

The purpose of a (nonzero) residual is to adjust the price of the security to new information. After the adjustment, an investor who holds the security can expect a rate of return that, on average, will cover the opportunity costs for waiting and for bearing risk, and no more.

An event for a particular security is an occasion on which investors acquire new information about the sequence of payments that will accrue to an investor who owns that security. An informationally efficient market will immediately adjust the price of the security to reflect the significance of that information. An event study is an analysis of the residuals surrounding an event to determine the direction, magnitude, and speed with which the market adjusts the prices of securities to reflect new information.

The calculation of the residuals required for an event study requires a model to adjust for risk. Consequently, the outcome of any event study is conditional on the investigator's choice of an asset pricing model. In his comprehensive review of event studies, MacKinlay reports that in most cases the conclusions of event studies are not sensitive to the asset pricing model used to calculate the risk-adjusted residuals.[8]

12.3.4 Using Portfolios to Eliminate the Effects of Irrelevant Information

The purpose of an event study is to isolate the effect of a well-defined piece of information on the (risk-adjusted) rate of return of a security. Unfortunately, nature rarely cooperates by generating information only one piece at a time. We would expect that several pieces of new information that are relevant to the price of a security could arrive simultaneously. Consequently, it is difficult to isolate the effect of any single piece of information.

For an example of this problem, suppose that on Monday afternoon, after the major markets close, there are two announcements. The House Ways and Means Committee announces that it has just voted to support a bill that would reduce the taxes on the profits of banks. Later that afternoon, a judge announces a decision against a particular bank in a major lawsuit. When the markets reopen on the following day, there is a negative residual for the security of the particular bank in question. Presumably, the residual is the joint effect, one positive and one negative, of the two announcements made on the preceding day. Without a more powerful analytical technique, we cannot resolve the joint effect into its components.

An event study overcomes this problem by calculating the average of the residuals across a portfolio of firms, with the residuals for each firm measured relative to the timing of the event for that firm. Using the example described in the preceding paragraph, the event study would calculate the average of the residuals for all banks for several days preceding, including, and following the announcement on Monday of the vote of the House committee. In addition, there would be positive information for some of the banks, negative information for other banks, and no additional information for the remaining banks. Arguably, the effects of the information other than the vote by the House would have a small effect on the average of the residuals across the banks on each of the several days covered by the study. Consequently, for any particular day relative to the day of the announcement of the House vote, the average residual across the banks for that day should be a good measure of the effect of the House vote on the banks' securities for that day.

In the preceding example, the event under study occurs on the same day for all the banks. There is no need to distinguish between event time and calendar time. Consider the following example in which the event times and the calendar times differ across firms.

Over a period of several years, groups of investors arrange takeovers of various firms. Each takeover is idiosyncratic. The takeovers do not occur simultaneously, nor do they occur in the same or related industries. For each takeover, however, there is a well-defined event, namely the announcement that the takeover has been completed.[9] The event day for a given takeover is the day on which the announcement occurs for that takeover. Economists use an event study to measure the effect of the takeovers on the equilibrium expected rates of return of the target firms. The average of the residuals across the target firms for a given day relative to the event day measures the effect of the merger for that day. For example, the average residual for event day -3 measures the extent to which the market anticipates the takeovers three days prior to the announcements. The potential confounding effects of other kinds of new information that might have arrived for some of the target firms on event day -3 is minimized because we are calculating the average of the residuals across the target firms for that event day.

12.4 Examples of Event Studies

In the remainder of the chapter, we present brief reviews of five event studies. In each case, we determine the magnitude and direction of a specific kind of information on the equilibrium return of the affected firms. We also examine the speed with which the market adjusts security prices to the new information. Finally, we comment on the implications of the event studies for public policy. A critical question for public policy is whether a particular event creates a net addition to wealth for the economy, or only redistributes the existing wealth.

12.5 Example 1: The Effect of Antitrust Action against Microsoft

In 2000, the economists George Bittlingmayer and Thomas Hazlett published an event study in which they measured the effect of antitrust action against Microsoft on both the value of the Microsoft Corporation and on the values of other firms in the computer industry.[10] The study demonstrated that new information that indicated an increase in the probability that the Department of Justice (DOJ) would prevail in court in its antitrust suit against Microsoft was immediately followed by a decrease in the market values of both Microsoft and other firms in the computer industry. Similarly, in response to new information favorable to Microsoft's defense against the suit, the market immediately increased the market values of both Microsoft and other firms in the computer industry.

This event study is significant for several reasons. First, the study evaluates the efficacy of the antitrust act against the criterion of economic efficiency in the software industry. The Sherman Antitrust Act of 1840 prohibits "combinations in restraint of trade."[11] In terms of economics, the purpose of the act is to prohibit monopolistic (or oligopolistic) concentrations of market power that have a substantial deleterious effect on competition. Under the act, the federal government may ask a court to order a monopoly to cease certain activities that are considered anticompetitive. An important part of a typical introductory course in economics is to show that an efficient allocation of resources requires that each firm produces the rate of output for which the price of the good is equal to the firm's marginal cost of producing it. To maximize profits, a perfectly competitive firm will choose the rate of output for which price is equal to marginal cost. But a monopolist (and indeed any imperfect competitor) will produce a rate of output for which price exceeds marginal cost. Consequently, the presence of a monopolist creates an inefficient allocation of resources. The economic rationale for the Antitrust Act is that by reducing the share of a market held by a monopolist, that firm will behave more nearly like a perfectly competitive firm, and the allocation of resources will consequently be more efficient.[12]

In the case of Microsoft (and in most antitrust suits), it is unlikely that the government thought that it could create perfect competition in the computer industry. One of the requirements for perfect competition is that all firms in the industry produce a homogeneous good. Consequently, each perfectly competitive firm must accept the market price for its product. In the computer industry, the products, such as software and laptops, are not homogeneous. Each firm in that industry can set its price above marginal cost by an amount determined by the extent to which consumers regard the firm's product as having close substitutes in the products of other firms.[13] The government did, however, intend to make the computer industry more competitive by redistributing some of Microsoft's share of the market to its competitors.

Bittlingmayer and Hazlett identified two competing hypotheses regarding the effect on both Microsoft and other firms in the computer industry of the government's lawsuit. Under both hypotheses, the market value of Microsoft should fall upon the arrival of information indicating an increase in the probability that the government would win its lawsuit. Conversely, the market value of Microsoft should rise on information indicating a setback for the government's lawsuit. The two hypotheses differ in their predictions of the effect of the lawsuit on the efficiency of the allocation of resources. Consequently, the hypotheses differ in their implications for public policy regarding the enforcement of the Antitrust Act.

Under the first hypothesis, information indicating that the government was making progress in its lawsuit against Microsoft would cause the market values of other firms in the computer industry to increase. Firms that compete with Microsoft would become more valuable because they would gain a larger share of the market. Firms that used computers and software as inputs would become more valuable because the increase in competition among firms that produce computers and software would drive the prices of these products downward. Under this hypothesis, a win by the government in its lawsuit against Microsoft would reallocate wealth from the shareholders of Microsoft to the shareholders of other firms in the computer industry and to consumers, who would pay lower prices.

Under the second hypothesis, information favorable to the government's case against Microsoft would decrease the market values of other firms in the industry. The rationale for this hypothesis is that the success of Microsoft creates a network effect. For example, an increase in the use of Microsoft products such as Microsoft Word and Microsoft's Internet Explorer increases the demand for computers, printers, and other ancillary products. Like many firms, Microsoft uses its profits to finance the development of new products. If the government wins its lawsuit, Microsoft would have smaller profits with which to finance the development of new products. The markets for ancillary products produced by other firms would be adversely affected, and thus the market values of the firms that produce those products would decrease.

Each of the two competing hypotheses is plausible. Under the first hypothesis, a win by the government would only redistribute wealth, leaving the aggregate level of wealth in the economy unchanged. Under the second hypothesis, a win by the government would reduce the aggregate level of wealth (at least in the sense that there would be a decrease in the rate of capital formation or investment in the computer industry, and therefore the aggregate level of wealth would grow less rapidly).

Bittlingmayer and Hazlett use an event study to determine which (if either) of the two hypotheses is correct. They conclude that data on residuals strongly favor the second hypothesis, namely that a win by the government would reduce both the market value of Microsoft and the market values of the other firms in the computer industry. Therefore, a win by the government would reduce the aggregate level of wealth. Conversely, a loss by the government would increase the aggregate level of wealth.

The implication for public policy is that, for industries in which dominant firms create strong network effects, a vigorous enforcement of the Antitrust Act can destroy wealth.[14]

Bittlingmayer and Hazlett conduct their event study by defining an event as an occasion on which there is information regarding the status of the government's lawsuit against Microsoft. These events are partitioned into three categories. A *proenforcement event* is a report indicating that the DOJ will pursue a more strict enforcement of the antitrust law against Microsoft. News that the DOJ has filed a lawsuit against Microsoft is a proenforcement event. News that the judge has ruled in favor of a motion filed by the DOJ is a proenforcement event because the judge's ruling suggests an increase in the probability that the government will prevail in its lawsuit. Similarly, an *antienforcement event* is a report that reduces the probability that the government will prevail.

An *ambiguous event* is either a report whose implication for Microsoft is unclear, or a report about the lawsuit that occurs within a few days of other news about Microsoft that could have a significant effect on the value of Microsoft. Bittlingmayer and Hazlett provide the following example of an ambiguous event.[15] On April 15, 1991, the Federal Trade Commission announced that it was broadening its investigation of Microsoft. This was clearly a proenforcement event, which would presumably decrease the price of Microsoft's stock. Two days later there appeared a report that Microsoft's earnings had increased by 65%. This report should increase the price of the stock. Since the two reports occurred within the same three days and presumably had opposite effects on the price of the stock, it is difficult to separate the effects of the two reports.[16]

Bittlingmayer and Hazlett identify 28 proenforcement events and 8 antienforcement events. For each event, the authors estimate the residuals both for Microsoft and for a portfolio of 159 other firms in the computer industry over a three-day window centered on that event. For the proenforcement events, Microsoft shares decline by an average of 1.2% over the three days; the average decline in the shares of the other firms is 0.71%. For the antienforcement events, Microsoft shares increase in value by an average of 2.36% over the three days; the average increase in the shares of the other firms is 1.18%. These results imply that the enforcement of the antitrust act against Microsoft destroys value in the entire industry, rather than redistributing wealth from Microsoft's shareholders to the shareholders of its competitors.[17]

12.6   Example 2: Regulatory Rents in the Motor Carrier Industry

In 1985, Nancy Rose published the results of an event study in which she determined that the effect of the deregulation of the motor carrier industry was to reduce the profits of firms in that industry.[18] After testing several competing hypotheses, Rose concluded that the regulation had the effect of creating economic rents for trucking firms. The deregulation of the industry redistributed wealth by reducing these rents.

12.6.1   Economic Rent

An economic rent is that portion of the income received by the owner of a resource that exceeds the owner's opportunity cost. Consequently, an economic rent generated by a resource in a particular employment could be taxed away without causing the owner of the resource to withdraw the resource from that employment.

The classic example of an economic rent is the rental payment received by the owners of unimproved land. The aggregate quantity of unimproved land is fixed by nature. If the market for land is perfectly competitive, each owner will offer a quantity of land that equates the marginal cost for supplying a unit of land to the price of a unit. Owners incur a zero marginal cost up to the quantity of land that they own. At that quantity, their marginal cost is infinitely large because they cannot produce land. Then the aggregate supply function of land is perfectly inelastic at the total quantity of land that nature has provided. We assume that the demand function for land is downward sloping, and that it intersects the vertical supply function at a positive price. A landowner's income will be equal to the price of a unit of land multiplied by the number of units that he or she owns. Graphically, his or her income will be equal to the area of the rectangle whose upper right corner is at the intersection of the demand and supply functions.

Let the equilibrium price of the land be $1,000 per acre per month, and suppose that Mr. Green owns 500 acres. Then Mr. Green's income is $500,000 per month. Now suppose that the government imposes a tax on landowners equal to $900 per month for each acre rented. Students will recall from their introductory course that Mr. Green's optimal response is to leave the price unchanged, pay the tax, and accept a reduction in his income equal to the tax. Since the market is perfectly competitive, any attempt by Mr. Green to pass on the tax by raising the price will reduce his income to zero. The tax has no effect on the quantity of land that Mr. Green will supply. In fact, the government could impose a tax up to $1,000 per month per acre without affecting the quantity of land that Mr. Green will supply.[19]

Assuming that Mr. Green has no interest in using the land himself, his opportunity cost of renting it to someone else is zero. Therefore, any positive income is a net gain for him. Consequently, the loss of any part of this income through a tax that does not affect his marginal cost will not cause him to change the quantity of the land that he supplies.

A second example of economic rent is the profit that a pure monopolist obtains by producing the quantity at which marginal revenue is equal to marginal cost, and charging a price determined by the demand function for that quantity. The size of the monopolist's economic rent is equal to the area above the marginal cost function and below a horizontal line whose height is equal to the price.[20] Suppose that this rent is $44,000 per month. The government could impose on the monopolist a monthly tax equal to $44,000 without causing the monopolist to change the rate of output or the price. If the rate of output does not change, the quantities of resources employed by the monopolist will not change either. Since no resources would be withdrawn from the monopolist's enterprise as a consequence of the tax, the entire $44,000 is an economic rent.

12.6.2 The Hypotheses

Among the several hypotheses that Rose tests, we consider two. Rose's Hypothesis 1 is competitive: "Regulation had no effect on firms; prices and profits were determined competitively."[21]

In this case, even under regulation, the number of regulated carriers was large. Moreover, a large number of carriers were exempt from regulation. This hypothesis claims that, despite regulatory constraints on prices, routes, and entry of new firms, the number of actual and potential competitors was sufficiently large to render collusion impracticable, with the result that prices, quantities, and qualities of service were determined as if the industry were perfectly competitive. The empirical implication of the competitive hypothesis is that deregulation would leave the prices of the stock of trucking firms unchanged because there were no monopolistic profits to eliminate.

Rose's Hypothesis 5 refers to monopoly rents. "Regulation enabled the industry to act collusively; prices and profits both increased as a result."[22] This hypothesis asserts that regulation of the trucking industry prior to the Motor Carrier Act of 1980 enabled firms in that industry to obtain economic rents by shielding those firms from competition. The regulators controlled two kinds of competition. First, the regulators set minimum prices, thereby preventing firms from undercutting each other. Second, the regulators restricted the entry of new firms. Under this hypothesis, the deregulation provided by the 1980 Act would, by increasing competition, reduce the economic rents enjoyed by existing trucking firms. In terms of the monopolist described in the preceding subsection, deregulation would replace the monopolist by an industry that more closely met the conditions of perfect competition. If this hypothesis is correct, we should observe the values of the stock of trucking firms to fall on news that the industry is about to be deregulated.

12.6.3 The Event Study

Rose conducted an event study by using an adjusted CAPM to define abnormal returns for trucking firms. In addition to adjusting the returns for sensitivity to the return on the market portfolio, Rose added three terms: one term to adjust for difference in the levels of debt among firms, a second term to control for the fact that some of the firms in the trucking business were conglomerates that had interests in other fields unrelated to trucking, and a third term to adjust the returns for changes in expectations about the future price of fuel.

Rose's event study calculated average abnormal returns (the risk-adjusted residuals) across firms in the trucking industry. Quoting from her conclusion: "Share price data indicate that regulatory reforms significantly reduced the expected future profits of firms in the motor carrier industry. The results are consistent with the presence of monopoly profits for trucking firms in the pre-1978 regulatory environment. . . . The results reveal an average loss of 31% of the prereform equity value of general freight carriers as a consequence of the Interstate Commerce Commission's deregulation campaign, beginning in 1978."[23] Notice Rose's use of the term *expected future profits*. The market reduces expected future profits by creating negative risk-adjusted residuals.

12.7   Example 3: Merger Announcements and Insider Trading

Arthur Keown and John M. Pinkerton conducted an event study to determine whether investors who possess nonpublic information about planned mergers affect trade on that information, and the speed and accuracy with which the market incorporates that nonpublic information into the stock prices of the affected firms.[24] "The results [of the event study] confirm statistically what most traders already know. Impending merger announcements are poorly held secrets, and trading on this nonpublic information abounds. Specifically, leakage of inside information is a pervasive problem occurring at a significant level up to 12 trading days prior to the first public announcement of a proposed merger."[25]

In chapter 13, we discuss some of the reasons why firms might create value for their shareholders by merging with other firms. In chapter 16, we examine the question of insider trading. We consider both questions against the criterion of economic efficiency. For now, we confine our discussion to the question of informational efficiency.

Mergers can create value for the shareholders of the firm that is to be acquired by another firm. An investor who expects that a merger is planned can obtain a capital gain by purchasing the shares of the firm to be acquired before the market has revalued the shares of that firm to reflect the effect of the planned merger. Trading on nonpublic information is illegal. Two questions arise. First, do insiders trade on private information? Second, if insiders do trade on this information, how speedily and how accurately does the market adjust the prices of the relevant stocks to reflect the insiders' information?

Using the market model,[26] Keown and Pinkerton conducted an event study of the (abnormal) residuals of firms that are merged with other firms. The average residuals for these firms are significantly positive for several days prior to the public announcement of the merger. A plausible inference is that insiders who know of the impending merger cause the positive residuals by purchasing the stock in larger quantities than they otherwise would.[27]

Turning to the question of the speed and the accuracy with which the market incorporates information about the proposed merger, Keown and Pinkerton show that the residuals are close to zero beginning the day after the pubic announcement. Since nonzero residuals indicate adjustments to prices to reflect new information, we conclude that the market speedily and accurately incorporates the insiders' information.

12.8 Example 4: Sudden Changes in Australian Native Property Rights

Well-defined property rights create value because they facilitate mutually beneficial exchanges. One of the most valuable aspects of a property right is salability. Landowners who have the right to sell their land have a stronger incentive to maintain it, and to improve it, than landowners whose rights are limited to using the land and bequeathing it to their descendents. The legal term for salability is *alienability*. A change in governmental policy that establishes new property rights has the potential to affect both the aggregate level of wealth in an economy and the distribution of that wealth among individuals. A decision by the High Court in Australia provided an unusual opportunity to study the economic consequences of creating property rights.

Robert Brooks, Sinclair Davidson, and Robert Faff used an event study to determine whether a judicial creating of enforceable property rights for the Aboriginals in

Australia affected the aggregate level of wealth in that country.[28] Their results demonstrate that while creating new property rights for the Aboriginals had an effect on the distribution of wealth, there was no effect on the level of wealth. Consequently, the judicial decision had no effect on economic efficiency. Brooks et al. describe the context for their study as follows:

> When Europeans colonized Australia, they ignored Aboriginal property rights and continued to do so until 1992. In the 204 years that passed between colonization in 1788 and 1992, a legal regime with respect to land developed that ignored any rights that the Aboriginals may have had.
>
> In 1992 the Australian High Court (which is the Australian equivalent to the US Supreme Court) ruled that not only did Aboriginals have land rights (native title), but also that these rights had survived to the present day. Native title, in this context, refers to, "the interests and rights of indigenous inhabitants in land, whether communal, group or individual, possessed under the traditional laws acknowledged by, and the traditional customs observed by, the indigenous inhabitants."[29]

Within the last half-century, several economists have concentrated on studying the economics of property rights. One of the central propositions of these economists is that many legally recognized (and thus governmentally enforceable) property rights arise from common law because these rights promote an efficient allocation of resources. Harold Demsetz has "the classic paper in this area [in which he argues] that property rights emerge to internalize externalities in response to changes in technology and relative prices. Property rights in this model are endogenous."[30] Richard Posner advances a "common law efficiency argument. [Posner] argues that judges have little power to effect distributional aspects of wealth and consequently are predisposed toward increasing the total amount of wealth in the economy."[31] Finally, Ronald Coase "has argued that once property rights are allocated, bargaining should ensure that the optimal allocation takes place. Once we accept that negotiation costs may inhibit bargaining, institutions that reduce these costs become important. The legal fiction [that the Australian continent was uninhabited, and therefore that all property rights belonged to the British Crown] had effectively reduced negotiation costs with the Aboriginals to zero. The court mandated institutional change [in granting property rights to the Aboriginals], in effect, could have infinitely increased negotiation costs. In effect, a bilateral monopoly situation was created."[32]

According to Coase, transferring property rights from the British Crown to the Aboriginals could well have affected the distribution of wealth (in favor of the Aboriginals) but should not have affected the level of wealth, except possibly through the deleterious effect of increasing the costs of negotiation. The empirical question, then, is: what was the net effect of the court's decision on the aggregate level of wealth in Australia?

Brooks et al. measured the aggregate level of wealth in Australia by the value of the Australian Stock Exchange (the market portfolio for Australia). Assuming that the market is informationally efficient, the effect of the level of economic efficiency of the court's transferring property rights from the Crown to the Aboriginals should be reflected in the value of the market portfolio immediately upon publication of the court's decision. Brooks et al. "do not find significant costs resulting from the change in property rights."[33]

| 12.9 | **Example 5: Gradual Incorporation of Information about Proposed Reforms of Health Care into the Prices of Pharmaceutical Stocks** |

Many of the event studies in economics investigate the market's response to a single, isolated event, such as the announcement of a merger between two firms. Information about changes in public policy, however, is more likely to be revealed gradually as proposals move through commissions, committees of the Congress, and eventually to a vote. Our last example of an event study comes from a paper by Sara Fisher Ellison and Wallace P. Mullin, who examined the market's response to the gradual revelation of information about President Clinton's proposal to reform health care.[34] These economists used a relatively new empirical technique, isotonic regression, to estimate the risk-adjusted residuals for pharmaceutical firms in an environment in which the information about a significant event is revealed gradually.[35]

> It is not clear a priori that increased government intervention in the form of health care reform should necessarily have negative consequences for the pharmaceutical industry. For instance, achieving the goal of universal coverage could lead to higher consumption of health care products and services, including pharmaceuticals. Alternatively, an emphasis on overall cost-effectiveness could result in a shift away from more costly surgical procedures toward cheaper drug therapies.
>
> As Burton A. Weisbrod points out in his discussion of the effects of diagnosis-related payment on pharmaceutical firms, not all pharmaceutical products would be equally affected. Many products, such as cholesterol-lowering drugs, can further overall cost-effectiveness goals, as they can substitute for higher cost procedures. Some may not, such as Prozac and Viagra, because they create treatment options where none existed before. Furthermore, some drugs, such as certain antibiotics, complement expensive surgical procedures. In addition, cost containment can be implemented not by capping overall expenditures but rather by separately capping individual categories of expenditures, thus not resulting in a substitution into pharmaceuticals.[36]

Ellison and Mullin presented three conclusions:

> First, investors thought health care reform was bad news for the pharmaceutical industry. The loss in the market-adjusted value of [a] pharmaceutical portfolio was sizeable. Consider an investment in a portfolio of brandname pharmaceutical company stocks on January 19, 1992, just before candidate Clinton issued a vague "five-point plan" during the New Hampshire presidential primary campaign. By October 4, 1993, when President Clinton had unveiled a more specific, and different, proposal before Congress, and Hillary Rodham Clinton had advocated it impressively at congressional

hearings, that investment would have lost 38 percent compared to buying and holding the value-weighted market portfolio.

Second, the decline in pharmaceutical values closely coincided with the Clinton plan's growing emphasis on containing costs rather than merely securing universal coverage.[37]

The third result discovered by Ellison and Mullins is particularly interesting because it bears on the question of whether Clinton's proposed reform would discourage research by pharmaceutical firms by inhibiting their ability to recover the costs of research through revenues from selling drugs. Ellison and Mullins demonstrated that a portfolio of pharmaceutical firms that did not conduct research suffered losses in value similar to those of a portfolio of firms that did specialize in research.

The study by Ellison and Mullins contributes much to our understanding of how the market adjusts the prices of securities to the gradual revelation of information about a significant event. We can conclude from their work that the market, at least in this area of a proposed change in public policy, is informationally efficient.

12.10   Conclusion

Economists assess the informational efficiency of a financial market by examining the behavior of risk-adjusted residuals that occur within an interval of time surrounding the publication of new information. An efficient market will adjust prices immediately to new information, with the result that the average of the risk-adjusted residuals over a portfolio of firms that experience similar events will be near zero immediately after the event. Indeed, if some of the information leaks to the public prior to the announcement, the residuals there will be nonzero prior to the announcement as the market anticipates the announcement. In addition to determining whether the market is informationally efficient, event studies can determine the net effect of proposed or announced changes in public policy.

Notes

1. Eugene Fama, Fischer Black, Michael Jensen, and Richard Roll conducted the first major use of an event study in finance by analyzing the effect of announcements of stock splits on rates of return.

2. A. C. MacKinley, "Event Studies in Economics and Finance," *Journal of Economic Literature* 35 (March 1997): 13–39.

3. For convenience, we shall follow convention by dropping the qualifier *risk-adjusted* and speak simply of residuals. We include both explicit payments, such as dividends and interest, and the implicit payments that occur as capital gains.

4. The ratio of the increase in the expected rate of return to the increase in the risk is the slope of the security market line.

5. More precisely, the characteristic line is the least squares regression line for the scatter diagram.

309

6. Recall that the rate of return from time t to time $t+1$ is $(P_{t+1}+D_{t+1}-P_t)/P_t$. If the price does not change, the rate of return is D_{t+1}/P_t. Then an increase in the payment, D_{t+1}, will increase the rate of return.

7. For some studies, the unit of time is as small as 15 minutes during which the exchange is open for trading.

8. MacKinlay, "Event Studies in Economics and Finance." We do not claim that the magnitudes of the risk-adjusted residuals are independent of the choice of asset pricing model. The assertion is that the conclusions of the event studies are robust with respect to the choice of asset pricing model. For example, in section 12.5 we describe an event study of the results for the computer software industry of the government's antitrust suit against Microsoft. The conclusions of this study are robust with respect to the choice of asset pricing model.

9. We discuss the procedures involved in takeovers briefly in section 12.7.

10. G. Bittlingmayer and T. W. Hazlett, "DOS *Kapital*: Has Antitrust Action against Microsoft Created Value in the Computer Industry?" *Journal of Financial Economics* 55 (2000): 329–359.

11. The Sherman Antitrust Act has been extended and modified several times. The chief statutory changes are in the Clayton Act and the Federal Trade Commission Act, both passed in 1914. Numerous decisions of the federal courts have affected the enforcement of the acts.

12. In fact, the matter is not quite so simple. There are several ways in which an imperfect competitor can mitigate the economic inefficiency that would otherwise occur. One way is to use discriminatory pricing.

13. Economists use cross-price elasticity of substitution to measure the extent to which two goods are close substitutes.

14. "Network effects arise when a product becomes more valuable as more people use it. Telephones and fax machines provide classic examples. When a single firm controls the underlying standard, the result may be a 'winner-take-all' outcome. Economic analyses (Declaration of Kenneth J. Arrow, U.S. v. Microsoft, Jan. 17, 1995) and popular treatments ('The force of an idea,' *The New Yorker*, Jan.12, 1998) of the Microsoft case have highlighted network effects. However, network effects can cut both ways. 'The theory of increasing returns (to scale) is crucial to the case against Microsoft . . . [but] increasing returns (to scale) are equally crucial to the case *for* Microsoft—as a reason why trying to break it up would be a bad thing' ('The legend of Arthur,' *Slate Magazine*, Jan. 14, 1998; see also 'Soft microeconomics: the squishy case against you-know-who,' *Slate Magazine*, April 23, 1998). Again, theory is inconclusive. Such ambiguity plagues nearly every other aspect of the nearly decade-old discussion about Microsoft and monopoly." Bittlingmayer and Hazlett, "DOS *Kapital*," 331–332.

15. Ibid., 338.

16. We cannot assume that the market adjusted the price of the stock fully and immediately to the effect of the first report before the second report appeared.

17. Bittlingmayer and Hazlett also present results based on the event day itself, and on an 11-day window centered on the event date. The conclusions based on these windows are the same as the conclusions based on the 3-day window. For an executive summary of the study by Bittlingmayer and Hazlett, see "The Stock Market's Verdict of Microsoft's Antitrust Case," *Economic Intuition* (Spring 2000): 1–2.

18. N. L. Rose, "The Incidence of Regulatory Rents in the Motor Carrier Industry," *Rand Journal of Economics* 16, no. 3 (1985): 299–318.

19. Strictly speaking, if the tax were equal to $1,000 per month per acre, Mr. Green would be indifferent between supplying all of his land and supplying none of it. Once the tax exceeds $1,000, Mr. Green will supply no land. The tax in this example is a constant unit tax, because it is assessed as a constant dollar amount per unit supplied. We encourage the reader to consider the optimal (i.e., profit-maximizing) response to a unit tax for a producer whose marginal cost

is positive, rather than zero. Rather than impose a constant unit tax of $900, the government could have imposed on each landowner a tax equal to 90% of that owner's monthly income from renting land. Since each landowner's marginal cost of supplying land is zero, the effect of the two taxes would be the same.

20. More precisely, the economic rent is equal to this area minus the monopolist's fixed cost.

21. Rose, "The Incidence of Regulatory Rents," 300.

22. Ibid., 302.

23. Ibid., 314–315.

24. A. Keown and J. M. Pinkerton, "Merger Announcements and Insider Trading Activity: An Empirical Investigation," *Journal of Finance* 36, no. 4 (1981): 855–869.

25. Ibid., 855.

26. Recall from chapter 9 that the market model is a variant of the CAPM in which the intercept term is not constrained to be equal to the rate of return on the risk-free asset.

27. The insiders could also contribute to positive residuals by postponing previously planned sales of the stock, knowing that the price will soon rise to reflect the insiders' private information.

28. R. Brooks, S. Davidson, and R. Faff, "Sudden Changes in Property Rights: The Case of Australian Native Title," *Journal of Economic Behavior and Organization* 52 (2003): 427–442.

29. Ibid., 428.

30. Ibid., 429.

31. Ibid.

32. Ibid. For an exposition of this argument, see the references in ibid., particularly A. Alchian and H. Demsetz, "The Property Rights Paradigm," *Journal of Economic History* 33 (1973): 16-27; H. Demsetz, "Toward a Theory of Property Rights," *American Economic Review: Papers and Proceedings* (1967): 347–359; R. Posner, "A Theory of Primitive Society, with Special Reference to Law," *Journal of Law and Economics* 23 (1980): 1–53; R. Posner, *Economic Analysis of the Law*, 5th ed. (New York: Aspen Law and Business, 1998).

33. Brooks et al., "Sudden Changes in Property Rights," 427.

34. S. F. Ellison and W. P. Mullin, "Gradual Incorporation of Information: Pharmaceutical Stocks and the Evolution of President Clinton's Health Care Reform," *Journal of Law and Economics* 44 (April 2001): 89–129.

35. Ordinary (least squares) regression produces a linear function to estimate the (risk-adjusted) expected rate of return for a firm. Isotonic regression allows the expected rate of return to be a step function, which is more appropriate to an environment in which the information about a significant event, such as a change in governmental policy, is revealed gradually in a large number of steps. See ibid.

36. Ellison and Mullin.

37. Ibid.

Part VI

The Informational and Allocative Efficiency of Financial Markets: Applications

13 Capital Structure

Introduction

Debt is bad, right? Persons who have not studied economics, particularly the economics of finance, are likely to agree that debt is bad. While it may sometimes be necessary for a firm to borrow money to finance a new project, clearly the sooner the debt is paid off, the wealthier the firm's shareholders will be. For a particular example, consider an individual who obtains a mortgaged loan to purchase a house. It would be obvious to many persons that the homeowner should put a high priority on paying off the loan as soon as possible. After all, the sooner the homeowner pays off the loan, the sooner he or she can stop paying interest.

In economics, propositions that on first glance seem obvious are often, on closer examination, incorrect. Often the error arises because of a failure to take full account of implicit costs and benefits. The analysis of the costs and the benefits of debt is no exception. In this chapter, we show that debt is not unambiguously bad. In fact, there are many cases in which firms and individuals can use indebtedness to increase the rate at which they accumulate wealth. The apparent contradiction in the foregoing sentence can be resolved by recognizing the distinction between the level of a person's (or a firm's) wealth and the structure of that wealth.

Consider Mr. and Mrs. Hudson, who own a house. The Hudsons make monthly payments on a mortgaged loan. The market value of the house is $600,000, and the unpaid balance on the loan is $140,000. In addition to their house, the Hudsons own a portfolio of financial securities that is worth $200,000. The Hudsons' net worth is the value of their assets minus the value of their liabilities. The total value of their assets is $600,000+$200,000, or $800,000; their single liability is the unpaid balance of $140,000 on the mortgaged loan. Consequently, the Hudson's net worth is $800,000−$140,000, or $660,000. Ignoring transaction costs, such as brokers' commissions and attorneys' fees, the Hudsons could raise $660,000 in cash by selling their assets (the house and the financial securities) and paying off their debt (the unpaid balance on the mortgaged loan). Their wealth, which is synonymous with their net worth, is $660,000.

Now suppose that the Hudsons decide to get out of debt by paying off the mortgaged loan. Again ignoring transaction costs, the Hudsons sell $140,000 worth of their financial securities and use the cash to pay off the loan. They are now wealthier because they own their home free and clear (of a mortgage). Right? Obviously not. The Hudsons will have changed only the structure of their wealth; the level of their wealth will remain at $660,000. The total of their assets is $600,000 (for the house) plus $60,000 (in financial securities), or $660,000. Having paid off the mortgaged loan, they have no liabilities. Consequently, their wealth (or net worth) is $660,000−$0, or $660,000.

The Hudsons cannot gain wealth by paying off the mortgaged loan any more than a young boy can gain wealth by exchanging four 5-dollar bills for one 20-dollar bill. The boy might feel wealthier because the 20-dollar bill has a larger numeral on it than do each of the 5-dollar bills, but clearly he is no wealthier. Similarly, the Hudsons might feel wealthier because they can now mount an emblem of an eagle on the garage (which is the popular way to indicate that your home is free and clear), but they are no wealthier. The amount of cash that they could raise by liquidating their assets and discharging their liabilities is still $660,000.

We can push this example further by considering the relationship between the structure of the Hudsons' wealth and the rate at which they can increase their wealth over time. The analysis involves opportunity costs. Specifically, if the Hudsons liquidate some of their financial securities to pay off the loan, they no longer pay interest on the loan, but they forego the earnings that those securities would have generated.

We can partition the Hudsons' portfolio of financial securities into two smaller portfolios. The first portfolio contains securities worth $140,000; the second portfolio contains securities worth $60,000. Since the value of the first portfolio is equal to the unpaid balance on the loan, the first portfolio and the loan exactly offset each other in their effects on the Hudsons' wealth. Specifically, for each $100 of assets in the first portfolio, there is an offsetting $100 worth of debt in the loan. In effect, each $100 of debt finances $100 of assets in the portfolio.

Suppose that the interest rate on the loan is 4% per year, and the (expected) rate of return on the portfolio of financial securities is 7% per year. Ignoring taxes, each $100 of the unpaid balance on the loan costs the Hudsons $4 in interest per year, and the corresponding $100 of assets in the financial portfolio earns (an expected) $7 per year. Consequently (ignoring taxes and transaction costs), paying off each $100 of the loan will save the Hudsons $4 in interest per year and cost them $7 in foregone (expected) earnings per year. The Hudsons can gain wealth over time by using the bank's money to finance their holdings of financial securities.

The purpose of the preceding discussion is to show that the analysis of debt requires more care than simply regarding debt as bad. In the following subsections, we examine the more important ways in which firms and investors can use debt to mitigate some of the impediments that would otherwise preclude some mutually beneficial exchanges. Investors' use of debt in the capital structure of their firms enables financial markets to increase the efficiency of intertemporal resource allocation.

13.2   What Is Capital Structure?

The capital structure of a firm is the relationship among the financial securities issued by the firm. As we have seen, these securities are saleable claims on sequences of payments that investors expect the firm to make over the future.[1] Initially, investors create a firm by providing resources with which the firm can undertake projects that will generate sequences of earnings. Usually, the investors provide financial resources (money) that the firm uses to purchase capital goods. Recall that a capital good is a good that is used as an input for the production of other goods (including both goods for households, or consumption goods, and other kinds of capital goods). The prices of the financial securities depend on the values of parameters determined outside the firm, such as the rate of return on the risk-free asset and the market price of risk, and investors' expectations about the firm's ability to generate earnings.

Economists, investors, and lawyers partition financial securities into two broad classes: debt and equity. For economic analysis, we use the classifications of contractual claims and residual claims. With a few exceptions, debt securities are contractual claims, and equity securities are residual claims. A contractual claim specifies the sequence of payments that the firm must make to the investors who hold those claims. The most common kind of contractual claim is a bond, and the required payments are called interest. A residual claim entitles its owner to a share of whatever assets the firm has, if any, that remain after the firm has made the required payments to the holders of the contractual claims. The most common form of a residual claim is a share of common stock.

With some exceptions, the firm must pay the contractual claimants in cash. The owners of the residual claims, however, usually delegate to managers the decision on what portion of the firm's assets should be paid out as dividends and what portion should be retained to finance new investment projects. The managers can produce implicit dividends for the residual claimants by using the retained earnings to finance projects. Whenever the managers retain a portion of the earnings, the residual claimants incur an opportunity cost. This opportunity cost is the net present value of the most profitable project that the residual claimants could have financed on their own had the managers paid out the retained earnings as dividends. Consequently, the managers should retain earnings if, and only if, they can invest those earnings in projects whose net present values are positive. In calculating the net present value of a project, the firm should discount future payments by the shareholders' marginal risk-adjusted rate of return.

In an informationally efficient market, the aggregate market value of a firm's stock will change by the net present value of a new project. Consequently, if the managers use the retained earnings to finance a project that has a positive net present value, the shareholders will receive a capital gain that exceeds the dividend that the managers could have paid with the earnings that they retained. Of course, if the net present value of the project financed by the retained earnings is negative, the shareholders will incur a capital loss.[2] In any event, the shareholders can convert their capital gains to (homemade) explicit dividends by selling the proportion of their shares that is equal to the proportional increase in the price of one share.

The residual claimants cannot compel the managers of their firm to pay dividends. But the managers must pay the contractual claimants. Typically, the firm will use its current earnings to meet these obligations. If current earnings are insufficient, the firm could try to raise cash by selling new shares of stock. The firm might be able to do this if investors expect that the firm's shortfall between its current earnings and the required payments to contractual claimants is temporary, and that the firm's future earnings will be large enough to cover both the contractual payments and the opportunity costs of the investors who purchase the new shares. Alternatively, the firm could sell some of its current assets. Of course, selling assets will inhibit the firm's ability to generate earnings.

A distinction between contractual claims and residual claims is that investors who hold contractual claims have the right, under bankruptcy, to acquire control of the firm. A second distinction between contractual claims and residual claims is that the contractual claimants will not have their payments increased if the firm's earnings increase. The market price of the contractual claims might increase if the firm's expected future earnings increase because the higher the firm's expected earnings, the greater the probability that the firm will be able to meet its commitments to the contractual investors without delay. But there is an upper limit to the value of the contractual claims. Once the firm's expected future earnings become large enough so that investors believe that the firm is virtually certain to make all the contractual payments on time, the contractual claims become risk-free assets. In this event, the price of a contractual claim is the present value of the promised future payments, discounted at the rate of return on the risk-free asset.

By contrast, the price of the residual claims has no upper bound. As the firm's earnings increase, the residual earnings increase because the contractual payments are fixed. Therefore, as the earnings increase above the level required to make the contractual payments, the payments to the residual investors can increase.

A third distinction between contractual claimants and residual claimants is that only the latter can vote for members of the firm's board of directors. By choosing the firm's directors, and thereby the senior managers of the firm, the residual claimants can, under some conditions, bring pressure on the firm to choose investment projects that will transfer wealth from the contractual claimants to themselves. Economists call this the problem of asset substitution, which we examine later in this chapter.

13.3 The Economic Significance of a Firm's Capital Structure

We have organized the analysis in this book on the concept of economic efficiency. An allocation of resources is economically efficient if there are no further opportunities for mutually beneficial exchanges. The capital structure of a firm determines the set of mutually beneficial exchanges that the firm can effect among various classes of investors. Therefore, there is a direct connection between capital structure and economic efficiency.

In earlier chapters, we analyzed a model in which (1) there is no uncertainty about future payments, (2) the managers of each firm always act to maximize the wealth of the firm's current shareholders, and (3) there are no taxes. Under these (idyllic) conditions, we demonstrated that the capital structure of firms has no bearing on economic efficiency. Each firm will undertake all projects that have positive net present values, and there will be no net transfers of wealth between a firm's current shareholders and new investors who finance the projects. Consequently, there will be an efficient allocation of resources because there will be no further opportunities for mutually beneficial exchanges.

In this chapter, we examine six cases that are more realistic. In all of these situations, neither investors nor managers of firms can be certain about the future payments that investment projects will generate. In each case, we show how changes in a firm's capital structure can create mutually beneficial exchanges that would otherwise be foregone.

The first case involves investors who differ in their willingness to tolerate risk. We then examine three examples of the problems of agency. In the first example, the managers of a firm invest some of the firm's earnings in projects whose net present values are negative. The managers do this because the projects provide valuable perquisites or self-aggrandizement for the managers, even though the shareholders lose wealth. In the second example, the managers refuse to liquidate the firm even though doing so would increase the shareholders' wealth. The third example is the case of asset substitution mentioned earlier.

For the fourth case of the economic significance of a firm's capital structure, we examine a situation in which the managers of a firm have better information about the probability distributions of future payments than the firm's current shareholders or potential new investors do. This is the case of asymmetric information.

We conclude by briefly discussing two cases in which a firm can affect the behavior of its competitors or the demand for its products by its choice of capital structure. In the first case we explain how, in an industry that has only two firms, each firm can use its own choice of capital structure to affect the quantity that the other firm will produce. Consequently, capital structure becomes a determinant of the equilibrium values of price and quantity produced for the industry.[3]

In our final case we discuss, again briefly, how a firm that produces a durable product can increase the shareholders' wealth by using the choice of capital structure to signal the firm's customers and suppliers of its intention to remain in business over the longer term.

We examine the six cases just described to determine the connections between a firm's capital structure and economic efficiency. Our analyses have the following common theme. Investment projects are the basis for mutually beneficial exchanges among investors. In an economy that has access to modern technology, most investment projects require so much capital and technical expertise that investors concentrate their capital in firms run by professional managers who operate these projects. In general, uncertainty about future payments will create conflicts of interests among investors that can preclude certain mutually beneficial exchanges. Under some conditions, investors can resolve those conflicts by using sophisticated financial securities to alter a firm's capital structure.

The firm's managers, acting as agents for the shareholders, choose the capital structure of their firms. In elementary economic analyses of the firm, we assume that the managers choose the capital structure so as to maximize the wealth of the current shareholders. This means that managers choose a capital structure that will enable them to finance all projects that have positive net present values. The problem of agency, described briefly above, is an important exception to this assumption.

Since the seminal work of Franco Modigliani and Merton Miller in 1958,[4] discussed in the next section, economists have produced a large volume of theoretical and empirical knowledge about capital structure. We do not present an exhaustive survey of this work. Rather, in keeping with our objective to provide an introduction to the economics of financial markets, we examine the six cases described earlier as representative examples of this work.

13.4   Capital Structure and Mutually Beneficial Exchanges between Investors Who Differ in Their Tolerances for Risk

The basis for a mutually beneficial exchange is that two (or more) persons have different rates at which they are willing to substitute between two goods. In particular, investors differ in the rates at which they are willing to substitute between expected levels of future income and the unpredictable variability in that future income. In this section, we examine how a firm might choose its capital structure so as to promote mutually beneficial exchanges between these investors. We first offer a brief digression on the economics of substitution for the purpose of placing our discussion of capital structure within the context of the general principles of economic theory.

13.4.1   The Economics of Substitution

One of the fundamental principles in economics is that a typical individual, let us call her Ms. Brown, is willing to substitute between any two goods, say Good X and Good Y.[5] We do not assert that Ms. Brown is willing to give up all of one good in exchange for the other good. Rather, the principle is stated in terms of the rates (per unit of time) at which she consumes or acquires Goods X and Y. Specifically, we assert that in exchange for a sufficiently large increase in the rate at which Ms. Brown consumes (or acquires) Good Y, she would be willing to decrease by one unit the rate at which she consumes (or acquires) Good X. Equivalently, Ms. Brown would accept an increase of one unit in the rate at which she consumes (or acquires) Good X in exchange for a sufficiently small decrease in the rate at which she consumes (or acquires) Good Y.

For example, define one unit of Good X as a meal in a particular restaurant, and one unit of Good Y as an evening at the movies. Suppose that Ms. Brown is currently consuming Good X at the rate of seven units per month and Good Y at the rate of three units per month. We do not claim that Ms. Brown is willing to trade seven meals in the restaurant per month in exchange for three visits to the movies per month. Rather, the substitution we have in mind is substitution at the margin. We assert that it is possible to persuade Ms. Brown to decrease the number of times that she goes to the movies each month from three to two by offering her a sufficiently large increase in the number of times that she may dine in the restaurant each month.

For an example in financial economics, define Good X as the level of spending for consumption in the current year, and let Good Y be the expected level of income in some future year. It would be ridiculous to claim that Ms. Brown is willing to forego all of her current spending on consumption just because by investing those resources she could increase her expected level of income in some future year. It is not ridiculous to claim that the typical shareholder is willing to substitute between current consumption and future income at the margin. Most persons make these substitutions all the time by allocating a portion of their current income to investment. Consequently, we assert that for a sufficient increase in the expected level of future income, Ms. Brown will decrease her current rate of spending on consumption by one unit (say $100). Similarly, she will increase her current rate of consumption if the consequent sacrifice of expected future income is sufficiently small.

We can restate the preceding discussion in terms of the rate of return on invested funds. For a sufficiently large expected rate of return on invested funds, Ms. Brown will decrease her current rate of consumption by $100. Similarly, for a sufficiently small expected rate of return foregone on invested funds, Ms. Brown will increase her rate of current consumption by $100.

The marginal rate at which Ms. Brown is willing to substitute between current spending and future income is not a constant. The rate depends on the location of her margin. Consider two alternative situations. In the first situation, Ms. Brown's current income is so low that she allocates almost all of it to current consumption; she invests very little each year. In the second situation, her current income is so large that she invests almost all of it. It seems plausible to assert that in either situation we could persuade her to decrease her current spending by $100 in exchange for a sufficiently large expected rate of return in invested funds. But it is also plausible that in the first situation (when her income is relatively low) she will require a much higher rate of return, before she decreases her spending on current consumption, than in the second situation (when her income is relatively high).

Individuals differ in the rates at which they are willing to substitute between Goods X and Y, whatever they are. Even if Ms. Brown and Mr. Green have identical combinations of current spending and expected future income, in general they will differ in the rates at which they are willing to substitute between current and expected future income. Most important for the present chapter, Ms. Brown and Mr. Green will likely differ in the rates at which they are willing to substitute between expected future income and unanticipated variability in that income. We will now examine how a firm might choose its capital structure so as to promote mutually beneficial exchanges between Ms. Brown and Mr. Green without changing its portfolio of investment projects. We also show that in some cases a firm might not be able to finance an investment project without accommodating the differences in the rates at which potential investors are willing to substitute between the level of expected future income and the variability of that income.

13.4.2 Merging Two Farms

Ms. Brown and Mr. Green each operate a farm on identical, adjacent plots of land. Each farmer plants corn every year. Each farmer's annual income varies unpredictably due to the effects of weather, insects, weeds, and the price of corn. Even so, each farmer's annual income is governed by a simple probability distribution. Specifically, each year is either a good year or a bad year. In a good year, each farmer's income is equal to $1,400; in a bad year each farmer's income is only $600. Good years and bad years each occur with a probability of .50, and the outcome for any particular year is independent of the outcomes for the preceding years. Consequently, each farmer's expected annual income is equal to $1,000.

Ms. Brown and Mr. Green differ in their willingness to substitute between their expected levels of income and the unpredictable variability of that income. For simplicity, we say that Ms. Brown and Mr. Green have different trade-offs between expected income and risk. Suppose that Ms. Brown would prefer to have a guaranteed annual income of $900 rather than an income that has an expected value of $1,000 but fluctuates unpredictably between $600 and $1,400. Ms. Brown is willing to trade away $100 of expected income in exchange for an elimination of risk.

Mr. Green is willing to tolerate a wider range over which his income will fluctuate in exchange for a sufficiently large increase in the expected value of that income. Specifically, Mr. Green would prefer an annual income whose expected value is $1,100 and that fluctuates unpredictably between $300 and $1,900, rather than an income whose expected value is only $1,000 and that fluctuates unpredictably between $600 and $1,400.

Both Ms. Brown and Mr. Green are risk averse in the sense that each person would choose to eliminate the fluctuations in his or her annual incomes if they could do so without any decrease in the expected values of those incomes. Ms. Brown and Mr. Green are, however, willing to substitute at different rates between the level of their expected income and the level of their risk. Ms. Brown is more risk averse than Mr. Green.

We will now explain how Ms. Brown and Mr. Green can create a mutually beneficial exchange by merging their farms into a single firm and then issuing two kinds of securities (or claims) against the firm's earnings.

The new firm will operate the two farms as a single enterprise. In a good year, each of the two farms will generate an income of $1,400, so the firm's income for that year will be $2,800. In a bad year, each farm will produce an income of only $600, and the firm's income will be $1,200. Since good years and bad years occur with equal frequency, the firm's annual income will fluctuate unpredictably between $1,200 and $2,800; the firm's expected annual income is $2,000. To keep the example simple, we assume that the firm pays out its entire net earnings each year.

The firm issues two securities. One is a bond, which is a contractual claim; the other security is a share of common stock, which is a residual claim. The bond is a perpetual bond. The terms of the bond (the contract) require the firm to pay $900 each year to whoever holds the bond that year. There is no maturity date for the bond. Hence, by issuing the bond, the firm is obligated to pay $900 per year forever. Ms. Brown, being more risk averse than Mr. Green, will hold the bond. As the contractual claimant, she will have a guaranteed income of $900 per year.

The second security is a share of common stock, which Mr. Green will hold. As a residual claimant, he is entitled to receive whatever earnings remain, if any, after the firm meets its obligation to Ms. Brown. In a good year, Mr. Green will receive $2,800−$900, or $1,900. In a bad year, he will receive $1,200−$900, or $300. Since good years and bad years are equally likely, Mr. Green's expected annual income is ($1,900+$300)/2, or $2,200/2, or $1,100.

By merging their farms into a single firm and by creating both contractual claims and residual claims in the capital structure of that firm, Ms. Brown and Mr. Green effect a mutually beneficial exchange that is based on their different tolerances for risk.

Note that the sum of the expected values of the two persons' incomes is the same as it was when they operated the two farms separately. Before the merger, each person's expected annual income was $1,000, so the sum of the expected incomes was $2,000. After the merger, Ms. Brown's expected (and guaranteed) income is $900; Mr. Green's expected income is $1,100. Thus the sum of the expected incomes for the two persons is still $2,000. But Ms. Brown and Mr. Green have made an exchange that moves each of them to a preferred position because they have different tolerances for risk. Ms. Brown has shifted to Mr. Green all of the risk that she bore when she operated her farm alone. The cost that she incurs for shifting this risk is a decrease of $100 in her expected annual income. By accepting the risk shifted from Ms. Brown, Mr. Green's risk has increased. His annual income now fluctuates unpredictably between $300 and $1,900. When he operated his farm separately, his income fluctuated over a smaller interval, namely from $600 to $1,400. Mr. Green's reward for accepting this increase in risk is an increase of $100 in his expected annual income.

The merger of the two farms into a single firm does not create an increase in wealth; the expected annual income of the firm is the sum of the expected annual incomes of the two farms operated separately. But the merger, combined with creating a capital structure that has both contractual claims and residual claims, does increase utility because both Ms. Brown and Mr. Green move to a preferred combination of expected income and risk. Since both persons gain utility, and no one else loses utility, the merger increases the level of economic efficiency by promoting a mutually beneficial exchange.

Now we consider the prices of the bond and the share of common stock. The bond is a risk-free asset because even in a bad year the firm's earnings are $1,200, which is sufficient to pay the required $900 to the bondholder. Assume that the risk-free rate of interest is .10 per year. Since the bond is a risk-free claim to a perpetual sequence of annual payments of $900, the equilibrium price of the bond is $900/.10, or $9,000.[6]

The share of common stock is a risky asset. If we use an asset pricing model such as the CAPM, we could obtain the equilibrium risk-adjusted expected rate of return on the stock, and thus its equilibrium price. Rather than using an asset pricing model, we will suppose that the risk-adjusted rate of return on the stock is .13 per year. We know that the expected annual payment to the stockholder is $1,100. Therefore, the equilibrium price of the stock is $1,100 (per year)/.13 (per year), or $8,462.

The value of the firm is the sum of the values of its outstanding securities. In the present example, the outstanding securities consist of one bond and one share of common stock. Accordingly, the value of the firm is (1)$9,000+(1)$8,462, or $17,462. An investor (or group of investors) who wanted to acquire the entire firm could do so by paying $17,462 to purchase all of the firm's outstanding securities.[7]

13.5   A Problem of Agency: Enforcing Payouts of Free Cash Flows

In this section, we describe a way that the shareholders of a firm can mitigate a problem of agency by placing debt in the firm's capital structure. In this case, the debt forces managers to pay out to shareholders in dividends that portion of the firm's earnings that cannot be invested in projects that will cover the shareholders' opportunity costs. Without the presence of the debt, the managers might create perquisites for themselves by investing in projects that do not cover those opportunity costs.

Consider Firm K, whose annual net earnings are $80,000. To maximize the shareholders' wealth, the firm's managers should undertake all projects whose rates of return exceed the shareholders' opportunity costs. The firm can use its net earnings to finance these projects, or it can use the capital markets to finance the projects by selling new securities. (In section 13.7 we examine a situation in which asymmetric information between the firm's managers and the prospective new investors would reduce the current shareholders' wealth if the firm were to finance the project by selling new securities.) However the firm finances the projects, it should undertake only those projects whose rates of return cover the shareholders' opportunity costs. Any earnings that exceed the requirements for financing those projects should be paid out to shareholders as dividends. The firm should not retain resources that its shareholders can invest by themselves at higher rates of return than the firm can earn.

Each year, Firm K invests in profitable new projects $50,000 of its annual net earnings of $80,000. By definition of profitability, each of these projects generates a rate of return that exceeds the shareholders' opportunity costs. The firm also invests $20,000 each year in projects that are not profitable; although the revenues from these projects might cover their explicit costs, the revenues do not cover the shareholders' opportunity costs. Firm K uses the remaining $10,000 of its annual net earnings to pay dividends to the shareholders.

The unprofitable projects in which the managers invest might include new products or new markets that enhance the managers' reputations even though the revenues from these projects are not large enough to cover the opportunity costs. The unprofitable projects could also be excessively sumptuous offices, excessively generous pension plans, and other perquisites.[8] Clearly, the shareholders would be better served if the managers paid the $20,000 to shareholders as dividends.

Economists define a firm's free cash flow as that portion of its net earnings that is not paid in dividends and is not invested by the firm in profitable projects. By this definition, Firm K's annual free cash flow is $20,000. The problem of the shareholders is to create a structure that will force the managers to pay out in dividends the earnings that they cannot invest profitably within the firm. That is, the shareholders want to force the managers to reduce the free cash flow to zero by increasing the dividends.

One way to solve the problem is to cause Firm K to sell a sufficient number of perpetual bonds so that the managers are forced to use $20,000 of the firm's net earnings to make the required annual payments of interest on the bonds. For convenience, suppose that the investors would discount the annual sequence of $20,000 of interest payments at the rate of .12.[9] Then the aggregate price of the bonds will be equal to ($20,000 per year/.12 per year), or $166,666.67. That is, Firm K could sell to bondholders for $166,666.67 a contractual right to receive a perpetual sequence of annual payments equal to $20,000. Firm K could use the $166,666.67 obtained from the sale of the bonds to make a special, one-time dividend to its shareholders. The shareholders could then invest the $166,666.67 themselves. In particular, individual shareholders could use their share of the special dividend to purchase some of these bonds, thereby obtaining a contractual right to their share of what is now Firm K's annual free cash flow.

The introduction of bonds into Firm K's capital structure imposes a constraint on the managers' use of the firm's earnings. When there are no bonds in the firm's capital structure, the managers are free to invest some or even all of the firm's earnings in new projects. If the firm uses earnings to finance profitable new projects, rather than pay dividends, the shareholders will gain wealth because the increase in value of their shares will more than offset the dividends that the firm could have paid. Analogously, if the firm uses earnings to finance projects that do not cover the shareholders' opportunity costs, the shareholders will lose wealth. The value of their shares will decrease by an amount that reflects the difference between the capitalized value of the investments that the shareholders could make on their own, if the firm paid out the free cash flow, and the capitalized value of the unprofitable investments that the firm finances by retaining the free cash flow. The shareholders have no right to compel their managers to pay dividends. The shareholders' recourse is to elect directors who will discipline the managers. As we have explained, the difficulties in electing a majority of the board of directors are often insurmountable.[10]

13.6   A Problem of Agency: Reallocating Resources When Consumers' Preferences Change

The managers of a firm increase the wealth of the firm's shareholders by operating investment projects that have positive net present values. The net present value of a project depends on the prices that the firm's customers will pay for its products. If the customers' preferences change so that the firm can no longer cover the shareholders' opportunity costs, the shareholders will lose wealth. To minimize this loss of wealth, the investors must reallocate their resources to more profitable projects. Sometimes the managers of the firm can do this for the shareholders by reallocating resources among projects within that firm. In other cases, the reallocation requires moving the resources to a different firm. Moving resources out of the current firm will reduce the size of that firm. In the extreme case, the current firm will be liquidated. The managers of the current firm will often resist a reduction in the size of the firm, or a liquidation. If the managers own some of the firm's shares, and if the remaining shares are owned in small quantities by a large number of investors, the managers can impede the reallocation of the investors' resources.

This is an instance of the problem of agency; the managers, as agents for the shareholders, pursue their own interests to the detriment of the shareholders' interests. In this section we provide an example of how the use of debt in a firm's capital structure can mitigate this problem of agency.

The situation is substantively different once there are bonds in the firm's capital structure. Bonds are contractual claims on the firm's earnings. If the managers do not make the contractual payments of interest to the bondholders, the bondholders can force the firm into bankruptcy. A bankruptcy can, but need not, cause a liquidation of the firm. In some situations, the bondholders will accept a reorganization of the firm in which they are allowed to fill a majority of the seats on the board of directors. The new directors will then require that the managers pay the interest on the bonds, even if this means foregoing investments in some projects. It is likely that the new directors will install their own team of managers, dismissing the former managers.

In any case, a bankruptcy (even a threatened bankruptcy) will force the firm to discontinue using earnings to finance unprofitable investment projects. Moreover, the managers will suffer a loss in their reputations as managers. Who wants to employ managers whose last position was in a bankrupt firm? The loss of reputational capital for the managers will constrain their use of earnings to finance unprofitable projects.

13.6.1   Two Firms That Have Different Ratios of Debt to Equity

Firm L and Firm H have different capital structures. Specifically, Firm L has a lower ratio of debt to equity than Firm H. We could also say that the leverage in the capital structure in Firm L is lower than it is in Firm H. In all other respects, the two firms are identical.

Each firm produces a product that generates net earnings equal to $100,000 per year. There are no taxes. The earnings are net in the sense that after the firm meets all of its costs, including wages and salaries, the costs of new materials, maintenance of equipment, and provision for periodic replacement of equipment as it wears out, the firm can pay a total of $100,000 per year to the bondholders and the stockholders. These two groups of investors together hold all the claims against the firm's net earnings. We assume that each firm distributes its entire net earnings each year to its bondholders and shareholders.

The net earnings of $100,000 per year for each firm are not certain. There is a chance that consumers' preferences will change, with the consequence that the firm's annual net earnings will be greater than, or less than, $100,000. If there were no uncertainty about the net earnings, there would be no substantive difference between the bonds and the stocks issued by the firm. Both securities would be risk-free assets; their prices would be the capitalized values of the sequences of interest and dividend payments, using the rate of return on a risk-free government bond to discount future payments.

Since the firm's net earnings are uncertain, each kind of security will be priced to allow for the effect of the uncertainty of the firm's net earnings on the payments to that security. This means two things. First, the rate of return (or the discount rate) that will be used to capitalize the sequence of future payments associated with each security will be higher than the risk-free rate of return. Second, since the bondholders' claim on the earnings takes priority over the stockholders' claim, the discount rate used to determine the price of the bonds will be lower than the rate used to determine the price of the stock. Consequently, relative to what the prices of the securities would be if the earnings were certain, the reduction in the price of the bonds will be less than the reduction in the price of the stock.

We now present a numerical example of how the bonds and the stocks of the two firms could be priced. We then use the example to illustrate how firms could adjust their capital structure so as to mitigate one of the problems of agency.

Firm L has issued 500 bonds and 10,000 shares of (common) stock; Firm H has issued 800 bonds and 10,000 shares of stock. The bonds issued by each firm have an annual coupon rate of .08 and a face value of $1,000. Therefore, each firm is committed to pay to the bondholders $80 per year on each of its outstanding bonds. Since Firm

L has issued 500 bonds, that firm must pay $40,000 per year to its bondholders. Firm H, which has 800 bonds outstanding, must pay $64,000 per year to its bondholders. Each firm generates net earnings of $100,000 per year. Firm L, which has only $40,000 of payments to make on its 500 bonds, has $60,000 for distribution to shareholders each year. By comparison, Firm H has only $36,000 for distribution to shareholders each year; the remaining $64,000 of its annual earnings is pledged to the investors who hold its 800 bonds.

To simplify the numerical example, assume that the bonds are perpetual bonds. As such, they have no maturity date. Each firm is committed to pay $80 per year on each of its outstanding bonds forever. This assumption has no substantive effect on the fundamental economic relationships that we want to illustrate.

We will now determine the prices of the securities issued by the two firms. Consider first the bonds issued by Firm L. The expected annual payment on each of these bonds is $80. But this payment is not certain. If Firm L's net earnings should fall below $40,000, the firm will not be able to meet its commitments to the bondholders. The payment on each bond would be less than $80. Since the firm will have defaulted in its contractual obligation to the bondholders, the investors who hold those bonds will presumably invoke the legal recourse to which the terms of the bonds entitle them. We will not pursue the possible consequences of this here. We simply state that since bondholders recognize that there is a possibility that they might not receive $80 per year on each bond forever, they will not pay as much for one of these bonds as they would pay for a risk-free asset that pays $80 per year. Equivalently, the investors will discount (or capitalize) the expected annual payments at a rate of return that is higher than the risk-free rate.

Suppose that investors capitalize the expected annual payments on Firm L's bonds at .11 per year. Let P_{BL} be the price of a bond issued by Firm L: Then

$$P_{BL} = \frac{\$80/\text{year}}{.11/\text{year}} = \$727.27. \tag{13.1}$$

We next consider the price of a share of the stock issued by Firm L. The price of a share is the risk-adjusted present (or capitalized) value of the sequence of dividends. Firm L's annual commitment to its bondholders is $40,000. Therefore, if the net earnings are $100,000 there will be $60,000 available for distribution as dividends over the 10,000 shares. Consequently, the dividend per share will be $6 in any year in which net earnings are $100,000. If earnings fall short of $100,000, the dividends will be reduced because the bondholders must be paid first. The firm is prohibited from paying any dividends unless bondholders are fully paid. (Symmetrically, if net earnings rise above $100,000, the dividend per share will increase above $6. Bondholders, as contractual claimants, are entitled to only $80 per bond per year; shareholders, as residual claimants, absorb all the fluctuations in the net earnings.)

Since there is more risk for the shareholders than for the bondholders in Firm L, the shareholders will capitalize the expected sequence of dividends paid by Firm L at a rate higher than the rate used by bondholders. Let P_{SL} be the price of a share of stock issued by Firm L. If shareholders capitalize the dividends at the rate of .14 per year, then

$$P_{SL} = \frac{\$6/\text{year}}{.14/\text{year}} = \$42.86. \tag{13.2}$$

The market value of Firm L is the total value of the claims on its earnings. This is the sum of the market value of its bonds and the market value of its stocks. Using the prices in (13.1) and (13.2) and the fact that Firm L has issued 500 bonds and 10,000 shares of stock, the market value of Firm L is

$$V_L = (500)(\$727.27) + (10,000)(\$42.86)$$
$$= \$363,635 + \$428,600 \tag{13.3}$$
$$= \$792,235.00.$$

An investor (or a group of investors) could purchase the rights to all of Firm L's earnings by purchasing all of its outstanding securities for $792,235.[11]

Let $(D/E)_L$ be the debt-to-equity ratio for Firm L. Using equation (13.3),

$$(D/E)_L = \frac{\$363,635}{\$428,600} = .85. \tag{13.4}$$

For every $1 worth of equity, there is $0.85 worth of debt.

We now turn to Firm H. Both Firms L and H have expected annual net earnings of $100,000. Both firms are committed to pay $80 per year to each of its outstanding bonds. But the bondholders of Firm H bear more risk than do the bondholders of Firm L. Since Firm H has more bonds outstanding than does Firm L, the bondholders of Firm H are more likely to encounter an occasion on which the net earnings will be insufficient to meet its commitments to the bondholders. Firm H has issued 800 bonds. Therefore its annual obligation to its bondholders is $80×800=$64,000. The comparable figure for Firm L is only $40,000 ($80×500). Consequently, Firm L can experience a larger decrease in net earnings before it defaults on its bonds.

Recognizing that the bonds of Firm H are riskier than those of Firm L, investors will capitalize the expected payments on Firm H's bonds at a higher rate than the rate used for Firm L's bonds. Suppose that this rate is .12. Then the price of a bond issued by Firm H is

$$P_{BH} = \frac{\$80/\text{year}}{.12/\text{year}} = \$666.67. \tag{13.5}$$

The price of the riskier bond issued by Firm H is $666.67; the price of the less risky bond issued by Firm L is, from equation (13.1), $727.27.

The price of a share issued by Firm H is the risk-adjusted present value of the expected dividends. If net earnings take their expected value of $100,000, Firm H will have $36,000 available to pay dividends after paying the $64,000 that it has committed to its bondholders. Since Firm H has issued 10,000 shares, the expected annual dividend per share is $3.60. The comparable figure for shareholders of Firm L is $6.00. The expected dividend for Firm H is riskier than the dividend for Firm L because Firm H has more bondholders to pay than does Firm L. Since Firm H's annual commitment to its bondholders is $64,000, a decrease in net earnings of only $36,000 is sufficient to eliminate the dividend for shareholders in Firm H; shareholders in Firm L will continue to receive some dividend so long as the decrease in net earnings does not exceed $60,000.

Table 13.1
Capital Structures of Firm L and Firm H

	Firm L	Firm H
Value of debt	$363,635	$533,336
Value of equity	$428,600	$225,000
Value of firm	$792,235	$758,336
Debt-to-equity ratio	.85	2.37

Recognizing that the dividend in Firm H is riskier than the dividend in Firm L, investors will discount the former at a higher rate than the latter. Suppose that the discount rate for dividends in Firm H is .16. Then the price of a share in Firm H is

$$P_{SL} = \frac{\$3.60/\text{year}}{.16/\text{year}} = \$22.50. \tag{13.6}$$

The market value of Firm H is therefore:

$$
\begin{aligned}
V_H &= (\$666.67)(800) + (\$22.50)(10,000) \\
&= \$533,336 + \$225,000 \\
&= \$758,336.
\end{aligned}
\tag{13.7}
$$

The debt-to-equity ratio for Firm H is:

$$(D/E)_H = \frac{\$533.336}{\$225,000} = 2.37. \tag{13.8}$$

For every $1 worth of equity in the capital structure of Firm H, there is $2.37 worth of debt.

Firm L and Firm H generate the same sequence of net earnings, but differ in capital structure. We summarize the capital structures in table 13.1.

13.6.2 Using Debt to Resolve a Problem of Agency

The purpose of the numerical example that we constructed above is to demonstrate how shareholders can use leverage to mitigate a problem of agency. A problem of agency will arise if a manager continues to operate projects whose rates of return do not cover the shareholders' opportunity costs. In such a case, the managers could increase the shareholders' wealth by liquidating the projects and either reallocating the capital to a profitable project or paying out the liquidated capital to shareholders as a special dividend. The shareholders could then invest the dividend in another firm.

We will now demonstrate how shareholders can choose the capital structure of their firm to mitigate this problem of agency. In particular, we demonstrate how the presence of debt in the firm's capital structure can increase the shareholders' wealth.

Suppose that a shift in consumer preferences causes each firm's net annual earnings to decrease from $100,000 to $60,000. Suppose further that it is impracticable to redesign the firms' products so as to conform to the consumers' new preferences. While there remains some demand for the firms' products, the most profitable decision is to cease operations, liquidate the firms, and thus return the capital to the shareholders, who can then invest it elsewhere. Finally, suppose that the managers of each firm have strong personal reasons to continue the current operations. For example, if the firms are liquidated, the managers (and their relatives who are now employed by the firm) will have to search for new jobs.

How can the shareholders make certain that their managers will liquidate the firm whenever it is in the shareholders' interests to do so? The shareholders could ask their directors to order the managers to liquidate the firms. If the directors refuse, the shareholders could elect a new set of directors. But this is not easy to do in the typical firm. In most firms, the directors and the managers own some of the shares themselves. The ownership of the remaining shares is widely dispersed among a large number of investors, each of whom owns a relatively small number of shares. Although each investor would gain wealth if the firm were liquidated, the incentive for any one investor to organize a replacement of the board of directors is usually too small to make the effort worthwhile.

One solution to this form of the agency problem is to place a sufficiently large amount of debt in the firm's capital structure so that the bondholders will force the firm to liquidate when its earnings no longer cover the shareholders' opportunity costs.

The annual net earnings of both Firm L and Firm H have decreased from $100,000 to $60,000. Suppose that if each firm were to liquidate, the bondholders and the shareholders of that firm could reinvest the capital in a new firm that would generate annual net earnings of $90,000. Call this new firm Firm N. (Firm N would produce a product that is more profitable than the products that Firms L and H are now producing.) Consequently, the investors in each firm have an interest in reallocating into Firm N the resources now located in Firms L or H. The bondholders of both firms would gain because the higher a firm's (expected) earnings, the less likely it is that a downward fluctuation in those earnings will cause the firm to fail to make the contractual payments of interest to the bondholders. The shareholders of both firms would gain because they are residual claimants. For any contractual obligation to the bondholders, the greater the net earnings, the greater the dividends to the shareholders can be.

The question is, which set of investors is more likely to see their capital reallocated to the new, more profitable, firm? It is easy to show that the firm with the greater debt-to-equity ratio will provide better protection to its investors.

Since Firm L has 500 bonds outstanding, it must pay its bondholders $40,000 per year ($80 per bond per year). Firm L's new annual earnings are $60,000, which will cover this obligation. Since the firm can meet its contractual obligation, the bondholders have no right to force the firm to liquidate. The reduction in Firm L's annual earnings from $100,000 to $60,000 will be borne entirely by the shareholders because they are the residual claimants. After Firm L pays the contractual $40,000 to its bondholders, only $20,000 will be available for distribution as dividends to shareholders.

Dividends per share in Firm L will now be ($60,000−$40,000)/10,000 shares, or $2 per share. When annual earnings were $100,000, dividends per share were $6 [($100,000−$40,000)/10,000 shares=$6 per share].

When the dividend was $6 per share, investors in Firm L capitalized this sequence of dividends at an annual rate of .14. Consequently, the price per share was ($6 per year/.14 per year), or $42.86. If investors use the same discount rate to capitalize the lower rate of dividends, the new price of a share in Firm L will be ($2 per year/.14 per year), or $14.29. The decrease in Firm L's annual net earnings from $100,000 to $60,000, coupled with the fact that Firm L does not use liquidation to allow its investors to reallocate their capital, imposes a capital loss on shareholders equal to $42.86−$14.29, or $28.57 per share. In percentage terms, the capital loss is $28.57/$42.86, or 66.7%.

The shareholders in Firm H suffer a smaller capital loss than do their counterparts in Firm L because the high debt-to-equity ratio in Firm H forces that firm to liquidate.

The annual net earnings of Firm H decrease from $100,000 to $60,000, just as is the case with Firm L. However, the higher debt-to-equity ratio in that firm enables its bondholders to force the firm to liquidate. Liquidation enables all the investors in Firm H to redeploy their resources into more profitable projects.

Since Firm H has 800 bonds outstanding, it must pay its bondholders $64,000 per year ($80 per bond per year). Since the firm's annual earnings are now only $60,000, the bondholders can force a liquidation. For ease of exposition, suppose that the bondholders and the shareholders of Firm H together redeploy their resources to the new firm, Firm N, and maintain the same capital structure that they had in Firm H. That is, the bondholders will hold 800 bonds, on each of which Firm N contracts to pay $80 per year. The shareholders hold 10,000 shares. We can now calculate the prices of the bonds and the stock issued by Firm N.

Firm N's total obligation to its bondholders is $64,000 per year, as it was in Firm H. Since the expected annual earnings of Firm N are $90,000, the bondholders can expect that the firm will be able to meet this obligation. If the bondholders use the same rate of discount that they did for the bonds of Firm H, the price of each bond issued by Firm N will be ($80 per year/.12 per year)=$666.67.

The dividend per share paid by Firm N will be ($90,000−$64,000)/10,000 shares=$2.60 per share. If the shareholders use the same discount rate to capitalize these dividends that they did for the dividends in Firm H, the price of a share in Firm N will be ($2.60 per year/.16 per year)=$16.25. Consequently, the decrease in the annual net earnings of Firm H from $100,000 to $60,000 will impose on its shareholders a capital loss equal to $22.50−$16.25, or $6.25 per share. The percentage of the capital loss is $6.25/$22.50, or 27.8%.

Both Firms L and H suffered the same reduction in annual net earnings. The shareholders in Firm L, who were not able to redeploy their resources, suffered a capital loss equal to 66.7%. By contrast, the shareholders in Firm H suffered a capital loss of only 27.8% because the higher ratio of debt to equity enabled them to overcome the agency problem and redeploy their resources into Firm N.

Of course there are also costs of including debt in the capital structure. In the preceding example, we saw that the contractual obligation imposed by debt could benefit the shareholders by forcing the firm to liquidate when it can no longer cover its opportunity costs. But in an uncertain and turbulent economic environment, shareholders might be best served by having very small levels of debt (or even no debt) in their firm's capital structure. If shareholders believe that their firm's current difficulty is temporary, while its longer-term prospects are strong, the shareholders might want to keep the firm intact so as to take advantage of an economic recovery.

As an example, consider the case of a software engineer who has a young family and who owns a home on which there is a large mortgaged debt. His personal capital structure is analogous to that of a firm that has a high debt-to-equity ratio; he has large contractual obligations in the form of monthly payments to the bank that holds his debt. Now suppose that the engineer has just lost his job due to an economic recession. He believes that based on his strong record of productivity it is only a matter of a year or so before the economy will recover sufficiently for him to be recalled by his former employer, or to find a comparable job in the same city. But his personal savings might not last long enough to support his family and make monthly payments. His high debt-to-equity ratio might cause him to lose his house before the economy recovers. The bank is unlikely to allow him to postpone payments on his loan. If the engineer had no mortgaged debt on the house, he could hold on much longer, even if he has to postpone routine maintenance. (Of course there are some costs, such as property taxes, that cannot be postponed without his eventually losing the house.)

We conclude that there are situations in which a high debt-to-equity ratio will not be advantageous to the residual claimants, be they shareholders in a firm or the owner of a house. The optimal debt-to-equity ratio for a firm depends on a variety of circumstances. Consequently, the simple assertion that debt is bad is false.

In section 13.8, where we discuss the impediments to economic efficiency caused by asymmetric information, we shall discover another disadvantage to a high debt-to-equity ratio.

13.7   A Problem of Agency: Asset Substitution

13.7.1   The Essence of the Problem

In most cases, the earnings of an investment project are stochastic.[12] Alternative projects differ in the nature of the stochastic processes that generate their earnings. In some cases, by substituting one investment project for another, a firm can transfer wealth from its bondholders to its shareholders. This transfer occurs because the bondholders and the shareholders hold different kinds of claims against the firm's earnings. Specifically, the bondholders hold a contractual claim, while the shareholders hold a residual claim. The managers of the firm serve at the pleasure of the shareholders (to the extent that the directors, whom the shareholders elect, represent the interests of the shareholders). Therefore, the managers have an incentive to choose projects that will maximize the wealth of the shareholders, even if the choice of one project over another will reduce the wealth of the bondholders.

Rational and informed investors will anticipate that when a firm sells bonds to finance a specified new project, there is a risk that the firm will substitute a different project in an attempt to transfer wealth from the new bondholders to the shareholders.

To protect themselves against this risk, the investors will reduce the maximal price that they are willing to pay for the bonds. To finance any project, a firm has three choices: use internal funds, use external funds, or use a combination of the two. Internal funds are current or previous earnings that the firm has retained, rather than paying as dividends to the shareholders. External funds are monies raised by selling new securities. We limit our consideration to stocks and bonds.[13] The smaller the portion of the project that new investors are willing to finance by purchasing bonds, the larger the portion that the firm must finance either by selling new shares of stock or by using retained earnings. If the firm is unwilling or unable to use retained earnings or to issue a sufficient number of new shares, the firm will forego the project, even though the project has a positive net present value. If a firm foregoes a profitable project, there is an inefficient allocation of resources.

In this section, we present a simple numerical example of how bondholders can lose wealth to shareholders through asset substitution and how this transfer of wealth can cause an inefficient allocation of resources.

13.7.2 Simplifying Assumptions; Definitions

We posit several conditions that will simplify the presentation without destroying the economic content. First, the rate of interest on the risk-free asset is equal to zero. Second, the correlation coefficient between the rate of return on each investment project and the rate of return on the market portfolio is equal to zero, so the value of beta for each project is zero. Therefore, the equilibrium expected rate of return on each project is equal to the rate of return on the risk-free asset, which is equal to zero.[14] Third, each firm exists for only one period, and undertakes a single project. At $t=0$, the firm raises the required financing and begins the project. One period later, at $t=1$, the project generates a value, which the firm immediately distributes to the bondholders and the shareholders. The firm is then liquidated.[15]

The three foregoing assumptions imply that the market value of the project at time 0 is the expected value of the outcome of the project that will appear at time 1. If markets are perfectly competitive, the cost of undertaking the project at time 0 will be equal to its expected value.[16]

Define the following:

S_i = The total market values at $t=0$ of the stockholders' claims to the earnings of Project i

B_i = The total market values at $t=0$ of the bondholders' claims to the earnings of Project i

$V_i = S_i + B_i$ = The total market at $t=0$ of the value of Project i

F = The aggregate face value of the bonds

B_i = Minimum (F, V_i)

S_i = Maximum $(V_i - F, 0)$

The bond is a contractual claim that requires the firm to pay F to the bondholders. If the value of the firm at $t=1$ is less than the firm's obligation to the bondholders ($V_1 < F$), the firm must pay the entire value of the firm to the bondholders. Hence, the market value of the bonds at $t=1$ is the minimum of F and V_1.

The shareholders hold a residual claim. At $t=1$, the market value of their claim is whatever value remains in the firm after the firm meets its obligation to the bondholders. Therefore, the market value of the stock at $t=1$ is the maximum of V_1-F and 0.

13.7.3   A General Example of an Investment Project

In this section, we present a simple, general example of an investment project. In the following section, we use this general example as a template to analyze four specific numerical examples of the problem of asset substitution.

The firm begins the project at $t=0$. One period later, at $t=1$, the firm liquidates the project and receives X. The liquidation value X is a random variable governed by a uniform probability density function over the interval (L, U), in which L and U are constants that are constrained by $0 \leq L < U$. The probability density for the random variable X is $1/(U-L)$. Let X_0 and X_1 be possible values for X, with $X_0 < X_1$. Then the probability that X will take a value in the interval (X_0, X_1) is $(X_1-X_0)/(U-L)$. Using a uniform density function for the outcome of the investment project makes the calculations easier without making the example vacuous.[17]

For the numerical examples in the following section, we use the following formulas; the derivations of these formulas are in the appendix to this chapter.

The expected value of X, $E(X)$, is equal to $(L+U)/2$, which is the midpoint of the range of possible values for X.

The standard deviation of X is equal to $(U-L)^2/2\sqrt{3}$.

The value at $t=0$ of the shareholders' claim to the earnings of the project is $S=(U-F)^2/2(U-L)$.

The value at $t=0$ of the bondholders' claim, B, to the earnings of the project is the difference between the expected value of the project and the value of the shareholders' claim. That is, $B=E(X)-S$.

13.7.4   Three Numerical Examples of Asset Substitution

We now examine three numerical examples using the general template presented in the preceding section. The examples differ in the values for L and U, the lower and upper boundaries of the probability density function for the project. We have drawn the probability density functions for four projects in figure 13.1. For each project, we indicate the values for L, U, the expected value, and the standard deviation. We compare these values in table 13.2. The details of the calculations appear in the appendix to this chapter.

We can illustrate the problem of asset substitution by comparing Projects B, C, and D separately with Project A. Suppose that the firm, acting for its shareholders, announces that it will undertake Project A, and that it will finance that project by selling bonds that have a face value of $90. Investors who purchase the bonds at time 0 will receive a payment at time 1 that will depend on the outcome of a random variable. The market value of the bonds at time 0 is the expected value of the payments that the bondholders will receive at time 1. If investors believe that the firm will, in fact, undertake Project A, the market value of the bonds at time 0 will be $82. The cost of undertaking Project A is the market value (at time 0) of that project, which is $100.

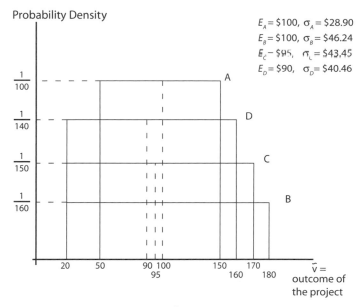

Figure 13.1 The probability density functions for projects A, B, C, and D, and the values of the associated parameters.

Table 13.2
The Values of the Parameters for Projects A, B, C, and D, and the Market Values of the Shareholders' Claims, the Bondholders' Claims, and the Firm

	Project			
	A	B	C	D
Upper bound for X	$150	$180	$170	$160
Lower bound for X	$50	$20	$20	$20
Face value of bonds	$90	$90	$90	$90
Expected value of the project	$100	$100	$95	$90
Standard deviation of the project	$28.90	$46.24	$43.35	$40.46
Market value at time 0 of the shareholders' claims	$18	$25.31	$21.33	$17.50
Market value at time 0 of the bondholders' claims	$82	$74.69	$73.67	$72.50
Market value at time 0 of the firm	$100	$100	$95	$90

Consequently, the firm can finance Project A by selling bonds for $82 and stocks for the remaining $18.

Now suppose that after the firm raises the $100 for the announced purpose of financing Project A, the firm substitutes Project B, C, or D for Project A. The probability density functions of Projects B, C, and D differ from the density function for Project A. Therefore, the expected values of the payoffs for both the bonds and the stock will change if the firm substitutes one of these projects for Project A. If investors learn of the substitution at time 0, the market values of the bonds and the stock will change, at time 0, to reflect the changes in the expected values of the payoffs for those securities.

Depending on which project the firm substitutes for Project A, the firm can effect a transfer of wealth between the bondholders and the shareholders. If the firm's managers are more sensitive to the interests of the shareholders (because the shareholders can vote for the firm's directors while the bondholders cannot), the firm will choose only those substitutions that increase the shareholders' wealth, even if the substitution causes bondholders to lose wealth.

If Project A has the same expected value as the project substituted for it, the aggregate level of wealth in the economy will not change; but the *distribution* of that wealth between bondholders and shareholders will change. If, however, the new project has a lower expected value than Project A, the aggregate level of wealth will decrease, imposing a deadweight loss on the economy.

We now consider the consequences for bondholders, shareholders, and the economy of substituting Projects B, C, or D for Project A.

The Effect of Substituting Project B for Project A

Although Project B has the same expected value as Project A, Project B is riskier. The probability density function for Project A extends over the interval ($50, $150); the interval for Project B is ($20, $180). Both intervals are centered at $100, so the two projects have the same expected value. The interval for Project B is wider than that for Project A, so Project B is the riskier of the two. Accordingly, the standard deviation for Project B is $46.24, as compared to a standard deviation of $28.90 for Project A. The bondholders' contractual claim specifies that the maximal payment they can receive at time 1 is $90. Substituting Project B for Project A increases the probability that the value of the firm at time 1 will be less than $90. Consequently, if investors learn at time 0 that the firm has substituted Project B for Project A, the market value of the bonds will immediately decrease from $82.00 to $74.69. Since the substitution of Project B for Project A does not change the expected value of the firm, and since the shareholders are residual claimants, the market value of the stock will increase from $18.00 to $25.31 to offset the decrease in the value of the bonds. That is, the substitution of Project B for Project A will transfer $7.31 in wealth from the bondholders to the shareholders. Since there is no decrease in the value of the firm, the substitution of the riskier project imposes no deadweight loss on the economy.

The Effect of Substituting Project C for Project A

Project C has both greater risk and a smaller expected value than Project A. Substituting Project C for Project A would increase the standard deviation of the earnings (from

$28.90 to $43.35), and reduce the expected value (from $100 to $95). Comparing the columns for Projects A and C in table 13.2 indicates that substituting Project B for Project A will decrease the market value of the bonds (from $82.00 to $73.67) and increase the value of the stock (from $18.00 to $21.33). Bondholders lose $8.33 (because they absorb the entire reduction of the firm's $5.00) and lose an additional $3.33 in wealth transferred to the shareholders. Substituting Project C for Project A transfers wealth from the bondholders to the shareholders *and* imposes a deadweight loss on the economy.

The Effect of Substituting Project D for Project A

Project D, like Project C, has both greater risk and a smaller expected value than Project A. Unlike Project C, however, substituting Project D for Project A will reduce the wealth of both the bondholders *and* the shareholders, and impose a deadweight loss of $10 ($100−$90) on the economy. The bondholders would lose $9.50 ($82.00−$72.50); the shareholders would lose $0.50 ($18.00−$17.50).

We conclude from the preceding numerical examples that if the firm can raise $82 from bondholders by announcing an intention to undertake Project A, the firm can transfer wealth from the bondholders to the shareholders by substituting Project B for Project A. The economy will incur no deadweight loss because Projects A and B have the same expected value. If Project B is not available, the firm could still transfer wealth to its shareholders by substituting Project C for Project A. In this case, the economy would incur a deadweight loss of $5.00. The firm would not substitute Project D for Project A; to do so would cause the shareholders to lose wealth.

Rational investors will recognize that the firm can transfer wealth from bondholders to shareholders by substituting Project B for Project A. Unless the firm can guarantee that it will undertake Project A, prospective bondholders will anticipate that they will have a contractual claim on the earnings of Project B and thus pay no more than $74.69 for the bonds. Consequently, to finance Project B, the firm will have to use $25.31 of retained earnings, or raise that amount from shareholders.

If Project B is not available, prospective bondholders will anticipate that the firm will substitute Project C for Project A and thus will pay only $73.67 for the bonds. Consequently, to finance Project C, the firm must either use $26.33 of retained earnings, or raise that amount in new capital from the shareholders. The economy will incur a deadweight loss equal to the difference between the expected values of Projects A and C.

Notice that the firm has no incentive to protect the economy from the deadweight loss created by undertaking Project C rather than Project A. To do so would impose a loss on the shareholders. Anticipating that the firm will proceed with Project C, the bondholders will contribute only $73.67 in new capital to the firm. Since the cost of Project A is its expected value, $100, the firm would either have to contribute $26.33 ($100.00−$73.67) from retained earnings, or raise $26.33 in new capital from the shareholders. But if the firm undertakes Project A, the market value of the shareholders' claims will decrease from $26.33 to $18.00, while the value of the bondholders' claim will increase from $73.67 to $82.00. The economy will avoid the deadweight loss of the difference between the expected values of Projects A and C, but there will be a transfer of wealth from the bondholders to the shareholders.

13.7.5 Mitigating the Inefficient Allocation by Using Restrictive Covenants

Firms and investors can avoid the inefficient allocation of resources that can occur from the substitution of riskier projects for less risky ones by writing, and accepting, restrictive covenants in the bonds. A restrictive covenant is a provision in the bond that restricts the firm to use the funds provided by the bondholders only for a specific project.

For example, suppose that the ES&D Railroad offers to sell bonds to finance the purchase of freight cars to be used only on the route between Cleveland and Boston. The railroad also has a route between Kansas City and Baltimore. The returns for the two routes are governed by different probability density functions. The expected value for the route between Kansas City and Baltimore is less than the expected value for the route between Cleveland and Boston, and the risk for the route between Kansas City and Baltimore is higher than the risk for the route between Cleveland and Boston. Under some conditions, the railroad will have an incentive to sell bonds to finance the purchase of freight cars for the route between Cleveland and Boston, and then use the cars on the route between Kansas City and Baltimore. Anticipating this, the bondholders will not pay as much for the bonds as they would if they could be certain that the railroad would use the new cars only on the route between Cleveland and Boston.

The railroad could avoid this problem by including a restrictive covenant in the bonds. The covenant would state that each new car would be identified by a serial number, permanently stamped into the frame of the car when it was built. Further, each car would be dedicated to service on the route between Cleveland and Boston. To use the car on any other route would be a default by the railroad. A default would transfer to the bondholders certain rights formerly assigned to the shareholders.[18]

13.8   Economic Inefficiencies Created by Asymmetric Information

Economists use the term *asymmetric information* to describe a situation in which the actors on one side of a market have better information about relevant future outcomes than the actors on the other side of the market do. There are numerous situations in which asymmetric information can create an inefficient allocation of resources. Consider the following example.[19]

It is not unusual for the managers of a firm to have better information about the firm's ability to generate earnings than the current shareholders or prospective new investors do. In particular, the managers might have superior information about a proposed new investment project. If the firm lacks sufficient internal funds to finance the new project, the firm must raise additional capital by selling new securities. The firm's managers and the prospective new investors who could buy the new securities are on opposite sides of the market. In this section, we demonstrate that if the asymmetry of information between the managers and the prospective new investors is sufficiently severe (in a sense that we define below), the firm will forego the project even though the project has a positive net present value. Clearly, this outcome is economically inefficient. We also demonstrate how a firm, again under some conditions, can overcome the effects of the asymmetric information by issuing a sophisticated kind of security. The purpose of this demonstration is to show a relationship between economic efficiency and the capital structures of firms.

13.8.1 A Brief Summary of Akerlof's Market for Lemons

The seminal paper on asymmetric information presented in 1970 by George Akerlof is the basis of many advances in economics.[20] Akerlof demonstrated that asymmetric information can cause a market to collapse, thereby precluding some mutually beneficial exchanges that would occur if the asymmetry were eliminated. In section 2.4.1 of chapter 2 we presented in some detail a simple version of Akerlof's model, and in section 2.4.2 we used Akerlof's model to demonstrate how asymmetric information between managers of firms and prospective investors could create an inefficient allocation of resources. We now summarize briefly our work in chapter 2 on asymmetric information, and then consider a more sophisticated analysis that involves bonds that are callable and convertible.

The usual introduction to Akerlof's model is to consider a market for used automobiles. There is a set of automobiles that are individually offered for sale. Each automobile has a certain quality, such as the number of miles of service that it will deliver per $100 of expenditure for maintenance and repair. The current owner of each automobile knows the quality of that automobile. Prospective buyers of the automobiles know only the probability distribution of the values of quality across the set of automobiles offered for sale. Thus, there is asymmetric information in the market for used automobiles; the prospective sellers have superior information relative to the prospective buyers.

The asymmetry of information between buyers and sellers creates an asymmetry of optimal behavior for buyers and sellers. The maximal price that a rational buyer will pay for any automobile depends on the average quality of the automobiles offered for sale.[21] On the other side of the market, the minimal price that a rational seller will accept for a particular automobile depends on the quality of that automobile. Consequently, owners of used automobiles will not offer for sale any automobile that has a level of quality greater than the average level of quality across the population of used automobiles. Rational buyers, knowing that sellers will withhold all the high-quality automobiles, will revise downward the maximal price that they will offer for a used automobile. The reduction in the price offered by buyers will cause owners to withhold even more automobiles, which will cause buyers to reduce further the maximal price that they will pay. This process is degenerative. In the end, the market collapses; no used automobiles are offered for sale.

The asymmetry of information between sellers and buyers creates an inefficient allocation of resources. Presumably, there are some current owners of automobiles for whom the marginal values of (retaining) those automobiles is less than the marginal values that some prospective buyers would place on (acquiring) those automobiles. If there were no asymmetry of information, some current owners and some prospective buyers could effect mutually beneficial exchanges.

In section 2.4.2, we used a simple version of Akerlof's model to demonstrate how asymmetric information between managers of firms and prospective investors could create an inefficient allocation of resources. We considered a population of firms. Each firm is either strong or weak. Only the managers of a firm know whether that firm is strong or weak. A strong firm has a larger net present value for its current operations than does a weak firm. Each firm has an opportunity to undertake a profitable new investment project, but only if the firm can finance that project by selling new shares of stock. The net present value of the project for a strong firm is greater than for a weak firm. The cost of undertaking the project is the same for each type of firm.

Prospective investors, who could finance the project in either type of firm, know the net present values of the current operations and the new project in each type of firm. Unfortunately, the investors cannot determine whether a particular firm is strong or weak. Consequently, if a firm attempts to raise capital to finance the new project, the maximal price that investors will pay for those shares depends on the average of the net present values of strong firms and weak firms, including the new project, with the two net present values weighted by the numbers of each type of firm in the total population of firms. That is, prospective investors regard each firm that offers to sell new shares as a random draw from a population that contains both strong and weak firms.

To recover their opportunity costs for financing the new project, the new investors must acquire a certain proportion of the ownership of the firm. The current shareholders in a firm retain the remaining proportion of the firm. The proportion that the investors must acquire of a strong firm is smaller than the proportion that they must acquire of a weak firm. From the perspective of a strong firm, the presence of weak firms contaminates the pool of firms. Because investors regard any firm as if it were a weighted average of a strong firm and a weak firm, the proportion of a strong firm that the new investors acquire is larger than it would be if the managers of the strong firm could credibly inform the new investors that they are, in fact, acquiring a strong firm.

Depending on the net present values of the two types of firms, with and without the new project, and on the cost of the project, the shareholders of a strong firm will forego the project because the new investors would acquire so large a proportion of the firm that the current shareholders would lose wealth. By definition, if a project has a positive net present value, the sequence of payments generated by that project will cover more than the opportunity costs of financing it. Therefore, it is possible for both the current shareholders and the new investors to gain wealth if the firm undertakes the project, but only if the new investors do not acquire too large a proportion of the firm. If the weak firms are sufficiently numerous in the population of firms, and if each firm must finance the project by selling new shares, the current shareholders of a strong firm will forego the project, thereby creating an inefficient allocation of resources.

13.8.2 A Numerical Example in Which There Is Symmetric Information between Managers and Investors

For comparison, we first present an example in which there is symmetric information between the managers of a firm and new investors who are being asked to finance a new project.

There are 10,000 firms in a particular industry. Each firm has only common stock outstanding. The price of one share of a firm's common stock is the present value of that firm's future sequence of earnings per share. The market value of a firm is equal to the price of its stock multiplied by the number of shares outstanding. Therefore, the market value of a firm is the present value of its future earnings.

Among the 10,000 firms are 1,000 strong firms and 9,000 weak firms. The market value of a strong firm is $600; the market value of a weak firm is only $100. Since there is no asymmetric information, all investors can determine with certainty whether a particular firm is strong or weak.

Each firm has an opportunity to invest in a new project. The cost of undertaking the project for any firm is $50. The net present value of the project in a strong firm is $80. In a weak firm, the net present value of the project is only $30. No firm has any excess internal funds with which to finance the project. Consequently, if a firm wants to undertake the project, it must sell new securities in a quantity sufficient to raise $50.

If a strong firm undertakes the project, the market value of that firm will increase from $600 to $730. The increase of $130 in market value consists of the $50 of additional capital that the firm raises to finance the project, plus $80 for the net present value of the project.[22] If a weak firm undertakes the project, the market value of that firm will increase from $100 to only $180. The increase of $80 includes the $50 worth of resources required to finance the project plus the net present value of the project, which is only $30 for a weak firm.

To finance the project, each firm must sell new shares in a quantity sufficient to raise $50. The number of new shares that a firm must sell to raise $50 determines the proportion of the firm that the new investors will acquire. Competition among investors will ensure that the proportion of a firm that the investors will acquire will be such that the new investors will recover only their opportunity costs. The greater the market value of the firm for which the new investors are providing the $50, the smaller is the proportion of that firm that the new investors must acquire to recover their opportunity costs. Since investors can distinguish with certainty between strong firms and weak firms, a strong firm can raise the $50 by granting a smaller proportion of the firm to new investors than a weak firm can. We can demonstrate this easily using the numerical characteristics of the two kinds of firms.

The market value of a strong firm including the new project is $730. If new investors finance the project by purchasing $50 of new shares, then the proportion of a strong firm that the new investors will own is $50/$730=.068 (after rounding). Assume (only for simplicity) that the rate of interest at a bank is equal to zero. Then the new investors need to recover only $50 to meet their opportunity costs. If the interest rate is zero, the value of the new investors' shares next period will be $50, and the value of the firm next period will be $730. Then the new investors can sell their shares next period and recover their investment (including zero opportunity costs).

If a strong firm can finance the project by ceding only .068 of the firm to the new investors, the current shareholders will retain the proportion 1.000−.068, or .932, of the firm. Including the new project, the market value of the strong firm is $730. Then the value of the current investors' holdings will be (.932)$730, or $680 approximately. The market value of the value of a strong firm without the new project is $600. The net present value of the new project in a strong firm is $80. Consequently, the current shareholders capture the full net present value of the new project. The new investors obtain only .068 of the firm in exchange for purchasing $50 worth of new shares. Since (.068)$730=$49, we conclude (after rounding) that the new investors recover only their opportunity costs.[23]

We have demonstrated that if a strong firm finances the project by selling new shares, the current shareholders obtain the entire net present value of the new project, while the new investors recover only their opportunity costs. The same result holds for a weak firm.

Including the new project, the market value of a weak firm is $180. The proportion of a weak firm acquired by new investors is $50/$180=.278. Consequently, the current shareholders retain 1.000−.278, or .722 of the firm. Once the weak firm undertakes the project, the wealth of the current shareholders increases from (1.000)$100 to (.722)$180, which is equal to $129.96, or $130 after rounding. The wealth of the current shareholders increases by $30, which is the full net present value of the project in a weak firm. The new investors recover only their opportunity costs.

13.8.3   A Numerical Example in Which There Is Asymmetric Information between Managers and Investors

We now modify the example of the preceding section by dropping the assumption that investors can distinguish between strong firms and weak firms with certainty. Consider first the situation before any firm undertakes the new project. As before, there are 1,000 strong firms and 9,000 weak firms. The market value of a strong firm is $600, and the market value of a weak firm is $100. Only the managers of a firm know whether their firm is strong or weak. Therefore, if a group of investors were to purchase a single firm, they would have a 90% chance of obtaining a weak firm and only a 10% chance of obtaining a strong firm. If the investors were to purchase 100 of these firms, the average value of the firms that they purchase would be equal to (.9)($100)+(.1)($600), or $90+$60, or $150.[24] Since only the managers know whether a particular firm is strong or weak, the maximal price that the investors should pay for a firm is $150.

We will now determine whether a firm should undertake the new project if the firm must finance that project by selling new shares. The answer depends on: (1) the difference in the market values of the strong firms and the weak firms without the project, (2) the difference in net present values of the project in the two kinds of firms, (3) the amount of new capital that a firm must raise to finance the project, and (4) the ratio of strong to weak firms in the population of firms.

The market value of a strong firm that undertakes the project is $730. The market value of a weak firm that undertakes the project is $180. If all firms undertake the project, the average market value of the firms will be (.90)($180)+(.10)($730), or $235. If new investors purchase $50 worth of new shares in each firm, the investors must acquire at least $50/$235, or .213 (after rounding) of each firm in order to recover their opportunity costs. Competition among investors will ensure that each firm can raise the $50 required to finance the new project by selling a quantity of new shares that will allow the new investors to acquire .213 of the firm. Consequently, the current shareholders will retain .787 of the firm.

When investors cannot determine whether a given firm is strong or weak, a strong firm should not undertake the new project. If a strong firm undertakes the project, the value of the current shareholders' stake will be (.787)($730), or $574.51. Without the new project, the market value of the strong firm is $600, all of which is retained by the current shareholders because, without the new project, there are no new shareholders. Clearly, the current shareholders in a strong firm lose wealth if their firm sells new shares to undertake the project. Selling new shares to finance the project will transfer $600−$574.51, or $25.49 in wealth from the current shareholders to the new shareholders.

To see this another way, consider the situation of the new shareholders who were fortunate enough to have drawn a strong firm in which to invest. The new shareholders acquire .213 of the firm. Since the market value of the strong firm with the project is $730, the value of the new investors' stake is (.213)($730), or $157.62. We can write $157.62 as $50+$80+$27.62. The value of the new investors' stake in the strong firm allows them to recover their opportunity costs ($50), capture the entire net present value of the project ($80), and receive a transfer of $27.62 from the current shareholders.

The current shareholders in a strong firm will lose wealth to the new shareholders because the number of strong firms in the population of all firms is so low that the average market value of a firm is much closer to the market value of a weak firm than to a strong firm ($235 is much closer to $180 than it is to $730). The smaller the proportion of strong firms, the lower will be the average market value of a firm with the project relative to the market value of a strong firm with the project. The lower the average market value of a firm with the project, the higher the proportion of a firm that the new investors must acquire if they are to recover their opportunity costs. In the present example, the proportion of strong firms is so low, and consequently the proportion of each firm that the new investors must acquire is so large, that those new investors fortunate enough to invest in a strong firm receive a transfer of wealth from the current shareholders.

We now consider whether a weak firm should finance the project by selling new shares. If a weak firm sells new shares, the current shareholders will retain (1.000−.213) or .787 of the firm, just as in the case of a strong firm. The market value of a weak firm that undertakes the project is $180. Consequently, the value of the new investors' stake in a weak firm that undertakes the project will be (.213)$180, or $38.34. This is less than the new investors' opportunity cost, which is $50. Hence, the new investors suffer a loss equal to $50−$38.34, or $11.66. It is easy to show that the $11.66 is transferred from the new investors to the current shareholders.

When a weak firm sells new shares to raise the $50 for the project, the value of the current investors' stake in the firm will increase from (1.000)$100 to (.787)($180), or from $100 to $141.66. We can disaggregate this by writing $141.66=$100+ $30+$11.66. The value of the current shareholders' claim increases by the full net present value of the project ($30) plus $11.66 in wealth transferred from the new investors.

13.8.4   The Collapse of the Market

In the preceding numerical example, there are net transfers of wealth between the current shareholders of a firm and the investors who finance the project. In strong firms, the new investors gain at the expense of the current shareholders. In weak firms, the current shareholders gain at the expense of the new investors. In each case, the transfers occur because the asymmetry of information between managers of firms and investors prevents the new investors from acquiring a proportion of the firm that will allow them to cover no more than their opportunity costs and no less. In our example, the new investors acquire .213 of the firm, whether the firm is strong or weak. For a strong firm, this proportion is large enough to effect a transfer of wealth from the current shareholders to the new investors. But for a weak firm, the proportion .213 is small enough to effect a transfer of wealth in the opposite direction, from the new investors to the current shareholders.

Since neither strong firms nor weak firms can finance the project by selling newly created shares without causing net transfers of wealth, the market for new securities will collapse. A market is a mechanism through which individuals can effect mutually beneficial exchanges. But in the example at hand, one party or the other always suffers a net loss of wealth. Consequently, unless the asymmetry of information between managers and investors is eliminated, neither strong firms nor weak firms will be able to finance the new project by selling new shares.

We will now demonstrate that the asymmetry of information will disappear because all investors know that only weak firms will attempt to sell new shares. Competition among investors will enable each weak firm to raise $50 from new investors by allowing them to acquire the proportion $50/$180, or .278, of the firm. The current shareholders will retain the proportion $1.000 - .278$, or .722, of the firm. The new project increases the market value of the firm from $100 to $180. Consequently, the market value of the current shareholders' stake in the firm increases from $(1.000)\$100$ to $(.722)\$180$, or from $100 to (approximately) $130. The current shareholders capture the entire net present value of the project, leaving the new investors to recover only their opportunity costs.

13.8.5   Economic Inefficiency Caused by Asymmetric Information

Recall from earlier chapters that an efficient allocation of resources requires that every potential for a mutually beneficial exchange is realized. In particular, every firm must undertake any investment project that has a positive net present value. In principle, the net present value of the project can be distributed across various parties in a way that allows at least one of the parties to gain wealth without imposing a loss on any party. That is, there need be no net transfer of wealth.

In the numerical example at hand, the net present value of the new project is positive in both weak firms and strong firms. Therefore, there will be an inefficient allocation of resources unless both kinds of firms undertake the project. But the asymmetric information between managers and investors permits only the weak firms to finance the project by selling new shares. Consequently, if a strong firm has no access to financing other than by selling new shares, that firm must forego the project. In this case, the asymmetric information creates an inefficient allocation of resources.

The shareholders of a strong firm would lose wealth to the new investors if the firm undertakes the project because the new investors would acquire too large a proportion of the firm. The ratio of weak firms to strong firms is so large that the average market value of a firm is too close to the market value of a weak firm. The weak firms contaminate the pool of firms from which the investors will draw when purchasing new securities. If the managers of each strong firm could credibly signal the quality of their firm to potential new investors, there would be no need to grant so large a proportion of the firm to the new investors in exchange for their financing the project. Knowing that they were acquiring a portion of a strong firm, the new investors would recognize that they could accept a smaller proportion of that firm and still recover their opportunity costs.

13.8.6 Using Callable, Convertible Bonds to Eliminate Economic Inefficiencies Caused by Asymmetric Information

We will now show how a strong firm can overcome the problem of asymmetric information if either type of firm can choose between issuing straight equity or issuing callable, convertible bonds to finance the project. Investors know the level of earnings that a strong firm can generate, both with and without the new project. Consequently, investors know how a strong firm's decision on how to finance the project will affect the wealth of that firm's current shareholders. Similarly, investors can predict how a weak firm's decision on how to finance the project will affect the wealth of that firm's current shareholders. Under some conditions, the managers of strong firms can set the terms of a callable, convertible bond so that investors will recognize that only a strong firm can use that security to finance the new project without imposing a loss of wealth on its current shareholders. Similarly, the managers of weak firms can set the terms of an offering of straight equity so that investors will recognize that only a weak firm can use that security to finance the project without imposing a loss on its current shareholders. Consequently, the managers of any firm can credibly distinguish their firm as strong or weak by their choice of how to finance the project.

Each firm's choice of which security to issue eliminates the asymmetry of information between managers of firms and investors who can finance the new project. Consequently, each firm is able to finance the new project without imposing net transfers of wealth between current shareholders and new investors. Economists call this outcome a *separating equilibrium* because, with the asymmetry of information eliminated, investors are able to separate strong firms from weak firms before committing funds to finance the firms' projects. In the preceding section, the presence of asymmetric information required investors to evaluate each firm as if it were a weighted average of a pool of weak firms and strong firms. Economists call this outcome a *pooled equilibrium*.

Following is a numerical example of how the managers of weak firms and the managers of strong firms can use their choice of securities to create a separating equilibrium in which both types of firms can attract additional capital from new investors to finance profitable projects.

Assume that the risk-free rate of interest is equal to zero. Assume also that the earnings of all firms are uncorrelated with the earnings of the macroeconomy; hence each firm's value of beta is equal to zero. These assumptions will simplify our calculations without affecting the fundamental principles of the separating equilibrium that we want to present.

The current value of the strong firm's assets is $600. The current value of the weak firm's assets is $100. At the moment, each firm has only common stock outstanding. Each firm has an opportunity to begin a new project at a cost of $50. Neither firm has any idle cash, so a firm that wants to undertake the project must raise $50 in new capital. The net present value of the project in a strong firm is $80; the net present value of the project in a weak firm is only $30. Since the net present values of the project are positive in both types of firms, it is possible, in principle, for each firm to construct a mutually beneficial exchange between its current shareholders and a set of new investors. We can easily calculate the bounds on the values of the claims of the new investors that will create a mutually beneficial exchange.

The market value of a strong firm that undertakes the project is $730, of which $600 is the value of the strong firm's current assets, $50 is the value of the new capital, and $80 is the net present value of the project in a strong firm. The new investors who provide the $50 of additional capital required to finance the project must obtain a claim against that firm that is worth more than $50 and less than $130. If the new investors are to gain wealth, they must obtain a claim that is worth more than $50. (Recall that the interest rate is equal to zero.) If the current shareholders are to gain wealth, the value of the new investors' claim must be less than $130. Otherwise, the value of the current shareholders' claim will be worth less than $600, which is their wealth without the project.

For a weak firm, the value of the firm with the project is $180, of which $100 is the value of that firm without the project, $50 is the new capital required to finance the project, and $30 is the net present value of the project in a weak firm. Proceeding as we did for the strong firm, we find that both the current shareholders and the new investors will gain wealth if the value of the new investors' claim exceeds $50 and is less than $80.

We can now show that a strong firm can effect a mutually beneficial exchange between its current shareholders and new investors by financing the project with a callable, convertible bond, and a weak firm can effect a similar exchange by using straight equity to finance the project. By knowing the characteristics of a strong firm, investors will infer (correctly) that a strong firm can use the bond to increase the wealth of its current shareholders, while allowing the new investors to gain wealth also. Similarly, investors will recognize that a weak firm can use straight equity to increase its current shareholders' wealth, again allowing the new investors also to gain wealth. More important, investors will recognize that neither type of firm will masquerade as the other type of firm by issuing the security associated with that type of firm. To do so would cause the current shareholders in the "masquerading" firm to lose wealth.

Events occur at time 0 and time 1. At time 0, each kind of firm has an opportunity to undertake the new project. At time 1, all investors learn which of the firms are strong and which are weak. Any firm that issued a bond at time 0 must pay the face value of that bond to whoever holds the bond at time 1.

There are two securities that a firm can issue at time 0 to finance the project. The first security is a bond that has a face value of $125, is callable (by the issuing firm) for $110, and is convertible (by the bondholders) into .16 of the equity of the firm. The second security is straight equity that represents .28 of the firm. We will now examine the effects on the wealth of current shareholders and the wealth of new investors for the several cases distinguished by the type of firm, the firm's choice of which security to issue, and the choices made by managers and investors with respect to calling and converting the bond.

Consider first what will happen if the strong firm issues the bond at time 0. At time 1, the bondholders (and everyone else) learn that the firm in which they hold the bond is a strong firm. The market value at time 1 of a strong firm that undertook the project is $730. The firm now must decide whether to call the bond.

If the firm calls the bond, the bondholders have a choice. They can accept the call, in which case they surrender the bond in exchange for a payment of the call price, which is $110. The bondholders' alternative is to convert their bond into equity. By converting to equity, the bondholders will acquire .16 of the firm. Since the market value of the firm at time 1 is known by everyone to be $730, the bondholders recognize that if they convert their bond into equity, the value of their position will be equal to (.16)$730, or $116.80. So in the event that the firm calls the bond, the bondholders will convert to equity, because the value of the converted bond ($116.80) exceeds the call value of the bond ($110). We say that the managers of the strong firms can force conversion of the bond at time 1 because the converted value of the bond exceeds the call price.

Since the value of the converted bond, $116.80, exceeds what the new investors paid for the bond, $50, the new investors will gain an increase in wealth equal to $116.80−$50, or $66.80. Since the new investors will have acquired .16 of the equity in the strong firm, the original shareholders will have retained the proportion 1.00−.16, or .84 of the firm. Then the value of the original shareholders' claim is (.84)$730, or $613.20. Had the firm declined the project, the original shareholders of the strong firm would have owned 100% of a firm worth $600. Therefore, if the strong firm undertakes the project, finances it by issuing a callable, convertible bond, and forces conversion of the bond, the original shareholders will increase their wealth by (.84) $730 −(1.00)$600, or $613.20−$600.00, or $13.20. Both the original shareholders and the new investors gain wealth, so the firm will have effected a mutually beneficial exchange. Moreover, the sum of the gains in wealth of the original shareholders and the new investors is $13.20+$66.80, or $80, which is the net present value of the project in a strong firm. Therefore, the net present value of the project is fully distributed between the original shareholders and the new investors.

In earlier chapters, we showed that in the absence of uncertainty and asymmetric information, the original shareholders capture the entire net present value of the project, and the new investors only cover their opportunity costs. In the present example, the original shareholders do not capture the entire net present value; in fact the new investors gain more wealth than the original shareholders do. Nevertheless, the firm does invest in the project, and each party does gain wealth. Therefore, we have an efficient allocation of resources.

We next examine what happens if the strong firm does not call the bond. If the strong firm does not call the bond at time 1, the bondholders may still choose to convert their bond to .16 of the equity in the firm. The value of the converted bond is (.16)$730, or $116.80. The bondholders' alternative is to hold the bond and receive its face value, which the firm must pay at time 1. Since the total value of the strong firm with the project is $730, the value of the original shareholders' claim will be $730−$125, or $605. But we showed above that if the firm forces conversion of the bond by calling it, the value of the original shareholders' claim will be equal to $613.20. Since $613.20>$605, we conclude that the firm will force conversion of the bond by calling it.

We next show that a weak firm will not offer the bond. Suppose that a weak firm does offer the bond at time 0 and does not call that bond at time 1. At time 1, everyone will learn that the firm is a weak firm, whose market value with the project is $180. If the firm does not call the bond, the bondholders can choose between converting their bond into the proportion .16 of the equity of the firm, or accepting the face value of the bond. If the bondholders convert, the value of their equity will be (.16)$180, or $28.80. If the bondholders do not convert, the firm must pay the bondholders $125. Clearly, if the firm does not call the bond, the bondholders will not convert because the face value of the bond exceeds its converted value. If the weak firm does not call the bond, the new investors will obtain $125, for a net gain in wealth equal to $125−$50, or $75. Since the total value of the weak firm is $180, the value of the original shareholders' claim will be $180−$125, or only $55. If the weak firm had declined the new project, the original shareholders would have had a claim worth (1.00)$100, or $100.

We conclude that if a weak firm finances the project by selling a bond at time 0, and does not call that bond at time 1, the new investors will gain $75, and the original shareholders will lose $45. Note that the sum of the gains in wealth of the new investors and the original shareholders is equal to $75+(−$45), or $30, which is the net present value of the project in a weak firm. In this case, it is the new investors who capture the entire net present value of the project ($30), plus a net transfer of $45 from the original shareholders. Clearly, the original shareholders will not want their managers to issue the bond at time 0, and then not call it at time 1.

Suppose that a weak firm issues the bond at time 0 and does call it at time 1. The bondholders can accept the call, in which case they will get the call price, or $110. Alternatively, the bondholders can avoid the call by converting their bond to equity. We know that the converted value of the bond issued by a weak firm is (.16)$180, or $28.80. Given this choice, the new investors will surrender the bond in exchange for its call value of $110, leaving the original shareholders with a value equal to $180−$110=$70. Once again, the original shareholders lose wealth. The new investors gain $110−$50, or $60, and the original shareholders lose $100−$70=$30. The sum of the changes in wealth equals the net present value of the project in a weak firm, since $60+(−$30) is equal to $30.

We have now demonstrated that if a strong firm finances the project by offering the bond, both the original shareholders and the new investors will gain wealth. On the contrary, if a weak firm finances the project by offering the bond, the original shareholders will lose wealth to the new investors. Consequently, any firm that offers the bond will be recognized immediately as a strong firm. Moreover, potential new investors will know that they can gain wealth by purchasing the bond. Therefore, any strong firm can finance the project by offering the bond.

We now consider the second kind of security that firms can offer, namely new equity that represents .28 of the firm. Suppose that at time 0 a weak firm offers the straight equity and begins the project. At time 1, everyone will learn that the firm is a weak firm, whose market value (including the new project and the additional capital) is $180. Since there is no bond to call or to convert, the value of the new investors' claim on the weak firm is (.28)$180, or $50.40. The value of the original shareholders' claim is [(1.00)−(.28)]$180, or (.72)$180, or $129.60. The new investors gain $50.40−$50.00, or (only) $0.40, and the original shareholders gain $129.60−$100.00, or $29.60. Both parties gain wealth, and the sum of their gains is equal to the net present value of the project in a weak firm ($0.40+$29.60=$30.00).

Suppose that a strong firm offers the straight equity. At time 1, everyone will learn that the firm is a strong firm, whose market value is $730. Since the new investors will hold .28 of the equity, they will gain (.28)$730−$50, or $204.40−$50, or $154.40. The original shareholders will hold the remaining .72 of the equity, making their net gain equal to (.72)$730−$600, or $525.60−$600, or −$74.40. The sum of the gain in wealth is equal to $154.40+(−$74.40), or $80, which is the net present value of the project in a strong firm. Clearly, the original shareholders in a strong firm will not tolerate managers who finance the project by issuing straight equity in the proportion of .28.

Our overall conclusion is this: each kind of firm can eliminate the asymmetry of information between itself and potential new investors by its choice of which kind of security to offer. Investors will recognize that there is a one-to-one correlation between the kind of firm and the kind of security that the firm will offer; strong firms, and only strong firms, will offer the callable, convertible bond; weak firms, and only weak firms, will offer the straight equity. Both kinds of firms will invest in the project. There will be no foregone opportunities to effect mutually beneficial exchanges, and resources will be allocated efficiently.

Investors know that a weak firm has an incentive to masquerade as a strong firm because if it does so, the current shareholders in a weak firm can retain a larger proportion of the firm for themselves. If new investors provide $50 in new capital to a weak firm in exchange for straight equity, the new investors must acquire at least the proportion $50/$180, or .28 (approximately), of the weak firm in order to recover their opportunity costs. If the current shareholders of a weak firm cede .28 of their firm to the new investors, the current shareholders will retain only .72 of the firm. If a strong firm could identify itself at time 0 to prospective new investors as a strong firm, it could raise $50 in new capital by offering new investors the proportion $50/$730, or (approximately) .07 of the firm. We know that a strong firm can raise the requisite $50 in new capital at time 0 by offering a bond that is callable and is convertible into equity that represents (only) .16 of the firm. Since .16 is smaller than .28, the current shareholders of a weak firm would have an incentive to masquerade as a strong firm by offering the bond.

But if a weak firm could successfully masquerade as a strong firm, managers of firms and potential new investors would no longer be able to eliminate the deadweight losses created by the asymmetry of the information. Therefore, all parties have an incentive to prevent weak firms from masquerading as strong firms. A weak firm will not attempt to masquerade as a strong firm if both the call price and the face value of the bond are sufficiently high.

The Effect of Capital Structure on the Equilibrium Values of Price and Quantity in a Duopoly

A duopoly is an industry in which two firms produce an identical product.[25] An industry in which only two firms produce a particular grade of coal would be a duopoly. The profits of each firm depend on the structure of its costs, the quantity that it produces, and the price at which it can sell that product. Since the two firms produce identical products, each firm will face the same price, which will depend inversely on the sum of the quantities produced by the two firms. Consequently, when deciding what quantity to produce, each firm must take into account the quantity that the other firm will produce.

Define Q_1 as the quantity of coal that Firm 1 produces each month. Similarly, Q_2 is the quantity produced by Firm 2. The quantity produced in the industry is $Q = Q_1 + Q_2$. The price of coal depends inversely on Q. Suppose that Firm 1 believes that Firm 2 will produce the fixed quantity, $\hat{Q}_2$. Then the price at which both firms can sell their coal will vary inversely with the quantity of coal that Firm 1 chooses to produce. Suppose that Firm 1 chooses the value for its output, Q_1, that will maximize its own profit, given the quantity, $\hat{Q}_2$, that Firm 2 will produce. Designate this quantity that Firm 1 will produce as $Q_1^*(\hat{Q}_2)$. The notation $Q_1^*(\hat{Q}_2)$ represents a rule that specifies the profit-maximizing quantity for Firm 1 to produce given the quantity that the managers of Firm 1 expect Firm 2 to produce. As Firm 1 changes its expectation about the quantity that Firm 2 will produce, Firm 1 will change the quantity, Q_1, that it will produce by consulting the rule represented by $Q_1^*(\hat{Q}_2)$.

The behavior of Firm 2 is symmetric to the behavior of its competitor, Firm 1. Firm 2 has a rule, $Q_2^*(\hat{Q}_1)$, that specifies the optimal quantity that it should produce, given the quantity, $\hat{Q}_1$, that Firm 2 expects Firm 1 to produce. The following condition determines the quantities, Q_1^E and Q_2^E, produced by the two firms in equilibrium:

$$Q_1^E = Q_1^*(Q_2^E), \text{ and}$$
$$Q_2^E = Q_2^*(Q_1^E).$$
(13.9)

The condition specified in equation (13.9) states that in equilibrium the two firms produce quantities that are mutually consistent with each firm's maximization of its own profits.

The optimal quantity of coal for Firm 1 to produce, $Q_1^*(\hat{Q}_2)$, is inversely related to the quantity, $\hat{Q}_2$, that Firm 2 produces. To see this, let Firm 2 produce $\hat{Q}_2$, and let Firm 1 produce its corresponding optimal quantity, $Q_1^*(\hat{Q}_2)$. Then the total quantity of coal produced by the industry is $Q_1^*(\hat{Q}_2) + \hat{Q}_2$. The price of coal is inversely related to the sum of the quantities produced by the two firms. Therefore, if Firm 2 increases its production from $\hat{Q}_2$, while Firm 1 continues to produce the quantity $Q_1^*(\hat{Q}_2)$, the price of coal will fall because the aggregate quantity of coal supplied will have increased. The decrease in the price of coal will decrease the amount of profit that Firm 1 can obtain by producing the quantity $Q_1^*(\hat{Q}_2)$. The optimal response for Firm 1 is to produce less whenever Firm 2 increases its rate of output.[26]

In general, the rules that appear on the right sides of the two equations in (13.9) contain several parameters. Some of these parameters define the industry demand function for coal and the cost functions for the two firms. There are also parameters that define the capital structures of the two firms. In particular, the rule for Firm 1, $Q_1^*(\hat{Q}_2)$, could contain as parameters the levels of debt in the capital structures of the two firms. Under plausible conditions, an increase in Firm 1's level of debt will increase the quantity of coal that Firm 1 will produce for any given quantity of coal produced by Firm 2. The converse also holds. This result is a form of the problem of asset substitution that we examined in section 13.7.

Bondholders hold contractual claims against the firm's earnings; shareholders hold residual claims. The shareholders' liability to the bondholders is limited to the minimal of the face value of the bonds and the firm's earnings. This limited liability of the shareholders creates an incentive for them to direct their firm to increase the level of risk in the firm's operations. For the purpose of this example, suppose that an increase in the level of risk increases the standard deviation of the probability distribution of the firm's earnings without changing the expected value of that distribution. As we demonstrated in section 13.7, this increase in the level of risk will increase the expected value of the return to the shareholders, and decrease the expected value of the return to the bondholders. Since the shareholders' liability to the bondholders is limited, the increase in the level of risk transfers wealth from the bondholders to the shareholders.[27]

In their model of a duopoly, Brander and Lewis show that an increase in the quantity produced by Firm 1 will shift the probability density function of that firm's earnings in a way that will transfer wealth from the bondholders to the shareholders. Consequently, the presence of debt in the capital structure of Firm 1 causes that firm to produce a larger quantity, given the quantity produced by Firm 2, than Firm 1 would produce if there were no debt. That is, the presence of debt in Firm 1's capital structure changes the rule, $Q_1^*(\hat{Q}_2)$, that determines Firm 1's optimal response to the quantity that Firm 2 produces. Consequently, the presence of debt in the capital structures of the duopolists causes a net increase in the total quantity produced by the industry, and thus a decrease in the price paid by consumers.

We conclude that the capital structure of a firm can affect both its own rate of output and that of its competitors.

13.10 The Effect of Capital Structure on the Firm's Reputation for the Quality of a Durable Product

Earlier in this chapter, in the sections on asymmetric information and asset substitution, we examined ways in which a firm can use its choice of capital structure to transmit information credibly to prospective investors. In the case of asymmetric information, a strong firm could use its choice of capital structure to distinguish itself from a weak firm. In the case of asset substitution, a firm could use its choice of capital structure to assure prospective investors that the firm will not transfer wealth from the bondholders to the sharcholders by substituting riskier projects for the projects that the bondholders intended to finance. Without the ability to overcome these problems of asymmetric information and asset substitution, there would be an inefficient allocation of resources. For our final example of the effect of a firm's capital structure on the allocation of resources, we consider briefly the matter of a firm's reputation for the quality of a durable product.

Consumers who purchase a durable product, such as an automobile or a household appliance, face a problem of asymmetric information between themselves and the firm that produces the product. The consumers cannot easily determine the quality (particularly the durability) of the product at the time of purchase.[28] Since the cost to produce a product of high quality usually exceeds the cost to produce a product of lower quality, the firm has an incentive to offer as a product of high quality what in fact is a product of low quality. This is analogous (but not identical) to the problem of a weak firm masquerading as a strong firm. Without some assurance that the firm is, in fact, a strong firm, prospective investors may be unwilling to purchase the firm's securities at prices that are high enough to prevent a transfer of wealth from the current shareholders to the new investors. Similarly, without some assurance that the durable product offered by the firm is of high quality, consumers will not pay a price that is sufficiently high to cover the cost of production.

The asymmetry of information between prospective investors and a firm that wants to finance a new project, and between prospective consumers and a firm that is willing to produce a high-quality product, can create an inefficient allocation of resources. Prospective investors will pay a high price for the securities of a strong firm that wants to finance a new project, if the investors can be sure that the firm is a strong firm, and not a weak firm masquerading as a strong firm. Similarly, prospective consumers will pay a price that is sufficient to cover the cost of producing a high-quality product, if the consumers can be sure that the firm is not substituting a low-quality product for what only appears to be a high-quality product.

Maksimovic and Titman explain how a firm can use the level of debt in its capital structure to transmit credible information about its intention to produce a high-quality product.[29] Suppose that the cost of producing a high-quality product, and the price customers will pay for that product, make it profitable for the firm to establish and maintain a reputation for producing high-quality products. If a firm defaults on its bonds, the market value of this reputation is lost to the shareholders because the ownership of the firm passes to the bondholders. We recall from our discussion of asset substitution that the higher the level of debt, the stronger the incentives of the shareholders to undertake risky projects and then default on the bonds should the projects fail. Substituting low quality for the high quality that customers have come to expect is one form of substituting riskier projects for less risky ones. Consequently, shareholders can credibly signal their intention to maintain the firm's reputation for high quality by causing the firm to carry low levels of debt.

In another application of the use of debt to transmit information, Sheridan Titman explains that firms that produce durable products impose costs on their customers by going out of business because those customers will then have difficulty obtaining parts and service for the products.[30] Titman explains that in considering whether to liquidate their firm, the shareholders ignore the costs that the firm's customers would incur. The risk that the firm will go out of business negatively affects the price that consumers will pay for the firm's product. Consequently, the shareholders have an incentive to reduce the likelihood, as perceived by the firm's customers, that the shareholders will liquidate the firm.

Titman demonstrates that a firm can use its choice of capital structure "to commit the shareholders to an optimal liquidation policy. Specifically, [the firm can arrange its] capital structure [so that] stockholders never wish to liquidate, bondholders always wish to liquidate when the firm is in bankruptcy, and the firm will default only when the net gain to liquidation exceeds the cost to customers."[31] We would expect that "firms for which this effect is more important, e.g., computer and automobile companies, will have less debt, other things equal, than firms for which this effect is less important, e.g., hotels and restaurants. In general, for [products that are unique, or durable, or both], the costs imposed on customers when a producer goes out of business are higher than for nondurable products or those made by more than one producer."[32]

13.11   Conclusion

The capital structure of a firm is the configuration of financial securities issued by the firm. These securities are claims held by investors against the firm's earnings. There are two classes of securities: equity and debt. Each class has several subclasses (e.g., common and preferred stock for the equity; straight bonds and callable, convertible bonds for the debt). Investors who hold the firm's equity securities are residual claimants; investors who hold debt securities are contractual claimants. The firm can choose its capital structure to promote mutually beneficial exchanges among various classes of investors. Therefore, there is a direct connection between capital structure and economic efficiency.

In chapters 3, 4, and 5, we demonstrated that if all future events are known with certainty today, and if managers of firms maximize the wealth of their current shareholders, the capital structure of firms has no bearing on economic efficiency.[33] Each firm will undertake all projects that have positive net present values, and there will be no net transfers of wealth between a firm's current shareholders and new investors who finance the projects.

In this chapter, we have examined several cases in which a firm can use its choice of capital structure to mitigate problems of asymmetric information and problems of agency. In many of these cases, the future outcomes of investment projects are uncertain, both for the firm's investors and for its managers. Uncertainty about future outcomes is not, however, the only impediment to economic efficiency. The problems of asymmetric information and agency compound the effects of uncertainty on efficiency. We demonstrated how a firm's choice of capital structure can affect the level of economic efficiency by creating mutually beneficial exchanges that would otherwise be foregone.

Our study in this chapter provides one possible explanation for why some firms maintain stocks of cash and other highly liquid assets at levels far larger than necessary to conduct daily operations. By maintaining large stocks of liquid assets, a firm can finance investment projects with internal capital, thus avoiding the inefficiencies that could be created by the problems of asymmetric information and asset substitution. The value of being able to finance projects internally also explains why some firms merge with other firms. Suppose that Firm A lacks sufficient internal capital to finance new projects, and cannot finance them by selling new securities without transferring wealth from the current shareholders due to problems of asymmetric information or asset substitution. Suppose also that Firm B has a stock of liquid assets, or generates a flow of earnings, that exceed its requirements to finance its own new projects. The shareholders of the two firms can effect a mutually beneficial exchange by merging the firms. The shareholders of the combined firm will have access to the projects of Firm A and to the financial resources of Firm B, thus avoiding the problems of asymmetric information and asset substitution.

Appendix

In this appendix we derive the values that appear in table 13.1.

The outcomes for each of the four projects are uniformly distributed random variables. The distributions differ across the four projects. Let the letter a designate the lower bound of a uniform probability density function, and let the letter b designate its upper bound. Then the expected value of the random variable is $(b+a)/2$, which is the midpoint of the density function. The expected values of the four projects are listed in the fourth row of table 13.1.

To obtain the values of the standard deviations for each project we use the fact that the variance of any random variable is equal to the expected value of the square of that variable minus the square of the expected value of that variable. In symbols:

$$\text{Var}(x) = E(x^2) - [E(x)]^2, \tag{13.A1}$$

in which x is a random variable, $\text{Var}(x)$ is its variance, and E is the expectation operator. Using elementary calculus, we find that the first term on the right side of (13.A1) is

$$E(x^2) = \int_{x=a}^{x=b} x^2 f(x)\, dx,$$
$$\frac{1}{(b-a)} = \frac{1}{3}(b^3 - a^3), \tag{13.A2}$$

in which we use the fact that the uniform density function is $f(x) = 1/(b-a)$.

The second term on the right side of (13.A1) is:

$$[E(x)]^2 = (b+a)^2/4. \tag{13.A3}$$

Using (13.A2) and (13.A3), and making some simplifications, we find that the variance of a uniformly distributed random variable is;

$$\text{Var}(x) = (b-a)^2/12, \tag{13.A4}$$

and thus the standard deviation of x is:

$$\sigma_x = \sqrt{\text{Var}(x)} = (b-a)/[2\sqrt{3}], \tag{13.A5}$$

in which the symbol $\sqrt{}$ designates the positive square root.

Using (13.A5) produces the values for the standard deviations of the four projects in the fifth row of table 13.1.

Assuming that investors are risk neutral, the market value of a security is the expected value of the payoff to that security. Since a bond is a contractual security, the bondholders will receive the face value of the bond, or the total value of the project, whichever is less.

Consider Project A. The face value of the bond is $90, and the outcome of Project A is uniformly distributed over the interval from $50 to $150. Hence, the probability that the bondholders will receive the face value of $90 is ($150−$90) / $100, or .6. The probability that the bondholders will receive less than the face value is ($90−$50)/$100, or .4. If the value of Project A turns out to be less than $90, the bondholders will receive a payoff that is uniformly distributed over the interval from $50 to $90. Combining the outcomes in which bondholders receive $90 and less than $90, the expected value of the payoff to bondholders from Project A is

$$(\$90)\,(.6)+[(\$90-\$50)/2](.4) \tag{13.A6}$$
$$=\$54+\$28=\$82.$$

The stockholders for Project A hold a residual claim. Consequently, the sum of the market values of the claims of the bondholders and the shareholders to Project A is equal to the expected value of the payoff to that project. Since the expected value of the payoff to Project A is $100, the market value of the shareholders' claims is $100−$82=$18.

The market values of the securities for Projects B, C, and D are found analogously.

Problems

1. Two entrepreneurs, Kevin and Mike, operate shoe shining businesses on identical, opposite street corners in a major city. Although each of their annual incomes varies unpredictably due to the effects of weather, consumer preferences, and the disposable income of their customers, each young man's annual income is governed by a simple probability distribution. Specifically, each year is either a good year or a bad year. In a good year, each man's income is equal to $700; in a bad year each man's income is only $300. Good years and bad years each occur with a probability of .50, and the outcome for any year is independent of the outcomes for the preceding years. The two young gentlemen differ in their willingness to substitute between the average level of their income and the unpredictable variability of that income. Specifically, Kevin is more risk-averse than Mike.

(a) Explain, by creating a hypothetical numerical example, how the two men can create a mutually beneficial exchange by merging their businesses into a single firm and issuing a bond and a share of stock against the firm's earnings.

(b) Using your answer to question (a), calculate the prices of the bond and the share of common stock, assuming the risk-free interest rate is .10 per year and the risk-adjusted rate of return on the stock is .13 per year. What is the value of the firm?

2. Firm A and Firm B have different capital structures. Specifically, Firm A has a lower ratio of debt-to-equity than Firm B. In all other respects the two firms are equal;

in particular, each firm generates net earnings of $1,000,000 per year. Firm A has issued 5,000 bonds and 100,000 shares of common stock; Firm B has issued 10,000 bonds and 100,000 shares of common stock. The bonds issued by each firm have a coupon rate of .07 per year and a face value of $1,000. The bonds are perpetual bonds; they have no maturity date.

(a) What is each firm obligated to pay to its respective bondholders every year? How much do they have left to distribute to their shareholders?

(b) Suppose that investors capitalize the expected annual payments on the bonds issued by Firm A and by Firm B at .12 and .14 per year, respectively. What are the prices of the bonds issued by each firm? What is the value of debt for each firm?

(c) Suppose that investors capitalize the dividends of Firms A and B at a rate of .15 and .16 per year, respectively. What are the prices of the shares of each firm? What is the value of equity for each firm?

(d) Calculate the debt-to-equity ratio for each firm.

(e) Calculate the total value of each firm.

Suppose the annual net earnings of both Firm A and Firm B decrease from $1,000,000 to $500,000.

(f) Evaluate the effect this will have on the ability of each firm to pay its bond-holders and shareholders. Will each firm be able to meet the contractual requirements? What effect will the decrease in net earnings have on the price of each firm's securities? What will be each firm's capital loss? Discuss the results numerically.

(g) Discuss the effect of each firm's debt-to-equity ratio on the capital losses of its shareholders. What are the implications for economic efficiency of the presence of debt in a firm's capital structure?

Notes

1. We define payments to include both explicit payments, such as dividends and interest, and implicit payments, such as capital gains (and losses) arising from changes in the prices of the securities.

2. For an obvious example, suppose that the firm uses retained earnings to accumulate a hoard of currency. If the shareholders' marginal opportunity cost is the rate of return on the risk-free asset, they will incur a capital loss equal to the present value of the interest foregone on that currency.

3. The example that we will discuss is a Cournot duopoly, in which each firm can use its own choice of capital structure to shift its competitor's reaction function. Most courses in intermediate microeconomic theory examine models of Cournot duopolies. Our presentation does not require a familiarity with intermediate microeconomic theory or the Cournot model.

4. F. Modigliani and M. Miller, "The Cost of Capital, Corporate Finance, and the Theory of Corporation Finance," *American Economic Review* 48 (1958): 261–297.

5. Some authors cite the willingness to substitute as one of the axioms of choice that form the foundation for microeconomic theory. Another axiom is that the marginal rates at which a

person is willing to substitute less of Good Y in order to gain one more unit of Good X diminishes as the person's quantity of Good X increases. See, for example, A. A. Alchian and W. R. Allen, *Exchange and Production: Competition, Coordination, and Control*, 3rd ed. (New York: Wadsworth, 1983), 13–15.

6. We assume that the bond is priced on an ex-interest basis. Accordingly, an investor who purchases the bond today will receive the first payment of $900 one year from today.

7. In the present example, there is only one unit of the bond and only one share of the stock. Therefore, it is reasonable to calculate the total cost of acquiring the entire firm as the sum of the products of the number of units (one) of each security multiplied by its price. In the more general case, the firm will have large numbers of several kinds of securities outstanding. It would be unlikely that a group of investors could purchase enough of the firm's securities to acquire control of the firm without driving up the prices of those securities.

8. By *excessive*, we mean salaries and other emoluments that exceed what the firm would have to pay to attract and retain the level of managerial talent required to maintain the firm's ability to generate annual net earnings of $80,000.

9. We assume that the bonds are not riskless. Hence, investors capitalize the sequence of payments at .12 rather than .10.

10. If the prospective gain from paying out the free cash flow as dividends is sufficiently large, some investors will borrow money to purchase a sufficient number of shares to acquire control of the firm. Once in control, these investors will employ managers who will pay out the free cash flow. The investors can use the increased dividends to repay the borrowed funds, retaining a profit for themselves. These investors are often called, pejoratively, raiders who take over the firm. Of course, all of the firm's shareholders, including the managers, if they own some of the shares, gain wealth when the firm pays out its free cash flow. The managers might, however, also lose utility that is worth more to them than their gain in wealth.

11. We ignore the fact that an attempt to purchase all of the firm's securities would likely increase the prices of those securities.

12. By stochastic, we mean that the terms in the sequence of earnings are generated by some probabilistic mechanism. A sequence of draws from a normal probability density function to generate the rates of return on a security is an example of a stochastic process.

13. More precisely, we consider only common (i.e., not preferred) stocks and ordinary bonds. We do not consider bonds that are callable, or convertible, or both, nor do we consider lines of credit, notes, and other debt instruments issued by banks and other financial institutions.

14. We use the CAPM to define the equilibrium expected rate of return.

15. This condition is not as restrictive as it might seem. We can regard the value generated by the project at $t=1$ as the net present value (as of $t=1$) of a sequence of values that the project will generate over several periods. Instead of receiving a single payment at $t=1$, and nothing thereafter, the bondholders receive at $t=1$ a payment of interest and retain ownership of the bond. The market value of the bond is the net present value of the sequence of future payments of interest that the project will enable the firm to make. Similarly, at $t=1$ the shareholders receive a dividend and retain ownership of the stock, the market value of which is the net present value of the future dividends. Finally, we can allow the firm to undertake additional projects as time passes by regarding the firm as a portfolio of projects.

16. In a perfectly competitive market, competition among investors will force the cost of undertaking a project to equality with its expected value. For example, if the project requires purchasing or leasing land at a particular location, or purchasing a license to use a patented process, competition among investors will drive the cost of the land or the cost of the license to values that will make the expected rate of return on the project equal to zero.

17. The interested reader who has some facility with normal probability density functions can easily extend our example to include projects whose outcomes are governed by those density

functions. More ambitious readers can consider more sophisticated density functions. The point is that the economics of asset substitution depend on the properties of the density functions of the alternative projects among which the firm can substitute.

18. For example, in the default in question, the bondholders might obtain the right to require the railroad to repurchase the bonds at a price specified in the bond.

19. We considered a simple version of the problem of asymmetric information in chapter 2. Here we analyze a more sophisticated version of that problem, and we analyze its resolution by the use of callable, convertible debt.

20. G. A. Akerlof, "The Market for 'Lemons': Quality Uncertainty and the Market Mechanism," *Quarterly Journal of Economics* 84, no. 3 (1970): 488–500.

21. We assume here that buyers are risk neutral, so that only the expected value of the probability distribution of qualities affects the price that buyers will offer.

22. The market value of a firm includes the resale value of the resources contained in it plus the net present values of the projects that can be operated with those resources.

23. Recall that for this example the interest rate is zero.

24. More precisely, by the law of large numbers discussed in chapter 7, for any preassigned probability (such as .98), and for any preassigned number (such as 1.5), the probability that the average value of N firms will be within the interval $\$150 \pm \$1.50$ will exceed .98 if N is sufficiently large.

25. For a full analysis of this problem, the reader who has a strong grasp of microeconomic theory should consult the following papers: J. A. Brander and T. R. Lewis, "Oligopoly and Financial Structure: The Limited Liability Effect," *American Economic Review* 76 (1986): 956–970; V. Maksimovic, "Capital Structure in Repeated Oligopolies," *Rand Journal of Economics* 19 (1988): 389–407.

26. The proof that the optimal quantity for each firm to produce is inversely related to the quantity produced by its competitor requires a familiarity with intermediate microeconomic theory.

27. In the context of the example in section 13.7, the uniform distribution of the firm's earnings becomes wider with no change in the center point. That is, the standard deviation increases with no change in the expected value.

28. By *easily*, we mean without incurring inordinate costs. For many products, an inspection sufficient to determine the durability of the product would require hiring an expert.

29. V. Maksimovic and S. Titman, "Financial Policy and a Firm's Reputation for Product Quality," *Review of Financial Studies* 4, no. 1 (1991): 175–200.

30. S. Titman, "The Effect of Capital Structure on a Firm's Liquidation Decision," *Journal of Financial Economics* 13 (1984): 137–151.

31. Harris and Raviv, p. 318, stating Titman's argument.

32. Ibid.

33. An additional condition that is necessary for independence between capital structure and economic efficiency is that there be no taxes.

14 Insider Trading

14.1 Introduction

Inside information is information that is not publicly known.[1] Inside information is economically significant if the current prices of securities do not reflect that information. In a market that is informationally efficient with respect to public information, the prices of securities will change once the inside information becomes public.[2]

Persons who trade on the basis of inside information purchase or sell securities whose prices do not yet reflect that information. These investors will obtain a capital gain when the market adjusts the prices to reflect the information. But unless the information becomes public, the prices of securities will not change to reflect the information, and there would be no reason to trade on it. That is, inside information that remains inside forever is of no use to investors who seek capital gains by purchasing or selling mispriced securities. Moreover, the information must become public soon enough to enable the investors to cover the opportunity costs they incur by holding the mispriced securities.

Most editorialists, columnists, and members of the public appear to agree (without much careful thought) that insider trading is wrong because it is unfair. After all, why should a privileged few investors be allowed to use inside information when trading with other investors who do not have that information? Public policy in the United States reflects this view; insider trading is illegal and has been vigorously prosecuted for the past two decades.

In this chapter, we analyze insider trading on the basis of economic efficiency. We do this by examining the several effects that insider trading can have on the ability of financial markets to promote mutually beneficial intertemporal exchanges. We argue that if economic efficiency is a proper criterion for evaluating public policy, much of the prohibition of insider trading is not well founded.[3]

There is a large literature, both theoretical and empirical, on the relationship between insider trading and economic efficiency. As is often the case in economics, the implications of this literature for public policy depend on the resolution of empirical questions. In the case of insider trading, these empirical questions involve the relative effects of insider trading on four groups of economic actors. Corporate insiders are the first of these groups. The second group contains those investors (Hu and Noe call them *market professionals*) who are not corporate insiders but who have invested their own resources to acquire information about firms that is not available costlessly to the general public. Investment bankers and market analysts are included in this group.

The third group contains investors who have no private information and who trade to adjust the sizes or the levels of risk in their portfolios. Economists call these persons *liquidity traders*. In the fourth group are the investors who plan to hold the securities for long periods of time.

We discuss the definitions of insider trading and inside information in section 14.2. In section 14.3, we establish a context for the remainder of the chapter by addressing the question: Who owns the inside information? In section 14.4, we provide a general treatment of the effect of insider trading on economic efficiency, and then consider several specific questions of economic efficiency in sections 14.5 through 14.8. We discuss in section 14.9 the implications of these analyses for the regulation of insider trading and present a brief summary in section 14.10.

Insider trading is one of several issues in economics that generate passionate and ill-informed opinions. One of these issues is the impact of foreign trade on the domestic economy. Despite the almost universal agreement among economists that two (or more) nations can obtain mutual gains by allocating resources according to the theory of comparative advantage, we still hear shrill arguments to "buy American," and Congress still imposes tariffs on imports to protect American jobs.

The national debt is also an inflammatory topic. The words *debt* and *deficit* carry such a strong negative message with the general public that it is difficult to conduct a rational and informed, substantive discussion regarding the national debt. For example, there is a widely and deeply held belief that deficits will cause interest rates to rise because to finance its deficit the government must compete with the private sector for borrowed funds. The increase in the demand for borrowed funds will drive interest rates up. The opinion that the size of the federal budget deficit and the level of interest rates are positively correlated persists despite numerous empirical studies that show that there is no reliable correlation between deficits and interest rates.

14.2   The Definition of Insider Trading

One of the problems in studying insider trading is that the definitions of *insider* and *inside information* are fuzzy. We can begin with the definition of an insider.

14.2.1   The Definition of an Insider

Following Hu and Noe, we distinguish between hard-core insiders and a more inclusive group of persons whom the Securities and Exchange Commission and the courts might regard as being prohibited from trading on inside information. The hard-core insiders are directors, officers, critical employees (such as the director of a laboratory in a pharmaceutical company), and major shareholders (usually defined as persons who own 10% or more of the outstanding shares). But the legally operable definition of an insider is more extensive.

The definition of an insider in legal practice is wider than the definition of a hard-core insider. The major extension of the definition is based on the idea of fiduciary duty and misappropriation of information. Directors, officers, and key employees of a firm bear a fiduciary duty to the firm, and any trading based on the confidential information obtained when they perform their corporate duties may be viewed as (1) breaching their fiduciary duties, and (2) misappropriating information that belongs to the firm. Using this rationale as the essential basis for banning insider trading, agents who are not directors, officers, or key employees of a firm but who do bear fiduciary duties to the firm (such as the firm's contracted lawyers, consultants, and investment bankers) would be banned from trading on any information about the firm that they obtain when performing their duties.

This argument can be carried further. "If the information obtained from a firm by someone with a fiduciary duty to the firm is not about the firm itself but about some other firm(s), and the individual trades on such information, is he or she liable for breach of fiduciary duty or misappropriating information?"[4]

14.2.2   The Definition of Inside Information

The law does not prohibit insiders from trading, only from using material nonpublic information when they trade. A piece of information is nonpublic if that information is not readily and inexpensively available to all investors. By contrast, any information that has been published in the *Wall Street Journal* or by a governmental agency, or that has been publicly announced, such as a firm's report of its earnings, is publicly available information.

A piece of information is material with regard to a financial decision if a typical investor would pay to acquire that information before making that decision. With specific reference to a financial security, a piece of information is material if publication of that information would affect the price of the security. Obviously, under this definition, an investor would pay to acquire material information.

For example, the ES&D Railroad is constructing a tunnel that, upon completion, will substantially increase the railroad's revenues. The price that investors will be willing to pay today for the railroad's securities will depend substantially on the railroad's progress in completing the tunnel. News that the railroad has unexpectedly encountered substantial flooding in the tunnel is information for which investors would presumably be willing to pay. The information would have a substantial effect in determining the price that the investors are willing to pay to hold the railroad's securities. By contrast, a formal written statement that confirms something that has been announced previously is not material information. Investors would pay little, if anything, to obtain that formal statement. More generally, information that is not material is usually available to investors without charge. Conversely, investors will pay only for material information because, by definition, that information is not yet reflected in the prices of securities.

14.3   Who Owns Inside Information?

The opinion that insider trading is unfair appears to arise primarily from the idea that information is a free good. The argument is that every investor should have equal access to this information. Often, this argument is expressed in terms of the notion of a level playing field. This argument is mistaken because information is not a free good. Treating a private good as if it were free distorts incentives to produce and to manage that good, and thus creates an economically inefficient allocation of resources.

Private individuals, acting by themselves or jointly through firms, commit resources to produce most of the information that investors find valuable, just as individuals commit resources to produce railroads. With few exceptions, information is not a free good, as is the warmth that nature provides on a sunny day. Information does not occur naturally any more than railroads do. Most persons would have little difficulty agreeing that the individuals who provided the resources to build the railroad should have the right to control the use of that asset. By extension, one could argue (and some economists do) that the individuals who provide the resources to produce information should control the use of that information. We will refer to this argument throughout this chapter.

One of the arguments against insider trading is that persons who trade without revealing that they have access to inside information are behaving fraudulently. Hu and Noe observe that "[a] basic question not addressed by the fraud rationale for prohibiting insider trading concerns the assumption that exploiting the informational advantages for the purposes of security trading is unethical. All sorts of economic agents profit from informational advantages in a market economy, and such exploitation is not in general viewed as unethical. Why then is exploiting an informational advantage in securities trading unethical?"[5]

Consider, for example, a person who has, by investing his or her own resources, acquired information, and suppose that this information takes the form of a skill. An electrician, a pilot, a carpenter, a dentist, and an obstetrician are examples of persons whose skills are based, in part, on the information that they acquired. No one would claim that an electrician is overpaid because "all she does" is attach wires to terminals. Everyone knows that a large part of her ability to produce value is her knowledge (information) of which wires to attach to which terminals. Or consider a dentist who inspects one's teeth after the hygienist cleans them. "All the dentist does" is to look inside the patient's mouth, tap on a few teeth with his probe, and charge $25 for an inspection, in addition to the charge for the cleaning itself. But everyone understands that the dentist is using his knowledge to perform the inspection, and that he invested considerable resources to acquire that information.

14.4   The Economic Effect of Insider Trading: A General Treatment

In keeping with the central objective of this book, we examine the economic effect of insider trading on the ability of financial markets to promote mutually beneficial exchanges. Recall from our discussion of capital structure in chapter 13 that problems of asymmetric information and agency can create economic inefficiencies by preventing firms from undertaking profitable projects. To the extent that it mitigates these problems, insider trading increases the level of economic efficiency. Conversely, to the extent that insider trading impedes the willingness of investors to finance firms, it makes the allocation of resources less (economically) efficient.

An allocation of resources is economically efficient if there are no further opportunities for mutually beneficial exchanges. Before entering into an exchange, economic actors will require information about the sequence of payments that they can reasonably expect from that exchange. Hence, the extent to which an economy can achieve an efficient allocation of resources is constrained by the costs of acquiring information. In a market economy, it is prices that transmit information about potential exchanges. Therefore, the extent to which a market economy can achieve an efficient allocation of resources depends on the informational content of prices. It then follows that insider trading will increase the efficiency of resource allocation if that trading increases the informational content of prices, and conversely.

In the next five sections, we provide a brief description of the primary ways in which insider trading can effect an efficient allocation of resources. There is a large and sophisticated literature, both theoretical and empirical, on the question of the optimal (with respect to economic efficiency) regulation of insider trading. We encourage the interested reader to pursue the references in the notes at the end of this chapter and in the bibliography at the end of the book.

14.5   The Effect of Insider Trading on Mitigating Problems of Agency

The problem of agency arises because the firm's managers, who operate the firm as agents of the shareholders, have incentives that are not fully compatible with the interests of the shareholders.[6] We consider three ways in which insider trading can mitigate problems of agency.

14.5.1   The Incentives to Create Value

An argument first advanced by Henry Manne holds that "permitting insider trading . . . can improve the alignment of interests between outside claimants and management by allowing managers to profit from the appreciation in firm value that their efforts engendered."[7] For example, suppose that there were no legal prohibition against insider trading. In such a legal environment, the shareholders of each firm would be free to set the conditions under which their managers could trade on inside information, just as the shareholders are free to set the levels and the forms of managers' compensation. In some cases, permitting the managers of a firm to trade on inside information might produce net increases in wealth for the shareholders.

Consider a firm whose earnings depend critically on the managers' ability to produce research that will support new products. A pharmaceutical firm is a good example. Clearly, the more rapidly the managers of the firm bring efficacious new drugs to market, the more rapidly the shareholders will gain wealth. When investors learn that a pharmaceutical firm has made progress in bringing an important new drug to market, the price of that firm's stock increases, often substantially. The managers of the firm have private information about the prospects for a drug as it moves through the several developmental stages of research and testing that precede the availability of that drug on the market. The managers could increase their own wealth substantially if they were permitted to trade on this private information. Therefore, allowing the managers to trade on inside information would strengthen their incentive to accelerate the process of bringing new drugs to market. Consequently, it is arguable that the shareholders of a pharmaceutical firm would choose to permit their managers to trade on inside information if the law allowed it. The critical step in this argument is that producing new information can increase the value of the firm and consequently the wealth of the investors who own that firm. Then the question for the shareholders is: in what form should they reward their managers so that the managers' incentive to produce information is compatible with the shareholders' desire to gain wealth?

We are not arguing that it is always the case that the shareholders will gain wealth by allowing their managers to trade on inside information. But it does seem unlikely that in the absence of legal prohibitions against insider trading there would be no cases in which shareholders would choose to allow their managers to trade.

One of the arguments against allowing a firm's managers to trade on inside information is that the managers have an incentive to produce bad outcomes for the firm as well as good outcomes. To take an extreme case, suppose that the managers of a pharmaceutical firm intentionally impeded the research and development for a new drug and simultaneously sold the firm's stock short. As investors learn that the firm's prospects for bringing the new drug to market before its competitors do have diminished, the price of the firm's stock will decrease. Since the managers hold short positions in the stock, they will gain wealth as a consequence of their producing a bad outcome for the shareholders.

There are at least two responses to this argument. First, the shareholders could require their managers to sign a contract prohibiting them from selling the firm's securities short. Violation of the contract would entitle the shareholders to impose costs on the managers through a lawsuit.

The second response to the argument that allowing managers to trade on inside information would give them an incentive to produce bad outcomes for the shareholders is that an important part of a manager's wealth is his or her reputation. Many managers gain wealth and prestige by moving from one firm to a more senior position at another firm. A reputation for producing, or even being associated with, bad outcomes at a firm could inhibit a manager's mobility to more desirable positions. Whether the reputational effect on a manager's wealth is strong enough to dissuade managers from intentionally producing bad outcomes is an empirical question. The answer likely depends on characteristics of the firm in question.

14.5.2 The Incentives to Take Risk

Recall from our discussion of capital structure in chapter 13 that managers have an incentive to choose for their firms a portfolio of projects that is less risky than the shareholders would choose. The reason is that the managers cannot diversify their wealth as readily as the shareholders can. A significant portion of the managers' wealth is based on their reputations as managers. Clearly, the managers cannot diversify this portion of their wealth by holding managerial positions in several firms. Since the shareholders have no reputational capital that depends on their investments in the firm, they can reduce the risk of holding an investment in any firm by holding a portfolio that is diversified across the securities of several firms. Consequently, because of their desire to protect their reputational capital, the managers have an incentive to choose for the firm a portfolio of projects that is less risky than the portfolio that the shareholders would choose.

To mitigate this problem of agency, the shareholders have an interest to provide an incentive for their managers to take on more risk. One way to do this is to allow the managers to trade on inside information. Depending on the characteristics of the firm, managers might be willing to operate riskier portfolios of projects in exchange for the right to trade on inside information. Once again, whether shareholders would offer this right to their managers, if it were legal to do so, is an empirical question, the answer to which will likely vary across firms.

14.5.3 The Evaluation of Prospective Managers by Shareholders

The evaluation of prospective managers by shareholders, or by directors acting for the shareholders, is difficult. Shareholders pay managers to evaluate the risks of proposed investment projects. One way to discriminate among prospective managers is to offer them the right to trade on inside information in exchange for agreeing to accept a relatively low salary. The value of the right to trade on inside information depends on the manager's ability to identify profitable projects when future costs and benefits are uncertain. Managers who are confident in their ability to do so are more likely to accept a position that offers the right to trade on inside information even though the salary is relatively low. The rationale here is analogous to the reason why firms usually compensate their salespersons with relatively high rates of commission and relatively low salaries.

14.6 The Effect of Insider Trading on Protecting the Value of a Firm's Confidential Information

14.6.1 A Brief Review of the Problem of Asymmetric Information

In section 13.8 of chapter 13, we explained how asymmetric information between investors and the managers of firms could prevent the firm from undertaking a profitable investment project. Consequently, the asymmetric information would create an inefficient allocation of resources. In the example that we developed, there are two kinds of firms, strong and weak. Both managers and investors know the market value of a strong firm and the market value of a weak firm. But only the managers of a particular firm know whether that firm is strong or weak. Investors know only the total number of strong firms and the total number of weak firms. Since investors cannot determine whether a particular firm is strong or weak, competition among investors will force the market value of every firm to be equal to a weighted average of the value of a strong firm and value of a weak firm. The weights will be the relative proportions of the two kinds of firms in the population of all firms. Consequently, no firm will be correctly priced; each strong firm will be undervalued and each weak firm will be overvalued.

The fact that no firm will be correctly priced need not deter investors from holding the securities of these firms. By diversifying their investments across a large number of firms, investors can earn the equilibrium rate of return on their portfolios. That is, the rate of return on a portfolio will exactly cover the opportunity costs.

Now consider the effect of asymmetric information on the incentives of each type of firm to undertake a new project. In chapter 13, we showed that if the difference in the values of strong firms and weak firms is sufficiently large, and if the net present value of a new investment project is sufficiently small (but positive), a strong firm that finances the project by selling new securities will transfer wealth from its current shareholders to the new investors. Consequently, the current shareholders of the strong firm will want their firm to forego the new project even though the project has a positive net present value.

The fact that the project has a positive net present value means that the gain in wealth by the new investors would exceed the loss in wealth for the current shareholders. Since the net present value is positive, it is possible in principle to divide the net present value of the project between the new investors and the current shareholders so that both groups gain wealth. But this requires that the firm's current shareholders and the new investors can overcome the problems created by the asymmetry of information. If this is impossible, and if the only way that the firm can finance the new project is to sell new shares, then current shareholders and the new investors will forego an opportunity for a mutually beneficial exchange.

The situation for weak firms is the reverse of what it is for strong firms. If a weak firm offers new securities to finance the project, there will be a transfer of wealth from the new investors to the weak firm's current shareholders. Consequently, the current shareholders of the weak firm will be eager to have their firm finance the project by selling new securities. Even though investors cannot determine whether a particular firm is strong or weak, the investors know that only the weak firms have an incentive to offer new shares to finance the project. Knowing that only weak firms will offer shares eliminates the asymmetry of information with the result that only the weak firms will be able to finance the project.

In the preceding analysis, a strong firm will forego the project because the investors who would purchase the new shares would acquire a fractional claim on the earnings of the entire firm. If the firm could sell rights to the earnings of just the project itself, the problem created by the asymmetry of information would not arise.

Suppose that a new firm acting independently of the original firm could operate the project. The original firm could sell to the new firm the right to operate the project. The new firm could purchase the right to operate the project by issuing shares in the new firm to the shareholders of the original firm. The market value of this right would be the net present value of the project. The new firm would then finance the project by selling shares to new investors. Since the new investors would have no claim on the earnings of the original firm, there could be no transfer of wealth from the shareholders of that firm to the investors who finance the project. Creating a new firm to operate a project that arises in a larger firm is often called spinning off the project.

In some cases, the earnings of the new project can be separated from the earnings of the original firm with sufficient precision that it is possible for the original firm to finance the project by offering a special class of shares. In 1984, the General Motors Corporation did this by issuing "E-class shares" to finance a project organized by Ross Perot.

14.6.2 Using Insider Trading to Mitigate the Problem of Asymmetric Information

The problem described in the preceding subsection arises because the managers of a firm cannot credibly indicate to prospective investors whether their firm is strong or weak. In the absence of this inside information, investors regard each firm as if it were an average firm. Strong firms are underpriced; weak firms are overpriced. As we saw, this situation imposes deadweight losses on both the current shareholders and the prospective new investors of strong firms. The current shareholders in a strong firm and prospective new investors in that firm lose an opportunity to increase their wealth.

Under some conditions, this problem could be resolved by permitting managers to trade on the basis of their inside information. Managers of each kind of firm would know whether the price of their firm's securities correctly reflects the ability of that firm to generate earnings. In particular, if the securities of all firms were priced so that the firms were uniformly of average quality, then managers of strong firms would know that their firms are underpriced. These managers could earn a rate of return in excess of their opportunity cost by purchasing shares in their firms. Similarly, the managers of weak firms would have an incentive to sell (or sell short) shares in their firms.

The attempts by the managers to exploit their inside information would cause the prices of each firm's securities to move toward values that correctly reflect the quality of that firm. The more closely the prices of each firm's securities reflect the quality of that firm, the smaller is the deadweight loss created by that asymmetric information. If insider trading by the managers causes the prices of their firm's securities to reflect exactly the quality of that firm, the problem created by the asymmetry of the information disappears. Indeed, the problem disappears because the trading by insiders will cause the price of the firm's securities to reflect fully the insiders' information. In short, the insiders' trading removes some, or all, of the asymmetry of information between insiders and outsiders.

14.6.3 Example: Discovery of a Large Source of Crude Oil

In this subsection, we present a second example of how insider trading might enable a firm to overcome a problem created by asymmetric information. In this case, the firm lacks sufficient internal funds to finance a profitable new project. Potential new investors cannot evaluate the new project without access to the firm's private information about the project. But the profitability of the new project depends on the firm's maintaining secrecy about certain information until the project is underway. The firm cannot finance the project without attracting new investors; new investors will not provide funds without first examining the firm's private information; if the firm publishes its private information, competing firms will use the information, with the result that the project will no longer be profitable. Consequently, the firm cannot undertake the project, and an opportunity for a mutually beneficial exchange between the firm's current shareholders and new investors is foregone. The inability of the firm to transmit its private information about the project to the potential new investors without destroying the profitability of the project creates a deadweight loss.

We can explain how this deadweight loss occurs by considering a concrete example.

Geologists employed by an oil company have identified several sites that are highly likely to contain large pools of crude oil. The information produced by the geologists is not publicly available. Consequently, the market values of these sites do not reflect the oil company's information. Unfortunately, the oil company does not own the sites that its geologists have identified. Worse, the company lacks sufficient internal funds to purchase these sites. Therefore, the firm must obtain external financing if it is to purchase these sites and drill for the oil.

The firm might be unable to raise external financing without publicly revealing information produced by its geologists. But making the geologists' information publicly available will destroy its value. Competition by other oil companies and speculators for the sites identified by the geologists will raise the prices of these sites until the net present value of purchasing the sites and drilling for oil decreases to zero.

Moreover, it is illegal for the oil firm's managers to assemble a small group of investors and privately inform them of the geologists' reports under an agreement that those investors may not reveal that information to other persons. This is true even if the group of investors is limited to persons who already own shares in the oil firm. To inform a limited group of investors privately about the geologists' information as a means of inducing these investors to finance the new project is to trade on inside information, which is illegal. We conclude that the firm cannot raise the requisite external financing by privately revealing the inside information produced by its geologists, and publicly revealing this information would destroy its value.

14.6.4 Resolving the Problem by Allowing Insiders to Trade

The problem is to persuade potential new investors to finance the new project without destroying its profitability by publicly revealing information about that project. Allowing insiders to trade on inside information, and publicly announcing the insiders' trades, might solve this problem. There are two reasons for this.

First, if outsiders observe that insiders are purchasing shares shortly before or during the time that the firm offers new shares to finance the project, the outsiders will have reason to be more confident that the project is profitable. As insiders, the firm's managers are "putting their money where their mouths are." This mitigates the problem of agency.

The second reason involves asymmetric information between a firm's insiders and outsiders. Outsiders include the firm's current shareholders and any investors who might become shareholders either by purchasing shares from current shareholders or by purchasing newly issued shares. Recall from chapter 13 that when investors cannot distinguish between strong and weak firms, the strong firms may be unable to finance profitable projects. Consequently, both current shareholders and new investors in strong firms incur deadweight losses.

Asymmetric information causes the firm's securities to be mispriced. That is, the price of the firm's securities does not accurately reflect the firm's ability to generate earnings. Selling new shares to finance a project necessarily reduces the proportion of the firm owned by the current shareholders, and increases (from zero) the proportion acquired by the new investors. The greater the extent to which its securities are underpriced, the larger the number of new shares the firm must sell to finance a project. If the proportion of the firm ceded to the new investors is sufficiently large, the current shareholders will lose wealth even though the net present value of the project is positive.

The problem described in the preceding paragraph would disappear if the price of the firm's securities accurately reflected the insiders' information. If insiders were allowed to trade on their information, the price of the firm's securities would more accurately reflect this information. The reason is that if the price of a firm's securities does not accurately reflect that firm's ability to generate earnings, an investor can obtain a net increase in wealth by trading in that firm's securities. If a firm's securities are underpriced, the firm's earnings will generate a rate of return (relative to the price at which an investor could purchase those securities) that will exceed the investor's opportunity cost. Similarly, if a firm's securities are overpriced, investors who sell those securities will forego a rate of return that is less than what they could obtain by investing elsewhere the funds obtained by selling those (overpriced) securities.

By definition, insiders can recognize some of the occasions when their firm's securities are mispriced. If the securities are underpriced, insiders will have an incentive to purchase these securities. Purchases of the firm's shares, whether currently outstanding or newly issued, will cause an increase in the price of these shares. The higher the price at which the firm can sell newly issued shares, the smaller the proportion of the firm that the current shareholders will have to cede to the new investors in order to finance the new project.

14.6.5 Limitations on the Effect of Insider Trading in Transmitting Private Information to the Prices of Securities

There are two reasons why insiders' trading might not cause the price of their firm's securities to reflect fully the quality of that firm. First, like any investors, insiders are sensitive to the levels of risk in their personal portfolios. Given the level of risk that insiders are willing to bear, there is a maximal amount of the securities of any one firm, including the firm in which they are insiders, that they will be willing to hold in their portfolios. To exploit the inside information, they must either purchase or sell (or sell short) the firm's securities. This will change the proportion of their portfolios allocated to the firm's securities. Assuming that they were optimally diversified among all firms' securities before they traded on the inside information, the act of trading on inside information will cause their portfolios to become unoptimally diversified.

For example, suppose that each manager initially distributes his or her wealth between the risk-free asset and the market portfolio in a proportion that creates the combination of expected rate of return and risk that the manager wants to bear. If managers of strong firms now trade on their inside information, they will purchase some of their firm's securities. This will cause these managers to hold their firm's securities in a proportion greater than the proportion defined by the market portfolio. In the context of the CAPM, these managers' portfolios will be inefficient. Presumably, there are limits to the extent of inefficient diversification that managers are willing to accept in order to exploit their inside information. Consequently, managers might trade in their firm's securities in quantities that are not sufficient to cause the prices of these securities to reflect fully the insiders' information.

The second reason why insider trading might not remove the asymmetry of information involves the adverse effect that insider trading could have on a firm's cost of capital as a consequence of uninformed investors' attempts to protect themselves from losses that will arise from trading with insiders. We discuss this effect further in the following section.

14.7   The Effect of Insider Trading on the Firm's Cost of Capital through the Effect on Liquidity

The prices of financial securities determine the terms on which investors can construct mutually beneficial intertemporal exchanges. In particular, these prices determine the terms on which investors are willing to finance investment projects that firms can undertake. To obtain an efficient allocation of resources, it is critical that the prices of financial securities accurately transmit information about the terms on which investors are willing to lend and to bear risk, and about the (risk-adjusted) sequences of earnings that investment projects will generate.

A firm's cost of capital is the rate of return that the firm must offer to investors to induce them to finance investment projects. This is true for both current projects and for proposed new projects. In particular, if the firm finances a project by selling new securities, the price of the securities now outstanding will affect the cost of capital for that new project.

For current projects, the price of a firm's securities will adjust to the expected earnings of the firm so that investors who hold the firm's securities will receive a (risk-adjusted) rate of return that is equal to their opportunity cost. If the firm's expected earnings decrease, the price of the firm's securities will fall to a level where the investors' rate of return remains equal to their opportunity cost. If the price of the securities does not change to preserve this relationship, investors would be unwilling to continue to hold them. But to sell these securities, the investors who now hold the securities must persuade other investors to purchase them. The only way for this to happen is for the price of the securities to fall to a level consistent with opportunity costs.

One consequence of a decrease in the price of the firm's securities is that the firm might have more difficulty overcoming the problem of asymmetric information when attempting to finance new projects.

For proposed new investment projects, the current price of the firm's securities determines the profitability of a new project if the firm seeks to finance that project by selling additional shares. We have examined this relationship in our several discussions of the problem of asymmetric information. If the price of the firm's currently outstanding securities and the expected earnings from the proposed project are sufficiently low, the firm might not be able to finance the project by selling new securities without transferring wealth from its current shareholders to the new investors. But if the earnings from the new project are sufficiently high, the current shareholders can gain wealth by financing the project with new shares, even though asymmetric information causes the shares to be underpriced, with the result that both the current shareholders and the new investors enjoy a net gain in their wealth.

To examine more closely the effect of the prices of securities on a firm's cost of capital, we must distinguish between two prices for a given security. These prices are the bid price and the asked price.

On many financial markets, trading occurs through a system of dealers who quote a bid price at which they will purchase a particular security, and a higher asked price at which they will sell that same security. Sometimes the asked price is called the offered price. The difference between the bid and the asked prices is called the spread.

Dealers are described as providing a service of predictable immediacy.[8] Anyone can purchase the good from the dealer without notice by paying the asked price. Similarly, anyone can sell the good to the dealer without notice by accepting the bid price. Providing predictable immediacy requires that the dealer maintain both an inventory of the good and an inventory of cash or a line of credit through which the dealer can borrow.

The spread is one of the costs incurred by investors and firms who buy and sell securities. Suppose that the dealers' bid price for shares of the ES&D Railroad is $16.00 and their asked price is $16.75. Consider an investor who sells 100 shares of the railroad, reconsiders, and repurchases 100 shares a few hours later. Suppose that between the time when the investor sold her 100 shares and the time when she repurchased them there is no change in investors' expectations about the ability of the railroad to generate earnings. Then it is plausible to suppose that the dealers in this security will not change their bid and asked prices. Under these conditions, the investor who sells and then repurchases 100 shares will incur a cost of $75.00 ([$16.75−$16.00][100 shares]=$75.00) due to the spread. This cost is in addition to any commissions that the investor must pay to brokers to transmit to the dealers her orders to sell and to buy. The important point here is that for some purposes it is not adequate to consider a security as having a single price. We must consider the size of the spread between the bid and the asked prices.

Now it is rare that an investor would sell a security and then repurchase (or purchase and then resell) that security a few hours later. Even so, we can expect that a rational investor will consider the sizes of the spreads on various securities as one of the factors in determining which security to hold as a long-term investment. Investors who purchase securities as long-term investments do sell them eventually. (Even if the investor dies without selling the security, her heirs might sell it.) The larger the spread on a particular security, the smaller the rate of return that the investor will obtain over the period that she holds that security.

To illustrate this point, consider two railroads, the ES&D and the UP. The prices of the common stock in these firms are as follows:

ES&D, bid: $20.00
ES&D, asked: $23.00
UP, bid: $50.00
UP, asked: $51.00

Considered as a percentage of the bid price, the spread for the ES&D is 15% ($3/20 = 15/100$, or 15%). The corresponding percentage for the UP is 2%.

Now suppose that an investor wants to accumulate wealth over a period of 10 years, at the end of which time he will liquidate his holdings to finance a college education for his son. He expects both railroads to prosper at the same rate over the next 10 years. Specifically, he expects an investment in either railroad to grow by 100%. For ease of exposition, we assume that for each railroad the increase in wealth for an investor takes the form of an increase in the price of that railroad's shares.[9] If there are no changes in the percentages between the bid and the asked prices, the prices of the securities 10 years from now will be as follows:

ES&D, bid: $40.00
ES&D, asked: $46.00
UP, bid: $100.00
UP, asked: $102.00

Suppose that the investor has $10,000 to invest. Below we compare the rates of return for an investment in the securities of the two railroads.

For an investment of $10,000 in the ES&D Railroad:

Number shares purchased at the asked price: $10,000/$23.00 = 434.78
Proceeds from selling 434.78 shares 10 years later at the bid price:
   (434.78)($40.00) = $17,391.20
Growth over the 10-year period: $17,391.20/$10,000 = 1.74
Rate of return for the 10-year period: 74%

For an investment of $10,000 in the UP Railroad:

Number shares purchased at the asked price: $10,000/$51.00 = 196.08
Proceeds from selling 196.08 shares 10 years later at the bid price:
   (196.08)($100.00) = $19,608.00
Growth over the 10-year period: $19,608.00/$10,000 = 1.96
Rate of return for the 10-year period: 96%

We conclude from the preceding example that the size of the spread between the bid and the asked prices can have a substantial effect on an investor's rate of return. An investor who purchases $10,000 worth of the securities of the ES&D Railroad could liquidate his position 10 years later for $17,391.20. If the investor instead purchased $10,000 worth of UP stock, he could liquidate that position 10 years later for $19,608.00. Measured at their bid prices, the values of both firms' securities increase by 100% over the 10-year period. Similarly, their asked prices also increase by 100%. But an investor cannot obtain this rate of return because he must pay the asked price, the greater is the reduction in the investor's rate of return. In the preceding example, the difference in the sizes of the spreads for the securities of the two railroads creates a difference of 22 percentage points in the investor's ra the asked price, the greater is the reduction in the investor's rate of return. In the preceding example, the difference in the sizes of the spreads for the securities of the two railroads creates a difference of 22 percentage points in the investor's raate of return.

There is no single price for a security. For many questions, we must recognize the effect of the size of the spread between the bid and the asked prices.

Continuing with the example of the two railroads, we would expect rational investors to prefer the securities of the UP Railroad to those of the ES&D Railroad as a vehicle for accumulating wealth. A likely consequence of this preference for the UP over the ES&D is that the bid and asked prices of the UP will increase and those for the ES&D will decrease. In equilibrium, the bid and asked prices for the two railroads would be such that an investor will be indifferent between holding the two securities.[10]

In subsection 16.9 we examine some reasons why the spread might be different for the two railroads. Here we examine the consequences of the spread for each railroad's cost of capital.

Suppose that each railroad has an opportunity to increase its earnings by purchasing new locomotives that can pull longer trains and that require less maintenance. Neither railroad has sufficient internal funds to purchase the locomotives; to finance the project, each railroad must obtain external financing by selling new securities. Purchasing the new locomotives will be profitable if the cost of obtaining the required funds is not too high. Recall from chapter 5 that if a firm finances an investment project by borrowing from a bank, the net present value of that project varies inversely with the interest rate that the firm must pay for the borrowed funds. More generally, the net present value of a project varies inversely with the rate of return that the current shareholders of the firm must pay to the investors who finance that project. If the firm borrows from a bank, the investors are the shareholders of the bank. If the firm uses internal funds, the investors who finance the project are the firm's current shareholders who incur an opportunity cost; the firm could have paid out in dividends the internal funds that it uses to finance the project. In fact, the firm should use internal funds to finance a project only if the rate of return on the project exceeds the rate of return that the shareholders could obtain by investing their dividends in other firms.

Finally, if the firm finances a project by selling new securities, the firm must sell the new securities at a price that is sufficiently low, relative to the dividends that the new investors can expect, so that the new investors will meet their opportunity costs. We know (from our work in chapter 13) that the selling of new securities reduces the proportion of ownership that the current shareholders retain of the firm, and increases (from zero) the proportion ceded to the new investors. We can regard the proportion ceded to the new investors as a measure of the cost of capital incurred by the current shareholders.

Now, the higher the spread between the bid and asked prices of the firm's securities, the larger is the number of new shares that the firm must sell to finance the project. But the larger the number of new shares that the firm sells, the greater is the proportion of the firm ceded to new investors, and the greater the cost of capital incurred by the firm's current shareholders. We conclude that an increase in the spread between the bid and asked prices for a firm's securities increases that firm's cost of capital for financing a project by selling new securities. If the spread is sufficiently large, the net present value of the project will be negative, and the firm will forego it.

Return now to the two railroads that are considering the purchase of new locomotives. To concentrate on the effect of the spread on the profitability of a project, suppose that the cost of purchasing and operating the new locomotives is the same for both railroads. Further, the locomotives would increase the revenues for both railroads by the same percentage. But the effect of the spread will cause the bid and asked prices for the ES&D Railroad to be low relative to these prices for the UP Railroad. Consequently, the current shareholders of the ES&D Railroad will have to cede a larger proportion of their firm to the new investor than will the UP Railroad. If this effect is sufficiently large, the shareholders of the ES&D Railroad will be unable to finance the purchase of the new locomotives at a cost of capital that is low enough to make the project profitable.

14.8   The Effect of Insider Trading on the Trade-Off between Insiders and Informed Investors in Producing Informative Prices

The informational content of prices depends on the activities of speculators. Recall from our discussion in chapter 11 that speculators are investors who specialize in acquiring information about future sequences of payments and then seeking to gain wealth by purchasing or selling securities whose current prices do not accurately reflect that information. The accuracy of the information contained in the prices of securities depends on the costs that speculators must incur to acquire information and on the benefits that they expect to gain by trading on that information. Hence, anything that either increases the costs or decreases the expected benefits of trading on information will reduce the accuracy of security prices in transmitting information about sequences of future payments. For example, a tax on short-term capital gains would decrease the informational content of prices.[11]

One of the costs that a speculator incurs is the risk that the person on the other side of the transaction is an insider, who presumably has superior information. Hu and Noe partition informed investors (speculators) into two groups: insiders, who acquire inside information without having to invest additional resources, and informed outsiders.[12] The latter are market professionals, such as investment bankers and security analysts, who invest resources to acquire information about the sequences of payments associated with securities. The insiders have an advantage over the informed outsiders, but it is not necessarily the case that the insiders will exploit their advantage to the point that outsiders will have no incentive to invest in acquiring information.

Recall that there are two reasons why insider trading might be insufficient to cause prices to reflect all the insiders' information. First, insider trading by itself will not cause prices to reflect fully the inside information. The insiders must trade in a sufficient volume to change the equilibrium price to a value that reflects the inside information. The effect of the insiders' trading on the level of risk in their own portfolios might impose a constraint on the extent to which the insiders will trade, even if prices still do not fully reflect the inside information. Second, the insiders might be concerned about the effect of their trading on the firm's cost of capital.

We conclude that the extent of trading by insiders will affect the costs and the benefits of speculation by informed outsiders. Whether the net effect of insider trading will cause prices to be more informative or less informative is an empirical question that depends on the firm in question.

14.9 Implications for the Regulation of Insider Trading

It is often, but not always, the case that the implications of economic theory for public policy depend on empirical characteristics of the economy.[13] Would permitting insider trading increase the level of economic efficiency? The answer is: It depends. Hu and Noe provide an excellent illustration of this point in a hypothetical example, which we quote in full:

> Two hypothetical situations illustrate how theory, with the help of empirical research, can be translated into policy. First, consider an economy that empirical research has identified as fast-developing, characterized by numerous positive net-present-value projects, a lack of experienced outside analysts, and insiders who tend to have major stakes in the firms' ownership. In such an economy, the theoretical consensus indicates that permitting insider trading may be optimal. Ensuring maximal price informativeness and thus optimal allocation of capital across sectors is especially important. Given the lack of other information sources, insider trading will have a strong positive impact on price informativeness and thus will strongly further this goal. Because of the abundance of good projects, an increase in the cost of capital will have little adverse effect on investment. Further, because insiders have major ownership stakes, their interests are closely aligned with the other owners' interests and thus any adverse effects of trading in terms of agency costs can be minimal.
>
> On the other hand, consider an economy characterized by a separation of ownership and management, a sophisticated system of security analysis, and a mature investment climate in which most projects return the average market rate. In this economy prohibiting insider trading may be optimal. The separation between ownership and management implies that investors will have an incentive to substitute cheaper compensation based on insider trading for expensive salary packages designed to ensure high performance. At the same time, managers have an incentive to manipulate project returns to increase risk. The adverse effects of insider trading on market liquidity can decrease investment. The presence of a sophisticated security analysis

industry, at the same time, can reduce the importance of insider trading for market efficiency. Thus, in this case the costs of permitting trading may be outweighed by the benefits of prohibiting it.[14]

<hr>

14.10   Summary

The topic of insider trading generates more passion than analysis. For economists, the analysis depends on the criterion of economic efficiency. Depending on the circumstances, insider trading can mitigate or exacerbate economic inefficiencies that arise from asymmetries of information.

Notes

1. In this chapter, we draw heavily on the excellent summary of the economic issues regarding insider trading written by Jie Hu and Thomas H. Noe ("The Insider Trading Debate," *Federal Reserve Bank of Atlanta Economic Review,* Fourth Quarter, 1997). We will integrate the observations of Hu and Noe with our work on economic efficiency.

2. Consistent with our discussion in chapter 11 of the efficient markets hypothesis, if the market were informationally efficient with respect to all information, access to inside information would have no value because the current prices of securities would already reflect that information.

3. We remind the reader that the criterion for economic efficiency is the absence of any further opportunities for mutually beneficial exchanges. Economic efficiency does not address questions regarding the fairness of whatever distribution of income and wealth emerges from these mutually beneficial exchanges.

4. Hu and Noe, "The Insider Trading Debate," 38. This citation provides two examples of how courts have applied this extended definition of an insider.

5. Ibid., 39.

6. The conflict of interest for the managers as agents of the shareholders is mitigated by the extent to which the managers own shares of the firm.

7. Hu and Noe, "The Insider Trading Debate," 40. H. Manne, *Insider Trading and the Stock Market* (New York: Free Press, 1966).

8. For a development of the concept of predictable immediacy, see H. Demsetz, "The Cost of Transacting," *Quarterly Journal of Economics* 82, no. 1 (1968): 33–54.

9. Recall from chapter 5 that shareholders can obtain the value of the project in cash by selling a portion of the appreciated shares. This process is known as a homemade dividend.

10. Of course, there might be reasons why the bid and the asked prices of both railroads will increase or decrease. For example, if congestion on the highways increases the time required to ship goods by truck relative to the time required to ship by rail, competition among investors will cause the prices of the railroads' securities to increase relative to the prices of the securities of trucking firms. In this event, the bid and asked prices of the UP would increase relative to those prices for the ES&D.

11. At various times, the law defined a short-term capital gain as a gain obtained by selling a security within six months of having purchased it, or purchasing it within six months of having sold it (or sold it short). Such short-term profits were attributed to speculation rather than to

investment and consequently taxed at a higher rate than gains arising from positions held for more than six months. Recall our discussion in chapter 15 of the economic function of speculators and the specious distinction between speculators and investors.

12. Hu and Noe, "The Insider Trading Debate," 37, 42.

13. The effect of property rights is one area in which the implications of theory for economic efficiency do not depend on empirical characteristics of the economy. Stronger and more complete property rights, complemented by informationally efficient markets, increase the level of economic efficiency. Inefficiencies created by externalities, such as pollution, arise because of insufficient property rights.

14. Hu and Noe, "The Insider Trading Debate," 44.

15 Options

15.1 **Introduction**

The purposes of this chapter are to explain the pricing of options and to demonstrate some of the ways in which investors use options to effect mutually beneficial exchanges that would otherwise not occur. An option is a financial security. Throughout this book, we have argued that financial securities, and the markets in which these securities are priced and traded, contribute to economic efficiency by promoting mutually beneficial exchanges. In this chapter, we explain how options contribute to economic efficiency.

At its most fundamental level, the relationship between options and economic efficiency is analogous to the relationship between economic efficiency and the capital structure of firms that we examined in chapter 13. We argued that a firm's capital structure affects its ability to create wealth for its shareholders. In particular, by choosing the capital structure of their firms optimally, investors can create mutually beneficial exchanges that will otherwise be foregone. We demonstrated this argument in three ways. First, we showed how investors who differ in their willingness to tolerate risk can effect mutually beneficial exchanges by including both bonds and common stock in their firms' capital structures. Second, we explained how a firm could use callable, convertible bonds to mitigate the economic inefficiencies that would otherwise occur when there is asymmetric information between investors and managers of firms. Third, we examined some of the ways that investors can use debt in a firm's capital structure to mitigate problems of agency.

Investors and managers of firms can also use options to expand the set of mutually beneficial exchanges. Prior to the appearance in 1973 of the formula created by Fischer Black and Myron Scholes for pricing options, the use of options was inhibited by the lack of a rigorous model that could explain the equilibrium price of an option.[1] The success of the Black-Scholes option pricing formula led to phenomenal growth in both the trading of options on organized exchanges and the use of options in the operation of firms.

In this chapter, we first explain what options are. We then present a simple model to demonstrate that the equilibrium price of an option is a sophisticated application of the fundamental economic principle that equilibrium is a configuration of prices and quantities with the property that no economic actor has an incentive to change his or her choices on the quantities of goods to purchase or to hold. In particular, if there is an equilibrium among the prices of financial securities, no investor has an incentive to reallocate funds among these securities. In the case of options, we apply this principle by first showing that an investor can construct a riskless portfolio that contains both an option and the stock on which the option is written. We can then infer the relationship between the relative prices of the option and the stock from the fact that, in equilibrium, the rate of return on a riskless portfolio must be equal to the rate of return on the risk-free asset. A particular application of this principle leads to the "put/call parity." We then use our simple model of the price of an option to develop an intuitive appreciation for the (much) more sophisticated Black-Scholes option pricing formula. A formal derivation of this formula is beyond the scope of this introductory text.

Next, we consider two ways in which investors can use options to increase the level of economic efficiency. The central idea is that anything that enables investors to estimate more accurately the risk-adjusted net present values of investment projects will increase economic efficiency by promoting mutually beneficial exchanges. Both of these applications use the concept of an *implicit option*. An implicit option is a right that is sufficiently similar to a traded option that an investor can use the option pricing formula for a traded option to determine the value of the implicit option. We first explain how the shareholders of a firm hold an implicit option to purchase the firm from the firm's bondholders. We can then use the option pricing formula to infer some information about the equilibrium price of that firm's bonds. Second, we demonstrate how a firm can increase its shareholders' wealth by using the concept of an implicit option to calculate more accurately the opportunity costs associated with a proposed investment project.

15.2   Call Options

There are two kinds of options: call options and put options. Since the definitions and the analyses of these options are symmetric, we provide a detailed treatment only for call options.

An option is a financial security. As such, an option is a saleable right to a sequence of future payments. Consequently, the equilibrium price of an option will provide an investor who holds it with a rate of return that will cover, but not exceed, the risk-adjusted opportunity costs. There is nothing new in the economic principles that determine the equilibrium price of an option. The application of these principles is, however, a bit tricky because the future payments represented by an option are complicated.

15.2.1   The Definition of a Call Option

A call option, or a call, is a conditional contract that is defined in terms of a particular security, called the *underlying security*. For example, a call option on IBM common stock is a contract between the owner of the option and the writer of that option. The owner of the call option has a right, but not an obligation, to purchase one share of IBM common stock from the writer of the option by paying to that writer a fixed price no later than a fixed date.[2] The fixed price is called the *exercise price* (or the *strike price*) of the option. The fixed date is the *expiration date*.

Suppose that Ms. Brown owns a call option on IBM stock that was written by Mr. Green. The exercise price for this option is $110, and the expiration date is December 31, 2005. Then Ms. Brown has the right to purchase one share of IBM from Mr. Green by paying $110 to him no later than December 31, 2005. The option is a call option because Ms. Brown has the right to "call away" from Mr. Green one share of IBM by paying $110 to him before the expiration date.

There is an asymmetry between Ms. Brown and Mr. Green. Ms. Brown has a right to call on Mr. Green to deliver one share of IBM in exchange for paying him $110 before the option expires. But Ms. Brown has no obligation to purchase a share of IBM from Mr. Green; Ms. Brown may allow the option to expire without purchasing the share from Mr. Green. In this case, we say that the option expires unexercised. Mr. Green has no right to compel Ms. Brown to exercise her option.

15.2.2 The Market Price of the Option, the Exercise Price of the Option, and the Market Price of the Underlying Stock

Students sometimes confuse the market price of an option with its exercise price. To illuminate the difference between these two prices, we review some facts about a financial security.

A financial security is a saleable right to a sequence of future payments. Accordingly, an investor who owns a share of IBM stock has a right to receive a share of IBM's future earnings. These earnings will increase the shareholder's wealth by generating dividends, capital gains, or both. Consequently, the current price of a share of IBM stock depends on investors' expectations about IBM's ability to generate earnings. More precisely, the current price of a share of IBM stock is the (risk-adjusted) net present value of the company's future earnings. Clearly, the market price of a share of IBM stock is a variable; its value changes over time as investors change their expectations about IBM's ability to generate earnings.

Economists define an option as a derivative financial security (or, more simply, a derivative) because the value of the option is derived from the value of another security. Since the market price of IBM stock depends on investors' beliefs about the ability of that firm to generate earnings, the market price of a right (but not an obligation) to purchase a share of IBM stock depends derivatively on the investors' beliefs about IBM's ability to generate earnings. Since the market price of a share of IBM is a variable that changes as investors' beliefs change, the market price of a call option on IBM stock is a variable for the same reason. The exercise (or strike) price of the option is, however, a constant whose value is specified in the contract that defines the option.

Since the call option is a financial security, the owner of the option can sell it to another investor at any time before the expiration date. (After the expiration date, the option is worthless.) Of course, the price at which the owner of the option can sell it to another investor is the market price of that option, and that market price varies with investors' expectations.

A second point of confusion arises over the relationship among the current market price of the option, the current market price of the underlying stock, and the exercise price of the option. We address some of this confusion here, and defer a full analysis to section 15.4, where we formally derive the equilibrium price of a call option.

Suppose that the exercise price of a call option written on IBM stock is $100, and that the current market price of a share of IBM stock is $125. Then an investor who owns a call option has the right to purchase for $100 a share of IBM stock that she could immediately resell for $125. Since the profit from exercising the option would be $25, we might conclude that the equilibrium market price of the option is $25. This is incorrect. It is true that the market price of the call option will not be less than $25 when the price of the underlying stock is $125, but the price of the option could be more than $25.

Suppose that the market price of the option is $24 at a time when the market price of the stock is $125. The (fixed) exercise price of the option is $100. Then an investor could obtain a riskless profit equal to $1 by purchasing the call option for $24, spending an additional $100 to obtain a share of IBM stock by exercising the option, and immediately selling the share of IBM at its current market price of $125.[3] Competition among investors would soon force the price of the option up to $25, thus eliminating any further opportunity for a riskless profit.[4]

If the current price of a share of IBM stock is $125, then the current market price of a call option that has an exercise price of $100 cannot be less than $25. But the price of the option could be more than $25. The reason is that the price of the stock might increase between now and the time that the option expires. If the current market price exceeds the exercise price of the option, then each $1 increase in the price of the stock will increase the value of the option by $1 because the exercise price of the option is fixed. Consequently, the current market price of the option will reflect investors' beliefs about the probability that the price of the stock will increase between now and the time that the option expires. Of course, the price of the stock could decrease between now and the expiration date of the option. But the argument in the preceding paragraph establishes that the current market price of the option cannot fall below the difference between the current market price of the stock and the exercise price of the option.

15.2.3 The Writer of the Option and the Firm That Issued the Underlying Stock

A third point of confusion occurs in the distinction between the writer of the option and the firm whose stock is the underlying security. Mr. Green, who writes the call option on IBM stock, does not issue shares of IBM stock. Only the IBM Corporation can do that. Mr. Green can, however, sell a contract to Ms. Brown, under which Mr. Green promises to deliver a share of IBM stock to Ms. Brown should she call upon him to do so by paying the exercise price no later than the expiration date.

Should Ms. Brown exercise her option, Mr. Green has three ways to meet his obligation. He could deliver to Ms. Brown a share of IBM withdrawn from his own portfolio. If he does not own shares of IBM, he could purchase a share in the open market and deliver it to Ms. Brown. If the writer of the option owns the underlying security at the time that he sells the option, we say that the option is covered. If the writer does not own the underlying security, the option is naked.

The third way in which Mr. Green could satisfy his obligation to Ms. Brown is to pay her the difference between the exercise price of the option and the current price of a share of IBM. In many cases, Ms. Brown will want the market value of the share of IBM rather than the share itself. In these cases, if Mr. Green delivered a share to Ms. Brown, she would immediately sell it. To simplify the transaction, Mr. Green could pay to Ms. Brown the difference between the current market price of the share and exercise price of the option.

15.3 Put Options

A put option is analogous to a call option. A put option (or a "put") is a contract between the owner of the option and the writer of that option. The put option has an exercise price and an expiration date. Suppose that Tom writes a put option on IBM stock, and that Jeff purchases that option. Then Jeff has the right, but not an obligation, to sell one share of IBM stock to Tom at the fixed exercise price at any time before the option expires. If Jeff exercises his option, Tom must pay to Jeff the exercise price of the option and accept one share of IBM stock in exchange.

As with a call option, the value of the exercise price of the put option is a constant, while the market price of the put option is a variable that depends on investors' beliefs about IBM's ability to generate earnings.

Using an argument analogous to our treatment of a call option, we can see that the current market price of a put option cannot be less than the difference between the exercise price of the option and the current market price of the underlying security. Suppose that the exercise price of the put option is $90 and that the current price of a share of IBM is $80. Then Jeff, who owns the option, could obtain a riskless profit of $10 by purchasing a share on the open market for $80 and immediately selling it to Tom for $90.[5] Consequently, competition among investors will prevent the price of the put option from falling below $10 when the price of the stock is $80.[6] But, analogous to the case of a call option, the current market price of the put option will reflect investors' beliefs about the probability that the price of the stock will decrease between now and the time that the option expires. Therefore, the current market price of a put option can be greater than the difference between the exercise price of the option and the current market price of the stock.

15.4 A Simple Model of the Equilibrium Price of a Call Option

In this section, we present a simple model of the equilibrium price of a call option. The central idea is that an investor can construct a riskless portfolio that contains a call option, the stock on which that option is written, and a bank account. The rate of return on this portfolio depends on, among other things, the price of the option, the price of the stock, and the rate of interest at the bank. Since the portfolio is riskless, the equilibrium values of the price of the option and the price of the stock must be such that the rate of return on the portfolio is equal to the interest rate. Otherwise, an investor could obtain a risk-free profit. We will provide numerical examples of this as we work through the model. Our analysis of the equilibrium price of an option is analogous to our analysis in chapter 8 of risk-free portfolios that an investor can create if the rates of return on two securities are perfectly positively or perfectly negatively correlated.

15.4.1 The F Model

In this model, time is discrete (rather than continuous). There are three equally spaced times at which transactions can occur, namely time 0, time 1, and time 2. The present moment is time 0. The rate of interest at a bank is r. Consequently, a deposit of \$100 in a bank at time 0 will be worth \$100$(1+r)$ at time 1, and \$100$(1+r)^2$ at time 2. Similarly, the present value (as of time 0) of \$100 payable at time 2 is \$100$/(1+r)^2$.

Let S_t be the market price of a stock at time t, and let C_t be the market price at time t of a call option written on that stock. Then S_0 and C_0 are the current prices of the stock and the option at time 0. Let X be the exercise price of the option, and let time 2 be the expiration date. We will derive the equilibrium price of the option at time 0 in terms of the price of the stock at time 0, the exercise price, the expiration date, and the interest rate. In particular, we will derive the equilibrium configuration of the prices of the stock and the option in terms of the parameters of the model. (Since we are dealing with a microeconomic model, we assume that the interest rate, r, is a parameter.)

The first step is to specify the mechanism that governs the changes in the price of the stock over time. Let u and d be positive constants, and define u as the "up factor" and d as the "down factor." We assume that between any two consecutive times t and $t+1$, the prices of the stock will be related by one of the following two paths:

$$S_{t+1} = (1+u)S_t \tag{15.1}$$

or

$$S_{t+1} = (1-d)S_t. \tag{15.2}$$

That is, starting from any time t and moving to time $t+1$, the price of the stock will either increase by a factor of $(1+u)$ or decrease by a factor of $(1-d)$. There is a probabilistic mechanism that governs whether the price of the stock follows the "up path" or the "down path" between times t and $t+1$. For this discrete time model, the equilibrium price of the option is independent of the probabilities with which the price of the stock follows the up path and the down path between any two consecutive times. This result is counterintuitive. Since the value of the option is derived from the value of the stock, one might expect that the current price of the option will depend on the probabilities that govern the evolution of the price of the stock from the present moment until the expiration date of the option. We will show that this counterintuitive result occurs because investors can use the option and the underlying stock to construct risk-free portfolios.

In figure 15.1, we display the several paths that the price of the stock can follow from time 0 to time 2. Starting from time 0, the price can follow either the up path or the down path. If the price follows the up path, the price at time 1 will be $S_1 = S_0(1+u)$. Alternatively, if the price follows the down path, the price at time 1 will be $S_1 = S_0(1-d)$. In the center column of figure 15.1, we show the alternative values for S_1 corresponding to the two paths that the price can follow from time 0 to time 1.

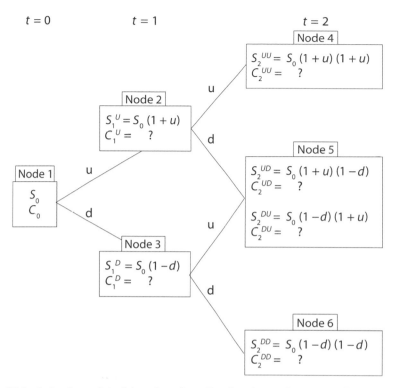

$t = 0$ $t = 1$ $t = 2$

Node 4

$S_2{}^{UU} = S_0 (1 + u) (1 + u)$
$C_2{}^{UU} = $?

Node 2

$S_1{}^{U} = S_0 (1 + u)$
$C_1{}^{U} = $?

Node 1

S_0
C_0

Node 3

$S_1{}^{D} = S_0 (1 - d)$
$C_1{}^{D} = $?

Node 5

$S_2{}^{UD} = S_0 (1 + u) (1 - d)$
$C_2{}^{UD} = $?

$S_2{}^{DU} = S_0 (1 - d) (1 + u)$
$C_2{}^{DU} = $?

Node 6

$S_2{}^{DD} = S_0 (1 - d) (1 - d)$
$C_2{}^{DD} = $?

Figure 15.1. A simple model of the price of a call option that expires two periods from now.

From each of the alternative outcomes at time 1, the price can again follow either an up path or a down path to reach a value for time 2. The column on the right in figure 15.1 displays the three possible outcomes for time 2, given the price at time 0. The largest outcome occurs if the price follows the up path successively twice in moving from time 0 to time 2. In this case, the price at time 2 is $S_2 = [S_0(1+u)](1+u)$, or $S_2 = S_0(1+u)^2$. Similarly, the smallest outcome for time 2 is $S_2 = S_0(1-d)^2$. The third possible outcome for the price at time 2 can occur in two ways. Starting from time 0, the price follows the up path once and the down path once in either order. Either combination of paths will produce a value for the price at time 2 equal to $S_2 = [S_0(1+u)](1-d)$ (if the price first goes up and then down), or $S_2 = [S_0(1-d)](1+u)$ (if the price first goes down and then up). Of course, either combination of paths produces the same result for the price at time 2.

We define a node as a point in figure 15.1 at which there is a possible outcome for the price of the stock. There are six nodes in figure 15.1, including the node for the price at time 0.

In figure 15.2, we have constructed a numerical example of the six nodes in figure 15.1. For this example, we set the initial price of the stock at $S_0 = \$105$, and the values of the factors at $u = .20$ and $d = .05$. At each node, we use superscripts to indicate the path over which the price moved to reach that node. For example, $S_1{}^{U}$ indicates the value of the price at time 1 if the price followed the up path from time 0 to time 1. Similarly, $S_2{}^{DU}$ is the value of the price at time 2 if the price followed the

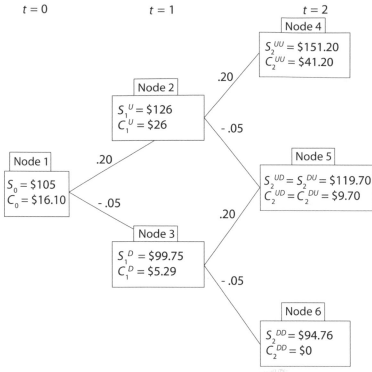

Figure 15.2. A numerical example of the price of a call option that expires two periods from now. The "up factor" is $u = .20$. The "down factor" is $d = .05$.

down path from time 0 to time 1, and then the up path from time 1 to time 2. We will demonstrate that as the price of the stock moves from one node to another, the equilibrium price of the call option changes so that the rate of return on the risk-free portfolio that an investor can construct using the stock and the option is equal to the rate of interest.

15.4.2 Deriving the Price of the Option at Node 3

Let the exercise price of the option be $110. Suppose that Kathleen wrote the call option, and that Adrian purchased it. Then at any time no later than time 2, Adrian can call upon Kathleen to deliver one share of stock in exchange for a payment of $110.

To determine the equilibrium prices of the option at each node, we begin at time 2 and work backward. Since the option expires at time 2, Adrian's optimal behavior at any of the nodes at time 2 depends only on the price of the stock at time 2 relative to the exercise price. Consider Node 4. The price of the stock is $151.20. If Adrian exercises his option at Node 4, he will obtain from Kathleen for a payment of $110 a share of stock worth $151.20. Therefore, he can obtain an immediate (and risk-free) profit equal to $151.20−$110.00, or $41.20, by exercising the option. If Adrian does not exercise the option at Node 4, the option will expire and Adrian will get nothing. Clearly, Adrian's optimal behavior at Node 4 is to exercise the option.[7]

There are two equivalent ways in which Adrian can obtain $41.20 at Node 4. First, he can exercise the option by paying $110 to Kathleen, receiving from her the share of stock, and then immediately selling that share for $151.20. Second, Adrian can sell the option to another investor. At Node 4, any investor will pay $41.20 for the option because she could recover that cost by immediately exercising the option. Competition among investors will prevent the price of the option from dropping below $41.20 at Node 4, and no investor will pay more than $41.20. Thus, the equilibrium price of the option at Node 4 is $41.20.

Proceeding similarly, we conclude that the equilibrium price of the option at Node 5 is $119.70−$110.00, or $9.70.

At Node 6, the price of the stock is $94.76, which is less than the exercise price of the option. Consequently, at Node 6 the option is worthless. Were Adrian to exercise his option at Node 6, he would pay Kathleen $110 to obtain a share of stock that is worth only $94.76. Clearly, Adrian will not exercise the option. Nor can he sell it. Since the option is about to expire, no investor will pay anything for the right to purchase for $110 a security whose current price is less than $110. Hence, the equilibrium price of the option at Node 6 is zero.

We have now determined the prices of both the stock and the option in each of the three nodes that can occur at time 2. These prices appear in the three boxes in the column under $t=2$ in figure 15.2. We can now use that information to determine the prices of the option in Nodes 2 and 3. We will do so by forming a different risk-free portfolio for each of Nodes 2 and 3. Consider Node 3 first.

Starting at Node 3, the prices of the stock and the option must travel either to Node 5 or to Node 6 during the next period. By knowing the prices of both the stock and the option in both Nodes 5 and 6, an investor can construct a portfolio that will generate a riskless rate of return during that period. That is, the investor's rate of return can be predicted with certainty at Node 3 even though he cannot predict whether the prices of the stock and the option will travel to Node 5 or to Node 6.

At Node 3, let the investor construct a portfolio that contains one share of stock and h_3 options. Since we know the price of the stock but not the price of the option at Node 3, the value of the investor's portfolio at Node 3 will be $(1)S_1^D+(h_3)C_1^D$, or $(1)\$99.75+(h_3)C_1^D$. That is, the investor must spend $(1)\$99.75+(h_3)C_1^D$ to construct this portfolio. The investor's rate of return on this portfolio from time 1 to time 2 depends on whether the prices of the stock and the option travel to Node 5 or to Node 6. To create a riskless rate of return, the investor chooses the value of h_3 so that the values of the portfolio in Node 5 and Node 6 are equal. Since we know the values of the prices of both the stock and the option in both nodes, this is easily done.

At Node 5, the value of the investor's portfolio will be

$$(1)S_2^{DU}+(h_3)C_2^{DU}=(1)\$119.70+(h_3)\$9.70. \qquad (15.3)$$

At Node 6, the value of the investor's portfolio will be

$$(1)S_2^{DD}+(h_3)C_2^{DD}=(1)\$94.76+(h_3)\$0. \qquad (15.4)$$

Let h_3^* be the value of h_3 that equates the values of the portfolio in Nodes 5 and 6. Then

$$h_3^*=(\$119.70-\$94.76)/(\$0-\$9.70)=-2.57. \qquad (15.5)$$

Since $h_3{}^*$ is negative, the investor constructs the risk-free portfolio at Node 3 by selling (or selling short) 2.57 options for each 1 share of stock that he purchases.[8] That is, his portfolio at Node 3 contains a long position in the stock and a short position in the option written on that stock. Recall that a long position in an asset is a position from which the investor will gain wealth if the price of the asset rises. If the investor holds a short position in an asset, he will gain wealth if the price of that asset falls.[9]

Let Robin create a risk-free portfolio at Node 3 by purchasing 1 share of stock and selling 2.57 call options. To sell these options, Robin uses an options broker to create the options, which the broker then sells to another investor, Don. Then Don has the right to purchase 2.57 shares of stock from Robin by paying her the exercise price of $110 per share any time before the option expires at time 2.

Robin can use her short position in the option to finance a portion of her long position in the stock. Since the price of the option at Node 3 is $C_1{}^D$, Robin will receive $2.57\ C_1{}^D$ by selling the options. Consequently, Robin's net cost to construct her portfolio at Node 3 is

$$(1)\$99.75 - (2.57)C_1{}^D. \tag{15.6}$$

To proceed, we need to define the liquidation value of a portfolio.

The liquidation value of an investor's portfolio is the amount of cash that she could raise by selling each of the long positions in her portfolio, and by simultaneously purchasing securities to offset each of the short positions. Consider the following example.

Maria constructed a portfolio one year ago by purchasing 100 units of Asset X and selling short 50 units of Asset Y. Maria's portfolio is long 100 units of X and short 50 units of Y. To establish her short position, Maria borrowed 50 units of Y from a broker and sold them for cash. Once she completed the construction of her portfolio, Maria owned 100 units of X and owed (to the broker) 50 units of Y. Maria's short position in Y obligates her to return 50 units of that security to the broker. The fact that she sold the 50 borrowed units of Y for cash has no bearing on her obligation to the broker. Typically, Maria would repay the broker by purchasing 50 units of Y in the open market and delivering them to the broker. When she does so, we say that she covers (or closes) her short position.

The liquidation value of Maria's portfolio is equal to the market value of her long position in X minus the market value of her short position in Y. Let the current price of X be $16, and let the current price of Y be $20. To liquidate her portfolio, Maria would sell her 100 units of X at $16 per unit, gaining $1,600 in cash. To complete the liquidation, she must deliver 50 units of Y to the broker from whom she borrowed them. Since she does not hold any units of Y in her portfolio (which is the essence of being short in Y), she must purchase 50 units of Y in the open market. This purchase will cost her $20×50 units, or $1,000. Consequently, the liquidation value of her portfolio is $1,600−$1,000, or $600.

We return to the question of determining the equilibrium value of $C_1{}^D$, which is the equilibrium price of the option at Node 3 in figure 15.2. Since Robin is at Node 3 at time 1, at time 2 she will be either at Node 5 or at Node 6. If she reaches Node 5, she can liquidate her portfolio by selling the share of stock that she owns and purchasing

2.57 options to offset her short position in that asset. Then the liquidation value of her portfolio at Node 5 will be (1)$119.70−(2.57) $9.70, or $94.77. Alternatively, if Robin reaches Node 6, the liquidation value of her portfolio will be worth (1)$94.76−(2.57)$0, or $94.76. At Node 6, the option is worthless, so Robin incurs no cost at Node 6 to cover her short position. Except for a rounding error, the values of Robin's portfolio are equal in Nodes 5 and 6. For definiteness, we use $94.76 as the common value of her portfolio at Nodes 5 and 6.

The portfolio that Robin constructs at time 1, at Node 3, is riskless because there is no uncertainty about its value one period later at time 2. Consequently, in equilibrium the rate of return on this portfolio must be equal to the rate of interest. We then have:

$$[(1)\$99.75-(2.57)C_1{}^D](1+.10)=\$94.76. \tag{15.7}$$

The first term in square brackets in equation (15.7) is the amount of her own money that Robin spends to construct the portfolio at Node 3. Solving equation (15.7) for $C_1{}^D$ produces the equilibrium price for the option at Node 3, namely:

$$C_1{}^D=\$5.29. \tag{15.8}$$

By comparing Node 3 and Node 6, we can see the distinction between the market price of the option and the value of the option if it were exercised immediately. Notice that the price of the option at Node 3 is not equal to the price of the stock minus the exercise price of the option, or zero, whichever is greater. At Node 6, the price of the option is zero because the price of the stock is less than the exercise price of the option, and the option is about to expire. No one would exercise the option at Node 6, and there are no future nodes for this option. At Node 3, the price of the stock is also less than the exercise price, so no one would exercise the option at Node 3 either. But the price of the option at Node 3 is greater than zero because there is a possibility that at time 2 the prices of the stock and the option will be at Node 5, where the price of the stock exceeds the exercise price of the option. At both Nodes 3 and 6, the value of exercising the option immediately is zero because the price of the stock at that node is less than the exercise price of the option. At Node 6, the market price of the option is zero because there is no possibility of reaching a further node. But at Node 3, the market price of the option is positive because the value of exercising the option could become positive as the system moves beyond Node 3.

15.4.3 Deriving the Price of the Option at Node 2

Proceeding as we did for Node 3, we first determine the structure of the riskless portfolio that Robin could form at Node 2. It is critical to recognize that the structure of this portfolio is different from the portfolio that she formed at Node 3. The reason is that starting from Node 3, Robin will move either to Node 5 or to Node 6; Node 4 is unattainable from Node 3. But starting from Node 2, Robin will move either to Node 4 or to Node 5; Node 6 is unattainable from Node 2.

To create a riskless portfolio at Node 2, let $h_2{}^*$ be the number of options that Robin should hold for each share of stock that she holds. The cost of her portfolio at Node 2 will be:

$$(1)\$126.00 + h_2{}^* C_1{}^U. \tag{15.9}$$

This portfolio will be riskless if its liquidation values in Nodes 4 and 5 are equal. Equating these liquidation values produces:

$$(1)S_2{}^{UU} + h_2{}^* C_2{}^{UU} = (1)S_2{}^{UD} + h_2{}^* C_2{}^{UD}, \text{ or}$$
$$(1)\$151.20 + h_2{}^* \$41.20 = (1)\$119.70 + h_2{}^* \$9.70. \tag{15.10}$$

Solving (15.10) for $h_2{}^*$ yields

$$h_2{}^* = -1. \tag{15.11}$$

Note that the structures of the riskless portfolios at Nodes 2 and 3 are different. The portfolio at Node 2 contains 1 option held short for each share of the stock held long. At Node 3, the portfolio contains 2.57 options held short for each share of stock held long.

The common liquidation value of the riskless portfolio at Nodes 4 and 5 is:

$$(1)\$151.20 - (1)\$41.20 = (1)\$119.70 - (1)\$9.70.$$
$$= \$110.00. \tag{15.12}$$

Substituting $h_2{}^* = -1$ into equation (15.9), the cost of the portfolio at Node 2 is $(1)\$126.00 - (1)C_1{}^U$. Since the portfolio is riskless, the equilibrium rate of return is .10, which requires:

$$[(1)\$126.00 - (1)C_1{}^U](1 + .10) = \$110, \tag{15.13}$$

which produces the equilibrium value for the price of the option at Node 2 as:

$$C_1{}^U = \$26. \tag{15.14}$$

In Node 2, we again see the distinction between the exercise value and the market value of the option. The exercise value of the option at Node 2 is the cash that an investor would receive by exercising the option when the price of the stock is $126. This exercise value is $126−$110, or $16. But the market value of the option at Node 2 is $26, which reflects the possibility that the system could move to Node 4 from Node 2. If an investor who owned an option at Node 2 wanted to liquidate that option, clearly he would sell it to another investor (for $26) rather than exercise it (which would yield only $126−$110, or $16).

15.4.4   Deriving the Price of the Option at Node 1

We can now use the equilibrium values for the prices of the option at both Nodes 2 and 3 to derive the equilibrium price of the option for time 0 (at Node 1). Let $h_1{}^*$ be the number of options that Robin should hold for each share of stock to form a riskless portfolio at Node 1. Then h_1^* is the solution to

$$(1)S_2^U + h_1^* C_2^U = (1)S_2^D + h_1^* C_2^D, \text{ or}$$
$$(1)\$126.00 + h_1^* \$26.0 = (1)\$99.75 + h_1^* \$5.29, \tag{15.15}$$

which yields:

$$h_1^* = -1.27. \tag{15.16}$$

The common value of the riskless portfolio at Nodes 2 and 3 will be:

$$(1)\$126.00 - (1.27)\$26.0 = (1)\$99.75 - (1.27)\$5.29, \tag{15.17}$$

or $93.00 (approximately).

The cost of the portfolio at Node 1 is:

$$(1)\$105.00 - (1.27)C_0. \tag{15.18}$$

Then equilibrium requires that:

$$[(1)\$105.00 - (1.27)C_0](1 + .10) = \$93.00, \tag{15.19}$$

so that the equilibrium price of the option at Node 1 (at time 0) is $16.11.

15.4.5   Extending the Binomial Model to N Periods

In the preceding sections, we analyzed a binomial model for the case in which there are two periods remaining until the option expires. It should be obvious that we could extend the analysis to the case in which N periods remain until the option expires. The larger the value of N, the larger the number of nodes. But so long as N is a finite integer, we can determine the prices of the stock and the option for each of the terminal nodes. Then for each node at which the system can be located when there is only one period remaining until expiration, there will be only two nodes to which the system can travel during the final period. We can then construct a riskless portfolio to obtain the equilibrium price of the option at each of the nodes that is one period away from the expiration date of the option. Proceeding backward through time, we can determine the equilibrium price of the option at time 0.[10]

By fixing the date of expiration and letting the number of periods increase without limit, we could obtain the formula for the equilibrium price of an option for the case in which the rate of return on the underlying stock is continuously compounded, rather than periodically compounded, as is the case in a binomial model. Instead of pursuing this further, we shall move immediately to the Black-Scholes formula, following a summary of the properties of the binomial model.

15.4.6   Summary of the Simple Model of the Price of a Call Option

The simple model that we have presented in this section is sufficient to illuminate the essential properties of the Black-Scholes option pricing formula that we discuss in the following section. To prepare for that discussion, we summarize briefly the features of the simple model. These features reflect the application to the pricing of options of the fundamental principles that we have used throughout the book.

First, equilibrium is a configuration of prices and quantities with the property that no economic agent has an incentive to change his or her decisions. In particular, if the price of a stock and the price of a call option written on that stock are in equilibrium, no investor will have an incentive to change the allocation of funds between the stock and the option.

Second, if an investor can construct a riskless portfolio by combining two or more assets in certain proportions, then the rate of return on that portfolio must be equal to the rate of interest available at a bank. The rate of return on a portfolio depends on the rates of return of its constituent assets and on the proportions in which the investor allocates funds among those assets. Further, the rate of return on an asset depends on the current prices of those assets. Consequently, requiring the rate of return on the portfolio to be equal to the interest rate imposes a condition on the relationship among the prices of the assets in the portfolio.

Third, the equilibrium price of the option has several properties that are apparent from the model presented above.

1. The most counterintuitive property is that the equilibrium between the price of a call option and the price of the underlying stock does not depend on the expected rate of return of the underlying stock. The price of the call does depend on the current price of the stock and on the variance of the rate of return on the stock. It is critical to recognize here that the model determines the equilibrium price of the call, *conditional* on the price of the underlying stock. The model does not predict the price of the call independently of the price of the stock. Finally, the model determines only the relative prices of the option and the underlying stock, not the absolute values of these prices.

In the simple model presented in this section, the magnitudes of the up and down factors are a proxy for the variance of the rate of return on the stock. If the up factor were to increase, the maximal possible value for the price of the stock at time 2 would increase. Similarly, if the down factor were to increase (so that the price of the stock could fall more rapidly on any of the down branches), the minimal value for the price of the stock at time 2 would decrease. The consequent increase in the range of possible values for the price of the stock at time 2 will increase the variance of the rate of return on the stock.[11]

An increase in the variance of the stock's rate of return increases the likelihood that on the expiration date of the option, the price of the stock will be significantly above, or significantly below, the exercise price of the option. The market value of the call option on its expiration date depends asymmetrically on the price of the stock on that date. The amount by which the price of the stock falls below the exercise price of the option on the expiration date is irrelevant; once the price of the stock falls below the exercise price of the option, the market value of the option is zero.[12] The converse is not true. On the expiration date, each $1 increase in the price of the stock above the exercise price of the option increases the market value of the option by $1. Consequently, an increase in the variance of the rate of return on the stock increases the current market value of the call. Increases in both the up factor and the down factor will increase the variance of the rate of return on the stock, and thus increase the current market value of the call option.

2. The longer the time until the option expires, the more opportunity there is for the price of the stock to move above the exercise price of the option before the option expires. Therefore, the more distant the expiration date, the higher the current price of the option.

3. As implied by the arguments above, the greater the amount by which the exercise price of the option exceeds the current price of the stock, the lower the current price of the option.

We used the model presented in this section to determine the equilibrium relationship between the prices of the call option and the underlying stock. There is an analogous model for a put option. Since the arguments in the two models are symmetric, we do not develop the model for put options. In our model for a call option, we used an extremely simple mechanism to govern the evolution of the price of the stock over time. In the next section, we describe the more realistic model produced by Black and Scholes to determine the equilibrium prices of options.

15.5 The Black-Scholes Option Pricing Formula

The model in the preceding section illustrates the economic rationale for the equilibrium price of an option. But that model is too simple to produce an empirically reliable formula. In this section we present, but do not derive, the Black-Scholes option pricing formula. This formula is widely used by both economists and investors. Prior to the appearance of this formula, the volume of organized trading in options was a small fraction of what it is today. By providing an intuitively rational and empirically verified procedure for determining the equilibrium price of an option, the formula reduced the risk of trading in options.

This does not mean that trading in options is not risky. Predicting the price of any security requires two steps. First, one must understand how specific kinds of information will affect the equilibrium price of the security. Second, one must predict how those pieces of information will change over time. For example, the Black-Scholes formula states the relationship between the equilibrium price of the option and the variance of the distribution of future prices for the underlying stock. The Black-Scholes formula does not, however, predict how that variance might change over time. Hence we have the distinction, first mentioned in section 9.5.2 of chapter 9, between predicting the equilibrium price that corresponds to a specific set of information and predicting that information itself.

15.5.1 The Differences between the Simple Model and the Black-Scholes Formula

In the simple model of the preceding section, transactions could occur only at equally spaced times. Treating time as discrete, rather than as continuous, facilitates analysis but sacrifices accuracy. Competition among investors adjusts security prices to new information, and information arrives irregularly through time. Moreover, in an efficient market the adjustment to new information is immediate.[13] A model that restricts transactions to discrete times is unlikely to produce accurate predictions, even though that model might produce valuable hints of how options would be priced in actual (as opposed to hypothetical) markets.

The Black-Scholes model is analogous to, but much more sophisticated than, the model in the preceding section. In particular, in the Black-Scholes model time is a continuous variable. The models are analogous in that they both recognize that an investor can use the option and the underlying stock to construct a risk-free portfolio. Then the equilibrium relationship between the prices of the option and the stock follows from the condition that the rate of return on the portfolio must be equal to the rate of return on the risk-free asset.

Whether time is discrete or continuous, the number of options that the investor must hold for each share of stock to construct a risk-free portfolio depends on the current prices of both securities and on the time remaining until the option expires. Consequently, if time is discrete, the investor must adjust the portfolio periodically over time. But if time is continuous, the investor must adjust the portfolio continuously over time. A rigorous derivation of the Black-Scholes option pricing formula is beyond the scope of this book. We instead present the formula and discuss its main properties.

15.5.2 The Black-Scholes Formula for the Price of a Call Option

In the Black-Scholes model, time is continuous. Investors can trade at any moment rather than being limited to trading periodically. Because time is continuous, we represent the rate of return on a stock as a continuously compounded random variable. The relationship between periodic and continuous compounding is easily explained, which we do in the appendix to this chapter.

Define the following:

C_0 = The current market price of a call option written on IBM stock.

E = The exercise price of the call option.

S_0 = The current market price of a share of IBM stock.

T = The number of years remaining until the option expires (since time is a continuous variable, T need not be an integer).

r = The continuously compounded annual rate of return on the risk-free asset.

σ = The standard deviation of the continuously compounded annual rate of return on a share of IBM stock.

$\ln(S_0/E)$ = The natural logarithm of (S_0/E).

$N(d)$ = The probability that a normally distributed random variable will take a value less than or equal to d. That is, $N(d)$ is the area under the normal probability density function to the left of the point d on the horizontal axis, expressed as a proportion of the total area under the density function.

The Black-Scholes option pricing formula is:

$$C_0 = S_0 N(d_1) - N(d_2)(E/e^{rT}),$$

in which

$$d_1 = \frac{\ln(S_0/E) + (r + \sigma^2/2)T}{\sigma\sqrt{T}}$$

$$d_2 = \frac{\ln(S_0/E) + (r + \sigma^2/2)T}{\sigma\sqrt{T}} \tag{15.20}$$

Although the problem of deriving the formula in equation (15.20) was intellectually formidable, the application of the formula is less formidable than it might appear. With the exception of the standard deviation, σ, all the terms on the right side of (15.20) are readily available. The financial exchanges post the current price of the stock, the rate of return on the risk-free asset, and the exercise price and the expiration date of the option. Once we have an estimate of σ, we can calculate the values of d_1 and d_2 from a table of probabilities for a normally distributed random variable. We can estimate the value of σ from historical data on the rate of return of the stock. Consequently, we can use equation (15.20) to obtain the equilibrium price of the call option, conditional on our estimate of σ. One indication of the value of the Black-Scholes formula in the investment community is that there are handheld calculators that include a program to evaluate the Black-Scholes formula. All the investor need do is enter the values for the variables and the parameters on the right side of equation (15.20), press a button, and obtain the corresponding value for the equilibrium price of the call option.

Using historical data on the rate of return on the stock to estimate the value of σ is problematic. Any formula for the equilibrium price of a security is based on information about the *future* rates of return for that security. The Black-Scholes formula is no exception. This formula establishes the equilibrium price of the call based on the standard deviation of the *future* rates of return on the stock. The probability distribution for future rates of return on the stock need not be identical to the distribution that generated the rates of return observed in the past.

There is an interesting twist to the problem of estimating the standard deviation. We can use the Black-Scholes formula to estimate the value of σ for the future rates of return on the stock, conditional on the current market prices of the call and the underlying stock and the current values of the other parameters. Since a financial security is a claim on a sequence of future payments, the current market price of the security depends on the future values of the parameters that will govern those future payments. If we have confidence in the Black-Scholes formula, it is reasonable to expect that speculators will keep the current market prices of the call and the underlying stock equal (or close) to the values specified by the Black-Scholes formula in equation (15.20), given the values of the parameters that will affect the future rates of return on the stock. Consequently, we can use the Black-Scholes formula to estimate the value of σ for the future rates of return on the stock that are implied by the current market prices of the option and the stock, and the values of the other parameters.

The sensitivity of the formula in equation (15.20) to the estimate of σ is understandable. Our analysis of the simple model in the preceding section showed that the current price of the call option depends significantly on the range of values that the price of the stock can reach on the date that the option expires. In the Black-Scholes formula, the larger the standard deviation of the rate of return on the stock, the wider the range of terminal values for the price of the stock.

15.6   The Put-Call Parity

In this section, we present and explain the relationship that will hold in equilibrium among the price of a stock and the prices of put and call options written on that stock. We know that an equilibrium in a financial market is a configuration of prices (and quantities) of securities with the property that no investor has an incentive to reallocate wealth among securities. In some cases, we can define the equilibrium as the absence of any opportunities for an investor to obtain a risk-free profit. The put-call parity is one of these cases.

Define the following:

S_0 and S_1=the prices at time 0 and time 1 of a stock

C_0 and C_1=the prices at time 0 and time 1 of a call option written on that stock

P_0 and P_1=the prices at time 0 and time 1 of a put option written on that stock

E=the exercise price for both options

r_f=the risk-free rate of interest

Assume that the stock pays no dividends between time 0 and time 1, and that both options expire at time 1.

The put-call parity states that in equilibrium, the prices of the stock and the two options must satisfy:

$$S_0=C_0+E/(1+r_f)-P_0. \tag{15.21}$$

We can develop the economic intuition of the put-call parity by regarding each side of equation (15.21) as the cost of a different portfolio at time 0, and then showing that the values of both portfolios will be equal to S_1 at time 1. If two different portfolios that an investor could construct at time 0 produce the same value at time 1, then equilibrium requires that the two portfolios have the same value at time 0.

The left side of equation (15.21) is the cost at time 0 of a portfolio that contains a long position in one share of the stock. At time 1, the value of this portfolio will be S_1.

The right side of equation (15.21) is the cost at time 0 of a portfolio that contains long positions in two assets and a short position in a third asset. The two assets held long are one unit of the call option and a bank account worth $E/(1+r_f)$; the asset held short is one unit of the put option. An investor, Michael, could construct this portfolio at time 0 by purchasing one call option, depositing $E/(1+r_f)$ in a bank, and selling (that is, writing) one put option. The sum of the first two terms on the right of equation

(15.21) is the value at time 0 of the long side of the portfolio. Michael would finance part of the cost of the long side of his portfolio by selling one put option. Consequently, the right side of equation (15.21) is the net cost to Michael at time 0 of constructing a portfolio that contains a long position in one call, a long position in a bank account worth $E/(1+r_f)$, and a short position in one put.

At time 1, the price of the stock will be greater than, less than, or equal to the exercise price of the options. We will now show that in each case the amount of cash that Michael could raise at time 1 by liquidating his portfolio will be S_1. Recall that to liquidate a portfolio is to sell the assets held long and purchase assets to offset the positions held short.

Suppose that $S_1 > E$. Consider first the long side of the portfolio. Since the call option expires at time 1, its market value will be equal to $S_1 - E$. That is, Michael could sell his call option for $S_1 - E$ in cash. Any investor will pay $S_1 - E$ for the right to purchase for E a security that can be immediately resold for S_1. The second asset that Michael holds long is his bank account. This account will have grown from $E/(1+r_f)$ at time 0 to $[E/(1+r_f)](1+r_f)=E$ at time 1. Then at time 1, Michael can liquidate the long side of his portfolio for $S_1 - E + E$, or S_1, in cash.

Alternatively, at time 1 Michael can exercise the call option to obtain a share of stock, using the funds in the bank account to pay the exercise price, E. He can then sell the stock, thereby raising S_1 in cash.

The short side of Michael's portfolio contains one put option. To hold a short position in an asset is to have an obligation to deliver that asset or its equivalent. If Michael's short position contained one share of stock, he would have to deliver one share of stock, or its equivalent, to liquidate that position. Consequently, the cost to Michael of liquidating at time 1 a short position in one share of stock would cost him S_1. (If Michael delivers the share from his own inventory, he incurs an implicit cost of S_1. If he purchases at time 1 the share that he delivers, he incurs an explicit cost of S_1.)

But Michael's short position is in the put option, not in the stock. The investor who purchased the put from Michael at time 0 has a right to require Michael to purchase one share of stock and pay the exercise price, E. But at time 1 Michael knows that the investor will allow her put option to expire unexercised because $S_1 > E$. To exercise the put at time 1 would be to sell to Michael for E a share of stock that is worth more than E. Consequently, the put is worthless at time 1, and thus Michael will incur no cost to liquidate the short side of his portfolio.

We conclude that if $S_1 > E$, the value of Michael's portfolio at time 1 will be S_1.

Suppose that $S_1 < E$. In this case, the call option that Michael holds long is worthless at time 1. No investor at time 1 will pay anything for the right to acquire for E a share of stock that is worth less than E. Hence, Michael will allow his call option to expire unexercised. His bank account at time 1 is again worth E. Then the long side of his portfolio at time 1 is worth $0+E=E$.

On the other side of his portfolio, Michael has a short position in one put option. The investor who purchased the put option from Michael at time 0 will exercise that option against him at time 1. By doing so, the investor will sell to Michael for E a share of stock that is worth, at time 1, less than E. Since Michael's bank account is worth E at time 1, Michael can use those funds to discharge his obligation under the put option. We conclude that after he covers his short position in the put option at time 1, Michael will own one share of stock that is worth S_1. Consequently, the value of his portfolio at time 1 is S_1.

Suppose that $S_1 = E$. In this event, both the call option and the put option are worthless. No one would bother to exercise a right to buy or sell, for E, one share of stock that is worth E. Michael's bank account is worth E at time 1. But in this case, $E = S_1$. Then the value of Michael's portfolio at time 1 is S_1.

We have established that for all three possible outcomes for time 1, the value at time 1 of the portfolio represented by the right side of equation (15.21) is S_1. Obviously, the value at time 1 of the portfolio represented by the left side of (15.21) is also S_1. Since the values of the two portfolios at time 1 are equal, their values at time 0 must also be equal, which establishes the put-call parity stated in (15.21).

15.6.1   Arbitrage and the Put-Call Parity

The put-call parity specifies a relationship among the equilibrium values of the prices of the put, the call, and the underlying stock. We can appreciate this relationship by considering how an investor could obtain a riskless profit whenever the prices of the stock and the two options do not satisfy equation (15.21).

Suppose that the stock is overpriced relative to the options. Then:

$$S_0 > C_0 + E/(1+r_f) - P_0. \tag{15.22}$$

If equation (15.22) holds, then we may write:

$$S_0 + P_0 > C_0 + E/(1+r_f) \tag{15.23}$$

Equation (15.22) states that a portfolio that contains the stock and the put option is overpriced relative to a portfolio that contains the call option and the bank account worth the present value of the exercise price. Under these circumstances, an investor could obtain a riskless profit by simultaneously selling the portfolio on the left side of equation (15.23) and purchasing the portfolio on the right.

The amount of risk-free profit will be equal to the value of the left side of (15.23) minus the value of the right side. We will now demonstrate this result.

At time 0, let Michael construct a single portfolio as follows:

1. Sell short one share of stock, obtaining revenue equal to S_0.
2. Sell one put option, obtaining revenue equal to P_0.
3. Buy one call option, incurring a cost equal to C_0.
4. Deposit $E/(1+r_f)$ in a bank account. [That is, purchase a bank account that has a balance equal to $E/(1+r_f)$.]

Using equation (15.23), the amount of cash that Michael will obtain at time 0 by constructing this portfolio is:

$$S_0 + P_0 - C_0 - E/(1+r_f) > 0. \tag{15.24}$$

We will now show that at time 1 the net value of Michael's portfolio will be zero with certainty. That is, the cash that he can raise by liquidating his two long positions will be equal to the cash that he will need to cover his two short positions.

Consequently, the positive net revenue in equation (15.24) is a risk-free profit for Michael at time 0.

Suppose that $S_1 > E$. On the long side of his portfolio, Michael owns a call option and a bank account. The call is "in the money"; by exercising the call, Michael can purchase for E a share of stock that is worth $S_1 > E$. The value of his bank account at time 1 is E. Then Michael can obtain a share of stock by exercising his call option, using the balance in his bank account to pay the exercise price. Consequently, Michael can convert the long side of his portfolio from containing one call and one bank account to containing one share of stock that is worth S_1. Alternatively, Michael can sell his call option for $S_1 - E$ in cash, and liquidate his bank account for E in cash. His net cash will then be $S_1 - E + E = S_1$.

On the other side of his portfolio, Michael is short one put option and one share of stock. Since $S_1 > E$, the put is worthless. The investor who purchased the put from Michael at time 0 will not exercise it at time 1; to do so would be to deliver to Michael a share of stock worth S_1 and accept $E < S_1$ in exchange. Then Michael's only obligation is to cover his short position in the stock. He can do this by delivering to the broker from whom he borrowed a share at time 0 the share of stock that he obtains at time 1 by exercising his call option. Or if Michael sells his call option for $S_1 - E$ and liquidates his bank account for E, he can deliver S_1 in cash to the broker, who could then purchase the share of stock himself. Then Michael's net revenue (and net cost) at time 1 is zero. Consequently, the net revenue in equation (15.24) that Michael obtained at time 0 is a clear profit; he never pays for it.

Suppose that $S_1 < E$. In this event, the put option is in the money at time 1 and the call option is worthless. The investor who purchased the put option from Michael at time 0 will exercise it against him at time 1 by delivering to Michael one share of stock (which is worth less than E) and collecting from Michael the exercise price, E. Michael can pay the exercise price by liquidating his bank account, which will be worth E at time 1. Michael can now use the share of stock that he obtains when the put is exercised against him to cover his short position in the stock by delivering the share of stock to the broker from whom he borrowed it at time 0. Michael's net gain at time 1 is zero, and therefore the revenue in equation (15.24) that he obtained at time 0 is a clear profit.

Suppose that $S_1 = E$. In this event, both the put option and the call option are worthless at time 1. As in all cases, his bank account is worth E at time 1. Michael can then liquidate his bank account, use the proceeds to purchase one share of stock at a cost of $S_1 = E$, and deliver that share to the broker from whom he borrowed it at time 0. Again, Michael's net gain at time 1 is zero; the positive net revenue in equation (15.24) that he obtained at time 0 is a clear profit.

15.7　Homemade Options

In several places in this book, we have provided examples of "homemade" items that individual investors can use to expand their opportunities for mutually beneficial exchanges and thus increase the efficiency of the allocation of their resources. The first example was a homemade dividend, presented in chapter 5. In the chapters on portfolio theory, we explained that a portfolio is a synthetic, or homemade, security. In the present section, we explain how an investor can construct a homemade option.

A homemade call option on Security X is a portfolio of securities that provides a sequence of payments that is identical to the sequence that a call option on Security X would provide. Suppose that at the present moment (time 0) there is active trading in both Security X and in a put option on Security X. The exercise price on the put is E, and the put expires one year from now (at time 1). There are, however, no investors or brokers who are willing to write call options on Security X that have an exercise price of E and that expire one year from now. Nevertheless, an investor can create a homemade call option that has these properties by purchasing one share of Security X, purchasing one put option, and borrowing the present value of the exercise price from a bank. We will demonstrate the equivalence between this portfolio of securities and a call option in table 15.1.

Suppose that the market did offer a call option on Security X that has an exercise price of E and that expires at time 1. In the first row of table 15.1, we show the values that the call option would have at time 1 conditional on the price of Security X relative to E at time 1. In the second, third, and fourth rows of the table, we show the values of each of the assets in the investor's portfolio at time 0 and the values of those assets at time 1 conditional on the price of Security X at time 1 relative to E. Each entry in the last row of the table is the sum of the entries in rows 2, 3, and 4 for that column. Thus the final row in the table shows the net value of the investor's portfolio at time 0, and the net value of that portfolio at time 1 conditional on the price of Security X relative to E.

If at time 0 there were a call option on Security X that had an exercise price of E and that expired at time 1, the market value of that option at time 1 would depend on the price of Security X at time 1 relative to E. If $S_1 \geq E$, the market value of the call at time 1 would be $S_1 - E$. If $S_1 < E$, the call would be worthless. The first row of table 15.1 shows these values.

To create a homemade call option at time 0, an investor constructs a portfolio by purchasing one share of Security X, paying S_0, purchasing one put option, paying P_0, and borrowing $E/(1+r)$ from a bank. Her net investment at time 0 is thus $S_0 + P_0 - E/(1+r)$. Were she to liquidate her portfolio at time 0, the funds that she

Table 15.1
A Homemade Call Option

		Market Values	
			Time 1
Asset	Time 0	$S_1 \geq E$	$S_1 < E$
Homemade call	—	$S_1 - E$	0
Buy 1 share of Security X	S_0	S_1	S_1
Buy 1 put option	P_0	0	$E - S_1$
Borrow $E/(1+r)$	$-E/(1+r)$	$-E$	$-E$
Portfolio	$S_0 + P_0 - E/(1+r)$	$S_1 - E$	0

would gain by selling her one share of Security X and her put option would be just sufficient to pay off her loan.

At time 1, the value of the investor's portfolio will be equal to the revenue that she could obtain by selling the two assets in her long position, minus the expenditure that would be required to repay her loan. Selling the one share of Security X and the one put option will generate revenue equal to $S_1 + P_1$. To repay her loan will cost E. Therefore, the net value of her portfolio at time 1 will be $S_1 + P_1 - E$.

The market price of the put option at time 1 depends on the value of S_1 relative to E. If $S_1 \geq E$, the put option is worthless. If $S_1 < E$, the put option will be worth $E - S_1$. We conclude that if $S_1 \geq E$, the value of the investor's portfolio at time 1 will be $S_1 + P_1 - E = S_1 + 0 - E = S_1 - E$. If $S_1 < E$, the portfolio at time 1 will be worth $S_1 + P_1 - E = S_1 + (E - S_1) - E = 0$. Thus, for any given value of Security X at time 1, the value of the homemade call option that expires at time 1 and that has an exercise price of E will be equal to the value of a conventional call option with those properties.

The value at time 0 of the homemade call option is $S_0 + P_0 - E/(1 + r)$. Since the homemade call option is economically equivalent to a conventional call option, the price at time 0 of a conventional call option must also be equal to $S_0 + P_0 - E/(1 + r)$. The alert reader will see that this assertion is equivalent to the put-call parity in equation (15.21).

15.8 Introduction to Implicit Options

The groundbreaking contribution that Fischer Black and Myron Scholes made to the economics of finance, and to the practice of finance, by producing their option pricing formula is well known. Less well known is their insight that some configurations of financial securities and capital structures of firms contain implicit options. An implicit option is an opportunity that is sufficiently like a conventional option that we can use the option pricing formula to infer some information about that opportunity that will enable investors to effect mutually beneficial exchanges that would otherwise be foregone.

Economic efficiency requires that firms and investors undertake all mutually beneficial exchanges. Some potentially beneficial exchanges are foregone because the costs of acquiring reliable information about future outcomes are too high. In situations that contain implicit options, we can use the theory of option pricing to increase allocative efficiency by reducing the costs of acquiring information.

We examine two uses of implicit options. First, we use the concept to determine the equilibrium allocation of a leveraged firm's total market value between its common stock and its bonds. Specifically, we explain how the common stock-holders of the firm hold an implicit option to purchase the firm from the bondholders. We can then use the option pricing formula to infer properties of the prices of both securities.

Second, we explain how a firm's decision on whether to invest in a new project can involve an implicit call option. Owning a call option on a security enables an investor to postpone the decision on whether to purchase that security while preserving the right to obtain the security at the fixed exercise price specified by the option.

The investor can use the time until the option expires to collect information that could reduce uncertainty about the future rates of return on the security. The market price of the call option is the investor's opportunity cost of continuing to hold the option, rather than selling it or exercising it.[14] Therefore, the market price of the option is the investor's implicit marginal value of information about the security (net of the explicit costs of collecting the information).

Under some conditions, the investor's situation just described is analogous to that of a firm that can postpone a decision to invest in a new project whose initial costs are irrecoverable (sunk) and whose future earnings are uncertain. A benefit of investing in the project without delay is that the firm will receive the revenues from the project sooner than if the firm postponed the project. A cost of investing in the project without delay is the value of the foregone opportunity to collect information that could lead the firm to reject the project and thus avoid losing the initial sunk costs. The value of the option to collect information by postponing the decision on the project is one of the opportunity costs incurred if the firm begins the project now. To maximize its shareholders' wealth, the firm should include this opportunity cost when deciding whether to begin the project now or postpone a decision on the project in order to acquire more information. A familiarity with options is useful for recognizing the existence of these implicit options and in calculating their values.

Consequently, recognizing implicit options and using option pricing theory to determine their values can increase economic efficiency by increasing the accuracy of the net present values of investment projects.

15.9   Implicit Options in a Leveraged Firm

In chapter 13, we explained that the capital structure of a firm can affect the extent to which investors can effect mutually beneficial exchanges. A simple but typical form of capital structure consists of common stock and bonds. The former are residual claims on the firm's earnings; the latter are contractual claims. In chapter 13, we provided several examples of how investors could expand their opportunities for mutually beneficial exchanges by including both residual claims and contractual claims in the capital structure of their firms.

We will now use option pricing theory to determine the equilibrium allocation of the total value of a firm between the investors who own the common stock and the investors who own the bonds. By definition, the sum of the market values of the stock and the bonds is the market value of the firm. That is, if an investor were to purchase all the shares of the common stock and all the bonds, that investor would hold a claim to all of the firm's earnings. But this fact does not tell us how the financial markets will allocate the total value of the firm between the shareholders and the bondholders.

We begin by recalling the distinction that we offered in section 13.2 of chapter 13 between the legal significance and the economic significance of the difference between shareholders and bondholders. By law, the shareholders own the firm; the bondholders are creditors of the firm. As owners, the shareholders elect a board of directors, who then hire professional managers to operate the firm. Ultimately, the shareholders control the firm's operations, including its choice of projects in which to invest.[15] As residual claimants, the shareholders own whatever remains of the firm's earnings after the firm discharges its contractual obligations. As residual claimants, the shareholders have no right to bring legal action against the firm, its managers, or its directors if the residual earnings fall below some threshold. If there is little or nothing left for the shareholders after the contractual claimants are paid, so be it.

As creditors, the bondholders hold a contract with the firm. In consequence, the bondholders do have a right to bring legal action if the firm fails to make the payments specified in the contract. The bondholders do not, however, own anything other than this contract.

A legal analysis of common stocks and bonds addresses the nature of the rights that pertain to the two kinds of securities. Accordingly, a legal analysis would determine how the rights held by the owners of each security are affected by various outcomes. For example, who has the right to determine whether the firm should invest in a project that would substantially increase the risk that the firm might fail to make the required payments to the bondholders on time? In contrast to a legal analysis, an economic analysis of common stocks and bonds is concerned with the market prices of the securities. The market price of a security depends ultimately on investors' perceptions of the probability density functions that govern the future payments generated by those securities, rather than on the legal definitions of the rights attached to those securities.

We will now construct a simple model of a firm to demonstrate how the existence of bonds in the firm's capital structure creates an implicit option. We then use option pricing theory to determine the equilibrium allocation of the total value of the firm between the bondholders and the shareholders.

15.9.1 An Implicit Option for the Shareholders Written by the Bondholders of the Mosquito Point Barge Company

The Mosquito Point Barge Company carries fertilizer and other agricultural inputs along the Seneca River. The company owns several barges and tugboats, financing these assets by issuing a sequence of one-year bonds. Specifically, at the beginning of each year the company sells 10,000 new bonds at a market price of $850 each. Each bond has a face value of $1,000 and matures one year after the company issues it. Consequently, the firm has a contractual obligation to pay the bondholders a total of $10,000,000 ($1,000 times 10,000 bonds) at the end of each year to redeem the bonds that were issued at the beginning of that year. The bonds are zero-coupon bonds. Accordingly, the firm makes no explicit payments of interest on the bonds. An investor's return from holding one of the bonds arises from the difference between the market price of the bonds and their face value. In the present example, the investor's rate of return would be ($1,000−$850)/$850, or $150/$850, or .177 (approximately

By selling 10,000 new bonds at the beginning of each year at a price of $850 p⟨ bond, the Mosquito Point Barge Company finances $8,500,000 worth of equipmen⟨ By redeeming the bonds at the end of each year for a total of $10,000,000, the con⟨ pany pays a finance charge equal to $1,500,000 per year. Since the company repea this process each year, the company is perpetually in debt. Before concluding that this is a bad arrangement, remember that the company's alternative to using bondholders to finance the equipment would be to have the shareholders finance it. If the shareholders financed the equipment by permanently contributing an additional $8,500,000 in capital, they would perpetually incur an opportunity cost on this capital. Thus, as we have learned, the shareholders must either pay interest explicitly, by having their firm issue a perpetual sequence of one-year bonds, or they must pay interest implicitly by contributing an additional $8,500,000 in capital that they could have invested elsewhere.

We turn now to the implicit option created for the company's shareholders by the existence of these bonds. At the end of each year, the shareholders must decide whether to continue operating their firm for at least one more year or to liquidate the firm. To operate for one more year, the shareholders must redeem the maturing bonds. The maturity (face) value of these bonds is $10,000,000. The shareholders can raise part of this $10,000,000 by issuing a new set of one-year bonds. If the new bonds have zero coupons and an aggregate face value of $10,000,000, as do the bonds that are now maturing, the shareholders will have to sell the new bonds at a discount from their face value. Consequently, the shareholders will have to use part of the revenue their firm earned during the year now ending to make up the difference between the receipts from the sale of the new bonds and the $10,000,000 they need to redeem the maturing bonds.

Alternatively, if the shareholders decide to liquidate the firm, they could simply abandon the firm to the owners of the bonds that are now due for redemption. That is, the shareholders could allow the bonds to go into default, in which case the bondholders would acquire the right to take over the firm and either operate it themselves or sell the equipment in an attempt to recover the $10,000,000 owed to them by the shareholders.

In effect, the shareholders have an implicit call option to purchase the firm from the bondholders at the end of each year by paying an exercise price of $10,000,000. If the shareholders expect that the firm's future earnings will be sufficiently high, the shareholders will exercise their option to retain control of the firm by redeeming the maturing bonds. Otherwise, the shareholders will let their implicit option to retain control of the firm expire by not redeeming the maturing bonds.

The shareholders have a sequence of implicit options. Each option expires at the end of a year. To exercise an option is to retain control of the firm for one more year. The exercise price of each option is the aggregate face value of the bonds that are now maturing. To operate the firm for a sequence of years, the shareholders exercise a sequence of implicit options by sequentially issuing new one-year bonds to finance the firm's operations one year at a time.

We can now use option pricing theory to allocate the total value of the firm between the shareholders and the bondholders of the Mosquito Point Barge Company. First, regard the shareholders as holding an implicit call option on the firm. The current market price of this implicit option is the current total market value of the outstanding shares. The firm itself is the underlying asset on which the option is written. The exercise price of the option is the face value of the bonds. By definition, the current market value of the firm is the sum of the current market values of the firm's outstanding securities. These securities consist of the bonds and the shares of stock. If it is correct to regard the shareholders as holding a call option on the firm, then the total market value of the shares should be equal to the market price of that (implicit) option as determined by the Black-Scholes option pricing formula.

In figure 15.3, we use the Black-Scholes model of the price of a call option to represent the current market value of the firm's stock as a function of the current market value of the firm. Let the current moment be the beginning of a year just after the firm has raised $8,500,000 by issuing a new set of bonds that will mature one year from now. The face value of these bonds is $10,000,000.

Let V be the current market value of the firm. We measure V on both the horizontal axis and the vertical axis in figure 15.3. From the perspective of the current moment, the value of the firm one year from now is the random variable, $\tilde{V}$. Assume that $\tilde{V}$ is uniformly distributed over a range that is centered on V and that is W units wide. If the current market value of the firm is V, the value of the firm next year will be uniformly distributed over the interval $[V-(W/2), V+(W/2)]$. The expected value of $\tilde{V}$ is the current market value of the firm, V. We measure both $\tilde{V}$ and W as present values.

Under the Black-Scholes model, the current price of a call option is an increasing convex function of the current price of the underlying asset, given the time remaining until the option expires, the exercise price of the option, the variance of the price of the stock, and other parameters.[16] Taking the entire firm as the underlying asset, we plot in figure 15.3 the value of a call option on the firm as the upward-sloping convex

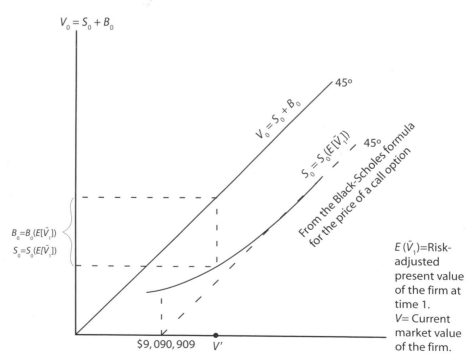

Figure 15.3. An implicit call option in a leveraged firm.

curve, $S_0 = S_0(E[\tilde{V}_1])$. Since we regard the stockholders as a group as having a call option on the entire firm, the height of $S_0 = S_0(E[\tilde{V}_1])$ is the current aggregate market value of the stock as a function of the current market value of the firm. The market value of the firm is equal to the sum of the market values of the firm's outstanding securities. Then for any value of V, the height of the 45° line from the origin above that value of V is equal to the sum of the current market values of the stocks and the bonds. Consequently, for any current value of the firm on the horizontal axis, the vertical difference between the height of $S_0 = S_0(E[\tilde{V}_1])$ and the 45° line from the origin is the current market value of the firm's bonds.

Let V' be a specific value for V. Then the range of values for $\tilde{V}$ is the interval between the points $V' - (W/2)$ and $V' + (W/2)$ on the horizontal axis in figure 15.3. The present value of the maturity value of the bonds is $10,000,000/[1 + .10]$, or $9,090,909. If the (present value of the) outcome next year for $\tilde{V}$ lies within the subinterval $[V' - (W/2), \$9,090,909]$, the shareholders will default on the bonds because the value of the firm will be less than the maturity value of the bonds. Using the terminology of options, the exercise price of the option will exceed the value of the asset on which the option is written. Consequently, the holder of the option will allow it to expire unexercised. Alternatively, if the value of $\tilde{V}$ lies in the subinterval ($9,090,909, $V' + W/2$), the shareholders will exercise their option to purchase the firm by paying off the bonds.

The fact that the shareholders will finance the payment to bondholders in part by issuing new bonds is irrelevant. The critical consideration is that the shareholders will "purchase" the firm from the bondholders by paying the maturity value of the bonds.

It is easy to understand why the height of the curve increases as the current market value of the firm increases. The height of $S_0 = S_0(E[\tilde{V}_1])$ is the current value of the implicit option held by the shareholders. For any current market value of the firm, the value of the option is the expected value of the difference between the value of the firm next year and the maturity value of the bonds.[17] This difference is a uniformly distributed random variable whose expected value is equal to the current value of the firm, V. An increase in the expected value shifts this distribution rightward. Since the maturity value of the bonds is fixed, any rightward shift of the range of the distribution of $\tilde{V}$ increases the range of positive values for the difference between the future value of the firm and the maturity value of the bonds. Consequently, an increase in the current value of the firm increases the current value of the implicit call option, and thus the curve $S_0 = S_0(E[\tilde{V}_1])$ has a positive slope.

The lower of the two 45° lines in figure 15.3 begins on the horizontal axis at $9,090,909, which is the present value of the maturity value of the bonds. At this point, the height of the upper 45° line is $9,090,909. Since the two 45° lines are parallel, the vertical distance between them is $9,090,909 for any value of $V \geq \$9,090,909$.

As the current value of the firm increases, the curve $S_0 = S_0(E[\tilde{V}_1])$ approaches the lower 45° line, becoming coincident with that line for $V \geq \$9,090,909 + W/2$. When $V \geq \$9,090,909 + W/2$, the lower bound of the distribution for $\tilde{V}$ is at least as large as the present value of the maturity value of the bonds. Once the current value of the firm is high enough so that there will be no default on the bonds, the value of the option is equal to the value of the firm minus the present value of the maturity value of the bonds. Moreover, once $V \geq \$9,090,909 + W/2$, each further $1 increase in the current value of the firm increases the value of the shareholders' implicit option by the same amount. Consequently, for all values of V that exceed $\$9,090,909+W/2$, the bonds are riskless.

Finally, we assert without proof that for any value of V, the slope of the $S_0=S_0(E[\tilde{V}_1])$ curve is the probability that the shareholders will exercise their option by redeeming the bonds on schedule.[18] As we explained earlier, if V is less than $\$9,090,909+W/2$, there is a positive probability of default. Accordingly, for $V < \$9,090,909+W/2$, the slope of $S_0=S_0(E[\tilde{V}_1])$ is less than 1. As V increases, the proportion of the distribution for $\tilde{V}$ that lies to the left of $\$9,090,909$ decreases, thus reducing the probability of default. Accordingly, as V increases, the slope of $S_0=S_0(E[\tilde{V}_1])$ increases. Once V reaches $\$9,090,909+W/2$, the probability of default reaches 0, and the slope of $S_0=S_0(E[\tilde{V}_1])$ becomes equal to 1.

The Black-Scholes option pricing formula provides valuable information about the equilibrium prices of the securities of a leveraged firm. By regarding the common stock as an implicit option, we can determine the equilibrium allocation of the total value of the firm between the shareholders and the bondholders. Moreover, we can determine the probability of default on the bonds. Of course, to do this we must estimate the values of the parameters required by the Black-Scholes formula. One of these required parameters is the variance of $\tilde{V}$, the future value of the firm.

15.10 An Implicit Option on a Postponable and Irreversible Investment Project

15.10.1 The Model

The ES&D Railroad has an opportunity to construct a branch line that would run 10 miles from its main line to a new factory being constructed now, at time 0, in an isolated rural area by the Genteel Furniture Company. The construction of the factory will be completed one year from now, at time 1. Construction of the branch line would require one year.

The managers of the furniture company plan to ship large quantities of rough lumber to the factory from distant locations, produce an unusual line of new furniture, and ship it to retail stores across the country. For a variety of reasons, the owners of the factory prefer to use the railroad to receive the raw materials and to ship the finished goods, assuming that the branch line is available. Shipping and receiving by trucks is an alternative because the factory is located 100 miles from an interstate highway.

The managers of the furniture company are reasonably certain that the demand for the new product will be strong enough to justify having constructed the factory. There is, however, a chance that the new line of furniture will flop. To reduce their risk, the managers will use the coming year to conduct test marketing of some samples of the new furniture. If the results are positive, the managers will begin producing the new line of furniture in the new factory at time 1. If the results are negative, the managers will sell the newly completed factory. There are no other plants located near the proposed branch line of the railroad, and there is little prospect that a new owner of the plant would use the branch railroad line.

The railroad is assured of a sufficient volume of traffic to justify constructing the branch line if the demand for the new line of furniture is as strong as the managers of the Genteel Furniture Company expect. But if the new line of furniture flops, the railroad will earn nothing on its investment in constructing the new branch line.

The managers of the ES&D Railroad have a choice:

1. Construct the branch line immediately so that it is ready for use by the time that the furniture company is ready to begin operations at its new factory.
2. Postpone for one year the decision on constructing the branch line. If the Genteel Furniture Company begins to operate their new factory at time 1 (having learned from their test marketing that the demand for the furniture will be strong), begin construction of the branch line at time 1. Otherwise, do not construct the line.

Each choice is risky.

Constructing the branch line at time 0 is risky because the new line of furniture might flop, in which event the railroad would earn nothing on its investment.

Postponing a decision on constructing the branch line is also risky. Without the new branch line in place when the factory begins operations, the managers of the factory will use trucks to receive lumber and to ship furniture during the first year of operation. Once the trucking companies begin serving the new factory, they might be able to provide incentives that would overcome the managers' preference to ship by rail. In this event, the railroad might have to offer a substantial discount to persuade the managers to switch from trucks to rail. The discount would reduce the rate of return on the railroad's investment in constructing the branch line.

The railroad's opportunity to construct the branch line has the characteristics required for an implicit option. First, the railroad can postpone its decision on constructing the line. Unlike some investments, the opportunity to construct the line is not a now-or-never proposition.

Second, there is no salvage value for the investment because there is little prospect that there will be other customers for the railroad on the new branch line. Should the railroad construct the new line, the value of the resources committed to that construction would be irrecoverable.

Third, at time 0 the net present value of an investment in the branch line is uncertain because no one knows how consumers will respond to the new line of furniture.

It is easy to see the analogy between the railroad's prospective investment and a call option on a stock. An investor who owns a call option on IBM common stock has the flexibility to postpone the decision on acquiring the stock at the fixed exercise price, E, in order to collect additional information. Of course, the investor cannot retain this flexibility beyond the expiration date of the option.

The current value to the investor of the flexibility to postpone the decision is the current market price of the option. Were this not so, a rational investor would sell the option rather than continue to hold it.[19]

An investor who acquires the stock now will pay two costs; one is explicit, the other is implicit. The explicit cost is the exercise price of the option. The implicit cost is the current market price of the option.

Once the investor exercises the option, he or she will own the stock for better or worse; the investor will no longer have the opportunity to postpone the decision in order to consider additional information. Consequently, to exercise the option now is to destroy an opportunity whose value is the current market price of the option.

The railroad has an option to obtain the new branch line (by constructing it). The branch line is analogous to the IBM stock; both assets are claims to uncertain future sequences of payments. The exercise price of the railroad's option to acquire the new branch line is the cost of constructing it.

The railroad's option on the new branch line has a value. In principle, we could imagine a market in which the railroad could sell its option to construct the branch line. If such a market existed, the railroad's option on the new branch line would have a market price, and this price would be the implicit component of the cost that the railroad would incur to acquire the new branch line. In fact, it is unlikely that there would be an organized market in which the railroad's option on the branch line would be traded. Consequently, there will be no market price for the option. But the absence of an organized market for the railroad's option does not mean that the option has no value. The challenge is to use option pricing theory to estimate the value of the option so that the railroad can more accurately calculate the net present value of acquiring the branch line. More accurate calculations of the net present values of prospective investment projects lead to a more efficient allocation of resources.

15.10.2 A Numerical Example

We will now present a simple numerical model of the railroad's implicit option on the investment project defined as constructing the proposed branch rail line. The revenues from hauling freight on the branch line depend on whether the test marketing of the new furniture is successful and on whether the branch line is ready for traffic when the furniture company begins to operate its new plant. Constructing the branch line requires one year. The railroad could begin to construct the branch line at time 0. If the test marketing of the new furniture between time 0 and time 1 succeeds, the furniture company will begin shipping by rail at time 1, and the railroad will receive annual revenues equal to $3,000,000 beginning at time 1 and continuing forever. If, however, the test marketing of the new furniture fails, the furniture company will not operate the plant, and the railroad will receive nothing.

Alternatively, the railroad could postpone the decision on constructing the branch line until time 1, when the furniture company will have the results of the test marketing of the new furniture. If the new furniture succeeds, the furniture company will begin to operate its new plant at time 1 and ship by truck. If the railroad then begins construction of the new branch line, it will be ready for traffic beginning at time 2, and the railroad will obtain annual revenues of $2,800,000 beginning at time 2 and continuing forever. The reduction in the annual revenues reflects the discount required to persuade the furniture company to switch its shipping from truck to rail. If the new furniture is not successful, the railroad will not begin to construct the proposed branch line. The (explicit) cost of construction is $20,000,000, which the railroad must pay at the beginning of the year in which the construction occurs.

The railroad's subjective probability that the new line of furniture will succeed is .8. The prospective revenues from freight traffic on the new branch rail line are uncorrelated with the performance of the macroeconomy. Hence, the systematic risk of the investment project is zero, and we can use the rate of return on the risk-free asset to calculate the net present value of the project. The risk-free rate of return is .10 per year.

The railroad has an implicit option to purchase the new branch line. The exercise price of the option is $20,000,000. The option has value because it allows the railroad to postpone its decision on purchasing the branch line pending additional information about the profitability of that line. Since there will be no additional information available beyond time 1, and thus no point in postponing any further the decision on constructing the branch rail line, the option expires at time 1. To begin constructing the branch line at time 0 is to kill the option to collect additional information. Consequently, the net present value of a decision to begin construction today should reflect the opportunity cost of killing the option.

To understand this, let $V_0(0)$ be the net present value (as of time 0) of a decision to begin construction of the branch at time 0, ignoring the opportunity cost of killing the option. Using the conventional calculation of net present value, we have:

$$V_0(0) = -\$20,000,000 + (.8)(\$3,000,000/.10)$$
$$= -\$20,000,000 + \$24,000,000 \qquad (15.25)$$
$$= \$4,000,000.$$

In words, if the railroad begins construction at time 0, it incurs a cost of $20,000,000. With a probability equal to .8, the new line of furniture will succeed, and the railroad will obtain annual freight revenues equal to $3,000,000, beginning at time 1 and continuing forever. The net present value of this sequence would be $3,000,000/.10, or $30,000,000, if the revenues were certain to occur. But since the revenues will occur only with a probability of .8, the expected net present value of the revenues is only (.8)$30,000,000, or $24,000,000. The railroad pays the construction cost with certainty at time 0. Then the expected net present value of beginning construction of the branch line at time 0 is $-\$20,000,000 + \$24,000,000$, or $4,000,000.

To maximize its shareholders' wealth, the railroad should undertake every project that has a positive net present value. Since $V_0(0)$ is positive, the railroad should begin construction of the branch line at time 0. We will now show that this conclusion is incorrect because the calculation of the net present value in equation (15.25) ignores the cost of killing the implicit option.

Let $V_0(1)$ be the net present value (as of time 0) of a decision to begin construction at time 1 if the furniture company begins to operate its new plant at time 1. We have:

$$V_0(1) = (.8)[-\$20,000,000 + (\$2,8000,000/.10)]/(1+.10)$$
$$= (.8)(-\$20,000,000 + \$28,000,000)/(1+.10)$$
$$= (.8)(8,000,000)/(1+.10)$$
$$= (.8)\$7,272,727$$
$$= \$5,818,182. \qquad (15.26)$$

With probability of .8, the railroad pays $20,000,000 at time 1 to begin construction of the branch line. Annual revenues of $2,800,000 begin one year later, at time 2, and continue forever. The present value of these revenues as of time 1 is $2,800,000/.10, or $28,000,000. Then the net present value of the project as of time 1 is $8,000,000. Dividing $8,000,000 by $(1+.10)$ produces the present value as of time 0. Finally, multiplying by .8 adjusts the net present value for the fact that the railroad will construct the branch line only if the test marketing of the new line of furniture is successful.

Equation (15.25) states that if the railroad begins construction of the branch line at time 0, the expected value (as of time 0) of the increase in the shareholders' wealth will be $4,000,000. From equation (15.26), the expected value (again as of time 0) of the gain for shareholders of delaying the decision on construction until time 1 is $5,818,182. Since the two projects are mutually exclusive, the railroad should choose the second one.

We can restate the railroad's opportunities in terms of two options. For each option, the underlying asset is the new branch line to be delivered one year after the option is exercised, and for each option the exercise price is $20,000,000, which is the cost of constructing the new line. The first option expires now, at time 0; the second option expires one year from now, at time 1. At time 0, the value to the railroad of the first option, the one that will expire momentarily, is $4,000,000. In chapter 3 we explained that the net present value of a project is the maximal amount of money that a firm would be willing to pay for the right to undertake the project.[20] By beginning construction of the branch line now, the railroad would increase the expected value of its shareholders' wealth by $4,000,000.[21]

But the value to the railroad at time 0 of the option that will not expire until time 1 is $5,818,182. To maximize its shareholders' wealth, the railroad should be willing to pay up to $5,818,182 for the right to postpone for one year the decision whether to purchase the (construction of the) new branch line for $20,000,000. As we learned earlier in this chapter, increasing the time remaining until the option expires increases the value of the option.

The conventional rule for choosing investment projects is to undertake any project that has a positive net present value. In equation (15.25), the net present value, $V_0(0)$, of the project in which the railroad begins construction now is positive, and yet we have demonstrated that the railroad's shareholders will gain wealth if the railroad rejects that project. The anomaly vanishes when we recognize that the calculation of $V_0(0)$ ignores an implicit cost, namely the cost of killing the option to postpone the decision. The value of this option is $5,818,182. Let $V_0'(0)$ be the net present value of the project net of the cost of killing the implicit option. Then

$$
\begin{aligned}
V_0'(0) &= V_0(0) - \$5,818,182 \\
&= \$4,000,000 - \$5,818,182 \\
&= -\$1,818,182.
\end{aligned} \tag{15.27}
$$

Since the net present value, properly calculated, of beginning construction now is negative, the railroad should reject this project.

We conclude that recognizing implicit options contained in proposed investment projects can enable firms and investors to calculate net present values more precisely and thereby increase the efficiency of the allocation of resources.

15.11 Summary

Options are financial securities because they are saleable rights to receive sequences of payments. We can determine the equilibrium prices of options relative to the equilibrium prices of other securities by using the same principles that govern the prices of all securities. One of these principles is that in equilibrium the rate of return on a risk-free portfolio must be equal to the rate of return on a risk-free asset. The Black-Scholes formula for the equilibrium price of an option is based on this principle and on the fact that an investor can construct a risk-free portfolio that contains an option and the underlying stock.

An efficient allocation of resources is one in which there are no further opportunities for mutually beneficial exchanges. A necessary condition for effecting these exchanges is an accurate evaluation of their net present values. The theory of option pricing contributes to these evaluations because some of the exchanges contain implicit options. A leveraged firm contains an implicit call option for the shareholders. Option pricing theory has implications for the allocation of the firm's total market value between the shareholders and the bondholders, and for the probability that the firm will default on the bonds. This information can assist investors in evaluating proposed exchanges by improving the accuracy with which the investors estimate the values of the securities that would finance those exchanges.

Investment projects that are both postponable and irreversible also contain implicit options. By increasing the accuracy with which firms can estimate the net present values of these projects, option pricing theory can facilitate mutually beneficial exchanges, and thus increase the efficiency of the allocation of resources.

Appendix: Continuous Compounding

In this appendix, we sketch the relationship between periodic and continuous compounding of the rate of interest.

Let r be the rate of interest per year. If interest is compounded annually, the value one year from today of an account that is worth $\$A$ today will be:

$$\$X_1 = \$A(1+r)^1. \tag{15.A1}$$

By extension, two years from today the account will be worth:

$$\$X_2 = \$X_1(1+r)^1 = \$A(1+r)^1(1+r)^1$$
$$= \$A(1+r)^2 \tag{15.A2}$$

In general, the value of the account t years from today will be:

$$\$X_t = \$A(1+r)^t. \tag{15.A3}$$

Suppose that the interest is compounded semiannually, and let $\$Y_t$ be the value t years from today of an account that is worth $\$A$ today. Then the value of the account one year from today will be:

$$\$Y_1 = \$A[1+(r/2)][1+(r/2)]$$
$$= \$A[1+(r/2)]^2. \tag{15.A4}$$

With semiannual compounding, there are two periods during each year in which the account earns interest. The rate of interest per period is $(r/2)$.

Over a span of t years there are $2t$ periods in which the account earns interest. Then the value of the account t years from today will be:

$$\$Y_t = \$A[1+(r/2)]^{2t} \qquad (15.A5)$$

Now suppose that interest is compounded n times per year, and let $\$Z_t$ be the value of the account t years from today. By analogy with equation (15.A5), we have:

$$\$Z_t = \$A[1+(r/n)]^{nt}. \qquad (15.A6)$$

Continuous compounding is the limit of equation (15.A6) as the number of compounding periods per year, n, increases without bound. Let $\$V_t$ be the value of the account t years from today when interest is compounded continuously. Then

$$\$Y_t = \text{Limit } \$A[1+(r/n)]^{nt}$$
$$n \to \infty \qquad (15.A7)$$
$$= Ae^{rt}.$$

Problems

1. A call option expires 2 periods from now. Given the following information, calculate the values of the stock at times 1 and 2, and the values of the option at times 0, 1, and 2.

$S_0 = \$30$
$U = .25$
$D = .10$
$R = .10$
Exercise price $= \$33$

2. A call option expires 2 periods from now. Given the following information, are the options correctly priced at Nodes 2 and 3?

$S_0 = \$10$
$U = .3$
$D = .05$
Exercise Price $= \$11$
$R = .10$
$C_1^+ = \$2$
$C_1^- = \$.80$

If not, what would one do to obtain a riskless profit? How large is the riskless profit?

3. Use the put-call parity to create at time 0 (a) a homemade put option that will expire at time 1, (b) a homemade call option that will expire at time 1, and (c) a homemade share.

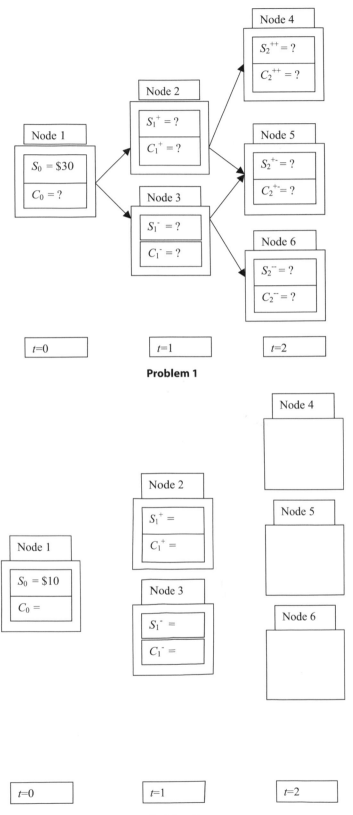

Node 4
$S_2^{++} = ?$
$C_2^{++} = ?$

Node 2
$S_1^{+} = ?$
$C_1^{+} = ?$

Node 5
$S_2^{+-} = ?$
$C_2^{+-} = ?$

Node 1
$S_0 = \$30$
$C_0 = ?$

Node 3
$S_1^{-} = ?$
$C_1^{-} = ?$

Node 6
$S_2^{--} = ?$
$C_2^{--} = ?$

$t=0$ $t=1$ $t=2$

Problem 1

Node 4

Node 2
$S_1^{+} =$
$C_1^{+} =$

Node 5

Node 1
$S_0 = \$10$
$C_0 =$

Node 3
$S_1^{-} =$
$C_1^{-} =$

Node 6

$t=0$ $t=1$ $t=2$

Problem 2

Notes

1. F. Black and M. Scholes, "The Pricing of Options and Corporate Liabilities," *Journal of Political Economy* 81 (1973): 637-659.

2. In practice, a call option is usually defined as a right to purchase 100 shares (or some other convenient round number). For convenience, and with no loss of generality, we define a call option as a right to purchase one share.

3. A riskless profit of $1 is trivial, but a riskless profit of $1 per option is not trivial. Purchasing 1,000,000 options and 1,000,000 shares of stock will generate a riskless profit of $1,000,000. We ignore transaction costs.

4. More precisely, competition among investors will reduce the difference between the market price of the stock and the market price of the option to equality with the difference between the price of the stock and the exercise price of the option, thus eliminating the opportunity for a riskless profit. Whether investors force the price of the option up, or the price of the stock down, or some combination of the two is immaterial for the question at hand. The point is that the equilibrium configuration of the market prices of the stock and the option, relative to the exercise price of the option, will provide no opportunity for a riskless profit.

5. We ignore transaction costs.

6. The demonstration of this riskless profit is analogous to the numerical example in section 15.2.2 for a call option. We encourage the reader to construct a numerical example for the put option.

7. The price that Adrian paid to purchase the option prior to time 2 is a sunk cost at time 2. Thus Adrian's optimal decision at time 2 on whether to exercise the option or allow it to expire does not depend on the price that he paid for the option. The level of his profit from having purchased the option depends on what he paid for it, but his decision on whether to exercise the option does not. Compare Adrian's decision to the irrelevance of a firm's fixed costs to its optimal behavior in the short run.

8. Again for convenience, we assume that investors can trade in fractional units of securities, including options. We could demonstrate our result by having the investor purchase 1,000,000 shares of the stock and selling 2,570,000 call options on that stock. Since the ratio is 2.57 options sold for each share of stock purchased, the portfolio will be riskless.

9. A detailed numerical example of long and short positions appears in section 8.3.3 of chapter 8.

10. Most, if not all, of the intermediate and advanced texts in finance present analyses of the binomial model of option pricing for N periods.

11. Recall from chapter 7 that the variance of a security's rate of return is the probability-weighted sum of the squared deviations that are possible between the rate of return and its expected value. Whatever the probabilities that govern whether the stock will follow the up path or the down path from one time to the next, an increase in the values of the up factor and the down factor will increase the variance of the stock's rate of return.

12. Recall that this statement does not hold for dates prior to the expiration date.

13. The reader might review chapter 11 on the efficient markets hypothesis for the economic interpretation of *immediate*.

14. More precisely, the opportunity cost of holding the option for one period is equal to the risk-adjusted interest rate (per period) multiplied by the current market price of the option.

15. In practice, because the ownership of the common stock is widely dispersed, individual shareholders or small groups of shareholders have virtually no control over their managers. Important exceptions occur if mutual funds or pension funds own sufficiently large blocks of shares. The California State Pension Fund is an example of a fund that frequently affects the decisions of firms in which it holds investments. In any case, the managers of a firm do have an

interest in increasing the value of the firm's shares. But (as we learned in chapter 13) problems of agency can create conflicts between the interests of the managers and the interests of the shareholders.

16. More advanced texts provide a derivation of this statement.

17. Subject to the condition that the value of the option cannot be negative.

18. Advanced texts in portfolio theory demonstrate this fact.

19. More precisely, the market price of the option is the marginal value to the investor of the right to postpone the decision.

20. If future costs and revenues are certain, the shareholders' wealth will increase by the net present value of the project, minus whatever the firm pays for the right to undertake the project. Equivalently, we could define the costs of the project to include any fee that the firm must pay for the right to undertake the project.

21. We assume that the railroad operates several investment projects. For example, each regularly scheduled train is a project that involves a sequence of uncertain costs and revenues. The shareholders are concerned with the expected rate of return and the risk on the railroad's portfolio of projects. If the systematic risks of these projects are zero, the railroad should undertake any project that has a positive net present value.

16 Futures Contracts

16.1 Introduction

A *futures contract* is a standardized version of a forward contract. A forward contract is an agreement under which one person agrees to deliver a specified quantity of a good to a second person at a specified future time in exchange for a price that is specified when the contract is made. For example, suppose that on March 16, 2005, Mr. X purchases a forward contract in oats from Mr. Y. The contract specifies that on September 30, 2005, Mr. Y must deliver one ton of oats to a designated location (such as Kansas City), and that Mr. X will accept delivery of one ton of oats at that location and pay $46 to Mr. Y. The $46 is the forward price to which Mr. X and Mr. Y agreed on March 16, 2005, for delivery of oats on September 30, 2005.[1]

The forward contract described above is a private agreement between Mr. X and Mr. Y, who negotiate directly with each other. For most forward contracts, there is no organized market in which the contracts can be traded continuously over time. The absence of an organized market for forward contracts substantially increases the transaction costs incurred by using forward contracts to effect mutually beneficial exchanges. The higher the transaction costs, the fewer exchanges will occur, with a consequent decrease in economic efficiency.

There are three ways in which the absence of an organized market for forward contracts increases transaction costs. First, both Mr. X and Mr. Y incur considerable costs to find each other and to negotiate the terms of the contract. Second, each man incurs a risk that the other man will not meet his obligations under the contract. Mr. X might refuse to accept delivery of the oats at the agreed price of $46. Similarly, Mr. Y might refuse to deliver the oats in exchange for $46.

Third, the lack of an organized market substantially increases the costs that each man would incur to cancel the commitment that he made under the contract, should changes in circumstances make it advantageous for him to do so. For example, after the contract is created in March, but before September arrives, Mr. X could decide that he no longer wants to accept delivery of oats in September and pay $46 per ton. If there were an organized market on which forward contracts were traded, Mr. X could easily find a third party, say Ms. Z, who would purchase from him the right to receive oats in September from Mr. Y, and pay Mr. Y $46 per ton. The price at which Mr. X could sell to Ms. Z his right to receive oats from Mr. Y would be set by negotiation between Mr. X and Ms. Z. Similarly, should Mr. Y's circumstances change, he would have an incentive to find a third party, say Mr. W, who, for a price, would agree to perform Mr. Y's obligation to deliver oats to Mr. X in September and accept $46 per ton in payment.

By increasing the costs incurred to reverse a position in a forward contract, the absence of an organized market increases the risk of entering into these contracts, thereby reducing the extent to which these contracts can promote mutually beneficial exchanges.

There is an additional deleterious effect on economic efficiency of the absence of organized trading in forward contracts. As we have stressed in earlier chapters, markets generate information about possibilities for mutually beneficial exchanges and transmit this information through prices. The prices at which persons agree to receive and deliver oats at a future date contain information about future events. As time progresses, there can be new information about these future events. An organized market would transmit this new information by promoting continuous trading in forward contracts.

A futures contract is a standardized forward contract that is traded continuously on an organized market, often known as a futures exchange. The exchange defines several kinds of contracts by specifying the commodities to be delivered, the quality of the commodity acceptable for delivery, where the commodity is to be delivered, and the date on which delivery is to occur. For example, the Chicago Board of Trade organizes trading in corn futures that have delivery months of March, May, July, September, and December. The corn may be delivered at Chicago, Burns Harbor, Toledo, or St. Louis.[2] The Chicago Board of Trade (with its affiliated organizations) also guarantees the performance of investors who buy or sell these contracts. Using a process called *marking to the market*, the Board of Trade causes the prices of futures contracts to reflect new information about future events. We will explain the process of marking to the market in section 16.6.2.

Markets for futures contracts promote economic efficiency by allocating risk among persons according to their comparative advantages in bearing risk. When the economy allocates resources according to comparative advantage, the economy expands the set of achievable mutually beneficial exchanges. In this chapter, we explain how markets for futures contracts promote mutually beneficial exchanges among producers, speculators, and consumers.

16.2   Futures Contracts as Financial Securities

In section 2.1 of chapter 2, we defined a financial security as a saleable right to receive a sequence of future payments. The practice of marking to the market makes a futures contract a financial security. "A futures price is something of a misnomer, for it is not a price at all. Rather, purchasing or selling futures contracts means making a legal commitment to accept a series of cash flows called *variation* margin during the period the contracts to deliver (or accept delivery) are held.[3] A futures exchange maintains an account for each investor who purchases or sells a futures contract on that exchange. Investors are required to deposit with the exchange an amount of money, called a margin, to increase the likelihood that they will meet their obligations to deliver, or to accept delivery, as specified by the contracts that they have purchased or sold. The variation margin is the amount by which the exchange adjusts the investor's account as the contracts are marked to the market.[4]

16.3   Futures Contracts and the Efficient Allocation of Risk

To achieve economic efficiency, the economy must do more than allocate the production of oats to those farmers who have a comparative advantage in producing oats. The economy must promote an efficient specialization and exchange in every aspect of the production of oats. For example, farmers who grow oats do not also produce the fertilizer that they use. Nor do they manufacture the tractors that they use, any more than they refine the gasoline that they use in their tractors. In an efficient allocation of resources, those persons who have a comparative advantage in the planting and harvesting of oats do only that; the production of fertilizer, tractors, and gasoline is left to persons whose comparative advantages lie in the production of those goods.

One aspect of the production of oats is the risk that farmers will overestimate in the spring, when they decide how much oats to plant, the price at which they will be able to sell the crop in the fall. An efficient allocation of resources will assign this risk to whoever has a comparative advantage in bearing it. It is plausible that farmers will not have a comparative advantage in bearing risk; their specialty is in determining how to combine land, seed, fertilizer, machinery, and time to produce oats. They are not skilled in predicting the price of oats several months in advance. But there are persons who do specialize in predicting future values of the price of oats. Some of these persons, called speculators, sell their knowledge to farmers through the process of insulating farmers from the risks involved in predicting the price of oats. A market in futures contracts for oats organizes this mutually beneficial exchange between farmers and speculators.

Suppose that Mr. Green is a farmer who produces oats. Mr. Green calculates that he will be able to obtain a profit by planting oats in the spring if he can sell the oats for at least $46 in September. Since the price of oats in September might be less than $46, Mr. Green will incur the risk of a loss by planting oats in the spring. He can transfer this risk to a speculator by selling to him on March 16, 2005, a futures contract for the delivery of oats for $46 on the following September 30. As the purchaser of the futures contract, the speculator is committed to accept delivery in September, and pay the $46 on which he and Mr. Green agreed in March. Consequently, the speculator will bear the risk that the price of oats in September will be less than $46. The speculator's profit (or loss) in September is the difference between the price at which he can resell the oats in September and the $46 that he is committed to pay for it.

Speculators are just as eager as anyone else to avoid losses. Therefore, speculators will purchase futures contracts in March for $46 only if they are reasonably sure that the price at which they will be able to sell oats in September will be greater than $46. If speculators have a comparative advantage relative to farmers in predicting the future price of oats, the speculators will incur losses less frequently than farmers would if they were to predict the future price of oats. A market for futures contracts in oats does not eliminate the risk involved in predicting the future price of oats. Rather, the market enables farmers to transfer that risk to speculators who, because of their comparative advantage in predicting future prices, can bear the risk at a lower cost than the farmers can.[5]

There is an analogous risk for persons who use oats as an input for production. Ms. Black could be a miller who signs a contract in March 2005 to deliver cereals at a fixed price to a chain of hotels for several months beginning in October 2005. If Ms. Black purchases in March the oats that she will require beginning in October, she will incur storage charges for six months.[6] Suppose that Ms. Black calculates that she can make a profit if she can purchase oats in September for no more than $46. If the price of oats in September is greater than $46, she will incur a loss in producing cereals for the hotels at the price agreed to in March.

Ms. Black can transfer this risk to a speculator by purchasing from him a futures contract for the delivery of oats for $46 on the following September 30. As the seller of the futures contract, the speculator is committed to deliver oats in September and accept in payment the $46 on which he and Ms. Black agreed in March. Then the speculator will bear the risk that the price of oats in September will be greater than $46. The speculator's profit (or loss) in September is the difference between the price at which he purchases the oats in September in order to make delivery to Ms. Black, and the $46 that he is committed to accept from Ms. Black for the oats.

We have seen how farmers and speculators, and millers and speculators, can use futures contracts to effect mutually beneficial exchanges. Consequently, through the intermediary participation of speculators, the farmers and the millers create mutually beneficial exchanges between themselves.

By reducing the risks that producers would otherwise incur, markets in futures contracts also create lower prices for consumers. Prices paid by consumers must cover producers' marginal costs; otherwise the producers will reduce their rates of output. Conversely, if producers' marginal cost curves shift downward, the producers will expand their rates of output, and reduce the prices that they charge consumers.[7] In most cases, producers must make commitments well in advance of learning the price at which they will be able to sell their product and the prices that they will have to pay for inputs. The unpredictability of these prices is one of the costs incurred by producers. To the extent that producers can use futures markets to transfer these costs to other persons who have a comparative advantage in bearing them, the producers can shift their marginal cost curves downward. Consequently, markets for futures contracts reduce prices paid by consumers by creating an efficient allocation of risk.

16.4   The Futures Price, the Spot Price, and the Future Price

It is critical to distinguish among the futures price for oats, the spot price for oats, and the future price for oats.

A *futures price* for oats is a price at which a buyer agrees to deliver, and a seller agrees to receive, oats at a specified future date. The futures price is a fixed number that is specified in the futures contract.

The *spot price* of oats is a price at which a buyer agrees to deliver, and a seller agrees to receive, oats immediately, that is to say, on the spot.

The *future price* of oats is the value that the spot price will take on a future day.

Consider the following example. On March 16, 2005, there are three contracts available for the delivery of oats. The first contract specifies immediate delivery of the oats; the second contract calls for delivery on June 30, 2005; and the third contract requires delivery on September 30, 2005. On March 16, 2005, there are three separate markets operating simultaneously. Each market corresponds to one of the delivery dates, and each market has its own demand for, and supply of, oats for delivery on the date that corresponds to that market.

On March 16, the spot market organizes trading between persons who offer to sell, and persons who offer to buy, oats for immediate delivery. On the same day, the second market organizes trading between persons who offer to deliver oats on June 30, 2005, and persons who offer to accept delivery of oats on that date. The trading in this market determines the price as of March 16, 2005, of oats for delivery on the following June 30. The expression for this futures price is the June (30, 2005) oat futures price on March 16.

Finally, the third market determines the price as of March 16, 2005, of oats for delivery on the following September 30. This price is the September oat futures price on March 16.

The *future* (without the *s*) price of oats for a given future date will (obviously) not be known until that date arrives.

16.5   The Long Side and the Short Side of a Futures Contract

The two sides of a futures contract are known as the long side and the short side. From chapter 10, recall that an investor who holds a long position in a security will gain wealth if the price of the security increases. Conversely, an investor who holds a short position will gain wealth if the price of the security decreases. We can easily apply these definitions to futures contracts.

Mr. Green, who sells a futures contract at $46 on March 16 to deliver oats in September, has a short position in the contract. Increases in the value of the spot price for oats in September will cause Mr. Green to lose wealth. As the seller of the futures contract, Mr. Green is committed to deliver oats in September and accept $46 as payment. His profit in September will therefore be $46 minus the cost of delivering the oats. The cost of delivering the oats in September is the spot price in September. To deliver oats in September, Mr. Green must either purchase the oats in September on the spot market or draw down his inventory of oats. If he purchases the oats on the spot market, he incurs the spot price as an explicit cost of delivering oats. If he draws the oats out of his inventory, he incurs the spot price as an implicit cost because he could have sold those oats in the spot market. Therefore, his profit in September will be the futures price at which he sold his contract ($46 in our example) minus the spot price in September.

Suppose that the spot price in September is $44. Then Mr. Green will obtain a profit of $2 because he will receive $46 for oats that will cost him only $44 to deliver.

If the spot price in September is $49, Mr. Green will incur a loss of $3, because he will incur a cost of $49 to deliver oats for which he will receive only $46. Since the price that Mr. Green will receive for the oats delivered in September is the futures price, which is fixed by the contract that he sold on March 16, we conclude that Mr. Green loses wealth as the spot price in September increases. We conclude that the value of a short position in a September futures contract for oats varies inversely with the spot price for oats in September.

Mr. Green's short position in the futures contract is analogous to an investor's short position in a share of IBM stock. The investor is obligated to return one share of stock to the person (or the broker) from whom he borrowed the share. To deliver a share back to the broker, the investor must either purchase a share on the open market or draw a share from his own inventory. In either case, the cost to the investor of delivering the stock is the current price of the stock. As the price of the stock increases, the investor who is short in that stock loses wealth.

Ms. Black has a long position in a futures contract. On March 16, she purchased a contract to accept delivery of oats in September and pay $46 at that time. It is easy to show that the value of a long position in a September futures contract for oats varies directly with the spot price for oats in September. Ms. Black can resell in the spot market the oats that she will receive in September. Her profit will be equal to the spot price in September minus the fixed price that she is committed to pay for the oats. The higher the spot price in September, the higher her profit (or the smaller her loss).

16.6   Futures Contracts as Financial Securities

A financial security is a saleable right to receive a sequence of payments. To show that a futures contract meets this definition, we must explain a bit more about how these contracts are traded and how the market determines their prices.

16.6.1   The Clearinghouse

An organized futures market uses a clearinghouse that acts as an intermediary between persons who buy and sell futures contracts. The main purpose of the clearinghouse is to reduce the risk of buying and selling futures contracts by guaranteeing the performance of persons who enter these contracts. The use of a clearinghouse is another example of how a financial market promotes mutually beneficial exchanges by allocating risk among persons according to their comparative advantages in bearing risk.

Continuing with our example involving Ms. Black and Mr. Green, on March 16 futures contracts for oats delivered on September 30 are trading at $46. Mr. Green places (through a broker) an order to sell a contract, and Ms. Black places an order to purchase a contract. Since the price at which Mr. Green is willing to deliver oats in September is equal to the price that Ms. Black is willing to pay in September for oats delivered then, the two orders can be crossed in a single contract. But this contract involves risk for each party because the other party might default. When September arrives, Mr. Green might fail to deliver the oats as promised, or Ms. Black might fail to pay for the oats as promised. Holding a contract with another person, and obtaining that person's performance under the contract, are not the same thing. Futures contracts promote economic efficiency by allocating risk among persons according to their comparative advantages in bearing risk. The greater the likelihood of defaults on futures contracts, the less useful these contracts will be in allocating the risks of predicting future prices. Consequently, prospective buyers and sellers of futures contracts will be willing to pay something to reduce the likelihood of defaults.

The clearinghouse reduces the likelihood of defaults by acting as an intermediary between those who purchase and those who sell futures contracts. Rather than creating a single contract between Mr. Green and Ms. Black, the clearinghouse creates two contracts. Mr. Green sells a contract to the clearinghouse, and Ms. Black purchases an offsetting contract from the clearinghouse. As a seller of a futures contract for $46, Mr. Green must deliver oats to the clearinghouse on the following September 30 and accept $46, minus a small commission, in payment from the clearinghouse at that time. Ms. Black, who purchases a futures contract for $46, must accept delivery of the oats from the clearinghouse in September, and pay $46, plus a small commission, to the clearinghouse at that time. The commissions are the price that the clearinghouse charges for guaranteeing the performances of Ms. Black and Mr. Green.[8]

If there is no default, Mr. Green will deliver oats in September to a location designated by the clearinghouse, and Ms. Black will accept delivery of the oats at that location. Ms. Black will pay the clearinghouse $46, plus a commission, and Mr. Green will receive from the clearinghouse $46, less a commission. Should Mr. Green fail to deliver the oats in September as promised, the clearinghouse will purchase oats on the open market in September and deliver the oats to Ms. Black, accepting from her a payment of $46, plus commission. There is, of course, no assurance that the clearinghouse will be able to purchase oats in September for $46. Should the price of oats for immediate delivery in September exceed the price of $46 on Ms. Black's futures contract, the clearinghouse will incur a loss.

Similarly, should Ms. Black fail to purchase oats in September as promised, the clearinghouse will purchase the oats that Mr. Green delivers and pay him $46, less the commission. The clearinghouse will then sell those oats on the open market, incurring a loss if the price of oats in September for immediate delivery is less than the $46 on Mr. Green's futures contract.

16.6.2 Marking to the Market

Marking to the market is a protocol under which each day the futures prices of all contracts that have a common delivery date are changed to the futures price on contracts established on the current day for that delivery date. Consequently, contracts that have the same delivery date are interchangeable. This interchangeability facilitates both trading in futures contracts and the transmission of new information about the estimated spot price on the delivery date.

Consider the following example. On March 16, competition on the futures exchange sets the futures price for delivery of oats on September 30 at $46. Mr. Green sells a contract and is thereby obligated to deliver oats in September and receive $46 at that time. Ms. Black purchases a contract and is thereby obligated to accept delivery of oats in September and pay $46 at that time.[9] The futures price of $46 is the consensus, on March 16, among investors and speculators, of what the value of the spot price will be on September 30.

March 17 is a new day. Competition on the futures exchange on that day will set the futures price for September delivery of oats based on all the information that was available through March 16, augmented by whatever new information has arrived on March 17. Suppose that the futures price for contracts established on March 17 is $49.[10] Now the clearinghouse has two sets of contracts to handle. Contracts established on March 16 have a delivery price of $46; contracts established on the 17 have a delivery price of $49. Indeed, there will be as many sets of contracts as there are days on which contracts trade for September delivery.

To facilitate trading in futures contracts for delivery in September, on March 17 the clearinghouse will change the delivery prices for the contracts established on March 16 from $46 to $49. Simultaneously, the clearinghouse will make offsetting adjustments to the financial positions of the persons who sold or purchased contracts on the 16. This practice is called marking to the market.[11]

Mr. Green sold a contract on March 16. Under the terms of that contract, he is committed to deliver oats in September and receive $46 at that time. Once the clearinghouse marks that contract to the price set by the market on the 17th, he is entitled to receive $49 in September, a gain of $3. Mr. Green maintains a cash deposit with the clearinghouse.[12] To offset the gain created when the clearinghouse marks his contract to the new price of $49, the clearinghouse reduces his cash balance by $3. Consequently, the net price that Mr. Green will receive for oats delivered in September is $49−$3, or $46, which is the price to which he committed when he sold the contract on March 16th.

Similarly, when Ms. Black purchased a contract on March 16, she made a commitment to accept delivery of oats in September and pay $46 at that time. When the clearinghouse marks her contract to the market on the 17, her commitment is to pay $49 in September. To offset this loss, the clearinghouse will increase her cash balance by $3, so that the net price that she will pay for the oats in September is $49−$3, or $46, which is the price that she agreed on March 16 to pay upon receiving delivery in September.

16.7 Futures Contracts as Transmitters of Information about the Future Values of Spot Prices

In an efficient market, the price of a financial security is continuously adjusted to reflect new information about the underlying sequence of payments. In particular, good news will create a capital gain for an investor who owns that security. The investor can realize that capital gain by selling a portion of her now more valuable security. In several earlier chapters, we described this process of realizing capital gains as creating a homemade dividend. Of course, bad news will impose a capital loss on the investor.

Futures contracts are financial securities because they are saleable rights to a sequence of future payments. The protocol of marking futures contracts to the market means that the prices of these contracts reflect current information about the future values of spot prices. Consequently, investors who own these securities will enjoy capital gains (or suffer capital losses) as new information arrives about the future value of the spot price.

Consider the following example for Ms. Black, who purchased a contract on March 16 for $46. In purchasing that contract, she made a commitment to accept delivery of oats in September and pay $46 at that time. Since Ms. Black can resell on the spot market the oats that she will receive in September, she will make a profit if the spot price on September 30 exceeds $46. On March 17, new information about the likely value of the spot price for oats in September causes the futures price for September delivery of oats to increase to $49. Based on this new estimate of the spot price in September, Ms. Black stands to make a profit of $3. Because the clearinghouse marks the futures price on Ms. Black's contract to $49, and makes an offsetting adjustment to her cash balance, she need not wait until September to realize the $3 in profit.

At the end of the day on March 17, the clearinghouse marks the contract that Ms. Black purchased on the 16th up from $46 to $49. She is now obligated to pay an additional $3 for the oats that she will receive in September. To offset this loss, the clearinghouse will increase her cash balance by $3, so that the net price that she will pay for the oats in September is $49−$3, or $46, which is the price that she agreed on March 16 to pay upon receiving delivery in September.

On March 16, Ms. Black purchased a contract for September delivery. Once this contract is marked to the market on the 17, she is committed to accept delivery of oats in September and pay $49. Suppose that on the 17th Ms. Black sells a contract for September delivery. Since the futures price on the 17th is $49, she is now committed to deliver oats in September and accept $49 in payment. The clearinghouse could now cancel her contract to deliver oats against her contract to accept delivery of oats, since both contracts have the same delivery price of $49. Once the two offsetting contracts are canceled, Ms. Black no longer has any commitments to deliver or accept delivery of oats, but she does have a cash balance of $3 in her account at the clearinghouse. By withdrawing this balance on the 17th, Ms. Black can realize on March 17 the capital gain generated by the new information on the 17th about the likely value of the spot price for oats in September.

We conclude this section with a comparison of options and futures contracts. Like options, futures contracts are derivative securities, or derivatives. The current price of a futures contract is derived from investors' current expectations about what the spot price will be on the delivery date specified in the contract. Similarly, the current price of an option is derived from investors' current expectations about what the price of the underlying security will be on the expiration date specified in the option. Unlike options, the parties to a futures contract must make delivery, or accept delivery, of the underlying commodity. The parties to a futures contract do not have an option to allow the contract to expire unexercised.

16.8 Investment, Speculation, and Hedging

Intelligent discussion of financial markets in the popular press is inhibited by the fact that many persons regard investment with approval, speculation with disdain, and display little or no understanding of hedging.[13] It is particularly unfortunate that speculation is so ill regarded, because speculation is essential to an informationally efficient market, and informational efficiency is a necessary condition for the efficient allocation of resources. Sometimes it seems that a person's willingness to condemn an activity as speculation varies inversely with that person's understanding of the financial security under discussion. Hence, one sees trading in futures contracts denigrated as "just a bunch of speculators playing financial bingo." Or a large and unexpected change in a price is "just the work of greedy speculators," with the implication that there is no acceptable reason for the price to change. In this section, we discuss the relationships among investment, speculation, and hedging in the context of economic efficiency. In chapter 14, we examined the consequences of insider trading for economic efficiency. Our argument reflects the position of Professor Michael Jensen, who stated in 1986, "Arbitragers provide important productive services to investors, and the supply of these services is threatened by the current outpouring of self-righteousness and legal action in the wake of the Securities and Exchange Commission's prosecution of [persons] accused of insider trading."[14]

16.8.1 Investment

To invest is to allocate resources out of activities that provide goods and services for current consumption, and into activities that will increase the quantities of goods and services available for future consumption. Examples come quickly to mind. A farmer increases the time spent clearing new fields and decreases the time spent weeding the fields currently under cultivation. The shareholders in a firm accept a reduction in current dividends so that the firm can use retained earnings to finance the development of a profitable new product. Taxpayers accept an increase in taxes so that the government can construct a more efficient air traffic control system.

Investment necessarily involves the accumulation of capital goods, which can be either tangible, such as a cleared field, or intangible, such as better computer software to assist air traffic controllers. Each capital good has an owner, which could be a single individual, a set of individuals (such as the shareholders in a firm), or the government (all members of the society). Ownership brings us to speculation.

16.8.2 Speculation

To speculate is to purchase a good in part because of a belief that the price of that good will increase, or to sell a good in part because of a belief that the price of that good will decrease. Consider the following example of a purchase that is, in part, speculative.

A young husband and wife who plan to begin a family five years from now purchase a home that is expensive because it has four bedrooms and a large yard, and is located in an attractive neighborhood with a good school district. Why purchase such an expensive home now? Why pay the additional property taxes, interest, insurance, utilities, and maintenance on a home that is far larger than two persons will use? With no children at the moment, what is the benefit of living in a good school district with its attendant high school taxes? Surely it would be more economical to postpone the purchase of this home for five years and either rent or purchase a less expensive home in the interim. By purchasing the expensive home now, the young couple is speculating that the price of the expensive home will not only increase within the next five years, but will increase by more than enough to cover the property taxes, interest, and so on that the couple could avoid by postponing the purchase.

A variation of this rationale is the belief that, while the young couple can afford the down payment on the home today, the price of the home will increase so rapidly within the next five years that the couple will no longer be able to afford the down payment. Of course, by postponing the purchase of the home, the couple could invest in the stock market the money that they have accumulated for the down payment. By deciding instead to purchase the home now, the couple is speculating that the rate of return on an investment in the stock market over the next five years will be less than the rate at which the price of the house will increase.[15]

Next consider a case in which a consumer speculates that the price of a good will go down. Mr. Wheeler owns an automobile that has 130,000 miles on the odometer. The vehicle is in excellent condition cosmetically, but Mr. Wheeler is not willing to trust it mechanically any longer for extended trips, so he purchases a new automobile. Should Mr. Wheeler trade his old automobile in for the new one, or should he store the old automobile until it becomes a valuable antique, at which time he can make a killing? If Mr. Wheeler trades his old automobile in for the new one, he is speculating that the value of his old automobile will not increase sufficiently over time to justify the explicit costs of storing it and the implicit cost of not using it as a trade-in.[16]

"To own is to speculate."[17] To own something is to speculate that its price will increase sufficiently rapidly (or decrease sufficiently slowly) to justify owning it now, rather than renting it now or purchasing it later.

Most persons earn incomes by specializing in an activity in which they have a comparative advantage. These persons do not purchase a home or trade in an automobile solely for the purpose of speculating on the future value of the price. Some persons, however, do specialize in collecting and analyzing information about the future values of the prices of certain assets. For example, some persons specialize in predicting the value of the spot price for oats in September. Speculators will use their comparative advantage to purchase futures contracts when the futures price for September delivery is less than the estimate of what the spot price will be in September. If the speculators' estimates are correct, the futures prices will increase as the time for delivery approaches, and speculators will obtain a profit on their futures contracts as those contracts are marked (up) to the market.

Similarly, speculators will sell futures contracts when the futures price for September delivery is greater than their estimate of the future value of the spot price. Again, if the speculators are correct, the futures prices will decrease as the delivery date approaches, and they will obtain a profit on their futures contracts as those contracts are marked (down) to the market.

By speculating in the market for futures contracts for September delivery of oats, those persons who have a sufficiently strong comparative advantage in predicting future values of spot prices for oats produce two services. First, the speculators publish their estimates of the future value of the spot price by trading in futures contracts, thus causing futures prices to reflect those estimates of the future value of the spot price. Second, the speculators enable producers and users of oats to transfer risk.

By purchasing futures contracts from farmers, the speculators guarantee a price at which farmers can sell their oats in September, thus insuring farmers against a low price. Of course, when farmers insure themselves against a low price in September by selling futures contracts to speculators, the farmers relinquish the opportunity to gain from a high price in September. Similarly, by selling futures contracts to millers, speculators insure the millers against having to pay a high price for the oats they will require to produce cereal.

We know that an efficient allocation of resources depends on financial markets that are informationally efficient. Speculators increase the informational efficiency of these markets. Unfortunately, speculators and speculation have an undeserved reputation as social parasites. The term *greedy speculator* is almost a redundancy.

16.8.3 Hedging

To hedge is to construct a portfolio that contains at least two assets whose rates of return are negatively correlated, with the consequence that the rate of return on the portfolio is less volatile than it would be if the portfolio contained only one of those two securities. Similarly, an investor would hedge a position in Asset A by holding that asset as part of a portfolio that contains some other asset whose rate of return is negatively correlated with the rate of return on Asset A.

A portfolio is *perfectly hedged* if the standard deviation of its rate of return is zero. We saw in chapter 8 on portfolio theory that an investor can construct a perfectly hedged portfolio by allocating funds in the correct proportions between two securities whose rates of return are perfectly correlated. If the rates of return on the two securities are perfectly negatively correlated, the investor takes long positions in both securities. If, however, the two securities are perfectly positively correlated, the investor takes a long position in one of the securities and a short position in the other. In chapter 15 we created perfectly hedged portfolios containing a share of stock and a call option written on that stock to derive the formula for the equilibrium configuration of the price of the stock, the price of the option, and the interest rate. Since the rates of return on the stock and the call option are positively correlated,[18] a long position in the stock must be hedged by a short position in the option if the portfolio is to be riskless. The converse is also true.

A farmer who has oats in the ground has a long position in oats (because he will gain wealth as the spot price of oats increases and lose wealth as the spot price decreases). He can hedge his long position in oats by taking a short position in oat futures contracts. We saw in section 16.4 that an investor who sells a futures contract holds a short position in that contract (because he will gain wealth as the spot price decreases, and lose wealth as the spot price increases). Similarly, a miller who has made a commitment to deliver cereals containing oats in the future in exchange for a price fixed by contract today has a short position in those cereals, and hence a short position in oats. The miller can hedge her short position in oats by purchasing an oat futures contract today.

The production of most goods and services requires time. Consequently, one of the costs that the producer incurs is that the spot prices of inputs or outputs can change unpredictably between the time that people make a commitment to produce a good, and the time that they can sell that good.[19] The existence of organized markets for futures contracts enables producers to reduce their costs by shifting to speculators some of the risk created by the difficulty in predicting future values of spot prices. By definition, speculators take unhedged positions in futures contracts. They are willing to take risks because they have a comparative advantage in predicting future values of spot prices.

Speculators who do not have a comparative advantage in predicting future values of spot prices will lose wealth on their unhedged positions. Eventually, these inept speculators will cease their activities, either because they become discouraged or because they are ruined financially. Speculators who lose wealth do so because they either purchase or sell futures contracts at prices that are not compatible with the future values of spot prices. Consequently, these inept speculators cause futures prices to mislead producers. An efficient market will discourage these speculators by imposing losses on them. More generally, an efficient market will allocate resources efficiently by encouraging each person to specialize in producing those goods or services in which he or she has a comparative advantage. This discipline imposed by an efficient market applies to speculators, farmers, millers, and everyone else.

16.9   Futures Prices as Predictors of Future Values of Spot Prices

Futures contracts provide a way for hedgers to insure themselves against unfavorable movements in the future values of spot prices. Persons who construct speculative positions in futures contracts therefore have an incentive to collect information about the likely future movements in spot prices. A natural question for financial economists is whether competition among speculators causes the current price of a futures contract to be an unbiased estimate of the value that the spot price will take on the delivery date specified in the contract.

This debate is unresolved. The answer depends in complicated ways on the relative sizes of the positions taken by speculators and by hedgers, whether speculators as a group are risk averse, whether the risk created by unpredictable fluctuations in commodity prices is diversifiable (with the result that speculators should expect no compensation for bearing this risk), and the investigator's choice of an asset pricing model to explain future prices. Assessing the state of the debate is beyond the scope of this book. For an introduction, the reader might consult the work of Stoll and Whaley.[20]

16.10   Conclusion

Futures contracts are financial securities because they are saleable rights to a sequence of future payments. Most of these payments occur as capital gains or losses that occur as the futures prices on existing contracts are marked to the market to reflect new information about investors' beliefs about the future values of spot prices. Markets for futures contracts increase the efficiency of the allocation of resources by promoting mutually beneficial exchanges between hedgers and speculators.

A hedger is an investor who seeks to reduce the risk of unpredictable changes in the future values of spot prices by taking a long (or short) position in a good and an offsetting short (or long) position in a futures contract in that good. A speculator is a person who specializes in collecting information on the probabilities of future values of spot prices. The speculator sells information by taking unhedged positions in futures contracts.

Notes

1. A futures contract is usually denominated in some convenient multiple, such as 100 tons of oats. For convenience, and without loss of generality, we will suppose the futures contract is for one ton of oats. If the date for delivery is not a business day, Mr. Y must deliver the oats on the last business day preceding the date for delivery specified in the contract.

2. J. C. Hull, *Options, Futures, and Other Derivatives*, 6th ed. (Englewood Cliffs, N.J.: Prentice Hall, 2006), 25.

3. D. Duffie, *Futures Markets* (Englewood Cliffs, N.J.: Prentice Hall, 1989), 11.

4. We explain in section 16.6.2 how marking to the market generates positive and negative flows of cash for the investor.

5. Consider the analogy between the example here, the simple example in chapter 1, and the more complex example in section 6.5 of chapter 6 in which two farmers who have different tolerances for risk effect a mutually beneficial exchange by merging their farms into a single firm that issues a contractual claim and a residual claim.

6. One form of storage cost is the depletion that might occur due to spoilage.

7. Students will recall from their introductory course that under both perfect competition and monopoly, a downward shift in the marginal cost curve will cause a profit-maximizing producer to expand the rate of output until marginal revenue is again equal to marginal cost. The producer cannot sell the higher rate of output without reducing the price paid by the consumer.

8. The clearinghouse also performs other services, such as record keeping.

9. These prices are net of commissions, which we will ignore from here on.

10. There are several reasons why the futures price for September delivery could increase from March 16 to March 17. Immediately after the market closed on the 16th, traders could have received information that an infestation of insects will reduce the size of the crop available for delivery in September, thus increasing the spot price in September. Or Congress might have passed a bill subsidizing the sale of oats to certain foreign countries, thus increasing the demand for oats for delivery in September. For whatever reason, if persons expect on the 17th that the spot price in September will be higher than they had expected on the 16th, they will be unwilling to agree on the 17th to deliver oats in September for only $46. Similarly, persons looking to acquire deliveries of oats in September will be willing to commit on the 17th to pay more than the $46 to which they would have committed on the 16th.

11. More precisely, the process is "marking (the price set for contracts established on the 16th) to (the price set by) the market (for contracts established on the 17th)."

12. Alternatively, the clearinghouse might require Mr. Green to deposit $3. The interest that he will forego by maintaining a deposit with the clearinghouse is one of the opportunity costs of trading in futures contracts. We ignore this cost in our calculations.

13. An old joke defines the difference between investment and speculation as follows: "When I make money in the stock market, that's investment; when my mother-in-law makes money in the stock market, that's speculation."

14. M. C. Jensen, "Don't Freeze the Arbs Out," *Wall Street Journal*, December 3, 1986, editorial page.

15. Suppose that banks require a down payment of 10%, and the current price of the home is $100,000. The young couple now has $10,000 with which to make the down payment. If the price of the house increases by 50% over the next five years, the down payment will be $15,000. But if the five-year rate of return in the stock market is sufficiently greater than 50%, the couple would be better served to rent a house for five years and invest their $10,000 in the stock market during that period rather than in the house.

16. Of course, the reason why most persons trade in their old automobiles is that most automobiles deteriorate to the status of scrap, rather than appreciate to the status of antiques.

17. Stated.

18. The correlation is not perfectly negative throughout the entire range of values for the stock because the range of values for the option is truncated at zero.

19. Although most services are produced and consumed instantaneously, many services require that the persons who produce them spend years acquiring sophisticated skills. Think of performing violin concerti or cardiac surgery. A person who invests time and money to acquire any of these skills has an unhedged long position in that skill because there might be a decrease in the future demand for those skills. The unanticipated availability of compact discs or new medication might reduce (but not eliminate) the demand for certain kinds of violinists or surgeons long after the investor has invested the resources to acquire those skills.

20. H. R. Stoll and R. E. Whaley, *Futures and Options: Theory and Applications* (South-Western, 1993), especially chapter 5.

17 Additional Topics in the Economics of Financial Markets

The analysis of the economic efficiency of financial markets involves many topics. This introductory treatment in this book omits several of these topics. The following sections describe briefly the more important of these topics. At the end of the chapter there is a selected bibliography for readers interested in a more comprehensive (omits more challenging) treatment.

17.1 Bonds

In our analysis of financial securities, we concentrated on common stocks, presenting bonds as an alternative way in which investors can hold claims against a firm's earnings and firms can raise capital to finance new projects. We demonstrated how the use of bonds can promote economic efficiency by organizing exchanges between persons who have different tolerances for risk and by mitigating problems of agency between the shareholders and the managers of a firm. There are many additional ways in which the use of bonds affects the efficacy of financial markets. For example, there is a substantial literature on the effect of callable and convertible bonds on economic efficiency. The contributions to this literature analyze the optimal behavior of firms and investors with respect to these bonds. There is also a large empirical literature on the relationship of the rates of return on bonds that have different amounts of time remaining until their dates of maturity.

17.2 Initial Public Offerings

Firms frequently raise capital to finance projects by issuing new securities rather than by relying on retained earnings. The proportion of the firm that the current shareholders will have to cede to the new investors depends on the price at which the firm can sell the new securities. As is the case throughout economics, setting the price at which the firm attempts to sell the new securities involves a trade-off. The higher the price, the smaller the proportion of the firm that the new investors will acquire, and thus the wealthier the current shareholders will be once the firm undertakes the new project.

There is, however, a benefit for the firm in selling the new securities at a lower price than the firm might otherwise receive. The probability distributions of the sequence of returns that an investor will receive from a firm depend both on the firm's capital structure and on the portfolio of projects that the firm has underway. By issuing new securities, a firm changes its capital structure. It is costly for an investor·to determine how the new capital structure will affect future returns. Similarly, by undertaking a new project the firm creates additional uncertainty for investors. A relatively low price for the new securities encourages speculators to collect information about the firm. In an efficient market, competition among these speculators causes the prices of all the firm's securities to reflect the speculators' information, thus making the securities less risky. The reduction in the levels of risk in the firm's securities will increase the price at which the firm can sell new securities in the future, which in turn will increase the profitability of future new investments. Economists have produced many studies, both theoretical and empirical, of the pricing of newly issued securities and the effect of new issues on economic efficiency. Some of these studies involve the economics of signaling, which we discuss below.

17.3 Mutual Funds

A mutual fund is a professionally managed portfolio of financial securities. A fund raises capital by creating shares that investors purchase, just as the IBM Corporation does. The difference between a mutual fund and IBM is that the mutual fund uses the capital provided by investors to purchase a portfolio of financial securities, whereas IBM uses the capital provided by its investors to construct and operate a portfolio of investment projects. By generating economies of scale, a mutual fund can operate a portfolio of financial securities at a lower cost than an individual investor could. Moreover, because the mutual fund is professionally managed, the investor might be able to obtain a higher average rate of return, for a given level of risk, by placing assets with the fund than by managing his or her own portfolio. That is, a mutual fund might enable an investor to obtain a combination of average rate of return and risk that lies above the capital market line, thus beating the market on a risk-adjusted basis.

Economists have conducted many empirical studies to determine whether managers of mutual funds can outperform the market as agents for their investors. The answer is clear: after subtracting the expenses of operating the fund, the managers cannot consistently produce results for their investors that outperform the market. In particular, the managers can neither identify mispriced securities nor predict movements in the rate of return of the market portfolio (after allowing for the expenses incurred in operating the fund). Empirical studies of the performance of mutual funds were the first tests of the efficient markets hypothesis. The use of mutual funds to test the efficient markets hypothesis involves complicated empirical problems, such as determining whether the fund's managers maintain a constant level of risk in the fund's portfolio.

17.4 Behavioral Finance

A fundamental postulate in economic analysis is that persons make rational choices. A person's choice is rational if it is compatible both with that person's values and with objective facts. The term *behavioral finance* designates a set of empirical studies of financial markets that show that investors (at least some of them) make irrational choices. Many of these studies show that the irrational behavior is compatible with some concepts and empirical data from psychology. Consider the following simple example of irrational behavior from financial economics.

Mr. Manor states that he prefers more wealth to less wealth. He has an opportunity to invest in a project that has a positive net present value, and he can borrow and lend at a bank at the risk-free rate of interest. (For this example, we ignore risk.) Mr. Manor declines to invest in the project, saying that the amount of cash that he would have to contribute to initiate the project would require too large a reduction in his current expenditures on consumption. Since the project has a positive net present value, Mr. Manor could simultaneously finance the project and obtain its net present value by borrowing from a bank. Consequently, by undertaking the project, he could increase his current level of consumption without reducing his levels of consumption at any time in the future. Given Mr. Manor's preferences (for more wealth rather than less), and the fact that he can borrow from a bank to finance a project that has a positive net present value, his decision to forego the project is not rational.

Richard Thaler and Werner deBondt produced the seminal study in behavioral finance. These economists documented that the market produces a systematic over-reaction for stocks that are winners or losers. Specifically, portfolios of stocks that have underperformed the market in one five-year period outperform the market in a subsequent five-year period, and conversely. Thaler and deBondt argue that if investors were rational, competition among them would diminish these overreactions to a level consistent with the transaction costs that speculators would incur in attempting to exploit them. But the overreactions persist. The literature on behavioral finance contains many other instances of apparently irrational behavior by investors.

17.5   Market Microstructure

Market microstructure is an encyclopedic term that represents the entirety of the mechanisms and institutions through which investors trade financial securities. A comprehensive analysis of the economic efficiency of financial markets must include a study of market microstructure because the level of allocative efficiency that a market can achieve depends on the quality of information contained in the prices of the goods that are traded in that market. Prices emerge from trading. Therefore, the microstructure of a market determines the extent to which that market can allocate resources efficiently.

17.6   Financial Derivatives

The Black-Scholes option pricing formula is a seminal contribution both to the economics of financial markets and to the professional management of risk. Following the appearance of the Black-Scholes formula in 1973, there has been a rapid development of options and futures contracts in financial markets. These securities are known as *financial derivatives*. Examples of financial derivatives include futures contracts and options on interest rates offered by government bonds, foreign exchange rates, and values of stock market indexes, such as the S&P 500. Both individual investors and firms use these securities to reduce the risks associated with future commitments. There is now a large literature of formal models on how these financial futures are priced and how investors and firms can use them to increase profits. A comprehensive analysis of the equilibrium trade-off between expected rate of return and risk in financial markets requires a sophisticated understanding of financial derivatives.

17.7   Corporate Takeovers

Corporate takeovers are likely a close second to insider trading as a popular (and populist) impassioned belief about unfairness in financial markets. Indeed, the word *takeover* of a corporation has a negative connotation. Discussions in the popular press of corporate takeovers are inflamed further by the use of expressions such as "corporate raiders" who "attack" a corporation by "making a run" at it.

The scholarly literature on corporate takeovers has made four major contributions. The first contribution is to recognize that the managers of a firm are agents for the shareholders, who own the firm. The job of the managers is to maximize the wealth of the shareholders. What the press typically represents as a takeover of a corporation by outsiders is, in fact, the outcome of competition among alternative teams of managers for the right to manage the shareholders' assets. The "outsiders" are not raiders who seize control of the corporation from its shareholders. Rather, the shareholders remain in control and exercise their rights of control to replace the current team of managers with a new team that is more to their liking.[1]

Now, a populist might argue that the outsiders are able to force the current management out of office only by purchasing enough shares so that the outsiders (or their agents) can acquire a majority of the seats on the firm's board of directors. But the outsiders can acquire shares only by offering prices that are high enough to induce a sufficient number of the current shareholders to sell their shares. Current shareholders who sell their shares do so voluntarily, presumably because these shareholders prefer the money offered by the outsiders rather than continuing to hold a portion of their wealth in the securities of this firm. Current shareholders who sell to outsiders voluntarily cede their portion of the control of the firm to the outsiders. The term *takeover* does not seem compatible with the voluntary sale of their shares by at least some of the current shareholders.

The second contribution that economists have made to the analysis of takeovers is to identify the reasons why investors might want to replace the current team of managers with a new team. One reason is to mitigate a problem of agency. Sometimes a group of investors believes that a different team of managers can operate the firm more profitably. If the current team of managers has the confidence of the current board of directors, the only way to install the new managers is to purchase a sufficient number of shares to gain a majority of the seats on the board. The price that the outsiders will offer to the shareholders to induce them to sell their shares reflects the increase in profit that the outsiders believe the new managers can produce. It is instructive to recognize that the outsiders are risking their own money, believing that their expectation of a higher profit is correct.

Problems of asymmetric information can create a reason for replacing the current team of managers. We recall that asymmetric information between managers and prospective investors can inhibit a firm from financing a profitable new project. One way to resolve this problem is to take the firm private. The board of directors can decide to withdraw the firm's securities from being listed on exchanges that are accessible to the public. The firm would then no longer be publicly traded and therefore no longer subject to the prohibitions against insider trading. For example, a group of investors could acquire a sufficient number of shares to gain a majority of seats on the board of directors. The new board could then cause the firm to offer a sufficiently high price to repurchase all the outstanding securities of the firm, except for those owned by the directors and a small number of large shareholders. With the firm no longer publicly traded, the managers can reveal private information to the remaining shareholders and thus finance new projects by raising capital from them.

Another way that a firm can finance new projects in the presence of asymmetric information is to acquire a second firm whose current operations generate more cash that it can profitably invest. In effect, each firm becomes a division of a single new firm. The new firm can then finance internally projects generated by one division by using the earnings of the other division. Having access to internal funds eliminates the problems of raising capital from new investors under conditions of asymmetric information.

The third major area in which economists have contributed to the analysis of corporate takeovers is the empirical determination of which parties gain and which parties lose in contests for the control of corporations. Using event studies (discussed in chapter 12), economists have established that the shareholders of corporations that are taken over almost invariably gain wealth. This fact invalidates the populist argument that the shareholders in a firm are harmed by the activities of "raiders." To the contrary, by replacing the firm's current managers with new managers, the raiders make the firm more profitable, which delivers an increase in wealth to the firm's current shareholders by increasing the market value of their shares. These event studies support the efficient markets hypothesis by showing that the prices of a firm's securities begin to increase at the first sign that a group of investors is attempting to take over the firm. Moreover, these prices fluctuate to reflect information about the probability that the new investors will succeed in acquiring control of the firm. The losers in battles to replace a firm's current management are, of course, the current managers.

Several studies have examined the distribution among bondholders and shareholders of the gains from replacing a firm's management. Some firms make a business of identifying and acquiring other firms that, in the view of the acquiring firm, would be more profitable with new management. The empirical evidence is that the shareholders of these acquiring firms neither gain nor lose as a consequence of their firms' acquisitions. A commonly accepted explanation for this is that the price of the acquiring firm's securities already reflects investors' expectations of the earnings that their firm will generate by its activities in acquiring other firms.

Finally, some economists have produced interesting results of the relationships among the ways in which investors finance a takeover of a firm and the consequences of that takeover for the current shareholders of that firm. Investors have several options for financing the purchase of a sufficient number of shares to gain control of the firm. For example, the new investors can offer cash to the current shareholders. Alternatively, the new investors can offer a contract under which any current shareholder can transfer ownership of shares to the new investors in exchange for receiving newly issued securities should the new investors succeed in gaining control of the firm. Shareholders who do not offer their shares to the new investors will receive a less valuable settlement. The contract between the new investors and the shareholders who offer their shares to the new investors provides in some way for the event in which the new investors fail to gain control of the firm.

The means by which new investors finance their attempt to gain control of a firm has consequences for the capital structure of that firm. Recall from chapter 13 that a firm's capital structure has, in turn, consequences for economic efficiency. Therefore, the analysis of the financing of a corporate takeover can be conducted in terms of economic efficiency, just as we did for the several topics considered in this book.

17.8   Signaling with Dividends

In our discussion of capital structure in chapter 13, we explained how asymmetric information between the managers of a firm and prospective investors can create an inefficient allocation of resources. We demonstrated how, under some circumstances, a firm can reduce the degree of asymmetry, and thus mitigate the inefficiency, by choosing the appropriate security to issue to finance a new project. The firm's choice of which security to issue credibly transmits the firm's private information to prospective buyers of the new securities.

A firm's choice of the kind of security to issue is an example of the general problem of signaling in economics. When there is asymmetric information between two parties who could effect a mutually beneficial exchange in the absence of the asymmetry, both parties have an incentive to find ways to eliminate (or at least reduce) the asymmetry. When one or both parties has an incentive to mislead the other, or when either party consists of numerous persons, the costs of gathering, analyzing, and verifying information can preclude the exchange, thus creating economic inefficiency.

To maximize the shareholders' wealth, the firm's managers must make optimal choices of which investment projects to undertake and how to finance them. Optimal choices of investment projects and the ways to finance them require optimal choices for transmitting private information to prospective investors. Economists have produced many theoretical and empirical studies of ways in which a firm might use the payment of dividends to transmit (or signal) credibly the firm's private information about its ability to generate future earnings.

17.9   Bibliographies

17.9.1   Bonds

Hotchkiss, Edith S., and Tavy Ronen. "The Informational Efficiency of the Corporate Bond Market: An Intraday Analysis," *Review of Financial Studies* 15, no. 5 (2002): 1325–1354.

Klein, Linda S., and Dogan, Tirtiroglu. "Valuation Process and Market Efficiency for US Treasury Bonds," *Financial Management* 26, no. 4 (1997): 74–80.

Lindvall, John R. "New Issue Corporate Bonds, Seasoned Market Efficiency and Yield Spreads," *Journal of Finance* 32, no. 4 (1977): 1057–1067.

17.9.2   Initial Public Offerings (IPOs)

Aggarwal, Reena, and Pat Conroy. "Price Discovery in Initial Public Offerings and the Role of the Lead Underwriter," *Journal of Finance* 55, no. 6 (2000): 2903–2922.

Derrien, Francois. "IPO Pricing in 'Hot' Market Conditions: Who Leaves Money on the Table?" *Journal of Finance* 60, no. 1 (2005): 487–521.

Loughran, Tim, and Jay Ritter. "Why Has IPO Underpricing Changed Over Time?" *Financial Management* (Autumn 2004).

Michaely, Roni, and Wayne Shaw. "The Pricing of Initial Public Offerings: Tests of Adverse-Selection and Signaling Theories," *Review of Financial Studies* 7, no. 2 (1994): 279–319.

17.9.3   Mutual Funds

Brown, Stephen J., William Goetzmann, Roger G. Ibbotson, and Stephen A. Ross. "Survivorship Bias in Performance Studies," *Review of Financial Studies* 5, no. 4 (1992): 553–580.

Elton, Edwin J., Martin J. Gruber, Sanjiv Das, and Matthew Hlavka, "Efficiency with Costly Information: A Reinterpretation of Evidence from Managed Portfolios," *Review of Financial Studies* 6, no. 1 (1993): 1–22.

Prather, Larry, and Karen Middleton. "Are N + 1 Heads Better Than One? The Case of Mutual Fund Managers," *Journal of Economic Behavior and Organization* 47, no. 1 (2002): 103–120.

17.9.4   Behavioral Finance

De Bondt, Werner F. M., and Richard H. Thaler. "Does the Stock Market Overreact?" in *Advances in Behavioral Finance*, ed. Richard H. Thaler. New York: Russell Sage Foundation, 1993.

Lee, Charles M.C., Andrei Shleifer, and Richard H. Thaler. "Investor Sentiment and the Closed-End Fund Puzzle," in *Advances in Behavioral Finance*, ed. Richard H. Thaler. New York: Russell Sage Foundation, 1993.

Malkiel, Burton. "The Efficient Market Hypothesis and Its Critics," *Journal of Economic Perspectives* (Winter 2003): 59–82.

Shefrin, Hersh. *A Behavioral Approach to Asset Pricing*. Burlington, MA: Academic Press, 2006, chapters 1, 28, 29.

Shefrin, Hersh, and Meir Statman. "The Disposition to Sell Winners Too Early and Ride Losers Too Long: Theory and Evidence," in *Advances in Behavioral Finance*, ed. Richard H. Thaler. New York: Russell Sage Foundation, 1993.

Shiller, Robert. "From Efficient Markets Theory to Behavioral Finance," *Journal of Economic Perspectives* (Winter 2003): 83–104.

17.9.5 Market Microstructure

Clarke, Jonathan E., C. Edward, Fee, and Shawn Thomas. "Corporate Diversification and Asymmetric Information: Evidence from Stock Market Trading Characteristics," *Journal of Corporate Finance* 10, no. 1 (2004): 105–129.

Harris, Larry. *Trading and Exchanges: Market Microstructure for Practitioners*. New York: Oxford University Press, 2003.

Hasbrouck, Joel. "Stalking the 'Efficient Price' in Market Microstructure Specifications: An Overview," *Journal of Financial Markets* 5, no. 3 (2002): 329–339.

Lipson, Marc L. "Market Microstructure and Corporate Finance," *Journal of Corporate Finance* 9, no. 4 (2003): 377–384.

17.9.6 Financial Derivatives

Amram, Martha, and Nalin Kulatilaka. *Real Options*. Boston: Harvard Business School Press, 1999, 3–45.

Bernardo, Antonio E., and Bhagwan Chowdhry. "Resources, Real Options, and Corporate Strategy," *Journal of Financial Economics* 63, no. 2 (2002): 211–234.

Dixit, Avinash, K., and Robert S. Pinkdyck. *Investment under Uncertainty*. Princeton, N.J.: Princeton University Press, 1994, 3–33.

Faff, Robert, and David Hillier. "Complete Markets, Informed Trading and Equity Option Introductions," *Journal of Banking and Finance* 29, no. 6 (2005): 1359–1384.

Hentschel, Ludger and S. P. Hothari. "Are Corporations Reducing or Taking Risks with Derivatives?" *Journal of Financial and Quantitative Analysis* 36, no. 1 (2001).

Howison, Sam, and David Lamper. "Trading Volume in Models of Financial Derivatives," *Applied Mathematical Finance* 8 (2001): 119–135.

Trigeorgis, Lenos. *Real Options*. Cambridge: MIT Press, 1996, 1–21.

17.9.7 Corporate Takeovers

Duggal, Rakesh, and James A. Millar. "Institutional Ownership and Firm Performance: The Case of Bidder Returns," *Journal of Corporate Finance* 5, no. 2 (1999): 103–117.

Griffith, John M., Lawrence Fogelberg, and H. Shelton Weeks. "CEO Ownership, Corporate Control, and Bank Performance," *Journal of Economics and Finance* 26, no. 2 (2002).

Holderness, Clifford G., and Dennis P. Sheehan. "Raiders or Saviors? The Evidence on Six Controversial Investors," *Journal of Financial Economics* 14, no. 4 (1985): 555.

Isagawa, Nobuyuki. "Callable Convertible Debt under Managerial Entrenchment," *Journal of Corporate Finance* 8, no. 3 (2002): 255–270.

Jensen, Michael C. "The Efficiency of Takeovers," *The Corporate Board* (September/October 1985): 16–22.

Jensen, Michael C., and Richard S. Ruback. "The Market for Corporate Control: The Scientific Evidence," *Journal of Financial Economics* 11, nos. 1–4 (1983): 5–50.

Kini, Omesh, William Kracaw, and Shehzad Mian. "The Nature of Discipline by Corporate Takeovers," *Journal of Finance* 59, no. 4 (2004): 1511–1552.

17.9.8 Signaling with Dividends

Christie, William G. "Are Dividend Omissions Truly the Cruelest Cut of All?" *Journal of Financial and Quantitative Analysis* 29, no. 3 (1994).

Crawfod, Dean, Diana R. Franz, and Gerald J. Lobo. "Signaling Managerial Optimism through Stock Dividends and Stock Splits: A Reexamination of the Retained Earnings Hypothesis," *Journal of Financial and Quantitative Analysis* 40, no. 3 (2005).

Gombola, Michael J., and Feng-Ying Liu. "The Signaling Power of Specially Designated Dividends," *Journal of Financial and Quantitative Analysis* 34, no. 3 (1999).

Kaestner, Robert, and Feng-Ying Liu. "New Evidence on the Information Content of Dividend Announcements," *Quarterly Review of Economics and Finance* 38, no. 2 (1998): 251–274.

Peterson, Steven P. "Some Experimental Evidence on The Efficiency of Dividend Signaling in Resolving Information Asymmetries," *Journal of Economic Behavior and Organization* 29, no. 3 (1996): 373–388.

Viswanath, P. V., and Yu Kyung Kim. "Dilution, Dividend Commitments and Liquidity: Do Dividend Changes Reflect Information Signaling?" *Review of Quantitative Finance and Accounting* 18, no. 4 (2002): 359–379.

Note

1. The new team of managers could increase profit in either, or both, of two ways. First, the new managers could operate the firm's current projects more efficiently. Second, the new managers could discontinue unprofitable projects and initiate new projects that are profitable. In particular, the managers could pay out as dividends any earnings that cannot be invested in projects that do not cover the shareholders' opportunity costs.

18 Summary and Conclusion

An Overview

The purpose of a system of financial markets is to facilitate mutually beneficial intertemporal exchanges. Financial markets promote these exchanges by organizing trading in a variety of financial securities. A financial security is a saleable right to receive a sequence of future payments. Economists assess the performance of any system of markets against the criterion of economic efficiency. A system of markets is economically efficient if it allocates resources so that there are no further opportunities for mutually beneficial exchanges.

The economic analysis of financial markets is a particular application of microeconomic theory. Equilibrium is the fundamental concept in the analysis of a system of markets. Equilibrium is a configuration of prices and quantities with the property that no one, whether a consumer, an investor, or a manager of a firm, has an incentive to change their current choices about the quantities that they wish to buy or sell. Equilibrium in a system of financial markets is a configuration of the prices and quantities of financial securities such that no person has an incentive to restructure his or her portfolio of securities. An investor's portfolio of securities contains stocks and bonds issued by firms, and options and futures contracts issued by other investors. Each investor constructs a portfolio to obtain the combination of risk and expected rate of return that he or she most prefers.

A firm's portfolio of securities consists of the stocks and bonds that the firm has issued to finance its operations. The configuration of these securities defines the firm's capital structure. A firm's capital structure can affect the wealth of its shareholders in two ways. First, the choice of capital structure can mitigate problems of asymmetric information that could reduce the shareholders' wealth by inhibiting the firm's ability to finance new projects. Second, a firm can use its choice of capital structure to reduce the costs of agency. Shareholders incur costs of agency because they cannot costlessly prevent their managers from operating the firm in ways that will transfer wealth from the shareholders to themselves. Since firms compete in the financial markets to raise capital to finance new projects, an efficient market will cause firms to choose their capital structures to reduce the costs of asymmetric information and agency.

18.2   Efficiency

An efficient intertemporal allocation of resources requires accurate information about the sequences of future payments generated by current and prospective investment projects. Consequently, informational efficiency is a prerequisite for economic efficiency. Financial securities are claims, however indirectly, on earnings generated by investment projects. Consequently, informational efficiency in financial markets requires that the current prices of the securities are compatible with all current information about the investment projects that underlie those securities. Prices are compatible with information if there are no opportunities for investors to obtain positive (risk-adjusted) profits. The information that the prices of the securities must contain (to support an efficient allocation of resources) includes the size, the timing, and the nature of the unpredictable variability of those future earnings.

The efficient markets hypothesis is a statement about the informational content of the prices of securities. Most information is not freely available; individuals produce the information and incur costs to do so. The financial markets themselves do not cause the prices of securities to reflect information about investment projects. Investors produce information. By submitting (or withholding) offers to buy and sell securities, investors cause the prices of those securities to reflect the information. The maximal level of informational efficiency in a system of financial markets is conditional on the costs of producing information about investment projects and the costs of trading on that information.

The empirical criterion for informational efficiency is the absence of risk-adjusted residuals that are sufficiently large and predictable to enable an investor to obtain profits that exceed her opportunity costs. A risk-adjusted residual for a security is the amount by which the rate of return on that security differs from the sum of the reward for waiting and the reward for bearing risk. The efficient markets hypothesis asserts that the residuals are unpredictable and small (relative to transaction costs). The calculation of the residuals depends on the economist's choice of asset pricing model. Consequently, any test for informational efficiency is a test of a joint hypothesis regarding the behavior of the residuals and the model for calculating those residuals.

18.3   Asset Pricing Models

The seminal asset pricing model is the capital asset pricing model. In the CAPM, the reward for bearing risk by holding Security i is the product of a market price of risk that applies to all securities and a quantity of risk that is specific to Security i. The quantity of risk for Security i is β_i, which is the slope of line obtained by regressing the rate of return on Security i against the rate of return on the market portfolio. The market portfolio contains all risky securities in proportions equal to the total market values of those securities relative to the sum of the total market values of all risky securities. The value of β_i is the marginal effect of the rate of return on the market portfolio on the conditional expected rate of return for Security i. That is, β_i is the amount by which the center point of the probability density function for Security i

shifts when the rate of return on the market portfolio increases by one percentage point.

The CAPM is a single-factor asset pricing model. The factor is the market portfolio. The purpose of the factor is to measure the quantities of risk in individual securities.

The empirical shortcomings of the CAPM led to a variety of multifactor asset pricing models. A factor is a portfolio of risky securities. Economists choose the factors based on the ability of the model to explain the trade-off between risk and expected return in individual securities. In a multifactor asset pricing model, the quantity of risk in Security i is multidimensional; Security i has a separate quantity of risk for each of the factors. Analogously to the CAPM, the quantity of risk contained in Security i with respect to Factor j is the marginal effect of the rate of return on Factor j on the conditional expected rate of return for Security i. This quantity of risk is measured by $\beta_{i,j}$. There is a separate market price of risk for each factor. The market price of risk for Factor j is λ_j. The reward for bearing risk by holding Security i is a sum of products, one for each factor. The risk attributable to Factor j incurred by holding Security i the product is $\lambda_j \beta_{i,j}$. Although multifactor models perform better than the single-factor CAPM, the seminal contribution of the CAPM has survived in the multifactor models. The quantity of risk contained in a security is the marginal effect of the rate of return on a portfolio on the conditional expected rate of return for that security, and the reward for bearing risk by holding Security i is equal to the product of that quantity of risk and a market price of risk that is independent of Security i.

With a notable exception, the consensus among economists who study financial markets is that the efficient markets hypothesis (constrained by the joint hypothesis) is sufficiently accurate to preclude systematic opportunities for a typical investor to obtain profits either by searching for mispriced securities or by anticipating major changes in the prices of all securities (timing the market). Investors who have a comparative advantage in obtaining information that is not contained in current prices, and in trading on that information, can obtain profits. The existence of such atypical investors is compatible with the fact that producing information and trading on it are costly.

The notable exception to the efficient markets hypothesis is the behavioral school, which provides some evidence that investors buy and sell securities based on unsupportable projections of recent trends in the rates of return on those securities. A consequence of this irrational behavior is that the prices of some securities can diverge significantly from values that are compatible with information about the abilities of the underlying firms to generate earnings.[1]

18.4   Market Imperfections

An important topic in the economics of financial markets is the nature and the significance of various market imperfections. A market imperfection is a situation in which the market fails to establish an efficient allocation of resources. That is, a market imperfection precludes mutually beneficial exchanges that would otherwise occur. We examined two kinds of imperfections: asymmetric information between the managers of a firm and the investors who hold that firm's securities, and problems of agency between the managers and the investors.

The managers of a firm usually have better information about the firm's prospects than investors do. This asymmetry of information can inhibit the firm's ability to finance profitable projects by selling new shares. The reason is that investors recognize that managers can offer new shares only when doing so will transfer wealth to the firm's current shareholders from the investors who purchase the new shares.

When a firm sells new shares, it transfers to new investors a portion of the equity previously held by the firm's current shareholders. The proportion of the equity that the firm must cede to the new investors depends on the profitability of the firm, including the new project. If the new project is profitable by itself, the total value of the equity (the sum of the current shares and the new shares) will increase when the firm undertakes the project.[2] The distribution of this value between the current shareholders and the new shareholders will depend on the proportion of the equity that the firm transfers to the new investors in order to induce them to finance the project. When there is asymmetric information, prospective new investors will protect themselves by insisting on acquiring a larger proportion of the firm than they would if information were symmetric. Under some conditions, the proportion of equity that the firm must cede to the new investors is so large that the current shareholders will lose wealth even though the project is profitable. In this event, the firm will not finance the project by selling new shares. If the firm has no alternative way to finance the project, there will be an inefficient allocation of resources. The project would have enabled the firm to increase the wealth of both the firm's current shareholders and the new investors who finance the project.

A firm can avoid this inefficiency by using a portion of its earnings to accumulate a stock of idle cash with which to finance new projects, rather than paying those earnings to its current shareholders as dividends. An alternative to using its own earnings to accumulate idle cash is to purchase, or merge with, a firm whose earnings exceed the cash required to finance profitable new projects in that firm. The idle cash insulates the firm from choosing either to forgo the profitable new projects or to raise capital from new shareholders under the disadvantages of asymmetric information.

There is a third way in which a firm can avoid the problem created by asymmetric information. Under certain conditions, the managers of a firm can credibly transmit their information to potential investors by offering to sell specific kinds of securities. In this event, the asymmetry of information disappears. Each firm can finance its projects without imposing losses of wealth on its current shareholders, and thus there is an efficient allocation of resources. To effect this credible signaling of information, there must be a relationship between the profitability of a firm and the kind of security that the firm can use to finance a project without transferring wealth from its current shareholders, and investors must understand this relationship. We presented an example in which strong firms could distinguish themselves from weak firms by using convertible, callable bonds to finance the project. The weak firms would identify themselves to investors by using straight equity to finance their projects.

We turn now to the problem of agency. To maximize the shareholders' wealth, the managers must make all of their decisions regarding capital structure, the selection of projects, and the financing of those projects subject to the criterion of maximizing the value of the shares held by the current shareholders.[3] The problem of agency is that the shareholders cannot costlessly monitor their managers. Consequently, the managers enjoy some opportunities to pursue their own interests to the detriment of the shareholders. Managers can reduce the shareholders' wealth by excessive consumption of perquisites and by reducing the risk, and thereby the expected rate of return, of the firm.

Excessive consumption of perquisites occurs in many forms, including plush offices, nepotism, and the use of aircraft and lodgings owned by the firm for vacations visibly disguised as seminars, to name only a few. The managers can also undertake projects that have negative (risk-adjusted) net present values but that provide the managers with personal satisfaction. For example, expanding the firm's line of products or acquiring another firm will increase the size of the enterprise under the managers' control, which might enable them to feel more important and accomplished.

Managers also have an incentive to operate their firms at lower levels of risk than the shareholders prefer because managers cannot diversify their wealth across firms as easily as shareholders can. According to modern portfolio theory, each investor will allocate funds across firms to achieve the most preferred combination of risk and return.[4] In effect, the investor is diversifying wealth across portfolios of investment projects because each firm is a portfolio of investment projects. The composition of the firm's portfolio determines the combination of expected rate of return and risk that the shareholders will receive on their investment in that firm. Shareholders can reduce (or increase) the level of risk to which they expose their wealth by changing the allocation of their funds across firms. A significant portion of a manager's wealth is reputational capital, which the manager cannot diversify by managing several firms simultaneously. Consequently, managers have an incentive to choose for their own firms a portfolio of projects that is less risky than the shareholders might prefer.

Another form of the problem of agency is the possibility that the firm's managers will transfer wealth from the firm's bondholders to its shareholders by substituting riskier projects for the projects that the bondholders intended to finance. We described this problem of asset substitution in chapter 13.

The several problems of agency inhibit the ability of firms to persuade investors to finance projects. To the extent that problems of agency prevent firms from financing profitable projects, there will be an inefficient allocation of resources. Competition among firms for investors' capital should cause firms to choose capital structures that will increase their shareholders' wealth by mitigating problems of asymmetric information and agency.

18.5 Derivatives

A derivative is a financial security that contains either a right or an obligation to purchase or sell another security or a commodity. Derivatives are special cases of financial securities. We discussed options and futures contracts.

The models for determining the price of options are an application of the proposition that in equilibrium the rate of return on a riskless portfolio that contains an option and the underlying stock must be equal to the rate of return on the risk-free asset. The pricing of options is a clear example that the analysis of sophisticated securities (or indeed the analysis of many sophisticated questions in economics) begins with the application of fundamental propositions presented in the introductory course. In the case of options, the fundamental principle is that in (perfectly competitive) equilibrium there are no opportunities to obtain positive profits net of opportunity costs.

We discussed two applications of implicit options. First, the shareholders in a leveraged firm hold an implicit option written by the bondholders; the underlying asset is the firm itself. Option pricing models have implications for the relationship between the values of debt and equity in leveraged firm, and for the probability that the firm will default on its bonds.

There is also an implicit option in an investment project that has an irreversible (sunk) initial cost and that allows the firm to postpone for a limited time its decision on whether to undertake the project. The option is the right to postpone a decision in order to obtain additional information on the profitability of that project. The exercise (or strike) price of the option is the initial cost of the project; the underlying asset is the project itself. To undertake the project before the time for making a decision expires is to exercise (or kill) the option to collect additional information. Consequently, the current value of the option is the value of the right to collect additional information, while retaining the right to undertake the project. We can use an option pricing model to determine the value of the implicit option. The value of the option then becomes part of the opportunity cost that the firm will incur by choosing to begin the project now.

Our treatment of futures contracts in chapter 16 is more descriptive and less analytical than our presentations in other chapters. We explained how futures contracts promote mutually beneficial exchanges by allocating the risks of adverse changes in future prices according to the comparative advantages of producers of commodities and investors who speculate in those commodities. We emphasized that speculators produce value by producing information about the future values of prices.

18.6   Implications for Public Policy

The analysis of the economics of financial markets has many implications for public policy regarding the regulation of those markets. The fundamental insight is based on the recognition that financial markets exist to promote mutually beneficial intertemporal exchanges. Therefore, to the extent that the objective of public policy is to promote an efficient allocation of resources (rather than to redistribute wealth), the regulation of financial markets should be evaluated against the criteria of informational efficiency and economic efficiency. Regulations that make it easier for investors and firms to mitigate imperfections such as asymmetric information and problems of agency should be preserved and, if possible, extended. Regulations that inhibit, or prohibit, mutually beneficial exchanges that would otherwise occur should be removed.

Insider trading presents a difficult question for public policy. In chapter 14 we explained how the effect of insider trading on economic efficiency depends on empirical questions such as the relative importance of traders who are insiders, traders who are informed outsiders, and liquidity traders. We emphasized that attempts to assess insider trading on the basis of fairness are likely to be futile.

| 18.7 | **A Final Word** |

The formal economic analysis of financial markets is a particular application of microeconomic theory. The concepts of equilibrium, opportunity costs, marginal analysis, and conditions of tangency that are used throughout microeconomic theory are as relevant to the analysis of financial markets as they are to any set of markets. Much of the analysis is necessarily complicated by the fact that the goods that are priced in financial markets are claims on uncertain sequences of future payments. Even so, we hope that the reader will appreciate that the application of microeconomic theory to financial markets produces an understanding of these markets that is analogous to many of the applications of economic theory presented in introductory courses in microeconomics.

Notes

1. The leading proponents of the efficient markets hypothesis and the behavioral school are Eugene Fama and Richard Thaler, respectively. Both are economists at the University of Chicago.

2. A project is profitable if its (risk-adjusted) net present value is positive.

3. If the managers do not issue new shares, maximizing the wealth of the current shareholders is equivalent to maximizing the current market price of the outstanding shares.

4. In the context of the CAPM, each investor will select a point on the capital market line at which there is a tangency between that line and one of her indifference curves. Since the capital market line is linear and her indifference curves are convex, this point of tangency is unique, and the tangential indifference curve represents the maximal level of utility that that investor can obtain.

Answers to Problems

Chapter 1

1. The price of the bond will decrease because there is an increased probability that the farm will default on its bonds.

2. All consumers would be better off because they have the choice of paying for the furniture today or one year from today. The consumers could acquire the furniture today, and deposit in a bank today the price of the furniture. One year from today the consumer could withdraw the initial deposit to pay for the furniture, and spend the accumulated interest.

ABC furniture will benefit if the increase in future revenue from current sales exceeds (1+the rate of interest) multiplied by what the current revenue would have been in the absence of the offer to allow customers to postpone payments for one year without interest.

3. No; there is an opportunity for a mutually beneficial exchange. Mr. Green can lend $100 to Mr. Brown at a rate of interest greater than 10% but less than 15%. Both parties will be better off.

4. Ms. Black can "buy" Ms. White's farm by agreeing to pay 1,000 tons of apples per year to Ms. White. Ms. White will still operate her farm, but she will receive 1,000 tons of apples each year, being insulated from the variations in productivity from one year to the next. Because good and bad weather occur with equal probability, Ms. Black's average yearly production will increase from 1,500 tons to 3,000 tons.

Ms. Black would hold a residual claim, similar to a common stock. Each year she will receive the output that remains after she pays Ms. White 1,000 tons of applies. Ms. White would hold a contractual claim, which is like a bond.

Chapter 2

1. A convertible bond enables its owner to protect herself against a decline in price of the stock, while also giving her an option to take advantage of a rise in the price of the stock. If the price of the stock rises, the value of the bond will increase because the investor can convert the bond into a fixed number of shares, the value of which has increased.

2. Suppose that the bonds issued last year have a face value of $1,000 and a coupon rate of 0.05 per year. The firm is obligated to pay to each bondholder $50 per year [(0.05/year) $1,000] until the bond matures, at which time the firm must redeem the bond by paying $1,000 to the bondholder.

Suppose also that the rate of return last year on securities that are comparable (in the levels of risk, timing of payments, etc.) to the firm's bonds was 0.0625 (6¼%). Assume that investors paid approximately $800 for these bonds last year. The bonds were sold at a discount from their face value because their coupon rate of 0.05 was less than the 0.0625 that was available by purchasing comparable securities. Since the firm must pay $50 per year for each $800 that it obtained from the investors who purchased the bonds, the firm is paying (and bondholders are receiving) a rate of interest equal to $50/$800, or 0.0625 (6¼%).

More precisely, the price of the bond last year would be somewhat greater than $800 because at maturity the bond holders will receive $1,000, not the price that they paid for the bond last year. Since comparable securities were generating a rate of return equal to 0.0625, which is equal to $50/$800, competition among the investors will have forced the price of the bond above $800. Consequently, the firm will pay somewhat less than 0.0625 for funds borrowed by issuing bonds. The amount by which the price of the bond will exceed $800 varies inversely with the time that remains until the bond matures.

If the Fed lowers interest rates, the prices of all bonds, whether newly issued or previously issued, will rise. If the bonds that the firm issued last year are callable, the firm can cancel those bonds by paying the bondholders a fixed amount of money that is less than the market price of those bonds. The firm can finance this canceling of its bonds by issuing new bonds at the lower interest rates generated by the Fed's action.

   3.

   A. $260−$90=$170, for a strong firm.

     $150−$90=$60, for a weak firm.

     ($170+$60)/2−$115=average market value of all firms' shares

     [($260−$150−$90)+($150−$50−$90)]/2=$15=average increase in shareholders' wealth per firms.

   B. The average value of a firm with the new project (inclusive of the $90 worth of new resources invested in the project) is ($260+$150)/2=$205. New shareholders will not provide $90 of new capital unless they acquire a sufficiently large proportion of the firm to enable them (on average across all firms) to recoup their investment. Since new shareholders cannot distinguish between strong firms and weak firms, the current shareholders of any firm must cede the proportion 90/205 of its ownership to the new shareholders. The old shareholders will retain the proportion (115/205) of the firm.

Levels of Wealth (Liquidation Value)

Strong Firm	With the Project	Without the Project
Old shareholders	(115/205)*($260)=$145.85	$150.
New shareholders	(90/205)*($260)=$114.15	$0.
Weak Firm	With the Project	Without the Project
Old shareholders	(115/205)*($150)=$84.15	$50.
New shareholders	(90/205)*($150)=$65.85	$0.

Strong firms will not undertake the project by issuing new shares because the firm's current shareholders would lose wealth. Conversely, weak firms would attempt to finance the project by issuing new shares because the current shareholders would gain wealth.

   C. Strong firms will finance the project by selling bonds, while weak firms will finance the project by issuing new shares.

Chapter 3

   1. The marginal cost to produce 15 units of gum in East Plant is 3 units of pops. Both plants have a comparative advantage. West Plant has a comparative advantage in producing pops; East Plant has a comparative advantage in producing gum.

2.

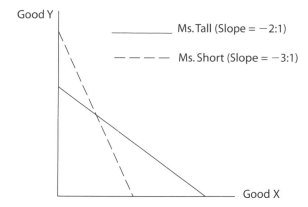

Good Y

Ms. Tall (Slope = −2:1)

Ms. Short (Slope = −3:1)

Good X

Ms. Short has a comparative advantage in producing Y; Ms. Tall has a comparative advantage in producing X.

3. Let X be the deposit required at $t = 1$. Then:

$$\$100\,(1+.1)^2 + X(1+.1) = \$275$$
$$X = \$140.$$

Let Y be the additional deposit required at $t=0$. $\$275/(1.1)^2 = \$206.46 =$ the next present value (at $t=0$) of $\$275$ payable at $t=2$. Then:

$$Y = \$206.46 - \$100 = \$106.46$$

4. Let X be the amount that Mr. Smith would be willing to pay today to buy the full four-year package. Then:

$$X = \frac{\$2200}{(1+.1)^1} + \frac{\$2420}{(1+.1)^2} + \frac{\$2662}{(1+.1)^3} + \frac{\$2928.20}{(1+.1)^4} = \$8,000$$

5.

Sequence of earnings: $\{\$5,000;\ \$5,000;\ \$5,000;\ ...\}$
Sequence of dividends/share: $\{\$50;\ \$50;\ \$50;\ ...\}$
Sequence for the project: $\{\$0;\ -\$1,100;\ \$330;\ \$330;\ ...\}$

Using *ex dividend* pricing, the equilibrium price of a share now (at time 0) before the firm announces the project is:

$$P_0 = \frac{\$50/yr}{.10/yr} = \$500.$$

NPV of the project=

$$\frac{-\$1,100 + \dfrac{\$330/yr}{.10/yr}}{1.1} = \frac{\$2,200}{1.1} = \$2,000.$$

Then the NPV of the project per original share is $\$2,000/100$ shares $=\$20$ per share.

Let P_1' be the equilibrium value of the price of a share at $t=1$ if the firm sells X new shares at $t=1$ to finance the project. Then:

$$P_1'X = \$1,100$$

$$P_1' = \frac{(\$5.000 + \$330)/\text{yr}}{100 + X}$$
$$.10/\text{yr}$$

The second equation above can be rewritten as:

$$100P_1' + P_1'X + \$53,300.$$

Using $P_1' X = \$1,100$ from the first equation, we have:

$$P_1' = \frac{\$53,300 - \$1,100}{100},$$

or

$$P_1' = \frac{\$52,200}{100} = \$522.$$

Then, using $P_1' X = \$1,000$, we find:

$$X = \frac{\$1,100}{\$522} = 2.11 \text{ shares.}$$

Hence, the firm must issue (approximately) 2.11 new shares at $t=1$. The new equilibrium price of a share at $t=0$ is

$$P_0' = \frac{\$50 + P_1'}{1.1}$$
$$= \frac{\$50 + \$522}{1.1}$$
$$= \frac{\$572}{1.1} = \$520.$$

Hence, as required, the wealth of the original shareholders increases at $t=0$ by $20, which is the net present value of the project per original share.

Chapter 5

(a) $\{-\$5,000,000, +\$800,000, +\$800,000, +\$800,000 ...\}$
(b) The net present value of the project is:

$$-\$5,000,000 + ([\$800,000 \text{ per year}/0.10 \text{ per year})$$
$$= -\$5,000,000 + \$8,000,000 = \$3,000,000.$$

(c) We recall that the fleet's regular annual net earnings are $15,000,000. The entire earnings are paid as dividends to the 1,000,000 outstanding shares, making the annual dividend per share equal to $15. Therefore, using an interest rate equal to 0.10, the (*ex dividend*) price of each share is $150.

At time 0 Captain Mo borrows $5,000,000 and purchases the boat. Beginning at time 1 and continuing yearly thereafter forever, he will owe $500,000 to the bank as interest on the loan.

Annual earnings will increase from $15,000,000 to $15,800,000, with the increase of $800,000 produced by the new boat. After using $500,000 to pay interest to the bank, the total annual net earnings available for payment to shareholders as dividends will be $15,300,000. Since the firm will not have issued any new shares, the dividend rate beginning at time 1 will be ($15,300,000 per year)/1,000,000 shares, or $15.30 annually. Since the interest rate is 0.10, the price of a share will increase at time 0 from $15/0.10 to $15.30/0.10. That is, the price of one share will increase from $150 to $153. Therefore, purchasing the new boat will deliver to each investor who owns one share a capital gain on that share equal to $3. We note that $3 is the net present value of the project per original share.

(d) Captain Mo could raise the $5,000,000 required to purchase the new boat by issuing X new shares at time 0. Let the new equilibrium price of a share at time 0 be P_0''. Captain Mo must raise $5,000,000 by selling X new shares at a price of P_0'' each.

Therefore, $P_0'' X = \$5,000,000$.

Beginning at time 1 and continuing forever, the net earnings available to pay dividends will be $15,800,000. The number of shares will be $1,000,000 + X$. Therefore, beginning at time 1 the dividend rate per share will be:

$$D'' = \$15,800,000 \text{ per year} / (1,000,000 + X)$$

Therefore, the (*ex dividend*) equilibrium price of a share at time 0 will be:

$$P_0'' = D''/.10$$
$$= [(\$15,800,000/1,000,000 + X)]/.10 \text{ per year}$$

Multiplying both sides of the preceding equation by $(1,000,000 + X)$ produces:

$$P_0''(1,000,000 + X) = \$15,800,000/.10 = \$158,000,000.$$

Using the fact that $P_0'' X = \$5,000,000$, and substituting, we have:

$$P_0''(1,000,000) + \$5,000,000 = \$158,000,000, \text{ so that}$$

$$P_0'' = \$153,000,000/1,000,000 = \$153.$$

Since $P_0'' X = \$5,000,000$, the number of new shares that the fishery must issue is:

$$X = \$5,000,000/\$153 = 32,680 \text{ shares (approximately).}$$

Therefore, the new dividend rate, which will begin at time 1, is:

$$D'' = \$15,800,000/1,032,680 = \$15.30 \text{ (approximately).}$$

The present value of a share held before the announcement of the project will increase by $3, which (again) is the net present value of the project per original share.

(e) Captain Mo will purchase the new boat at time 0 by reducing current dividends by total of $5,000,000. The earnings available at time 0 for distribution as dividends will then b $15,000,000 − $5,000,000, or $10,000,000. Therefore, the dividend per share at time 0 will b $10,000,000/1,000,000, or $10.

Beginning at time 1 and continuing forever, Captain Mo's net earnings per year wi increase to $15,800,000. Therefore, the dividend per share starting at time 1 is $15,800,00(1,000,000 or $15.80 per share.

The *ex dividend* equilibrium price of a share at time 1 is $15.80 per year/0.10 per year, or $15&

The new equilibrium value for the price of a share provides a capital gain, at time 0, equa to $8.00 per share. Of this capital gain, $3.00 is the net present value of the new project per orig inal share, and $5.00 offsets the reduction by $5.00 in the dividend per share caused by Captaii Mo's using retained earnings to finance the project.

Chapter 6

1.

(a) The reward for waiting is .10. The quantity of risk in Security K is 2.5.

(b) Let E_K be the equilibrium average rate of return for Security K. Then,

$$E_K = \text{reward for waiting} + \text{reward for bearing risk}$$
$$= .10 + [.05][2.5]$$
$$= .225$$

(c) Since the market price of risk is .05, the investor must accept an increase equal to .2 in the standard deviation of the rate of return on his portfolio. (Change in average rate of return = .05 times the change in the standard deviation of the rate of return.) Hence, to increase the average rate of return on his portfolio by .01, the investor should increase the proportion of funds allocated to the market portfolio (thereby reducing the proportion allocated to the risk-free asset) so that the standard deviation on his portfolio increases by .2.

2. The investor could purchase the security using $19,000 borrowed from a bank. One year later the investor would realize a profit equal to $100 because he would receive $2,000 from the security and owe only $1,900 in interest to the bank [(0.10)$19,000=$1,900]. If the bank were willing to leave the principal of the loan outstanding, and collect only the interest each year, the investor would realize a profit of $100 per year. If the bank insisted on having the loan paid off at the end of one year, the investor could do so by selling the security for $19,000. Whether or not the investor pays off the loan at the end of the first year, he still realizes a profit of $100 for that year.

The investor would certainly not purchase the security using borrowed funds from the bank as he did before. To do so would incur a loss for the investor equal to $100 every year, because the interest owed to the bank each year would exceed the annual payments generated by the security.

Chapter 7

1.

(a) Capital gain:

$$\frac{P_{A,t} - P_{A,t-1}}{P_{A,t-1}} = \frac{\$1,100 - \$1,000}{\$1,000} = .10$$

(b) Dividend yield:

$$\frac{D_{A,t}}{P_{A,t-1}} = \frac{\$50}{\$1,000} = .05$$

(c) Total rate of return:

$$R_{A,t} = \frac{(P - P_{A,t-1}) + D_{A,t}}{P_{A,t-1}}$$
$$= \frac{(\$1,100 - \$1,000) + \$50}{\$1,000}$$
$$= .15.$$

2. Since the distribution for Security A is symmetric, the expected return for r_A is its middle value, .30. The standard deviation of a random variable is the probability-weighted average of the amounts by which the values for the random variable can deviate from its expected value. Using the entries from the matrix, and the expected value for Security A, the standard deviation for Security A is:

$$\sigma_A = \sqrt{\sigma_A^2}$$
$$= \sqrt{[(0-.30)^2(.3)+(.30-.30)^2(.4)+(.60-.30)^2(.3)]}$$
$$= \sqrt{[(-.3)^2(.3)+(0)^2(.4)+(.3)^2(.3)]}$$
$$= \sqrt{[2(.3)(.09)]}$$
$$= \sqrt{.054} = .232,$$

in which we take the positive square roots.
     For Security B:

$$\sigma_B = \sqrt{\sigma_B^2}$$
$$= \sqrt{[(.07-.14)^2(.4)+(.14-.14)^2(.2)+(.21-.14)^2(.4)]}$$
$$= \sqrt{[(-.07)^2(.4)+(0)^2(.2)+(.07)^2(.4)]}$$
$$= \sqrt{(2)(.4)(.0049)} = \sqrt{00392} = .0626$$
$$= \sqrt{(2)(.00196)} = \sqrt{00392} = .0626.$$

Chapter 8

1.
     (a) Let G designate the portfolio that contains Securities H and B. Then the rate of return on Portfolio G for January is $r_G = X_H r_H + X_B r_B = (.60)(.09)+(.40)(.15) = .054+.06 = .114$.
     (b) Let J designate the portfolio that has a short position in Security H equal to 20 percent of the investor's initial funds. Then $X_H = -.20$, and $X_B = 1.20$. Therefore, the rate of return on Portfolio J for January is:

$$r_J = X_H r_H + X_B r_B = -(.20)(.09)+(1.20)(.15) = -.018+.18 = .162.$$

2. Let δ be the number of the standard deviations of Security B by which the rate of return on that security is displaced from the expected rate of return of that security.

$$E(\tilde{r}_A | \tilde{r}_B = E_B + \hat{\delta}\sigma_B)$$
$$= E_A + \rho_{AB}\hat{\delta}\sigma_A$$
$$= .35 + (.668)\,\hat{\delta}(.1622)$$
$$= .35 + .1083\hat{\delta}.$$

$$\sigma[\tilde{r}_A | \tilde{r}_B = E_B + \delta\sigma_B]$$
$$= \sqrt{\sigma_A^2[(1-(\rho_{AB})^2]}$$
$$= \sqrt{(.1622)^2[1-(.668)^2]}$$
$$= \sqrt{.01456}$$
$$= .1207.$$

3. The required expected rate of return on the portfolio is 13%. Then we have the equation:

$$.13 = X_H(.09) + X_B(.15) = X_H(.09) + (1 - X_H)(.15)$$
$$= X_H(.09) + .15 - .15X_A$$
$$= .15 - .06X_A, \text{ or}$$
$$.06X_H = .02, \text{ so that}$$
$$X_H = 1/3.$$

Therefore $X_B = (1 - X_H) = (1 - 1/3) = 2/3$.

4. For Portfolio P to be riskless, the standard deviation of its rate of return must be equal to zero. Since the standard deviation is the (positive) square root of the variance, the variance of the rate of return must also be zero.

The variance of the rate of return on a portfolio that contains Securities H and K is:

$$(\sigma_P)^2 = (X_H)^2(\sigma_H)^2 + 2\rho_{HK}(X_H)(1 - X_H)(\sigma_H)(\sigma_K) + (1 - X_H)^2(\sigma_K)^2$$

Substituting the value of -1 for ρ_{HK}, and recognizing that the expression on the right-hand side is the square of a difference, we have:

$$(\sigma_P)^2 = [(X_H)(\sigma_H) - (1 - X_H)(\sigma_K)]^2.$$

To set the variance, and hence the standard deviation, of Portfolio P equal to zero, we choose the value for X_H that will set the right-hand side of the preceding equation equal to zero. Then:

$$X_H = \frac{\sigma_K}{\sigma_H + \sigma_K} = \frac{.08}{.04 + .08} = 2/3,$$

and

$$X_K = (1 - X_H) = 1/3.$$

Since the standard deviation on Portfolio P is equal to zero, the guaranteed rate of return on that portfolio is its expected rate of return, namely:

$$E_P = X_H E_H + X_K E_K$$
$$= (2/3)(.08) + (1/3)(.010)$$
$$= .057.$$

Chapter 9

Firm	Proportions That Define the Market Portfolio		
1	10,500,000,000/43,000,000,000	=10.5/43	=0.244
2	7,500,000,000/43,000,000,000	=7.5/43	=0.1744
3	25,000,000,000/43,000,000,000	=25/43	=0.5814
			1.00 (after rounding)

Therefore, Kaitie will allocate as follows:

Security 1	(.244) ($45,000)	=$10,980
Security 2	(.1744) ($45,000)	= $7,848
Security 3	(.5814) ($45,000)	=$26,163
		$45,000 (after rounding)

Chapter 10

(a) The term $\beta_{19,1}=5$ indicates that the conditional expected rate of return for Security 19 will increase by five percentage points when the rate of return on Factor 1 changes by one percentage point. Similarly, the term $\beta_{19,2}=.8$ indicates that the conditional expected rate of return for Security 19 will increase by 0.8 percentage points when the average rate of return on Factor 2 changes by one percentage point.

The terms $\beta_{84,1}=7$ and $\beta_{84,2}=3$ have analogous interpretations for Security 84.

The term $\lambda_1=.11$ indicates that for each percentage point of risk generated in a security by Factor 1, the market will increase the expected rate of return on that security by .11 percentage points over the rate of return on the risk-free asset. Similarly, the term $\lambda_2=.25$ indicates that for each percentage point of risk generated in a security by Factor 2, the market will increase the expected rate of return on that security by 0.25 percentage points over the rate of return on the risk-free asset.

(b)

$$E_{19}=.10+(.11)(5)+(.25)(.8)=.10+.55+.20=.85$$
$$E_{84}=.10+(.11)(7)+(.25)(3)=.10+.77+.75=1.62$$

The risk-adjusted equilibrium expected rates of return for Security 19 and Security 84 are 0.85 and 1.62, respectively.

Chapter 13

1. (a) Because Kevin is relatively risk-averse, he would prefer (for example) a guaranteed annual income of $400 (that is, he is willing to trade away $100 of expected income in exchange for an elimination of risk). Mike, on the other hand, is willing to tolerate a wider range over which his income will fluctuate in exchange for a sufficiently large increase in the expected value of that income. For example, Mike prefers an annual income whose expected value is $600 even though that income fluctuates unpredictably between $200 and $1,000.

Therefore, Kevin and Mike could combine their businesses into a single firm. Kevin, being more risk-averse than Mike, will hold a contractual claim on the firm's earnings. As the contractual claimant he will have a guaranteed income of $400 per year.

The firm will also issue a share of common stock, which Mike will hold. As a residual claimant, he is entitled to receive whatever earnings remain, if any, after the firm meets its obligation to Kevin. In a good year, Mike will receive $1,400−$400, or $1,000. In a bad year, he will receive $600−$400, or $200. Since good years and bad years are equally likely, Mike's expected annual income is ($1,000+$200)/2, or $600.

By merging their businesses into a single firm, and by creating both contractual claims and residual claims in the capital structure of that firm, Kevin and Mike effect a mutually beneficial exchange that is based on their different tolerances for risk.

(b) Because the bond pays a guaranteed $400 per year, and assuming the risk-free interest rate is 0.10, the equilibrium price of the bond is $400/0.10, or $4,000.

The share of common stock is a risky asset. Assuming that the risk-adjusted rate of return on the stock is 0.13 per year, and that the expected annual payment to the stockholder is $600, the equilibrium price of the stock is $600/.13, or $4,615.38.

The value of the firm is the sum of the values of its outstanding securities. Therefore, the value of the firm is (1) ($4,000)+(1) ($4,615.38)=$8,615.38.

2. (a) Firm A is obligated to pay 5,000(0.07)($1,000), or $350,000 to its bondholders. Firm B is obligated to pay 10,000(0.07)($1,000), or $700,000 to its bondholders. Firm A has

$650,000 remaining to distribute to its shareholders. Firm B has $300,000 remaining to distribute to its shareholders.

(b) Firm A's bonds are priced at $70/0.12, or $583.33. Firm B's bonds are priced at $70/0.14, or $500. The value of Firm A's debt is 5,000($583.33) or $2,916,650. The value of Firm B's debt is 10,000($500)=$5,000,000.

(c) Firm A pays dividends of $650,000/100,000 shares, or $6.50 per share. Therefore, the price of a share of Firm A is $6.80/.15, or $43.33.

Firm B pays dividends of $300,000/100,000 shares, or $3.00 per share. Therefore, the price of a share of Firm B is $3.00/0.20, or $15.00.

Ignoring problems of liquidity, the market value of the equity in Firm A is $43.33(100,000 shares), or $4,333,000. The market value of the equity in Firm B is $15.00(100,000 shares), or $1,500,000.

(d) The debt-to-equity ratio for Firm A is $2,916,650/$4,333,000=0.673. The debt-to-equity ratio for Firm B is $5,000,000/$1,500,000=3.33.

(e) The total market value of Firm A is 5,000($583.33)+100,000($43.33)=$4,683,000. The total market value of Firm B is 10,000($500)+100,000($15.00)=$6,500,000.

(f) Even with the reduction in earnings, Firm A will be able to fulfill its obligation to its bondholders. That is, it can continue to pay the required $420,000 per year. Consequently, it will have only $150,000 remaining to pay to its shareholders. Since there are 100,000 shares outstanding, the firm will pay a dividend of $1.50 per share.

The reduction in Firm A's annual earnings from $1,000,000 to $500,000 will be borne entirely by the shareholders because they are the residual claimants. If investors use the same discount rate of 0.15 to capitalize the lower rate of dividends, the new price of a share will be ($1.50/0.15), or $10.00.

The decrease in Firm A's annual net earnings, coupled with the fact that Firm A does not use liquidation to allow its investors to reallocate their capital, imposes a capital loss on shareholders equal to $15.00−$10.00, or $5.00. In percentage terms, the capital loss is $5.00 / $15.00=33%.

Firm B, on the other hand, will not be able to fulfill its contractual obligations to its bondholders. That is, the higher debt-to-equity ratio in that firm enables its bondholders to force the firm to liquidate. Liquidation enables all the investors in Firm B to redeploy their resources into more profitable projects. This will reduce the capital loss the investors in Firm B incur following the reduction in its annual earnings.

(g) The higher debt-to-equity ratio in Firm B enables its investors to overcome a problem of agency and redeploy their resources in a more profitable project, thus reducing their capital loss.

Chapter 15

1. $C_0=\$4.05$
    $S_1^+=\$37.5$
    $C_1^+=\$7.5$
    $S_1^-=\$27$
    $C_1^-=\$.39$
    $S_2^{++}=\$46.88$
    $C_2^{++}=\$13.88$
    $S_2^{+-}=\$33.75$
    $C_2^{+-}=\$.75$
    $S_2^{--}=\$24.3$
    $C_2^{--}=\$0$

2. The equilibrium price of the call option at Node 2 is $3.00. Therfore, the option at Node 2 is underpriced. The equilibrium price of the option at Node 3 is $0.52. Therefore, the option at Node 3 is overpriced.

At Node 2 the hedge ratio for a riskless portfolio is −1; the investor should sell (short) 1 call option for each share of stock purchased (held long). Since the option is underpriced, the investor should reverse the portfolio by purchasing 1 call option and selling short 1 share of the stock. The net cost at time $t=1$ of constructing this portfolio is +$2.00 (to purchase the call)−$13.00 (obtained by shorting the share), or −$11.00. That is, the investor will enjoy a net inflow equal to $11.00 at $t=1$ by forming this portfolio. Depositing the $11.00 in a bank at time $t=1$ will yield $12.10 at time $t=2$.

Between time $t=1$ and time $t=2$, the system will move either to Node 4 or to Node 5.

At Node 4 the investor can liquidate her portfolio by paying $16.90 to purchase a share of stock with which to cover her short position and selling the call for $5.90. Thus the net cash flow from liquidating the portfolio at time $t = 2$ is +$5.90 − $16.90, or −$11.00. But the value of the investor's bank account at time $t = 2$ is $12.10. Therefore, the investor has a profit at time $t = 2$ in Node 4 equal to $12.10−$11.00, or $1.10.

The investor will also have a profit equal to $1.10 should the system move to Node 5. At Node 5 the net cash flow generated by liquidating the portfolio is +$1.35 − $12.35, or −$11.00 (as at Node 4). Since the bank account is worth $12.10, the investor's profit is again $1.10.

We conclude that if the price of the call option is equal to $2.00 at Node 2, the investor can obtain a guaranteed profit equal to $1.10 by purchasing 1 call option and selling 1 share of the stock short at time $t = 1$. Ignoring problems of liquidity, the investor can obtain a riskless profit equal to K times $1.10 by purchasing K call options and hedging those options by selling K shares short.

Now consider Node 3. The equilibrium price of the call option at Node 3 is $0.52; therefore, the option is overpriced at $0.80.

At Node 3 the hedge ratio for a riskless portfolio is −2.46. To create a riskless portfolio at Node 3 the investor should sell 2.46 call options for each 1 share of stock purchased (held long). Since the option is overpriced, the investor should sell the option and purchase the stock.

Selling 2.46 options at Node 3 will raise (2.46)$0.80, or $1.968. Purchasing 1 share will cost $9.50. Thus, the net expenditure required to construct the portfolio at Node 3 is $7.532. Borrowing $7.532 from a bank at time $t = 1$ will require the investor to repay (1.1) $7.532, or $8.285 at time $t = 2$.

If the system moves to Node 5 at time $t = 2$, the investor's 1 share of stock will be worth $12.35, and the call options will be in the money. To cover her short position in the calls, the investor will have to purchase 2.46 calls at $1.35 each. Thus, upon liquidating her portfolio in Node 5 the investor will receive $12.35 by selling her share of stock, and pay 2.46($1.35), or $3.321 to cover her short position in the calls. Her net revenue from liquidating the portfolio will be $9.029. Subtracting the $8.285 that she will owe the bank at time $t = 2$, her profit will be equal to $0.744.

If the system moves to Node 6 at time $t = 2$, the call options will be worthless, and her 1 share of stock will be worth $9.025. Subtracting the $8.285 that she will owe the bank at time $t = 2$, her profit will be equal to $0.740.

We conclude that at Node 3, the investor can obtain a riskless profit equal to (approximately) $0.74 by selling 2.46 of the overpriced calls and purchasing 1 share of the stock.

3. (a) To create a homemade put option at time $t = 0$, the investor constructs a portfolio by selling short 1 share of the stock, receiving S_0, purchasing 1 call option, paying C_0, and lending $E/[1 + r]$ to a bank. This is equivalent to paying $P_0 = C_0 E/[1 + r] − S_0$, which is a form of the put-call parity.

To establish that the portfolio will replicate the payoffs to a put option, note the following:

If the price of the stock at time $t = 1$, S_1, exceeds E, the put option will be worthless. But the portfolio will also be worthless because the value of the call option, which the investor owns, will be worth $C_1 = S_1 - E$, the bank account will be worth E, and the investor will have to pay S_1 to cover her short position in the stock.

If the price of the stock at time $t = 1$, $S = 1$, is equal to E, both the put option will be at the money, and hence worthless. The portfolio will be worthless, because the call option will be worthless, and the bank account will be worth E, which is the cost that the investor will incur to cover her short position in the stock.

Finally, suppose that the price of the stock at time $t = 1$, S_1, is less than E. Then the put option is worth $E - S_1$. The portfolio is also worth $E - S_1$, because the call option is worthless, the bank account is worth E, but the investor must pay S_1 to cover her short position in the stock.

(b) To create a homemade call option at time $t = 0$, the investor constructs a portfolio by purchasing 1 share of the stock, paying S_0, purchasing 1 put option, paying P_0, and borrowing $E/[1 + r]$ from a bank. This is equivalent to paying $C_0 = S_0 + P_0 - E/(1 + r)$, which is a form of the put-call parity.

An argument analogous to that for part (a) will establish that the portfolio replicates the payoffs to a call option.

(c) To create a homemade share of the stock, the investor constructs a portfolio by purchasing 1 call option, paying C_0, selling 1 put option, receiving P_0, and lending $E/(1 + r)$ to a bank. This is equivalent to $S_0 = C_0 + E/(1 + r) - P_0$, which is a form of the put-call parity.

An argument analogous to that for part (a) will establish that the portfolio replicates the payoffs to a share of stock.

Glossary

Agency Problem   By administering the enterprise so as to favor its own interests rather than those of its principal, the agent might exploit the flexibility provided by the principal. In a corporation, the *principal* is the group of shareholders; the *agent* is the team of managers employed by the shareholders to operate the firm. The presence of agency problems creates economic inefficiencies (deadweight losses) in the allocation of resources.

Arbitrage Pricing Theory (APT)   A multifactor model in which the investigator uses a mathematical technique called *factor analysis* to choose the factors (portfolios) of an asset pricing model. The technique chooses the factors to maximize the accuracy with which the model can explain the expected rates of return on individual securities by using the sensitivities of the securities' rates of return to the rates of return on the factors. These sensitivities are the securities' quantities of risk with respect to the factors.

Asset Substitution   The substitution by a firm of a riskier project for a less risky one as a means of transferring wealth from the contractual claimants (e.g., bondholders) to the shareholders, who are the residual claimants.

Asymmetric Information   Information that is not available equally to all parties of an exchange. If the parties to a proposed exchange have asymmetric information, the parties with the superior information have an incentive to enter the exchange only in circumstances that are likely to transfer wealth to themselves from the parties with the inferior information. Being aware of this possibility, the latter parties might refuse to enter the exchange *even though* the exchange, properly structured, could be mutually beneficial. The presence of asymmetric information, unless mitigated, can thus create deadweight losses.

At the Money   An option on an underlying security is "at the money" when the strike price of the option is equal to the market price of the stock.

Beta   A numerical measure of the sensitivity of the expected rate of return on a specific stock to changes in the rate of return on the market portfolio. Graphically, the value of beta for a security is the slope of that security's characteristic line.

Bond   A saleable debt security (contractual claim) issued by a corporation or government guaranteeing to the holder a finite number of interest payments for a specified period of time, plus a final payment equal to the face value of the bond when the bond matures.

Book-to-Market Value of a Firm   The ratio of a firm's book value to its market value. The average book-to-market value of a portfolio of firms is often used as one of the factors in a multifactor asset pricing model, such as the models of Fama and French.

Book Value   The estimated amount of money that a firm could raise by selling all of its assets. Sometimes the book value of a firm is known as the firm's liquidation value, or its salvage value. The book value usually includes a term called "good will," which is an estimate of the value that the firm's management contributes to the ability of the firm to generate earnings. Due to the difficulty of separating the contributions of the firm's saleable assets and the firm's management to the firm's ability to generate earnings, the "good will" is entered as an arbitrary figure, such as $1,000,000, or even $1.

Callable Bond   A bond that the issuing firm has the right to cancel by paying to the bond's current owners a fixed price (the call price) that is specified in the definition of that bond.

Call Option   A contract that gives the holder the right (but not the obligation) to buy a given security at a fixed price within a specified period of time.

Call Price of a Bond   The amount of money a firm must pay to bondholders in order to cancel a callable bond.

Capital Asset Pricing Model (CAPM)   A model that defines the relationship in equilibrium between the expected rate of return on a security and the quantity of systematic risk contained in that security. The graphical representation of this relationship is the Security Market Line.

   The central idea of the CAPM is that in equilibrium each investor will adjust the levels of expected return and standard deviation on her portfolio by choosing the proportion in which to split her funds between a risk-free government bond and a unique efficient portfolio that contains the risky securities of every firm in the economy. This unique efficient portfolio is called the *market portfolio*. Within the market portfolio, the proportion of funds allocated to each firm is equal to the ratio of the market value of that firm's securities to the aggregate market value of all firms' securities.

Capital Gain   The amount by which the current market price of an asset exceeds the original cost of that asset.

Capitalized Value (of a sequence of payments)   The net present value of the sequence. The capitalized value of a firm is the total market value of the firm's common stock. Since the price of a share is the (risk-adjusted) net present value of the firm's earnings per share (as perceived by investors), the capitalized value of a firm is the (risk-adjusted) net present value of the firm's residual earnings.

Capital Market Line   The line in the CAPM that defines the tradeoff in equilibrium between expected rate of return and standard deviation for efficient portfolios. The Capital Market Line extends from the risk-free rate of return on the vertical axis to a point of tangency on the concave locus of efficient combinations of expected rate of return and standard deviation for portfolios that contain only risky assets. This point of tangency defines the market portfolio.

Capital Structure   The configuration of claims on the firm's earnings held by investors. These claims are partitioned into contractual claims (e.g., bonds) and residual claims (e.g., common stock). The capital structure of a firm can affect economic efficiency by mitigating or exacerbating problems of agency and asymmetric information.

Characteristic Line   Each security has its own characteristic line that defines the conditional expected return on that security for period t as a linear function of the rate of return on the market portfolio for period t. The slope of a security's characteristic line is the value of beta for that security.

Comparative Advantage   The amount by which the cost incurred by one person (or firm) to produce some Good X is less than the cost incurred by a second person (or firm) to produce that same Good X. For each person, the cost of producing Good X is measured in terms of the quantity of some Good Y *foregone*. That is, the cost of producing Good X is the *real cost*, as measured in terms of Good Y foregone.

Concavity   A measure of the curvature of line for which the chord between any two points on the line lies below the line.

Conditional Expected Rate of Return   The expected rate of return (on a security) when the value of some other variable (such as the rate of return on the market portfolio) is pre-specified.

Conditional Probability Density Function   The probability density function of a random variable (such as the rate of return on a security) when the value of some other variable (such as the rate of return on the market portfolio) is pre-specified.

Conversion Ratio   The fixed number of shares of a firm's stock that the holder of a convertible bond issued by that firm receives by surrendering the bond and paying a fixed price specified in the convertible bond.

Convertible Bond   A bond that gives the bond's owner an option to convert the bond into a fixed number of shares of the firm's common stock at a fixed price.

Convexity   A measure of the curvature of line for which the chord between any two points on the line lies above the line.

Correlation Coefficient ("closeness of fit")   An index of the average proximity of a set of data points to their regression line. If all the data points lie on the regression line, the correlation coefficient is equal to $+1$ if the line has a positive slope, and -1, if the line has a negative slope.

Coupon Rate of a Bond   The percentage of the face value of a bond that the issuing firm must pay periodically to the investor who holds the bond.

The coupon rate of a bond is the rate of return on the bond *if and only if* the market price of the bond is equal to the face value of that bond.

Covariance   The covariance between any two random variables is the probability-weighted sum of the products of the amounts by which the value of each random variable can deviate from its expected value.

Dead Weight Loss   The value of potential mutually beneficial exchanges foregone as a consequence of an inefficient allocation of resources.

Debt   A contractual claim on a firm's earnings. Also, the totality of the contractual claims on a firm's earnings.

Debt/Equity Ratio   Also known as leverage. The ratio of the market value of firm's debt securities (contractual claims) to the market value of a firm's equity securities (residual claims).

Economic Efficiency   An evaluation of an allocation of resources in terms of mutually beneficial exchanges. An allocation is economically efficient if there exist no alternative allocations that would provide at least one person with a gain in utility (or wealth), without imposing a loss on any person. Equivalently, an allocation is economically efficient if there are no *further* opportunities for mutually beneficial exchanges, that is, if there are no deadweight losses.

Economic Equivalence   Two sequences of payments are economically equivalent if they have the same present value. Consequently, an investor who can borrow from and lend to a bank can convert any sequence of payments to any other sequence that is economically equivalent to the first sequence.

Economic Rent   That portion of the income received by the owner of a resource that exceeds the owner's opportunity cost. Hence, if the owner of a resource were to incur a fixed cost (i.e., a cost that does not depend on the rate of output) that does not exceed her economic rent, she would continue to produce the same rate of output that she did before the cost was incurred. (A change in a marginal cost would induce a change in the owner's choice of the quantity of output to produce.) Economic rent is synonymous with economic profit and producer's surplus.

Efficient Allocation of Resources   *See* Economic Efficiency

Efficient Markets Hypothesis   The assertion that the current prices of securities reflect all information that is currently known about the future payments that the owners of the securities will receive. An implication of the Efficient Markets Hypothesis is that the net marginal benefit of searching for mispriced securities or attempting to predict movements in the general level of prices of securities (i.e., "time the market") is equal to zero.

The prices of securities reflect the willingness of investors to buy, sell, and hold positions in those securities. Therefore, if the prices are to reflect information, there must be some investors whose trading causes the prices to change when information changes. For *these* investors, the net marginal benefit of searching for mispriced securities must be positive, else these investors would have no incentive to search for information. Consequently, the Efficient Markets Hypothesis cannot be true for every investor; if the Efficient Markets Hypothesis is true, there must be some investors who have a comparative advantage in analyzing information about the prices of securities.

Equilibrium   A configuration of prices and quantities for which the quantity supplied of each good is equal to the quantity demanded. The goods can include financial securities.

Equity   A residual claim on a firm's earnings. Also, the totality of the residual claims on the firm's earnings

Exercise (Strike) Price   The fixed price at which the owner of a call (put) option can buy (sell) the underlying security at any time before the option expires.

Expected Rate of Return   The expected value of the rate of return on a security. *See also* Expected Value.

Expected Value   The sum of the values that a random variable can take, with each value weighted by the probability that the variable can take that value.

Face Value (of a Bond)   The amount of money that the issuer of the bond must pay to the holder of the bond on the maturity date of that bond. The face value of a bond is specified by the contract that defines the bond. The price of a bond is not necessarily equal to the bond's face value; as is the case for any financial security, the price of a bond is set by the willingness of investors to hold that bond in their portfolios.

Financial Asset   A claim on the earnings of a real asset. Sometimes used interchangeably with "financial security."

Financial Security   A saleable right to receive a sequence of payments over time. The payments can continue for a finite number of periods (as in a bond) or for an indefinite number of periods (as in a share of stock). The size of the payments can be specified in advance (as in a bond) or be determined by a probability density function (as in a share of stock).

Homemade Dividend   A payment that a shareholder can create, for each share that she owns, by selling a portion of that share. The concept of a homemade dividend is most commonly used to illustrate how a shareholder can obtain the net present value per share of a new investment project that the firm finances by retained earnings. If a firm finances a project by retaining earnings that it would otherwise have paid to its shareholders as dividends, the increase in the price of a share will be equal to the sum of the net present value of the project per share plus the amount by which the current dividend decreases. [The preceding statement holds without qualification if there is no uncertainty about future events. When there is uncertainty about future events (such as the outcomes of a new investment project), the preceding statement must be qualified.]

Idiosyncratic (Firm-Specific) Risk   A measure of the amount by which a firm's earnings are affected by factors other than the level of macroeconomic activity, such as the prices that it pays for inputs, the strength of the demand for its products, litigation, resignations of critical executives, and the actions of regulatory authorities. In the CAPM, the variance of the vertical distances between the data points for a security and the characteristic line for that security is the idiosyncratic risk of that security.

Imbedded Option   Synonymous with an implicit option.

Implicit Option   An opportunity to postpone for a fixed amount of time a decision to acquire at a fixed price an asset other than a financial security. The option is *implicit* because the underlying asset is not traded on an organized exchange. Consequently, the use of the Black-Scholes option pricing model is not as transparent as in the case of a conventional option, such as a call option or a put option. By contrast, a conventional option is *explicit* because the underlying asset is traded on an organized exchange.

     An example of an implicit option is the opportunity of a firm to postpone a decision to undertake an investment project in order to collect additional information about the future outcomes of the project. The option to postpone the decision has a value, which can be analyzed by using versions of the Black-Scholes model. Recognizing implicit options enables one to include in the calculation of the opportunity cost of a project the value foregone by beginning the project now rather than postponing the project in order to collect additional information.

     A second example of an implicit option arises in the case of a leveraged firm. Rather than regard the shareholders as the owners of the firm, we can regard the firm's bondholders as owning the firm and as giving shareholders an option to acquire the firm by making the contractual payments of interest and face value to the bondholders. Viewed in this way, the shareholders have an option to postpone a decision to pay the bondholders until the shareholders learn whether the firm will be profitable in future periods. The exercise price of the implicit option is the set of promised payments of interest and face value. If the firm will be profitable, the shareholders will "exercise" their option to acquire the firm by causing the firm to pay the bondholders. If the firm will not be profitable, the shareholders will allow their option to expire unexercised by causing the firm to default on the bonds.

Information Trading   Trading by investors who believe that the current price of a security does not correctly reflect the risk-adjusted net present value of the sequence of payments associated with that security. Distinguished from liquidity trading.

Internal Rate of Return (of a sequence of payments)   The discount rate for which the net present value of the sequence of payments is equal to zero. Consequently, the internal rate of return of a sequence is the maximal rate of interest that an investor could afford to pay on funds borrowed to finance the purchase of the sequence, assuming that the investor could earn interest at that same rate by depositing in the bank the payments generated by that sequence. *See also* Yield-to-Maturity (of a bond).

In the Money   An option is "in the money" if an immediate exercise of the option would create a gross profit for the owner of that option, excluding any consideration of the price that the owner paid to acquire the option. A call option is in the money if the current price of the stock exceeds the exercise price specified by the option. A put option is in the money if the current price of the stock is less than the exercise price specified by the option.

Joint Hypothesis   If investors could outperform the market by using a particular strategy, there are always two competing explanations between which the economist can not distinguish. One explanation is that the Efficient Markets Hypothesis does not hold; there is information about future earnings that is not accurately reflected in current prices. The competing explanation is that the economist is using the wrong model to define the equilibrium relationship between expected rates of return, waiting, and risk.

Similarly, if there is evidence that investors cannot outperform the market, either the Efficient Markets Hypothesis holds, or economists are using the wrong model to define the equilibrium tradeoff between expected rate of return and risk.

Lambda   The market price of risk associated with a specific factor in a multifactor asset pricing model. A multifactor asset pricing model has as many market prices of risk as the model has factors.

Leverage   The ratio of the total market value of a firm's debt securities to the total market value of its equity securities. Also known as the firm's debt/equity (or d/e) ratio.

Liquidity   A measure of the increase in the cost that one would incur as a consequence of increasing either the size of a transaction in that asset or the speed at which the investor wants to conclude the transaction.

Liquidity Trading   Trading by investors to adjust either the size or the level of risk in their portfolios. Distinguished from information trading.

Long Position   A long position in an asset is a position in which the investor will lose wealth if the price of the asset falls and gain wealth if the price of the asset rises.

Market Portfolio   A portfolio consisting of every risky security in the economy. The proportion in which a particular security appears in the market portfolio is equal to the proportion of the total value of the outstanding shares of that security relative to the sum of the total values of the outstanding shares of all the risky securities in the economy. The market portfolio is an essential feature of the CAPM.

Market Price of Risk   The increase in the average rate of return on an efficient portfolio that an investor can obtain if she accepts an increase of one percentage point in the standard deviation of the rate of return on that portfolio. Therefore, the market price of risk is the rate at which the market compensates an investor for bearing risk.

Market Value of a Firm   The total market value of the firm's securities. Ignoring considerations of liquidity, the market value of a firm is the amount of money that investors would have to pay to purchase the totality of the claims on the firm's earnings (and thereby purchase the firm itself).

Maturity Date (of a bond)   The date on which the issuer of the bond must pay to the holder of the bond the face value of the bond. On the maturity date the periodic payments of interest cease.

Multifactor (Asset-Pricing) Model   An alternative to the CAPM in which there is more than one source of systematic risk. In a multifactor model the equilibrium expected rate of return on a security is equal to a reward for waiting plus a sum of terms to adjust for risk. Each adjustment for risk is a product of two terms. One of these terms is the quantity of a particular type of systematic risk; the other term is the market price for that type of risk. The quantity of risk contained in a security relative to a given factor is the beta of that security for that factor. The market price of risk for a factor is the lambda for that factor.

Net Present Value (of a sequence of payments)   The amount of money that, if deposited in a bank today, would enable the depositor to make a sequence of withdrawals that would exactly replicate the timing and the sizes of the payments in the sequence.

Out of the Money   An option is "out of the money" if an immediate exercise of the option would create a gross loss for the owner of that option, excluding any consideration of the price that the owner paid to acquire the option. A call option is out of the money if the current price of the stock is less than the exercise price specified by the option. A put option is out of the money if the current price of the stock exceeds the exercise price specified by the option.

Perfect Negative Correlation   If the rates of return on Securities A and B are perfectly negatively correlated, the correlation coefficient between two securities is equal to -1. If the rates of return are jointly normally distributed, the values of the two rates of return will always lie on opposite sides of their respective expected values by the same number of their respective standard deviations. For example, suppose that at time t the rate of return on Security A is displaced from its expected value in a given direction by a distance equal to z of its standard deviations. Then at that same time t the rate of return on Security B will be displaced from its expected value in the opposite direction by a distance equal to the same value, z, of its standard deviations.

Perfect Positive Correlation   Analogous to perfect negative correlation. For perfect positive correlation, the correlation coefficient between Securities A and B is equal to $+1$. The paired deviations of the rates of return on Securities A and B are in the same direction from their expected values.

Portfolio   A collection of securities in which the proportions of the total value of the portfolio allocated to the constituent securities are specified.

Probability Density Function   A function that specifies the densities with which a continuous random variable takes various values. The values of the random variable are plotted on the horizontal axis; probability densities are plotted on the vertical axis. The area under the density function between any two given values for the random variable is the probability that the random variable will take a value between the given values. By definition of probability, the total area under the density function is equal to 1.0. A normal density function is a bell-shaped curve that is symmetrical around the expected value of the random variable.

Probability Distribution   A list of the probabilities with which a random variable will take its possible values.

Put Option   A contract that gives the holder the right (but not the obligation) to sell a given security at a specific price within a specific time period.

Quantity of Risk   The quantity of systematic risk contained in a security is proportional to the sensitivity of the rate of return on that security to variations in the rate of return on the market portfolio. The market portfolio is a proxy for the level of macroeconomic activity. In the CAPM the quantity of systematic risk in a security is the value of the beta for that security.

Real Asset   A factor of production that can generate earnings by producing a valuable good or service.

Real Option   An option to purchase or sell a real asset.

Regression Line   A straight line whose slope and vertical intercept summarize the relationship between paired values for two variables. In the CAPM, the characteristic line for a security is the line obtained by regressing the rate of return on that security (plotted on the vertical axis) against the rate of return on the market portfolio (plotted on the horizontal axis).

Risk-Adjusted Residual   The vertical distance between the rate of return on a security and the characteristic line for the security. Equivalently, in the CAPM, that portion of the rate of return at time t that can not be attributed to either the reward for waiting or the reward for bearing risk.

Risk Aversion   An investor is risk averse if the average rate of return that she must have to hold a security increases as the level of unpredictable variability in the rate of return on that security increases.

Risk-Free Portfolio   A portfolio that has a guaranteed rate of return because the proportions in which the constituent securities are held guarantees that the random variations of each security's rate of return will be mutually offsetting.

Risk-Free Rate of Return   A rate of return that has a zero probability of deviating from its expected value. A U.S. government bond that has a guaranteed rate of return is regarded as risk-free, because the government has the power to tax and to print money. A corporate bond is not a risk-free asset because the issuing firm may be unable to make the promised payments.

Risk Neutrality   An investor is risk neutral if she evaluates a security based only on its expected rate of return; measures of dispersion (or unpredictable variability in the rate of return on that security), such as the standard deviation and beta, are irrelevant to the investor.

Security   *See* Financial Security.

Security Market Line   A linear relationship that defines the set of alternative combinations of systematic risk (beta) and expected return for individual securities when the market is in equilibrium. The Security Market Line is the essence of the CAPM.

Security Market Plane   A plane (or hyperplane) that is analogous for a multifactor model to the Security Market Line for the CAPM. The plane has as many "horizontal" dimensions as there are factors in the model. For a given security, the values of the betas for each of the factors are plotted in these horizontal dimensions. The expected rate of return on the security is measured in the "vertical" dimension. The value of the lambda for each factor is the slope of the hyperplane in the "horizontal" dimension in which the beta for that factor is plotted.

Short Position   A short position in an asset is a position in which the investor will gain wealth if the price of the asset falls, and lose wealth if the price of the asset rises.

Short Selling   The process of selling a borrowed asset in order to acquire a short position.

Standard Deviation   The positive square root of the sum of squared deviations from its expected value that the variable can take, with each deviation weighted by the probability that it can occur.

Stock   A saleable right to receive an indefinitely long sequence of future payments, with the size of each payment contingent on the firm's future earnings, on the firm's future opportunities to identify and finance new investment projects, and on the firm's decisions on what portions of earnings to distribute as dividends. *See* Homemade Dividend.

Systematic Risk   The sensitivity of the rate of return on a security to fluctuations in the rate of return on the market portfolio.

Transaction Costs   A term used to describe any and all costs that individuals incur to make exchanges.

Variance   The square of the standard deviation.

Volatility   A measure of the magnitude and the rate at which the value of a random variable can change unpredictably.

Yield-to-Maturity (of a bond)   The rate of return that would set the net present value of the sequence of payments generated by the bond equal to the current price of that bond. The yield to maturity on a bond is therefore the maximal rate of interest that an investor could afford to pay on funds borrowed to finance the purchase of the bond, assuming that the investor could earn interest at that same rate by depositing in the bank the payments generated by that bond.

Equivalently stated, consider the purchase of a bond as an investment project. The expenditure required to initiate the project is the price of the bond, and the periodic payments of interest and the payment of the face value when the bond matures are the earnings of the project. Viewed as an investment project, the bond has a net present value. The internal rate of return of the bond is the rate of interest for which the net present value of the bond viewed as an investment project would be equal to zero. Consequently, the internal rate of return of a bond is the maximal rate of interest that an investor could afford to pay on funds borrowed to purchase the bond.

Zero (coupon bond)   A bond on which the coupon rate is equal to zero. Consequently, the issuer of the bond (the borrower) makes no periodic payments of interest. The issuer does pay the face value of the bond to the bondholder when the bond matures. The investor (the lender) obtains interest implicitly because the price at which the investor purchases the bond is less than the face value of the bond.

Bibliography of Nobel Laureates

What follows is a selected bibliography of the works of Nobel laureates who have contributed to the economics of financial markets.[1]

1985   Franco Modigliani

For his pioneering analyses of saving and of financial markets.

Modigliani, Franco (with Merton H. Miller). "The Cost of Capital, Corporation Finance, and the Theory of Investment." *American Economic Review* (June 1958).

1990   Harry M. Markowitz, Merton H. Miller, William F. Sharpe

For their pioneering work in the theory of financial economics.

Markowitz, Harry. "Portfolio Selection." *Journal of Finance* (1952).
———. "Portfolio Selection: Efficient Diversification of Investment" (1958).
———. "Foundations of Portfolio Theory." *Journal of Finance* (1991).
Miller, Merton (with F. Modigliani). "The Cost of Capital, Corporation Finance and the Theory of Investment." *American Economic Review* (June 1958).
———. "Dividend Policy, Growth and the Valuation of Shares." *Journal of Business* (October 1961).
Miller, Merton (with E. F. Fama). *The Theory of Finance*. New York: Holt, Rinehart and Winston, 1972.
Miller, Merton (with Kevin Rock). "Dividend Policy under Asymmetric Information." *Journal of Finance* (September 1985).
Miller, Merton. "Financial Innovation: The Last Twenty Years and the Next." *Revue de la Banque* (September 1986). [An expanded version appears in *Journal of Financial and Quantitative Analysis* 21, no. 4 (December 1986).]
———. "The Modigliani-Miller Propositions after Thirty Years." *Journal of Economic Perspectives* (Fall 1988).
———. "Leverage." Nobel Prize Lecture, December 7, 1990, Stockholm, Sweden. [Reprinted in *Journal of Finance* 46, no. 2 (June 1991).]

---

[1] NobelPrize.org, Nobel Foundation web group, 1994; available at http://nobelprize.org.

——. "Index Arbitrage: Villain or Scapegoat?" *Journal of Financial Engineering* 1, no. 3 (December 1992).

Sharpe, William. "Capital Asset Prices—A Theory of Market Equilibrium Under Conditions of Risk." *Journal of Finance* (September 1964): 425–442.

——. "Mutual Fund Performance." *Journal of Business* (January 1966): 119–138.

——. *Portfolio Theory and Capital Markets.* New York: McGraw-Hill, 1970.

——. "The Capital Asset Pricing Model: A 'Multi-Beta' Interpretation." *Financial Decision Making Under Uncertainty*, Haim Levy and Marshall Sarnat, eds., 127–136. New York: Academic Press 1977.

——. "Capital Asset Prices with and without Negative Holdings." Nobel Prize Lecture, December 7, 1990, Stockholm, Sweden. [Reprinted in *Journal of Finance* (June 1991): 489–509.]

1997   Robert C. Merton, Myron S. Scholes

For a new method to determine the value of derivatives.

Merton, Robert C. "An Intertemporal Capital Asset Pricing Model." *Econometrica* 41 (September 1973).

——. "On Market Timing and Investment Performance Part I: An Equilibrium Theory of Value for Market Forecasts." *Journal of Business* 54 (July 1981).

Merton, Robert C., and R. D. Henriksson. "On Market Timing and Investment Performance Part II: Statistical Procedures for Evaluating Forecasting Skills." *Journal of Business* 54 (October 1981).

Merton, Robert C. "Financial Economics." In *Paul Samuelson and Modern Economic Theory*, E. C. Brown and R. M. Solow, eds. New York: McGraw-Hill, 1983.

——. "A Simple Model of Capital Market Equilibrium with Incomplete Information." *Journal of Finance* 42 (July 1987).

——. "In Honor of Nobel Laureate, Franco Modigliani." *Economic Perspectives* 1 (Fall 1987).

——. "Applications of Option-Pricing Theory: Twenty-Five Years Later." *American Economic Review* 88, no. 3 (June 1988): 323–349.

——. "Capital Market Theory and the Pricing of Financial Securities." In *Handbook of Monetary Economics*, B. Friedman and F. Hahn, eds. Amsterdam: North-Holland (1990).

——. *Continuous-Time Finance.* Oxford, U.K.: Basil Blackwell, 1990. (Rev. ed., 1992.)

Merton, Robert C. (with A. Perold). "Theory of Risk Capital in Financial Firms." *Journal of Applied Corporate Finance* (Fall 1993).

Scholes, Myron M. (with Fischer Black and Michael Jensen). "The Capital Asset Pricing Model: Some Empirical Tests." In *Studies in the Theory of Capital Markets,* Michael C. Jensen, ed. New York: Praeger, 1972.

Scholes, Myron M. (with Fischer Black). "The Valuation of Option Contracts and a Test of Market Efficiency." *Journal of Finance* (1972).

——. "The Pricing of Options and Corporate Liabilities." *JPE* (1973).

——. "The Effects of Dividend Yield and Dividend Policy on Common Stock Prices and Returns." *Journal of Financial Economics* (1974).

Scholes, Myron M. "Taxes and the Pricing of Options." *Journal of Finance* (1976).

Scholes, Myron M. (with Merton H. Miller). "Dividends and Taxes." *Journal of Financial Economics* (1978).

2001   George A. Akerlof, A. Michael Spence, Joseph E. Stiglitz

For their analyses of markets with asymmetric information.

Akerlof, George. "The Market for 'Lemons': Quality Uncertainty and the Market Mechanism." *Quarterly Journal of Economics* (August 1970).

———. *An Economic Theorist's Book of Tales.* Cambridge, U.K.: Cambridge University Press, 1984.

———. "Gift Exchange and Efficiency Wage Theory: Four Views." *American Economic Review* (May 1984).

———. "Introduction." In *Efficiency Wage Theories of the Labor Market,* George A. Akerlof and Janet Yellen, eds. Cambridge, U.K.: Cambridge University Press, 1986.

Akerlof, George, and Janet Yellen. "The Fair Wage-Effort Hypothesis and Unemployment." *Quarterly Journal of Economics* (May 1990).

Spence, Michael, and Richard Zeckhauser. "Insurance, Information, and Individual Action." *American Economic Review* 61, no. 2 (1971): 380–387.

Spence, Michael. "Job Market Signaling." *The Quarterly Jounal of Economics* 87, no. 3 (1973): 355–374.

———. "Informational Aspects of Market Structure: An Introduction." *The Quarterly Journal of Economics* 90, no. 4 (1976): 591–597.

———. "Investment, Strategy, and Growth in a New Market." *Bell Journal of Economics* (1979).

———. "Competition, Entry, and Antitrust Policy, Strategy, Predation, and Antitrust Analysis," Federal Trade Commission (September 1981).

———. *Competitive Structure in Investment Banking.* Cambridge, Mass.: Harvard University Press, 1983.

———. "Signaling in Retrospect and the Informational Structure of Markets." *American Economic Review* 92, no. 3 (2002): 434–459.

Stiglitz, Joseph. "Modigliani, the Modigliani-Miller Theorem, and Macroeconomics." Paper presented to a conference, "Franco Modigliani and the Keynesian Legacy." New School University, New York, N.Y., April 14–15, 2005.

———. "Information and the Change in the Paradigm in Economics." *The American Economist* 47 nos. 2 and 3 (Fall 2003 and Spring 2004). Also published in *Les Prix Nobel*, Tore Frangsmyr, ed., 472–540. Stockholm, Sweden: The Nobel Foundation, 2002; and in *Revista Asturiana De Economia* 25 (December 2002): 95–164.

———. "The Contributions of the Economics of Information to Twentieth Century Economics." *Quarterly Journal of Economics* 115, no. 4 (November 2000): 1441–1478.

Bibliography

Akerlof, George A. "The Market for 'Lemons': Quality Uncertainty and the Market Mechanism." *Quarterly Journal of Economics* (March 1984): 488–500.

Alchian, Armen A., and William R. Allen. *Exchange and Production: Competition, Coordination, and Control*, 3rd ed. Belmont, Calif.: Wadsworth, 1983.

Alchian, Armen A., and Harold Demsetz. "The Property Rights Paradigm." *Journal of Economic History* 33 (1973): 16–27.

Arrow, Kenneth J., declaration of, *U.S. v. Microsoft*, January 17, 1995.

Barbour, Brad M., and Terrance Odean. "Trading is Hazardous to Your Wealth: The Common Stock Investment Performance of Individual Investors." *Journal of Finance* 55, no. 2 (April 2000): 773–806.

Bittlingmayer, George, and Thomas W. Hazlett. "DOS *Kapital*: Has Antitrust Action against Microsoft Created Value in the Computer Industry?" *Journal of Financial Economics*, no. 55 (2000): 329–359.

Black, Fischer, and Myron Scholes. "The Pricing of Options and Corporate Liabilities." *Journal of Political Economy* 81, no. 3 (1973): 637–659.

Brander, J. A., and T. R. Lewis., "Oligopoly and Financial Structure: The Limited Liability Effect." *American Economic Review* 76 (1986): 956–970.

Brooks, Robert, Sinclair Davidson, and Robert Faff. "Sudden Changes in Property Rights: The Case of Australian Native Title." *Journal of Economic Behavior & Organization* 52 (2003): 427–442.

Chen, N., R. Roll, and S. Ross. "Economic Forces and the Stock Market." *Journal of Business* 59, no. 3 (1986): 383–403.

Ching W. K., and M. S. Lee. "A Random Walk on a Circular Path." *International Journal of Mathematical Education in Science and Technology* 36, no. 6 (2005): 680–683.

deBondt, Werner, and Richard Thaler. "Does the Stock Market Overreact?" In *Advances in Behavioral Finance*. Edited by Richard H. Thaler. New York: Russell Sage Foundation, 1993.

Demsetz, Harold J. "Toward a Theory of Property Rights." *American Economic Review: Papers and Proceedings* (1967): 347–359.

——. "The Cost of Transacting." *Quarterly Journal of Economics* 82, no. 1 (1968): 33–53.

Duffie, Darrell. *Futures Markets*. Englewood Cliffs, N.J.: Prentice Hall, 1989.

Ellison, Sara Fisher, and Wallace P. Mullin. "Gradual Incorporation of Information: Pharmaceutical Stocks and the Evolution of President Clinton's Health Care Reform." *The Journal of Law and Economics* 44 (April 2001): 89–130.

Elton, Edwin J., Martin J. Gruber, Stephen J. Brown, and William N. Goetzmann. *Modern Portfolio Theory and Investment Analysis*, 6th ed. New York: John Wiley & Sons, 2003.

Fama, Eugene F. "Efficient Capital Markets: A Review of Theory and Empirical Work." *The Journal of Finance* 25, no. 2 (1970): 383–417.

——. "Efficient Capital Markets: II." *Journal of Finance* 46, no. 5 (December 1991): 1575–1617.

Fama, Eugene F., and Kenneth R. French. "Common Risk Factors in the Returns on Stocks and Bonds." *Journal of Financial Economics* (February 1993): 3–56.

Fama, Eugene F., and Merton H. Miller. *The Theory of Finance*. New York: Holt, Rinehart and Winston, 1972.

"The Force of an Idea." *The New Yorker*, January 12, 1998.

Harris, Larry. *Trading and Exchanges: Market Microstructure for Practitioners*. New York: Oxford University Press, 2002.

Hilsenrath, Jon E. "Stock Characters: As Two Economists Debate Markets . . . Mr. Thaler Takes on Mr. Fama." *The Wall Street Journal*, Monday, October 18, 2004, A1.

Hu, Jie, and Thomas H. Hoe. "The Insider Trading Debate." *Federal Reserve Bank of Atlanta Economic Review* (Fourth Quarter 1997).

Hull, John C. *Options, Futures, and Other Derivatives*, 6th ed. Englewood Cliffs, N.J.: Prentice Hall, 2006.

Jaffe, Jeffrey. "Special Information and Insider Trading." *Journal of Business* 47, no. 3 (July 1974): 410.

Jensen, Michael C. "Don't Freeze the Arbs Out." *The Wall Street Journal*, December 3, 1986, editorial page.

——. "Risk, the Pricing of Capital Assets, and the Evaluation of Investment Portfolios." *Journal of Business* 42, no. 2 (1969): 167.

Jensen, Michael C., and William H. Meckling. "Theory of the Firm: Managerial Behavior, Agency Costs and Ownership Structure." *Journal of Financial Economics* (October 1976): 305–360.

Keown, Arthur, and John M. Pinkerton. "Merger Announcements and Insider Trading Activity: An Empirical Investigation." *Journal of Finance* 36, no. 4 (September 1981): 855–869.

Landsburg, Steven E. "Random Walks and Stock Prices." In *The Armchair Economist: Economics and Everyday Life*, 188–196. New York: The Free Press, 1993.

"The Legend of Arthur." *Slate Magazine*, January 14, 1998.

Leland, Hayne E. "Insider Trading: Should it be Prohibited?" *The Journal of Political Economy*, no. 100 (1992): 859.

Lintner, John. "The Valuation of Risk Assets and the Selection of Risky Investments in Stock Portfolios and Capital Budgets." *The Journal of Economics and Statistics* 47 (1965): 13–37.

MacKinley, Craig A. "Event Studies in Economics and Finance." *The Journal of Economic Literature* 35 (March 1997): 13–39.

Maksimovic, V. "Capital Structure in Repeated Oligopolies." *The Rand Journal of Economics* 19 (1988): 389–407.

Maksimovic, V., and S. Titman. "Financial Policy and a Firm's Reputation for Product Quality," *The Review of Financial Studies* 4, no. 1 (1991): 175–200.

Malkiel, Burton G. *A Random Walk Down Wall Street*, 8th ed. New York: W.W. Norton, 2004.

Manne, Henry. *Insider Trading and the Stock Market*. New York: The Free Press, 1966.

Markowitz, Harry. *Portfolio Selection: Efficient Diversification of Investments*. New York: John Wiley & Sons, 1959.

Modigliani, F., and Merton H. Miller. "The Cost of Capital, Corporate Finance, and the Theory of Corporation Finance." *The American Economic Review* 48 (1958): 261–297.

Myers, S. C., and N. Majluf. "Corporate Financing and Investment Decisions When Firms Have Information That Investors Do Not." *The Journal of Financial Economics* 13 (1984): 187–122.

Posner, Richard. *Economic Analysis of the Law*, 5th ed. New York: Aspen Law and Business, 1998.

——. "A Theory of Primitive Society, with Special Reference to Law." *The Journal of Law and Economics* 23 (1980): 1–53.

Rose, Nancy L. "The incidence of Regulatory Rents in the Motor Carrier Industry." *The Rand Journal of Economics* 16, no. 3 (Autumn 1985): 299–318.

Seyhun, Nejat H. "The Effectiveness of the Insider-Trading Sanctions." *The Journal of Law and Economics* 35 (April 1992).

——. "The Information Content of Aggregate Insider Trading." *The Journal of Business* 61, no. 1 (January 1988): 1–24.

——. "Insiders' Profits, Costs of Trading, and Market Efficiency." *The Journal of Financial Economics* 16, no. 2 (1986): 189–212.

——. *Investment Intelligence from Insider Trading.* Cambridge: MIT Press, 1998.

——. "Why Does Aggregate Insider Trading Predict Future Stock Returns?" *The Quarterly Journal of Economics* 107, no. 4 (November 1992): 1303.

Seyhun, Nejat H., and Michael Bradley. "Corporate Bankruptcy and Insider Trading." *The Journal of Business* 70, no. 2 (1997): 189–216.

Sharpe, William F. "Capital Asset Prices: A Theory of Market Equilibrium under Conditions of Risk." *The Journal of Finance* 19 (1964): 425–442.

Shiller, Robert J. *Irrational Exuberance*, 2nd ed. Princeton, N.J.: Princeton University Press, 2005.

——. "The Volatility of Long-Term Interest Rates and Expectations Models of the Term Structure." *The Journal of Political Economy*, no. 81 (1979): 1190–1219.

Siegel, Jeremy J. *Stocks for the Long Run: The Definitive Guide to Financial Market Returns and Long-Term Investment Strategies.* New York: McGraw-Hill, 2002.

"Soft Microeconomics: The Squishy Case against You-Know-Who." *Slate Magazine*, April 23, 1998.

"The Stock Market's Verdict of Microsoft's Antitrust Case." *Economic Intuition* (Spring 2000): 1–2.

Stoll, Hans R., and R. E. Whaley. *Futures and Options: Theory and Applications.* Belmont, Calif.: South-Western Publishing Company, 1993.

Summers, Lawrence H. "Does the Stock Market Rationally Reflect Fundamental Values?" *The Journal of Finance*, no. 41 (1986): 591–601.

Thaler, Richard H. *Advances in Behavioral Finance.* New York: Russell Sage Foundation, 1993.

Titman, Sheridan. "The Effect of Capital Structure on a Firm's Liquidation Decision." *The Journal of Financial Economics* 13 (1984): 137–151.

Weisbrod, Burton A. "The Health Care Quadrilemma: An Essay on Technological Change, Insurance, Quality of Care, and Cost Containment." *The Journal of Economic Literature* no. 523 (1991).

Index